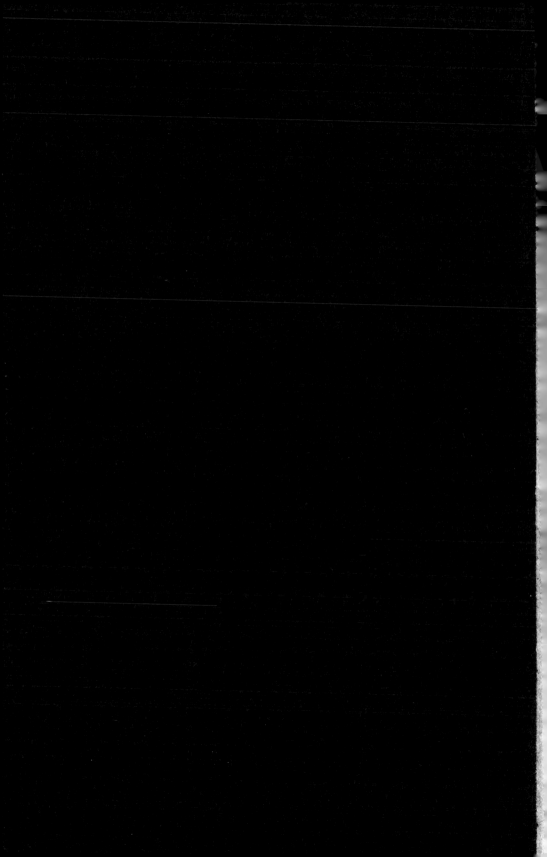

The Return of
Comrade Ricardo Flores Magón

The Return of
Comrade Ricardo Flores Magón

Claudio Lomnitz

ZONE BOOKS · NEW YORK

2014

© 2014 Claudio Lomnitz
ZONE BOOKS
633 Vanderbilt Street
Brooklyn, NY 11218

Printed in the United States of America.

Distributed by The MIT Press,
Cambridge, Massachusetts, and London, England.

Frontispiece: The corpse of Ricardo Flores Magón
displayed in Mexico City. Courtesy of the Casa
de El Hijo del Ahuizote, Mexico City.

Library of Congress Cataloging-in-Publication Data

Lomnitz-Adler, Claudio.
    The Return of Comrade Ricardo Flores Magón /
    Claudio Lomnitz—
        p.   cm.
    Includes bibliographical references and index.
    ISBN 978-1-935408-43-7
        1. Flores Magón, Ricardo, 1873–1922. 2. Flores
Magón, Ricardo, 1873–1922—Friends and associates.
3. Mexico—History—1867–1910. 4. Mexico—History—
Revolution, 1910–1920. 5. Anarchism—Mexico—History.
6. Anarchism—United States—History. I. Title.

F1234.F663L66 2014
972.08'16092—dc23
[B]
                                    2013037470

Contents

Odysseus and Circe. Dialectical image:
Anglo-America, *Ulises criollo*, and his
hyphentated-American crew. Photo
by Olef Haupt. Courtesy of Ny Carlsberg
Glyptotek, Copenhagen.

Dedication

To the Mexican People; and to the memory of my uncle Ilya, free spirit of the sixties.
—From Aeaea, with love (Oink!)

She led them in and seated them on couches and on chairs, and made a potion for them—cheese, barley, and yellow honey, stirred into Pramnian wine—but mingled with the food pernicious drugs, to make them quite forget their native land. Now after she had given the cup and they had drunk it off, straight with a wand she smote them, and penned them up in sties; and they took on the heads of swine, the voice, the bristles, and even the shape, yet was their reason as sound as heretofore.
—*The Odyssey*, book 10

Writing his enthralling memoir *Ulises criollo* from the United States—a country whose culture he deeply disliked—José Vasconcelos, Mexico's self-styled *Übermensch*, identified with an Odysseus writing from exile, still plotting to destroy the suitors who plundered his country's treasures and to put Ithaca to rights.

For many years, I harbored similar illusions, albeit with a more modest horizon of expectation. Vasconcelos was the Saint Peter of Mexico's cultural revolution. In 1929, he even presented himself as a presidential alternative to Mexico's emerging dynasty of revolutionary strongmen. Vasconcelos's was the exile of a king.

Mine has been the exile of a Jew, haunted by a long-foretold Jerusalem that I have never actually known. Although I have loved Mexico as much as anyone, I have aspired only to be known there, to return and be among friends, to teach and write and participate in public life.

xi

And I have never been denied these things. In fact, I have been embraced by the dearest friends and have had true and faithful students. Despite occasional obstacles, I have participated in Mexican public life. Yet there has never been a proper return. The scars of exile linger, even for those who do go back.

Indeed, the taste of exile gave Vasconcelos an ironic distance from Mexican affairs, even at the moment of his triumphal return, at the helm of Francisco I. Madero's revolution, in 1911. Vasconcelos was made head of the Maderista party in Mexico City. His family was reunited. Except that his little brother, Carlos, had returned to Mexico only just to die there. He had contracted tuberculosis working in Philadelphia's steel mills while José labored for the Madero cause. José used every influence to get his brother healed, but Carlos was beyond the powers of medical science, and his life slipped away.

Like all mourners, José turned to little things to numb his pain and guilt. He read the papers…a habit that was second nature to him. One of these had published a story noting Carlos's death: "It characterized my brother as an intelligent young man, full of promise. We were no longer obscure and uninteresting rustics [*provincianillos*]. Fortune's whim had made us prominent. If, on the contrary, Don Porfirio had snuffed out the revolt, my brother would have died at a hospital in Philadelphia, without giving work to any typesetters. I looked away from the paper in disgust."[1]

The panegyric of a press that had so easily cast off its loyalty to its old masters once the revolution triumphed—out with the old, in with the new—was a bitter pill to swallow alongside the irreparable loss of Carlos, a blow sustained in the penury of political commitment and self-sacrifice. This bitterness distanced Vasconcelos from glorying in his own apotheosis. There was not enough sincerity among his acolytes. His triumph itself was a vanity, a memento mori.

Perhaps my many returns to Mexican professional life have been blighted by similar frosts.

Or has the American Circe slyly given me one of her potions and transformed me into a member of that half-breed mass, the hyphenated American? (Oink! Oink!) Maybe. At times, I fail to find fortitude in the wily Odysseus and begin to cast a wary eye on the unfortunate members of his crew. Am I, perhaps? (Grunt! Oink!)…Who knows? Pigs can never see themselves. Only others.

Berlin, January 19, 2012

Introduction

The revolutionaries' worst enemy is the revolution itself, because it is an implacable selectionist.
—Francisco Bulnes

It seems to me that historians of the Revolution have, and always will have, to make a choice between Michelet and Tocqueville.
—François Furet

This is the story of a transnational revolutionary network that thought of itself collectively as the servant of an ideal. It could be told in the mold of Don Quijote—the story of a group of men and women who read books and acted on them, only to run up against a society that was entrenched in its coarsest concerns. Their acts were seen as wild. Like Don Quijote, they seemed to be out of place—utopian—or more precisely, out of time. Unlike Don Quijote, though, they knew *why* they were being singled out. "The theory of competitive individualism," Peter Kropotkin reminded his followers, "is the religion of the day, and to doubt of its efficacy is to be a dangerous Utopian."[1] And still reality overwhelmed them, reducing some to lashing out against betrayal and others to serenity in skepticism, or else to a lifelong wait for the revolution's Second Coming.

In the American mainstream, this group of people has largely been forgotten. They were a fraction of a fraction—the "Mexican" portion of an American socialist and anarchist movement that was put down during the Red Scare of 1917–1918, when Woodrow Wilson betrayed his campaign promises and led the country into World War I. Within the international socialist movement, their ideology was eclipsed by Bolshevism, a movement that purged and persecuted anarchists, yet again for being utopian and especially because they opposed the Bolsheviks' routine abuse of the *raison d'état*.

Summing up the reasons for his own disillusion with the Russian Revolution, one of the members of this group, Librado Rivera, explained that "the Bolsheviks played the same role in the Marxist Church as the Jesuits had played with the Christians."[2] Bolshevism was to libertarian communism what the Counter-Reformation had been to primitive Christianity. And just as the Jesuits had crushed the values of the primitive Christians, so, too, did Bolshevism push alternative movements of libertarian communism to the margins.

In Mexico, our group met a different fate. Its most vocal leader, Ricardo Flores Magón, was enshrined as a symbol of purity amid the muck of compromise, bribery, and murder that was rife in the so-called revolutionary family. But only after he was dead. On November 22, 1922, fellow radical Antonio Díaz Soto y Gama, by then a representative in the federal Chamber of Deputies, delivered Ricardo's funeral oration in Congress, giving voice to a deeply resonant sentiment of survivor's guilt:

> Perhaps no one has been greater among Mexico's revolutionaries than Ricardo Flores Magón. Ricardo Flores Magón—always modest. Ricardo Flores Magón, who had the luck, the immense joy of never being a victor. Ricardo Flores Magón who knew only the thorns and pains of the Revolution. All of us revolutionaries who have had the disgrace of tasting the delicacies that are served up in the banquet of the Revolution ought to bow our heads before this man.[3]

Like other symbols of purity, Ricardo and his closest collaborators were solemnly set apart. Soon they would be referred to reverentially as "Precursors of the Mexican Revolution," despite the fact that they were its contemporaries. Along with this displacement in time—the denial of this group's contemporaneity—the radical group's binational makeup was played down in favor of a patriotic reading that allowed the Mexican Congress to celebrate the national hero with little mention of his foreign collaborators.

In short, while in the United States the group is but the vaguely recalled fringe of a dimly remembered margin, in Mexico, the group was hallowed in national history, but only after being placed safely outside—"prior to" and "above"—mainstream revolutionary history, and then only after being "brownwashed," that is, made Mexican, with its foreign ties expunged. Only thus could Ricardo Flores Magón be safely placed in the hallowed niche of the sacred ancestor.

However, a contemporary audience that is aware of this movement is the Mexican-American reading public, particularly since the Chicano movement of the 1970s. This is because the story of Ricardo Flores Magón is susceptible to being told in the mold of the *Aeneid*, as a foundation myth. Rome, after all, was the phoenix that rose from the transplanted ashes of Troy. It was founded by the orphaned children of a survivor's survivors, so distant from the security of city and lineage that they were nursed and raised by a wolf. In the 1970s and 1980s, young Chicano intellectuals could see themselves as long-orphaned descendants of Ricardo Flores Magón. Ricardo's story was told as an opening chapter of the epic of the foundation of the Mexican-American people, a tale that lacks the grandeur of the founding of Rome, perhaps, but that is nevertheless a proper subject for an epic.

Following this tendency, early Chicano historians such as Juan Gómez-Quiñones referred to Ricardo Flores Magón's generation as *sembradores*, the planters of Chicano political culture.[4] Except that unlike Aeneas, our Mexican protagonists did not believe that their homeland had been irreparably lost to them.

Virgil tells that Romulus and Remus's great ancestor, Aeneas, was so heart-stricken when he left his destroyed city that he envied the dead that he was leaving behind: "O, three and four times blessed were those who died before their fathers' eyes beneath the walls of Troy." There was no sentiment like this among the Mexican exiles who arrived to Texas in 1904 and started to hatch their plans for revolution. This is why more than a few secretly modeled themselves on Odysseus or on any of the masked avengers who were his popular avatars. Or else on Moses, leading their people from slavery to freedom. I've never read any of them who thinks of himself or herself as an Aeneas figure. They did not see themselves as creators of a new nation, but as a regenerative force, there to ring in a new time. Indeed, their most famous journal was not titled *Mexican America*, or *Aztlán*, or anything like that, but rather *Regeneración*. If they saw themselves as planting something, it was the seed of revolution, rather than of a new Mexican American identity.

For their part, the Americans who worked with these men and women thought of themselves as collaborators in the "Mexican Cause," a movement that had taken the lead in the universal struggle for emancipation. The Mexican struggle for freedom was seen as not only eminently just, but also as a moral example to Americans. As Ethel Duffy Turner put it:

> What notion have we of real bravery? We search our minds and find a few foggy ideas about the "hero of San Juan Hill," or Dewey at Manila Bay, or some other petty actor in a petty cause. But those who possess the courage to risk all for no other reward than the joy of fighting for Liberty, with the odds all against them, often with the almost certain expectation of death—such are the heroes of the Mexican revolution.[5]

This story is an exalted one, to be sure, but it is not about the origin of a new nation. The history of the Mexican-American people is a barbarian's history of Rome. Its popular heroes are either tricksters or martyrs whose triumphs cannot be measured in traditional nationalist terms. There is no Mexican-American Washington or Benito Juárez, no founder or liberator of the nation. Rather, theirs has been a contribution to civilization that emerges, painfully and joyously, from friction between nations, and nations not only as ideals, but also as lived human relationships.

It is because of this uneasy relation to nation that our small and very international group has been denied its place in time and treated as an anachronism—hallowed as "pure" or discarded as "mad," like Don Quijote. But like Don Quijote, too, with the strength of their right arms, our heroes managed to make a small tear in the collective unconscious.

Return and Sacrifice

It is, indeed, with a wink to Cervantes, or more precisely, to Cide Hamet Benengeli, Cervantes's fictional author of Don Quijote, that one of our heroes, Mexican worker and anarchist Blas Lara, begins his memoir, presenting his book as if it were an arcane manuscript written by somebody else and found by yet another, a tourist in a Northern California city.

After spending the day visiting the town's principal establishments, especially its university, the document's putative finder, one Mariano Gómez Gutiérrez, wanders to the outskirts of the city until he comes upon the municipal dump. "It seemed to be a business in which workers unloaded trucks loaded with old things: rags, shoes, furniture, automobile parts, books, magazines, and all sorts of papers belonging to industries, offices, and commerce. Residues that had been handled by technicians and then resold by collectors [*garreros*] of the capitalist corporation known as Junk Company."[6]

While he contemplates this collection of discarded artifacts, a truck unloads bundles of old paper. One of the reams rolls to the feet of "Mariano Gómez Gutiérrez," who picks it up and takes it back to his hotel. "On the way back, I thought that maybe among the packages there might be drafts composed by the people who made the Atomic Bomb, since it was in that university that the process of the atom had been analyzed and where they developed the explosive that killed more than 100,000 people in two Japanese cities in 1945, quicker than a cock's crow."[7] But when he opens the package, he finds that it is "a kind of autobiography of historical events in which the names of the family of the author had been changed in order to avoid any question of self-promotion."

The fantasy is revealing. Blas Lara wrote his memoir as an old man in Berkeley, where he had lived since the end of World War I. He published it with an unnamed printer in a cheap edition, bereft of professional copyediting, leaving his many spelling mistakes as proudly uncorrected as his remarkable prose. Blas Lara's life as a Mexican migrant turned agitator and revolutionary did not leave a mark in Berkeley's monuments or institutions. Instead, Blas imagined encountering its traces near the city limits, in the junkyard, where obsolete objects are discarded, dismembered, and recycled.

In case the gallows humor of finding the story of his life in a heap of industrial waste did not make his own proletarian marginality sufficiently clear, Blas added a second fantasy to his book's introduction. When Mariano Gómez Gutiérrez first takes the ream of paper home, the fictional finder of his autobiography excitedly hopes that he has found a relic of the grand and terrible event, the invention of the Bomb, that tied Berkeley to the history of the world and that first created a common, global time by making the biblical idea of Armageddon real. Instead, he finds a curiosity, the convoluted life of a minor figure, a work whose only claim to stylistic merit is that "it has sought to suppress the superfluous verbiage and abstract terms that exist in the work of some professional novelists." As to content, the manuscript's pseudonymous author, whom Lara named "Edmundo," wishes only to share an account of his life with the modest hope that it "will please the lovers of times spent for the sake of setting an example, and of duty accomplished."[8]

Despite his keen sense of marginality, however, Blas was not despondent about the significance of his life. He presented it as a contribution to the history of human emancipation, albeit in a minor key. Like so many of his comrades, Blas Lara's intimate conviction of the eternal return of revolutionary horizons expressed itself in many ways. One of his daughters was named Floreal, after the second month of spring in the French revolutionary calendar. Another was Voltairine, like American feminist and anarchist Voltairine de Cleyre, and of course after Voltaire himself. His boys were named Orbe and Américo.

The bastard peasant daughter of the Great Revolution, the Mexican Revolution, had spawned a California spring.

But in the two pseudonyms that he used in his memoir, there is also another example of Blas's claim to the persistence of his revolutionary ideals. Mariano Gómez Gutiérrez, the document's putative finder, is named after Mariana Gómez Gutiérrez, a schoolteacher and colonel in Pancho Villa's army, whom Blas affectionately called "Marianita" in his personal correspondence. Thus, while Blas Lara's pseudonym veiled his own identity, it perpetuated the memory of another, equally minor revolutionary comrade. The second pseudonym, "Edmundo," which means "protector of victory," invokes the name of the big-hearted and grievously wronged hero who escaped from prison and returned to society as the mysterious Count of Monte Cristo to savor a most elaborate revenge, bit by delicious bit—a nineteenth-century Odysseus.

Time, Place, and Mutual Aid

The continued uneasiness that I have described with regard to placing in time the movement that Ricardo Flores Magón led—the insistence that it was "utopian" (nowhere) or anachronistic (either "before its time" or simply untimely)—was related to the fact that this movement arose in a novel context marked by the economic reorientation of Mexico to the United States and that it was led by a new population: Mexican émigrés and exiles and their American and European friends, allies, and comrades. Although Magón's organization carried a Mexican name, the Partido Liberal Mexicano, and a legacy that had deep roots in Mexico, its radical form flourished in the border region, and it depended crucially on new relations of mutual aid.

Following the arguments of the Russian naturalist and anarchist Peter Kropotkin, the protagonists of this book subscribed to the idea that humans rely on mutual aid for survival, welfare, and enjoyment. Contrary to the Social Darwinist credo of survival of the fittest, which posited competition between individuals within a species as key to evolutionary success, these Mexican and American radicals believed that for the most part, predatory behavior runs against collective interests and that it should be checked, rather than celebrated.

Kropotkin believed that the modern state had led a sustained assault on the great institutions of mutual aid that had been developed in the Middle Ages and in prior periods. Village lands had been confiscated, guilds repressed, communities deprived of their courts and councils, cities stripped of their sovereignty, parishes cheated of their autonomy. Individualism was the result, rather than the cause, of the war that the state—and its ally, the bourgeoisie—had carried out against communal institutions. Acquiescing to the war cry that the state alone is entitled to the "monopoly over legitimate violence," society had been violently reduced to a collection of individuals. Helpless before the wreckage of their cooperative institutions, individuals were left to compete with one another and to rely on the state for policing and on its unfair and insufficient systems of taxation for the distribution of beneficence.

Making virtue of necessity, individualism developed as an ideology that was used deliberately to misrecognize the collective defeat wrought on humanity by the unholy alliance between capitalist classes and the state. It exalted selfishness and made competition into a mystical principle.

On the eve of its revolution, Mexico's social conditions corresponded to a remarkable degree to Kropotkin's interpretation of the relationship between the history of the state and war on cooperative structures. The consolidation of the Mexican state came at the expense of Mexico's cooperative traditions: village commons were under attack, local governments were controlled from the top, and protesters were conscripted into the army and sent to Yucatán, where they often starved or died of illness. This was exactly the kind of situation that Kropotkin had so vigorously decried.

A kind of social isolation was one palpable result. New forms of bonded labor emerged in areas of rapid capitalist development, especially in the Mexican tropics. Slavery, masked as debt peonage, became prominent in plantations that sprang up around new export commodities: rubber, coffee, tobacco, chicle, henequen (agave raised as the raw material for twine and rope), and precious woods. Artisans were ruined by changing tax legislation and by economies of scale made possible by the railroad. Thanks to the railroad, too, dispossessed people began streaming into cities, where vagrancy, criminality, prostitution, alcoholism, and above all, misery reached dismal lows.

Consumption of tequila more than doubled in the course of the duration of Porfirio Díaz's government, from 1876 to 1911, known as the "Porfiriato"; *pulque* production more than tripled.[9] Porfirian public health official Luis Lara Pardo pointed out that in 1905, Mexico City had more than twice as many registered prostitutes as the famously dissolute city of Paris and in a population that was one-fifth the size.[10] The numbers of unregistered and casual prostitutes were many times that figure.

The desperate situation of the poor was manifested in the enormous popularity of gambling. Writing in 1901, Julio Guerrero noted just how slim were the chances for advancement by observing caustically that a number of Mexico City parishes had taken to organizing raffles to extricate souls from purgatory. Earning your way into Heaven did not seem as feasible a route to parishioners.[11]

When the socialist journalist John Murray, one of the characters in this book, was on his way back from his first visit to Mexico in 1908, he groped to find an image to sum up his impressions. Riding on a Pullman car on the Texas-bound Mexican Central Railroad, he wrote: "I kept my face glued to the carriage window and asked myself this question: 'Mexico, Mexico, Mexico is—what?' The answer seemed to rise from the passing throng of bent-backed, human burden bearers, 'Mexico is a land of *cargadores*.'"[12] Seen from the viewpoint of the international labor movement, Mexico had been reduced to a nation of mules (Figure I.1).

Figure I.1 *Cargadores*, postcard purchased
in Mexico by John Murray. This is the key
emblem for Murray's parable "What is
Mexico?" Courtesy of the Bancroft Library,
U.C. Berkeley, John Murray Papers.

The Relevance of the Liberal Party

But human cooperation will find a way, and alongside rampant degradation and social dissolution, new forms of mutual aid developed, painfully, but surely. In Mexico, these new forms of cooperation—labor unions, utopian communities, peasant leagues, political clubs, reading clubs, and political parties—were either outlawed or closely watched. Nonetheless, the ideal of bringing alive a modern version of cooperative traditions did gain a foothold.

Writing from Leavenworth Federal Penitentiary in Kansas during the closing years of Mexico's revolution, Enrique Flores Magón wrote to Teresa, his wife, back in Los Angeles, that "we can at least take solace from the fact that we are civilized, though we are enslaved and hungry. It would be still worse if we returned to the era when our fathers and mothers of two generations back lived on their communal lands in 'our' fatherland." But then, he immediately reconsidered: "But, speaking seriously, our grandparents working on their communal lands were free of the master's yoke . . . they were happier and lived more peacefully than us. . . . If to that society of our Indian grandparents we could add all of the comforts and scientific advances of today, for everyone's benefit, then life would really be worth living!"[13]

The difference between revolutionary time and ordinary time is that revolution has the power to make this sort of palimpsest of the old and the new seem attainable: graft the material progress that Enrique saw in Los Angeles—and even in Leavenworth Penitentiary—onto the (somewhat idealized) communal habits of his grandparents, and you have a plan for human happiness. The Mexican Revolution was that moment of accounting and of cleansing, when modern progress was to be shed of exploitation and greed and the communitarian life of the past would be revived and enriched with all the benefits of progress.

But revolution is also a fleeting moment, a possibility that must be seized before it becomes a murky and unintelligible past that must be painstakingly explained and vindicated, because it has been distorted by every sort of reality. Thus, Jules Michelet began his famous history of the French Revolution with such an attempt at vindication. In the 1840s, the Revolution needed to be told again, rerembered:

The peaceful, compassionate, and loving character of the Revolution seems a paradox today.... We so ignore its origins and so misrecognize its nature that after only a short time, its tradition has been obscured!

The violent and terrible efforts that she was forced to make so as not to perish—against a world that conspired against it—have been mistaken by a blind and forgetful generation for the Revolution itself.

And this confusion bred a deep and grave malady in that people, very difficult to heal: the adoration of force.[14]

For the actors themselves, the moment and the timing of revolution was not always easy to recognize. Thus, Ricardo Flores Magón made the controversial decision of remaining in California at the helm of *Regeneración*, his party's official organ, rather than move into Mexico and participate directly in the armed struggle. His motives are still debatable. Ricardo claimed that his role as writer and as ideologue was more valuable to the revolution than a role as soldier, while his detractors attributed the decision to cowardice. William C. Owen, editor of the English-language page of *Regeneración* and one of the leading lights of the group's inner circle, wrote to fellow anarchist Rafael García shortly after Ricardo's death that he attributed the decision to the influence of María Brousse, Ricardo's lover and companion: "You may know, perhaps, that I was most anxious that we should all move to Mexico—some 10 years ago—and I have always thought it would have been very much better. My own idea was that María's influence did much to prevent it."[15]

Whatever his reasons, though, Ricardo tried to direct the revolution from Los Angeles, but his activity there landed him in prison. He spent the years from 1907 to 1910 in prisons in Los Angeles and Arizona, from 1912 to 1914 at McNeil Federal Penitentiary in Washington state, four months of 1916 again in the L.A. County Jail, 1918 and part of 1919 at McNeil again, and from 1919 until his death, in November 1922, at Leavenworth Federal Penitentiary in Kansas.

Remarking on his rift with Ricardo over the matter of staying on in the United States, one-time comrade Jesús González Monroy wrote: "Ricardo himself must have understood his mistake.... But by then that intransigent revolutionary was prisoner number 14,596 at Leavenworth Federal Penitentiary and had no hope of obtaining freedom. And there was no other Revolution on Mexico's horizon, as indeed there has been none since then."[16]

In other words, according to González Monroy, Ricardo had missed the Mexican Revolution. But had he? That was certainly not Ricardo's own diagnosis. For him, the revolution was to be a drawn-out process, and working as a critic and bellwether was crucial to its ultimate success. Only ideological work—propaganda—could oppose the ploys of the politicians who wanted nothing but to hijack the revolution and use it for their own benefit. Ideology was more useful to the proletarian cause than providing it with yet another *caudillo*.

A revolution's guiding intellect cannot be said to have missed "the revolution." And yet it is no less true that in order to remain unrestricted by narrow political interests and true to those of the proletariat, Ricardo proffered his propaganda from beyond the nation's confines. He therefore was and was not a part of the "Mexican" revolution.

But something similar might be said of the revolutionary party in Mexico that Ricardo helped found, the Partido Liberal Mexicano (PLM). Thus, historian Alan Knight's rigorous study of "the" Mexican Revolution makes a bold point concerning the PLM's marginality, even with respect to political life late in the Porfirian era, to say nothing of its practical irrelevance in the revolution itself. Knight warns against distortions caused by reading later revolutionary developments back into the ideals of the PLM and so inflating that movement's importance simply because their ideas prefigured later developments. The PLM had ceased to be a major political actor in Mexico as far back as 1908 and so could not be said to have been at the root of the revolution.[17] And following Knight, professional historians have regularly expressed doubts as to the significance of the work of the exiled PLM for Mexico's revolution, while, conversely, many of the men whom Ricardo was to accuse of betraying PLM went on to become relevant players in the revolution. At the same time, a parallel historiographical trend has emerged to justify the movement's significance by turning to the American side of the border, where the PLM is somewhat problematically cast as forerunner of the Chicano movement. Caught between the movement's lack of political muscle in the "Mexican" revolution and its critical stance toward identity politics in the United States, the movement that produced the Liberal Party is difficult for historians to justify as an object of historical inquiry, beyond hero worship for its most vocal leaders.

The Partido Liberal Mexicano was in fact more of a movement than a party and more an ethos than a movement. Though Liberals shared a common Jacobin sensibility, in the sense that they were both anticlerical and believers in popular democracy, the core of the movement soon veered into socialism and to anarchism. The label "Liberal" was kept for strategic reasons and to underline a common Jacobin origin that had roots in earlier Mexican history.

It originated in 1901 at a congress that was meant to bring clubs with similar political leanings from across the Mexican Republic together into a single movement. The Liberal Party (or movement) was the only oppositional force in Mexico that openly attacked Porfirio Díaz, and it was quickly subjected to persecution. For this reason, it cannot be said to have operated as a political party in its early years, and we cannot calculate its membership, beyond noting the proliferation of such clubs, of which there were perhaps one to three hundred by the end of 1901.[18] The "party" was initially no more than a loose social movement founded on autonomous local organizations that had a set of ephemeral newspapers as their focal point.

This situation changed after 1904, when the (now-) exiled party leadership tried to create a formal political party, complete with membership dues, party rolls, and a detailed program that was launched from St. Louis, Missouri. The trouble was that this new, bold structure was set hurriedly in motion as part of preparations for revolutionary action in 1906, and that attempt failed completely. As a result, the PLM went underground in Mexico, while the party leadership in the United States was imprisoned. These conditions provided the Liberal Party with something like a spectral presence in Mexico: It was an oppositional force that was immanent and repressed. Indeed, its diffuse and ethereal nature is not a reflection of its lack of significance, but rather of the context in which the movement gestated.

A second stumbling block for assessing the Liberal Party's significance to the revolution stems from its own standard for defining loyalty. Thus, many apostates from the Liberal Party went on to become prominent players in the revolution. Antonio Villarreal was the first revolutionary governor to sack churches and make public burnings of confessional boxes. During his brief tenure as minister of agriculture, he ratcheted up the rhythm of land distribution. Juana Gutiérrez de Mendoza organized several revolutionary women's associations, was one of the first female suffragists during the revolution, and was an officer in Emiliano Zapata's army. Manuel Sarabia, Lázaro Gutiérrez de Lara, and Antonio Díaz Soto y Gama were among the founders of Mexico's first anarchosyndicalist labor federation, the Casa del Obrero Mundial. Francisco Madero himself was a moderate Liberal before going on to become president of the republic.

Even Ricardo ended up recognizing the significance of the PLM's diffuse influence. Thus, during one of the journal's many moments of crisis, while reminding his readers of *Regeneración*'s accomplishments, he credited not only its role in preparing the ground for the revolution, but also in retaining the people's focus on their true interests against those of the politicians, regardless of whether or not they identified as Liberals. Thanks to this work, he argued, "there is today in Mexico a revolutionary environment. Even government officials now make revolutionary proclamations. The people have lost their respect for their masters and their confidence in the goodness of government. Isn't all of that due to *Regeneración*'s propaganda and to the action and propaganda of the members of the Partido Liberal Mexicano?"[19]

The U.S. government seems to have agreed with this assessment. Thus, in its 1913 hearings geared to evaluating the question of how American interests and citizens were aiding the revolution in Mexico, the Foreign Relations Committee of the Unites States Senate ascertained that although the Liberal Party was no longer a military threat, the effects of its propaganda had nonetheless been considerable. Asked specifically about this matter, Dudley W. Robinson, assistant U.S. district attorney for the Southern District of California, told the Senate committee that:

> I think that undoubtedly the propagation of that bunch of ideas throughout practically all of Mexico for a number of years, most of it coming from the United States, has placed the Mexicans in such a state of mind, considering their mental development...that undoubtedly the great mass of them will continue to revolt until they get to the point where there are a large enough class of intelligent people there to support a strong Government, or until some arrangement is made by which they divide up the land and go through a period when they realize that they cannot hold onto it."[20]

Ideology and the Sacred

Octavio Paz once pointed out that ideology was underdeveloped in Mexico's revolution and that for this reason, its key movements were identified with leaders more than with ideological programs. The only true force and originality of the revolution was its clamor for a return—a return of lands to native communities. That is why Emiliano Zapata—represented as a peasant, reclaiming land for the community—was the revolution's purest symbol.[21]

This primacy of leaders over ideological principles, known in the political parlance of the period as *personalismo*, has sometimes been marshaled in support of a view of the revolution as a conflict between elites in which the peasant and the worker were but pawns. Others have argued that the prominence of *personalismo* (or *caudillismo*) is a reflection of the fact that the revolution was powered by a disarticulated and cacophonous agrarian revolt, with elites scrambling to place themselves at the head of movements that they could never really control.

Either way, revolutionary ideology seems of secondary importance, conjured up opportunistically by revolutionary leaders or latent as underdeveloped potential in the grievances of agrarian masses. The revolution was pure experience. It was its own sovereign—it was its own explanation. "La revolución es la revolución" was Luis Cabrera's famous formulation.

What is less commonly observed is that the tension between clientelistic and ideologically motivated movements was a prominent theme in revolutionary politics itself. Indeed, the Mexican Liberal Party had a tradition of denouncing *personalismo* that dated back to its very gestation in 1901, when, in order to deflect Porfirio Díaz's repression, Liberals under Camilo Arriaga's leadership carefully emphasized that their movement (for it was not yet a political party) was there to uphold the principles of the 1857 Constitution and not to back any particular candidate for the presidency. The PLM was in fact born under the banner of advancing principles, not following leaders.

In 1903, arguments against *personalismo* were again brandished, this time in response to tensions within the Liberal Party itself. On that occasion, Antonio Díaz Soto y Gama, Camilo Arriaga, and Juana Gutiérrez de Mendoza opposed a motion by Santiago de la Hoz, Ricardo Flores Magón, and Juan Sarabia, who had called for the party openly to oppose Porfirio Díaz in the upcoming reelection. Soto y Gama argued that if the PLM opposed Díaz, it would ipso facto betray its single-minded commitment to revive the 1857 Constitution and would become a personalist party instead: again, the PLM's aim was to uphold principles, not to support or reject candidates.[22]

This somewhat contrived use of the PLM's antipersonalist discourse to reject a potentially disastrous confrontation with Díaz reflects the prestige of the antipersonalist idea among its leaders. A few years later, when the Liberals tried (unsuccessfully) to compete against Francisco I. Madero at the outset of the 1910 revolution, they again cast that contest as a contrast between support for principles (Liberalism), and support for a person (*Maderismo*).

Indeed, the rejection of *personalismo* had by then become a key point of identification for the Liberals. Thus, in his obituary for Calixto Guerra, an assassinated Liberal chieftain, Antonio de P. Araujo wrote: "An intransigent enemy of all personalista parties, Calixto Guerra fought the same against Díaz as against De la Barra, Madero, Huerta, and Carranza."[23]

Given the premium it put on principles, it is not surprising that one of the labels that most disgusted the Liberal Party was "Magonismo." Thus, Tomás Sarabia reproached his cousin Juan for referring to the members of the PLM as "Magonistas": "Among us, Ricardo Flores Magón is simply a fellow comrade. He is not our 'leader,' nor our master, nor our chief, nor our idol.... Simply and succinctly, Ricardo is our comrade. For that reason the 'Magonista' label is not for us."[24]

Liberals understood the "Magonista" epithet as a deliberate perversion of the essence of their movement, which was not to enshrine Ricardo Flores Magón, or even to champion an ideology that he authored, but rather to promote a set of principles that had been collectively shaped. Liberalism was seen as an ideology, sustained by a network of like-minded militants.

This book takes Tomás's viewpoint very seriously. Revolutionary radicalism was generated by a network in interaction with other networks, not by a single ideologue or leader. At the same time, though, that network's own insistence on the primacy of ideology over personal loyalty paradoxically directed much attention to the selflessness of its members. Indeed, internal factions placed such a premium on ideological purity that the leadership careened toward an increasingly stern asceticism, with a marked propensity to expel the apostate and denounce the traitor, a dynamic that eventually became uncontrollable.

Ironically, emphasis on a selfless attachment to the ideal created room for a personality cult, and it is for this reason that the figure of Ricardo Flores Magón is a leitmotif in our story. This book is not a biography of Ricardo, and yet his figure best articulates the biography of the larger network with which the book is concerned because it was held up by some as the purest living example of uncompromising commitment to the ideal.

The story of the Liberal network as a whole is characterized by a mixture of robust ideological commitment and the ever-present fear of betrayal—of militants' lapses into self-interest or *personalismo*. Indeed, dread of fragmentation and treason reached such a pitch that the best way to describe it is as a form of vertigo. To inhabit the ideal was also to live in a hall of mirrors that recursively projected and refracted suspicions of treason.

As an example, here is the case of Lázaro Alanís. Alanís had been among the leaders of the Liberal uprisings of 1906 and 1908, and he was one of the party's most successful military leaders early in 1911. But when he made his peace with Francisco Madero after the latter's triumph over Porfirio Díaz, the party's central committee, the Junta Organizadora, now in exile in Los Angeles, branded him a traitor, an accusation that was coined in the "golden calf" imagery that was a staple of the antipersonalista rhetoric: Alanís had "prostrated himself at Madero's feet."[25]

Nevertheless, there were a number of Maderista politicians in Chihuahua who still mistrusted Alanís, despite his alliance with Madero, and the man was soon landed in jail, accused of being a troublemaker and a "Magonista." At that point, former Los Angeles junta secretary Antonio Villarreal, who had also allied himself with Madero and been branded a traitor, took an interest in rescuing Alanís.

Responding to Villarreal's efforts on Alanís's behalf, Chihuahua's revolutionary governor, Abraham González, warned that contrary to Villarreal's assertions, Alanís was still a Magonista. Abraham González claimed to have intercepted a letter from Ricardo Flores Magón in which Ricardo revealed that *Regeneración* was calling Alanís a traitor in order to fool the Madero government into releasing him from prison: "We might rescue him from jail if we keep loudly calling him a 'traitor'" was what Ricardo allegedly had written.[26]

Thus, Alanís remained susceptible to being accused of being a Magonista even though he had been denounced by Ricardo as a traitor. Indeed, he would and would not be a Liberal for the rest of his career, rising up against tyrant after tyrant, making opportunistic alliances with whomever was available in support of his social ideals. Alanís rose up against Díaz as a Magonista, then against Madero himself with Pascual Orozco, then against Madero again with Victoriano Huerta, then with Venustiano Carranza against Huerta and with Álvaro Obregón against Carranza.... In 1923, Alanís again rose up in arms with Adolfo de la Huerta against Plutarco Elías Calles and Obregón and was finally put before a firing squad. Historian José Valadés published the story of his execution in *La Opinión* in Los Angeles: Alanís "placed his cap on the ground, asking the leader of the firing squad to place it over his face [after his death] to protect it from the dirt, and raising his voice, he shouted: 'Soldiers! I am on old Liberal....'"

The commanding official interrupted Alanís and forbade him to address the troops. But Alanís started again, "Soldiers, you are going to shoot an old Liberal...." At that point, one of the soldiers came up to his side and dug a bayonet into his back.[27] In his final moment, this agrarian leader, who had rebelled time and again, allying himself with leaders of every political stripe as the occasion presented, wished to speak of his lifelong ideals. He had always been a Liberal.

As Alanís's example suggests, revolutionary ideology was neither underdeveloped nor incapable of guiding personal action. It was, rather, such an elevated ideal that few ordinary mortals could make credible public claims to following it consistently. Indeed, it can be said without exaggeration that revolutionary ideology belonged to the realm of the sacred: it was ubiquitous, but never in profane control.

Ideology was the truth that Alanís chose to speak at the moment of his death, but in life, it was not easy convince others of his sincerity. Thus, when Enrique Flores Magón prepared to return to Mexico in 1922, he sent his close friend Rafael García on ahead of him, and García contacted General Alanís in Mexico City. García thought Alanís a sincere comrade, though not deeply schooled in the ideal. Enrique, however, was careful to remind Rafael that Alanís had betrayed the cause back in 1911 and was not to be trusted.[28]

Today, there are two dominant positions on the question of ideology in the Mexican Revolution. One, championed by Mexican political philosopher Arnaldo Córdova, defines the ideology of the revolution as a particular kind of project for the state. The other, developed by numerous social historians, argues that because the revolution was powered by an agrarian class struggle, it gave rise to a rather underdeveloped ideological field that had two common goals: land distribution and increased local autonomy.[29]

Neither position deals squarely with the conditions that gave ideology its sacred (and spectral) character. Rather than being merely "underdeveloped," ideology was a constantly invoked absence: too pure for ordinary mortals to embody, it was also the revolution's most cherished transcendental object.

It is indeed for this reason that when revolutionary ideology is seen as a diffuse popular common ground, it appears to surface only in fleeting eruptions, like epiphanies, that, when absent, again take on the qualities of the specter: their absence is always felt and lamented. And when, on the contrary, the so-called ideology of the Mexican Revolution is viewed as an ideology of the state, then it is the people that it means to represent who take on a spectral quality, always invoked, always absent.

Regeneración

In addition to its obvious Christian sources, the exaltation of ideological purity in Mexico also rested on economic conditions. Regional diversity within Mexico fomented *personalismo*, because heterogeneous political constituencies could more readily be represented in the person, body, and kindred of a leader than in consensually approved ideological programs. But Mexico's economic integration with the United States provided exiles with a kind of backstage area in which ideological coherence could be reconstituted and projected back onto the national stage.

Magonismo (or Liberalism) was the first social movement to develop a coherent revolutionary ideology and program. Not coincidentally, that development turned crucially on Mexico's northern borderlands, for although Liberalism began squarely within Mexico, as a movement for the recovery of a once-dominant ideology ("pure" or "Jacobin" Liberalism), it soon faced such harsh repression that its leaders were driven into exile. The United States was the only place from which these militants might aspire effectively to continue their propaganda efforts. But once there, they faced some stark alternatives: assimilation to a foreign land in which they had neither weight nor consequence, fighting for revolution in Mexico from without, or an abject and humiliating return as subordinates to Mexico's politicians.

Ricardo Flores Magón chose the second option. Much ideological innovation occurred along that road of uncertain return. But precisely because it was innovative, fired in the furnace of exile, Liberal ideology became at once immanent in and external to Mexican political life. As a radicalized branch of the tradition of Mexican Liberalism, it had roots trailing back to the nation's independence, but because ideological radicalization could thrive only along the border, Liberalism was also always something foreign or alien.

Up until the outburst of the Mexican Revolution in 1910, Mexican Liberals thought that the outbreak of revolution itself would be the moment in which their ideology would be repatriated, but the Mexican Liberal Party was not strong enough to lead the revolution at the moment of its outbreak, so repatriation again presented the risk of subordination to regressive political forces, guided by aims that were at odds with the ideological ideal.

Understanding this full well and wary of the dangers of declining to the status of a mere *politiquillo*, a minor politician, Ricardo Flores Magón kept the revolutionary junta in Los Angeles through the entire revolutionary era. Thus, Ricardo refused to become a politician or a *caudillo* and preferred to safeguard the Liberal junta's role as ideological bellwether. That decision was a gamble that sought to perpetuate the Liberal movement's prerevolutionary situation of being at once immanent in and external to the revolutionary process.

In such a situation, the movement's journal, *Regeneración*, became a kind of droid or prosthetic, a phantom body, managed by the junta from Los Angeles to operate within Mexico and orchestrate conditions for an eventual full-bodied return of the ideologues. But as the revolution plowed forward in a counterpoint of violence and silence, the triumphal return of the ideologues became impossible, and with that, too, the ideologues' droid—*Regeneración*—began to falter.

Revolutionaries are either thought of as being "ahead of their time" or else they are seen as women and men possessed and consumed by a collective frenzy—prisoners of their time. Once revolution is raging, images of possession and consumption by revolution, of being swept up by the revolutionary gale, abound. Mexican popular culture represented the revolutionary movement as a rolling avalanche, *la bola*, and its leaders were at times thought of as lacking in everything but cunning and instinct. Martín Luis Guzmán, one of Pancho Villa's erstwhile intellectuals, represented Villa himself as a gun. Villa *was* his gun.[30]

Of Ricardo Flores Magón, one might say with equal justice that he *was* his journal. Its title, *Regeneración*, came to represent the utopian moment of return, when the body of the ideologue could at last take its place in the nation that had cast it out. That moment never came. But eventually, Ricardo was paraded back to Mexico in triumph, as a corpse, a gesture that reflected a will to perpetuate the presence of his absence.

El Yugo

Yugo in Spanish means "yoke"—the kind used for oxen or for a workhorse. Mexican anarchists used the term to refer to jobs. "When you write, you need only send a few lines," Rafael García wrote, shortly after Enrique Flores Magón's release from prison. Enrique should take proper care of his health. Holding two *yugos* (jobs) and then attending to such a volume of correspondence was too much. But then Rafael went on to congratulate Enrique "for the 'spectacular' arrival of that *bone* [Mexican slang for "job" or "gig"]. No yoke is pleasant, but being on the eternal lookout for a *bone* is even less so, and your yoke is not the worst, and it will undoubtedly bring you some benefit."[31]

The tension between work as externally imposed subjection (a "yoke") and work as a craving (a "bone") is the tension between the subjective reality of the individual worker, who needs, desires, and seeks a job as greedily as a dog wants a bone, and the collective reality of all workers, who have been subjected and yoked as a class. But the tension also expressed the relationship between living *in* the United States (an imposed sacrifice) and living *for* Mexico (a desire).

Among militants, these contradictions were resolved by eagerly seeking a *yugo* in order to pay for revolutionary activity. Mexico's exiled revolutionaries frequently referred to themselves as "fighters" or "gladiators," but their fight implied a life of something like what feminists call "double duty": they worked in their *yugos* for long hours, then used the money gained there for their collective emancipation and return. If they were women, they sometimes did triple duty. A few weeks after his brother Ricardo's death, Enrique complained to his closest friend of his physical state and attributed his condition to the wear of this double life: "I've had a constant pain in my heart for about a month now.... Disappointments, disillusions, miseries, great anxieties, and deep sorrows in my twin struggle for the cause and for the loaf of bread—excessive labors, for the master by day, for the slave by night.[32]

This is what Enrique and Ricardo meant when they figured their lives with a paradox: They were slaves of freedom, a condition that required a disciplined ability to endure physical and mental punishment, but also a keen sense of the immediacy of emancipation.[33] Both forces—slavery and emancipation, exile and return—were immanent in these fighters' daily lives.

Jack London's short story "The Mexican," set in the very same social circle as the subjects of this book, is about this powerful combination of slavery and freedom in the day-to-day management of the *yugo*.[34] It is the story of a mysterious young Mexican named Felipe Rivera who offers his services to the revolutionary junta in Los Angeles. The members of the junta don't initially trust Felipe Rivera. He is quiet and secretive. "'His soul has been seared,' said May Sethby. 'Light and laughter have been burned out of him. He is like one dead, and yet he is fearfully alive.'"[35] The young Rivera is a mystery to the junta, because he keeps both his past and his *yugo* a secret. No one knows what he does when he is not working for the revolution.

As the revolution is about to explode, the junta is in desperate need for cash for arms, and Rivera mysteriously offers to bring in the large sum that is needed. It is then revealed that he is making the revolution's money as a boxer. London's story culminates in a prizefight, where Rivera, who is brought in as a handicapped substitute, demands a winner-take-all fight with a Great White Hope–type boxing champion.

Rivera is vituperated by the crowd and underestimated even by the hired caretakers on his side of the ring. It is to Jack London's credit that he made the connection between slavery and emancipation, exile and return, *yugo* and revolution, the pivot of the one story that he wrote about the Mexican revolutionaries in Los Angeles: "Rivera forgot to look his usual hatred. A vision of countless rifles blinded his eyes. Every face in the audience, far as he could see, to the high dollar-seats, was transformed into a rifle. And he saw the long Mexican border arid and sun-washed and aching, and along it he saw the ragged bands that delayed only for the guns." It is also fitting that London chose boxing, "the hated game of the hated Gringo," as his hero's *yugo*. Rivera, London wrote, "despised prize fighting, in itself it was nothing to him."[36]

But did the fact that Rivera was a natural boxer really mean nothing? Not to Jack London, certainly, since the story turns on the drama of the prizefight, rather than on the drama of the battlefield. But revolutionaries also cared about their jobs and about their lives in the United States. These were, ultimately, radical spaces of self-fashioning and change—not always welcome, but always transformative.

Revolution has a rhythm, and it is a double counterpoint: past/future and present/future. Past and present are alternative sources of possibility and strength for the future. Jack London's Mexican hero is haunted by the image of his father and mother, murdered by the dictator's troops at the Orizaba textile workers' strike of 1907. This memory is the fire that steels him through the prizefight. But his success in "the hated game of the hated Gringo" is what makes him indispensable to the revolution.

Why I Wrote This Book

Exile and return, ideological purity and pragmatic accommodation, *personalismo* and its principled refusal. These are the three antipodes that shaped this book. They have also been at the heart of my relationship with Mexico and with Latin America.

Latin American political life is still plagued by *personalismo* and the cult of the state. And reactions against this disturbing tendency veer, yet again, toward old-style liberalism, now complete with an exaltation of private over public property and of the rights of the individual over collective rights. I was touched by the characters who shaped the "Mexican Cause," because they dared to explore a third alternative. It was cooperativist, but not personalista; internationalist, and deeply critical of the state.

How I Wrote This Book

The historian of revolution François Furet once wrote that all histories of revolution follow either Tocqueville or Michelet. What he meant by this was that accounts of revolutions are either structural

(Tocqueville) or phenomenological (Michelet), either critical (Tocqueville) or epical (Michelet), either focused on secular processes of transformation (Tocqueville) or focused on the irruption and interruption of hope and possibility (Michelet). The Mexican Revolution has not been excepted from this dialectic. Sadly, though, the historians' professional penchant for synthesis has produced an ever more reasonable, calibrated, and evenhanded narrative that moves through Mexico's history of violent convulsions with the parsimoniousness of a dentist working on a root canal.

Today, with the Mexican and U.S. historical academies operating at full capacity, writing about this or that aspect of the revolution has become a professional pursuit. While previous generations wrote their histories to the tune of the "Marsellaise," the "Internationale," or the "Adelita," ours seems as if it can't stop humming "Fixin' a hole, where the rain gets in," even while doing its damnedest to eroticize its dulled routines with a boyish fascination with trains, guns, and bandits and the homoerotics of men singing *corridos* around a campfire while they grease their guns and stroke their mustaches, complemented, for the girls, by the pleasurable palming of tortillas around a hot *comal*.

And yet Michelet's indignation about the ways in which the revolutionary generation in France had been forgotten still pops up sometimes in accounts of the Mexican Revolution. Except that the problem in this case is not so much that the revolution has been forgotten as that the phenomenology of the revolution has been incomplete. It has ceased to touch us, because it appears as a thing of a Mexico that has declined—call it "Peasant Mexico." In fact, though, the Mexican Revolution is a foundational moment in Mexico's contemporary history—it erupted when Mexico had only just become economically integrated into the United States.

The Mexican Revolution has been told principally as national history, and at times as international history, but analysis of the revolution as a transnational phenomenon has not yet made a deep mark. This is especially true for the study of revolutionary ideology, and not merely because there were intense transnational conversations and influences, a fact that is as trivial as it is well known. Transnationalism had structural implications for revolutionary ideological production that cannot be understood simply by tracking international dialogue and intellectual influences.

Mexico became the biggest source of migrant labor for the United States only after it had become the single largest foreign destination of American capital. As a result, Mexico's politicized migrants—starting with its exiles—had much to learn from American politics, since American interests were part and parcel of Mexican affairs. Meanwhile, the Americans who became part of the Mexican circuit of expats, too, came to understand the underbelly of their own government and corporations by seeing how they operated in Mexico.

For this reason, a number of the revolution's key ideologues were at once major and minor figures, which is an uncomfortable fact that has not yet been analyzed or even named. Movement across the U.S.-Mexican border turned protagonists of Mexican political life into minor figures. I don't mean to say that it diminished their worth, but rather that it shifted their subject position from one who identifies with the language of national prestige to that of an easily disregarded member of a minority. As intellectuals, these exiles went from being readers of and writers for major Mexican papers to devotees of the arts that philosophers Gilles Deleuze and Felix Guattari identified as the literary practices of the "minor," characterized by political immediacy, linguistic displacement, and heavy reliance on *bricolage*.[37] When a person is at once an impoverished miner living in a barracks with forty other workers with no privacy or place in which to store anything and a leader and organizer of a revolutionary movement in another country, as Librado Rivera briefly was, shifting between linguistic registers and speaking out opportunistically becomes both a bane and an art.

Thus, though the heroes of this book can safely be called "intellectuals," in the sense that they sought to represent their communities with the help of their cultural accomplishments, they were anything but mainstream professionals. When he was once asked for advice and criticism of a piece of poetry, Ricardo Flores Magón, a man who had had "ink as his passion" from his teenage years on, wrote back sincerely: "You want me to be a critic, my good comrade, and I think it sensible to decline such a function. I cannot judge your productions for one simple reason: to wit, that I have forgotten all about rhetorical rules."[38]

Ricardo was not lying when he said that he had "forgotten" those rules. At one time he knew them so well that he had taken it upon himself to guide his kid brother, Enrique, on their use: "At home, there's a little treatise on rhetoric and poetics by Campillo y Correa—learn that book well, it will serve as a stepping stone," Ricardo wrote.[39] He then instructed Enrique to read a lot of history and to learn geography, as well as general notions of physics, the natural sciences, and Spanish grammar.

But after years of living, printing, and struggling in the United States, Ricardo no longer had the stomach for that sort of advice. His minority position—surrounded by speakers of other languages and in constant exchange with clumsy readers and writers of Spanish—had taught him a different kind of writing, at once more precarious and more vital.

Venustiano Carranza, Pancho Villa, Plutarco Elías Calles, Álvaro Obregón—all of them avoided residence the United States, insofar as they could. They were Northerners, and they knew very well what living in the United States might do to them. They tried always to keep a gingerly distance from a country that they knew would transform them into minorities—quaint or vile Mexicans, Wild West attractions, singers in bars, assistants to a local consul, ghostly personages in a segregated Mexican section of town. Indeed, when Mexican revolutionaries went into exile, they became shadows, existing only in Spanish-language newspapers such as *La Prensa*, or *La Opinión* on the U.S. side of the border and rarely meriting even a passing reference in the egregious pages of America's mainstream press.

For borderland radicals, though, corruption was also perceived as a risk when moving in the opposite direction, from the United States to Mexico. So, for instance, Antonio Rincón, leader of a Liberal clan from San Gabriel, California, penned a violent denunciation against a former comrade, Emilio Campa, calling him a traitor to the cause for having made peace with the Madero government. "What a great step he's taken," Rincón wrote. "He was a soaring eagle in the United States, in the Capital of Mexico he's become a despicable insect."[40]

Similarly, writing from a San Antonio exile in the heat of Mexico's civil war, Santiago de la Vega wrote that "from afar, with distance from all of the repugnant intrigues and meanness of our politicians of every faction, one thinks of the true needs of the nation and sees the crime of *personalista* contention, where the only ones who benefit from the chaos are the traffickers in human hides who have used the revolution as if it were a dirty pimp."[41]

And yet this book is about a network whose very existence depended on movement across the border and on a willingness to shift between major and minor keys. Instability between these two registers is found all over the writings and in the working lives of these revolutionaries, divided as they were between their role as domesticated workers, harnessed into their *yugos* by day, and as warriors of freedom by night. Their paradoxical self-description as slaves of freedom underscores the indivisibility of these two ways of living.

In the face of exile, mainstream Mexicans were turned into minor figures. By 1915, many key ideologues of Mexico's revolution were writing and thinking from this American exile—José Vasconcelos, Martín Luis Guzmán, Juan Sarabia, and Santiago de la Vega, to name a few. From exile, they understood that their role was to define something like the general interest: "To form opinion," Martín Luis Guzmán wrote privately to Antonio Villarreal, "that is what we need to do. And to form it not around personalities, not as the program of a specific group—that would provoke the ire and opposition of those who now have the power and the money—but rather from a viewpoint that appears entirely disinterested and foreign to any possible political movement."[42] True national opinion could be formed only from the position of the minor.

The Liberals' American allies, for their part, cultivated the culture of the minor by choice. For them, learning about Mexico and the Mexicans was like learning the lower dialect in the sort of linguistic situation that Mikhail Bakhtin called "disglossia"—situations in which two languages or dialects form part of a single unit, with one of the two occupying the position of prestige in the face of a vulgar vernacular. This made some of these Americans honorary "major" figures within Mexico, not only by virtue of the services they rendered to the revolution, but also, more importantly, by virtue of their role in the translation of Mexican social and political demands from the minor to the majority register in both countries. This bifocality between major and minor registers is key to a comprehensive understanding of ideology in the Mexican Revolution, and yet it has been passed up in favor of buttressing the revolution's own (commendable) aim to claim for itself the language of the major. Like their subjects, historians of the revolution have feared the transposition of the revolution into the minor key.

For several years, I have lived with the letters and writings left by

the women and men of this major/minor transnational revolutionary network. That cohabitation with their traces has itself been a
lesson in the nature of writing in the major/minor network, for we
find intimate love letters written from the Los Angeles County Jail
in the archives of Mexico's Ministry of Foreign Relations, picture
postcards made for American tourists turned into incriminating
evidence in the pages of Socialist muckraking magazines, and tensions between American citizens over actions in Mexico recorded in
the archives of the U.S. State Department. Pieces and more pieces
of our story appear in various family papers, housed in a variety of
repositories on both sides of the border ... the Bancroft Library, the
Huntington Library, the library of the Instituto Nacional de Antro-
pología e Historia in Mexico, the Mexican Foreign Ministry, its
National University, the Enrique Flores Magón Archive, the Ricardo
Flores Magón online archive, and more.

In the course of this readerly pilgrimage, I moved from a feeling of intimate attraction to these intellectuals' modes of writing—which I also claim for myself—to the conviction that these
women's and men's existential openness, beyond nationalism, is
timely, for it shakes the foundations of a North American order that
is blighted by lack of imagination for a collective future of cooperation and mutual aid.

Dramatis Personae

When I began to write this book, I felt that I needed a guide.
That guide could not be Ricardo Flores Magón himself—he was too
much at the epicenter of the revolutionary circuit's key fractures
and cleavages. Indeed, in order to bring perspective to Ricardo's
strange story, I needed to understand the collective that made him
what he became. This therefore is a collectivist account of a social
movement. There is no telling the story of its greatest leader except
through relationships between friends and enemies, collaborators
and detractors. So I sought them out: friends, kin, rivals.

At first, I settled on a couple of friends as my guides: an American
muckraking journalist by the name of John Kenneth Turner and a
Mexican lawyer, agitator, and author called Lázaro Gutiérrez de Lara.
I confess that I was especially taken by the idea of using Lázaro as
guide because of his name. Since the publication of the picaresque
novel *El Lazarillo de Tormes* in the mid-sixteenth century, the name

"Lázaro," in Spanish, is used to refer to any guide for the blind. I could hardly resist the coincidence. In 1908, Lázaro Gutiérrez de Lara had guided John Kenneth Turner through a perilous and politically consequential journey to the slave plantations of Yucatan and Valle Nacional; now he would guide me, posthumously, through the secrets of Mexican-American collaboration in Mexico's revolution and through that to an interpretation of the significance of Ricardo Flores Magón's core paradox: ideological centrality and political marginality.

John Kenneth Turner's exposé of Mexican slavery became so famous in its time that writer Ernest Gruening compared it to Thomas Paine's writings on the American Revolution. But guide Lázaro's work through all of it had pretty much been forgotten. Turner's book relied absolutely on close Mexican-American collaboration, but the mechanics of how these collaborative relations operated—even their very existence—had never been fully investigated.

I had also chosen Lázaro as my guide for two other reasons. He had authored a history of the Mexican Revolution, published in 1914 and adapted for an English-speaking audience with the help and collaboration of a British socialist, Edgcumb Pinchon, a man who would later write works that would become the basis for Hollywood scripts on Pancho Villa and Emiliano Zapata. Lázaro, in short, had guided Turner, whose book spurred and framed the Mexican Cause in America, and he had later guided Pinchon, whose writing contributed to Hollywood's prolific treatment of the subject. For all these reasons—poetic and historical—Lázaro seemed to be a guide of choice.

The trouble was that following him was like tracking a skiff on the open sea. As my research progressed, I found that I had to rely on other guides as well. And I found them soon enough, in people such as Ethel Duffy Turner, Enrique Flores Magón himself, Blas Lara, Antonio Villarreal, and several others, who left traces—sometimes entire archives—as well as personal reflections of times and events transpired. Slowly, I realized that I was no longer being guided by a pair of friends, but rather by characters that formed part of a "circle."

Or, more precisely, of two overlapping circles. The first of these had at its core the central committee of the Mexican Liberal Party, the Junta Organizadora, with its president, the famous Ricardo Flores Magón, his lover, María Brousse, his brother Enrique, and their closest collaborators—Librado and Concha Rivera, Antonio I. Villarreal, and his two sisters, Juan and Manuel Sarabia, and later

Anselmo Figueroa, Praxedis Guerrero, Antonio de P. Araujo, William C. Owen, Blas Lara, Jesús M. Rangel, and many others, including, for a time, Lázaro Gutiérrez de Lara. This group was mainly Mexican, mostly in exile in the United States, and mainly, but by no means exclusively composed of communist anarchists.

The second circle pivoted around a small group of American Socialists who committed themselves to "the Mexican Cause" early in the year of 1908. This was a tight group that met regularly at the home of Frances and P. D. Noel in Los Angeles. Initially, their leader was a lawyer, Job Harriman, who was defending Magón, Villarreal, Sarabia, and Rivera, then imprisoned at the Los Angeles County Jail. Harriman was a prominent public figure. The other members of the circle were John Kenneth Turner, who would become the most famous of the lot; his young wife, Ethel Duffy Turner, a writer who was very active in the Mexican conspiracy; union activist and journalist John Murray; and Boston heiress and Radcliffe graduate Elizabeth Trowbridge. Frances Nacke Noel was a suffragette and a union leader, and her husband, P. D. Noel, was a businessman who was active in the Socialist Party.

These two groups came together early in 1908 around the public defense of the Mexican exiles, who were being hunted down, deported, or imprisoned for "violation of the neutrality laws." A set of crisscrossing relationships between the two circles developed the framework of what became, in effect, the first major grassroots Mexican-American solidarity network.

The Return of
Comrade Ricardo Flores Magón

PART ONE

Cultural Origin of the "Mexican Cause"

CHAPTER ONE

Ethel and John

Cuernavaca, Mor.—On Saturday, August 30, Mrs. Ethel D. Turner passed away in this city. Mrs. Turner was a North American writer who, in the company of her writer husband, Mr. John Kenneth Turner, collaborated with Ricardo Flores Magón.
—*El Correo del Sur,* Cuernavaca, September 7, 1969

A modest entry in a local paper of Morelos state.

The last living member of our group, Ethel Duffy Turner passed away on August 30, 1969. Her funerary cortege was attended by a few government officials, in recognition of Ethel's status as a "Precursor of the Mexican Revolution." A group of peasant leaders carried her casket to its final resting place.

Ethel lived out her final years in Cuernavaca at a place called Las Catorce Casitas, far from her daughter, Juanita, her sisters and brother in San Anselmo, California, and her friends and comrades in San Francisco, in Carmel, where she and John Turner eventually had settled, and in Los Angeles. She had lived modestly. Her bungalow at the Catorce Casitas was rented. Its contents were mainly files, about two hundred books, and some photos.

The local news emphasized that she received a pension from the Mexican government. She had indeed, though only during the final years of her life. Ethel's correspondence is littered with notes from friends and family sending her small amounts of cash. They knew that she got by on a meager income, and a number among them spontaneously sent assistance. To share the flavor of these donations, here is a note from one John Langdon, who wrote: "You say, in your letter 'spent your money.' Dearest Ethel, when we sent it was no long *our* money but *yours* to do with as you wished, and whatever

4

Figure 1.1 Ethel Duffy. A trace, an elegiac memento from her scrapbook. Courtesy of the Bancroft Library, Ethel Duffy Turner Papers.

you saw fit to do with it, that is what we would want."[1] Old comrades such as Ralph García and Alma Reed also occasionally sent money that never seems to have been required, but that was spent and appreciated.

In January 1964, Juanita wrote: "Dear Mom: Enclosed is $100 for plane fare. If you need more, let me know."[2] Juanita sent Ethel small checks sporadically in those years—ten dollars here, twenty-five there.

Money was never Ethel's thing. When her late husband John Kenneth Turner's great classic *Barbarous Mexico* was finally translated into Spanish in 1954, it sold by the thousands before anyone thought of giving some compensation to the elderly lady who had been that author's companion, collaborator, and coconspirator during the years when he wrote that book (Figure 1.1).[3] During her final years, Ethel eked out a living by designing and selling crafts for tasteful Americans—Maya silhouettes done in gold leaf on ceramic plates—supplemented by money that she received from her daughter, from friends from California, and her modest Mexican government pension as a *precursora* of the Mexican Revolution.

But there was nothing depressing about her existence. At eighty-three, Ethel was still lucid and passionate in her commitments. She was working on a book that was to be an "account of the participation of Americans in the preparation for and execution of the Mexican Revolution."[4] It was never finished.

The One-Way Ticket

Ethel Duffy and John Kenneth Turner met as students at Berkeley in 1904. Ethel was the eldest of seven children. Her father was an official at San Quentin State Prison. At the time that Ethel was born, he and his wife, Eugenia Amanda Palmer, were farmers in San Pablo, Contra Costa County. Their families were among the early Anglo setters of California: "My father," Ethel recalled, "was a farmer and also justice of the peace in that little pioneer town. My mother was born there. Her family had crossed the plains, and my father's family had gone from New York to Panama, then crossed the Isthmus of Panama and got another boat to San Francisco."[5]

In her autobiographical novel *One-Way Ticket*, Ethel described her childhood surroundings by way of a fictional alter ego, Veronica Bourne, who is described as being of Irish descent and as having lived in San Quentin all her life, in a home on the front row of officer's houses, just steps from the penitentiary's entry gate (Figure 1.2). That home vibrated with the sensibility of a family that had a romantic appreciation for nature: overgrown vines and a quiet beauty of interiors standing almost as an objection to confinement in the penitentiary.

> The Bourne dwelling was a one-story bungalow of seven rooms. It had been painted green, with a red roof, but time had drained and mellowed its color. Vines of honeysuckle, rose and moonflower smothered its eaves. There was a white rose climber over the side door leading from Veronica's bedroom to the garden, and at one of her windows an ivy straggler forced its way through a gap between the screen and the window casing.[6]

Indeed, the prison gate and the bleakness of the fortresslike penitentiary coexisted with a carefully cultivated wholesomeness—gardening, prison sports, school life. And Ethel's issue with the penitentiary was not the guards' cruelty—in *One-Way Ticket*, at least, those are good men, doing their jobs. Indeed, Ethel was proud both of her father and of her brother, who would later lead California's prison reform movement as warden of San Quentin. The problem, as she saw it, lay not with the guards, but with captivity itself and the society that had made these men captives: "Walls built around human passion.

That was what a prison was. Concentrated human passion. Hate, lust, remorse, tenderness of memory—all stretched beyond the normal."[7]

In Ethel's novel there is a recurring contrast between freedom and confinement—between the inside of the penitentiary and the houses of the officers, between the view of the bay from San Quentin and the fixity of that place, where prisoners arrived with their "one-way tickets" (Figure 1.3):

> Across the water were the El Campo hills, green turning to fawn. The full flood of the bay ran beyond them to the shores of Contra Costa and Alameda counties, where the foothills of the Coast Range shimmered and folded in the noonray sun. A white sail moved down the bay toward San Francisco. Another sail followed, and then another—the leaders in a yacht race coming from the north, from Vallejo or Suisun.[8]

But despite this open view, movement to and from San Quentin was so constricted that its prisoners *smelled* of stuffiness. Ethel remembered the bus riders who traveled on evenings to San Quentin: "A few tired commuters, a later shopper or two returning from the City, a white-faced prisoner with an indescribably stuffy jail smell—these were her usual bus companions in the evening. The prisoner was always shackled to a deputy; the deputy had a round-trip ticket for himself and a one-way ticket for the convicted man."[9]

When a prisoner was released, he was sent out with a one-way ticket, same as he had had coming into prison. The fluidity of movement, symbolized in one-way versus round-trip tickets, became the key symbol of Ethel's 1934 novel, because it represented her own existential choices so well. Prisoners got one-way tickets, commuters—people who moved in a routine connection with the prison—got the round-trips. Ethel's heroine, though, ended up taking something like a one-way ticket—from the prison world to freedom. The life of the prisoner was closer to her own existential position than the conformity of the commuter.

Ethel and her fictional double, Veronica Bourne, both broke with social expectations that would have them retain normal ties with the prison and the world that sustained it. Veronica Bourne ends up leaving her local boyfriend, helping a prisoner escape, and going to study at Berkeley.

We don't know whether Ethel herself assisted any San Quentin prisoners to escape. It seems unlikely that she would have. But later,

Figure 1.2 Panoramic view, San Quentin Prison. The panorama is a shot from a builder's point of view. The photo identifies the public's perspective with the gaze of the builder. Prisoners enjoyed no such panorama – they could not stand outside the confines of the prison, except only once, on their way in. Ethel's own views of the prison move between these two subjective positions. Bancroft Library, U.C. Berkeley, from the Online Archive of California.

Figure 1.3 Officers' houses, San Quentin State Prison. Dialectical image: Walls within walls; bourgeois interiority flourishing within the confines of the penitentiary institution. Bancroft Library, U.C. Berkeley, from the Online Archive of California.

she would help the Mexican political prisoners held in the Los Angeles County Jail in illegal ways, and her experience might have helped Ethel imagine that possibility and develop it in her novel. What Ethel really did do is leave San Quentin and go to Berkeley, where she met and married the nonconformist John Kenneth Turner.

Ethel's matriculation at Berkeley was made possible by Hugo Karl Schilling, a professor in Berkeley's German Department and a Goethe specialist, who was scouting for talent at nearby schools and saw her perform in her English class (Figure 1.4).[10] She was supported in this endeavor by the school principal, also a German humanist, who in Ethel's novel shows her protagonist his library before sending her off to college:

> "Durer, Holbein, Hogarth—everybody," he said. "Miss Bourne, clean all that X equals Y rubbish out of your head and put these great men there. I say this because there is in you something—what we Germans call *der Geist*. I know you are not the valedictorian of your class. I know you are lazy sometimes, and day dream too much. But I don't care for valedictorians. And as for dreamers—well, I asked you to come in here, didn't I? May you always live a little inside the dream, Miss Bourne!"[11]

One-Way Ticket also describes the young woman's social world in San Quentin in some detail. Bachelors were divided between inmates—who were socially off-limits—and men who presented a narrow range of life choices for a young woman like Ethel. The closest friend of the protagonist gets pregnant and then marries a Mexican. She is severely beaten by her father and criticized in the Anglo prison community for that deviation. Maybe the prison community's reaction in *One-Way Ticket* is exacerbated by the fact that San Quentin's officers and guards live in close proximity with low-status ethnics. There are Chinese, Poles, Filipinos, Greeks, Mexicans, Swedes, Chileans and Japanese who are either inhabitants or occasional visitors, a diversity that mirrors the racial milieu inside the prison: "In Chiny Alley, in Crazy Alley, in Hoodlum Alley, among the niggers and the Mexicans and the Filipinos, throughout the incalculably diverse mixture that is called white, the heart strains over the great wall toward anything whatever, so long as it is not a cell with bolts and bars, and a couple of cots and a table and a toilet, and a barred space for air" (Figure 1.5).[12]

Figure 1.4 Ethel Duffy's Schoolhouse at San Quentin. Emblem in Ethel's parable of escape to freedom. A house for free children, nursed by a German romantic. Bancroft Library, U.C. Berkeley, from the Online Archive of California.

Figure 1.5 Crazy Alley. "Walls built around human passion" is how Ethel described prison. The institution's essence is revealed in the tension between unadorned architectural functionality and the exuberance of inmate naming practices. Bancroft Library, U.C. Berkeley, from the Online Archive of California.

There is a kind of equality in incarceration, and San Quentin's guards and officials are keen to avoid being leveled by that same razor. Following the conventions of her social world, the novel's protagonist finds the most desirable of the young prison guards for her beau—a handsome young man who had studied agriculture at the "cow school" (now U.C. Davis), and who wants to take Veronica Bourne as his wife to live on his ranch. It is against this option, and for Berkeley and freedom, that the Ethel character buys her own "one-way ticket," out to the great world beyond the prison walls.

Once she's on the outside, the novel describes her sense of shame for being connected to the San Quentin community. Recalling this same sentiment as an elderly lady, Ethel told the *San Francisco Chronicle*'s Judy Stone that she "had grown up disturbed about the hangings at the prison, embarrassed about telling people where she lived, and imbued with a secret desire to join the Salvation Army until she began reading books like Edward Bellamy's utopian socialist romance, *Looking Backward*."[13]

It is perhaps because of this sense of shame that the protagonist of Ethel's novel finds herself irrepressibly drawn to a convict whom she helps escape, and it is around the time of the prison break that she herself leaves for Berkeley, where she discovers freedom (Figure 1.6):

> Paradise, it is conceivable, may be a glitter of green lawns among crooked oaks; it may be white walls joining around test tubes and plotted curves and seventeenth century prose; it may be a stag line at Sather Gate and coffee-and-doughnuts at four in the Coop, and football talk in the air; it may be a campanile caught in the sky's blue, and lovers climbing Grizzly to the Big C, and a Greek theatre growing old under the sun.[14]

Veronica Bourne's closest friend at Cal, Hazel, is free in a way that the novel's protagonist had never been before, and she easily frees Veronica of the weight of her past, even to the point of renaming her—"Veronica" becomes "Vera": "Vera. It was—in a way—a metamorphosis."[15] For the first time, Vera has found a friend on the outside with whom she can share her San Quentin background freely, without the stigmatizing effect that she compares to having a harelip.

It was in Berkeley's emancipated environment that Ethel Duffy met John Kenneth Turner (Figure 1.7), who was a schoolteacher back then, taking classes at Cal in some sort of continuing education program. Ethel, for her part, wanted to be a writer and was majoring in English.

To that young pair, the world of the prison was the innermost layer of a system of confinement that had conventional marriage as its outermost layer. Respectability was definitely not freedom. Indeed, Ethel's relationship with John, despite its considerable difficulties, would at least avoid the captivity of female American domesticity, a condition that had been aptly captured by a Latin American traveler, the Argentine Faustino Domingo Sarmiento, who already in 1847, remarking on the comparative liberty of the unmarried American female (or, as he colorfully put it, of the "men of the female sex"), noted that this freedom ended abruptly with marriage, at which point:

> The bride has forever said goodbye to the world of pleasure that she had until then so freely enjoyed: goodbye to the green forests that witnessed her lovers' trysts; goodbye to the waterfall, to roads and to rivers. From here on, a closed domestic sanctuary is her perpetual prison; the roast beef

COPYRIGHT 1898 BY EDW. H. MITCHELL, S. F.

Figure 1.6 U.C. Berkeley, 1898. Paradise lost. Bancroft Library, U.C. Berkeley, from the Online Archive of California.

Figure 1.7 John Kenneth Turner. Courtesy of the Bancroft Library, Ethel Duffy Turner Papers.

is her eternal accuser; the brood of children—blond and rompish—her continuous torment; and an uncivil husband—though "good natured"—sweaty by day, a snorer by night—is her accomplice and her ghost.[16]

The young couple married in March 1905. John was twenty-seven then; Ethel had not yet turned twenty. We may never know much about Ethel and John's marriage, which ultimately ended in divorce in 1916. Ethel seems to have saved few of John's letters—perhaps they were given to their daughter. John's papers remain lost. And Ethel did not like to write or even talk about their divorce. Her extensive personal archives include biographical sketches of the major figures of her circle (John among them), genealogies of her own family, and autobiographical notes of various portions of her life, but not one mention of the divorce, its circumstances, or its causes. The most that Ethel seems to have said about it was pronounced just three years before her death, in an interview with Ruth Teiser for the Bancroft Library's Oral History Project: "I have to tell you this, I don't like to, but we did separate."[17]

The only account of the circumstances that I could find is in a 1918 letter from John to his and Ethel's old comrade (and by then, a general), Antonio Villarreal in which John responded to Antonio's query about Ethel and their daughter, Juanita, writing that "I have to tell you a painful thing, that after I left New York two years ago Ethel deserted me, returning to Carmel later only in order to get some personal possessions." The circumstances of her departure, John wrote, "were such that a reconciliation was impossible."[18]

John added that Ethel had moved to San Francisco (545 Turk Street), that she had deposited their daughter, Juanita, with a sister at San Quentin, where Juanita was going to school, and that Ethel was working in an art store. John sent money to support Ethel and Juanita and said that she and John were friends, "as far as that is imaginable." John had since remarried to the socialist writer Adriana Spadoni, a novelist and regular collaborator to *The Masses* with the likes of Louise Bryant, Mabel Dodge, and Agnes Smedley, among others.[19] John claimed that Ethel, for her part, "realized her blunder when too late, and is not happy." Given John's comment regarding the impossibility of reconciliation and the studied silence that Ethel observed regarding the divorce, it seems possible that she might have fallen in love with somebody else. But regardless of what sparked Ethel's decision to abandon John, it does appear that she felt some sense of remorse for having done so.

The one letter that we have from Ethel to John from this period is a 1919 note thanking him for a check for a raincoat and dentist fees for Juanita. In that letter, Ethel also thanks John for his offer of financial assistance for her health bills, "but I do not want you to do another thing for me as long as you are poor. If you are ever the proud possessor of plenty of dollars, then I would truly appreciate your help." Ethel let John know that she was working hard to become more independent and so be united with their daughter—she was only seeing her on weekends at that point: "Am going to try to rustle up some typing to do in the afternoons and evenings. If I work up some business, then I can have Juanita over here. Am also going to try to get Spanish and French translations."

Finally, with reference to her state of health, Ethel acknowledged that beyond her chronic catarrh, "the chief trouble all along has been mental, and that is not easily cured."[20] To Antonio Villarreal, John had expressed worry and concern for Ethel's future, about which he said he could do nothing beyond providing financial assistance, and John confided that for some time, Ethel had been more like a daughter than like a wife or companion—a second responsibility, along with their daughter, Juanita.[21]

From this and from everything else, it is clear that Ethel and John's marriage was not a conventional affair. Neither was their divorce. Theirs was a circle in which people, in Ethel's words, "liked to be individuals and not conform to the pattern."[22] This included much independence and self-reliance, as well as solidarity and support. Thus, unlike many divorcees, Ethel and John maintained a cordial relationship. Ethel visited John in Carmel occasionally, and she conferred with him when she was thinking of going to live in Mexico in the 1940s, a plan of which John approved: "I used to see John once in a while in Carmel," she told an interviewer in 1966, "and I told him what I was doing [going to Mexico]. He seemed very enthusiastic, but he wouldn't do it himself. He should have. His relatives always said that I was the one behind him who made him tick about Mexico."[23]

In short, theirs was a connection between free individuals, reminiscent in some ways to the relationship between John Reed and Louise Bryant that has been set to film in the movie *Reds*. This was the generation that subscribed to Edna St. Vincent Millay's philosophy of "burning the candle at both ends." And Ethel and John represented the best of that tradition. Interviewed by Judy Stone, I. F. Stone's sister, in 1965, Ethel, who was by then eighty, characterized herself as "a wild one" and identified with the youth movement of the sixties: "Just the way the kids today are concerned about civil rights, we had to be concerned about something and it was poverty."[24]

Given their ambition to change the world, it is little wonder that Ethel and John left Berkeley without giving too much thought to graduation. Possibly Ethel already had the impression of Berkeley academics that she would attribute to her protagonist in her novel: "They talked smoothly of breaking down prejudices, these beautifully cultured young Ph.D.'s with the brave minds, the faultless personal behavior, the Harvard, if not the Oxford, accent. Their lives were shaped to a gentle routine; it was not difficult for them to follow a clean trail through books to an easy and charming freedom."[25]

Rather than pursuing such a life, the young couple went to live in San Francisco. John was a stringer for the *Fresno Republican*, a paper then under the direction of the progressive editor Chester Rowell. They were in San Francisco when the great earthquake of 1906 hit. It was this tremor that eventually took them to Los Angeles.

We were staying in a hotel at Sixth and Market. I was thrown out of bed, I remember. The plumbing was all twisted and torn. We managed to get down the stairs. We were adventurous and wandered all over the central part of the city. We saw ruins and dead bodies being taken out of different places. The City Hall had fallen. That was a great adventure, but we got out that morning on the last ferry boat."[26]

The earthquake in San Francisco was a formative event for an entire generation. It was the worst peacetime disaster that the United States had suffered, and—together with the sinking of the *Titanic*—it was the greatest media event of its time. Thanks to the transatlantic telegraph cable and the invention of the telephone, the San Francisco earthquake was an instantly reported global media story that laid bare the social fault lines of the city, suggesting ways in which a committed journalist might move from the surface details of tragedy, destruction, and chaos to a broad exposure of social injustice.[27] It is likely that it provided John with his first experience of what might be involved in action reporting with true national reverberations.

But John was not yet in a position to take journalistic advantage of this opportunity. When he and Ethel toured a destroyed San Francisco, then left the city, along with a river of refugees, the young couple went to Ethel's family home in San Quentin and from there to John's relatives in Portland, Oregon. John got a job there as sports editor of the *Oregon Journal*, but as a Californian, Ethel objected to the Portland rain.[28] So the couple decided to return to California, and John took a job with the *Los Angeles Herald*.

Although the paper was interested in appealing to the working man, its editors did not take long to throw John out for being too literary. This is how Ethel explained the episode: "Somewhere in the tumultuous period that followed, the newspaper job vanished. I believe that John, in a feature article, had called a whale a leviathan. Figures of speech were taboo in those sternly matter-of-fact days of journalism. An argument arose, and John, hotly defending the literary approach, was on the losing end."[29]

John

As the "leviathan" incident suggests, there was religion in John Turner's background. His grandfather on his mother's side, a Methodist minister by the name of Clinton Kelly, was one of the founding fathers of the city of Portland. John combined the evangelizing zeal of his grandfather with a passion for the press that came to him from his father, Enoch Turner, who was a printer. He became a school-teacher and then a journalist. His creed was socialism.

Born on April 5, 1879, John Kenneth Turner and his parents moved from Portland to Stockton, California, when John was six. His father set up a printing shop. At the age of sixteen, John had joined the Socialist Party and traveled to Los Angeles, where he met practically every active member of the party. At seventeen, John published his own weekly, the *Stockton Saturday Night*, dedicated to exposing corrupt politicians and businessmen.[30]

By the time of her 1966 interviews with Ruth Teiser for the Bancroft Library's Oral History Project, Ethel was, as she put it, "really ancient." But even then, with sixty years' distance and a divorce between them, she still described John with admiration. "John was good looking. He had an aquiline nose and an olive complexion, dark eyes and black hair. George Sterling used to say that an Indian got into the family somewhere.... he was about 5 feet 11, and slender."[31]

John Turner exuded a kind of authority that stemmed from his impressive writerly and analytical talents, but also from his substantial political experience, his courage, and his sense of situation and direction. Turner shared some qualities with other writers of those generations, such as Jack London, who would later earn Turner's disdain. Turner knew how to fish and to hunt, and he was a champion tennis player. During Mexico's revolutionary outbreak, he ran guns to Baja California, and he risked his life more than once on his Mexican reporting missions. In other words, Turner was a "man's man." Reflecting on the period when they met, Ethel drew a contrast between them. John had been overtly political, independent, and networked into Socialist circles from his teenage years. "He was seven years older than I was, but he seemed a lot older than that."[32]

THE BORDER

A Monthly Magazine of Politics, News and Stories of the Border

VOLUME ONE ❧ JANUARY, 1909 ❧ NUMBER THREE

Tucson, Arizona, U.S.A.　　　　　　　　　　　One Dollar a Year

MANUEL SARABIA
SECOND VOCAL OF THE JUNTA

LIBRADO RIVERA
FIRST VOCAL OF THE JUNTA

R. FLORES MAGON
PRESIDENT OF THE JUNTA

ANTONIO I. VILLARREAL
SECRETARY OF THE JUNTA

POLITICAL PRISONERS HELD IN THE UNITED STATES

THE MEN DIAZ DREADS

Mexico's Revolutionists and Their Third Uprising

John Murray

THE warm clasp of Tom's hand tempted me to talk—in a moment, and my loose tongue let slip enough to give hint of my errand to Mexico. Now Tom Hart was the last man that I should have supposed would show the white feather—a bear hunter, mind you, and grizzlies at that.

"Look here, Bud," he spoke with a down-drop of his eyes that was new to me, "don't be so foolish as to rub the President's hair the wrong way. You don't know Mexico—it's prison or death down here. You're fooled if you think for a moment that this is the United States. Why, I have seen a bunch of rurales ride into a village before sun-up, where things were not going to suit the Diaz government, and call out the whole population, line 'em up and shoot down every tenth man. No trials. Nothing. That's Mexico. And don't you go for to stand on your dignity as an American citizen, thinking that you're safer than a native to speak your mind free. I've seen Americans—yes, and there's three of 'em right now in the prison of San Juan de Ulua—who might just as well be Esquimaux for all the protection that their nationality gives 'em. For God's sake, old man"— Tom's pleading startled me, for if he were possessed of such a crushing fear of Diaz what chance had I to escape contagion?—"don't do anything to offend the Mexican government."

"It's too late, Tom, I'm into it now—up to my neck. You never held back when we were after the big-footed grizzly that killed our cattle in the pines back of the Loma Pelon ranch. The game I'm after now is news—the true story of Mexico's sandaled-footed burden-bearers and their nearness to revolt."

For several minutes he said nothing, and the grind of the car wheels got on my nerves. We were racking through that strip of sandy desert which lies between the Rio Grande and the fertile cattle ranges of General Terrazas' three-million-acre ranch. It was hot to suffocation and I made a motion as if to rise from the seat, but his hand checked me.

"How are you goin' to do it, Bud? What's your plan?"

I had to think for a moment before answering. From now on, until I recrossed the line back into the United States, I must trust people—people whom I had never seen before, whose native tongue was not my tongue, and whose lives would lie in my hands, as mine would be in theirs. So why should I not trust my old partner, although he was not a member of the Mexican Liberal Party?

The car seats next to us were vacant—I made certain of this with a glance—and opening my check book I extracted from a slit in the cover a thin, closely written sheet of paper, dated from the Los Angeles county jail, which was to pass me through forbidden paths of Mexico. Tom read my introduction to the revolutionists, slowly, from the first word to the last:

"El portador del presente documento es Sr. John Murray, periodista Americano de indiscutibles ideals"—being the first line, and winding up with—"su hermano que os desea—

"R. Flores Magon."

Refolding the letter he handed it back to me without a word, and I rebedded it securely in the leather cover of my check book.

"Tom, you've heard of Magon, the leader of the Liberal Party?" I dropped the sound of my voice to the last notch and the answer came back in the same key:

"Every peon in Mexico knows him, Bud. He's worshipped next to Juarez—but he's got no chance. If it was Texans, now, that were coming over the border, I'd say 'yes' and oil my rifle with the rest, but however willing these poor Mexicans are to fight, I've got just one question to ask, and that's a corker: 'where's the guns?'"

"Well, Tom, maybe the guns are coming. I know that preparations—. With a quick, upward motion of his finger Tom signified silence as the train came to a sudden stop and three Mexican officials entered the far end of the car.

I was dumb.

"Open your baggage for inspection," called out the first of the three. The last man in this uniformed bunch gave silent emphasis to the demand by shifting his carbine from one hand to the other. He was a rurale with sugar-loafed sombrero, grey-coated, grim.

Pulling my suit-case out from under the seat I unlocked it and threw back the lid. There was nothing inside to make me nervous; that I had made certain of before leaving my hotel room at El Paso. Every scrap of paper that might give a clue to my purpose in Mexico had been carefully burnt, all—except the one thin sheet hidden in the lining of my check book.

Figure 2.1 The four prisoners, in *The Border*, January 1909. The eyes of the junta are on Díaz. Exile has become a space for hostile witnesses, plotting beyond the assassin's reach. Courtesy of the University of Arizona Libraries.

CHAPTER TWO

The Mexican Cause

In the L.A. County Jail

Upon the young couple's arrival to Los Angeles, John got in touch with the most active members of the Socialist Party. Job Harriman, a lawyer and politician, and John Murray, editor of the Socialist Party organ *Common Sense*, were prominent among them. It was through them that John Kenneth Turner first heard about a group of Mexican radicals who were languishing in prison for the curious crime of trying to invade their own country.

John had a good nose for a story, and he liked to see things firsthand, so he asked John Murray to arrange a meeting with the prisoners. The Mexican radicals had discovered that the American press was a potential ally—they had actively sought press attention to their cause since they had led the failed 1906 revolt that had landed them in jail for violation of the U.S. neutrality laws.[1] Murray and Harriman, for their part, were eager to attract the interest of journalists, because they had committed themselves to those men's defense—Harriman as their attorney, Murray as a propagandist. So the appointment was set.

The prison meeting was a transformative event for John, just as these meetings had been for Harriman and Murray. When John met with the four men, in February 1908, Ricardo Flores Magón, Librado Rivera, and Antonio I. Villarreal had been in the Los Angeles County Jail for about a year. Manuel Sarabia had joined them more recently, on December 31, 1907 (Figure 2.1). As a result of a collective decision to go into exile in the face of hardened political repression, these four men and several compatriots had arrived in Laredo, Texas, in early February 1904, shortly after being released from prison in Mexico City. Moving to San Antonio, they had brought

19

back to life the Flores Magóns' political journal, *Regeneración*, which had been closed by Díaz, and then, in 1905, after only four months, they moved again, to St. Louis, Missouri, because Texas had its own extradition treaty with Mexico and a cozy relationship with Porfirio Díaz, where in 1906, the group of exiles named themselves the Junta Organizadora, the central committee of the new Partido Liberal Mexicano, and *Regeneración* the official organ of that party.[2] Their aim was to raise a revolution in Mexico. In 1906, they had tried, failed, and been driven further into hiding in Los Angeles, where Ricardo, Librado, Antonio, and Manuel were arrested.

Formation of the American Circle

The prison meetings with the Mexican exiles were deeply moving—so powerful that they triggered the formation of a circle of U.S. supporters of what came to be known as "The Mexican Cause," a group that began as a kind of committee for the defense of the political prisoners being held in the L.A. County Jail.

The circle consisted of Job Harriman, Frances and P. D. Noel, John Murray, Elizabeth Trowbridge, the Turners, and, less consistently, a young law student named Jimmy Rouche. They had their informal headquarters in the Noels' house, a "brown-shingled bungalow, which had lovely gardens and a view of high mountains"[3] (Figure 2.2). For a time, that house became the social center of the American defenders of the Mexican Cause.

What was it about those prisoners that sparked the committed action of this small circle? Certainly, the intensity of the organizational endeavor taken on by the junta, the intellectual effort and political work that went into shaping a politically coherent and ambitious program, which they had published in 1906 before launching their failed revolution, and the hardship and persecution that they had faced in both Mexico and the United States endowed the imprisoned men with an aplomb that impressed the American Socialists.

They were men who had sacrificed everything. Exiled by a brutal dictator, they had lived a frugal life in America, dedicated exclusively to overthrowing Porfirio Díaz. The Mexicans shared in the social ideals of the men and the women of the American circle, but they had sacrificed much more deeply for them. In this regard, the men in prison were role models. "The two chief characteristics of the

Figure 2.2 The Noels' place, Los Angeles. An elegiac tribute to the brown-shingled bungalow on the L.A. hills, with a romantically gowned Frances Nacke Noel on the veranda. P. D. and Frances Noel Scrapbook, Huntington Library.

man," Elizabeth Trowbridge wrote of Ricardo Flores Magón, "are his perfect mastery over self, and his courage and devotion in the cause of the oppressed."[4]

When Elizabeth Trowbridge interviewed Manuel Sarabia, the man she would later marry, she wrote that "in spite of the hardships through which he had passed, it was not of himself that Sarabia wished to talk, but of the people, for working on whose behalf he is now imprisoned—really by the Mexican Government, held though he is in the United States."[5] According to Elizabeth's first impression of Manuel, he "was short, lithe and slender, yet with an easy grace of speech and manner that in spite of his dark blue prison suit...showed him to be a man of education, refinement and intelligence. His brown eyes looked at us clearly and honestly, and his smile was singularly winning. He appeared to be very young—probably not five and twenty" (Figure 2.3).[6]

21

Figure 2.3 Manuel Sarabia. Courtesy of the Casa de El Hijo del Ahuizote, Mexico City.

The prisoners were Mexicans who in every way transgressed American national stereotypes: They were neither illiterate peons nor venal and corrupt overlords. Their very existence in a U.S. prison suggested that there was something sinister and contrived about Mexico's famously debased society.

Thus, in the early pages of his blockbuster exposé of what he called "The Díaz System," John Kenneth Turner acknowledged the consciousness-raising role of his first meeting with the prisoners:

> My special interest in political Mexico was first awakened early in 1908, when I came in contact with four Mexican revolutionists who were at the time incarcerated in the county jail at Los Angeles, California. Here were four educated, intelligent Mexicans, college men, all of them, who were being held by the United States authorities on a charge of planning to invade a friendly nation—Mexico—with an armed force from American soil.
>
> I talked with those Mexican prisoners. They assured me that at one time they had peacefully agitated in their own country for a peaceful and constitutional overthrow of the persons in control of their government.
>
> But for that very thing, they declared, they had been imprisoned and their property had been destroyed.

Figure 2.4 Ricardo Flores Magón. There is no photographic trace of Ricardo in exile that is not also already an emblem. He was famous in Mexico – his pictures were flashes from a morality tale. This photograph has Ricardo with a lapel pin, probably PLM. Courtesy of the Casa de El Hijo del Ahuizote, Mexico.

Finally, hunted as outlaws beyond their national boundaries, denied the rights of free speech, press and assembly, denied the right peaceably to organize to bring about political changes, they had resorted to the only alternative – arms.[7]

Again and again, commentators who met the junta leaders stressed their combination of modesty and unbending commitment. Thus, William C. Owen described the Magóns as "lions when it came to work" and recalled how Ricardo and Enrique Flores Magón were back at their typewriters in *Regeneración*'s offices barely one hour after being released from a two-year stint in federal prison.[8]

Even Ricardo's enemies grudgingly recognized his integrity. In a mortuary notice written from his own exile after the revolution, Victoriano Salado Alvarez, a senior Porfirian diplomat, condemned Flores Magón's acts, ideas, and legacy, but still called him a man of character and honor, unlike the bulk of Mexico's revolutionaries (Figure 2.4).[9]

The Mexican Cause

And yet, although crucial for their appraisal of the worth of these men, dignity and readiness to sacrifice were not the only factors that attracted the American women and men who committed to the Mexican Cause. Indeed, the attraction requires some explanation, because the American group would itself sacrifice deeply for its commitment.

So, for instance, just a few months after meeting the prisoners, John Kenneth Turner risked his life for the Mexican Cause; Ethel supported her husband's involvement and took additional risks on her own account. Elizabeth Trowbridge spent the whole of her substantial inheritance on the cause. She also married a junta leader and so embraced the stigma of being an (outlawed) Mexican's wife. John Murray, for his part, also took a few risks. Tracked by detectives in the United States and always wary of the Mexican police, Murray traveled to Mexico to do investigative reporting. Later on, his protests and journalistic activities made him a watched man, and he was also briefly jailed in Texas. And although Job Harriman, Frances Noel, and P.D. Noel did not suffer comparable risks, they did face costs to their careers and reputations for defending such a radical group.

In short, the small group of American supporters gave up a lot for the cause. Personal admiration for the four Los Angeles prisoners served to vouchsafe their motivations by making them certain that the cause was in good hands. But what moved these Americans to sacrifice so much?

It was not any prior love for Mexico—that is certain. As I sifted through the papers left behind by the various members of this group, it became clear that in each case, commitment to the Mexicans' cause came first, and learning about Mexico and Mexican culture followed.

For instance, one of the surviving texts that we have from the pen of Elizabeth Trowbridge is a short story that she published in *The Border*, a magazine that she, John Murray, and Ethel published late in 1908 and early 1909, during their months in Tucson. The story, titled "Topacio," is in the form of a Western romance, complete with beautiful señorita, gallant Mexican boyfriend, and coarse and corrupt Anglo sheriffs. Elizabeth should not be treated too harshly for her story's trite and commercial qualities. The idea that Murray, Elizabeth, and Ethel had had for *The Border* was to put out a glossy magazine that they could sell to tourists while raising consciousness about the political conditions that raged across the border. So the cocktail that Elizabeth prepared for her readers was a love story, complete with good guys and bad guys, that had the Liberal revolution of 1908 and its violent repression as a backdrop.

Romance, therefore, can be forgiven, but what stands out, even given *The Border*'s editorial policy, is the contrast between Elizabeth's familiarity with Mexican revolutionary politics and her shaky knowledge of the Spanish language and of Mexican culture. Thus, the protagonist of the story, who is given the odd name of Faquita, is made to utter these lines to her dog (named after Elizabeth, John Murray, and Ethel's own Tucson dog: Topacio): "Oh! Topacio. Topacio, little dog,' she whispered, 'what is happening over there? Over there beyond the mountains, where lies Mexico? My father—is he dead? And Rodrigo—what of him?'"

We have, in short, the exalted story of a girl whose name, though Spanish sounding, is not quite Spanish. Her boyfriend is christened with the noble name of Rodrigo, more resonant perhaps with the Castilian classic *El Mío Cid* than with naming practices in rural Sonora, but this might still be credible, were it not for the fact that Rodrigo is then given the (nonexistent) last name of Estrado, rather than Estrada, suggesting that Elizabeth was still a bit confused by the use of feminine and masculine endings in Spanish. Faquita's relationship with her dog, too, would be difficult to recognize for Sonoran revolutionaries, most of whom were miners and ranchers who adhered to a strict line of separation between man and dog: "She dropped upon her knees, hiding her face against the beast's silken coat, her slender body shaking with sobs. The dog whined gently, lapping her tear-stained cheek with his warm, soft tongue, his liquid, topaz eyes shining with almost human affection."[10]

Neither were these linguistic and cultural lapses into stereotypes or ignorance Elizabeth's alone. When major political exposés by John Murray and John Kenneth Turner were published, in the course of 1909, they, too, were littered with small mistakes that revealed the authors and their editors' limited acquaintance with the Spanish language and frequent confusion between Spanish and Italian. Even after years of intense collaboration with the Mexican Cause, Ethel Duffy still spoke rudimentary Spanish, and she was not immune to indulging in national stereotypes, either. Thus, in her 1934 novel, a Mexican character makes a cameo appearance:

Paul Escobar, the young Mexican guard from the Horse Post, galloped by on his black mare. As he passed her, he leaned far out from his saddle, flourishing a felt sombrero with a snakeskin band.

Veronica watched his spectacular gallop down the road. He thinks himself *muy caballero*, this fellow![11]

The fact is that not one of the members of the American group entered the cause because of a prior love of Mexico. And none of them spoke Spanish before joining the cause, as far as I can tell. The group as a whole recognized this when it committed to the cause, and very soon, Elizabeth, Ethel, John Kenneth Turner, and John Murray began taking private Spanish lessons with Socialist agitator and Liberal Party collaborator Lázaro Gutiérrez de Lara.

I don't think that any of these women and men would have been ashamed of admitting how new Mexico was to them. If Mexico itself was unknown, there were aspects of the Mexican situation that were disturbingly familiar.

Tolstoyans

All seven members of the Noel circle were college educated, and half of them came from well-to-do families. John Murray and Elizabeth Darling Trowbridge came from the eastern seaboard elite, and there are aspects of their biographies that deserve attention.

John Murray came from a prominent Quaker family that gave its name to the Manhattan neighborhood that is still known as Murray Hill.[12] J. P. Morgan's Park Avenue mansion, today the Morgan Library and Museum, stands opposite a charitable organization that is still called the John Murray House, after John Murray, Jr., Johnny Murray's great-grandfather. George Washington drank beer brewed by John Murray, Jr. During the Civil War, the Murrays were active in the underground railroad that brought runaway slaves into the North.

Our John Murray was born in Orange, New Jersey, on November 27, 1865, but his family moved west in 1876 (Figure 2.5). He went to school in Oakland and Berkeley, and for a time in New York City, too, but he had incipient tuberculosis, and this brought him back to California. In 1891, he married Gertrude Etchinson in San Francisco and had two children by her. He took up ranching. Murray and Etchinson were divorced in 1899. Given the relative rarity of divorce

26

Figure 2.5 John Murray. Noel scrapbook, Noel-Harriman Papers, courtesy of the Huntington Library.

in those days, it seems likely that theirs was at least in part an effect of Murray's conversion to socialism, though that is speculation.

What is certain is that moved by the writings of Leo Tolstoy, Murray renounced his inheritance and took up the cause of the working man. Exactly when he arrived in Los Angeles is not known, but by 1901, Murray was active in the Socialist Party there and, like Job Harriman, he became a supporter of the fusion between that party and the local union movement. In 1902, Murray joined Los Angeles Federal Labor Union 9614. He remained a union man, mostly as a member of the printers' union, until his suicide in 1921. During those early years, Murray was the editor of *The Socialist*. He married Olga Wirthschalt in Los Angeles on May 22, 1903, and they had a son, John, born September 22, 1904. But we never hear of Olga or John Murray, Jr., in the Mexican conspirators' correspondence. Judging from the mobile life that Murray led in those years, he must not have lived with them much, if at all.

In 1903, John Murray began to do work with Mexican unions during a beet thinners' strike in Oxnard. By 1907, he was deeply involved in the Mexican Cause. He supported Harriman's controversial decision to take up the legal defense of the radical agitators Ricardo Flores Magón, Antonio I. Villarreal, and Librado Rivera.[13] At that point, Murray was quite well known. Ethel described him as "an outstanding figure of the day who was engaged in trade union work and editing trade union papers, but was very volatile with a lot of fire and enthusiasm."[14]

Harriman's decision to defend Magón and friends was controversial, even within the Socialist Party. First off, they knew that for the most part, the Mexican Liberals did not approve of American trade unionism. The American Federation of Labor and most other unions of the period were reformist organizations that did not seek radical social change. Moreover, many of their unions were racist and did not welcome Mexicans. The California Socialist Party itself had supported Chinese exclusion in 1906, and vocal anti-Mexican sentiments routinely were expressed by members of the union movement. These issues might have been of some consequence to Job Harriman's political career. Harriman had repeatedly run for office: in 1898, as the Socialists' candidate for state governor and in 1900 as Eugene Debs's running mate for the vice presidency of the United States. Harriman continued to seek elected office after that until his run for mayor of Los Angeles in 1911, which he lost because of the bombing of the *Los Angeles Times* building by disgruntled union men.[15]

Thus, Murray's and Harriman's decisions to back the Mexican Liberals were controversial not only for the Los Angeles conservative establishment—most prominently the *Los Angeles Times* and the Hearst-owned *Los Angeles Examiner*, which were staunch defenders of Porfirio Díaz—but even inside the Socialist Party itself, where there was ambivalence with regard to defending Mexicans generally and toward defending anarchists such as Ricardo Flores Magón in particular.

Nonetheless, Murray was committed to denouncing labor conditions in Mexico. In the Southwest, some unions were beginning to admit Mexicans. The Mexican miners' strike in Morenci, Arizona, in 1903, had proved to skeptics in the Western Federation of Miners that Mexicans could organize.[16] As a result, the Western Miners aided the strikers across the border, at Cananea, Sonora, in 1906, and generally supported unionization in Mexico, which was illegal under Díaz. In fact, labor organizing in Mexico was critical to supporting the integration of Mexicans into unions in the United States. Since the Partido Liberal Mexicano had the only prolabor program for Mexico at the time, Murray and Harriman decided to throw their support behind the Liberal junta, even despite misgivings from within their own party.

28

Elizabeth

The other high-class easterner in the Noel conspiratorial salon was Elizabeth Darling Trowbridge. A Boston heiress who had studied English at Radcliffe, Elizabeth had joined the Socialist Party at eighteen. She came to Los Angeles early in 1908 with her mother, the redoubtable Mrs. Shultis. She was twenty-nine years old then. Through socialite friends in Santa Barbara, Elizabeth contacted the Noels, who combined respectability (P. D. Noel worked in finance) with strong Socialist commitments. Frances Nacke Noel was active as an organizer and as a writer, both in the union movement and for women's suffrage, a cause that would finally pass the ballot in California in 1910. Her husband always went by the highfalutin acronym P. D., but not so much because he was a power-mongering, cigar-puffing financier as because his given name was Primrose. So, as Ethel once wryly remarked, "who could blame him?"

Frances and P. D. Noel became intimate friends and protectors of Elizabeth, who moved into their home and made it hers. Through the Noels, Elizabeth met Harriman, and through him, the Mexican prisoners. She was so powerfully drawn to their plight that in a matter of days, she committed to the Mexican Cause.

There were thus three women in the American group: Frances Nacke Noel, an educated, German-born American who, in addition to her political militancy, was married, had a son, and ran a household; Elizabeth Trowbridge, a college graduate with a substantial inheritance and needing only emancipation from her mother; and Ethel Duffy Turner, the youngest of the group, who was an artist and writer and married to John Kenneth Turner, who was about to risk his life for the cause.

Naturally, Elizabeth took the lead. She was older and more experienced than Ethel and had no marital duties, the way Frances did. Elizabeth was well educated and old enough to stand her ground among men of the intellectual stature of Murray, Turner, and Harriman. She had already stood up to her mother, the crusty Mrs. Shultis, and to her rigorous social expectations.

According to Ethel, Elizabeth took after her father, Almarin Trowbridge, an engineer and social reformer who had died before Elizabeth was born. His absence had left Elizabeth in the power of her mother, a stern and convention-bound lady, and yet Elizabeth took her own path. Ethel, who loved Elizabeth, painted her like this:

The girl refused to become a debutante, nor would she conform to the expected standards. She had brown curly hair, good features and large blue eyes; she might have been attractive had she made an effort. But she was painfully shy. She rode horseback, but she did not dance. She had no close friends and shrank from the opposite sex. After her Radcliffe College days, she spent her time in charity work among the very poor. The mother was distracted, and when the girl continued to spend money on the indigent, she threatened to have her committed for insanity.[17]

Like other unconventional women in that sort of society, Elizabeth was confined to home for her rebellious acts. Her health began to decline as a result, and she was then taken to Europe—on the well-trodden "European tour" to make elite women forget and to rebuild strained social ties. That was a familial strategy often discussed in American literature of the era. Henry James, Edith Wharton, and others wrote works where the European tour was so employed—whisking away a rich but scandalous woman for the relief of the family and with hope of reform.

And indeed it was this that confronted Elizabeth, except that unlike the characters in James's and Wharton's novels, Elizabeth's scandal stemmed from her social convictions, rather than from rumors of a disadvantageous romantic attachment. That would come later.

Upon her return from Europe, Elizabeth's health was still faltering, so Mrs. Shultis took her to California, hoping to effect a cure. But I believe that Elizabeth's mother was exasperated by her daughter, so by the time that they reached California, the lady accepted Elizabeth's excuse regarding the benefits of the local climate and left her in the care of the Noels, who, though respectable, were nonetheless known Socialists.

It seems possible that Mrs. Shultis was relieved by the prospect of leaving her daughter far from Boston and in a place where she herself might be perceived as having discharged her duties as a mother, given the healthy benefit of the California weather. That, however, is speculation. What we know is that the lady left Elizabeth in Los Angeles, much to that girl's relief.

As soon as she was on her own, Elizabeth transferred her entire trust fund to P. D. Noel's bank and threw herself and her money into her newfound passion: the Mexican Cause. The girl had the financial resources to make a difference in the cause, and she was more than willing to use them. Elizabeth's education, age, marital status, character, independence, and money put her in a position of some ascendancy: "At first," Ethel recalled, "Elizabeth was shyly in the background, but she had taken fire, and before long she was leading all of us except, perhaps, Harriman. Even the incandescent John Murray, always ready to do battle for the downtrodden, learned to defer to her when she set her stubborn chin."[18]

Why was Elizabeth so drawn to the Mexican Cause? This question has at times been badly mangled. Thus, historian Lowell Blaisdell has characterized the American supporters of the Mexican Liberal Party in the following terms: "In addition to the usual radicals, there were a number of prosperous American donors, such as people misled by the innocuous-sounding name of the party (Mexican Liberal Party), ardent sympathizers of obvious underdogs, and cloistered radicals, some of whom were well-educated but maladjusted women."[19]

Certainly, Elizabeth, who was the Liberals' biggest donor in 1908 and 1909, was both well educated and maladjusted, at least with regard to her natal family, but her support for the Mexican Liberals was not the irrational act of an isolated hysteric, as Blaisdell implies. Though eccentric, Elizabeth's commitments had social roots. They were shared by an identifiable current.

The Women's Sensibility

In addition to the prisoners' compelling character, the Liberals' denunciation of Mexican slavery was a strong factor of attraction for the three women who were at the core of the American group.

Certainly, the connection between slave emancipation and feminine politicization was a central tenet for the Bostonian Elizabeth Trowbridge. Convinced of the need to seek a deeper unified meaning to life than what was upheld in dominant conventions, Elizabeth had earlier refused to be a member of the Church of England and cultivated a friendship with Theosophist Evangeline Adams instead.[20] The esoteric teachings of Theosophy were founded in the conviction that the universe as a whole has a ciphered, but coherent meaning and purpose, and indeed, Elizabeth was committed to the exploration of a panoply of interconnected philosophies concerned with human morality and freedom. Thus, in addition to being a Theosophist, she was a Socialist, a feminist, a defender of animals, a vegetarian, and even an amateur astrologist. Such combinations were not unusual for progressives of her generation.[21]

Indeed, the connection between the American feminist tradition and the fight against slavery in the Mexican Cause was anything but random or fortuitous. There was a deep historical connection between feminism and emancipation, from Harriet Beecher Stowe, Lucy Stone, and Susan B. Anthony forward. It is thus no coincidence that when Ricardo Flores Magón was in Leavenworth Penitentiary, where he died, one of the people who regularly inquired after him was Lucy Stone's daughter, Alice Stone Blackwell, an editor, author, and suffragist, who despite never having met Ricardo, supported his release and made special inquiries to the prison physician on his behalf: "I am interested in Ricardo Flores Magon, who is in prison under the Espionage Act," she wrote. "A friend of his in New York tells me that his health is seriously broken.... Will you kindly tell me just what the state of his health is, and much oblige, Miss Alice Stone Blackwell."[22]

Moreover, although Elizabeth's diet of reading and her concerns may not have found much reinforcement in Radcliffe's curriculum (the college was conservative in its approach to what constituted suitable reading for young ladies), students there were open to America's women writers, and the overall environment at Harvard was by no means devoid of radicals. Thus, just a few years after Elizabeth studied there, John Reed also majored in English and got involved in the Mexican Revolution (albeit a little later, in 1914). Reed went on famously to join the Russian Revolution and was a founder of the American Communist Party.

To my knowledge, no one has ever called Reed a maladjusted, overeducated hysteric. Elizabeth Trowbridge deserves the same courtesy. Moreover, the constellation of concerns that brought Elizabeth to the Mexican Cause applied just as powerfully to Frances Nacke Noel and to Ethel Duffy Turner. They were, in short, part of an identifiable trend (Figure 2.6).

Democracy in America

A final factor that drew the American circle to the Mexican Cause was their sense that basic American rights were being trampled. Elizabeth's decision to stay in California was clinched when Job Harriman persuaded her that Ricardo, Antonio, Librado, and Manuel

Figure 2.6 Frances Nacke Noel, suffragette (*on right*). Noel scrapbook, courtesy of the Huntington Library.

had been illegally detained by private Furlong detectives in the employ of the Mexican government. Thus, Ethel explained,

> Elizabeth, grounded in the faith that the Constitution of her country, with the Bill of Rights, guaranteed civil liberties to all without prejudice, was shocked to the bottom of her heart. When she heard, furthermore, that the Attorney General in Washington had telegraphed to authorities in California that the men in jail must be held at all costs, as they were "wanted in Mexico," that was the final turn of the screw. She would not go back to Boston. The Mexicans needed all the help they could get. She would stay in California and fight.[23]

Connected to this feeling of civic indignation was the comparison between Mexico and Russia. Russian writers—Gogol, Dostoyevsky, and Tolstoy—were influential in educated circles, and they wrote incisively about the relationship between family disintegration, individual character, and social movements. Tolstoy's *War and Peace* showed how the people and nature were the driving forces of history, and his subsequent work detailed how vacuous an "upright life"—as it was conventionally defined—really was. As Tolstoy matured, he became an inspiring example of renunciation and political courage.

In addition to their aesthetic influence, the Russians also had philosophical weight. Russian populism coincided on certain points with an ideological current that had been developing in the United States, a movement known as "Nationalism" that was at the root of the American Socialist Party. This current had as its motto "Production for use, not for profit." It was, in short, a communitarian movement, and that sort of political inclination had best been theorized by Peter Kropotkin, who went further than American Nationalists, into the realm of science and history, to shape a coherent cooperativist ideology. Harriman, Murray, Turner, Duffy, Trowbridge, and the Noels had all read and participated in this indigenous American tradition, and there was in this populist connection some common ground with the Mexican Liberals.

There was, finally, yet another way in which Russia influenced Elizabeth, Frances, and Ethel's proclivities to support the Mexican prisoners, and this was through current events. The 1905 revolution in Russia had publicized the brutal face of czarism: violent charges of Cossacks against workers in St. Petersburg, the persistence of near-slave conditions of the peasantry, the ample use of the Siberian wastelands for political dissidents, and the scapegoating of Jews subjected to pogroms. By 1905, the Russian regime was a paradigm of brutality, in vivid contrast with the work of an admired intelligentsia that had showed in sensitive detail that the true heroes of Russia's tragic history were its people.

Like the czar, Mexico's ancient autocrat surrounded himself with obsequious sycophants. His immediate circle bore some resemblance to Russia's decayed autocracy. Social conditions in the countryside paralleled those of Russia's serfs, and the Mexican Army's repression of strikes in Cananea and Rio Blanco in 1906 and 1907 recalled the Cossack charges against students and workers in St. Petersburg the year before. Prison conditions at Belem and San Juan de Ulúa were reminiscent of the czar's infamous dungeons, while territories on the Yucatán peninsula seemed to be a kind of tropical counterpart of Siberia. Finally, the Mexican Army itself was a kind of miniature and brown version of Russia's army, stocked with peasant conscripts, with the elite corps of *rurales* playing the part of the Cossacks (Figure 2.7). For all of these reasons, the comparison between the czar and Porfirio Díaz was a stock image in the pages of *Regeneración* and had indeed already been in use for some time even before then. Catarino Garza had deployed the comparison as far back as 1895, for instance.

But there was one aspect of the Mexican Cause that made it more attractive to this particular circle than the cause of the Russian Revolution, and this was that Mexico was next door to the United States, and U.S. capital was the key source of support for the Díaz autocracy. This fact was poignantly reflected in the imprisonment of the Mexican exiles. Russian radicals exiled in the United States were free to engage in efforts to emancipate their mother country. They were teeming in the tenements and coffee houses of Manhattan's Lower East Side, where they published their papers and organized support committees and political parties freely. But because of U.S. involvement in Mexico, the Mexicans were constantly harassed. Moreover, vested interests in Mexico led to heightened racism in the United States against Mexicans, whom American travelers to Mexico routinely represented as ungovernable except by a dictatorship.

This racial dimension was decried by Ricardo himself. Writing from prison in Arizona to his lover, María Brousse, he expressed

Figure 2.7 Mexican officers and recruits. Dialectical image: the moment of recruitment is a dangerous instant of freedom and play. Courtesy of the Bancroft Library, John Murray Papers.

skepticism regarding a Chicago organization for the protection of political refugees. In his view, the organization was bound to privilege support for Russian over Mexican, exiles: "The Chicago organization does not defend us. It has no other purpose than to defend the Russians; and we are poor Mexicans. We are revolutionaries and our ideals are very advanced, but we are Mexicans. That is our flaw. Our skin is not white, and not everyone is able to understand that underneath a dark skin there are nerves, there is heart, and there are brains."[24]

Although Ricardo was wrong in this particular instance, since the organization had been founded by John Murray with Mexicans specifically in mind, his suspicions were amply justified. Russian émigrés in the United States were well organized, with forceful and vocal leaders. In contrast, Ricardo and his group were in severe need of representation and help. "How many citizens of the United States know that we have political prisoners in this country just as in Russia?"[25] This was Elizabeth, writing indignantly for the American public. Ricardo spoke insufficient English to do public speaking. His brother Enrique, who spoke better English, was at that time insufficiently prominent for the role. The best-known Mexican public speakers supporting the cause in the United States were Lázaro Gutiérrez de Lara and, to a lesser degree, Manuel Sarabia, Fernando Palomares, and Anselmo Figueroa, but all told, the Mexican leaders were in need of spokespersons, translators, and American interlocutors. "Too much American money has gone to the defense of Russian or Polish refugees," wrote Elizabeth, "too many Americans have died for Cuba's liberties, for one to believe that the people of the United States desire to persecute these Mexicans who have broken none of our laws, and whose only offense is to oppose a tyranny worse than that of Persia itself."[26]

There was, in short, a real conjunction between the political paths of the American circle and the situation of the Mexican prisoners, from the politics of unionization to women's suffrage, from the protection of American liberties to the promotion of a kind of neo-Christian philosophy of selfless love. Describing the Mexican political prisoners, Elizabeth wrote that: "their personal privations were mentioned only in answer to persistent questioning. Their self-effacement is carried to an extreme."[27] She might as well have been writing about the American circle that she had just helped to found.

Figure 3.1 Coronel Teodoro Flores and
Margarita Magón. Flores is represented as a
man of the Republic. Portraits were costly
investments, and so photographic studios
were equipped with props designed to serve
as background and support for the subject's
aspirations. Courtesy of the Casa de
El Hijo del Ahuizote, Mexico City.

CHAPTER THREE

Hermanos Flores Magón

In addition to the various practical points of convergence between the Socialists' political programs and the Mexican Cause there was also much attraction to the magnetic personalities of the prisoners. Who were those men? What education did they have? In what ways did they stand apart from the general prejudice toward Mexicans that was current in the United States at the time? These questions can be explored in part by way of the story of the Flores Magón brothers themselves.

Class Origin

Jesús, Ricardo, and Enrique Flores Magón were the children of Colonel Teodoro Flores and Margarita Magón (Figure 3.1). Historians and hagiographers have often represented Teodoro as an Indian and Margarita as a mestiza.[1] Enrique, in his memoir, wrote of his family that they descended from Aztec conquerors of Oaxaca's upper Mazatec region and that Teodoro was the leading elder of his "tribe." It is worth looking closely at Enrique's account, because it reveals much about the ways in which ideals of purity bend facts to shape historical memory.

> "You should remember," Teodoro is supposed to have said to his three boys, "that we descend from a member of an Aztec military expedition. It was sent to Oaxaca by the Aztec emperor in order to collect tribute.... But we are Oaxaca natives nonetheless, because we were born there.
>
> "All the land around each of our villages belongs to the community. Every morning we all go out to work the land, except the sick, the invalids, the elderly, and women and children. Everyone who is able goes joyously, and uplifted by the thought that the work that each does is for the benefit of all.... *Each receives according to his needs.* There are

neither rich nor poor among us"—and he lifted a finger to emphasize this observation.

"Supposedly, I was the one who gave them orders," my father smiled, "because I was the *tata*. True, I was the chief. But I never gave orders or exerted coercive authority. I only gave advice and provided arbitration. We have no imposed authority. It is unnecessary, dear children. We have no judges, no jails, not even a single policeman. We live in peace, love and mutual esteem as friends and brothers."[2]

This fanciful story—parts lifted from Marx's idea of "primitive communism" and parts from B. Traven's novel *The White Rose*—suggests that Enrique was keen to promote an image of Indian nobility for his family, even despite a number of facts that were known to him. Claiming Aztec origins was a way of endowing Enrique with a genealogy that stood as an alternative to modern Mexican class hierarchy.

The members of the 1892 student movement, which included all three Flores Magón brothers, viewed the Aztecs as a flourishing and splendorous empire where "art and artists, science, literature, and industry shone everywhere." The oppressive regimes that followed degraded all of that, so that contemporary Indians could barely "count to 100, pray an Our Father—often only in their language or dialect, because they speak no Spanish—and weave a rough sack in which to wrap their bodies."[3] Enrique's fantasy of his family as being descendants of Aztec warriors whose dignity had been preserved in the distant mountains of Oaxaca was a way of imagining his lineage as an alternative source of national authority.

But Teodoro Flores would not have been considered an Indian during the time in which he lived. He was literate and wrote Spanish very competently, as regards not only orthography and grammar, but also penmanship. Teodoro was, in short, well schooled, and that was itself the harshest dividing line between being "Indian" and being "civilized" in the nineteenth century. Matías Romero published a compilation of Oaxaca statistics for 1883, which was a more prosperous time than the 1850s, when Teodoro was growing up. But even then, the District of Teotitlán had only six, with one teacher in each and a grand total of only 425 students in a population of over twenty-seven thousand.[4] Moreover, the quality of Teodoro's writing strongly suggests that he had education beyond the basics provided in Teotitlán's schools, probably education he received in the state capital.

Matías Romero also calculated the cost of Indian labor in the region by way of a study of the yearly material needs of an Indian family. Predictably, these did not include a single cent spent on education, books, paper, or pencils. Moreover, the Indians' dressing needs did not coincide with Teodoro's apparel. In short, and to repeat: by the standards of his day, Teodoro was not an Indian.

It is true, though, that Teodoro was a leader in his natal region, so the description of him as a *tata*, or elder, may not have been far off the mark: Teodoro also owned two ranches, one of them large enough to be called a hacienda, and though they seem not to have been all that lucrative, they were neither communally owned nor communally worked. In 1883, there were only six ranches in the entire Teotitlán district.[5]

In other words, there was a class line that elevated Teodoro Flores above the Mazatec-speaking peasants of his native Mazatlán, Oaxaca. This distinction was a source of both pride and discomfort for Enrique (and possibly for Ricardo, as well, though we do not know this). The easiest way to resolve his ambivalence was to claim that Teodoro's distinction had remote Aztec origins. To an anarchistic communist such as Enrique Flores Magón, this seemed more noble than to say that Teodoro was simply a member of Oaxaca's provincial elite. Above all, Enrique wanted to be a *hijo del pueblo*, a son of the people.

It is for that reason that Enrique insisted on invoking such a perfect picture of communitarian harmony and of his father as a guiding elder in a community of equals. But despite its stunning beauty, the village and region that Colonel Flores came from was not so very harmonious. Indeed, acrid internal divisions are at the very heart of Teodoro's story, and they play a key part of the Flores Magón family history. It is not insignificant that Enrique chose to leave those stories out of his memoir.

During the war against the French intervention (1862–1867), the wife, father, and mother-in-law of Captain Teodoro Flores were killed by pro-Imperialist militias from his own village. This is how Teodoro's military commander, General Pérez Figueroa, reported the incident:

> On August 8, 1865, Commander Teodoro Flores had an encounter on the road to Huautla. The traitors ambushed him from an advantageous position in order to take the arms that he was transporting, but they

41

were dispersed, and in order to take their revenge, they went to the commander's ranch to murder his family, and they shot and killed his father, his mother-in-law, and his wife, and they ransacked the place, leaving the commander in poverty and with no papers. This horrible event took place...while Commander Flores, after his triumph, was proceeding on his march to Huautla.[6]

In addition to losing such dear family members, Teodoro's house was burned down, and with it, his documents, including proof of the dates of his entry into and promotion in the various military corps to which he belonged. Later in life, Teodoro would spend time and money trying to get his seniority recognized and full pension paid.

Teodoro's first military appointment was as second lieutenant (*subteniente*) of the National Guard in 1859, and he was also commander of a volunteer force that he had put together in the Sierra de Teotitlán. The fact that he began his military career with an officer's rank again confirms that Teodoro was a member of a middling or higher class in his remote and poor region. On the other hand, the fact that he was ratified as commander of a volunteer militia suggests that Teodoro was also a popular leader. Though his leadership was sanctioned by the army, it did not emanate exclusively from it, but rather from his ability to amass a corps of volunteers among his *paisanos*.

In 1860, the *jefe político* of Teotitlán promoted Teodoro to first lieutenant of the National Guard. One year later, he was made captain by the state governor and asked to form two companies from his native Mazatlán in order to meet the foreign invasion that was then being prepared. Captain Flores accomplished the task and attached himself and his militia to the command of General Luis Pérez Figueroa. In 1864, General Figueroa named Flores *jefe de la línea* of Oaxaca State's Sierra Norte and military commander of the Cantón of Huehuetlán. Those were war years. The Liberals were fighting French Imperialist and Mexican Conservative forces that had crowned Maximilian of Hapsburg emperor. In 1865, Flores was put in charge of a full battalion, which came to be known informally as the Batallón Flores.[7] In 1867, when the Liberals finally defeated the French and Conservative forces, President Benito Juárez ratified Captain Flores's appointment, but because of the raid on his home, Teodoro Flores was still paperless and impoverished.

Legitimacy

There is a second important omission in Enrique's memoir: Teodoro Flores did not have three children—he had five. The two who are rarely mentioned, Aniceto and Paula, were offspring from Teodoro's first marriage. The three Flores Magón brothers had, in short, two half siblings on their father's side.

We don't know the dates of birth of Aniceto and Paula Flores or even the name of Teodoro's first wife. Both Enrique Flores Magón and historian Jacinto Barrera Bassols say that Teodoro and Margarita met during the Imperialist Army's siege of the city of Puebla in 1863. If they did, then Teodoro and Margarita met while Teodoro still had a wife living back in Teotitlán del Camino, Oaxaca.

Here again, the memories of an aged Enrique provide a telling (and entertaining) counterpoint to the documentary record: "Margarita Magón, a twenty-two-year-old *criolla*, had a mane of light brown hair that almost touched the floor, a rose-and-milk complexion, and beautiful soft eyes. Teodoro, for his part, was thirty-four, straight as a pine, six feet tall, and enormously powerful. 'This is a *man*'—Margarita said to herself. And her heart went to him."[8] In Enrique's story, Margarita Magón, the beautiful señorita, meets the dashing Captain Flores in the heat of the combat for the city of Puebla—during the famous battle of May 5, which the Mexicans won. Margarita also risks her life to encourage Captain Flores's men: "'Since I can't serve as a soldier,' she yelled, 'the least that I can do is to encourage our heroic defenders. You always lead your men on their attacks on the trenches—you never linger behind, like some commanders. So then why shouldn't I, too, take risks for the sacred cause of liberty?'"[9] The couple was supposed to have married after that epic encounter and had their three children: Jesús, Ricardo, and Enrique.

But several uncomfortable facts are excised from this memory, and it must be said that they seem not to have been memorialized by Ricardo, either. The first is that Teodoro Flores was still married in 1863, when he and Margarita are supposed to have fallen in love. The second is that he had two children, Aniceto and Paula, who were also alive and well then. The third is that possibly because of Teodoro's marital status, Margarita and Teodoro were in fact not married, so that Jesús, Ricardo, and Enrique were registered as the natural children of a common-law union.

43

Finally, the last oft-omitted item is that Margarita was a widow when she met Teodoro. She had been married to a Mr. Perea, and she had two children by that marriage, Enrique and Josefa Perea Magón. [10] We do not know who raised Enrique and Josefa Perea once Margarita went to live with Teodoro Flores, but those two children lived and were probably raised either by Margarita's Puebla family or by the Pereas.

Many of these facts can be ascertained from documents that were among the Flores Magón family papers, and given Enrique's meticulous care of the family documents, it seems likely that his omissions in his memoir were deliberate. In an earlier biographical interview, Enrique had expressed concern with restricting who was legitimately entitled to the Flores Magón family name and legacy: "Beware of the counterfeits!" Enrique warned. "The last name of Flores Magón is productive in the hands of people with no scruples."[11] This concern with false Flores Magón heirs may have led Enrique to omit the existence of two half siblings on the Flores side and another two on the Magón side, although this motivation strikes me as unlikely, in particular because these half siblings are also generally missing from Ricardo's accounts, and Ricardo died before anyone would dream of "cashing in" on his last name.

The explanation, I think, lies elsewhere. It is not difficult to speculate about the motive for discretion regarding a set of facts with the potential for causing polemical damage. Interestingly, in the first era of *Regeneración* (1900–1901), Jesús and Ricardo Flores Magón published articles arguing for the right to keep birth-status information private in Mexico City.[12] Though those articles were not written to protect the brothers' own private information, which would not have been publicized by the Mexico City law that they criticized, it is still interesting that they had strong feelings on the advisability of keeping birth status confidential.

Elsewhere, Ricardo also pointed out that in Mexican constitutional law, free unions had the same legal status as church marriages: "The law does not forbid unwedded unions [*mancebía*]. It tolerates them, just as it tolerates Catholic marriages.... Unwedded unions may be condemned on moral grounds, but not on legal grounds."[13]

But despite the young men's tacit defense of their parents' matrimonial status, it is difficult to be sure about the psychological effect on them of the existence of prior marriages for both parents, the existence of half siblings on both sides, and the fact that these other children were not raised within their family. Enrique's exalted celebration of his parents as a romantic couple and all three brothers' deep commitment to romantic love may have been a way of sublimating the guilt that came along with the exclusion of their half siblings from their family lives. But this is speculation.

The young men's attitudes toward their maternal half siblings are also intriguing, because the only mention by them that I have been able to track is in Ricardo's and Enrique's 1912 prison records at McNeil Island, Washington, where they acknowledge having one sister, Margarita's daughter, Josefa, who is listed as being four years older than Jesús and as living in the same address as Ricardo's consort, María Brousse, in Los Angeles.[14] Enrique and Ricardo thus shared at least one brief portion of their adult lives with one of these half siblings, and that makes the brothers' discretion about their complex family structure even more difficult to interpret.

What is certain, in any case, is that the Flores Magón brothers were legally "natural children"—*hijos naturales*: that is, "illegitimate." Thus, Ricardo Flores Magón's birth certificate reads:

> In the town of San Antonio Eloxochitlan on September 22, 1873 at 9AM there came before me the citizen Teodoro Flores, of forty-four years of age, resident and originary of Mazatlán, widower and agriculturalist, who asked, in accordance with the law, for registration of the birth of a boy whom he assures is his illegitimate child [*hijo natural*] born of Margarita Magón Grajales, widow, in his home on the 16th of this month."[15]

Teodoro appears to have courted and possibly to have lived with Margarita Magón while he was still married back in Teotitlán, but if that was in fact the case, the situation was of short duration: Teodoro and Margarita met in Puebla in 1863, and Teodoro's wife and family were massacred in August 1865. Moreover, all of this occurred in conditions of war and while Teodoro was involved in military actions. Even if they fell in love in 1863, it is unlikely that Teodoro and Margarita could have lived a settled life in those early years.

The departure of Teodoro, Margarita, and their three children from Oaxaca to Mexico City is usually explained with reference to Margarita's desire to see her children educated.[16] There were, however, additional factors. One of these was the Tuxtepec Revolution

(1876) that brought Porfirio Díaz into power. Teodoro had supported his fellow countryman (Díaz) in that venture, and he may have judged it a good idea to move to Mexico City under the circumstances. Teodoro was in fact promoted from captain to lieutenant colonel in recognition of his support of the Tuxtepec rebellion. This, again, is discreetly underplayed in Enrique's memoir.

But there may also have been complicated sentiments on Margarita's part with regard to Teodoro's two children and to the fact that Margarita herself had abandoned her own two children by her previous marriage, whether she did so willfully or was forced to do so. It is possible that Margarita saw a move to Mexico City as a chance for a fresh start for the new family. Judging from Teodoro's relative lack of financial success in Mexico City, it would seem that Margarita positively desired to make her family home in the capital, rather than in Teodoro's home in Teotitlán del Camino.

Margarita's identity is difficult to track, even to this day, so her motivations for preferring to be in Mexico City are unclear. She came from an urban, middle-class background—that, at least, is certain. According to Barrera Bassols, Margarita was born in Puebla; her father was Spanish and a skilled artisan (glasswork); her mother was an Indian.[17] Although it is always worth being skeptical of any claim of Indian identity in the case of the Flores Magóns, still, it seems plausible that Margarita was indeed a mestiza. In Mexican society of the time, she would have been considered a *criolla*, that is, as nonindigenous, for not only was she white and the daughter of a Spaniard, but she could also read and write, and her handwriting and spelling, though not as good as Teodoro's, demonstrated what was then a high level of education in a woman. An inscribed 1884 photograph of Margarita's brother, Justo Magón, confirms the image that hers was an urban, middle-class birth family (Figure 3.2).

But though we have a sense of the class and ethnic origins of the lady, we know nothing of her marriage to Mr. Perea, or how her first husband died, or what became of Enrique and Josefa Perea Magón. Did Margarita abandon those two children? We do not know. The fact that she named her youngest son in her second marriage Enrique—in other words, that she had two sons named Enrique—suggests that she felt a sense of loss with regard to her two original children and that her family with Teodoro was in some way restitution for those whom she had lost. If Margarita's first-born,

Figure 3.2 Justo Magón. Courtesy of the Casa de El Hijo del Ahuizote, Mexico City.

Enrique, had died young, which is a possibility, the feeling that her new family was restitution for the old would have been even keener.

Had the Magón or Perea families shunned Margarita for falling in love with Teodoro and taken her children from her? It is possible. Did Teodoro compel her to leave her children behind to accompany him back to his home in Oaxaca? That is also possible—though unlikely, since the relationship between Teodoro and Margarita appears to have been a very good one. Did Margarita voluntarily leave her two children to be raised in her family home or in the home of her in-laws? That is a third possibility.

It is certain that Margarita went to live in Teodoro's home without them. Jesús, Ricardo, and Enrique were all born in Eloxochitlan, and the nuclear family left for Mexico City right after the triumph of the Tuxtepec Revolution, in 1877, while Aniceto Flores, Teodoro's eldest, remained in Teotitlán and was left in charge of administering the family interests there. In 1877, Aniceto acted on his father's behalf in a lawsuit against José Candelario,

> resident of Mazatlan, trying to promote a civil law suit against him for damages caused by the robbery and murder of his family, which he committed together with others at his father's ranch on the edge of Mazatlan in the year of 1865. At the preliminary hearing, the aforementioned person [José Candelario] agreed to cede to him [unreadable extension

47

of a property] of *ganado menor y mayor* and in addition some farm land measuring four *maquilas de sembradura* on the edges of Mazatlan, with the properties of José Ruperto Cid on one side, and the lands of Mazatlan on the other.[18]

In short, the man who had killed Teodoro's wife and family was a neighbor from his same village. In compensation for those damages and because the Conservatives had lost their war, José Candelario "voluntarily" offered Aniceto, who acted on his father's behalf, a cattle-and-sheep ranch and some agricultural land, all of which had boundaries with the communal lands of Mazatlán itself. Given the timing of this transaction, a full eleven years after the end of the war but scarcely months after the triumph at Tuxtepec, and given Teodoro's promotion to colonel, it is likely that José Candelario's "voluntary concession" was only technically voluntary.

In any case, though, the properties known as the Hacienda de Tres Cabezas and La Laguna may not have been very lucrative, given the distances to markets, and they were certainly not communal, as Enrique claimed, nor did they have ancestral origins dating back to "time immemorial." Rather, they were given to Teodoro in recompense for war damages inflicted in 1865, probably because Teodoro's promotion after the 1876 ascent of Porfirio Díaz made it advisable for his neighbors to placate him.

Memory and Sublimation

But if Enrique's vision of the Indian community and of his parents' story was idealized, it nonetheless provides useful clues to the family's background. Indeed, it would be a mistake to discard the memories as simple lies.

Teodoro Flores had sacrificed his family for his country—there was no more exalted act than this—but he also had failed to defend his family. Teodoro defended the law and the sacred Constitution of 1857, but he also participated in the 1876 uprising at Tuxtepec to instate Porfirio Díaz as president against the legally reelected President Sebastián Lerdo de Tejada. He was a hero of resistance to the French intervention, but he received his last promotion, from captain to lieutenant colonel, because of his support for Díaz. Teodoro had believed in the Tuxtepec Revolution, but he had later been forgotten by the Díaz government and was not given a full pension for his sacrifices in the military. He had lost his wife, father, and mother-in-law in war, but he had also found a new love before their death.

Always wishing to preserve one aspect of his father's legacy and to bury the other, Enrique composed a dramatic final death-bed scene for his father. In it, Teodoro declared his unfailing love to Margarita, saying to her: "I could have given you a beautiful house and good clothes. Everything that money can buy. But I could not have done that without giving up my character." And then, turning to his three sons, he declares:

> "Do not allow the tyrant to strip you of your manhood! Always remember that you are the sons of a man who served Benito Juárez honorably, in the sacred cause of the people's liberty."
>
> "Remember!" His voice resounded, and then he fell back, dead.[19]

The injunction for his sons to remember seems to have been taken by Enrique to signify that they should work to vindicate injustices from the past, and this meant forgetting, even sometimes deliberately obliterating, facts that might distract from the main points of vindication. Thus, Enrique crossed out the evidence of Porfirio Díaz's patronage of his father in the two photographs that the general bestowed upon his loyal subordinate (Figures 3.3 and 3.4), and after the revolution, Enrique conveniently skipped over the fact that his father had actually supported Díaz in the 1876 revolt that brought Díaz to power.

Margarita, for her part, was remembered by her boys as a protecting angel and as a wife who had doted on her husband and who was, in turn, honored by him. By all accounts, these recollections were true to the facts, but phantoms of Margarita and Teodoro's earlier relationships and of their abandoned children were also cast aside with the insistent assertion of complete exclusivity of maternal and spousal dedication.

The Flores Magón children's tendency to exalt their parents' love match may have been all the more vehement because Teodoro and Margarita were not married and Teodoro had suffered his children being registered as "natural sons," though it is equally clear that the boys were raised with a strong moral education that exalted every sort of virtue, including marital love. So, for instance, we still have Enrique's youthful (1895) "Definiciones y Pensamientos" in which he wrote down moralistic adages with his finest penmanship, defining

Figure 3.3 Photo of Díaz with crossed-out inscription to Teodoro Flores in the back. Courtesy of the Casa de El Hijo del Ahuizote, Mexico City.

Figure 3.4 Second inscribed Díaz portrait with the inscription crossed out. Courtesy of the Casa de El Hijo del Ahuizote, Mexico City.

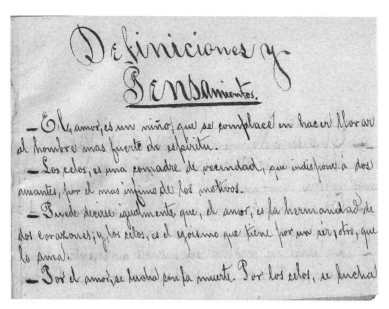

Figure 3.5 "Definiciones y Pensamientos" from Enrique's boyhood, Mexico City, August 3, 1895. The schoolboy's moralism is continuous with his elaborate penmanship. Each sentiment is carefully defined. Courtesy of the Casa de El Hijo del Ahuizote, Mexico City.

love, jealousy, wisdom in choosing marriage partners, greed, pride, and so on (Figure 3.5).[20]

Whatever the boys' attitude was toward their half siblings, it was clear that there was at the very least a division of labor between them: Aniceto Flores ran, controlled, and eventually seems to have inherited the Hacienda de Tres Cabezas and La Laguna. He stood as a kind of local heir of Teodoro Flores, while the three Flores Magón brothers went to Mexico City, gained a first-rate education, studied law, and had exclusive rights to their mother. One group of Flores children thus remained with the land, and the other was offered to the law.

CHAPTER FOUR

The Generation of 1892

Chancletismo intelectual

Just as the Flores Magón brothers made much of the fact that they were from Oaxaca, most other Liberals claimed ties to one Mexican province or another. A substantial contingent was from San Luis Potosí—indeed, the movement got started there and in Mexico City. Liberals Camilo Arriaga, Juan and Manuel Sarabia, Librado Rivera, Antonio Díaz Soto y Gama, and Filomeno Mata were all from San Luis Potosí. Santiago de la Hoz was from Veracruz; Alfonso Cravioto from Hidalgo; Antonio, Andrea, and Teresa Villarreal were from Lampazos, while Lázaro Gutiérrez de Lara was from nearby Monterrey; Juana B. Gutiérrez de Mendoza was from Durango...but the kernel of Liberals that came together around 1901 can be understood better in generational rather than in geographical terms. Although the approach has some limits, since the founding group was rather heterogeneous, it is nonetheless helpful to think of them as being spearheaded by the Generation of 1892.

The year 1892 was a watershed for Mexico's intellectual and political classes. It was the year when a political clique of known as the *científicos* came into their own as Díaz's technocratic and financial elite, while a second, younger, generation—Ricardo's generation—was first confronted with a wall and a ceiling that barred them from political and social advancement. Dialogue between these two generations was limited. They knew one another, but they had very different prospects. Thus, writers in the Generation of 1892 crowed: "Our youth knows that it can find nothing to emulate or to glorify in the generation that rules today."[1]

The significance of this rift was not apparent to the older generation until it was too late. After Díaz's death, Francisco Bulnes, a prominent member of the *científico* establishment, wrote a book about him. The Mexican Revolution was still raging, and Bulnes wrote from deprivation and exile in Cuba. He identified lack of generational turnover and Díaz's corruption of the intellectual class as core causes of the regime's cataclysmic finale.

Bulnes's analysis laid bare the subtle governing principles of the Díaz system, which relied extensively on the practice of governing for one's friends and on keeping men of talent on a short leash. At the apex, the dictator's personal command was a sacrosanct principle. In his characteristically colorful language, Bulnes wrote that after the 1886 assassination of presidential hopeful General Trinidad García de la Cadena, "being called a presidential candidate was feared more than being accused of parricide, arson, or treason."[2]

Once his own position became untouchable, Díaz worked to check all autonomous forms of power, most particularly those based on intellectual merit and the independence of the press. According to Bulnes, Díaz degraded men of intellectual talent, using public employment as his weapon.

> He strived to attract men of great talent because he feared them. As a result, they were also disagreeable to him, so he placed them in second- or third-rank positions, beneath nonentities, so that the public would not notice them. Díaz's system was to provide intellectuals with congressional posts that were under check [*curul con freno*], naming them the substitute deputies of military men and then offering them, in addition, a professor's salary and some other government commission so that they could live comfortably, but not achieve independence by way of their private fortunes, either.[3]

All of this was true, but from the vantage point of a younger generation, the picture looked quite different (Figure 4.1). Prominent intellectuals of Bulnes's age had managed to get the combination of posts that he described: the compromised congressional post, together with the poorly paid, but prestigious teaching position in the university, combined with a special governmental commission, and so on, a combination that allowed them to live very well indeed. Insecurely, perhaps, without the share of influence and independence that was their proper due, certainly, but live well they did, and they received honors and awards that were scarcely available to Ricardo's generation. In the specific case of Bulnes, it was not until he was

Figure 4.1 Jesús, Ricardo, and Enrique Flores Magón. Courtesy of the Casa del Hijo del Ahuizote, Mexico City.

exiled to Cuba that he experienced living conditions comparable to those that the Flores Magón family experienced in Mexico City during the so-called golden years of the *pax porfiriana*, the 1890s.

Whereas in his early twenties Bulnes was already a favorite of President Sebastián Lerdo de Tejada and had been sent on interesting governmental missions; whereas at that same age fellow *científico* José Yves Limantour was a professor at the Escuela Nacional Preparatoria and a rising star in the Ministry of Foreign Relations; and whereas Justo Sierra was a poet laureate, member of congress, and director of an influential newspaper, Ricardo Flores Magón, who was arguably their peer in sheer intellectual ability, had a brother in prison and a mother who had been compelled to move to an impoverished Mexico City neighborhood while he himself held a string of low-level positions in various Mexico City newspapers, not to mention having had to do a brief, but potentially stigmatizing stint as domestic servant.[4]

Lázaro Gutiérrez de Lara, for his part, did not undergo quite such hard times, but he still graduated from Law School only in 1898, a full ten years after his initial enrollment. This protracted period of study contrasted with the meteoric rise of the generation that was in power. Whereas Lázaro graduated at twenty-eight, by that age, the principal members of the *científico* generation had long ascended to national prominence. Lázaro's was a generation of students stringing out long careers before graduation and holding odd jobs while their families eked out an insecure living.

As far as jobs went, Lázaro fared somewhat better than Ricardo. "After my expulsion from school," he wrote, "I served variously as a clerk in the Military Court of the capital, as a student in the diplomatic school in the Department of Foreign Relations, and as a judge in the city of Parral, Chihuahua."[5] Nevertheless, these jobs were still in low-to-middling echelons of government bureaucracy, and Lázaro ended up with a position—provincial judge—that proved to be morally untenable. Given the prominence of his family name—Lázaro's great-grandfather had been a leader of Mexico's struggle for independence and governor of Texas—this career trajectory cannot be described as resoundingly successful.

And yet, despite the difficulties faced by the young generation, Bulnes did not present them with a sympathetic eye. To him, they were demagogues: ferocious, hungry, and without scruples. Bulnes did, however, identify them as the true authors of the Mexican Revolution of 1910, a claim that he explained thus: the intellectuals agitated the masses, because hunger agitated the intellectuals.[6]

Nodding to their doubly proletarianized character (hungry demagogues), Bulnes dubbed the authors of Mexico's revolution "sandal-wearing intellectuals" (*intelectuales chancletudos*). The sartorial reference is significant, since it underlined the fact that these "mongrels" were half aristocrat, half vagabond: "General Díaz used a Judaic sentence to justify the existence of these Apaches of the intellect [*apachería mental*]: 'a dog with a bone in its mouth can't bite or bark.' But the prince incurred a serious error when he equated the dog, which is the gentlemanly animal par excellence—noble, loyal, passionate, and sincerely affectionate—with the denizens of gambling houses and taverns that are the demagogues."[7]

Bulnes argued that the multiplication of this class of "demagogues" was a direct result of Díaz's selfish policies: he used government employment to degrade the noble virtue of the intellectual while training people for jobs that could exist only in an industrial setting. The Mexican economy was built on agriculture and mining, so Porfirian progress produced cohorts of useless intellectuals, hungry *intelectuales chancletudos* who knew only how to agitate.

The Generation of 1892

Though there was some truth in these conclusions, Bulnes's critique of revolutionary intellectuals was shortsighted, since it was written long after the damage was done. The generation of underemployed intellectuals first came into public view in 1892, more than twenty years before Bulnes wrote his book, and it burst onto the scene with open disdain for the generation of Porfirio Díaz's Tuxtepec Revolution, which it portrayed as decrepit and lacking in moral authority: "Tuxtepec is a sick ward of politicians."[8] Establishment politicians put on airs, yet its judges were corrupt and ministers subservient, while congressmen slept through their sessions.[9]

Porfirio Díaz's third consecutive reelection occurred in 1892. There was widely shared understanding that this reelection signaled Díaz's perpetuation in office, now unambiguously as dictator. It was also a year of widespread rural unrest. Peasant alliances with local landowners were frayed or severed, because landlords now tended to align themselves with the central government in order to make a concerted push to build up their fortunes in a budding export economy that was being made possible by the railroads. Building these fortunes involved terminating long-term rental and sharecropping agreements, shutting down access to communal resources such as pastures and forests, extending landholdings, and exploiting peasants as laborers, rather than as tenants or sharecroppers. The new arrangement also led to rising land prices and to higher taxes for peasants and ranchers.

In other words, 1892 was a year in which the dictatorship was consolidated while its social implications hardened, particularly for the peasantry. In a few years, things would get worse for artisans, too. Class conflict was starting to take shape.

In Mexico City, it was the year in which students organized to protest Díaz's reelection. Jesús, Ricardo, and even the fifteen-year-old Enrique Flores Magón were involved, as was Lázaro Gutiérrez de Lara, along with a number of other future radicals. The Escuela Nacional de Jurisprudencia, where Jesús, Ricardo, and Lázaro studied, was one center of agitation. On April 4, its director, Justino Benítez, banned students from gathering on the patio of the school, while government officials called on students to join pro-Díaz reelection forces. But the pressure had a contrary effect: on April 7, students came together in the Alameda park to begin the movement against reelection and then congregated outside the offices of two newspapers that had shown independence with respect to Porfirio Díaz—*El Monitor Republicano* and *El Hijo del Ahuizote.*

On April 24, the students founded the Comité de Estudiantes Antirreeleccionistas. By then, the movement had become sufficiently loud for the government to tighten the screws. Joaquín Baranda, the minister of justice and public instruction, banned political meetings in educational facilities, and Díaz issued private instructions to his governors to be wary of student movements in the provincial capitals. These instructions were carried out, but in Mexico City, the politicization of the student body increased.[10]

By May 1, the movement had gathered enough steam for the government to send the police to tear down anti-reelectionist signs that the students had put up all over the city.[11] Officials also spurred students at Mexico City's College of Mining to create a committee supporting Díaz's reelection that might be used to provide an image of complementary and opposed political leanings in the student body. This was done, but the committee garnered only nine members.[12] Meanwhile, the pro-Díaz press decried student unruliness and implied numerical symmetry between the adherents of the movements supporting and opposing reelection while painting the progovernment students as more sober and more fair-minded.[13]

Student ferment burst into public protest on May 15 with a rally that began at the tomb of President Benito Juárez and swelled as it moved to the city center, where students clashed with the police. A group of students tried to ring the bells of the cathedral, crying "Death to Centralism!" "Down with Reelection!" and "Long Live No Reelection!" They were arrested for forcing their way in.

The rally at Juárez's tomb is an early example of a political tactic that would become routine. The 1892 student rallies were among the first to try to steal the cult of the nation's heroes from Díaz's grip. Francisco Bulnes complained about that strategy, too: "Juárez was made into a divinity not because the sandal-wearing intellectuals believed in his glories as a magician or in his celestial essence, but simply to humiliate Díaz—all the while still drawing salaries from Díaz. Some people called July 18 the Day of the *Juarazo* against Díaz."[14]

The politics of appropriation of founding fathers was not confined to the preeminent figure of Juárez, either. A few days prior to the rally at Juárez's tomb, student leader Antonio Rivera concluded his speech by inviting everyone to accompany him to the monument to Miguel Hidalgo in order to "deposit a humble offering of admiration and of gratitude." The opposition paper *El Diario del Hogar* described the resulting procession in glowing terms: "From Campo Florido, the students and workers advanced in compact files, two by two, in orderly fashion and possessed by noble sentiments, these seven or eight hundred patriots crossed the city. They went to call forth the shades of our liberators, now that our rights expire on the altars of ambition."[15]

On the next day a second rally came together at the Alameda. That demonstration was suppressed by the police, though the dispersed students continued to rally in Santa Anita and in other working-class neighborhoods. Finally, on May 17, a third consecutive rally was held, this time inside the cloister of the Escuela Nacional Preparatoria, with small groups setting up flash demonstrations in various parts of the city, but police and military repression grew much stronger, and twenty-six leaders of the movement were detained. The *Monitor Republicano* and the *Hijo del Ahuizote*, which had supported the students, were temporarily shut down.

Ricardo Flores Magón had chosen that very day to give his first public speech:

> I had just begun to make a speech protesting against the dictatorship when the barrels of a couple of cocked revolvers touched my chest, ready to go off at my slightest move, thus cutting off my first attempt at public speaking. Surrounded by henchmen, I was taken to the roof terrace of the Municipal Palace, where I found a dozen comrades from the various schools who had also been detained.[16]

Many students were held temporarily in police precincts; others were expelled. The mounted police also shot into the crowd. The number of demonstrators killed or wounded is not known (Figure 4.2).[17]

The effect of this repression was palpable and generated sympathies for students that probably saved many lives. "The news of the students' arrest and their probable late-night execution struck everyone like an electric current," Ricardo recalled.[18]

In one of his final letters, from prison in Leavenworth, Ricardo still gave pride of place to this experience in his formation as a militant. "Did I ever tell you that on May 16, 1892, an indignant mob saved me and another seventy students from being shot? The crowd threatened

Figure 4.2 José Guadalupe Posada, "Continuación de las manifestaciones anti-reeleccionistas," in *Gaceta Callejera*, undated (May or early June, 1892).

to attack Mexico City's Municipal Palace, where we were being held as a result of our demonstration against the dictatorship. That was my first experience in the struggle."[19] But the student movement had been effectively repressed, and Díaz was reelected without a hitch.

The riots did not get much play outside of Mexico City. The student movement failed to forge effective alliances with the peasant uprisings that were raging at the time. It is likely that Mexico City's students were unaware of many of these, and when they were aware, they lacked effective ties with them in any case. At the same time, the city's support for the students, the hardened system of social exclusion that followed the repression of the peasant uprisings, and the students' own experiences with raw repression convinced many of the members of the Generation of 1892 that they were up against a wall.

First Taste

Jesús and Ricardo Flores Magón were arrested at the May 17 rally and then released. The movement was snuffed out. Peace in continuity seemed guaranteed. Nonetheless, there were a few aftershocks, and it was around those that the Flores Magón family would get its first taste of the longer-term hardships derived from political agitation, following the adrenaline rush of political rallies.

Late in October 1892, federal troops finally vanquished the sturdy peasant rebels of the town of Tomochic, in Chihuahua. That was only one of many local revolts that had been crushed in the year, but

59

with a difference: Tomochic made a deep mark on Mexican public consciousness. It achieved that through channels that were being developed by the students in the Generation of 1892.

On February 1, a group that included Jesús Flores Magón had founded a newspaper, *El Demócrata*, and a little over one month later, it began publishing a series of articles on the massacre at Tomochic. Their author, Heriberto Frías, had witnessed the events as a young army officer and published the pieces anonymously. Moreover, during the weeks in which it was publishing the Tomochic articles, *El Demócrata* announced that it would soon move on to narrate the "terrible devastations" and the "unheard-of assassinations" that the soldiery had wrought on another rebel population, at Papantla, Veracruz.[20] A couple of weeks later, the students announced the start of yet another rebellion, at Temósochic, Chihuahua, and promised to send a reporter to cover it.[21]

The Díaz government was sensitive to preempting connections between rural uprisings and urban discontent, and all the more so when the link included army personnel, as it did in the case of Heriberto Frías. So it was quick to react. Though *El Demócrata* was at first allowed to continue publication, its editors, Joaquín Clausell and Querido Moheno, and its owner, Francisco Blanco, were thrown into Belem Prison in March. Early in April, Minister of Education Joaquín Baranda laid out strict ordinances regarding activism in the national schools, ordering police presence outside the schools and granting wide authority to combat student immorality. Student insubordination would be met with expulsion, and the notion of "insubordination" explicitly included attacks by students in the press.[22] On April 26, accusations of libel were brought against *El Demócrata*. The paper was closed down, and its remaining staff members were imprisoned. Jesús Flores Magón was among them.

Jesús spent around nine months in Belem Prison. For the Flores Magón family, his detention could hardly have come at a worse time. The boys' father, Teodoro, had died on April 22, that is, barely four days before Jesús was taken to jail, and the family now depended on Jesús for its upkeep. Ricardo, who was eighteen, was unemployed.[23] Enrique, who had just turned sixteen, was still in school. To make matters worse, barely one month after Teodoro's death, with Jesús in prison, the army general and *compadre* who had leased the Flores family home to Teodoro decided to terminate the long-standing arrangement and asked Margarita to vacate the house.[24] Whether the general did this out of disgust for Jesús's anti-Porfirian politics or simply because he felt no obligation toward the family after Teodoro's death is uncertain.

The fact was that Jesús's confinement compelled the family to move to a poorer neighborhood and pushed Ricardo urgently into the labor market in the midst of the family's mourning and during the economic crisis of 1890–1893. It was during this time that Ricardo did his brief stint as a domestic worker while Jesús scrambled among his contacts to find Ricardo something better.

One valuable source on the family's experience of Jesús's imprisonment is a set of undated messages exchanged between Margarita and Jesús while the latter was in Belem Prison (Figures 4.3 and 4.4). Though they are barely fragments, these missives help round out a picture of the effects of repression on the Flores Magón family.[25]

The messages have been arranged in logical order by Casa de El Hijo del Ahuizote curator Hugo Sánchez Mavil, beginning with a note from Jesús informing his mother that he and the other students are being held in the Patio de los Encausados and asking her to bring him his personal effects. In the course of the correspondence, Jesús asks his mother to bring his father's cot, fresh clothes, newspapers (*El Hijo del Ahuizote*), and, in what seems to me to be a very Flores Magón gesture, to collect his black tie, which he had loaned to Enrique. Margarita also took him towels, handkerchiefs, a needle and thread, a stool, food, and money.

Several matters are clear in these exchanges. The first is that the student prisoners were not treated too harshly. They were kept in the Patio de los Encausados, rather than in the more secluded portions of the prison. In other words, they were never convicted, but held instead in an ambiguous situation that could either be stretched out indefinitely or abruptly cut short, depending on the superior power's whim. In that purgatory, the students were allowed communication with the outside, though some messages sent by Jesús were never received by Margarita. This access to the outside world allowed the young prisoners to enjoy certain amenities, such as sleeping on cots, having a stool to sit on, reading papers, and so on.

The messages also show that Jesús, as eldest brother, was indeed the acting head of the family, even from prison. Thus, Jesús admonished Enrique to study hard and reminded him that he was not to

Figure 4.3 Belem Prison, symbol of Porfirian
repression, was built in an old convent.
Like the Catholic vision of the afterlife, it
had its limbo, purgatory, and hell. From
Charles F. Lummis, *The Awakening of a
Nation: Mexico of To-Day* (New York: Harper
and Brothers, 1904), p. 64.

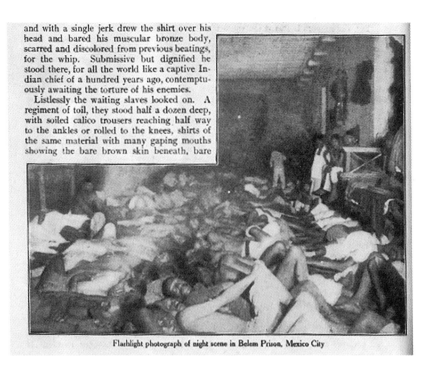

and with a single jerk drew the shirt over his head and bared his muscular bronze body, scarred and discolored from previous beatings, for the whip. Submissive but dignified he stood there, for all the world like a captive Indian chief of a hundred years ago, contemptuously awaiting the torture of his enemies.

Listlessly the waiting slaves looked on. A regiment of toil, they stood half a dozen deep, with soiled calico trousers reaching half way to the ankles or rolled to the knees, shirts of the same material with many gaping mouths showing the bare brown skin beneath, bare

Flashlight photograph of night scene in Belem Prison, Mexico City

Figure 4.4 Flash photograph of one of the overcrowded Belem Prison sleeping quarters. The flash technique allowed Turner to offer an original and poignant view into life in the prison and in the Mexico City tenements (*mesones*). From John Kenneth Turner, "The Tragic Story of the Yaquis," *American Magazine* 69 (November 1909), p. 44.

betray the family's expectations that he gain admission into the military academy. He expressed concern about Ricardo's lack of work, while he asked his brother not to suffer too much anguish while searching for jobs. Jesús corresponded with Francisco Blanco, *El Demócrata*'s owner, in order to get Ricardo placed, and instructed his mother not to give up a set of unpaid family photographs that they had ordered, but to ask rather that the studio hold off on their debt. Jesús was, in short, consulted on the details of all significant family decisions during his imprisonment.

Concordant with this responsibility, Jesús worried about the health and the psychological state of his mother and siblings and instructed them on how to face the current hardships: "You need to be brave now," he wrote to his mother, "You must understand that it is necessary to take risks in order to secure our sustenance, even if it means that there will be no food for now."

The family's first taste of political repression put pressure on each of its members to act responsibly and strengthened the family's sense of struggle for a common cause. The combination of individual steadfastness, resourcefulness, and the ability to forge strong ties of solidarity would be a lasting trait of the three siblings. The government would later have to harden its repressive strategy in the face of this resilience.

Meanings

In its day, the 1892 student movement was not perceived as a very threatening affair. The students did not even have an alternative candidate for the presidency, so their opposition to Díaz's reelection was a form of remonstrance, rather than offering a positive political alternative. The mainstream press viewed their rallies as a bawdy protest whose mood and tenor stood somewhere between Mardi Gras and a food riot. "El pequeño Motín del Pambazo fue nada más un San Lunes," as one witty critic put it.[26]

Curiously, it is this sort of bitingly sarcastic coverage that provides the most insight into the social significance of the movement. Prostudent papers such as *El Diario del Hogar* and *El Monitor Republicano* painted the opposition to Díaz's reelection with such exultation that they glossed over the painful class distinctions that were central to it. In those papers, each anti-reelectionist leader was a veritable Pericles, and speeches were invariably "eloquent" if not *elocuentísimos*. The students' poetry was "magnificent," and their ceremonies were brimming with "patriotic devotion" and "solemnity."

The pro-Díaz press, on the contrary, took a harsh look at the people in the rallies, and what they saw was a mixture of proletarianized students and a hodgepodge of hangers-on taken mostly from Mexico City's markets and from its seedier neighborhoods. The working and artisanal classes were not present, they claimed, but rather the crowds were composed of the *"populacho"*—the people who could not be civic, the rabble: "The rabble was the hero of this ridiculous street-corner adventure, and the rabble is neither a student, nor a worker, nor a citizen; it is an amorphous mass of hatred and ignorance that writhes and convulses in impotence."[27]

The result of this mixture of students and rabble was precisely the kind of hybrid monstrosity that Bulnes invoked twenty years later when he conjured the image of *chancletismo intellectual*—"intellectual sandalism." It is indeed no coincidence that a critical editorialist paused to comment on the apparel donned in the May 17 rally, the very one that had landed Ricardo in jail. There were few honest workers there, the reporter said, because no one was wearing a clean shirt, although it was a Sunday, but the leader of the rally, intent on compensating for that deficiency, donned an exuberant "double breasted frock coat, a top hat, and yellow gloves."[28] The image is all carnival: a *lagartijo* (dandy), king of the plebes.

In a still more burningly classist remark, another editorialist offered a kind of thumbnail satirical sketch and urban cartography of the poverty and vulgarity of the student activist:

> The wit of the so-called students is always sticky and greasy from the chophouse [*figón*]. It is the wit that sleeps on rented floor space at the tenements [*mesones*] of Parque del Conde, that breakfasts—if it can—at the food stalls of Balvanera and the Callejón de los Parados. Its symbol is the TORTA COMPUESTA [a heaping "everything" sandwich, popular when you are hungry—also greasy] put on the tab; its sauce is the *salsa borracha*. Its main ingredient is lard, and it has a barrel of pulque for its podium.[29]

The pro-Díaz press consistently emphasized the movement's lack of political relevance. This was, after all, a movement without an alternative political candidate in the election, a student initiative that had failed to mobilize broad-based popular support, a civic-minded initiative that degenerated into insult, defacement of property, vagrancy, and petty larceny.

But in its effort to belittle the movement's civic pretentions and to probe beyond the movement's outer layer of patriotic fervor, the conservative press revealed that social rifts ran deep, even despite the movement's very real political weakness. And the fact was that menacing or not, students had been expelled or imprisoned for standing up for what they believed. Commenting on the expulsion of one student, *El Demócrata* protested: "Our youth does not have the right to be virile, or honest, or patriotic; it is compelled shamefully to accept a tyranny that kills every noble and patriotic sentiment."[30]

The Generation of 1892's denunciation of violent repression in the countryside, of the lack of democratic expression, and of a comfortable and useless political class composed of pretentious and venial judges and lazy congressmen who slept through their sessions did leave its mark.

CHAPTER FIVE

La Bohème

It became fashionable to adopt the manners of the *sans culotte*, and not a few people added the word "citizen" in their salutation. The gloomy faces of the beaten-down masses now donned daring gestures. Withered brows were rejuvenated by a heroic wind. The "Marseillaise" was being sung in student boarding rooms, while on the streets and squares, you could guess by plain sight who styled himself a Marat, who a Robespierre, and who a Saint Just.
—Ricardo Flores Magón, on the 1892 student movement

The Latency Period

We know only a little about the Flores Magón brothers' economic activities in the 1890s. We know that they studied law, in addition to accounting, in Enrique's case. Ricardo was unable to finish his law degree, though he dragged out his studies and retook exams for a number of years. We know that Jesús was in prison for several months in 1893, at which time the family fell on hard times due to the compounded effects of Teodoro's death and Jesús's imprisonment, and that Ricardo scrambled for jobs then. We know that Jesús was involved in the editorial board of *El Demócrata* in its off-and-on career through the mid 1890s and that Ricardo worked at typesetting for several newspapers. Beyond this, there is only a faint glimmer. Hard facts about the brothers' activities are few and far between. There is, however, at least some reconstruction that can be attempted.

For this, it is useful to begin with a discussion of Teodoro's situation. As we have seen, Teodoro was given an estate in recompense for his losses during the French intervention—the Hacienda Tres Cabezas and the property known as La Laguna. These lands were left in the charge of Teodoro's oldest son, Aniceto, and seem to have been employed partly in agriculture and partly in sheep ranching, though it is unclear whether they generated a very substantial revenue. For many years, Teodoro tried to increase the pension that he received from the army. Part of his problem stemmed from difficulties in proving the length of his tenure in the militias back to 1859, because his house had been burned down, and his papers were destroyed. Teodoro had his superior officers testify in his favor, but it appears that his efforts were subjected to much red tape, and he seems only to have gained a portion of the amount that was his due.[1]

A second source of income for Teodoro appears to have been commerce. We know almost nothing of this. Jacinto Barrera Bassols writes that when the family came to Mexico City from Oaxaca in 1877, Teodoro Flores had a shop that sold and bought corn on the Calle Ancha, between Callejón San Antonio and Ayuntamiento, near the San Juan Market in central Mexico City.[2] But how long Teodoro remained in commerce is uncertain, as is the connection between his commercial activities and his landholding in Oaxaca. It seems likely that there were economic links between the family's Oaxaca concerns and their livelihood in Mexico City, since the family regularly spent the boys' school vacation period in Teotitlán, a habit that the lads relished.[3] That might also have been an occasion to transport corn back to Mexico City.

In addition to commercial entrepreneurship, Teodoro made some earnings as a power broker. Thus, beginning in the late 1870s, he served as a legal intermediary for processing land litigation for a number of Oaxaca communities.[4] Teodoro would continue to have this kind of work through his Mexico City years.

The picture that emerges from the documents left by Teodoro and Margarita and their children, then, is that Teodoro's livelihood was cobbled together from a mixture of resources gained from his Oaxaca properties, commerce in Mexico City, legal and political brokerage between his local district and Mexico City, and his military pension. But by 1890, three years before his death, Teodoro had fallen on hard times. For some reason, he was no longer receiving his military pension. Two letters written to Margarita from Oaxaca show that he was anxious about sending money back to the family.[5]

On that trip, Teodoro spent several months trying to get his Oaxacan affairs in order. The letters suggest that he had not been getting much revenue from his lands in recent times, because he writes that "the business of Gabriel, who arbitrarily occupied the lands of La Laguna—was settled—though not with that much profit. On the 30th of this month he will pay $53.... He should have paid $70, but he said that I owed him $10, plus the $7 for Aniceto's receipt, that left a debt of $53."[6] In other words, his lands at La Laguna were being rented out at that point, but with scanty funds flowing to the Mexico City family, because the rent was hard to collect. The letter also shows that Teodoro continued to make a bit of money from legal intermediation for local communities' land titles.

By the time of Teodoro's death in 1893, Jesús was already the main breadwinner of the family. Unfortunately, it's unclear when Jesús began his law practice or what jobs he held in the early 1890s, but by the final years of that decade, he was at the head of a commercial business, in addition to his law practice. It is possible, but not certain, that this was his father's commercial business. It is also possible that Enrique studied accounting, which he finished in 1896, in order to help out, particularly in light of the fact that the other career to which the family had aspired for Enrique—the military—was also in some sense a "family business."

Jesús's business was built on the family's back-and-forth movement to and from Teotitlán and the numerous relationships that had been built through those connections, though the exact nature and volume of the business handled is unclear. The company's name was "Siordia & Flores Magon. Comerciantes, Importadores, Exportadores y Comisionistas," and it was established enough to have letterhead stationary and at least one permanent employee in Oaxaca, in addition to Ricardo, who also was stationed in Oaxaca (Amapa) in 1899 and 1900. There is only one letter remaining in Enrique's papers connected to this business, sent by an agent to Jesús during an outbreak of cholera around Valle Nacional and the Papaloapan River, where the company operated. The letter suggests that the company relied on agents, but the nature of its exact business—what it imported and exported and in what volumes—is unclear.[7]

One of the interesting aspects of this business is that it confirms that Ricardo had first-hand knowledge of Valle Nacional and of the entire Isthmus and Mazatec regions, since he worked for his brother there in 1899. The few glimmers that one has from the letters that Ricardo sent to Enrique from Amapa show that both brothers were politicized, that Ricardo was guiding Enrique's early attempts to develop his writing, and that Ricardo was already committed to devoting his life to the press. That Ricardo was bored in Amapa was also made clear in a remark expressing his anticipation for his return to Mexico City: "And how happy we'll be then! I'll just remember the stupid parties [*estúpidos guateques*] of these black folk here, who don't add even a bit of style [*ni tantita sal*] to their dances. Everything becomes just a lot of hollering in nasal voices and a fooling tap dance [*zapateado*] on the boards. That is what they do for fun here."[8]

This picture confirms what we have pieced together thus far. The 1890s were a time when the brothers were politicized, but also dedicated to the family business. It was also a time when tastes developed around an urban life that combined reading, writing, politics, and a somewhat dandified aesthetic.

It is, in part, against a few features of this "latency period," a liminal or transitional stage in which development appears to give way to stasis, that the obsession with "regeneration" was later directed. The group's call for "regeneration" referred mainly to official Mexico's corruption and to the nation's political apathy, but it also had their own generation's immediate past of bohemian dissipation in the backdrop. Thus, one of the first documents that systematized the political ideas of the Generation of 1892, the 1903 *Manifiesto del Club Liberal Ponciano Arriaga*, included among its articles, a telling declaration: white-collar "employees lead a life of humiliation and misery. The privileges and prerogatives of the times have plagued us with a [political] class that is vice ridden and useless and who are spongers of the whole society." Thus, "Virtue no longer predominates; instead it is gold and power, the priest and the foreigner who predominate. The talent of the so-called middle and humble class vegetates, ignored or despised."[9]

La Bohème

After the dispersal, incarceration, and intimidation of the student movement, no opposition party was formed, nor was there clandestine activity against the dictatorship. Thus, Ricardo closed his account of the 1892 student riots by noting that they were a swan song of revolutionary activity, followed by a prolonged slumber of acquiescence. "That is how the days that might have been the beginning of a revolutionary movement ended; in fact they turned out to be the final

69

shudder of a body that was about to give itself up to a long slumber."[10]

Indeed, Díaz's fourth reelection inaugurated an era that can be thought of as the golden age of his thirty-year reign. On the economic front, 1892 is the date of the ascent of José Yves Limantour to the Finance Ministry, the end of the ancient *alcabala* sales tax, the vertiginous rise of direct foreign investment, and exponential growth of the railroad system. The Porfiriato was the first period of prolonged and sustained growth in postindependence Mexican history, with a doubling of per capita income over a thirty-year span.[11] The 1890s were the high point of confidence in that system.

The combination of rapid growth, modernization, hardened class lines in the countryside, and peace under a dictatorship also spawned a rich bohemian life in Mexico City. The educated youth could not ascend too high in the ranks of government, but it could nonetheless lead a life of some excess. In those days, the "825 steps" of the Calle Plateros were Mexico City's counterpart of the Parisian *Belle Époque* boulevards and arcades. They were the place to strut, to dine or have a drink, to shop for elegant accoutrements, to see and to be seen. But there was also a life of indulgence beyond that golden district—*pulquerías*, eateries and brothels, beckoning from the city's seedier districts, and some of those districts were expanding, thanks to a growing stream of migrants. Thus, poet Manuel Gutiérrez Nájera, one of Mexico's most famous *flaneurs*, seems to have found it necessary to remind his readers that "the City of Mexico does not start at the National Palace and end at the Calzada de la Reforma. I give each of you my word that it is much bigger than that. The city is like a great turtle that extends its disjointed legs outward toward each of the four cardinal points."[12] There was much to explore in the disjointed geography of the growing city.

The historian José Valadés, who interviewed a number of Ricardo Flores Magón's closest collaborators and had access to papers that have since been lost, wrote that Ricardo had been one of these young bohemian explorers. According to Valadés, Ricardo had been a womanizer in the 1890s, a man who had frequented the brothels and low life in Mexico City. He is said to have contracted a sexually transmitted disease at the time that is thought to account for his sterility.[13] Valadés is the only historian to have discussed this aspect of Ricardo's life (however briefly), though he imputes considerable importance to it:

70

Why not talk about that period, when it was then that Ricardo Flores Magón's spirit, his integrity, and his love for the poor were forged? That was when the young Flores Magón knew the reality in which the Mexican people lived—when he went into their houses, which were opprobrious for both their economic and their moral conditions. That was where he saw rape and incest...where there was neither respect, nor love, nor any reward for those who lived in misery; where there was no peace, or light or health for the poor. All of that produced an indelible wound in Ricardo's spirit that etched in his soul a panorama of a dark and satanic Mexico.[14]

Valadés paints an image of a Ricardo whose youth was marked by a personal history very like the one portrayed by diplomat and novelist Federico Gamboa in *Santa*, a Mexican adaptation of Emile Zola's *Nana*. Whereas Zola's novel has the courtesan Nana stand for the degeneration of the Third Empire, in the Mexican version, the prostitute is pure and innocent. She is a victim, rather than a corrupted representative of society. And in this, Gamboa's view was very like Ricardo's—despite their having been on opposite ends of the political spectrum. Both men shared the position of the bohemian whose remorse was channeled to the vindication of the prostitute. By the end of the decade, though, Ricardo had steeled himself for a truly forceful intervention in public life, beyond sentimental moralization.

Santiago de la Vega, one of the young companions involved in *El Hijo del Ahuizote* who went to jail with Ricardo in 1903, also invokes the bohemian image in his striking portrait of Ricardo Flores Magón in 1902: "Swollen eyelids, lively eyes that searched in their nearsightedness. Tall. Always dressed in black and fastidious in his care for his necktie. A Bohemian in the end—always clean and tidy. He wrote hunched down, with his eyes close to the paper. His script would then run and turn, thin and elongated, like a ballerina, on the back of the unpayable bills of *El Hijo del Ahuizote*."[15]

In fact, a certain fastidiousness with regard to personal appearance would be a shared trait of members of this group—it was part of their flair and their dignity.[16] So, immediately after his arrival to Leavenworth penitentiary in 1918, Enrique Flores Magón wrote to his wife, Teresa Arteaga: "Please send me two of my undershirts, of those short-sleeved ones, and one of my plain black neckties—

either long or short. Could you send my watch and chain? They allow it here."[17]

Nor were other members of the generation so very different in this respect. So, for instance, U.S. reporter Timothy Turner published a book of portraits and interviews with key members of the Maderista revolt, done mostly in El Paso while the fight with Díaz was still raging. One of these was with Lázaro Gutiérrez de Lara, whom he described as "a poetic individual, with romantic mustaches and an aesthetic expression on his face" (Figure 5.1).[18]

Práxedis Guerrero, for his part, was described by John Kenneth Turner, in an emotional obituary written upon that great captain's death as "a man of refinement and taste" (Figure 5.2). Turner recalled that "Guerrero refused to buy himself a new suit of clothes, saying that the Cause needed the money more than he. I remember the first time I invited him to supper at my home. He glanced down a little shyly, a little sadly, at his clothes, then, scorning a bourgeois apology, he shrugged his shoulders and said: 'All right.'"[19]

Bohemian dandyism was a mark of pride in the face of the indignities to which the militants were subjected. The first of these, as we've seen, was underemployment and limited chances for status recognition, visible in the 1892 movement itself, where pro-Díaz journalists constantly harped on the theme that the anti-reelectionists were either mainly the "underfed" (*destripados*) or students who "are wholly unknown in the National Schools."[20] As political involvement intensified at the start of 1900, repression hardened, and the dignity of the dandy was set against much harsher forms of debasement: the stench of urine at Belem Prison or at Yuma Penitentiary or against racial discrimination in Texas and Arizona.

In a potent set of articles exposing the conditions that they had encountered in the penitentiaries in Arizona, Antonio I. Villarreal described their entry and registration at Yuma: "We were put through the inevitable and inexpressibly repugnant ordeal of being stripped, examined for future identification, photographed, and clad in stripes" (Figure 5.3).[21] The degradation meted out by the state was met with stoic dignity.

Obviously, there was more to this dignity than a flair for fashion. There was also refinement, cultivation, and taste. So, for example, the editor of *El Demócrata*, who was also 1892's most visible student leader, Joaquín Clausell, was a law student who went into exile in

Figure 5.1 Lázaro Gutiérrez de Lara, revolutionary dandy, posing with women revolutionists after the fall of Ciudad Juárez (and
Porfirio Díaz), May 1911. The writing on
the postcard reads "Women ready to receive
Rábago." Given Lázaro's union activities, perhaps these women were members of a union.
We don't know whether they were armed as
a show of force for or against General Rábago
(who was in the federal army). Courtesy of the
Bancroft Library, John Murray Papers.

Figure 5.2 Praxedis Guerrero as a dandy. Courtesy of the Casa de El Hijo del Ahuizote, Mexico City.

Paris and became Mexico's most renowned Impressionist painter. Alfonso Cravioto became a member of Mexico's Academy of Letters. Juan Sarabia and Santiago de la Hoz were published poets. Antonio Díaz Soto y Gama, Lázaro Gutiérrez de Lara, and Querido Moheno wrote memoirs or histories. In addition to his newspaper articles, Ricardo Flores Magón wrote two plays and a number of short stories.

The pages of *El Demócrata* are punctuated by brief nods that indicate that its contributors belonged to Mexico's high intellectual culture. Here's one, for instance: "Miss Doña Gertrudis Nájera, aunt of the well-known writer, Mr. Don Manuel Gutiérrez Nájera, just passed away in this capital; we wish to convey to him our deepest regrets."[22] The writers for *El Demócrata* were of the same social world as the era's intellectual aristocracy.

In other *El Demócrata* articles, Jesús Flores Magón blasted Colonel Vidal Castañeda y Nájera, the director of the Escuela Nacional Preparatoria, and accused him of suppressing the patriotic and libertarian Jacobin impulses of the student body in favor of an obsessive concern with propriety. He complained that Castañeda had proscribed *El Demócrata* from school premises. But he also protested, with satire, Vidal Castañeda's ban on student use of canes and hats.[23] Because this generation was developing a process of self-fashioning that flaunted a kind of youthful dandyism in the face of the glass

Figure 5.3 Antonio I. Villarreal in Yuma
Penitentiary. The state penal system presents
its Delilah-esque power of emasculation by
way of the haircut and the imposition of
a drab uniform. The ideal of prisoner reform
is also asserted in the ritual removal of all
removable personal accoutrements. Courtesy
of the National Archives.

ceiling presented to them by the establishment, the sartorial prohibition is as significant as the censorship of reading material. The limited economic prospects of a generation that had been accused by its critics of leading "a rally of the vagrant and the indolent" were met with an aristocracy of spirit, and so the personality of the young rebel was reflected in clothes and demeanor, as much as in his reading material.

After the Generation of 1892 began to suffer harsh political persecution, cultivation was critical for maintaining a sense of self and sanity. So, for instance, writing from Leavenworth, a prison that, unlike Yuma, was committed to reform, Enrique Flores Magón cheered his wife up (in English, for the benefit of the prison censors) with news of prisoner musicians: "I'd say that I enjoy their playing, although I am so fastidious in my artistical taste that I must hear real good music and these must be well interpret to suit me. The band will play tomorrow my old friend 'Poet and Peasant.' I'll be all ears."[24]

Indeed, transforming oppressive conditions into creative action was of the utmost importance. Almost all, if not all, of the major militants, and very many of the minor ones, wrote poetry. Some of it became well known, at least within the movement, and sometimes beyond. Juan Sarabia, Santiago de la Hoz, Alfonso Cravioto, and Práxedis Guerrero were all decent poets, and their verses circulated widely. Writing from Belem Prison in 1903, for instance, Juan Sarabia made his call for revolution in a verse that might as well have been written for Mexico's national anthem:

> Ya tiembla el despotismo agonizante
> Y se hunde la caduca tiranía;
> Ya de la Patria en el azul Levante
> La Libertad triunfante
> Se yergue como el sol de un nuevo día.
> Para el César altivo es un ocaso
> Para el humilde pueblo es una aurora;
> La Justicia inmutable se abre paso:
> ¡ha sonado la hora!

> [Despotism trembles in agony
> The decrepit tyranny is sinking
> And from the fatherland's blue east

Triumphant liberty rises
Like the light of a new day.
It is twilight for they haughty Caesar,
But a dawn for the humble people.
Immutable Justice has found its way.
Now is the time!]

The form, rhyme, and meter of such poetry was forged in the literary world of Mexico City through intimate acquaintance with the work of favorite poets such as Manuel Gutiérrez Nájera, Manuel José Othón, Manuel Acuña, and Rubén Darío. The content of the poetry, though, was political, although occasionally the poems turned to romantic love or combined the two themes. So, for instance, on the occasion of Teresa's birthday, Enrique Flores Magón sent her a romantic-combat poem from prison and signed it with his prisoner number (12839). Its title, "Amor púgil" (A boxer's love), is itself a fusion of the two themes of these militant poets.

Podré ser gladiador que en épicos torneos,
Animado por bélicos deseos,
Sepa quebrar mi lanza
Luchando con pujanza;
Pero eso nunca impide
Que en mi pecho anide
El dulce sentimiento
Que yo, querida Tere,
Por ti siento
En mi púgil corazón que bien te quiere.

[I may well be a gladiator
who knows how to break his lance
fighting with vigor and strength
spurred on by martial intent
in epic tournaments.
But that has never prevented
Sweet feelings from nesting
In my breast for you, dear Tere,
In my prizefighter's heart
That loves you.]

In the more private realm of epistolary correspondence, dandyism was also cultivated as a form conducive to camaraderie by way of shared trysts and adventures. Juan Sarabia again provides some flavor and spice. After the fall of Porfirio Díaz, Francisco I. Madero decided to remove Antonio Villarreal from the local political scene by naming him Mexico's consul in Barcelona. While Villarreal was there, Sarabia, who was by then editor of *El Diario del Hogar*, began a letter to his old friend by saying that he and his comrades believed that Antonio deserved any hardship that he might complain of, since he was now gallivanting about, "crushing the most beautiful Barcelonian women—the ones that I'd wanted myself—in your satyrlike arms, instead of grabbing hold of a gun and eating Terrazas' cattle in the fields of Chihuahua, next to the many revolutionaries that have risen up against the not very respectable government of Don Panchito [Madero]."[25]

In short, questions of taste were also important for expressing and developing affinities and conflicts. Sensitivity was important to the group as a whole, because, as Ricardo once put it, "only he who suffers can understand the suffering of others." This, perhaps, was the ultimate reason why aesthetic sensibility played such an important role in the lives of these men and women.

We know a little about Ricardo's literary and musical preferences from Librado Rivera's foreword to the book by Ricardo's first biographer, the Argentine anarchist Diego Abad de Santillán. According to Librado, Ricardo knew Spanish, English, French, Italian, and Portuguese, and he could read a little Latin and Greek and knew a bit of Náhuatl. He spoke Mexico City argot with ease. Ricardo could recite by heart from the key poets who shaped the sensibilities of his generation: Rubén Darío, Díaz Mirón, Carpio, Manuel Acuña, and could also recite King Nezahualcóyotl's poetry.[26]

According to Librado, Ricardo was disgusted with Antonio I. Villarreal, for instance, because "that octopus" (*ese pulpo*) had referred to music as "that noise." One might read this aesthetic clash as the chasm between the high culture of Mexico City, represented by Ricardo, and the bumptious northern "sincerity" of a man from Lampazos, Nuevo León (Antonio Villarreal), but in fact, Ricardo's sense of aesthetic repugnance was also a manifestation of a consequential rift between the two men. Indeed, Villarreal, too, had standards that were no trifling matter, and in 1900, he fought a duel and killed José Flores in his native Lampazos, ostensibly over a difference of opinion on literary matters.[27]

Conocidos

One effect of transitioning between jobs, of taking years to graduate from the nation's top schools, and of leading active recreational lives is that the members of the Generation of 1892 were known in elite circles, though they were often not intimately known. So, for instance, when Lázaro Gutiérrez de Lara died, in 1918, Federico Gamboa, who had been Mexico's senior diplomat, wrote an entry in his diary: "[Lazaro Gutiérrez de Lara] was once an employee of our Ministry of Foreign Relations that I barely knew, though I knew his feats as agitator of Mexican workers in the United States and as rabid enemy of General Porfirio Díaz."[28]

This sort of fleeting recognition—garnered from shared school years, connections in the bureaucracy, or from casual encounters in bars or theaters—placed Lázaro, Jesús, and Ricardo in the category of person that in Mexico was known as *conocidos*: they had been classmates, students, or employees, or they had distant family connections with members of the elite, and some of them felt naturally entitled to access to it. So, for instance, El Demócrata's editors offered readers a chronicle of a (at the time very fashionable) bicycle excursion that they made to Toluca, where they found it most natural to stop by the governor's palace to pay their respects to the man.[29]

Student activism was often the first place where these lads entered the political sphere. So, for instance, Lázaro Gutiérrez de Lara had joined Jesús Flores Magón and others in forming a student organization in 1895, the Gran Comité Nacional de Estudiantes (GCNE). These students—who, though talented, were either relatively poor, or from provincial backgrounds, or both—competed in elections with a platform run by scions of the Porfirian elite, such as Jorge Vera Estañol, who would later serve in Victoriano Huerta's cabinet.

Some of the youngsters of the Generation of 1892 came from a long line of vaguely remembered *conocidos*—their parents, too, had been known and forgotten by the barons of the age. That was certainly the case of the Flores Magón brothers. Thus, when she fell on hard times, Margarita Magón repeatedly appealed to Porfirio Díaz for help—her husband had been a *conocido* and a military ally. Margarita had two photographs inscribed to her husband by the young Porfirio Díaz to prove it. So she wrote to the president for help, but bonds between *conocidos* could be ignored, and Díaz did not respond.[30] He may later have come to regret his negligence.

There were times, however, when relations between more powerful *conocidos* and less powerful members of the same class were honored. When Antonio I. Villarreal, who was from a well-known family in Nuevo León, was wasting away in jail after the duel in which he killed a man, General Bernardo Reyes, governor of that state, intervened to cut his sentence short and so allowed a man from a *conocido* family to escape to the United States.[31] Similarly, when Lázaro was thrown in Cananea's jail during the famed 1906 miners' strike there and was in line for summary execution, a friend got a telegram out to Lázaro's brother in Mexico City, Dr. Felipe Gutiérrez, who as a midlevel official in Mexican public health and was able to call Porfirio Díaz's attention to the matter. Díaz sent the Cananea officials a telegram of inquiry regarding the cause of Lázaro's imprisonment, and that gesture was enough for local authorities to set the prisoner free, no further questions asked.[32] In sum, this was a generation that had tenuous, but real connections with the governing elites.

True Heirs

While the Generation of 1892 made lateral moves through the bureaucracy and confronted the realities of growing social inequality, impoverishment, and a glass ceiling preventing their own ascent, they became impassioned by public affairs and increasingly viewed themselves as the true heirs of the nationalist spirit that Díaz and his friends had betrayed. So, for instance, Lázaro's law thesis on maritime commerce—written as a formality for graduation—contained some characteristic elements.

That rather rudimentary document was an argument in favor of Mexico developing its own merchant marine. The thesis was defended during the Spanish-American War and thus at a time when the rise of American naval power was much on people's minds. It propounded an active mercantile policy for Mexico, imitating the French model, wherein all shipping internal to Mexican waters would be conceded exclusively to national companies, while the state supported the (longer-term) development of a Mexican deepwater seafaring marine. Focusing on the deformities of colonial dependency, Lázaro decried "the system of absolute protectionism that Spain and England adopted in their New World possessions."[33] His concern was with the completion of a project of national sovereignty that independence itself had not achieved.

One implication of this kind of argument was that Mexico's elite had been auctioning the country off to foreigners while capable Mexicans were been kept out of the upper echelons of the economy. Greater national autonomy implied employment for skilled Mexicans, since a nationalized merchant marine would mean jobs for Mexican engineers, pilots, builders, sailors, and so on. The guiding goal was national development, as against making unlimited concessions to foreigners who were involved in an extractive economy: "México para los mexicanos," as this was later formulated. Thus, the Generation of 1892 saw itself as the true champion of the national interest.

CHAPTER SIX

A Passion for the Press

When the students rallied in downtown Mexico City, they were joined by an anonymous mass—the *pueblo*—made up of workers and artisans, vagrants and drunkards, and even perhaps a few policemen or soldiers. It is precisely because of this mixture that Ricardo Flores Magón would recall those heady days with such exaltation:

> All of Mexico City came enthusiastically to witness the march. Every-one was shouting "*Vivas!*" to Liberty, and "Death" to tyranny. The flags shone in the sun. Music bands moved the multitude with heroic chords. On every cornerpost, on every cart, and wherever you might find an object that could serve as an improvised podium, there was an orator, sometimes in a frock coat, sometimes in a blouse; sometimes elegant, others as rugged as the tempest itself.[1]

Government toleration for this sort of interclass agitation was low, and so it unleashed troops on the riot. After that, retreat from public space to protesting in print was a logical development, so the passion for the press among students, which was high to begin with, naturally was bolstered.

Governmental forbearance toward the press was greater than for free association in public spaces. Given Mexico's low literacy rates—according to the census, in 1895, literacy was at barely 17.9 percent—many fewer people could join a paper's readership than could mob a public square.[2] Plus, the timing of news reporting and newspaper circulation loaned itself to a more nuanced strategy of regulation. As a result, the Porfirian papers were more open to political debate than is sometimes assumed, and the press was a regular, if difficult and insecure refuge for malcontents.

The coercive expression of the regime's limits of toleration deepened the generation's immersion in the press. By 1899, Ricardo was describing his passion for the press in an arresting fashion: "Paper is an idol to me, and I think that it will soon be my great weapon: the newspaper.... I know the business through and through."[3]

And in fact, in the course of the 1890s, Ricardo and Jesús Flores Magón had indeed learned the business. Jesús served several years on *El Demócrata*'s editorial desk, which reopened after the 1893 repression, and he also collaborated closely with the main opposition editor of the period, Filomeno Mata. Ricardo, for his part, set type in *El Demócrata* and *El Universal* and served as editor in a couple of short-lived journalistic ventures, *El Ideal* and *El Azote*. By August 1900, the combination of political experience—including prison, for Jesús—immersion in the working and social life of Mexico City, and rich experience in the press had put the two older Flores Magón brothers in the position of launching an editorial project that would have a mercurial history.

Regeneración

On August 7, 1900, Jesús and Ricardo Flores Magón put out the first issue of a new weekly journal, *Regeneración*. By May 15 of the following year, the two brothers were in jail. *Regeneración* struggled on for a few months, until it was compelled to close in October 1901. The first era of *Regeneración* was thus barely fourteen months long—but it catapulted the Flores Magón brothers to national fame.

The life of *Regeneración* in its first incarnation can be divided into two periods: from August to early December 1900 and from mid-December to the journal's closure in October 1901. During its first few months, *Regeneración* studiously avoided making direct criticisms of Díaz and presented itself as a forum for the denunciation of breaches in the operation of the system of justice. In the second period, *Regeneración* took on a more openly combative role, attached its criticism to a nascent political movement, and scorched the upper echelons of the Díaz establishment, including, very scandalously, Díaz himself.

In its first issue, *Regeneración* proclaimed its editorial mission, which was to "seek remedies and, when necessary, to point out and denounce all of the misdeeds of public officers who do not follow the precepts of the law, so that public shame brings upon them the justice that they deserve."[4] The paper thus confined itself to the public discussion of failures in the administration of justice. Its editors were Jesús Flores Magón, Antonio Horcasitas (both lawyers), and Ricardo Flores Magón, who was still officially a law student then. With Jesús at its head, the work of the journal was presented as a public service offered by a young generation of lawyers who appealed to the court of public opinion because the system of justice itself had been corrupted.

The journal made a public call for readers to denounce infringements of justice from any corner of the republic. The editors picked cases from the correspondence that began to pour in and then redacted denunciations for the general public. The journal's motto, "Periódico Jurídico Independiente," reflected its core aim, which was to offer an independent forum for airing injustice. At the end of each issue, *Regeneración* offered free legal advice to correspondents writing in with queries.

The journal proved to be a resounding success. *Regeneración* did not need to bother building a reporting staff, since the editors could rely on their copious correspondence for eye-catching and often scandalous news items, and it quickly developed a network of regular voluntary correspondents. This helped make the venture economically viable, and because the editors initially adhered to the fundamental rule of tolerated journalism of the period—never attack the dictator directly—*Regeneración* garnered a lot of readers from within the political class, who followed with interest when one or another of its members was singled out for criticism.

Moreover, the timing of *Regeneración*'s appearance was excellent. Díaz's fifth consecutive reelection occurred in the midst of rumors concerning his possible retirement and speculation about potential alternative candidates. Some of those rumors had been fanned by Díaz himself. As a result, governmental infighting was close to the surface of public life, with one faction gravitating toward the figures of the justice minister, Joaquín Baranda, and the governor of Nuevo León, Bernardo Reyes, and the other toward the finance minister, José Yves Limantour. For their part, midlevel officials also tended to gravitate toward one faction or another, and this meant that denunciation of wrongdoing, even by minor officials, could spark interest higher up.

The fact that *Regeneración* was edited by members of the Generation of 1892—in other words, by the generation that was not in power—gave its claim to independence credibility. The Flores Magón brothers were neither *científicos* nor followers of Reyes or Baranda. Moreover, Díaz had just turned seventy, which was a ripe old age at the time. In January 1901, rumors circulated about his state of health and whether retirement was not close at hand, and by February, Jesús and Ricardo boldly proclaimed the need for searching for a true Liberal as a presidential candidate, since "news of President Díaz's illness travels ear to mouth, from one end of the country to the other."[5]

For all of these reasons, *Regeneración* made Jesús and Ricardo famous way beyond Mexico City. On the other hand, the very electoral logic that had catapulted the journal to fame also accelerated these young men's confrontation with the harder side of power, a side that they had successfully avoided since Jesús's imprisonment in 1893.

On December 1, 1900, Porfirio Díaz began his sixth consecutive term in office. In that same month, *Regeneración* made its distance from the dictator more explicit. In its November 30 issue, it published a piece on censorship in monarchies, ostensibly about Germany, but with obvious implications for Mexico, given Díaz's perpetuation in power. In the January 7, 1901, issue, it argued that Díaz's government had not been characterized by its much trumpeted "poca política, mucha administración"—"not much politics, plenty of management"—but rather by the opposite.[6] Even more poignantly, the journal said that the people had not voted in the last election, because (and they quoted Díaz as their authority in this) impoverished peoples "are almost entirely denied autonomy and liberty, and so are practically proscribed from democracy and all things public [*la república*]."[7] At the same time that they made these criticisms of the president, *Regeneración* had been hailing the birth of new liberal political clubs and newspapers wherever they appeared, laying the groundwork for the formation of a national network extending all the way into Texas.

By the December 15 issue, *Regeneración* had changed its philosophy and orientation, manifested, first, by the exit of one of its editors, Licenciado Antonio Horcasitas, leaving only Jesús and Ricardo on the journal's masthead, and second, by a change in the journal's motto, from "Periódico Jurídico Independiente" to "Periódico Independiente de Combate."[8] The implication was clear: *Regeneración* had moved from being a journal dedicated to a kind of ombudsman role into a journal militantly commited to political change.

If any doubt remained regarding the tenor of the transformation, the lead article in the first issue of the journal's new era proudly proclaimed that *Regeneración* had refused to join the "Procesión de la Paz" that had been convened by the Círculo de Amigos del General Porfirio Díaz to celebrate Díaz's reelection on December 1.[9] Two weeks later, Jesús and Ricardo offered readers an explanation of their decision to change the orientation of the paper. Their interest in judicial matters had always been a reflection of deeper principles, and they recognized that systematic defects in the judiciary were related to defects in the two other branches of government. The brothers' principles compelled them to move to a broader sphere of engagement, even while they retained *Regeneración*'s interest in justice and the law: "Our struggle for Justice was an aspect of our principles, which in the end were hemmed in by such a constrained field of action."[10]

There is one dimension of this transformation that bears some pondering, and that is its timing. Unlike the 1892 student movement, the politicization of *Regeneración* sidestepped Díaz's reelection. Indeed its combative and confrontational phase began after Díaz's inauguration for a sixth term, and not before. Why?

Several considerations are relevant. The first is that like the many other newspaper editors and founders of political clubs in 1900, Jesús and Ricardo did not believe that they could successfully oppose Díaz's reelection. Indeed, *Regeneración* was careful not to cross the dictator during the delicate months between August and December, before Díaz was installed for yet another term in office.

The second consideration is that Mexican society generally was starting to prepare for Díaz's death or retirement from political life. Díaz was quite ancient for the standards of the day. Few people expected that he would last long enough to be considered for yet another reelection after 1900. So the formation of a new political block built out of a web of political clubs and newspapers was calculated to capitalize on the prestige that political exclusion had garnered the for the Generation of 1892 and to achieve public visibility for that cohort as an alternative political force to the two insider factions, the *reyistas* and *científicos*.

By mid-February, *Regeneración* was openly proclaiming the rumored sickness of Díaz and the advisability of preemptively putting forth their own presidential candidate for succession: "we declare undisguisedly that all of us who claim to be patriots should propose a candidate for the Presidency of the Republic, in case General Díaz's grave illness should have a fatal outcome."[11]

By the time that it printed this bold declaration, *Regeneración* and the new leaders of the Liberal Party movement had established themselves as political outsiders, braver, truer, and more patriotic than the establishment. The image of themselves that they sought to project is apparent in the words used by Ricardo and Jesús when they accepted an invitation to join San Luis Potosí's Club Liberal Ponciano Arriaga:

> Born under the splendid skies of the Oaxaca mountains, we began to breathe the liberty of that savage nature, far from the populous towns where adulation thrives and where subservience does its wormlike deeds. Educated, later, outside the official circle and preserving our independent character, we have been unable to understand the shameful complacency or the falsely imputed utility of that serious illness that is known as the Politics of Conciliation [between church and state].[12]

Club Ponciano Arriaga

On August 30, 1900, just weeks after the launching of *Regeneración*, Camilo Arriaga, an engineer born of a rich San Luis Potosí family, issued an invitation for a national congress of true Liberals to be held in San Luis Potosí on February 5, Constitution Day, 1901. Calculated to avoid any contention over the reelection of Díaz, the convocation of the Gran Congreso Liberal was thoughtfully timed to begin after the start of the new presidential term. Its aim was to achieve three core goals: to form a new Liberal Party out of a network of new political clubs and newspapers, to develop a distinctive ideological platform for that party, and, to instill the idea that Díaz's successor did not have to be elected from his inner circle of collaborators.

The first goal, the development of a network and political party, is key to our story, since the core group of Mexican exiles that we have been tracking originated in that effort. The new Liberal network had two key components: the oppositional press (the so-called *prensa de combate*), and the political club. There was, indeed, a connection between printing papers and organizing political clubs. By no means does this imply that each club had its own paper or that each oppositional paper stimulated the formation of a corresponding political club, but having a paper was an ideal of many clubs, and stimulating political organizations was an ideal of many newspapers.

One result of this dynamic was a vast multiplication of newspapers in these years. Historian James Cockcroft documented this trend many years ago. Citing Moisés González Navarro, Cockcroft framed the process in terms of a general surge of newspaper distribution, which had skyrocketed from one paper per 53,858 inhabitants in 1884 to one per 9,337 in 1907.[13] I can offer no reliable statistic regarding the exact number of papers that were founded during the 1900 effervescence, but in the fourteen months of *Regeneración*'s short first life, it printed notices signaling the formation or decried the forced closing of *Onofre* (Toluca); *El Gorro Frigio, Pro-Patria*, and *El Hijo del Ahuizote* (Mexico City); *El Paladín, Jalisco Libre*, and *El Despertador* (Guadalajara); *El Heraldo* (Aguascalientes); *El Demócrata, El Sol*, and *El Combate* (Hermosillo); *Renacimiento* (San Luis Potosí); *El Reproductor Campechano* (Campeche); *Excelsior* (Veracruz); *La Democracia* (Puebla); *El Pensamiento Libre* (Mérida); *La Flor de la Esperanza* (Tulancingo, Hidalgo); *La Idea Liberal* (Tlacotalpan; *Guelatao* (Tampico); *Vésper* (Guanajuato); *La Corregidora* (Laredo, Texas); *El Corsario* (Morelia); and *El Centinela* (Zacatecas). In addition to entries on these papers, a good many other Liberal journals from all regions of Mexico and Texas were mentioned incidentally in *Regeneración*'s articles.

Cockroft's classic study of the formation of the Liberal Party shows that when one looks closely to a single region, such as San Luis Potosí, the number of papers open and shut in this brief period multiplies still more. Indeed, one indication of the effervescence around printing and its connection to organizing is the high number of Liberal newspapers closed down and journalists jailed when the government decided to react against the movement. In his prison interview with John Kenneth Turner in 1908, Ricardo provided a list of fifty papers and hundreds of journalists imprisoned in the 1901–1902 crackdown.[14]

Several leaders of our core group first came to know one another by reading each others' papers, which engaged in exchanges from city to city. Ricardo was inducted into the San Luis Potosí Club Ponciano Arriaga because of *Regeneración*. The Club Literario Liberal of Veracruz put out *Excelsior*, edited by poet Santiago de la Hoz, who became a core member of the group. The Club Ponciano Arriaga, which became the pivotal political organization of the new Liberal Party movement, published *Renacimiento* in San Luis Potosí, edited by Juan Sarabia, who was to become one of the most charismatic leaders of the group. Juan's cousin, Manuel, also worked at that paper.

Newspapers were also an important venue for the women in the movement. Juana Gutiérrez de Mendoza and Elisa Acuña's paper, *Vésper*, brought them to the attention of the group; Sara Estela Ramírez first appeared by way of her paper, *La Corregidora*, published out of Laredo, Texas. Dolores Jiménez y Muro directed the *Revista Potosina*. Finally, figures such as Librado Rivera and Antonio I. Villarreal, who were important first as school teachers and organizers, moved into the press as a natural extension of their activities.

Most Liberal papers had small runs and were short-lived, since they were subjected to pressures from state governors or local *jefes políticos*. Mexico City papers could at times count on a more variegated set of political linkages for protection. The principle of avoiding direct attacks on Díaz while attacking government officials was one way of trying to carve out a space of tolerance there. But even in Mexico City, most papers had short lives.

On the other hand, the compounded effect of media density, proximity to the national elites, and relative independence gave the papers from the capital city much more prestige than their provincial counterparts. Thus, the director of the Chiapas *Revista del Soconusco* respectfully wrote to Jesús Flores Magón: "I've been told that provincial newspapers aren't much read in big cities like the one that you live in and that exchanges between city and provincial papers are done only for the sake of courtesy."[15] Given their priviledged position, Mexico City papers were key to any national movement.

Two Mexico City papers were crucial for the Liberal network that was emerging around Camilo Arriaga's initiative: the *Diario del Hogar* and *Regeneración*. The *Diario del Hogar* was a well-established and more moderate paper that had proved able to survive the dictatorship's pressures and moments of repression for many years. True, its editor, the Potosino Filomeno Mata, was often in and out of Belem Prison, but the paper survived nonetheless, and its stability and influence made it a source of support for *Regeneración*, which was initially printed in the presses of the *Diario del Hogar*. Meanwhile, *Regeneración*'s strident attacks galvanized the emerging political network. The groundswell of new clubs and newspapers prompted by the call for anational Liberal congress led to the formation of a new political party, the Liberal Party, in 1901.

CHAPTER SEVEN

The Wall

Liberalism

When Camilo Arriaga convened the Gran Congreso Liberal late in 1900, Mexican liberalism was everywhere and nowhere. It was everywhere, because there was no organized conservative opposition. It was nowhere, because there was no Liberal Party and because positivism, dictatorship, and the politics of reconciliation had blurred liberalism's ideological contours. For this reason, the Gran Congreso Liberal was convened at a time when it could to stake a credible claim to the prestigious capital-L "Liberal" mantle in Mexican politics. A little background is required to understand why this was so.

After its war with the United States (1846–1848), the struggle between Mexico's Liberals and Conservatives intensified. While Liberals of the 1820s had been content to uphold Catholicism as Mexico's official religion, the radicalized Liberals of the following generation drafted a constitution in 1857 that drew a strict separation between church and state, expropriated church property, and banned clerics from participation in public life.

But the triumph of the Liberals in the so-called Wars of Reform (1856–1861) was short-lived. Capitalizing on the entanglement of the United States in its own civil war, Mexico's Conservatives managed to forge an alliance with Napoleon III, and a Mexican Empire was instated by combined French and Conservative Mexican forces. This empire and its Hapsburg prince, Maximilian, finally succumbed to Liberal forces in 1867.

The effects of the Liberals' triumph over the French were counterintuitive, though. The Conservative Party had invited a foreign power to invade Mexico, and for this it was proscribed from political life. As a result, the Liberals no longer faced an organized Catholic opposition—merely a deeply entrenched popular religion—a combination that led inevitably to the blurring of liberal ideology. As long as civil strife had raged, Liberal ideology had become increasingly exalted and "pure." Once Liberalism became the only game in town, its ideology became increasingly compromised and diffuse.

Reconciliation—the promotion of peace and of a policy of reintegration of the defeated Conservative elites—occurred under the ideological frame of positivism. Mexican philosopher Leopoldo Zea showed that positivism became useful because it combined the Liberals' traditional rejection of Catholicism with an equally firm rejection of radical politics—and in particular of the Jacobin romance with revolution and political formulas that favored unmediated forms of popular sovereignty.[1] Mexican positivists such as Justo Sierra argued that the Liberal ideals of liberty and popular sovereignty had as their precondition peace and a degree of economic development, and they justified dictatorship as a transitional formula that was needed in order to achieve them.

Thus, Liberalism under Díaz developed a kind of religion of peace and progress that would supposedly adumbrate liberal freedoms by laying down the foundations of progress. This ideology was also a formula for reconciliation with the members of the old Conservative Party, who were brought into Díaz's ample political tent. Indeed, Justo Sierra favored the formation of a single, united Liberal Party that might guide Mexico through its transition to modern life.

This strategy—the attempt to form a unified Liberal Party—had been tried in 1892. While Jesús, Ricardo, and youngsters of their generation protested Díaz's reelection, Justo Sierra and his group of liberal positivists called the first Congress of the Unión Liberal, styled as a kind of Mexican version of a U.S. primary election. The Congreso de la Unión Liberal received representatives from Mexico's federal states and launched Díaz's candidacy for reelection while asserting party guidance. Justo Sierra delivered the speech naming Díaz as the Unión Liberal's candidate for the presidency. Sierra justified the objective, positive need for Díaz's third consecutive reelection, despite its negative implications for democracy, but he also tried to set limits on Díaz's power.

Porfirio Díaz adopted the language of Sierra's program to justify his perpetuation in office, but he shrugged off the limitations that Sierra's group had tried to foist on him, including their proposed transformation of the Unión Liberal into a genuine independent political party. As a result, the group that crafted the regime's ideology was condemned to remain a political clique, the so-called *científicos*.

Arriaga's Gran Congreso was astutely designed to jump into the breach. The new liberal movement sought democratic reform against the wishes of the dictatorship. And since it established itself as an oppositional force, it could develop sharp and identifiably Liberal ideological contours in a way that the pro-Díaz Liberals, who were always mired by political compromise, could not. Camilo Arriaga, the Sarabias, the Flores Magóns, and others thus cast their Liberal Party as standing in opposition to the status quo, which they proceeded to redefine as conservative. The Gran Congreso Liberal, in other words, had one clear advantage over all of the establishment factions within the Díaz establishment: it could claim (Liberal) ideological purity.

In order to drive the point home, Arriaga and his team claimed the mantle the Liberal brand for themselves with punctilious attention to detail. Not only did they hold the Gran Congreso on February 5, the Day of the (1857) Constitution (Figure 7.1), they billed the event as the First Liberal Congress of the Mexican Republic, thereby demoting the 1892 Congress of the Unión Liberal to less-than-Liberal status.[2] With delegates listed from forty-four associations coming from fourteen states, Arriaga's congress could give the 1892 Unión Liberal a run for its money, since the Unión Liberal had been attended by a comparable number of delegates (seventy), despite having enjoyed full official support.[3]

Pursuing this same effort to revive the old Liberalism, *Regeneración* presented the Liberal Congress at San Luis Potosí with a language reminiscent of the exalted cult of the founding fathers of the 1857 Constitution. Thus, the paper introduced the Gran Congreso delegates one by one, supplementing background biographical information with signature personality traits. They were fashioning new patriotic heroes.

Of Antonio Díaz Soto y Gama, *Regeneración* said "His speech is a masterpiece"; Manuel Antonio Facha was introduced as a "poet of the new school" who "uses satire with notable effect"; Diódoro Batalla was "without a doubt the best orator of the Republic. He hates tyranny, like a good *veracruzano*"; Francisco Naranjo "was born in the great expanses of the borderlands, breathing freedom.

Figure 7.1 Constitution Day, February 5, 1904: *El Hijo del Ahuizote* staff commemorate the death of the 1857 Constitution.

He has never known a yoke of any kind, which is why he loves wild liberty"; Luis Lajous was "a polyglot and encyclopedist. His knowledge [*ilustración*] is both extensive and deep, acquired in the best European universities"; young Lázaro Villarreal was consistently the best student at the Escuela Nacional de Jurisprudencia, and attracted to positivism, he was "the speaker of the future." The Brumellesque Federico Flores was a man who "appears to be a misanthrope, but in fact he loves humanity," and "when he speaks, it sounds like he is mocking everyone."[4]

What the new Liberal movement could and did not do was risk head-on confrontation with Díaz in the 1900 election. Instead, its strategy was to benefit from the factionalism, boredom, shame, and discontent that this sixth reelection generated. Once at the Gran Congreso, the Liberals made radical pronouncements against the church and against any official policy that might be construed as violating the separation between church and state. That strengthened their claim to the Liberal mantle while providing some cover for the group's attempt to build an organization that might soon be in a position to compete for Díaz's succession after his (supposedly immanent) demise.

The Wall

Despite the cares that the Liberals took to avoid the 1900 presidential election, the Díaz regime took steps to repress the new Liberal movement. In the weeks preceding and the months that followed the Gran Congreso Liberal, activists, newspapers, and political clubs faced much hardship. The Gran Congreso itself was subjected to harassment, with the Federal Army's Fifteenth Battalion patrolling the streets outside San Luis's Teatro de la Paz and with delegates fearing that the troops might crack down any minute.[5]

The orators stood their ground, though, emulating their heroes, the constitutionalists of 1857. Indeed, it was a moment when a turbulent sentiment was born: righteous indignation in the face of government troops conjured an image of a national network of healthy and "virile" (as they put it) patriots who were ready to stand up and demand their rights, facing an establishment composed in equal parts of stupefied, slumbering, indifferent and obsequious servants of dictatorship.

The main speeches, given by Diódoro Batalla, by the three *potosinos*, Juan Sarabia, Díaz Soto y Gama, and Camilo Arriaga, and by

Ricardo Flores Magón were all inspired in the rhetorical tradition of the "pure" Liberals of the mid-nineteenth century. The most obvious case was that of Ricardo, who, emulating Ignacio Ramírez, the young indigenous intellectual who had scandalized Mexican society by proclaiming loudly, in 1836, that God does not exist, called out that "the Díaz administration is a den of thieves." This unpronounceable transgression, spoken loudly in the elegant Beaux Art Teatro de la Paz, provoked giddy nervousness and outright fear in the audience, part of which tried to boo Ricardo into silence. But like Ramírez before him, the inflamed Liberal repeated his claim more loudly, twice, until the delegates tamed their fears and finally exploded into applause.[6] Ricardo's courageous accusation against Díaz himself was what sealed the group's claim to the prestige of being "pure" Liberals, and it was what made *Regeneración* an object of veneration. Ricardo and Jesús had succeeded in channeling the spirit of the deified saviors of the Mexican nation, Benito Juárez, Melchor Ocampo, Ignacio Ramírez, and Miguel Lerdo de Tejada Lerdo.

But although the army did not disrupt the Gran Congreso, the Liberal movement soon came up against a wall of repression. Liberal clubs, which kept springing up in the course of 1901, were being shut down and banned in many states, particularly in the north, but also elsewhere, and by May 21, that is, three months after the congress, Jesús and Ricardo were in prison. *Regeneración* continued to run, operated by Enrique Flores Magón and Ernesto Arnoux, until October, when it was definitively shut down. In November 1901, Arriaga, Sarabia, and Librado Rivera were imprisoned in San Luis Potosí. A number of Liberal clubs and papers were raided, journalists were imprisoned on charges of libel, and leaders were jailed or conscripted into the army. In short, the Liberals failed to build an organization that could be tolerated by the Díaz government.

Good Club, Bad Club

Political clubs had an ambivalent standing in Porfirian Mexico. The "good clubs" were formed around the personality cult of the dictator or of state governors or ministers. Those clubs had the Círculo de Amigos del General Porfirio Díaz as their prototype and model. They brought together ambitious members of the political class and provided occasions that could garner recognition. Twice, in 1896 and 1900, the sycophantic Círculo de Amigos was bestowed the opportunity of launching Díaz's reelection campaigns. Beyond that, they regularly made themselves visible at the birthdays of Porfirio Díaz and his wife, Carmelita, and at other patriotic occasions, serving as a ceremonial arm of the dictatorship.[7]

Related to these clubs were the patriotic and civic juntas of the nation's state, district, and municipal seats—organizations that brought together the members of local elites who had been empowered by Díaz or who had at least managed to maintain a working arrangement with him. However, civic associations that alleged nonpolitical purposes occupied a more ambivalent position with regard to supporting the status quo. They included officially sanctioned literary and scientific societies, as well as civic societies that often donned names such as Benito Juárez, Melchor Ocampo, or Miguel Hidalgo—patriotic heroes often mobilized by antigovernment groups, but who were also key figures of the state's official pantheon. These associations often brought together people who were on the outs with regard to local elites. Some were organized by Protestants or Freemasons. Others were organized by Spiritists. Spiritists believed in the reality of s spirit world and in the reincarnation of spirits in progressively greater states of consciousness, a doctrine that contrasted with the crusty scientism of the Positivists that dominated in official circles, while offering up a form of spirituality that was not in the control of the Catholic Church. Yet others were nondenominational associations that assembled artisans, notables, ranchers, or farmers with no peculiar religious convictions who wished to come together in circles not controlled by local *jefes políticos*.[8] This sort of organization tended to be seen as "troublemaking" from the Díaz perspective, particularly when it rallied around political campaigns to support independent candidates for local office.

Indeed, Díaz had a long history of trying to control these associations. Most dramatically, in 1890, he stymied the oppositional potential of Freemasonry by working to consolidate all Mexican lodges into a single organization, of which he became head.[9] However, because of Díaz's policy of appeasing the Catholic Church and that institution's crucial role in preserving the status quo, a few lodges refused to join, and Freemasonry continued to offer space in which to harbor opposition.

So, for instance, future PLM leader and Mayo Indian Fernando Palomares joined the Freemasons as a youth in his native Sinaloa.

The utopian socialist colony of Topolobampo, where he was raised, had been founded by Freemasons. By 1901, Fernando subscribed to *Regeneración*, and he wrote the editors asking them to publish a complaint against the bishop of Sonora, who was breaking the law by participating in local politics.[10] Like all future members of the Partido Liberal Mexicano, in 1900, Fernando was a militant secularist. When he went on to take part in union activities at Cananea, he joined a local lodge that had other key agitators as members, including 1906 strike leaders Manuel Diéguez and Esteban Baca Calderón.[11]

It is true that when Palomares asked Ricardo Flores Magón, already in exile in California, his opinion regarding the Masons, Ricardo wryly remarked that "Porfirio Díaz is a Mason, and he's no good," or something to that effect.[12] Before that, during dark days of persecution after the Liberal junta's failed attempt at revolution in 1906, Field Marshal Aarón López Manzano wrote to Ricardo signaling concern over the Masons' trustworthiness: "I've noticed that there are many Masons among our correligionaries. Don't you think that [Nuevo León Governor Bernardo] Reyes might pry inside our ranks? A number of people have asked me if you are a Mason. For convenience's sake [*por política*], I've told them that I think so. I distrust them a lot."[13] Ricardo replied by recommending care: "Beware of certain Masons who are just toadies [*lacayuelos*] of *Canana*," Reyes's nickname.[14]

But it may have been easier for Ricardo to shun Freemasonry than it was for most Liberal militants, because Ricardo did not have to travel as widely as a clandestine agent—he was either in jail or managing a paper most of the time. Moreover, as the hunted leader of a clandestine party, Ricardo was obsessed with spies, and that led him to see Freemasonry as a vulnerable link. In any case, Ricardo's opinion was not generally shared by the Liberal leadership. Thus, Enrique Flores Magón, Antonio Villarreal, Librado Rivera, Antonio de P. Araujo, and Camilo Arriaga were all Masons.

Finally, all of the leaders who came together in 1900 and 1901 had prior experiences in one club or another—anticlerical clubs, student organizations, literary associations—and the pages of *Regeneración* in 1900 and 1901 are generously sprinkled with news items greeting the formation of this kind of society: the Club Liberal Regenerador Benito Juárez of Cuicatlán, Oaxaca; the Club Liberal Melchor Ocampo of Puebla; the Club Liberal Literario Sebastián Lerdo de

Tejada of Veracruz; the association of political clubs of Sonora; and a long etcetera.

For this reason, as the government began to crack down on the Liberal clubs that had multiplied after 1900, a Liberal exiled from Lampazos, Vidal Garza Pérez, and his associate, Sara Estela Ramírez, started to organize a network of Mexican Liberal clubs in Texas with the purpose of sustaining the Liberal cause from there.[15] They did this in consultation with Ricardo Flores Magón and under the ideological and organizational umbrella provided by San Luis Potosí's Club Ponciano Arriaga. Thus, organizing on the U.S. side of the border was an available strategy practically from the beginning of the movement.

The principal rival factions for succession within the Díaz establishment also developed political clubs. General Bernardo Reyes, in particular, fostered a network of newspapers and clubs. As minister of war, he also organized a voluntary militia in 1900, the Segunda Reserva, which was an ambitious move to gain organizational clout at the national level. The putschist potential of the militia was denounced by *Regeneración* and understood by Díaz, who soon disbanded it and demoted Bernardo Reyes from the War Ministry back to the governorship of Nuevo León. Interestingly, several leaders of the Liberals, including Práxedis Guerrero, Manuel Diéguez, and Esteban Baca Calderón, had their first military training in Reyes's organization.

Catholic working and artisanal classes also had associations. Mutualist groups had sprung up in response to the new social orientation propounded by Pope Leo XIII's 1891 encyclical *Rerum Novarum*, responding to challenges coming from socialist and anarchist unions. Catholic artisan organizations developed in dynamic tension with the dictatorship—supporting Díaz, at least nominally, but often clashing with this or that policy or official. Thus, of three newspapers that refused the invitation to join the Marcha de la Paz celebrating Díaz's 1900 reelection, two were Liberal—*Regeneración* and *El Diario del Hogar*—but the third was the Catholic-nationalist *El Tiempo*.

Finally, there were the Protestants. Like the Masons, they represented a miniscule portion of the population. Historian Jean-Pierre Bastian writes that there were around six hundred Protestant congregations in Mexico in 1911.[16] Unlike the Masons, however, Protestants were a recent addition to the religious landscape, and they were often associated with American missionaries. This latter fact facilitated adverse public reactions from the Catholic populace. On the other hand, the very virulence of Catholic reaction made Protestant churches attractive to new generations of the disgruntled, in particular because Protestant churches offered educational opportunities for their brethren, along with a community that was free from the complicities that often existed between priests and local political bosses. As discontent with the dictatorship rose, Protestant churches also found a place in the constricted margins of Mexico's growing civil opposition. A number of Liberal Party members or Liberal sympathizers, including some prominent ones, such as Librado Rivera and Pascual Orozco, came from Protestant backgrounds.

All of these associations provided space for a kind of rumble of local opposition, but they were not in themselves sufficiently robust to give shape to a viable political party, at least not yet, especially because the Díaz government gave the new Partido Liberal little time to forge a union between all of these elements.

The Dynamics of Repression

Why did the Liberal movement and the Liberal Party come up against such stern repression fully three years before the next presidential election? The explanation has traditionally been to blame Díaz's intolerance, but the matter is rather more intricate.

The strategy of claiming the space of "pure" Liberalism and of painting the Díaz government as conservative was very successful. New clubs and newspapers sprang up like mushrooms. James Cockcroft cites the conservative *El Estandarte*, which claimed that there were 150 publicly recognized Liberal clubs in operation by October 1901 and around twice that number operating in secrecy.[17]

That dynamic concerned Díaz, since it implied the sort of positive synergy between political organization and the opposition press to which he had long been attentive. But soon his worries were aggravated by an even more dangerous development, a peasant uprising in the mountains of Guerrero, following the imposition of an unpopular candidate for state governor. Díaz responded brutally to that movement, waged in support of the candidacy of Rafael del Castillo Calderon, by sending in Colonel Victoriano Huerta, who burned villages, shot prisoners, held hostages, and was accordingly promoted to the rank of general.[18]

The combination of ideological effervescence in towns and cities and peasant revolt in the countryside was toxic. Díaz knew this, so he was implacable in repressing the Guerrero movement and either sent direct instructions or at least acquiesced as his subordinates moved to repress the Liberal clubs.

But even this was not the entire problem. The calculations of Arriaga had been that building a party immediately after the 1900 elections would buy the movement time. Along with most members of Mexico's political classes, the group calculated that 1900 would be Díaz's final term, due to his age. As a result, the group's aim was not to defeat Díaz (though attacking him might help establish their ideological credentials), but rather to defeat his intended successors, particularly General Bernardo Reyes, whom they believed to be the most serious threat.

By April, *Regeneración* was entirely explicit about its motives with regard to succession. In an open letter to Porfirio Díaz, Jesús and Ricardo defended the Liberal movement against a crackdown that had already made itself felt in many Liberal clubs, with particular violence in the northern town of Lampazos. "We're not revolutionaries," the men protested and then reiterated. They were for legality and for peace. The nation, however, was uneasy and on the verge of violence. The revolution in Guerrero proved that: "It is important to take popular discontent into consideration. The uprising in Guerrero State could echo in any one of the many oppressed states, and it could find sympathies amongst many humiliated citizens." It was precisely to avoid such a scenario, to avoid revolution—and the American invasion that they claimed would follow inevitably—that the Liberals were organizing, peacefully and legally. The movement also specifically sought to preempt General Bernardo Reyes from becoming the next president: "Fearing renewed bloodshed, we have tried to prove how imprudent it would be for General Reyes to become President of the Republic."[19]

As Porfirio Díaz's minister of war and the former governor of the state of Nuevo León, General Bernardo Reyes was a formidable figure and an implacable enemy. Reyes was the most powerful figure of Mexico's northeastern region, comprising the states of Nuevo León, Coahuila, and Tamaulipas, and so also influential on the Texas side of the border. Like Camilo Arriaga, Reyes, too seemed to believe that Díaz's succession was close at hand and was preparing for it. Reyes was therefore sensitive to the threat posed by an alternative national organization, and he reacted strongly against it, shutting down Liberal clubs throughout the border region, mobilizing a political club of his own in Monterrey, the Club Unión y Progreso, against the Liberal movement, and bringing the army down hard against the Liberals of the town of Lampazos, Nuevo León, which was home to an old elite, including General Francisco Naranjo, who would become one of the founding delegates of the Partido Liberal Mexicano, that stood in competition to his own clique.

And since Reyes was a national figure, his hounding of the Liberals was not confined to Nuevo León or the Texas border. Reyes very probably had a direct hand in shutting down *Regeneración* in October 1901, judging from the fact that *Regeneración*'s final articles were dedicated to denouncing Reyes's organization. He would again imprison Ricardo and Enrique in 1902 and temporarily shut down their editorial venture with *El Hijo del Ahuizote*.

The Flores Magón brothers, for their part, did manage to do Bernardo Reyes harm by airing and lambasting his presidential aspirations in public and by denouncing the use of the Segunda Reserva as a political organization and possibly as a platform for a military coup. As we've seen, these accusations stuck, and Díaz removed Reyes from the War Ministry and sent him back to govern Nuevo León in 1903.

By then, Liberal sentiments in the north were relatively strong, and there was a student movement in Monterrey against Reyes's reelection as governor. But as the 1900 uprising in Guerrero State had proved, the government would not brook opposition to Díaz's candidates for state government. Reyes and his supporters decided to make a quick show of force of their own and staged a massacre on April 2, 1903, that effectively shut down the Liberal movement in the region, at least for some years.

On a lesser scale, the Liberal movement faced similar kinds of problems with other governors and *jefes políticos*. As a rule, members of Liberal clubs came from emerging middle-class sectors (school teachers, journalists, artisans, ranchers) or else from elite families who were on the outs, as was the case of the Arriaga family in San Luis Potosí and of General Francisco Naranjo in Lampazos. The latter element was always closely watched by governors in power.

Thus, San Luis Potosí governor, Blás Escontría, came down against the Club Ponciano Arriaga and their paper, *Renacimiento*, and ended up throwing Camilo Arriaga and his associates in prison.

The Puebla governor, Mucio Martínez, was implacable with the Liberals in Izúcar de Matamoros, murdering and jailing several of them. The Sonora governor, Rafael Izábal, too, had his own beef with local Liberal clubs. And so forth.

Back in Mexico City, it was Joaquín Baranda who took the lead against Ricardo and Jesús. Baranda, who was a former governor of Campeche and who had had presidential ambitions for the 1900 election, had been regularly targeted by *Regeneración* from the very beginning because he was then the minister of justice. The situation with Baranda had parallels with what would happen with Reyes in anticipation of the 1904 election, since *Regeneración*'s attacks on the system of justice made Díaz's decision to remove Baranda from the Ministry of Justice that much easier. Baranda avenged himself on Jesús and Ricardo, orchestrating their imprisonment.

His strategy, which would later be used over and over again, was to encourage a libel charge against *Regeneración* from an obscure, low-level official and then to find a judge who would admit the charge and deal with it in a harsh and arbitrary manner. Because Baranda had been minister of justice, he had such a judge, a certain Wistano Velázquez, whom Baranda had used earlier to shut down other opposition papers. Thus, in March 1901, the *jefe político* of Huajuapam, Oaxaca, a Mr. Luis G. Córdoba, brought a suit for defamation against Jesús and Ricardo, who had printed an article in which they had (accurately) reported that *jefe político*'s abuses.

Judge Velázquez put the men in prison on May 15 and denied them bail. On January 22, 1902 (after *Regeneración* had closed down), Jesús and Ricardo were convicted and handed a two-year prison term, which was commuted, and the two brothers were released in March 1902.[20] Jesús and Ricardo thus spent ten months in Belem. Velázquez also took advantage of the occasion to confiscate the printing press of *El Diario del Hogar*, where the article against Córdoba had been printed, and briefly imprisoned its editor, Filomeno Mata, for good measure. While in prison, Jesús and Ricardo were allowed to continue to communicate with the outside, and thanks to Enrique and to Jesús's partner, Ernesto Arnoux, they were able to continue publishing *Regeneración* until October.

In sum, the Liberal Party faced a number of enemies, many of whom were emboldened against it by *Regeneración*'s brash attacks on Díaz himself. It was indeed for this reason that several prominent

Liberals, including Camilo Arriaga, had not been eager to confront Díaz directly. However, *Regeneración*'s direct criticisms of Díaz were also the only truly convincing way to wrench the Liberal mantle from the state, so there was a genuine political dilemma there.

Regeneración's strategy earned the movement attention, respect, and even veneration, but it also contributed to undermining the advantage that the Liberals sought to reap by avoiding the 1900 election. State governors, Díaz's cabinet members, local *jefes políticos*, and judges who had grudges against this or that Liberal group or individual could move against them and then take cover behind *Regeneración*'s attack on Díaz. Furthermore, the coincidence of Liberal civic activism with revolutionary agitation in Guerrero made any and all members of the movement vulnerable.

Finally, Díaz himself was not particularly interested in checking the crackdown on Liberals by Baranda, Reyes, or any of his governors. Although the dictator occasionally profited from *Regeneración*'s attacks on potential contenders, Díaz had probably made up his mind to die in office by then, and contrary to popular rumor, he was in excellent health. Getting the Liberals out of the way of the 1904 elections early was not such a bad idea, even for him.

Margarita's Death

Doña Margarita Magón died in Mixcoac, Federal District, on June 14, 1901. Just four days before, she had visited her two boys in Belem Prison. According to the press, it was her anguish over their situation that caused her health to deteriorate. So, for instance, *Las Dos Repúblicas*, a Laredo newspaper, noted that "maybe the sadness of seeing her sons in prison shortened the life of that honorable woman."[21]

The death of Doña Margarita became a rallying point for the opposition Liberal papers. The files in the Archivo Jesús Flores Magón contain a flood of personal notices and published obituaries for Margarita from thirty-one different newspapers from all over the country and from Texas. Ricardo and Jesús were famous by then. They had called Díaz a dictator and consistently decried violations of justice, citing specific instances and using real names. Now they were being held on trumped-up charges. This had general implications for freedom of the press.[22]

The death of Margarita Magón made the drama of the Flores Magón brothers at once more public and more personal. The dictatorship had imprisoned them for their courageous defense of liberty and justice, and that sentence was the cause of their mother's death. To make matters more painful to them, but also more appealing to the public, imprisonment had kept the noble brothers from receiving the final embrace and benediction of their dying mother. Jesús and Ricardo had been deprived of a precious moment, laden with metaphysical consequences.

Thus, in Laredo, *La Crónica* proclaimed that "we need not vent our feelings of indignation against the cause that kept those men from running to the deathbed of the person they loved so much."[23] The Mexico City *El Demócrata* added that indignation was high, because "everyone knows that those gentlemen were imprisoned on the order of an arbitrary judge and that they have not yet gained their freedom, despite the fact that justice and reason are both on their side."[24] Interestingly, the participation by the family of the news of Margarita's passing has her dying within the fold of the Catholic Church, signaling the children's respect for her belief, even while they themselves were so pointedly atheistic and anticlerical.[25]

For its part, *El Diario del Hogar* published a note remarking on the respect that the Magón brothers commanded inside Belem Prison: "There are about 30 men in the convicts' wing where the Flores Magon brothers are being held. In order to express their respect for the pain of the two orphans, those men kept the deepest silence on the night when the news of their terrible disgrace came, and also on the following night. You could even hear the buzzing of the occasional fly."[26]

The young men's failure to attend their mother at her deathbed echoed the tension between duty to country and duty to family in their own father's story. Teodoro Flores had left his wife and family vulnerable to attack while he was out fighting against the French. They were murdered while he protected his country. It is no coincidence, I think, that Enrique's memories of these events gave pride of place to the conflict between family and country. According to his version, Porfirio Díaz had sent an emissary to the dying Mrs. Magón: the president would free her two sons if they would agree to stop attacking him. Margarita, in Enrique's story, tells the Díaz emissary that "I'd rather see them hang from a tree or hanging post, than for them to retract or repent."[27]

Like so much in Enrique's memoir, it is likely that this anecdote, too, is apocryphal. The whole story rings false, at least to me. Nonetheless—again like so much in that memoir—the scene is revealing. The passion for politics that landed Jesús and Ricardo in prison could be conceived as a sacrifice of their most sacred relationship, to their mother, for political life (Figure 7.2). Enrique, who was alone at his mother's side at the time of her death, describes her as spurring his brothers on and providing them with a sublime example—transforming governmental extortion into a moment of feminine courage, with Margarita rising above the cowardly acts of dictatorship.

I believe that the varying attitudes of Jesús, Ricardo, and Enrique toward the circumstances surrounding their mother's death were consequential. Jesús emerged from this bout in prison deciding to marry the woman he loved, Clara Hong, and to remove himself from clandestine political activities. He had been sent to prison the first time barely four days after his father's death, leaving his mother and his younger brothers unprotected; now he found himself removed from his mother in her final hour. He would not do this again.

Ricardo, for his part, threw himself into political revolt single-mindedly, absolutely. It was, indeed, this fervor that gained him such respect among his peers and ultimate leadership of the group of young bohemians who came together to publish *El Hijo del Ahuizote* in 1902, who were subsequently imprisoned together in Belem, and who made their way to Texas in 1904. José Valadés paraphrases one of Ricardo's comrades, who paints Ricardo's inner state quite exactly: "Though Ricardo Flores Magón was not the very smartest of the group of prisoners, he was, according to Alfonso Cravioto, the prototype of the apostle. His ends and means were absolutely incorruptible.... Flores Magón dazzled his comrades with his character of iron."[28]

Enrique wavered between the positions of his older brothers, and indeed, he wavered between them for much of his life. Unlike Jesús and Ricardo, Enrique was with his mother in her final hour. He could not reproach himself on that score, the way the older two boys might have done. But on the other hand, neither did Enrique receive the public admiration that Jesús and Ricardo got, despite his own very considerable sacrifices. Like so many little brothers the world over, Enrique might well have wished to prove to the public that he, too, was capable of doing what his older siblings did—sacrificing everything.

Enrique had an artistic and lighthearted temperament. There is one letter surviving from him to his brothers from the time of their

Figure 7.2 Veneration for Margarita and Teodoro was the foundation of these siblings' ethical makeup. Ricardo would later go so far as to claim that "the child who does not love his parents cannot be a good person." To Margarita, from the boys. Courtesy of the Casa de El Hijo del Ahuizote, Mexico City.

imprisonment, written before their mother's illness, in which he tells of a bicycle tour to Texcoco with his friends. The letter is all levity and innocence, starting with the heading "Queridos Gordos" (Dear Fatsos), followed by a cartoon image of his brothers and signed at the end with a cartoon drawing of himself (Figure 7.3).[29] It is hardly the writing of the single-minded boy militant that Enrique chose for his self-image in his memoir, but it speaks instead of a different sort of life— a life with schoolmates and with a family, striving to continue living an everyday existence, even in the face of having two siblings in prison.

But it was that very lad, in those very months, who was in charge of keeping *Regeneración* going. Soon, Enrique would inch closer to Ricardo's sphere, which landed him in jail, first, briefly, in 1902, alongside Ricardo for articles printed against Bernardo Reyes in *El Hijo del Ahuizote* and then, together with the entire editorial group of *Hijo del Ahuizote* (Alfonso Cravioto, Juan Sarabia, Santiago de la Hoz, Santiago de la Vega, and Ricardo), in 1903. And from that prison, he, too, went directly into exile.

However, even then, the nature of Enrique's long-term plan as regards the connection between his private and political life is unclear. A rare missive, sent from Enrique to Jesús and his wife Clara from St. Louis, Missouri, barely one year after his exile, in 1905, suggests that Enrique may well have had Jesús as his longer-term model.

In that letter, Enrique wrote to his "*hermanitos*" (Jesús and Clara) to tell them that his fiancée in Mexico City, Guadalupe Rocha ("Lupita"), had cut off their engagement. Lupita had allowed her aunts to influence her and was now demanding that they undergo a Catholic Church wedding, which was impossible for any member of the Liberal Party. Indeed, the 1901 Liberal Congress prohibited Liberals from sending their children to Catholic schools and from supporting the church in any way.[30] But reading between the lines. it is also clear that Enrique's exile in the United States was a critical factor: "Being so far away, I had little—almost no—influence on her feelings and so could not correct her retrograde inclinations with regard to emancipation from the odious and stupefying Catholic Church or counter the influence of her prudish and imbecilic aunts, since they believe in the ridiculous farce of an ecclesiastic marriage."[31]

At two points, the letter spirals downward into despondency and despair: "This has been a folly of hers that damages both of us, because I know that she still loves me as ardently as I love her.... It

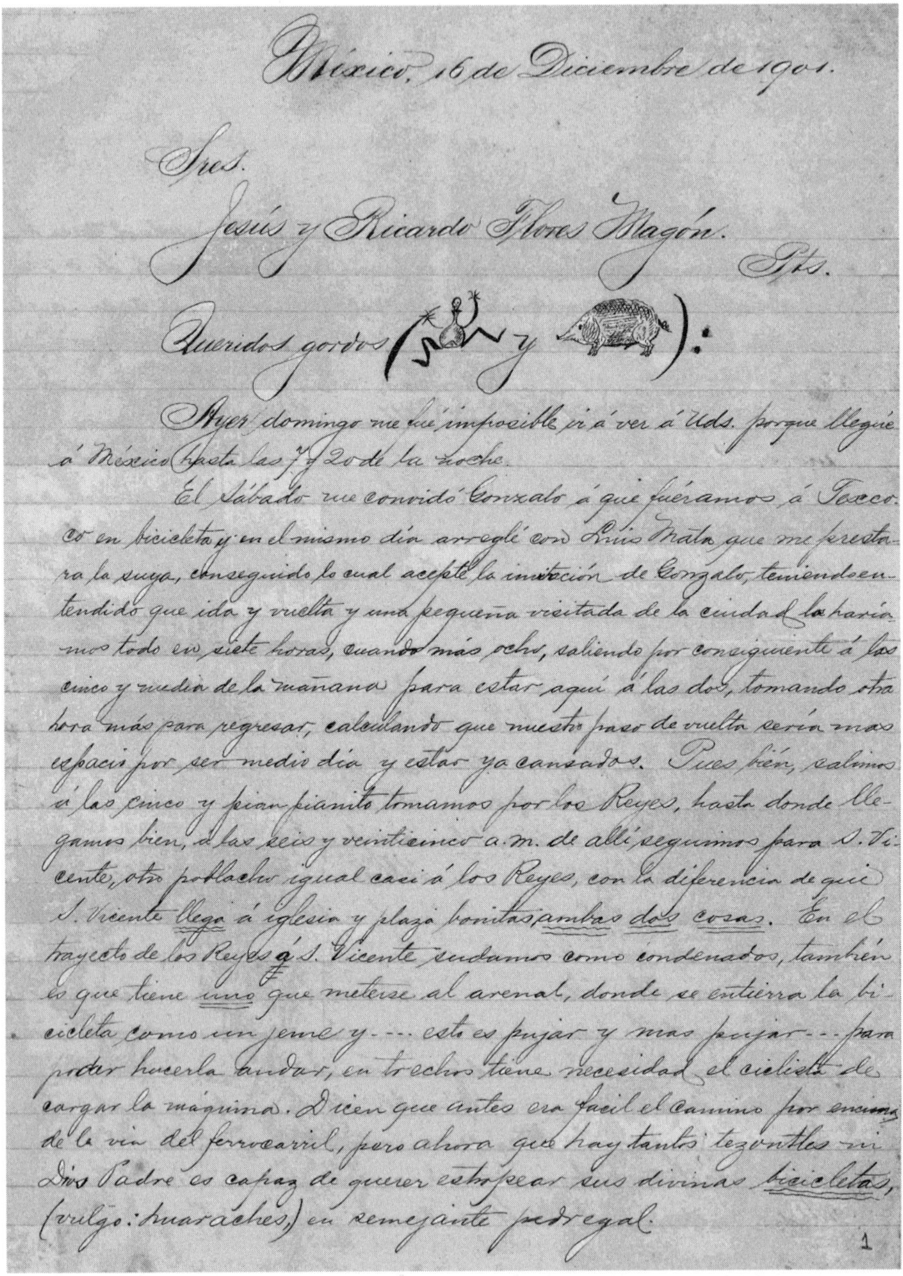

México, 16 de Diciembre de 1901.

Sres.

Jesús y Ricardo Flores Magón.

Pts.

Queridos gordos (🐀 y 🦔):

Ayer domingo me fue imposible ir á ver á Uds. porque llegué á México hasta las 7 y 20 de la noche.

El Sábado me convidó Gonzalo á que fuéramos á Texcoco en bicicleta y en el mismo día arreglé con Luis Mata que me prestara la suya, enseguida lo cual acepté la invitación de Gonzalo, teniéndose entendido que ida y vuelta y una pequeña visitada de la ciudad la haríamos todo en siete horas, cuando más ocho, saliendo por consiguiente á las cinco y media de la mañana para estar aquí á las dos, tomando otra hora más para regresar, calculando que nuestro paso de vuelta sería más espacio por ser medio día y estar ya cansados. Pues bien, salimos á las cinco y pian pianito tomamos por los Reyes, hasta donde llegamos bien, á las seis y veinticinco a. m. de allí seguimos para S. Vicente, otro poblacho igual casi á los Reyes, con la diferencia de que S. Vicente llega á iglesia y plaza bonitas, ambas dos cosas. En el trayecto de los Reyes á S. Vicente, sudamos como condenados, también lo que tiene uno que meterse al arenal, donde se entierra la bicicleta como un jeme y .... esto es pujar y mas pujar .... para poder hacerla andar, en trechos tiene necesidad el ciclista de cargar la máquina. Dicen que antes era fácil el camino por encima de la vía del ferrocarril, pero ahora que hay tantos tezontles ni Dios Padre es capaz de querer estropear sus divinas bicicletas, (vulgo: huaraches) en semejante pedregal.

1

Figure 7.3 Enrique to Jesús (pictured here as fat with a bow tie) and Ricardo (pictured as pig). AJFM caja 9, exp. 16, December 16, 1901. Courtesy of the Biblioteca Daniel Cosío Villegas, El Colegio de México.

is so sad to lose everything. Everything. And maybe forever." And then, farther down: "I hope that she forgets me if she has no intention of changing her ideas! She'll suffer less the sooner she forgets me. Oh, but if she could change her ideas! Then it would be beautiful if she could save a place in her heart for me!"

When Enrique had reached these points, which are dead ends, both from the viewpoint of his intended readers (Jesús and Clara) and from Enrique's own existential position, he drew two thick lines on the paper and started afresh, trying to back out of the narrative cul-de-sac and lighten the load: "¡Bah!," he wrote at one point, "I'm getting too dense. Forgive me!" At another point it is this: "I'm definitely being an ass [*un jumento*], and I'll stop writing any more foolishness. I don't know where my head is today."[32]

The broken engagement came at a pivotal time, because along with his love, Enrique lost his lifeline to a settled family life in Mexico City. In that moment of deep exile, in faraway St. Louis, Enrique's existential orientation turned decisively to Ricardo.

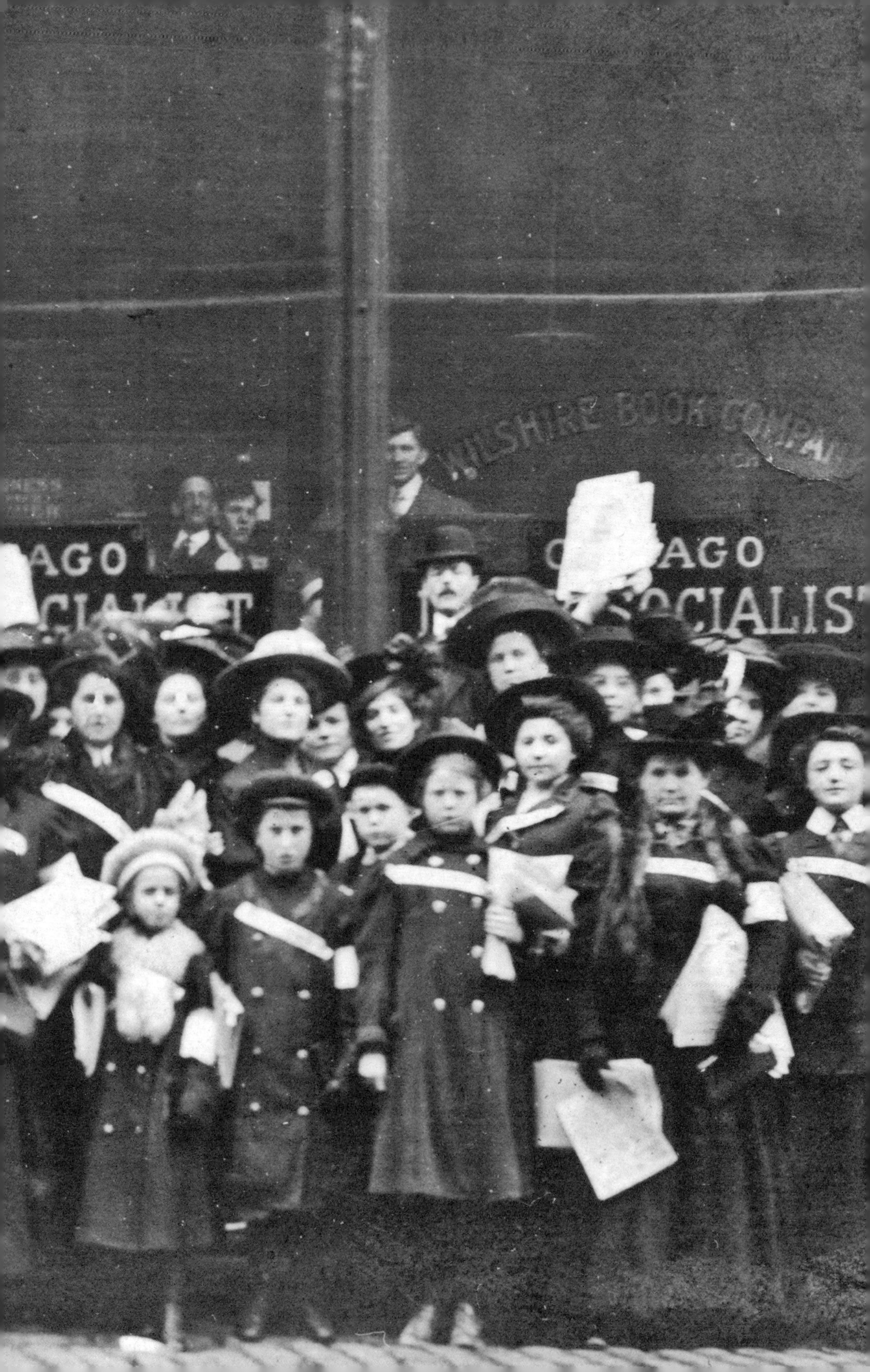

ILSHIRE BOOK COMPA
AGO
CIALI
AGO
OCIALIST

PART TWO

Changing American Opinion (1908–1909)

CHAPTER EIGHT

Slavery

The Valle Nacional is as accessible as Wall Street and beset with less dangers, and thousands of Americans have visited there.
—"The American Colony in Mexico," *American Magazine*, December 1909

Hidden in Plain View

Even on his first interview with the junta, John Kenneth Turner already realized that the issue that would awaken the American public with regard to the Mexican Cause must be slavery. Thus, John recalled his incredulous reaction when the prisoners first spoke to him of these conditions: "Human beings bought and sold like mules in America! And in the twentieth century. 'Well,' I told myself, 'if it's true, I'm going to see it.'"[1]

Turner knew instinctively that the scandal could not be poverty. Not corruption. Not dictatorship. Slavery and only slavery would do. Why? Was Mexican bonded labor really such a shocking discovery?

The image of slavery was a recurrent theme of Mexican combat journalism. For the Liberals, political and civil rights were dead in Mexico, and because of that, the Mexican worker was a slave, and the Mexican soldier was a slave. Even the tireless, freedom-loving Liberals sometimes referred to themselves as "slaves of freedom" or "slaves of the cause."

The lack of freedom and justice, the degree of power abuse that existed in Mexico, made slavery a kind of continuum, rather than an absolute state. Slavery was imminent in the tribulations of the worker who was denied the right to organize, and the conscripted peons in Mexico's tropical plantations were in a state of full-blown chattel slavery (Figure 8.1).

The figure of the Mexican slave was not an invention of the Partido Liberal Mexicano—it had developed over a protracted period. Slavery in Mexico's southeast—that is, bonded plantation labor—had been a regular aspect of U.S. public debate over the implications of American investments in Mexico, for instance. Thus, Mexico's senior diplomat and ambassador to the United States, Matías Romero, wrote articles in 1891 to dissipate American fears regarding the effect that miserable Mexican wages and Mexican slavery might have on American salaries. Romero summarized American misgivings in the following terms: "I've often heard that the main reason to block free trade with Mexico is that Mexican laborers—who are sometimes referred to as 'paupers' or 'peons'—are poorly paid and that in order to maintain the high wages that are paid here, Mexican products must be banned from entering the United States."[2] He then provided an extensive argument against such a position, arguing that Mexico's high transportation costs tended to offset low wages and that Mexican workers were four times less productive than American workers, so that lower wages corresponded to lower productivity.

This, of course, was a delicate argument for an ambassador to make, since it could be taken as justification for the racial denigration of Mexicans and, implicitly, as supporting discriminatory labor practices. At the time when Romero wrote his article, Mexican workers in mines, on railroads, and in other industrial concerns were paid around half of what Americans were paid for the same jobs, both in the American Southwest and in Mexico itself.[3]

However, courting foreign investment had priority, despite the obvious risk of national denigration. At the same time, Matías Romero was at least a little hesitant about offering the U.S. public a racially degraded view of the Mexican worker. Claiming that Mexicans were four times less productive than Americans needed some justification, and Romero offered an explanation that steered away from the racial question:

> In my view, the main causes of this differential in labor productivity are, first, that the Mexican laborer is not as well paid or as well fed as the American; second, that he usually works to exhaustion, which makes him less productive; third, he is usually not as well educated as the American worker; fourth, he has fewer needs to fulfill, and therefore fewer incentives to work. In addition to these causes there may be, in some locations, a climatic factor.

SOME OF THE SLAVES ON

Figure 8.1 Each plantation worker has a number stamped on his clothes, suggesting that workers were outfitted by the company store and that they were accounted for by number, rather than by name. It is often difficult to establish the provenance of the photos in Turner's *American Magazine* articles. Many are picture postcards, purchased in Mexico City. This photo may have been taken by Turner, although the use of the camera by John or Lázaro was severely constrained. The photos that seem most clearly to have been taken by Turner or by a Turner assistant — interiors of Belem prison and interiors of Mexico City tenements — were shot during John's second trip, when he worked as a sports editor for the Mexican Herald. From Herman Whitaker, "The Rubber Slavery of the Mexican Tropics," *American Magazine* 69 (February 1910), pp. 546–47.

But Mexican diplomacy was doing a tightrope act. Mexicans were less productive than Americans because they earned less, and they earned less because they were less productive. Americans need not fear Mexican imports, because although wages in Mexico were cheaper, lower labor productivity and higher transportation costs offset the difference. The Mexican government wanted to protect and increase U.S. investments in Mexico against arguments coming from American labor, but the only way to achieve this was either publicly to denigrate the Mexican worker or to make the Mexican economy appear uncompetitive.

As a result, a story of progress was needed: Mexico's labor productivity would improve gradually, alongside salary increases, improved education, and changing habits. All of these changes were

ONE RUBBER PLANTATION

being promoted by the patriotic and enlightened government of General Porfirio Díaz.

But none of these gradual and progressive changes could possibly occur if there was actual slavery. Slavery, if it existed, meant that there was unfair competition with America's free workers. It also implied that Mexican labor conditions would never improve. That is why official Mexico needed to dispel its specter: the matter had practical consequences in the policy debate over Mexican exports to the United States. Indeed, slavery in Mexico was as much a foreign-policy liability as it was an internal political problem.

Interestingly, the Mexican government's champion of the cause of Mexican free labor in the American press, Matías Romero, had himself pioneered the establishment of coffee *fincas* in the Soconusco (Chiapas) that ran on debt peonage. So the arguments that Romero used for the American public were one and the same as those that "slave owners" in Mexico used more broadly. Specifically, Romero argued that debt peonage existed in the Mexican tropics because commercial agriculture was developing quickly, and so those regions did not have enough laborers to stock new enterprises. As a result, Romero said, wages were higher in the tropics than elsewhere, and special provisions were granted to entice workers to go there. These provisions included advance payments or loans.

Thus, debt peonage was supposed to be an expression of the leverage that peons had over proprietors in the tropics and to be of a piece with higher salaries and better working conditions. The cradle-to-grave expenses that are part and parcel of slavery were presented by Romero as the equivalent of a modern-day benefits package.

True, the ambassador conceded, there were cases of abuse. But these were isolated cases. More than anything, debt peonage was misunderstood, misrecognized, and misinterpreted. The misunderstanding stemmed from the fact that when a worker changed jobs, his or her new employer most often had to pay the old employer the sum of that worker's debt. "I speak of this matter out of personal experience. I spent several years as an agriculturalist in the Department of Soconusco, Chiapas, where such conditions prevailed, and I saw the system of peonage there first-hand. There you cannot hire either a domestic or a farm laborer without first paying the debt held with his most recent employer. Debts range between $100 and $500."[4] Slavery, in other words, was an illusion. A misunderstanding.

Experience, however, suggested otherwise. The term used for debt-induced labor recruitment, *enganchar*, "to hook," itself suggested that loans were a prelude to captivity. And, indeed, popular lore was rife with stories of labor recruiters (*enganchadores*) making loans to drunkards in bars or misleading workers with lies and half truths. At times, *enganchado* workers knew that they were selling themselves into slavery from the moment that they took their advanced pay and passed the amount to their families for their most pressing needs. In many cases, however, workers were tricked—unless they were captured outright (Figure 8.2).

So, for instance the *American Magazine* reproduced the story of a German who had been drifting through Mexico and making his living fixing broken sewing machines. In Oaxaca City, he ran out of work and signed a six-month labor contract after receiving a $10 advance.

> Needing clothes, I invested most of the ten dollars in wearing apparel before I knew what I was really doing, and was then admitted or rather thrust into the courtyard of the *meson* [where the laborers were penned].
>
> The company which met me was more numerous than select, and very hilarious, being for the most part drunk. The next morning, having changed my mind, I decided to return the clothes I had bought, and the remainder of the ten dollars that had been advanced to me, and leave, but no such thing was allowed me. A bargain was a bargain, and

unless I could return the ten dollars in actual coin my contract would hold good.[5]

Workers received their advances and spent at least some of the money immediately, either on clothes and equipment for the job or in drink or to pay for a family emergency. Workers were then locked up and sent to the plantations with an armed escort. From that point forward, they were captives. The notion that the advance payment or loan was proof of the relative bargaining power of workers in the tropics was an obfuscation.

In Mexico's Southeast, denunciation of slavery became a leitmotif of the opposition press almost in perfect symmetry with the rise of the various euphemisms that were used to mask the working conditions in coffee, henequen, tobacco, rubber, chicle, and tropical logging plantations.[6] The trouble was that local papers

" We saw a procession of fourteen men crossing the platform, two in front and two behind with rifles, ten with their arms tied behind them with ropes, their heads down "

Figure 8.2 *Enganchados*. Illustrations for Turner's *American Magazine* articles include a number of drawings that stood in lieu of photographs, probably drafted in New York with visual coaching from John and aided by photographs and post-cards for information on costume and ambience. From John Kenneth Turner, "With the Contract Slaves of the Valle Nacional," *American Magazine* 69 (December 1909), p. 253.

and newspapermen who were prone to denounce bondage were often persecuted. Thus, British archaeologists Channing Arnold and Frederick Tabor Frost published a letter to Porfirio Díaz denouncing conditions in Yucatan in which they mention a specific case of citizens who had protested the murder of Maya slaves and who had been put in prison as a result.[7]

Despite planters' allegations, the reality of bonded labor kept resurfacing in rumors and in fleeting visions, and it periodically popped into the open. In Chiapas, for instance, reformist writer Angel Pola denounced conditions as constituting de facto enslavement as early as the 1880s. Nor was Pola shy about details, decrying the use of chains, whips, and the use of peons as beasts of burden. When he prodded the state's governor, Miguel Utrilla, about the justification for the planters' use of the stocks, shackles, and chains for peons, the governor replied that "it can be explained only by the servants' lack of education, by their rough and severe character, and by their proverbial laziness."[8]

Within Mexico, there was even less ambivalence about justifying labor conditions on the basis of racial inferiority than Mexican officials expressed in the United States. Perhaps this is because in the United States, "Mexicans" as a whole were thought of at the time as a "race," whereas racist justifications such as those of Chiapas's governor were directed only to an underclass of Indians, and not to all "Mexicans."[9]

Indeed, the *American Magazine*'s German worker who unwittingly sold himself into slavery was rescued from the hardest peon labor by one of the tobacco planters of Mexico's infamous Valle Nacional, who bought up his debt and then moved the German into a bookkeeping job for which he was, in fact, not qualified, because "he did not like to see a white man of some culture working as a peon." At the new plantation, the German worker was moved out of the heavily guarded *galeras* where the slaves were locked up every night and was instead asked to work as an enforcer: "I was given a huge .44 calibre Colt six-shooter and belt.... Then I gave my word not to take French leave, and was thereupon domiciled in the 'Galera de la Reconcentración.'... My meals I took with the clerks in the main dining-room."[10]

The dehumanization of the *enganchado* workers was achieved by dint of public beatings, inhuman toiling conditions, underfeeding, and by locking up men, women, and children together at night, in close quarters, with no privacy, toilet, or bathing facilities. According to the German slave, the process of denigration was effective, at least among plantation administrative personnel: "'These are not people,' one of the clerks said to me, 'they are animals without a spark of honor.'"[11]

In the case of the Yucatán Peninsula, the stream of slaves had four main sources: the debt bondage of local Maya villagers, the enslavement of Cruzob Maya rebels from Quintana Roo, the importation of "coolie" indentured servants from the Korean peninsula and China, and deportees from the rest of the Mexican Republic, sent either as entrapped military conscripts to build railroads and to exterminate Maya rebels or, in the case of the Yaqui Indians of Sonora, taken as captives and sold as plantation slaves.

Even friends and supporters of Díaz recognized that the image of Indian slavery in Yucatan was widespread. Thus, in 1891, Yucatecan reformer Manuel Sierra Méndez wrote to Díaz to proclaim his position on the matter, beginning with a commonplace genuflection that reflected a general impression, even as it rejected it: "Far be it for me to share in the frequently held belief that in this land the Indian is a slave."[12]

Like witchcraft, slavery in Yucatan seemed never to exist on one's own plantation. Always, it was across the way, always somewhere else. There was indeed a ritual disavowal of slavery: peonage, it was said, was misrecognized as slavery; slavery existed only as an exception.

At times, these rituals of disavowal were elaborate. So, for instance, Arnold and Frost told of the pains taken by the Yucatecan planter class to hide plantation slavery from Porfirio Díaz when he announced his first and only tour of the peninsula: "Díaz, they knew very well, cared little or nothing for the Indians *qua* Indians. But Díaz cares immensely about the fair name of Mexico.... If money and bribery were of any avail, those slave-owners would see to it that their terrible ruler should be fooled."[13] The anecdote is interesting, because the conceit that Porfirio Díaz did not really know about slavery in Yucatan seemed credible even to this pair of British archaeologists who denounced the practice as being extensive in Yucatan.

To make what was everywhere in evidence invisible, Yucatecan planters took their president to a plantation that was ninety miles away from Merida. Díaz's plantation visit was then presented as the culmination of his "fact-finding mission." He had gone to the "source" of all rumor, to a henequen plantation, where agave was raised to make rope:

> At the station where the President alighted for the drive to the farm, the roadway was strewn with flowers. Triumphal arches of flowers and laurels, of henequen, and one built of oranges surmounted by the national flag, spanned the route.... Having inspected the henequen machinery he...visited the hospital of the finca, and the large chapel where the Catholic laborers worshipped...and during his tour of inspection, he honored several laborers by visiting their huts thatched with palm-leaf and standing in their own grounds well cultivated by the occupants. More than two hundred such houses constitute the beautiful village of this hacienda, which breathes an atmosphere of happiness."[14]

After a most elaborate search, Díaz had failed to discover an institution that was all around him. He had visited the homes of the workers, where he made his definitive pronouncement on the matter: "Some writers who do not know this country, who have not seen, as I have, the laborers, have declared Yucatan to be disgraced with slavery. Their statements are the grossest calumny, as is proved by the very faces of the laborers, by their tranquil happiness."[15] But Díaz needn't even have gone so far to find slaves. He could have seen them around the corner of the National Palace.

The "Purloined Letter Effect"

One of the interesting things about the work of our American conspirators is the lengths to which they had to go, the talent, resources, and risk that they had to expend, to prove the existence of something that was in plain view. The phenomenon of something that is hidden in plain sight is sometimes recognized as a kind of "purloined letter effect," after Edgar Allan Poe's story.[16]

In the early 1900s, the United States was undergoing a revolution in its consumer culture, with new products, new standards, and new habits being adopted at an incredible rate. Edison's labs were producing patented inventions right and left; the country had just been electrified; the motor car was beginning to be mass produced; refrigerated cars were opening the way for the consumption of exotic tropical products.

All of that added up to a race for economic control over the tropics. Thus, in 1898, the British Social Darwinist Benjamin Kidd made a famous pronouncement to the effect that:

> The great rivalry of the past has been determined—decided on the whole overwhelmingly in favor of the English-speaking peoples. It has been for the inheritance of the white man's land of the world. The great rivalry of the future is already upon us. It is for the inheritance of the tropics, not indeed for possession in the ordinary sense of the word, for that is an idea beyond which the advanced peoples of the world have moved, but for the control of these regions according to certain standards.[17]

A growing array of American consumer products—rubber tires, copper wiring, umbrellas, hemp cord, vanilla and chocolate ice cream, and a long etcetera—was made from commodities produced south of the border and especially in Mexico. There was, however, some reticence about knowing too much about the conditions in which those products were made. They were, after all, goods that improved the daily lives of American consumers.

It was unpleasant to think, for instance, that the pacifier that a mother lovingly placed in her baby's mouth was made by the emaciated hands of a political prisoner, condemned to die in a Yucatecan rubber plantation, or that American corn, wheat, and alfalfa was being harvested, bundled, and tied by machines that used twine purchased from that same place.

The idea of progress went hand in glove with the notion that the American continent was a land that had cast off the fetters of oppression. Autocracy and slavery, in particular, were supposed to have been extirpated. Their horrors were on conspicuous display in Russia, for autocracy, and in the Belgian Congo, for slavery. Both of these places erupted in scandal around 1905—Russia with its failed Japanese war and its revolution, and the Congo with searing journalistic and literary exposés regarding the violence and human degradation behind the rubber and ivory boom fostered by Belgium's King Leopold. But these places were safely remote from the aw-shucks innocence of the American consumer. Read from the comfort of the America's living rooms, newspaper headlines about Russia and the Congo served as morality tales that reaffirmed the nation's chosen course.

But Mexico's situation was different. American investment there had preceded and then launched all U.S. foreign investment in Latin America; Americans held major positions there in mining, ranching, banking, and railroads and were sending thousands of investors, managers, and specialized workers south.[18] As a result, no one was eager to find ignominy there. Indeed, it was only once the cat was out of the bag—after the publication of John Kenneth Turner's exposé—that the silence about Mexico was shown to be cultivated and even deliberate. John managed to expose the various U.S. interests that worked to hide Mexico's reality from American opinion or else to make it seem natural.

Discovering the Obvious

The strategies used inside the United States to hide Mexican slavery paralleled those used in Mexico to some degree, but there were also differences. Indeed, hiding slavery in plain view benefitted from a kind of doubling, a game of mirrors that was made possible by the international border. Communicators sometimes used diverging strategies when they tried to legitimate debt peonage and slavery to Mexican and to American audiences. Thus, when Ambassador Matías Romero defended debt peonage before a U.S. audience, he explained it as an effect of labor scarcity in the tropics and the universal laws of supply and demand. But when, on the contrary, Chiapas planters such as Romero came together to discuss the matter in Chiapas, they included the need to discipline the lazy Indian as a core cause.

Armando Bartra has described the debates that Chiapas landowners and politicians held on these questions in the 1890s and early 1900s: all invoked the alleged indolence of the Indian—his refusal to work except through compulsion—as a significant legitimating factor.[19] Moreover, it was not only the "lazy Indian" who was being taught the virtues of work and wage: debt peonage also worked to flush out the vagrants from Mexico's cities. Thus, in 1902, Mexico's *Heraldo Agrícola* defended a "well-regulated" system of agricultural labor contracting, calling it a "powerful instrument for policing and hygiene in the great cities that extracts from them multitudes of men, women, and children who roam through the streets at all hours—ragged, hungry, lazy, useless—or else they are just sitting in the sun in their filthy districts... where they vegetate and ferment like putrid scum."[20]

But this argument was no reasoned proposition in support of some novel policy, nor was it spoken ironically, as if in Jonathan Swift's *Modest Proposal*. It was, rather, a post hoc justification of an established practice: the deportation of vagrants to forced labor in the tropics, often to their premature deaths, had been practiced in central Mexican cities for ten years by the time this "theoretical" debate about it hit the Mexico City press.

One can think of these two registers—one based on universal economic laws, and the other on the compulsory redemption of an inferior race—as "stage front" versus "backstage" justifications. Stage front, the more presentable argument involved an economic explanation that insisted on distinguishing debt peonage from slavery—in other words, it placed the institution of debt peonage squarely within the logic of contractual transactions between rational and free individuals. The second, less universally presentable argument was based on the alleged racial inferiority of Mexico's *clases ínfimas*. Coercion was for the good of the slave. This backstage argument, in turn, had two distinct justifications: physical punishment was an educational corrective to the racially inferior Indian or vagrant, and physical punishment was the only way to keep an inferior class of vagrants out of trouble.

What is interesting about this threefold system of justifications is that its first, most open, aspect was entirely progressive: debt peonage was the result of labor scarcity in the tropics, and it was in fact advantageous to the worker. The initial advance payment was a benefit and recompense used to entice the worker freely, and not a lure or pretext used to entrap and enslave. The second aspect, used internally in Mexico, was at once progressive and oppressive: the worker was cast as racially inferior and naturally lazy; coercion was required to change those bad habits, but the native's habits, once changed, would lead to the improvement of the worker's fate and of that of the society as a whole. The final aspect, however, did not retain even the veneer of progressive reason: workers were racially inferior and potentially dangerous; they could be controlled only via repression. Finishing them off was, in the end, a service to the nation and to civilization.

So the argument for debt peonage oscillated between a liberal set of claims about markets, a racist but still vaguely progressive paternalism, and an argument about the raw survival of the upper caste in the face of potential racial warfare. The use of one argument or another was finely attuned to context. In the slave plantations, hard racist positions were common currency and accompanied reliance on coercion and corporal punishment.

It was only when planters had to interact with gentlemen of other regions that the racial degradation of the slave was substituted for or at least supplemented with arguments founded on a universal market logic. This, no doubt, is why the archaeologists Arnold and Frost noted that "the Yucatecan millionaires are very sensitive on the question of slavery.... You have but to mention the word 'slavery,' and they begin a lot of cringing apologetics as to the comforts of the Indians' lives, the care taken of them, and the fatherly relations existing between the hacendado and his slaves."[21] This sort of paternalist racism gave way to an abstract argument about market logic when justifications were brandished in respectable venues that were far removed from the plantation areas—in the liberal Mexico City press, for instance, or in the pages of American newspapers.

It was this threefold system of argumentation and the system of complicities that went with it that allowed Mexican slavery to be hidden in plain view. The shock came only when citizens who usually heard only the abstract argument about market logic, which allowed no justification for slavery, were confronted with the fact that their daily comforts were supporting that slavery.

Thus, in his 1909 novel titled *The Planter*, Herman Whitaker's hero broods over American complicity in the degradation of Mexican slaves on a Veracruz rubber plantation:

> Yet—and it seemed horrible to David sitting in darkness palpitant with sorrow—these iniquities had been done in their name.... The spinning wheels of the automobiles then carrying luxurious women on errands of pleasure, the rain-coats and rubbers that protected shapely shoulders, and dainty feet, from the wet, each and all of a thousand articles, down to the nipple in the mouth of an innocent babe, the water-bag in the hands of the merciful nurse, were splashed with the blood of the Yaqui.[22]

The gendered dimension of this excerpt is relevant. The consumers who are splashed with Yaqui blood represent the most innocent and purest interior of American society: fashionable women with shapely shoulders and dainty feet, protecting themselves from the rain; mothers with babies and baby carriages and nurses. They are the very picture of insulation, like Kurtz's fiancée in Joseph Conrad's *Heart of Darkness*.

Published early in 1909, Herman Whitaker's *The Planter* was one of the first widely circulated denunciations of Mexican slavery written for an American living-room audience, and yet it did not succeed in creating a true scandal. It did not, in other words, puncture the spell that Mexican slavery had cast on the American public.

Although Whitaker's novel described conditions of slavery—terrible conditions—in rubber plantations of the Mexico's Isthmus of Tehuantepec, and although Whitaker had himself witnessed those conditions, the novel's conceit was that the problem could be set to rights by its hero, a true-blue New Englander who marries a beautiful señorita who happens also to be the daughter of an *enganchadora*, in other words, of a slaver. Moreover, the evil driving force of Mexican slavery in Whitaker's book is concentrated in the person of a German-Jewish planter, Herz, and secondarily in some American swindlers who sell stock for rubber plantations to clean out the pockets of honest, hardworking Americans. In other words, Whitaker's novel left American investors themselves innocent, with the exception of a few wiseguys in finance whose business it was to bilk innocent townsfolk of their savings and keep them in the dark about true conditions in Mexico.

Whitaker's novel is the story of a swindle—the speculative sale of Mexican rubber stock at bloated prices and on false pretenses. It leaves the general question of American complicity in Mexican slavery untouched and fails to link American consumer habits with the policies of respectable American companies and the government. As a result, the scandal of Mexican slavery remained muted.

Only a politicized and knowledgeable Mexican and a capable and savvy American writer, working together, could move effectively, step by step, from the inner aspects of Mexican class relations through to the great American consumer public. It fell to John Kenneth Turner and the guide who led Turner through a land where the American journalist was a stranger, Lázaro Gutiérrez de Lara, to do that hard and risky work.

CHAPTER NINE

John Turner's Guide

Lázaro's Background

Lázaro Gutiérrez de Lara was in some ways representative of the combustible mix of political exiles that the Porfirian dictatorship had edged out of the country. He first arrived to Mexico City from his native Monterrey in 1889, when he was eighteen.[1] Lázaro's branch of the family was downwardly mobile. His father inherited only a fraction of the family estate and died when Lázaro was young, leaving his wife a little money, which she carefully nursed in order to send her children to school.[2] In fact, the small Gutiérrez de Lara family moved to Mexico City so that Lázaro, who was the eldest of the brothers, might enroll at the Escuela Nacional de Jurisprudencia.

Although Lázaro avoided prison while participating in the 1892 student movement, he was expelled from school in June 1893 for the publication of an article that Lázaro described as a critique of "the antics of our cheap aristocracy."[3] Lázaro warned that Mexico's elite had lost its sense of patriotic duty, leaving the country open to foreign invasion: "a people exposed to oppression is a corpse; and a corpse cannot be a soldier," he wrote. The article had been published after Education Minister Baranda issued his ban on student insubordination, including attacks in the press.[4] Lázaro's expulsion came shortly after *El Demócrata* had been shut down for its articles on the revolt by peasants in Tomochic.

Lázaro came from a distinguished family. His great-grandfather, Bernardo Gutiérrez de Lara, was born in Revilla (now Ciudad Guerrero, Tamaulipas), joined in Miguel Hidalgo's independence movement, and received the rank of colonel. In 1811, he had traveled on horseback from Natchitoches, Texas, all the way to Washington, D.C., to persuade Secretary of State James Monroe to support Mexican independence. Indeed, Bernardo was the first Mexican national to visit the American capital, seeking support for Mexico's freedom.

It was a different world back then—with no border between New Spain and the United States, only a vast frontier inhabited by a mixture of Native American tribes and settlers. Bernardo's travel log describes an environment that would not have been recognized by his great-grandson Lázaro, who traveled through those same places one hundred years later.

On November 12, 1811, for instance, Bernardo spent the night at the house of an Indian couple. Those Indians wore "a shirt of very fine Holland long enough to reach their feet, without anything else." Nevertheless, Bernardo "was pleased to see the dexterity with which they used the knife and fork." Some days later, after crossing the black waters of the Bear River, Bernardo spent the night at the house of a rich Indian "whose slave quarters looked like a little village." By the time Lázaro arrived to the United States, though, all of those tribes had been reduced to reservations, if not exterminated, and there were no more rich, slave-holding Indians.

Other differences between the two nations were perhaps less deeply transformed. Thus, Bernardo was impressed by the prices of goods once he crossed the Cumberland River: "An arroba of superior tobacco is worth a dollar; a pair of pantaloons made of a kind of cotton that lasts a long time I have seen sell for a dollar and a half; a fine handkerchief at three or four *reals*. The cost of food for man and beast, however, is very great."[5]

Eventually, Bernardo reached Washington and was received by the president. as well as by several cabinet officers, for many of whom Bernardo was the first Mexican they ever met. One hundred years later, Lázaro, after having suffered prison and persecution by American police, was summoned by Congress to Washington to testify against the deportation of Mexican political refugees back to the very country that Bernardo Gutiérrez de Lara had supposedly liberated. *Mexico's Fight for Freedom*—the title of one of Lázaro's books—was for him a family affair.

An Aztec

Lázaro's family pride was entwined with the history of Mexico, a history that, for Lázaro, had only two sorts of actors: heroes and traitors. The rift between good and evil in Mexico ran so deep, for him, that Lázaro thought of it in racial terms: "The history of Mexico is the history of a class struggle in which the opposing classes, master class and working class, are of distinct bloods, traditions, and psychologies."[6] Moreover, Lázaro went on, "all that we know of the evil that is Mexican is the product of a small, parasitic and originally alien section of the nation; and all that we know of the good that is Mexican (and the world in general knows little enough)—the arts, the crafts, the poetry, the gentleness and good faith, the heroic struggle for democracy—is the product of the working class native races."[7]

It is no surprise, then, that when Lázaro presented himself to American audiences, he proclaimed proudly that "the blood of the Spanish conquistadors runs but thinly though my veins. I am almost pure Aztec."[8] This claim was believed and repeated by Lázaro's American friends. Here, for example, is Ethel's description of the man who first introduced her to the Spanish language: "De Lara had a striking personality; he was gentle and fiery almost in one breath. Tall, large-boned, with a handsome, rather heavy face, he always wore a black Windsor tie in a loose bow-knot, after the fashion of artists in that period. He repudiated even a trace of alien blood, claiming to be of pure Aztec origin."[9]

Lázaro's Mexico was divided in two castes, masters and workers; two races, Spaniards and Indians; and two parties, traitors and patriots. However, the traitors had tried to cloak themselves in the noble cause of the republic. "Bearing these simple facts in mind," said Lázaro to his American readers, "the maze of Mexican history may be threaded with ease." The history of Mexico was the history of "a struggle for racial expression and economic freedom on the part of an oppressed people, unusually gifted, of abandoned valor, of wonderful human kindness and gentleness—a struggle carried on against the most bloodthirsty and depraved master class the world has ever witnessed."[10]

In order to underscore the noble origin and worth of Mexico's working class, Lázaro insisted to his American audiences that the great native races of Mexico—Aztecs, Toltecs, Zapotecs, and Mayas—"are not Indians," by which he meant that they were civilized. Indeed, they were much more civilized than the Spaniards, whom he saw as members of a degenerate race, the worst of Europe, for "while Spain was exhausting her best blood in the incessant strife with Mohammed, the rest of Europe conserved their best blood for the enrichment of society, casting only their social offal to the dogs of war."[11]

Lázaro thus echoed eugenicist thinking of the day and made it his own while inverting its valuation of Spanish and Indian races.[12] The influence of Stanford's president, David Starr Jordan, comes to mind. Jordan, who was an influential public figure in California at the time, opposed entering World War I on eugenicist grounds almost identical to what Lázaro deployed as his explanation of Spain's racial inferiority: entering such wars meant losing the cream and flower of the nation's genetic pool.[13] Lázaro thus had racial ideas that could be convincing to American progressive reformers.

The grandeur of pre-Columbian civilization was proof that the Mexican people could govern themselves. It was certainly for this reason that when he was already a well-known agitator, public speaker, and union organizer, Lázaro still took time to do public lectures on pre-Columbian civilization, such as the one that he offered on ancient Mexican art in El Paso, Texas, in March 1915, in the midst of the most violent period of the revolution. On that occasion, Lázaro declared to the press that "in giving this conference, his aim was to destroy the preponderant opinion among Americans, which is that the Mexican people cannot govern themselves."[14]

Lázaro saw himself as belonging to a line of patriots who had been involved in unmasking traitors from the very time of independence. He was proud that his great-grandfather had taken part in the capture and execution of Agustín de Iturbide, the man who had usurped the patriot cause to style himself Agustín I, Emperor of Mexico. Lázaro's was a noble lineage whose rightful leadership had been stolen by a "cheap aristocracy" that had "exchanged the nation's legacy for a bowl of lentils." In this, Lázaro was typical of the Generation of 1892, who saw themselves as the guardians of the tradition begun by Mexico's great heroes Miguel Hidalgo and Benito Juárez against betrayal at the hands of a line of traitors that culminated in the person of the tyrant Porfirio Díaz.

On the other hand, strident appeals to indigenous identity like Lázaro's were more commonly made in the United States than south of the border. In Mexico City, Lázaro's claim to "pure Aztec" blood would have raised eyebrows. He was, after all, from Monterrey, which was never even conquered by the Aztecs. Moreover, Lázaro's famed ancestor's name, rank, deportment, wealth, education, and political standing all indicated that he was of European origin: Bernardo Gutiérrez de Lara was every bit a *criollo*. Finally, Lázaro's own appearance and deportment also would have distinguished him from those who in Mexico were called Indians. In those days, being an Indian meant being a peasant. It meant having little or no schooling and existing in a rather closed communal existence. Francisco Bulnes, though strident in his racism, nevertheless offered a characterization of the Indian that resonated widely: "Indians are unselfish, stoic, and with no education [*sin ilustración*]; they despise death, life, gold, morality, work, science, pain, and hope. They love four things: the idols of their old religion, the earth that feeds them, their personal liberty, and the alcohol that affords them a deaf and mournful delirium."[15]

This was hardly a striking likeness of any student at the Escuela Nacional de Jurisprudencia, an institution that was thought of at the time as a veritable cathedral of positive science, liberal values, hard work, and morality. Not surprisingly, then, none of the publications that Lázaro authored in Mexican newspapers presented him as an Aztec.

But seen from the borderlands, this sort of objection to Lázaro's self-presentation might have seemed a bit pedantic. The real point was that Lázaro's family history and national history were one. If the Porfirian elite was Esau, then the opposition was Jacob. It was they who were the guardians of faith, the true patriots. The sense of returning political power to a lost lineage is what identification with "Aztecs" encoded.

After graduation in Mexico City, Lázaro moved north. First he took a job as a judge at Parral, Chihuahua, but for reasons that are still unknown, he left that position and turned to private practice to defend the victims of Porfirian "progress," instead. He moved to nearby Sonora. In Arizpe and Ures, he defended Yaqui Indians of the district who were then being dispossessed of their land and deported to Yucatan. Ethel made the only notes we have on this subject:

Lázaro Gutiérrez de Lara spent some time in the Yaqui country handling law cases for the dispossessed Indians. At some time in 1906... he was standing on the wharf at the port of Coatzacoalcos, near a

Mexican steamer which had come from Vera Cruz. Then he heard a woman shouting:

"Black Horse! Hello, Black Horse! Come here, women! Here is Black Horse, the lawyer of Arizpe!"

Lazaro saw between the decks about a hundred women, and children. They were standing among horses and pigs, with whom they had been sharing the space.

At first he did not know the women who had called out the name the Yaquis had given him. She was so terribly emaciated that he did not recognize her. Then she told her name. She had been a small peasant landholder of Baviacora, County of Arizpe, Sonora. Those people had lived peacefully for years and years in one spot. Suddenly a squad of soldiers descended upon them, and for the crime of being Yaquis, dragged them away. Wives were here with newborn babies—where their husbands were they did not know. These people could not believe they were going to Yucatan to be worked to death.[16]

At Arizpe, Lázaro also briefly edited a newspaper, *El Porvenir*, but he soon moved a bit further north to Cananea, attracted, most likely, by the economic opportunities emerging there. At Cananea in 1903, Lázaro defended some ranchers who were being fenced out of their lands by the Cananea Copper Company's owner, the infamous William Greene, who had amassed close to half a million hectares in the region.[17] It was due to Lazaro's defense of one of those ranchers, a widow, that he did his first brief stint in jail at Cananea, accused of stealing thirty dollars' worth of Colonel Greene's kindling wood, an accusation that would be revived five years later by the Mexican government as part of its attempt to extradite Lázaro and take revenge for the help he had afforded John Kenneth Turner.

Finally, also at Cananea, Lázaro was hired to defend Antonio de Pío Araujo, a local journalist and leader of the Mexican Liberal Party who was thrown in Cananea prison under trumped-up charges due to company suspicion that he had sent inside information on Cananea to *Regeneración* in St. Louis and that was then published.[18]

Cananea

Porfirio Díaz once referred to Mexico City as "the balcony of the republic." It was only from there, and not from the provinces, that Mexico's political landscape could be inspected. But that was back in the days when Porfirio was merely a presidential hopeful; by 1903, the "balcony of the republic" had been turned into a catwalk for Mexico's prostituted elite to lure foreign investors. Primped up in the latest in Parisian fashion, Mexico City had become a display case. It was easier to read the nation's predicament from Cananea, a town that was barely seven years old. Located barely twenty-five miles south of the Arizona border, Cananea could serve as a token of all what was wrong with the "new Mexico."

The hideous copper mining boomtown was like a memento mori to Porfirian progressivism, its deep mineshafts gaping blankly at the vanities of the age like empty eye sockets. The cause of embarrassment was that while Mexican wages in Cananea were around half of what American workers made, and while Americans hogged the better jobs, to boot, wages there were still among the very highest in the country. Even educated white-collar workers—schoolteachers such as Esteban Baca Calderón and Manuel Diéguez—were attracted to manual labor in the mines because of its superior wages. Sitting in plain view of the American border, Cananea was a kind of monument to relative deprivation.

Moreover, Cananea was a new kind of place. It was an American-owned company town. By 1900, a rail line connected the mine to the new town of Naco, Arizona, barely four years after the Cananea Consolidated Copper Company was created and years before Cananea was connected by rail to any Mexican city.[19] By 1901, the municipality of Cananea had been created, and to mark the occasion, the sprawling copper miners' camp, which had mushroomed since it first was settled in 1896, tried to acquire a more civilized appearance. For this, too, Cananea relied on the company, which supplied the new municipality with electricity and telephone service and donated the property that was needed to build a town center and a municipal building. Plots for the slaughterhouse and even for the town cemetery were also donated by the Cananea Copper Company.[20] The entire venture was owned by "Colonel" William C. Greene and his fellow stockholders.

In order to hold sway over Cananea, Greene incorporated two companies, one in Mexico (the Cananea Consolidated Copper Company, S.A.) and one in the United States (the Greene Consolidated Copper Company). Because the Cananea Consolidated Copper Company was allegedly Mexican and had former Sonora governor (and current Mexican vice president) Ramón Corral as a partner, it had the rights of a Mexican national, a situation that was liberally interpreted both by Greene and by Sonora's governor, Rafael Yzabal, who allowed company officials to govern the municipality at their whim. During the years that Lázaro Gutiérrez de Lara lived in Cananea, between 1903 and 1906, the company's treasurer, Ignacio MacManus, originally an American citizen, was Cananea's municipal president.

Concern and consternation about Cananea went beyond the question of territorial sovereignty into practically every aspect of social life. In terms of labor rights, Cananea was an abomination. Mexicans were second-class citizens in their own country. Writing from St. Louis, *Regeneración*'s editors complained that "the people have to put up with the insolence of the three thousand Yankees who live in Cananea and with the disgusting filth of the two thousand Chinese there, part of whom have monopolized the grocery business, while the others give themselves to their parasitic and ignoble lives."[21]

Moreover, Mexicans working in copper mines across the border in Arizona had better conditions than workers in Mexico, and these miners knew one another, even came from the same villages. U.S. mining engineer Ralph Ingersoll made an enlightening reflection regarding this contrast. It was based on observations made in 1919, rather than in 1905. As Ingersoll colorfully put it, by then, "copper, which is the life-blood of the community, was deader then than the glory that was Egypt, and everybody seemed to be very busy drowning the memory of it."[22] Even so, the contrast that Ingersoll makes regarding the "elevation of the Mexican race" was already in place in the early era of Sonoran copper mining:

> In southern Mexico no attempt is made to change the status of the peon laborer: he is taken for what he is. He is fed and given money to buy alcohol, and his shortcomings are sworn at but accepted. Over the line, to the north, in camps that employ nothing but Mexican labor, where a Mexican city is literally transplanted from its own soil to ours, systematic attempts are made to raise the standard of living. I was told that it takes just four years to complete the Americanization of the Mexican—to teach him to bathe every day, to sleep in clean rooms with plenty of air, and to curb, in a measure, his ferocious appetite for spirits.[23]

Thus, not only were Mexican workers seen as inferior on both sides of the border, but Mexico as a whole was seen as inferior to the United States, since collective working conditions in the United States included some "Americanization" through measures that included urban planning, hygiene, dry laws, and so on and that were either entirely absent or much less intense on the Mexican side.

The blatant inequalities between Mexican and American workers proved that Mexicans were being put down with the complicity of their own government, a collusion that generated the worst kind of debasement of the Mexican in Mexico and fostered Mexican emigration to the United States, as well as Mexican second-class status in that country. Thus, Práxedis Guerrero, who was soon to become one of the main leaders of the Partido Liberal Mexicano, consistently blamed Mexicans for their passivity and insisted on a Mexican solution to Mexico's problems: 'The Mexican people must clean the Porfirian stain from their country."[24]

The editors of *Regeneración*, for their part, argued that urban squalor in Cananea was a result of discrimination, rather than a cause and justification of it: "Mexican workers who go to Cananea looking for improvement are soon disappointed. They are forced to live in dirty wood shacks, where they pay six, twelve, fifteen, or twenty pesos per month's rent. The better lodgings, which are at a separate location, are exclusively for the many Yankees who work there."[25] In short, being part of an enclave, part of a company town that was near the international border, to boot, put local workers in a field of invidious distinctions that made it clear that Mexicans were racially inferior and that Mexico as a whole was inferior to the United States.

These distinctions fanned tensions between Mexican and American workers in Cananea—and in every other enclave like it. The tensions were fired by U.S. workers' fears that management might supplant them with Mexican workers. Mexicans did, after all, come cheaper. As a result, the unions of U.S. specialized workers were tightly knit, and racist sentiments of American workers toward Mexicans could reach a higher pitch even than those of their employers.

Historian Jonathan Brown, who studied racial tensions between American and Mexican workers in this period, cites the 1911 diaries of Gordon Campbell White, a skilled and educated railway employee who was stationed in Empalme, Sonora: "I am inclined to classify the Mexicans as follows: Bastards 70%, syphilitics 80%, thieves and whores 90%, pure Indians 85%, Brainless 95%, 1000 years distant from real civilization 97%. And God help the other 3%." Brown shows that racism against Mexicans was most acute among supervisors and skilled laborers, who thought that they could protect their jobs and their privileges by demeaning Mexicans as a class.[26]

A second source of tension between Mexicans and Americans in Cananea related to public deportment. Causes of tension ranged from real or perceived lack of respect in day-to-day interactions, to differential treatment in commercial establishments, to differential access to justice, and finally to the proliferation of mores that were seen as corrupting public life. In the Mexico of the 1900s, the degradation of the Mexican people by alcohol, moral laxity, and lack of hygiene was discussed by every group on the political spectrum—divisions existed only on the matter of blame. For parties close to Porfirio, it was racial degradation and the depravity of the lower classes; for the opposition, it was the corruption of the political class. But blame needed to be meted out, one way or the other.

Seen from Cananea, Mexico's politicians had primary responsibility for the debasement of Mexican conditions, and it was easy to blame the Mexican government for negligence. Thus, *Regeneración* complained in 1905 that "we've received a flood of complaints from Cananea, Sonora, about the complicity between local authorities, gambling houses, and brothel owners, a relationship that in no way benefits the people, but that does line the pockets of all of the parasites."[27]

The scandal of prostitution and gambling houses had several dimensions that involved the relations between Mexicans and Americans. First, prostitution was regulated in Mexico, and gambling was illegal there. The very existence of numerous gambling houses in Cananea, including Proctor, a large establishment that was open day and night, implied connivance with local and perhaps state and federal authorities. That in itself might not have been so very scandalous, but since Cananea was a company town, and its municipal president was considered a *gringo*, connivance in this case implied national debasement.

Moreover, the petitions and complaints of Cananea's *gente decente* had fallen on deaf ears. Citizen committees had gone first to Cananea's municipal president, then to Sonora's governor, and finally to Porfirio Díaz himself, but their petitions were ignored. Why? According to *Regeneración*, it was because the owner of the gambling houses, Pedro Alvino, was a protégé of General Luis Torres, ex-governor and grandee of Sonora.

Implicit in the case is a demeaning complicity between Mexican authorities and American capitalists: Mexican officials gave Colonel Greene a free hand to extract wealth from the earth and blood from the people, and in exchange, these authorities got a free hand to rob Mexican workers of their hard-earned wages by tempting them with gambling, drinking, and prostitution: "Everything that the workers earn after a hard month's labor ends up at the gambling table. The salaries of white-collar employees go the same way...producing ruin, desolation, and misery in the families and the commerce of that unfortunate mining town."[28]

Thus, *Regeneración* complained, Mexican authorities gave concessions to American capitalists instead of developing the Mexican mining industry: "Cananea is a rich mining district that would have been the happiness of thousands of people, if Porfirio Díaz had not set himself on placing in public office immoral individuals capable of bringing ruin even to the most flourishing town."[29]

It was just a couple of months after the Cananea mining strike was violently put down, in September 1906, that the Junta Organizadora, now in exile in St. Louis, launched its first revolutionary uprising. In preparation for that revolt, Ricardo wrote instructions to Tomás Espinosa, the man whom the junta had named chief of the revolution in the towns of Cananea, Nacozari. and Douglas. In those instructions, Ricardo wrote:

> We should not forgive [Isidro] Castañeda, or [Arturo] Carrillo, or [Pablo] Rubio [all municipal officials], but we need to be wary of one thing: not to attack the Americans. We must get rid of our own rulers first and foremost; there will be time later to rein in the foreigners. We must avoid U.S. intervention at any cost. Our own officials are the cause of our ills, so it is they who we must hang.[30]

Another way in which gambling and prostitution heightened tensions between Mexicans and Americans had to do with regulation and zoning. Like all foreign-owned company towns at the time, Cananea had segregated housing, an arrangement that did not exist in older Mexican cities and towns, where the rich often lived cheek by jowl with the poor and where wealthy Mexicans lived in proximity to foreigners. The segregation of the American colony in Cananea also meant that prostitution was inevitably zoned into the Mexican neighborhoods.

Already social reformers such as Luis Lara Pardo were concerned with the high numbers of prostitutes in Mexico City.[31] But Cananea's situation was even more scandalous, for not only was prostitution rife there, but it was located in the center of town, making for a stark contrast between the manicured homes of the American sector and the degradation of the Mexican sector. And all of this was managed by the municipal president and his cronies.[32]

The visual effect of the contrast between virtue and vice presented by the American and Mexican quarters is outlined in Lázaro Gutiérrez de Lara's *Los bribones* (The scoundrels), a novel that he wrote in 1907, shortly after fleeing Cananea and going into exile in the United States. The novel ends with its heroine, Luisa, despoiled of her husband, her home, and her reputation, though not of her honor. She staggers out of the prison where she has long been entrapped on trumped-up charges. It is night, and Luisa doesn't know where to go, torn as she is between two impossible alternatives:

> On her left, sinking into a canyon, was the maze of alleys of the town of vice—submerged in waves of rot and corruption. It slept a sickly sleep, exhausted by degradation and moral abandon.... On the other side of the poor woman, to her back, a heavy slumber floated over the "homes" [in English in the original]—a calm that was circled and constrained by cold and hostile selfishness.[33]

Luisa is left with no honorable choice but the rejection of all local "society." Cananea's only healthy element is labor, and only labor can redeem all that corruption: "The mysterious and omnipotent force of labor emerged from the pit of the mines. There muscles contracted in a superhuman effort, in a real and effective struggle that created a portent of wealth, energy, and useful and rich material. From the healthy and virile soul of those muscles there also sprouted a wave of good and wholesome strength that was like a promise of redemption."[34]

Los Bribones
Immediately before moving to Sonora, Lázaro was briefly a Second Circuit judge in Parral, Guerrero District, Chihuahua. Although we know nothing of how he got the job or why he left it, we do know how he felt about the work. In his novel *Los bribones*, Lázaro's principal obsession is with justice—or, more precisely, the lack of

justice—with lots of attention lavished on the law, lawyers, prison conditions, and judges, including judges of the Second Circuit, which had been Lázaro's job.

Los bribones is a work of denunciation based on real facts, and Lázaro fully expected to pay a price for the exposé: "If anyone is skeptical about what is told in this novel, he will not find it hard to ascertain its veracity.... Indeed, it is likely that the novel's author will suffer persecutions for it...but no matter. For him. it is 'come what may.'"[35]

One of the novel's key characters—Isidoro Castañeta—transparently is a reference to Cananea's judge of the same period, Isidro Castañeda. The miniscule changes that Lázaro made to the names of Cananea's corrupt officials are perhaps traces of a lawyerly impulse to avoid a possible defamation sentence in Mexico, should Lázaro have sought to return there from exile, or even a suit for libel in the United States, should the Mexican government seek the legal route for revenge.

Lázaro begins his description of the judge with a physiognomic study that reveals him, to contemporary readers, as a brute, a degenerate, and an alcoholic:

> Flabby lips, with the lower lip hanging; a dirty, graying moustache with its convex tufts sticking to the—usually frowning—mouth. A blunt and bulbous nose poking forward, as it if were constantly trying to sniff something out. His skin had the red and bluish blotches that are the diagnostic sign of a deeply rooted alcoholism. His eyes disappeared behind thick glasses; his forehead was widened by baldness, while the few hairs that he had on it formed a dirty, scrawny arc that made him look apish, with this head going up and then back.[36]

This close attention to the debased ("degenerate") human specimen that had been chosen for the position of judge is, of course, deliberate. Like most of his comrades, Lázaro was convinced that there was a positive effort to select government officials for cruelty, pettiness, complacency, and selfishness. The generation's scathing views on the character of Mexican judges went all the way back to the 1892 movement. Thus, *El Demócrata* referred to its judges ironically as los *honrados* (the honest ones) and lampooned their conceit of propriety and impartiality.[37] There is an unbroken thread of acerbic criticism of Mexican justice in the Generation of 1892 from that point forward.

In the Liberal Party Manifesto of September 23, 1911, Ricardo Flores Magón put the matter very clearly. In the current system of private property, those who win all the competitions and accrue all the gains "are neither the best, nor the most dedicated, nor the most talented—physically, morally, or intellectually; rather, they are the most astute, the most selfish, the least scrupulous, the hardest of heart; the ones who place their own welfare above any consideration to human solidarity and justice."

According to Lázaro's account, Castañeta's career might have served as a paradigmatic case. It had begun in the brothels of Cananea, where his job was to entice visitors to enter, drink them into a stupor, and then rob them. Castañeta then began roping minors into prostitution, built a prostitution ring, and served as a provider for the sexual appetites of "rich degenerates"—a matter that caused enough of a scandal to force him to leave Sonora temporarily for Baja California. Upon Castañeta's return, he had renewed his ties to prostitution and trickery, but also had taken up a position as scribe, which allowed him to indulge in various forms of legal chicanery. He also began printing a newssheet dedicated to public scandal. It was indeed, this combination of "accomplishments"—providing sexual favors, understanding the simple procedures with which laws could be corrupted, and participation in public life by way of blackmail, ridicule, and extortion—that finally had brought him to the attention of a prominent general, who in turn recommended him to the governor of Chihuahua.

After Castañeta had performed untold services there, the governor had conferred a law degree on him (for unlike Lázaro, Castañeta never went to law school). Finally, he had come to the attention of the American owner of the Cananea mines (Colonel William Greene is unnamed in the novel, because even using a proxy for his name would have been legally risky—Greene had already sued *Regeneración* for libel), who had asked the governor to name him judge.

In short, the position of judge was untenable for Lázaro because he felt that there was a positive and very deliberate policy of corrupting the law. It is not surprising that he either resigned or was fired.

The likely scenario is that Lázaro got the position of circuit judge of Parral through his Mexico City connections at the Escuela Nacional de Jurisprudencia and that having arrived, he came into conflict with local authorities that he was expected to serve. As a result, he left that job and moved to Sonora, where he published a newspaper and set up a law practice, and then to Cananea, where he set up as a lawyer, but also as a prospector. One El Paso paper suggested that Lázaro made an important find:

> An ancient gold mine of fabulous richness, which, according to tradition, was operated more than 300 years ago, has been discovered, thirty miles south of the town of Sahuasipa, in the state of Sonora, Mexico, by Gutiérrez Lara, an attorney of Sahuasipa.
>
> Mr. Lara was exploring one of the numerous caves in the Santísimo mountains when he came upon the rich ledge of gold. It has long been superstitious belief of the natives of that section that the Santísimo caves are inhabited by supernatural beings, and they have been little explored on that account.[38]

It is doubtful that Lázaro's find was all that rich—he never became a wealthy man—but he did sell a mining property in order to survive after he went into exile, late in 1906, and he used the revenue to write his novel denouncing corruption in Cananea. Like so much oppositional literature of the Generation of 1892, it was printed on the U.S. side of the border.

CHAPTER TEN

"The People Were the Sacrifice"

Beginnings

Late in August 1908, around 7:00 p.m., Lázaro Gutiérrez de Lara and John Kenneth Turner set off separately to the Southern Pacific station in Los Angeles. They left surreptitiously. Neither man risked buying a ticket. Instead, they rode "the vestibule of a passenger train from Los Angeles to El Paso, a practice of the more daring 'hoboes.'"[1] Their unannounced departure and the modesty of their chosen means of transportation were in tune with the circumstances. These men were heavily watched.

The Mexican government was exploring all available means of neutralizing key members of the Liberal Party residing in the United States, and Lázaro was among the party's best-known agitators. And it was not only the Mexicans who were being watched. So were their supporters in Los Angeles—and they knew it.

In the spring of 1908, the circle that met at the Noel home had set up an office dedicated to making propaganda for the Mexican cause, to the liberation of the Mexican political prisoners, and to purchasing guns for the revolutionists who rose up in June of that year. They rented a space in the San Fernando Building, on the corner of Fourth and Main, and called themselves the Western Press Syndicate, with John Murray as president and John Kenneth Turner as treasurer. Financial support came from Elizabeth Trowbridge, whose name did not appear in order to avoid trouble with her family.[2]

The operation was pretty much run by Elizabeth Trowbridge and Ethel Duffy Turner, though, because on May 8, John Murray had secretly left to Mexico in an attempt to make a journalistic exposé that would be a blow to Díaz for American public opinion. Murray managed to give the detectives of the Furlong Agency the slip, but

Elizabeth, Ethel, and John were constantly being watched:

> Spies...they followed us everywhere. Elizabeth was more spy-conscious than I was. They enraged her, but they also made her jumpy, over-cautious. My method was to ignore them, hers to be violently aware of their every move. Sometimes I'd get tired of crossing streets in the middle of the block, darting around corners or into buildings. I'd protest, or try to ridicule. But nothing could change Elizabeth. After all, her way was probably more fun.[3]

At bottom, Elizabeth was more worried about her family than about the spies.[4] But the young women soon became well aware that the spying had serious consequences for their Mexican friends and for the movement as a whole. Their experience with the spies, which became increasingly more threatening, brought home the degree of collusion that existed between their government and the Mexican dictatorship.

By June 1908, the two women had begun taking serious risks:

> Rapidly Elizabeth and I were losing our romanticism and becoming realists. In the days after our jail experience [when they helped smuggle out Ricardo Flores Magón's marching orders for the 1908 insurrection] we had said farewell to Fernando Palomares and Juan Olivares separately in the San Fernando Building as they prepared to leave for Mexico and take part in the uprising. Elizabeth furnished money to buy guns. She spent her time between the Noel home and the Western Press Syndicate, with spies on her trail, the last ominous letter from her mother in her purse, and a vast purpose in her heart.[5]

The activists for the Mexican Cause had been under a lot of stress prior to Lázaro and John's departure. On June 25, the very day that John Murray returned from the Mexican trip he began in May, the Liberals launched an attack on the border towns of Viesca and Las Vacas, led by Práxedis Guerrero and Francisco Manrique. As in 1906, this attack was meant to trigger a widespread revolt. Unlike 1906, though, key members of the junta—Ricardo Flores Magón, Librado Rivera, Manuel Sarabia, and Antonio I. Villarreal—were in prison during both the planning and execution of the revolt. Ethel and Elizabeth played a cameo role in the plot: they had accompanied María Brousse, Ricardo's lover, on a prison visit and had helped her smuggle secret instructions to Enrique Flores Magón. These instructions were later intercepted. Indeed, the Mexican Liberals were deeply infiltrated, their rebellion was expected, and it was easily put down, with Liberals imprisoned and summarily shot in a number of Mexican towns. Ricardo and his comrades were put in isolation from the outer world at the Los Angeles County Jail ("incommunicado"), and the American group had to act on its own, with no consultations with the junta.

John and Lázaro's trip was a bold attempt to keep the movement alive politically and to move onto the offensive at the level of public opinion and propaganda. John Murray's articles on Mexico for the *International Socialist Review*, though impressive in some ways, failed to have a substantive impact on public opinion. There was despondency and despair in the Liberal camp. This is how Ethel recalled that period:

> John Kenneth Turner was doing some hard thinking those days. He spent a lot of time talking to de Lara. Then he consulted Elizabeth. Before long the plan that was to work, and that incidentally would help to shape Mexico's future history, was born. John and de Lara would go to Mexico together. John would present himself as a buyer from a New York firm—as a tobacco buyer in Valle Nacional, a buyer of sisal hemp in Yucatan and Quintana Roo. De Lara would go along as his paid interpreter and guide. Elizabeth agreed to pay all expenses.[6]

John and Lázaro were cognizant of the persecution that their movement faced, and their mission was kept completely secret, known only to the closest circle of collaborators—Ricardo, Antonio, Librado, and Manuel (all in prison), and Ethel, Elizabeth, John Murray, the Noels, the Harrimans, and Hattie Shea, who was Lázaro Gutiérrez de Lara's American Socialist wife. Even so, skipping town quietly was of utmost importance. Lázaro was a wanted man in Mexico, and he needed to enter the country with an assumed identity. So skipping town was a way of giving the slip to the consular spy network.

But there was also a second attraction for "riding the rails." In those days, the image of American freedom had come to be connected with free travel. As historian Frederick Jackson Turner had declared, the colonization of the West was over. There was no more homesteading, and there were no more Indian wars. The lawlessness of the "Wild West" had given way to development, the power of the trusts, and the rule of law.

But there was still some freedom left in the American West, and it was expressed, at least in part, in freedom of movement. Intense union activity occurred alongside vast labor migrations, not only because of the tremendous influx of migrants from abroad, but also because of the way in which people hopped between jobs. In such a context, "riding the rails" came to stand for a kind of freedom. Many veterans of the Spanish American War hopped on freight trains as hobos, looking for a new life after having seen the wider world. So, too, did the radicals of the Industrial Workers of the World—the IWW, known as the Wobblies—and the Western Federation of Miners, looking for brighter prospects. They rode the rails to flee the site of a strike, to look for new opportunities, or simply for the adventure. Mexican immigrants, too, learned to ride the rails as soon as they gained confidence in their new lives as American workers.

Indeed, this image of freedom and self-reliance had become as important for Mexican members of the Liberal Party as it was for the true-blue American hobo. So, for instance, in her portrait of the Mayo Indian radical Fernando Palomares, Ethel emphasized precisely this aspect:

> Sometimes he was a worker and sometimes a vagrant. He picked cotton in Texas near Austin. He went from Dallas to Shawnee, Oklahoma, still spreading the "powder" among Mexican workers. He rode the rails. He found that American tramps did not discriminate against Mexicans, but that they were all brothers. They would sleep in jungles, cook mulligans in cans, fry eggs on a shovel. He went to Nebraska. Slept in jungles until the police came with their clubs. He was a member of the IWW and went to their halls in the large cities.[7]

The campsites where the rail vagrants slept, known as "jungles," were places of equality between the races where an individual might seek out new opportunities, as well as "spread the powder"—propagandize. These facets of a free life led Mexican union men such as Blas Lara to refer to the cars of the Southern Pacific Railroad as "my trains." When he was once asked whether he needed money to go from California back to his native Jalisco to help his sick sister, Blas responded: "Not at all—I've got plenty of money. I'm going to ride on 'my trains.' Won't be giving a cent to the Southern Pacific Railroad."[8] The same language was used some years later by Liberal organizer Rafael García, who rode the rails from California to Texas and from there to Washington, D.C.

When crossing West Virginia, Rafael was caught and beaten up by the railroad guards. This is what he had to say about that:

> I missed "my train" in West Virginia because I was arrested by the rail companies' "dogs" there. Perhaps because of the constant friction between miners and local authorities in that state, their dogs are even wilder than the ones down south. In the South, the cops at least listened when I explained why workers are compelled to travel as tramps; here, they tried to beat me when I started making the same explanations or whenever I responded to their insults. Even so, they released me, after giving me heat and after inspecting the letters and papers I had with me, demanding that I leave town at once.[9]

Among Mexican radicals, riding the rails as *trampas* came to symbolize a class and a political identity. The term *trampa* rolls the English term "tramp" and the Spanish term for cheating (*trampa*) into a single image, the worker as free-roaming trickster, and it was also used to form a new verb that referred specifically to riding the rails, *trampear* (to tramp). Poor workers had to know how to "viajar de trampa" if they wanted to survive, and the ties of solidarity between those who did were a mark of belonging. So, for instance, when Liberal organizer Teodoro Gaitán was accused of bilking his comrades, one of the miners testified that "López and Gaitán were at the station in Lourdsburg, N.M., when a mail train approached, and Gaitán said: 'Tramp it [*trampéalo*]; I'm taking the passenger train.' That sort of arrogance is unseemly in a person who is traveling with money garnered from his comrades' contributions and especially when that person presents himself as a proletarian who has to tramp the trains to travel."[10]

The divide between the true worker and the opportunist thus was expressed in the class division between those who took the risk and hardship of traveling for free—hiding between or underneath the cars or in empty freight cars—and those who enjoyed the comfort of legality, and a paid seat. By "tramping it" from Los Angeles to El Paso, John and Lazaro gave the slip to a net of spies, police, and private detectives, but they also took the opportunity to immerse themselves in their radical, populist political identity of choice, because they were about to disguise themselves, instead, as enemies of the people.

The Disguise

This is how Ethel told it: "When they reached El Paso they shaved, bathed, changed clothes and stepped out of the hobo role to become a buyer for a large exporting and importing house in New York and his interpreter."[11]

John presented himself as an American investor interested in purchasing a plantation in the Mexican tropics—perhaps a henequen plantation in Yucatan or a tobacco plantation in Valle Nacional, maybe even an investment in Isthmus rubber. Lázaro played the part of John's translator and assistant. Their disguises were not too difficult to assume. John had read up on tropical agriculture, enough to make a few intelligent questions to would-be sellers. He was, in any case, familiar with agricultural economics, having grown up in Stockton and Fresno. Playing the millionaire may have been a bit more of a challenge, but John was a confident, educated man and well-rounded in his abilities, from sports, to academics, to politics. These qualities, in addition to his talent as an actor, allowed him to play his part with such conviction that he opened doors, even among the most jealous and suspicious groups of Mexican planters.

Lázaro's role, in its turn, was close to the part that he was in fact playing in the expedition: translation, explanation, guidance. He was indeed John Turner's guide, as Ethel said. When they set out on their trip, Turner had only had four or five months of training in the Spanish language, and Lázaro had been his teacher from the start. The more complicated aspect of Lázaro's disguise was that he was well known in certain circles, coming, as he did, from a distinguished family, having been schooled in the capital's most prestigious institutions, the Escuela Nacional Preparatoria and the Escuela Nacional de Jurisprudencia, and having worked in various government offices.

How did Lázaro avoid recognition? We cannot be entirely sure. It is possible that he changed his hair, shaved his moustache, or changed his romantic and poetical style of dress. What he did do for sure was avoid lingering in the Mexican north, where he had lived between 1901 and 1906 and where he became a wanted man. Lázaro did not take John to Cananea, for instance, despite John's interest in Díaz's repression of that strike. (John in fact wrote about that episode, based on information from interviews with Lázaro and Fernando Palomares done in Los Angeles.) Lázaro also did not take

John through Yaqui country, despite his contacts in that region. Neither did the pair stop in Monterrey, where Lázaro's family was from and where governor Bernardo Reyes took a deep personal interest in keeping a lid on border *revoltosos*.

In short, Lázaro reduced the risk of recognition to the one place that he and Turner could not avoid, Mexico City. We do not know what he did exactly to avoid recognition there. To some degree, Lázaro was protected from risk by his brother, Dr. Felipe Gutiérrez de Lara, who housed the pair of agitators in Mexico City. It is also likely that Mexico City police had little interest in Lázaro. He was wanted in faraway Sonora and for activity in a strike that had transpired two years prior.

This interpretation of the strategy used to protect Lázaro from the great risks that he faced finds indirect support in John's reporting. There are few observations in *Barbarous Mexico*, the book that resulted from this journey, on anything that transpired before the pair's arrival to Mexico City. Only one vignette stands out, though it is a significant one:

> It was in a second-class car on the Mexican Central, traveling south. They were six, that family, and of three generations. From the callow, raven-haired boy to the white-chinned grandfather, all six seemed to have the last ray of mirth ground out of their systems. We were a lively crowd sitting near them—four were happy Mexicans returning home for a vacation after a season at wage labor in the United States. We sang a little and we made some music on a violin and a harmonica."[12]

Turner then elaborated on the twin image of a broken family of Chihuahua farmers who were traveling south, on the verge of selling themselves into slavery, contrasted with a group of joyous Mexican workers returning from the United States on a home visit.

The anecdote suggests that Lázaro might have attached himself to the group of returning migrants. Although Lázaro and John both had first-class tickets, Lázaro's status as Turner's assistant allowed him to move freely into the second-class cabin and then to invite his (alleged) employer there. Although Lázaro was a man of much greater educational accomplishment and familial distinction than most Mexican migrants, he had worked as a laborer and with laborers since his arrival in the United States, so building connections in that sphere was easy enough. And indeed, John was to move freely between first-class and second-class compartments in his Mexican trip in order to do his interviewing as he saw fit.

In *Barbarous Mexico*, John does not tell stories of railway conversations with American investors, though it is likely that he had them. That kind of encounter was a staple of American travel writing on Mexico during those years. Conversations with Americans on the Mexican railroad played a significant part in John Murray's reporting on Mexican conditions, for instance, because he did not have a chance to observe plantation conditions directly. Thus, one American railway passenger interrogated Murray suspiciously before offering up a revealing perspective:

> "You're not opposed to 'contract labor,' are you?"
> He leaned forward and studied my face.
> "Why, not if it pays," I slowly answered.
> With a look of relief and pleased appreciation of my viewpoint, he lowered his voice to a confidential pitch, saying, impressively, "All wealth comes from labor (this startled me a bit, for it sounded the commencement of a socialist speech), and here, in Mexico, you can buy more labor for less money than any place in the world."
> "The Mexican government has warned all employers not to raise wages—and a warning from Díaz means an order."[13]

Stories like this are common in American travel books. Perhaps their absence in Turner's reportage reflected actual experience. It is possible that Turner and de Lara kept to the second-class car, with its singing migrants. But that is unlikely. The train from Juárez to Mexico City took several days, and trains and ships were sites of elaborate socialization, among elites as well as among plebeians. So it is much more likely that Turner met American investors and plantation managers on the train and that he had affable and informative conversations with them, but that he chose not write about them in his book because, unlike Murray, Turner was able to do first-hand reporting on actual plantation conditions. There was no point burning powder on hearsay when he was going to present direct testimonial evidence.

In short, Lázaro's presence on the expedition is audible even from the start of Turner's reporting mission, on the train to Mexico, where John was able to socialize freely with the Mexican migrants and workers, rather than keep exclusively to the English-speaking travelers in first class.

A second difference between Turner's reportage and John Murray's occurs upon arrival at Mexico City, and it, too, is attributable to Lázaro's presence and guidance. Murray's trip, which had been undertaken only a few months prior, had helped John and Lázaro to plan their strategy. Murray had faced difficulties that Turner and Lara sought to avoid. Murray had presented himself in Mexico as a tourist, a strategy that made him somewhat suspicious to American investors in tropical labor.

On the other hand, hidden in the lining of his checkbook, Murray had carried a letter of introduction written and signed by Ricardo Flores Magón. According to Murray (whose Spanish at the time was probably not much better than Turner's), the letter read: "The bearer of this document is Señor John Murray, an American journalist [misspelled and anglicized] of advanced ideals [both anglicized and misspelled]." That was Murray's mangled rendition of Ricardo's first line, and the letter supposedly wound up with "su hermano que no desmayo [*sic*]. R. Flores Magon."[14]

Murray had taken the precaution of burning union pamphlets, newspapers, and correspondence that he carried before leaving Texas into Mexico. He did, however, carry a list of potentially incriminating contacts and their addresses in Mexico City, written in code. He had therefore undergone the risk of police searches on the train to Mexico City, because, as Murray correctly explained: "If the Furlong Detective Agency, which had been following the members of the Mexican Junta all over the United States, already knew of my connection with the enemies of Díaz, the most likely place to hold me up would have been at the border."[15]

Murray also had felt some risk upon his arrival in Mexico City. Like most American tourists, he had stayed at a hotel on the Alameda, but he had needed to be careful with the use of Ricardo's letter of introduction and with his list of contacts. Murray felt watched, and he saw spies and police everywhere: "The first lantern I barely glanced at—the gendarme with his revolver in the shadow, I did not see—but when another, and another, and another in the center of all the main street-crossings flashed their signal lights back and forth, I saw the point. It was the military eye of Díaz burning in the night for fear the revolution might slip up and catch him in the dark."[16]

John and Lázaro's situation in Mexico City was quite different. They arrived at Lázaro's brother's house, and not at a hotel, and thanks to Lázaro, they had little need of letters of introduction or elaborate lists of underground contacts. There was thus not much risk for John, even if he was frisked or questioned by a policeman. For his part, Lázaro knew that in Mexico City he risked being recognized by old classmates or work or family friends, but probably not by the police.

The chances of being turned in by former classmates was low, given the forms of sociability in Porfirian Mexico, and Lázaro had, in any case, been prosecuted for his role in far-off Cananea, and not for the life that he had led in Mexico City. Moreover, Lázaro had Felipe and other friends who could advise him if they felt that he should avoid one place or another, and there were alternative guides who could take John here or there, if it was best for Lázaro to stay home. Once having left Mexico City for points farther south, Lázaro would be free from any significant risk of identification. He was not known there socially, or to the police in Veracruz, Yucatán, and Oaxaca, which is where they were headed.

The Road to Yucatan

One of the first articles that John Kenneth Turner published in the "Barbarous Mexico" series in the *American Magazine*, which was the first result of his trip, showed a map of the route that Yaqui captives took to Yucatan (Figure 10.1): from the Sonoran port of Guaymas to San Blas, Nayarit, and there by foot to San Marcos, Jalisco, where they boarded a train that stopped in Guadalajara, Mexico City, and Veracruz. At Veracruz, the Yaqui prisoners boarded ships that stopped at Coatzacoalcos and arrived finally at Progreso, Yucatan. The Yaquis that were headed to the tobacco fields of Valle Nacional got off the train between Mexico City and Veracruz, around Tehuacan, and took a smaller train through the mountains to El Hule, Oaxaca, and their deaths. John and Lázaro followed the same itinerary, though the story that Turner tells begins in the farthest extreme of their travel, in Yucatan, rather than recapitulating the slow and gradual immersion into Mexico's "heart of darkness."

Armando Bartra, in his study of Turner, reminds us of the stations at which John and Lázaro had to stop after taking the Ferrocarril Mexicano at 7:00 A.í. from Mexico City's Buenavista Station: across the central plateau through San Cristóbal, Tepexpan, San Juan, Otumba, La Palma, Ometesco, Irolo, Apan...and then, hours later,

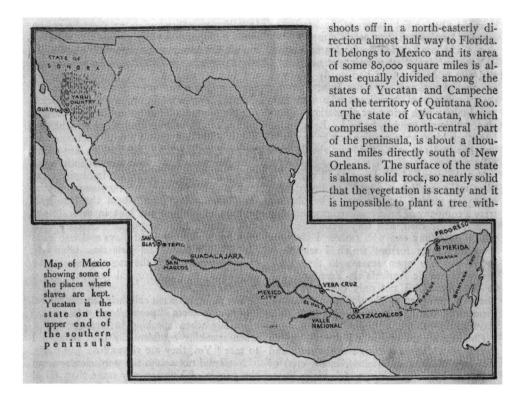

shoots off in a north-easterly direction almost half way to Florida. It belongs to Mexico and its area of some 80,000 square miles is almost equally divided among the states of Yucatan and Campeche and the territory of Quintana Roo.

The state of Yucatan, which comprises the north-central part of the peninsula, is about a thousand miles directly south of New Orleans. The surface of the state is almost solid rock, so nearly solid that the vegetation is scanty and it is impossible to plant a tree with-

Map of Mexico showing some of the places where slaves are kept. Yucatan is the state on the upper end of the southern peninsula

Figure 10.1 The trajectory of Yaqui deportation. From John Kenneth Turner, "The Slaves of Yucatan," *American Magazine* 68 [September 1909], p. 529.

downhill toward the gulf through Maltrata, Nogales, Orizaba, Sumidero, and Fortín . . . until the train finally reached Veracruz.[17]

But none of this is mentioned by Turner himself. *Barbarous Mexico*'s lack of descriptive attention to the picturesque details of the train ride was certainly deliberate. The places that Turner passed after his departure from Mexico City were remarkable enough for the American living-room audience: pyramids at San Juan Teotihuacan, strange and colorful pulque haciendas in Hidalgo State, and the dramatic drop into the tropics from the peaks at Maltrata. . . . These images were the stock in trade of Mexican travel writing, and it is for that very reason that Turner used them so sparingly. The raison d'être of his reportage, as the editors of the *American Magazine* announced, was that "the real news of Mexico does not get across the border." In the United States, they said, "a great Díaz-Mexico myth has been built up through skillfully applied influence upon journalism." Mexico, they said, had its tropical Siberias, and they needed to be brought to public attention.

So Turner had no intention of dwelling on what was quaint or picturesque about his trip. Instead, he began with a discussion of the geography and the demography of slavery as he found it in Yucatan. The extreme of Mexico, its "Siberia," was the place where Turner's reportage began, and his exposé worked from there in the opposite direction, toward Mexico City, toward Porfirio Díaz, and finally to American complicity and support for Mexican slavery.

> Here we find the city of Merida, a beautiful modern city claiming a population of 60,000 people, and surrounding it, supporting it, vast henequen plantations on which the rows of gigantic green plants extend for miles and miles. The farms are so large that each has a little city of its own, inhabited from 500 to 2500 people, according to the size of the farm. The owners of these great farms are the chief slave-holders of Yucatan; the inhabitants of the little cities are the slaves.[18]

That is vintage John Kenneth Turner, going straight to the point. But in another way, Turner's trajectory was also rather loopy. It began with what was hidden, the Mexican Siberia at Yucatan. But in Yucatan, Turner discovered things that were eerily familiar to his American audience.

I speak here of two things. First, Turner found slavery in Mexico's extremities—a slavery that was as much a part of American consciousness as totalitarianism is to ours. Indeed, slavery was central to the ethical makeup of Turner's generation. Mexican slavery, so cunningly hidden from view and yet so crucially supported by the American establishment, was like the return of the repressed for the progressive American reading public—America's reactionary slaving tradition pushing yet farther south under the shadowy cover of a dictatorship that they enthusiastically supported.

But there was also a second thing that Turner found in Yucatan and that Americans of his generation had repressed, and that was a final living scene of the Native American's Trail of Tears, represented here by the Yaqui.

The End of the Yaqui Nation

Turner was following the trail of the Yaqui nation to its final end, in slavery in Yucatan. He was unable to begin the pilgrimage in Yaqui country, because his guide, Lázaro, was wanted there. Had this not been so, Lázaro and John could have taken a train from Los Angeles to Tucson and from there into Yaqui country in Sonora, then followed the captive trains and steamers to key points south, at Guaymas and Guadalajara, all the way to Yucatan.

American residents in Arizona had begun to wonder aloud about the fate of the Yaqui around the time of John and Lázaro's trip. Up until the mid-1900s, Arizonans were in broad support of Sonoran authorities' war against the Yaquis, who were seen as deterring American prospectors, ranchers, and merchants. But by the middle of the decade, public sentiment had begun to be more mixed.

Thus, Nogales consul Albert Morawetz wrote a horrific report to Secretary of State Francis Loomis on September 23, 1904, telling how Sonora's governor, Rafael Izábal, had used the killing of two Americans by Yaqui Indians to wreak havoc on a political rival, an American landowner named Carlos Johnson, who had previously won a lawsuit against the governor. The consul explained the situation thus:

> There is a large amount of American capital invested in Sonora in mining and other enterprises, which are situated in that part of the state now made unsafe by this Yaqui uprising.
>
> Many of the enterprises have come to an absolute stand-still on account of the manner in which the governor is attempting to suppress the revolt. Not only are few, if any, really hostile Indians apprehended,

but the peaceable ones, of whom there are many and who are the best laborers and miners in the state, are, by his acts, compelled to either join the hostile Indians or to be hanged or deported to Yucatan.[19]

Regarding the action taken by Governor Izábal personally on Carlos Johnson's ranch, Morawetz summarized the situation in the following terms: "I am convinced that thirteen innocent Indians have been tortured and hanged, and that the guilty ones have not been apprehended."[20]

A few months later, four more Americans were killed by rebellious Yaqui Indians, and Consul Morawetz provided a broader and more general assessment:

> There have been many Indians hanged, shot and deported since [the four murders], but they have been gathered at various plantations and towns and have not been brought out of the mountains, where the really fighting Indians are.
>
> It is claimed by the Mexican government that the Indians who have been punished and who worked for wages, had supplied the fighting Indians with money to buy arms and ammunition and for that reason they were just as guilty as those that did the actual murdering and robbing. This may be true in some instances, but the measures so far taken have not decreased the number of actual fighters but it is the general opinion, that they have driven many peaceable Yaquis into the hostile ranks.
>
> No Indians have yet been followed and caught immediately after committing a crime or who have resisted arrest with arms in their hands. I am convinced that the government of Sonora has not the desire, nor have its troops the necessary courage nor other soldierly qualities, to follow and fight the real perpetrators of the crimes committed. If the present conditions continue a very large amount of invested American capital must be abandoned or many more lives will be lost.[21]

As 1905 came to a close, it was increasingly clear that the Sonora government was bent on the extermination of peaceful Yaquis. Sometimes the governor and his friends and family used the Yaqui war as a pretext to destroy rival landowners such as Carlos Johnson. Sometimes they killed to make a show of finding culprits that menaced American investments and sometimes to occupy Yaqui lands directly (Figure 10.2). In addition to these inducements, Mexican

Figure 10.2 "Yaquis After the Execution." The inscription on the bottom left reads: "W. L. Grey's Souvenirs of Guaymas." Most American tourists in Sonora did not witness the execution of Yaqui Indians, so the word "souvenir" is a bit of a stretch for this particular image, but the fact that photos such as this circulated as picture postcards suggests that visitors felt the immediacy of the war with the Yaqui, and that many approved of the government's extermination policy. Courtesy of the San Diego History Center.

military escorts for Americans in Sonora were charging five dollars per soldier per day and so were in effect profiting from a protection racket. High-level corruption was even more flagrant. By November, Consul Morawetz summarized the increasingly dire situation:

> This government has consisted for many years of a triumvirate, Rafael Yzabal, the present governor, General Luis E Torres, commander of the military zone, and Ramón Corral, now vice-president of Mexico. One of these three has alternately been governor for the past twenty years. What one has done, no matter what it was, has always been upheld, sanctioned and ratified by the other two. I am informed that they have made millions of dollars out of the money that has been sent for the purchase of rations, horse-feed and other supplies and that they have no desire to decrease their incomes by crushing this Yaqui war.[22]

The brutality and corruption of this Indian war had finally begun to turn border opinion on the U.S. side in favor of the Yaqui and against the Mexican and Sonoran governments.

Nonetheless, the Sonora government's Yaqui policy still enjoyed official U.S. support. So, for instance, the U.S. consul in Hermosillo,

Louis Hostetter, reported to the State Department that he had spoken with General Luis Torres, commander of the federal troops in Sonora, who reported that he and Governor Izábal were "very highly pleased at the action of our government in taking steps to stop the entrance of the Yaqui Indians into Arizona under the immigration law, as that if carried out, will certainly end the Yaqui trouble in a short time."[23] Moreover, there was no question that both the Hermosillo consul and the State Department were apprised of the exact meaning of "ending the Yaqui trouble." Thus, in another letter, Consul Hostetter wrote approvingly that agents of the "Mexican government are doing what they can to apprehend the Yaquis, and those found guilty of being on the war path, are being punished and the balance are being shipped to Yucatan, as they desire to rid the country of the entire lot."[24]

Still, there was also a growing sense of sympathy for the Yaquis on the Arizona side. By 1908, around the time when John and Lázaro were hatching their plan to expose the Díaz regime to American public opinion, border sentiment had reached such a pitch that even some of the *Yaquis broncos*, as the rebel Yaquis were called, found local support. Thus, at one of the points when the Yaqui War was declared ended, in May of 1908, Arizona notables were outraged by the U.S. federal government's acquiescence to the Mexican government's petition to extradite Yaqui rebel chiefs, the Matus brothers.[25]

Border sympathy for the Yaquis was also enhanced by peaceful coexistence with refugee *Yaquis broncos* on the Arizona side. As early as 1901, Nogales, Arizona, had a small colony of Yaqui refugees. Tucson's colony, which was to be significantly larger, got started just a few years later. By 1909, the community was sufficiently large for their "Barrio Libre" to have been known colloquially as "Yaqui Town" and for the Tucson Yaquis to have performed their collective traditional Easter celebrations there. The Yaquis who first came to Tucson, anthropologist Edward Spicer tells us, "were broncos, or at least their sympathies were with the broncos."[26]

It seemed clear to Arizona residents that these Yaquis were not the redoubtable force that the Sonoran government had made them out to be. A somewhat anachronistic, but nonetheless telling anecdote illustrates this point. In 1917, a group of Tucson Yaquis responded to a call for help from their kin, who were being hunted down yet again, this time by the revolutionary troops of Sonora governor

Plutarco Elías Calles. The Tucson group was caught near the border by the U.S. cavalry, jailed, and tried for violation of the U.S. neutrality laws. This was the first and only attempt by Tucson Yaquis to organize an armed expedition into Sonora. It was described by the *Arizona Daily Star* in the following terms: "The Yaqui 'army of liberation,' eight men and one child, disbanded yesterday in the federal court and gave its promise that if the court deemed it desirable to deal with it leniently, it would return to the fields and ranches from which it had gathered and think no more of Mexico and the outrages it heard that the Mexican government was inflicting upon its tribesmen."[27] The group was not exactly a great military menace, and it indeed was let go on the promise of a peaceful return to Tucson.

In short, Turner's questions regarding the fate of the Yaqui were shared by a good number of Arizona residents:

> In common with thousands of other Americans who have lived for years in our Southwest and near the border line of Mexico, I knew something of the sufferings of the Yaquis in their native state . . . of the methods of extermination employed by the army, of the indignation voiced by the decent element of Sonora, finally of President Díaz's sweeping order of deportation.
>
> But what fate was awaiting them there at the end of that exile road? The answer was always vague, indefinite, unsatisfactory. Even well-informed Mexicans of their country's metropolis could not tell me. After the Yaqui exiles sailed from the port of Veracruz the curtain dropped upon them.[28]

However, what Turner found in Yucatan and Valle Nacional went beyond what citizens on the border had imagined. It was not just that the Sonoran oligarchy was using troop rations and military budgets to line their pockets. They were double-dipping for profits by selling off Yaquis and other Indians—Pimas, Opatas, Papagos, Seris—anyone who could easily be confused with a Yaqui (Figure 10.3). Moreover, Turner showed that contrary to Consul Morawetz's impression, rather than being hoodwinked by the Sonoran elite, Porfirio Díaz knew all about this slave trade. Indeed, Díaz was Mexican slavery's chief accomplice.

And Turner's concern for the Yaquis resonated with American public sentiments beyond the Arizona border. This was because, like slavery, the Yaqui case named an American sin of the recent

Figure 10.3 Yaquis being herded through Tepic. This photo is probably a picture postcard. Lázaro and John did not witness this particular scene because they were not in Tepic. From John Kenneth Turner, "The Tragic Story of the Yaqui Indians," *American Magazine* 69 [November 1909], p. 34.

past—the extermination of Native America—and it replayed that chapter of history over, in all of its horror, at a time when the American public wanted an opportunity to redeem itself.

It is interesting to consider that the publication of Turner's *Barbarous Mexico* preceded the "discovery" of Ishi, the last survivor of the California Yahi Indians, by only about eighteen months. At the time of Turner's reporting, California was steeped in the melancholic sense that its native past was slipping beyond its grip. The power of modernization made the native world a thing to be rescued, rather than exterminated. After being brought in from the wild, Ishi was housed, studied, and even preserved for posterity at the University of California.[29] But in Mexico, Indians like the Yahi were being slaughtered for the most venial and vile extraction of profits: "I went to Yucatan in order to witness, if possible, the final act in the life drama of the Yaqui nation. And I witnessed it," Turner wrote.[30]

Mexico's heart of darkness—its slavery, its extermination of Yaqui and Maya Indians—was disturbingly familiar to Turner's readers, for in it, the sins of America were revived and made current in an alien form that was easy to condemn. Mexico provided Americans with a chance to redeem sins of the past and to stop their contemporaries—be they simple adventurers or owners of the great trusts—from exporting old

American sins. Mexico, as the *International Socialist Review* put it, had become "Our Capitalists' Slave Colony."[31]

Calling a Slave a Slave

If Mexican slavery was hidden in plain view, why did Lázaro and John have to go so far to find it? And how did John manage to prove that he had in fact discovered it? The answer to the first question is related to the answer to the second.

As we have seen, Turner took the opposite strategy of most travel writers. Rather than describe slow and increasingly exotic progress into the "heart of darkness," he moved quickly to its epicenter: "Slavery in Mexico! Yes, I found it. I found it first in Yucatan."[32]

Turner stated straight off that in Yucatan there were around fifty great slaveholding "kings," eight thousand enslaved Yaquis, three thousand enslaved Koreans, and between one hundred thousand and one hundred and twenty-five thousand enslaved Mayas. He then moved briskly to establish the fact that the slaves were indeed slaves and the masters, masters. Turner achieved this not by pulling on the reader's heartstrings and describing the wretched conditions of the slaves and the wickedness of the masters, but by putting sentiment aside in favor of economic analysis.

Turner began by defining his terms: "Slavery is the ownership of the body of a man, an ownership so absolute that the body can be transferred to another, an ownership that gives the owner a right to take the products of that body, to starve it, to chastise it at will, to kill it with impunity."[33] He then pointed out that all the workers on Yucatan's henequen plantations were bought and sold and that they had a standard price. This latter fact, the standard price, meant that the monetary transactions that were required to transfer a person who was allegedly an "indebted peon" to a different "employer" were not determined by that individual's debt, but by the value of the laborer as a commodity.

This fact, and this fact alone, established that the people in question were in a strict and technical sense, slaves. And that their so-called employers were in fact masters. Of course, the economic fact of a standard price for a slave went alongside the rest of the degradation that is connected to the institution of slavery. Yucatecan slaves did not receive monetary wages. True, plantation company stores kept accounts tallying the value of beans given, or lodging provided, but no money changed hands between the employer and his so-called employee. Instead, owners—for that is what they were—held their slaves by force, often locking them up at night. Lacking any provision for financial incentives to increase productivity, taskmasters routinely punished their bodies. Owners even had the de facto entitlement to kill slaves with little fear of prosecution.

The key to Turner's analysis, then, was that Yucatecan peons were slaves because they had a fixed price—$400 in Mexican silver pesos at the time of Lázaro and John's visits to Yucatecan plantations. "'If you buy now you buy at a very good time,' I was told again and again. 'The panic has put the price down. One year ago the price of each man was $1000.'"[34] The fact of the fixed price, though not unknown, was not so readily visible to travelers, because the "slave sharks," as Turner tellingly dubbed the *enganchadores*, operated discreetly. They generally served a select number of landowners and did not advertise their presence.

For this reason, Turner was unable to interview any *enganchadores* in Yucatan. He was told that they would not speak to anyone they did not already trust. Instead, the price of the slaves was given to him by plantation owners and their association president, Don Enrique Cámara Zavala, all of whom were ready to share this information because they were courting Turner as a potential investor. The economic crisis that followed the Panic of 1907, which was triggered by a failed attempt on Wall Street to corner the market of on the stock of the United Copper Company, had hit them hard, and they were eager for cash.

By the time John and Lázaro had moved from Yucatan to Valle Nacional, in Oaxaca, Turner had learned to establish his false credentials so convincingly that he was finally able to interview an *enganchador*. The person in question, named by Turner Señor P—, probably for fear of being sued for libel in U.S. courts by Mexican government proxies, was a relative of Félix Díaz, who was a nephew of Don Porfirio himself and at the time the chief of police in Mexico City. The political connection was important, since a good many *enganchado* slaves were vagrants and destitute migrants rounded up by police chiefs in central Mexican cities and then sold off to the tropical plantations, with government-subsidized railroad costs for the planters thrown into the bargain. Thus, Turner reports Señor P— as saying:

The fact that I am a brother-in-law of Félix Díaz as well as a personal friend of the governors of the states of Oaxaca and Veracruz, and of the mayors of the cities of the same name, puts me in a position to supply your wants better than anyone else. I am prepared to furnish you any number of laborers up to forty thousand a year, men, women and children, and my price is fifty pesos each.[35]

Proving the existence of slavery by showing that the price of a peon was not governed by a putative individual debt, but that it was, in fact, a standard price, differentiated by age and sex, but no more, had been a major a challenge. Because slavery was illegal in Mexico, there were no public auctions, so Turner needed to go to regions whose economies were dominated by a single, slave-dependent activity in order to show the mechanism behind price standardization beyond a shadow of a doubt. That is why Turner had to travel from the northern extremities of Mexico all the way to its southeastern tip. Once the fact of slavery was established, though, Turner was free to describe the horrific conditions that the slaves suffered under and how broad in scope the phenomenon really was.

Mexican Extremes

John and Lázaro knew from the start that they must get into a specific kind of plantation, preferably in Yucatan or Valle Nacional, to succeed in their propaganda mission. But if Yucatan and Valle Nacional were in some way exceptional, was it fair to use those places as the jumping-off point for a broad condemnation of Díaz and his regime? Mexican tropical slavery was a specific phenomenon, part of a broad international circuit of tropical commodity production that was deeply reliant on various modalities of slave labor.

Tobacco production in the infamous Valle Nacional is perhaps the most direct example of this connection. Valle Nacional planters were generally Cubans who had moved to Mexico during Cuba's protracted revolution (Figure 10.4). Those planters had strong feelings about slavery and its connection to success in the tobacco business. Cuba's famous tobacco fields of Vuelta Abajo had begun to decline in production during the 1880s, due mostly to slave emancipation. As Alsatian engineer E. Schenetz, who set up the Compañía de Tabacos Mexicanos in Oaxaca, wrote in the late 1890s:

The final abolition of slavery in Cuba precipitated a social crisis. Now they had to pay a lot to retain the black.... The residents of Vuelta Abajo perfectly understood this sad situation and began emigrating to Mexico.... A free man is incapable of tending more than 20,000 plants, and a freed black man does even less...because it is a proven fact that the freed slave works little, since he's no longer forced to do it."[36]

Cuban planters in the Valle Nacional decided to exploit a different sort of slaving system than the one that they had in Cuba— a system that was based not on owning African slaves for generations, but rather on constantly replenishing their stock of workers, shipped down from central Mexico by government agents. The Valle Nacional's tobacco fields became central Mexico's debtor's prison, its solution for both vagrancy and political resistance, all rolled into one.

Other tropical products were also involved in slaving. Rubber comes most immediately to mind. The horrendous conditions of slaving in Congo had been exposed and decried internationally just four years prior to Lázaro and John's Mexican expedition, and the exploitation of rubber in the Isthmus of Tehuantepec also depended almost entirely on forced labor and enslavement. Coffee, too, involved modalities of labor coercion, though they were distinct from the year-long sapping of slave life that was occurring on the tobacco and rubber plantations. The coffee plantations of the Soconusco region in Chiapas relied on seasonal labor. Like workers on the henequen and rubber plantations, coffee pickers were also kept in pens at night during their working months, and their working conditions were deplorable. However, it was to the advantage of the plantations to support a system of seasonal migration from highland villages, which were tightly squeezed economically, but remained at least partially free.

If the international conditions of tropical agriculture founded modalities of labor coercion and slavery, was Turner justified in condemning the Díaz regime as the cause of these conditions? He was, and these were his reasons. It was true that Yucatán was a Mexican extreme, both geographically and in terms of labor exploitation, but it was an extreme that revealed something fundamental about what Turner skillfully analyzed as "the Díaz system."

Turner described slavery as an extreme of the peonage system,

Figure 10.4 One of the chief operators of the prisoner racket on the tobacco plantations. Direct identification of local officials was a risk for Turner and the *American Magazine*. It was this level of officialdom that was mobilized by the Díaz government to bring lawsuits for libel against *Regeneración* and other U.S.-based newspapers. From John Kenneth Turner, "With the Contract Slaves of the Valle Nacional," *American Magazine* 69 [December 1909], p. 255.

a system that menaced the entire agricultural population and a good proportion of the artisanal classes.[37] Although the sources of Turner's statistics are unclear—presumably they were "guesstimates," formulated on the basis of broad judgments made from the study of official censuses and reports—John's claims did reflect one palpable reality faithfully, which was the vulnerability of Mexican lower classes, and particularly the peasantry, to various processes of dislocation, labor coercion, pauperization, atomization, and premature death. Turner tracked these displaced persons not only in the Yucatecan plantations, but also in the streets and boardinghouses of Mexico City and in and around several working-class districts.

But beyond these broad points, there was a more subtle way in which Turner's findings for Yucatan and the Valle Nacional revealed the existence of a *system* that tainted the whole of Mexican society. Turner demonstrated beyond any question that Mexican slavery was enforced by government agents, and was impossible to sustain without their support. Plantation owners relied on *jefes políticos* to provide a legal foundation for their indentured servants, as well as for protection in cases of local revolt. They also depended on urban police chiefs and army officers for their labor supply. Some planters even received transportation subsidies for slave transport on the Mexican railroad.

Indeed, the whole repressive apparatus of the Díaz government could be seen as an extraction machine that profited investors and politicians at the expense of the Mexican masses and, indirectly, of the American worker, who could only stand to gain from the improvement of Mexican conditions and the weakening of the power of the great robber barons who owned so much of Mexico—the Rockefellers, the Guggenheims, the Hearsts, and more.

Mexican progress was built on Mexican slavery. The deportation and slaughter of the Yaquis benefitted both American and Mexican landowners in the Yaqui Valley and corrupt Mexican politicians. The exploitation of the Mayas in Yucatan benefitted Yucatecan planters, but also the American cordage trust that purchased their product. American capital was complicit with Porfirio Díaz in a happy marriage with a dirty little secret. That secret was, as Turner put it, that in the case of Porfirio Díaz's alleged miracle of progressive development, "the people were the sacrifice."

CHAPTER ELEVEN

The Border

On the evening they left LA, I remember, Elizabeth and I decided to
visit Hattie de Lara, Lázaro's wife. In front of their house we paused to
talk to some Mexican friends. A pale, greenish-skinned youth of the
Mexican creole type sidled up to me.

"Where did John go?" he asked me, in a breezy, confidential tone.

I walked away. I had never laid eyes on the man before. But by this
time I knew a spy when I saw one.

—Ethel Duffy Turner, "Ricardo Flores Magón y el Partido Liberal"
(typescript)

Tucson

When John Lázaro left Los Angeles for Mexico, Ethel moved to the
Noel's house, where she felt less lonely and a little more protected.
Ethel and Elizabeth were teaching English to foreigners at a night
school on a voluntary basis,[1] and Elizabeth was writing articles about
Mexico for the *Appeal to Reason* and the *Miner's Magazine*, published by
the Western Federation of Miners. Because of the failed June revolt,
Antonio I. Villarreal, Librado Rivera, and Ricardo Flores Magón were
now being held incommunicado in the Los Angeles County Jail. No
prison visits or mailing privileges were allowed. Manuel Sarabia was
transferred to Tucson to await his trial there for violation of the neutrality laws. Soon, the other three men would follow.

The nerves of the American group were raw, given the risks
involved in Lázaro and John's mission. It was clear that Díaz's policing strategy was not to be underestimated. The letter planning the
1908 revolt that María Brousse, Elizabeth Trowbridge, and Ethel
Duffy had smuggled out of jail had been captured and even had

been published in several Mexico City newspapers just a few weeks before John and Lázaro's departure. It was hard to know the extent to which Liberal sympathizers were infiltrated by Mexican police.

Still, for this group, the best remedy for raw nerves was action, and the man with the plan was John Murray, who suggested to Elizabeth that she, Ethel, and Murray move to Tucson and establish a magazine there dedicated to raising awareness for the Mexican Cause and especially to defending the Mexican political prisoners. Murray even had a name for the magazine, *The Border*. He reasoned that the three of them should move to Tucson in any case, because Ricardo, Antonio, Librado, and Manuel would soon be held for trial there, and they would probably be convicted. The plan was perfect, or so Murray thought.

Elizabeth was a bit hesitant about whether a journal was the wisest investment—she did not spend a penny if it was not for the cause, according to Ethel. Her funds were dwindling, thanks to the expenses paid out for the legal defense of the political prisoners, the two reporting trips to Mexico, various propaganda efforts, and apparently some investment in guns for the failed 1908 revolt. But Elizabeth was won over to the idea in the end.[2] It is impossible to say whether her sentiments for Manuel Sarabia played a role in her decision; probably, they did. Elizabeth had had a private interview with Manuel in the Los Angeles County Jail, and she had been sufficiently impressed to write a long article about him. It is possible that her feelings for Manuel were already known to Murray and Ethel. Ricardo Flores Magón, in any case, was aware that Elizabeth was being courted by Manuel while the members of the junta were still in jail in Los Angeles.

Whether or not her love for Manuel played a role in the decision, the fact is that Elizabeth paid the hefty amount of $1,000 to bail Manuel Sarabia out of jail almost immediately after their arrival in Tucson, though she and Ethel insisted that her action was to save Manuel, because he had tuberculosis and was too frail to survive Arizona prison conditions. The question of whether Manuel had been rescued for reasons of health or for sentimental reasons was later to become a point of contention with Ricardo. What was relevant now was that Elizabeth agreed to Murray's proposal, and late in September 1908, a few weeks after Lázaro and John's departure from Los Angeles, the three friends said goodbye to the Noels and

left for Tucson. "In the cool, somnolent dawn we
Ethel recalled, "the desert stretched around us, s(
holding the age-old enchantment. Our spirits w(
would carry the fight to a finish, not only for the r(
Díaz, as well. We felt like a couple of superwome

Some days after their arrival, John Turner join
from Mexico. Lázaro had continued on to Los An
recalled, was deeply depressed by what he had see
"in a state of nervous tension."⁴ "He had a big stor
what he had seen was almost more than a human be
De Lara, he said, was all broken up. Not only what t
told us was true, but they had understated the tru
know the worst of it. They had not seen it with the

Turner's presence added a sense of urgency an(
Tucson operation. Elizabeth had rented an office in
son, at 140 Convent Street, as well as a "roomy bung
entire group lived. She paid for everything, of cours(
set up shop, Elizabeth and Ethel got busy selling ad
the magazine, which in theory was designed to su
cially. *The Border* was glossy, well designed, and nic(
like the Socialist rags that Murray had published in
say nothing of *Regeneración* (Figures 11.1 and 11.2).
was a monthly was certainly a mistake, given the rhy
that was pouring out of Mexico in those months. *Th*
fact, an experiment that sought to introduce the Me
a middle-class audience in a subtle fashion. "As a con
run Southwest allure articles—desert magic and so o

John Kenneth Turner and Manuel Sarabia also joi
The Border, albeit on a limited basis. Though he wrote
article, John was important mainly for advice and i
was obsessively working on his first two *American M*
on Mexican slavery and deeply affected by what he ha(
Mexico. Manuel took a more active role. While worki
in Douglas, Arizona, on the night of June 10, 1907, Ma
detained at gunpoint, with no warrant, by an Arizon
a Douglas policeman. He was taken to the local jail
constable Shorpshire turned him over to Pinkerton d(
were in the employ of the Mexican government. Th
shoved Manuel into their car, while he shouted out that

idnapped, and spirited him across the border, where a force of *urales* received him, tied him up, and took him to the Hermosillo prison. But because the kidnapping was witnessed, and Manuel was a well-known activist in Douglas, a public outcry got Manuel released and returned to the United States.

Manuel wrote up the story of his kidnapping for *The Border*, and it was published in the second issue. With Elizabeth's financial support, Manuel also began to edit a Spanish-language newspaper, *El Defensor del Pueblo*, of which there seem to be no copies extant.

The Tucson months would be the first and last time that Murray, Elizabeth, Ethel, John, and Manuel Sarabia were all together. They seem to have been heady and wonderful days.

> We rented a house, and the four of us lived there—the two Johns, Elizabeth and myself. A Papago Indian woman was hired to do the work. Before long we had another member in our household. Elizabeth had managed to get Manuel Sarabia, who was in the Tucson jail, out on a thousand dollar bail. Manuel was ill; a doctor reported that he had contracted tuberculosis. His only hope of life was freedom—good food, good fresh air.[7]

"Those were good days to remember," Ethel wrote. "John Kenneth Turner pounded the typewriter at home, writing his articles about slave conditions in Mexico. The rest of us spent many hours in the office. Elizabeth and I would walk home in the waning sunlight of the late autumn days."[8]

Ethel was not alone in her sense of nostalgia for those Tucson days. In the final years of her life, at the start of the Great Depression, Elizabeth wrote a note of congratulation to Ethel on the publication of her novel, reminding Ethel of her promise to write about their Tucson days: "Don't forget that the third [novel] is to draw inspiration from our old days in California and Arizona."[9]

In fact, the border itself was a place that was charged with nostalgia as much as it was loaded with future prospects. So, for instance, preening about how in the Rio Grande Valley, "alfalfa fields and irrigated farms now cover the region which was formerly a cactus-covered desert" and about how gunfights and banditry had virtually disappeared, the *Washington Post* somewhat melancholically remarked that "the cowboy hat and chaps have been abandoned in Hidalgo County. The Sherriff of Hidalgo would be mistaken for a

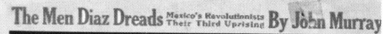

The Men Diaz Dreads Mexico's Revolutionists By John Murray
Their Third Uprising

COPY TEN CENTS   JANUARY, 1909

THE BORDER

RICARDO FLORES MAGON
PRESIDENT *of the* ORGANIZING JUNTA
of the
MEXICAN LIBERAL PARTY
(A POLITICAL PRISONER IN THE U S)
Drawn by
E·A·BURBANK
The Border Publishing Company. Tucson. Arizona. U. S. A.
Branch Office. 741 South Spring Street. Los Angeles. California

IN OLD ACOMA WHEN THE SPANIARD FLORENCE E. BROOKS
Conquered the Cliff Dweller

Figure 11.1 The movement to liberate the political prisoners was also the time when their photos began to be mass-reproduced and transformed into revolutionary emblems. Cover of *The Border*, January 1909. Courtesy of the University of Arizona Libraries.

LIST OF CONTENTS

NOVEMBER, 1908

THE BORDER

A Monthly
Magazine
of Politics

News and
Stories of
the Border

Application for entry as second-class matter at the postoffice at Tucson, Ariz., pending.   The contents of this magazine protected by copyright.

THE BORDER PUBLISHING COMPANY, TUCSON, ARIZONA, U.S.A.

BRANCH OFFICE, 741 S. SPRING ST., LOS ANGELES, CALIFORNIA

Figure 11.2 Native American iconography was a staple ornament in the Western radical or progressive press. *The Pacific Monthly* led each of its articles with an engraving with an Indian in headdress witnessing a sunset. In addition to uses of native images for ornamentation, *The Border* devoted feature articles and cover images to prominent native figures. Inside cover of *The Border*, November 1908. Courtesy of the University of Arizona Libraries.

bank cashier or a man of business."[10] The work and excitement that Ethel, Elizabeth, Murray, and John poured into *The Border* was a creative aesthetic and political response to this combination of future possibility and elegiac attachment to a vanishing world.

The Border

As an elderly lady and historian of the Liberal movement, Ethel looked back on *The Border* as an ill-conceived project. "The brainchild of Johnny Murray was delicate from the start," she wrote.[11] It was too costly, and circulation for a magazine of this kind could be raised only by years of hard work. This particular editorial group was not operating within that kind of time frame. They were committed to a cause that was about to blow up, and there was no way that they could stay long in Tucson.

Still, Murray, Elizabeth, Ethel, and Manuel took a while to see things that way, and they poured their hearts into the project. Murray served as editor, and Ethel and Manuel as associate editors. Elizabeth's name did not figure, because she was still afraid of her mother, who knew only that she had gone to the desert for health reasons. Mrs. Shultis had not been keeping close tabs on Elizabeth in those months, suggesting to Elizabeth and Ethel that perhaps she was coming to accept Elizabeth's independence. But Elizabeth could not be sure.[12]

The group's strategy was to combine reader-friendly Western themes alongside coverage of Mexico's situation, which was often on the cover. Murray wrote stories about a vagabond. Ethel wrote "Seven Prison Days," about her hometown of San Quentin, illustrated with her drawings (Figure 11.3). Elizabeth wrote stories and editorials against Díaz. From a psychological viewpoint, these were days of growth, particularly for the two women: "We were certainly digging deep into ourselves and, discovering new talents, and we were comical figures at times."[13]

And the magazine started to do reasonably well. Ricardo Flores Magón read it approvingly from prison and asked María Brousse to bring him new issues.[14] When the magazine was later put up for sale, it found a buyer.

As far as the work of production went, Murray traveled regularly to get material and sometimes also to meet his union-organizing obligations. He was often absent. The two women and Manuel kept long hours at the journal's offices. They also hired a business

SEVEN PRISON DAYS
A Woman's View of the Men in Stripes

Ethel Duffy Turner

I.

Thursday
August Third

OW calm and still things are today! The bay has a surface of polished glass, and even the white-winged sailboats doze and doze and never move. About the prison front the blue-coated forms of half a dozen guards, and an occasional striped figure carrying messages to and fro from the captain's to the warden's office, are the only signs of life.

From my veranda the prison appears for all the world like a huge walled castle of some proud baron of the middle ages. Would one ever think, to look at its sleepy gray walls, that it held eighteen hundred human lives? Eighteen hundred lives, toiling, sweating, talking gesticulating, rushing hither and thither—threading the looms of the jute mill, tending each cog and wheel of its vast machinery, sewing the sacks, sorting them, binding them, planing and sawing in the carpenter shop, working in shoe shop, kitchen, laundry or hospital. Yes, or waiting—waiting in lonely solitude, with idle hands and fevered brain—for the gallows and death-trap to claim one more victim for their own.

The afternoon is waning, and the bay grows pearl-gray like the wing of a sea gull. I have just watched the "line" go in—the "con" gardeners returning from their work at the officers' homes to their cells inside. How often have I watched them, in the seven years in which I have been an officer's wife, and have lived in this little brown bungalow within the shadow of the prison walls! It has grown to be as inevitable as the tide which ebbs and flows in the bay below.

At a quarter past four the guard blows his whistle, and the striped figures step out of their respective gardens all along the street and fall into line, their arms folded high upon their breasts. With faces immovable and stolid, and uniforms alike but for varying degrees of wear and tear, they move mechanically toward the prison front, to be mechanically searched at the gate, ere the keeper's ponderous key turns in the lock, and the iron door swings open to let them in.

I counted them as they passed by, as one involuntarily counts the stairs one has climbed unnumbered times. They were all there as they have always been for years and years. The men themselves change, it is true. One goes, but another falls into his place. Why does one not hide, or escape, or do something to vary the terrible monotony of the thing? Always the same—always the same, like clockwork that never runs down!

Alice, my pretty, timid cousin from the city, asks me if I am not afraid a prisoner will try to escape some day. Afraid! Oh, Alice, afraid of a thrill that would send the blood pounding through my veins once more, afraid of stripping myself of this weight of ennui which chains me to the earth, and to know, though it be only for a moment, the fast beating heart and the pulses that throb to the wild clanging of the alarm bell and the rushing of armed guards to the call!

No, I am not naturally cruel that I would glory in a man hunt. But in all this little world that teems with human activity about me, I—I, alone, seem not to live. And to live, with mind alert and heart blood-warm, and muscles leaping in joy to act—that is everything!

II.

Friday
August Fourth

Frank's old boyhood chum came today—Mark Prentiss, a man whom middle age has robbed of none of the boyish enthusiasm of youth.

A little before five o'clock this afternoon we three went upon the terrace to see the lock-up. From the terrace one can look down over the whole prison yard. The yard itself, cement-paved, is as neat as a well-kept floor, with a fountain in the center, and an umbrella shade tree here and there, and rows of scarlet geraniums raising their sunny heads from their beds of cool green.

Mr. Prentiss fairly bubbled over with questions. I looked at him in amazement till I remembered my own eager interest and feelings of fascination when I first came here, seven years ago. Frank explained glibly what each thing signified, sandwiching in anecdotes and bits of history, to the intense delight of Mr. Prentiss.

Immediately within the walls below the terrace are the women's quarters, where an occasional blue-clad figure can be seen peering curiously from behind the iron bars, feeding the chittering canary hung at her window, watering the geranium pots on the inner sill, chatting with her invisible neighbors on her right and left, or passing messages on note paper tied to the end of a long stick.

Straight ahead, beyond the women's quarters, are the four three-story buildings which contain the cells of the men. On the second row of the building which faces us are seven doors, closed when at this hour all else is open. This is "Murderers' Row," where the men who are condemned to be hanged await the day of execution.

Up the winding stairs from tier to tier we saw scores of striped figures hurrying to take their places before their own cell doors, ready for the lock-up. What a collection of huge striped swarming human ants! Some walked briskly, with shoulders back and head held high, some rolled and swaggered like sailors on land, while others drooped their heads and shuffled their lagging feet, broken reeds which could never stand straight again.

Frank pointed out "Crank" Alley, "Kid" Alley, and "Chiney" Alley to his friend, showed him where the incorrigibles lie in solitary confinement, marked the spot in the mill where a prisoner hid for three days while the guards scoured the hills and brush for miles around in search of him, pointed out the iron-barred gate of the dungeon, where a rebellious group of ill-doers, confined there at one time, had wrested the iron door open, and had made a "break," only to have the Gatling gun from the hill-post turned upon them.

And then Frank turned toward the long, wooden stairs which creep up the side of the big brick building on the right—a building used only for storage, with the exception of the rooms at the head of those long wooden stairs, where the frosted windows glare opaquely from the dull red walls like two blind eyes, expressionless, yet ominous, chilling, terror-inspiring in their very blindness. This is the Death Room, where the gallows, the death trap, and all the rest of that hideous contrivance has taken its toll of human flesh for years and years.

One week before the execution the condemned man is put in the Death Chamber below, under armed guards, who watch his every move to see that he does not cheat the gallows by spilling his own life-blood. On the final day he is taken up into the gallows room, and if he is too weak from fear to stand, a board is strapped to his back. He is offered the rites of the church if he desires them, and is given a chance to say a few last words. Then the drama goes on. The black cap is dropped over his head and face, the hangman's noose is slipped over his neck, and the signal is given.

Three men stand in little box-like booths awaiting the signal. Each holds in his hand a knife, and when the sign is given, each slashes furiously at a string stretched taut before him. The death trap falls, and all is over. Of the three men in the booths, no one knows which string it is, when cut, releases the trap, and not one of the three can be sure that his was the stroke which severed the life-cord.

As we waited, of a sudden the prison bell clanged loud in the belfry. It was the signal for the lock-up!

At the first sound the yard swarmed with life, scurrying to make its way up the crowded stairs, clattering rapidly along the balconies, and standing in place before the open cell doors. A flaming scarlet shirt or two among those throngs of gray-clad men, attracted Mr. Prentiss' attention. He was informed that the "red-shirt" men were those who at some time had attempted to escape, and were now so marked among their fellows.

manager to help out. But it was Elizabeth who carried the heaviest workload, staying on regularly to midnight and then walking home alone down Tucson's poorly lighted streets.

> Manuel sometimes waited for her, but not always. He would come home about ten o'clock, exhausted, for he was ill, to find me hugging the fire, Topacio beside me. I would teach him phrases in English, and he would recite poetry in Spanish or sing songs like *Los Ojos Negros* and *La Golondrina*. For the latter he used the words his father had written, saying they were much better than the original. When Elizabeth came home we'd make hot chocolate and go off to bed.[15]

It was in Tucson that Ethel, Elizabeth, John, and Manuel developed a truly close friendship. Turner was working feverishly, and his gravity and sense of purpose inspired the group as a whole. They thought of nothing but Mexico, Ethel recalled. Even their dreams and nightmares were colonized by Mexican symbols. At the same time, the struggle was also a time of companionship.

> Realizing the sensational nature of his material, [John] had worked day and night in an effort at completion. But I can still remember him with a kitchen apron around his neck and a small Belgian pistol in his hand, trying to get a bead on a large-sized rat that ran around the wainscoting in the dining room. We stood at various corners, cheering him on, but the rat succeeded in diving into its hole.[16]

At night, Manuel sang Mexican songs and recited poetry, or else the group took walks through "Yaqui Town" and "marveled at the regal grace of the women with heavy basket loads on their heads."[17] Because they worked such long hours, they generally took Sundays off for recreation, and these outings, too, were accented by the cultivation of an old Indian and Spanish world that was in some way flourishing alongside the dream of revolution:

> Sometimes we would walk along the dry river bed looking for arrowheads. At other times, in a hired carriage, we would take trips to the ruined adobe stronghold, Fort Lowell, or to the beautiful Sabina Canyon in the Santa Catalina mountains. Or, got in the other direction, we would visit the Mission San Xavier del Bac or climb the cactus-covered Santa Rosa Mountain. John Murray seldom accompanied us. He, like Manuel, was a tuberculosis victim, and felt he needed those hours for complete rest.[18]

Elizabeth, the lover of animals, found a yellow mongrel, brought him home, and bathed him. The dog became their constant companion and also kept watch over them and their home. They needed it.

Spies

Despite its moderate success, *The Border* did not gain too much political traction. Nor did Manuel Sarabia's *Defensor del Pueblo* exist long enough to become very notorious. That is, except to the "Díaz-American spy machine." Díaz was not letting down his guard on the border, and his spies "all but slept on our doorstep," Ethel recalled.[19] Murray, Elizabeth, Manuel, Ethel, and John were constantly watched.

In the first days of December 1908, John finished his first three pieces on Mexican slavery (one on Yucatán, one on the Yaquis, one on Valle Nacional) and set out for New York to meet with the editors of the *American Magazine*, Ida Tarbell and Ray Stannard Baker. About ten days later, Díaz's agents ransacked the offices of *The Border*, broke windows and machinery, stole the type, took about a thousand copies of *El Defensor del Pueblo* and whatever there was of *The Border*, and destroyed as much furniture as they could.[20]

The episode spooked Murray, who tried to persuade Elizabeth to give up the magazine. Murray might have been feeling the heat of persecution from other sources, as well—we do not know for sure, but a few months after this episode, the Department of Justice queried the Mexican Embassy regarding a rumor, denied by the ambassador, that Díaz had put a $10,000 bounty on Murray's head.[21] Regardless of the details of the broader context, though, the fact that Elizabeth refused to budge. She had poured too much money into the venture, and the political prisoners still needed its support. So Murray resigned and moved to Chicago, where he founded the Political Refugee Defense League, while Elizabeth, Ethel, and Manuel were left alone in Tucson. Elizabeth was bitterly disappointed by Murray's departure, Ethel recalled, but she, Manuel, and Ethel mended *The Border*'s offices and got back to work.[22]

The magazine's days were nevertheless numbered. Elizabeth and Manuel had fallen in love, and in her characteristically unconventional style, Elizabeth asked Manuel to marry her. She was very worried about Manuel having to return to prison. He was out on bail, but it was clear that the men of the junta would be convicted.

Manuel's tuberculosis was a serious concern, and Elizabeth felt certain that if he returned to prison, he would die there, so Elizabeth persuaded Manuel to marry and then skip bail with her to England.

Elizabeth Darling Trowbridge and Manuel Sarabia Labrada were married in Tucson on December 28, 1908. The wedding was a modest and unconventional affair. Elizabeth's family was not notified, lest they try to intervene. Manuel's closest relatives and friends—his cousin, Juan Sarabia. and his brother, Tomás, Práxedis Guerrero, and the men of the junta—were either in jail or on the run. His ailing mother was back in Mexico City. Murray was in Chicago, and John Turner was in New York. So the wedding began with a brunch with Ethel at the cottage.

> Elizabeth had invited one of the friends of the Mexican cause, an old time prospector and cattleman named Fuller. At the table he told some longwinded yarn about a cow. I thought it would never end and stared at him, open-mouthed, thinking him the most unromantic person in the world.... Finally Elizabeth in her timid way, always with a blush, announced that it was time to go to the Justice of the Peace, and would he mind being a witness? Poor Mr. Fuller was chagrined over his behavior; he had not dreamed there was a wedding on hand. He and I "stood up" with Elizabeth and Manuel, after which he went home and we three went back to the cottage.[23]

The modesty of this ceremony was in inverse proportion to the significance of the transgression. Elizabeth cabled her mother with the news and left with Manuel to Phoenix for their honeymoon. Overcome with distress, Mrs. Shultis took to her bed, sending one of Elizabeth's cousins to Tucson to pursue an annulment. Manuel, the family argued, was, as Mexican, "an inferior person," a fortune hunter, and a criminal under indictment to boot.

Elizabeth's cousin arrived to the Tucson bungalow when the newlyweds were off in Phoenix, so it fell to Ethel to face him. Ethel, who was by that time twenty-two and entirely part of the dreamworld of the Mexican Cause, made a fiery defense of Manuel and of the marriage. "Annulment," she said, "was out of the question." Elizabeth's family, Ethel said, should be proud of her, and she explained Manuel's devotion to the Mexican people, his opposition to the tyrant Díaz, and his unfair imprisonment in the United States. "I think Manuel emerged as a super-human being, and Elizabeth might well consider herself a lucky girl," she recalled.[24] Ethel did not reveal the young couple's whereabouts or yield to pressure, so the cousin returned to Boston in frustration.

The marriage was also transgressive in a much broader circle. Ricardo Flores Magón, for one, was not happy with the union and would later also accuse Manuel of being a fortune hunter. But his sentiments were not known to anyone at that time but María Brousse and probably Librado Rivera and Lucía Norman, María's daughter. Still, Manuel and Elizabeth had strong apprehensions about how their marriage would be received by the Liberals, especially given the newlyweds' intention to jump bail and flee to England together. Their wedding could surely be interpreted as a selfish indulgence and a betrayal of the cause, since it involved abandoning the United States and Mexico.

Elizabeth, who was the stronger-willed of the pair (though Manuel was no milquetoast), convinced Manuel that their departure was a matter of life or death, as it very likely was, and that his skipping bail would in no way alter the sentences meted out to Ricardo, Librado, and Antonio, as indeed, it seems not to have done.[25] Still, from the viewpoint of the junta, the case was an example of putting romantic self-interest before the interests of the cause.

Práxedis Guerrero, who had been Manuel's roommate and close collaborator in Douglas, Arizona, stopped communicating with Manuel due to this decision, and he did not renew the connection until he saw Manuel and Elizabeth's continued work for the cause from Europe. There was, in other words, a tear in the social fabric both on Elizabeth's side and on Manuel's side. Indeed, only the Noels, Ethel and John, and Manuel's Mexican family fully approved of the marriage.

On the public front, the story was also a sensation. It told of a breach in racial and class relations prompted by radical political beliefs and ideals, including feminism and Socialism, and it brought the plight of the political prisoners back into relief. Above all, it was romantic. As a result, the Sarabia-Trowbridge wedding was a news item, with articles appearing in a number of papers.

The most extensive of these, in the *Tucson Citizen*, identified Elizabeth as a wealthy and educated heiress from one of Boston's oldest families who had been a Socialist for ten years. Sarabia, for his part, was an "alleged Mexican revolutionist," among the most famous men of the revolutionary junta, whose kidnapping in Douglas and subsequent imprisonment in Mexico had caused a sensation that had forced the Mexican government to set him free.

The prison romance was highlighted, as were Elizabeth's ideals and her convictions regarding Manuel's innocence. Elizabeth declared in the piece that "I really became interested in Mr. Sarabia when I was at home in Boston" and "I am a Socialist and have spent a number of years in studying economics and history. I took a special course in economics at Radcliffe College, which is a department of Harvard University."

The *Citizen* concluded by noting that Elizabeth was an "ardent advocate of women's suffrage." The implication was, of course, that she was acting independently of her family. Elizabeth confirmed the paper's statement by declaring that "I firmly believe that a woman has the same right to vote that a man has.... I have been aiding the suffrage cause in every way possible, and I shall continue my labors in that direction."[26]

Departures

After Manuel and Elizabeth returned from their honeymoon, in January 1909, they and Ethel renewed their editorial responsibilities. They hired a woman to lend a hand with some of the chores at *The Border*, but soon fired her, fearing that she might be a spy. They hired no replacement. The group's situation was too unstable.

At the end of January, John telegraphed Ethel, asking her to join him in New York. The *American Magazine* was eager to print his stories. Because they recognized just how big they were, they wanted Turner to return to Mexico for a bit of reporting on the upper classes in Mexico City—to round out the picture that he had gotten on the plantations in Yucatan and Oaxaca. Editors Ray Stannard Baker and Ida Tarbell and John would keep the whole project in absolute secrecy, then emerge with a fully blown exposé of slavery and the "Díaz system."[27] The magazine helped set up a good cover for John in Mexico City, as sports editor of the English-language *Mexican Herald*, and Ethel was to accompany him. So Ethel prepared to leave.

On the other hand, there was Manuel's situation. His illness was serious. Even with all of Elizabeth's cares—good food, good medical attention—tuberculosis would in fact kill him just a few years later.

And Manuel's trial date had been set for April. Despite its success, *The Border* would have to close. So the couple made their plans for escape, and Manuel skipped town quietly and took a ship to England on the first week of February.

Elizabeth stayed on to around the time of Manuel's trial. She had wanted to postpone suspicions of his escape as long as possible. Elizabeth declared to local papers that Manuel was in Arizona on a reporting mission. Some of the Spanish-language border papers, barely hiding a sentiment of schadenfreude toward an uppity Mexican and the rich white girl who married him, claimed that Elizabeth had been jilted.[28] But, despite this unpleasantness, Elizabeth seems to have managed to inspire confidence in Manuel's return for the trial, judging from the surprise expressed when he in fact failed to make his appearance there.[29]

By early April, the Tucson chapter of this story was over. John Murray was in Chicago with his Defense League. Elizabeth and Manuel were in London. Elizabeth had spent down almost all of her father's inheritance, and her mother had disinherited her for the rest. Ethel and John had gone to Mexico City. The group would never come together again.

CHAPTER TWELVE

Mexico in the Headlines

American Opinion

During the months before going to trial for violation of the U.S. neutrality laws in the abortive uprising of 1906, Ricardo predicted to María that he and his companions would be condemned to prison terms of ten to fifteen years. The only thing that could hinder such an outcome was mass mobilization, and he saw none of that on the horizon: "None of those friends sends articles to the press, or contributions, or organizes protests or meetings in our favor. Nothing effective or practical is being done. We're as badly off now as we were a year ago."[1] Without external pressure, Ricardo, Librado, Manuel, and Antonio were doomed to rot in jail. What Ricardo did not yet realize was just how effective the Socialist group that Elizabeth Trowbridge and Job Harriman marshaled actually was.

At first, the effects were few, but they began to add up. Propaganda initiatives such as *The Border*, which had several issues devoted to the prisoners, had already appeared, as had John Murray's *International Socialist Review* articles on his trip to Mexico, along with the chorus of pro-Liberal Mexican papers printed on the U.S. side of the border. Upon his return to the United States late in 1908, Lázaro Gutiérrez de Lara accelerated his preaching against the Mexican dictatorship and for the liberation of the prisoners. It took Ricardo time to appreciate the compounded effect of these efforts, but by late February 1909, he had begun to appreciate the impact of the campaign that was being led from the Noel residence in Los Angeles. "If this agitation continues, we're saved," he wrote to María "Violeta [Elizabeth Trowbridge] is working tirelessly, as is Mother Jones, John Murray, and other friends."[2]

By March 1909 the Socialist Party had begun a campaign for the release of the prisoners. Eugene Debs's *Appeal to Reason* issued a "liberty edition" that was said to have run more than two million copies.[3] These campaigns received enough play in the mainstream press to put Mexico's ambassador in Washington into damage-control mode. In August, León de la Barra wired the minister of foreign relations asking for instructions on how to counter persistent rumors of a looming revolution in Mexico.[4]

Still, neither Ricardo nor anyone else foresaw the enormous effect of the publication of John Kenneth Turner's "Barbarous Mexico" articles. The first of these appeared in October 1909, causing an immediate and absolutely massive scandal. The effects of these pieces were compounded by much on-the-ground activism. Lázaro Gutiérrez de Lara went to Arizona and led public meetings in Tucson, in Phoenix, and in Yuma itself. On September 16, at the public celebrations of Mexican Independence in Tucson, Lara took the podium and launched an incendiary speech against Díaz. Despite having opened the podium to speakers, Teodoro Olea, the master of ceremonies and leader of the Tucson Mexican community, had Lázaro forcibly dragged off the stage.[5]

Similarly, Andrea and Teresa Villarreal—Antonio's sisters—who were well-known editors and public speakers, went to Phoenix and spoke at a rally organized by the IWW in support of the prisoners. The Mexican consul reported that the Mexican community in Phoenix was very favorable to the prisoners and to the Socialist cause, though he claimed that his activity since his arrival had contributed to diminish those sentiments.[6]

The fact remained that anti-Díaz activities such as Lázaro's in the environs of the Mexican prisoners worried the Mexican consul and Foreign Ministry. No charges were actually made against Lázaro at that point, though, because the consulate could find no legal grounds. But as soon as the first "Barbarous Mexico" article was published in the *American Magazine*, in October 1909, the Mexican Embassy in Washington formally pushed for extradition, based on a hastily put-together charge. The Los Angeles district attorney seized Lázaro, put him in jail, and initiated the extradition process.

Lázaro Gutiérrez de Lara's extradition provided a perfect occasion for active and effective Socialist Party propaganda against Díaz and for the liberation of the men who were imprisoned in Arizona.

Figure 12.1 Crowd of Chicago women, girls, and boys who sold newspapers to raise money to help the Mexican political prisoners. Murray's efforts in favor of Mexican political refugees effectively mobilized opinion in favor of the cause in major U.S. cities, many of them far removed from the Southwest. Courtesy of the Bancroft Library, John Murray Papers.

The case brought into focus all of the uneasiness that had been build-ing up with regard to the collaboration and aid that the American government was providing Díaz.

Lázaro was held for extradition based on the frivolous charge of having stolen twenty-eight dollars' worth of chopping wood from Colonel William C. Greene's properties in Cananea back in 1903. The charge against Lázaro was stereotypically absurd and poorly documented. And yet the U.S. judiciary held the man for months on end and set bail at the exorbitant price of $3000. Moreover, indig-nation was much intensified because Lázaro had collaborated with John in the sensational denunciation of slavery in Yucatan that was then resounding throughout the country.

The Socialist Party was ready to rally around Lázaro's case, since it had been rallying support for the Mexican political refugees for almost two years. In December 1908, John Murray had founded the Political Refugee Defense League in Chicago. Contrary to Ricardo's expectations, placing the case of Mexico, which had until then had very little traction in American public opinion, next to that of Rus-sia, which commanded widespread sympathy, seems to have helped draw national attention (Figure 12.1). In any case, the national media campaign that the Socialists engineered was effective and succeeded to some degree in casting policies toward Mexico's political refugees as "un-American."

So, for instance, among the letters that went back and forth between the Mexican consul in Tucson and Mexican Foreign Ministry there was an article published in the *Arizona Democrat* that called for giving Mexicans in the United States a "square deal." De Lara, the paper claimed, was going to be transported to Old Mexico, where the *rurales* would cut justice short and apply the *ley fuga*—"disappear" him, to employ a term that later became notorious. "The judge is also going to be called in as a witness. His name is Ridgway and he's the Chief Immigration Inspector. The Mexican government insists that De Lara is an anarchist." But Lara had said that he was not an anarchist, but rather a "worker of the world," and in any case, he had only exercised free speech at his various Arizona rallies. Thus, although the paper thought that Lara was strident, said a lot of rubbish, and the public mostly laughed at him, it concluded that he did no one any harm and that "sending men to Mexico or to prison just to please the Mexican government goes entirely against American principles of liberty, and it is starting to get irksome."[7]

And thanks to Turner's writings, Lázaro's arrest garnered attention beyond the Southwest. The Mexican Embassy noted with some alarm that the *Washington Post* carried the news of Lara's arrest under the heading "Mexico May Get Him: De Lara, Backer of Slavery Charge, Risks Deportation."[8] The *Post* wrote that immigration Inspector A. C. Ridgeway had said that Lara was accused of uttering words against the United States—against all governments, in fact—and of being undesirable. "De Lara," the paper continued, "is one of the national Socialist leaders of the United States, having been appointed from Socialist headquarters in Chicago." His case, in other words, was clearly political—he was a political refugee who had left Mexico after publishing a book; he was a member of the American Socialist Party and was married to an American citizen. The case for deportation stank to high heaven, and so, by implication, did the violation of neutrality cases against Flores Magón, Villarreal, Sarabia, and Rivera.

The Mexican Consulate in Los Angeles was flooded with queries and complaints regarding the attempt to extradite. "I've had to dissuade them by declaring that the Mexican government is not concerned with the case," the consul reported.[9] On that same day, the *Los Angeles Herald* noted that "funds for De Lara's defense are coming in from all quarters of the United States, and it is certain now that a proper defense will be provided."[10]

And indeed, Lara had the benefit of excellent lawyers from Harriman's Socialist team—Clarence Meilly and A. R. Holston—who now represented the newly constituted De Lara Defense League. Holston discredited the plainclothes policemen who were also witnesses in the case, Rico and Talamantes, arguing that they bore a grudge against Lara because they had sued *Regeneración* for libel the previous year. Moreover, the lawyer argued that the "anarchistic charge was disproved absolutely." Anarchism had been illegal in the United States since the McKinley assassination in 1900 and was sufficient cause to expel a foreigner, but Lázaro was a card-carrying member and official of the Socialist Party, which was legal.[11]

Defense attorney Meilly concluded:

> The trial would have been an opera bouffe had it not been for the fact that a man's liberty was at stake. It is a serious matter to put a man in jail and hold him there for days without bail, and when he is put on trial, have him fearing a farce. It looks to me like persecution of the very worst sort and savors of Russian police methods, not Americanism.[12]

The Socialists were yet again comparing Mexico's oppression to Russia's and calling collaboration with that oppression un-American. And at least some in the mainstream press were listening. "Letters are reaching the league [the De Lara Defense League] written by persons in Mexico. One of the writers in the City of Mexico urges the league to tell the American people of the dire necessity of keeping political refugees from the clutches of despotism. 'The horrors of hell await any political offenders who are returned here,' writes the correspondent."[13] One of the speakers at a Los Angeles rally in support of Lázaro was former California Supreme Court judge John D. Works, who said: "When a man may be seized on the streets of Los Angeles and incarcerated without authority of law, what is it but a despotism?"[14]

Lázaro's future as an American citizen was also introduced to the arguments in his favor. "If I am released from prison, which I believe will be the case, and if I am not deported to my death in Mexico, I shall at once make application for my first papers of naturalization as a citizen of the United States," he declared.[15] Further corroboration of the sense that Lara was practically an American came by way of the person of Lara's American wife, Hattie. "Mrs. De Lara, who is an American woman of education and refinement, is working night and day in her husband's behalf.... 'Mr. De Lara is no more an anarchist than President Taft,' said Mrs. De Lara last night."[16] Confirmation of Lázaro's upright character came also from Reverend D. M. Gandier of the State Anti-Saloon League, who testified that Lara had sought his assistance to protect Mexicans from gamblers and saloon sharks. Lara, an unselfish and educated man, was a Socialist and not an anarchist, and "that is no crime."[17]

The thuggish arrest of Lara and the general incompetence of the prosecution also provided a modicum of entertainment. Lázaro had been detained on October 10 while speaking at the so-called "Plaza de los Mexicanos," which was a free-speech zone that had a string of radical orators on the stump every weekend, so picking especially on Lara seemed arbitrary. And the Mexican-American detectives who made the arrest might have served well for a vaudeville show: "Young Rico," the *Los Angeles Herald* reported, "said he learned Spanish when he was a child, yet could not read or write the language, attempted to quote De Lara, giving a free translation as he went along. According to linguists present, the policeman made a most pitiable mess of it."[18]

The Socialist Party was able to supplement national press coverage with mass mobilization. Rallies and mass meetings were held to protest the deportation of Lázaro in Los Angeles, San Francisco, Seattle, Portland, Stockton, Denver, Chicago, and New York.[19] The Los Angeles meeting, held at Simpson Auditorium, had more than two thousand people in it. Speakers included John Kenneth Turner, Mrs. Lara, Judge John Works, and Job Harriman.

In his remarks, Harriman declared that "they want this man, because he dared to tell the Mexican people of the murder of 35,000 Yaqui Indians by the Mexican government. They want him because he dared to make public the story of slavery and oppression in that nation." The lawyer then proceeded to decry the abuse of immigration law:

> The immigration laws are such that a political reformer seeking a haven in the United States can no longer find it.... De Lara's greatest offense

against his government has been raising his voice for the weak and the oppressed. His mission has been one to the poor. Is that a crime? Meek, and gentle, a scholar and a lover of liberty—that is the man who is now in the county jail charged with being an anarchist."[20]

Less than one week later, on November 1, 1909, a second blockbuster article by John Kenneth Turner appeared in the *American Magazine*, "The Tragic Story of the Yaqui Indians." The December issue then carried the most haunting and horrifying piece of all, "Contract Slaves of Valle Nacional." The scandal reached such vast proportions that although the *American Magazine* ceased publishing Turner's pieces under pressure from the State Department, the cat was out of the bag. The noise that the Socialists made about the cases of Lázaro's extradition and of the imprisonment of Ricardo, Antonio, and Librado was such that by the start of 1910, the U.S. House of Representatives made its first inquiry into the imprisonment of the men.[21]

The Truth Comes Out

The Mexican government was very concerned to act against the articles in the *American Magazine* and to identify and persecute the Mexican who had been involved in the affair, with Mexico's ambassador in Washington leading the effort.[22] Very soon, Lázaro would again be jailed and another extradition proceeding attempted, while Mexico explored the possibility of bringing libel charges against Turner. It would fail in both.

But the Mexican government was not the only offended party. The State Department files in the National Archives contain a number of letters and documents that prove that American financial interests were deeply affected by John and Lázaro's exposé. So, for instance, in 1913, two years after the toppling of Díaz, when the U.S. ambassador, Henry Lane Wilson, orchestrated the expulsion of Turner from Mexico, he described John to Secretary of State William Jennings Bryan as "an American correspondent of doubtful morals but considerable notoriety, whose unpatriotic conduct in Mexico provoked condemnatory resolutions by the Society of the American Colony."[23]

In one such resolution, the American colony had pretended to be defending the honor of Mexico in the United States against Turner and the *American Magazine*:

We do not claim for the Government of Mexico that perfection not even found in many other governments, but we protest that the economic conditions of this country do not justify the sweeping assertions made by your correspondents, any more than a special exposition of lynchings, sweat-shop abuses, employment of convict labor or race riots, would justify the title of "Barbarous United States" to be applied to a series of literary efforts to describe the backward conditions of our own native land.[24]

This feeling of patriotic indignation was mobilized quite broadly in Mexico. Thus, the students who rallied in the streets of Mexico City to protest the lynching of a Mexican, Antonio Rodríguez, in Rock Springs, Texas, in November 1910 stridently declared that "with his feet in the furnace, Rodríguez died for the country he loved; for his Mexico, whose borders were so far; for his 'barbarous Mexico' where justice still reigns; for his 'barbarous Mexico' where murderers are not burned alive; for his Mexico where sentiments of humanity exist, and where tribunals are supplied to punish offenders against the law."[25] Mexico City students thus compared a Mexican migrant who had murdered his employer and was then dragged out of prison and burned alive by a lynch mob to the plight of the Aztec king Cuauhtémoc, whose feet were burned under torture by the Spaniards, all in order to say that Mexico was not barbarous and that the evidence presented by Turner regarding Mexican slavery and ethnocide should be ignored, because the United States, too, had much of which it should be ashamed.

Alongside attempts to rehabilitate Mexico and its American investors in the court of public opinion, there were powerful executives who tried to use the American government covertly to stop Turner's message from spreading. So, for instance, in 1910, Charles Q. Davis, president of the Bankers Mining and Development Company, wrote to Secretary of State Philander Knox suggesting that he "find some way to prevent these publications, by denying this magazine the use of the mail or possibly bringing a criminal action for libel."[26] As we will see, the secretary of state appears to have complied. And the Mexican government followed suit, encouraging its employee, the Furlong Detective Agency to file a libel suit against Turner and his publishers.[27]

In other words, after the "purloined letter" had been found and its contents publicly exposed, all defenders of the status quo—Mexicans and Americans—rallied to try to deny the reality of Mexican slavery. But this was no longer possible.

In her later years, Ethel reflected back on what had transpired during the months of publication of her husband John's incendiary articles:

> Newspapers were leaping to the Dictator's defense. But there was something about the article that rang true. Letters began to pour into the magazine's editorial rooms, to the press. The inarticulate, those who knew what the real Mexico was, but had no means of expression, began to verify John's findings. College professors and ministers were making statements. And this was only the beginning; the clamor was to increase day by day, until John's name was a byword, and "barbarous" a catch-phrase for local oppression—"barbarous Texas"—"barbarous Mississippi"—even "barbarous Washington DC."[28]

The purloined letter had been found, and its contents had been read aloud.

Congressional Hearings

The agitation for the Arizona prisoners, for the freedom of Lázaro Gutiérrez de Lara, and to expose and decry the cozy relationship between the American and Mexican governments occurred at a complicated moment in U.S.-Mexican relations. On October 16, 1909, Presidents William Howard Taft and Porfirio Díaz had a historical meeting on the bridge between El Paso and Ciudad Juárez. It was supposed to reaffirm the ties between the two governments and to guarantee continued Mexican support for American investment. It was also to supposed be a show of control and strength for Díaz in the area where opposition was strongest, the Texas border.

The prosecution used the looming Taft-Díaz meeting to paint Lázaro as a dangerous anarchist. Thus, detective Rico said "that he remembered well what De Lara had said, and quoted thus: 'The two presidents (meaning Taft and Díaz) will soon meet in El Paso. There will be a meeting on Maple Street to raise funds to send two men to El Paso. It will be a good time to fix Díaz.'"[29] But the bogeyman of anarchist assassination was countered by the increasingly convincing image of Díaz as a venal autocrat.

The Taft-Díaz photo opportunities didn't help Díaz in this regard. They provided a visible contrast between Taft's sober dress and

Díaz's chest full of medals. Moreover, the press harped quite a lot on the lavishness of the banquet served in Ciudad Juárez: the two-hundred-thousand-dollar cut glass that was brought from Chapultepec Castle, the three train carloads of flowers brought from Guadalajara, the transformation of the Juárez customshouse building, where the banquet was held, into a reproduction of a Versailles salon. Lavish displays of power such as these were easily interpreted as an expression of the kind of callousness of which that Díaz was being ever more loudly accused.

So the Socialist group used the Díaz-Taft meeting to continue to publicize their case. John Murray made his way toward El Paso from Chicago to report on the event, and he and some other Socialists were nabbed and held by security forces. But Murray was nothing if not an able newspaperman, and his arrest quickly made national news. Thus, the *Washington Post* reported:

> Preceding the arrival of President Taft in San Antonio, Sunday, several "undesirable citizens," as they were classified, were arrested, to be held during the visit of the President.... A committee of local socialists reports that a member of the Political Refugee Defense League and another local socialist are missing. The latter, it was learned, is in the city jail. The committee telegraphed to the Chicago socialist headquarters concerning the prisoner: 'Think he is incommunicado.'"[30]

Ten days after the Taft-Díaz meeting, an action for libel was brought in a New York court by the Díaz government against an Italian journalist who had edited a paper in Mexico City, Carlo de Fornaro, for the publication of his book *Díaz, Czar of Mexico*. Fornaro was condemned to one year in prison.[31] By that point, it had become abundantly clear that a battle was raging for American opinion about Díaz's Mexico. Thus, when Lázaro was discharged and his deportation proceeding was halted, his wife, Hattie, declared:

> It was the noble work of the newspapers that helped so much in our case.... We have hundreds of clippings, and many of these are editorials from all over the country. I want to say that some of them are far from complimentary to the Los Angeles police who entered this case in the spirit they did. Almost every editorial is outspoken in denunciation of the Spanish methods adopted in an American city.... Let all women be grateful that our country is not disgraced by delivering over a political

refugee who sought sanctuary here because he believed it to be the land of the free.[32]

As soon as Lázaro was free, he began a tour of American cities, lecturing on Mexican conditions. The archives of Mexico's Foreign Ministry attest to the fact that the consular service tried as best it could to stop these lectures, but found no legal basis to do so.[33] The combined offers of the various defense leagues and the scandal caused by Turner's exposé finally succeeded in garnering the nation's attention.

On June 10, 1910, the United States Congress called a set of witnesses to the House Rules Committee to discuss the persecution of Mexican political refugees. They were John Kenneth Turner, Lázaro Gutiérrez de Lara, John Murray, and the labor organizer "Mother" Mary Jones. The committee considered a resolution, put forward by Pennsylvania Representative William Wilson, a Democrat, calling for an investigative committee to inquire into the treatment of Mexican political refugees and the acceptance of money from the Díaz government by American customs and peace officers along the border to act as Mexican secret service agents.

Lázaro's part in the congressional hearings was to bear testimony as both a victim and Mexican government informant—he had been persecuted by the Mexican government on several occasions, with support from U.S. authorities, but he claimed also to know the consular spy network from within. John Turner's declarations went to the general features of the case.

> Immigration officials, forest rangers, custom agents, members of the Secret Service and soldiers in the regular army are implicated in the accusations made by Mr. Turner. He said that a United States forest ranger had seized a Mexican printer named Sarabia, a refugee, at Douglas, Ariz., and carried him, bound and gagged, in an automobile across the frontier, where he was given up to Mexican government agents.
>
> The witness said that three Mexicans, Villarreal, Magon and Rivera, who were later convicted, were held "incommunicado" in the Los Angeles jail on the orders of Attorney General Bonaparte, who had given as a reason the fact that the Mexican Government wanted the prisoners, and that the United States wanted to favor that Government.[34]

The labor leader "Mother" Jones, who had led the protests decrying the kidnapping of Manuel Sarabia in Douglas and then actively had defended Magón and company, presented her testimony in this regard, and John Murray told of the apprehensions suffered by Mexican Liberals in Texas.

It is true that the overall impact of these pressures on close collaboration between the U.S. and Mexican governments is easily overstated. Thus, Mexican ambassador León de la Barra, who met twice privately with Attorney General George Wickersham to discuss the situation, summarized the import of the congressional hearings to Mexican Foreign Minister Federico Gamboa by saying that Wickersham believed that the U.S. government would prove that it acted fairly and that Turner, Murray, Lara, and Mother Jones were untrustworthy witnesses. Wickersham "believes that this inquiry will only increase the good name of Mexico and of its government in the eyes of the American public." Ten days later, Ambassador De la Barra met again with the attorney general, who deemed that "the inquiry has served as a pretext for Congressman Wilson and the witnesses to attack the U.S. government, and Mr. Wickersham especially, because of the way in which the law has been applied in the case of Flores Magon and associates, but that it will have no real consequences."[35]

And indeed, there was still overwhelming support for Díaz in American newspapers, especially in those owned by the great moguls who had large moneyed interests in Mexico, such as William Randolph Hearst and Harrison Gray Otis. So, for instance, the Hearst-owned *San Francisco Chronicle* agreed that Díaz was a despot, but claimed that he was a necessary despot. Lara, on the other hand, was an anarchist and "a typical representative of the filibusters who would take the administration of Mexico out of President Díaz's hands. He is a man of mixed blood, part Indian, part Spanish. He says he has been a spy for Mexico and a recreant one. He is now an agitator."

Insisting on the respectability of the Díaz regime, the *Chronicle* waxed indignant with Congress for even having admitted testimonies of the likes of Lara, Turner, and Mother Jones: "As to a Committee of Congress giving a man like De Lara time to come before it and abuse President Díaz, it seems as inadmissible as it would have been to ask Johann Most, in his time, to address such a body about the political character of the Emperor of Germany."[36]

It was clear, though, that Díaz supporters were, for the first time, on the defensive, and the case of Flores Magón, Rivera, and Villarreal had become prominent. The judiciary was under close scrutiny, and it let the prisoners go sooner than the Mexican government would have liked.

PART THREE

Eve of Revolution

CHAPTER THIRTEEN

Learning from 1906

Clandestinity

On the run from the law, Ricardo wrote to Manuel Sarabia: "It seems that misfortune pursues us and that it is fated that we won't even be able to start the movement of our dreams."[1] The revolt that they had initiated in September 1906 was an unmitigated disaster.

Immediately after its relocation in St. Louis, in 1905, the junta reorganized the PLM around a radical platform. The PLM's new program committed party members to organize for the violent overthrow of Porfirio Díaz, so it was now a clandestine organization.

The junta then divided Mexican territory into five zones, each led by a party delegate. Together, they were supposed to stage a simultaneous, multisited uprising. Historians place the number of local PLM organizations that were ready to rise up in arms at around forty.[2] Most of these were located near the U.S. border, although there was an important armed contingent in southern Veracruz, as well.[3]

When the date of the uprising approached, the men of the junta traveled to Texas to participate in the assaults planned on the border towns of Ciudad Juárez (Chihuahua), Nogales (Sonora), and Jiménez (Chihuahua). But the Mexican and U.S. governments were appraised of these actions. The attack on Jiménez was defeated, while other border raids were preempted, and a number of militants and leaders were captured, including, most prominently, junta vice president Juan Sarabia and secretary Antonio Villarreal. Ricardo and Enrique Flores Magón, Librado Rivera, and Manuel Sarabia managed to escape, but they were driven into clandestinity, and communication between them broke down.

The files at *Regeneración* were impounded, and they included sensitive correspondence, as well as the PLM's registration rolls—

complete with addresses. The persistent and internationally coordinated work of spies and police continued to threaten most active PLM networks, and many suffered subsequent crackdowns.

Despite these devastating setbacks, though, field commanders Aarón López Manzano and Antonio de P. Araujo regrouped and worked tirelessly to launch a new offensive. Key junta leaders managed to reestablish contact from their new hideouts and began to coordinate these efforts. But the situation was still desperate: in addition to losses in personnel, there was no money left to support the fight.

In February 1907, Pascual Rodríguez, one of the field captains who was helping to prepare an assault on Matamoros, Tamaulipas, out of Browsnville, Texas, wrote to his superior about the group's lack of resources. In his group of seven committed militants, five had full-time commissions for the revolution, which meant that only two could hold down paying jobs for the upkeep of all. "The lack of funds has been such that we've been forced to take our children's sustenance for our own upkeep. In other words, we've asked our families to send us funds to keep us alive."[4] And other Texas rebels were in much the same situation. Tomás Sarabia wrote to Araujo explaining that in order to eat, he had had to take one of the three pesos that his brother Manuel had sent for their mother's sustenance; he reported that field comander Mendiola had no resources to sustain his men in Mexico and that they would soon be returning to San Antonio. Tomás, for his part, needed "55" (unclear whether they were cents or dollars, possibly cents) a day plus postage to keep printing their paper, *El Progreso.*[5]

True, there were still a few rays of light that encouraged the men to keep working on their offensive. On February 15, 1907, Antonio Villarreal escaped from his captors in El Paso and went into hiding, trying to reconnect with the remaining men of the junta. The El Paso police put a $1000 reward on his head (Figure 13.1).[6]

Another (relative) bright spot was that Juan Sarabia's trial in Mexico was a public-relations coup for the Liberal cause. Sarabia had defended himself eloquently and had succeeded in getting the judge to read the 1906 Liberal Manifesto out loud to prove that their movement was political and that prisoners such as Juan Sarabia and César Canales should not be tried as mere bandits. The people of Ciudad Juárez, where the trials were held, and where Juan Sarabia

ANTONIO I. VILLARREAL.

Age: about 31

Height: about 5 feet 6½ inches.

Color of eyes: black.

Color of hair: black.

Complexion: fair, slightly pale.

Build: medium.

Weight: about 160 lbs.

The above represents a Mexican alien who escaped from the custody of the Immigration Office at El Paso, Texas, on February 25, 1907·

A warrant for his arrest is in the hands of the Immigration Inspector at El Paso, Texas, and a liberal reward will be paid for his location. Please notify the nearest Immigration Officer, or the undersigned, by telegraph, collect, and hold at the expense of the United States Immigration Service.

T. F. SCHMUCKER,

U. S. Immigration Inspector in charge

EL PASO, TEXAS.

Figure 13.1 Wanted: Antonio I. Villarreal. Villarreal had not been in the United States for three years when he was caught for his participation in the 1906 uprising. That allowed U.S. authorities to prosecute him for violation immigration laws. Courtesy of the Archivo Histórico de la Secretaría de Relaciones Exteriores.

was convicted, had shouted *Vivas!* as he was escorted through the streets on his way to prison at San Juan de Ulúa. The trial, Ricardo wrote privately to Manuel Sarabia, proved that "the people are on our side. The public sympathy that has accompanied our *Charalito* [Juan Sarabia] is the best sign that they understand our mission, and that it is good, honest, and just."[7] The text of Sarabia's defense was dilligently printed by the Liberals in Texas and distributed widely. Juan Sarabia became the Liberals' first popular "martyr," a poster boy for revolutionary self-sacrifice and civic courage. Sadly, he would not be their last.

Encouraged by this news, the leadership of the Liberal Party felt that revolution might still be within its grasp. In January 1907, textile workers in Río Blanco, Veracruz rioted during a lockout, prompting a violent crackdown. Hundreds of workers were killed. Such events seemed to prove the potential for revolution in Mexico. Thus, Ricardo wrote to Manuel Sarabia about their plan for an offensive on Matamoros, Tamaulipas:

> This is going to be our second offensive, and if our lack of foresight on our first offensive can be forgiven—since we had no practice in revolutionary matters—this time no one will forgive us. For this reason, let's make a proper revolution [*una revolución bien hecha*].
>
> We don't have the money that is needed, but we do have the will of those who have remained true to the cause, and we have all of those who were injured by recent events, from the 1 of June 1906 [the Cananea strike] to the massacres at Orizaba. In other words, we have a lot of moral support. Let's make use of it![8]

But raising a revolution with no material base and with two governments on their tails was not so simple. On the day after the letter above, Ricardo wrote a second missive, about expenses and costs. They needed money to send to Juan Sarabia in prison, they needed money to print copies of their manifesto and other dispatches, they needed money to eat (since the leadership was in hiding and could not work to earn its keep), they needed money for lawyers in order to defend militants such as Modesto Díaz, who was being sued for libel, and to try to recover *Regeneración*'s papers, which had been impounded by Colonel Greene. They needed money for arms. They needed thousands of dollars, and they had no access to resources except by way of donations.

But seeking donations was also a public-relations vulnerability. The Liberals had known this from the very time of their arrival to the United States as exiles, and they had been careful to craft their letters asking for contributions with extensive explanations of the sacrifices that they'd made to devote themselves to the struggle, beginning with the sacrifice of exile itself, which they framed as the ultimate sacrifice: "Now that the imponderables of our struggle have heaved us onto foreign soil; now that we have arrived to our ultimate sacrifice, which is to abandon our country in order to fight for it; now it is the turn of our compatriots and coreligionaries to help us with the funds that we lack, and that are needed to renew our work."[9]

Still, pleas for money became a constant refrain, and they laid the group open to accusations of deception and chicanery. So, for instance, *El Puerto de Matamoros* printed a broadsheet revealing details of the 1906 "Revolución de ópera bufa" (farcical revolution) with a whole section on how "the bandits who dressed up as revolutionaries" bled their compatriots with collections.[10] Most importantly, funds received from collections were simply insufficient to reestablish the movement on firm footing.

At the end of February, Ricardo had to relocate from one unnamed place to another (actually, from San Francisco to the Imperial Valley), because he had been betrayed. "I don't know how I'll fare now," he wrote to Manuel. "I don't have anything here, not one friend. The vagabond's life is a sad one." He was exhausted, hungry, and wracked with worries.[11]

Ricardo was especially uneasy about his brother Enrique, who had been unable to contact any member of the junta for months. By late February, Ricardo was despairing: "What has become of my poor Luis [Enrique's code name]? I dream of him almost every night. Ah, there are few men who have suffered as much as I!"[12] Ricardo was also very worried that the junta's impounded papers might have fallen into the hands of the Díaz police. Those papers "were full of compromising information for many of our party members and for the future of the struggle."[13]

Other leaders were also down to one or two meals a day. By March, Antonio de P. Araujo wrote to the junta, "Your situation is critical, but mine is disastrous. I had neither lunch nor dinner today. I don't have five cents, nor any hope." He had pawned his assistant's watch the week prior and was going to pawn his own watch on the following day.[14] The men of the junta were not much better off. Thus, Ricardo wrote to Manuel that he and Villarreal were "really broke [estamos muy brujos]. We don't even eat in food stalls—we buy bread and luncheon meat in order to save. We've spent days of truly dogged hunger, because we've not had enough money even for that humble sustenance." Ricardo wrote that he and Antonio had almost been forced to go to the Salvation Army's soup kitchen and that if things continued this way, they would soon leave town to go work as miners. "When you're hungry, you don't even want to write. You feel faint, weak, and irritable."[15]

Librado Rivera, who was on the run from the law at this time, also described his painful circumstances. Librado was living in a community of forty poor workers. Their rooms were cells that barely fit a bed, the walls in the barracks did not reach the ceiling, and no one's belongings were safe. Librado kept no baggage and owned only the clothes on his back. Any letters or newspapers that arrived he burned after reading.[16]

On the other hand, the Mexican government had mobilized troops on the border (Figure 13.2). The towns where the Liberals wanted to strike—Matamoros, Piedras Negras, Las Vacas—were full of mochos (soldiers), and although Liberal strategists entertained the hope that these troops might switch over to the Liberal side, that did not happen. Nonetheless, as Ricardo wrote to field commander Aarón López Manzano, the Liberals needed to establish a foothold in Mexico urgently, because the network of spies and policing within the United States made the movement vulnerable to being betrayed a second time.[17] In short, they needed to gain a base in Mexico—but with no money for guns, well-watched garrisons in Mexico, and the disarticulation of networks in the United States, this was impossible. Falling into the hands of the American government was only a matter of time.

In April, Araujo was betrayed at Piedras Negras. Several of his men were jailed, and he was forced to flee back to El Paso.[18] Another group was caught in Torreón and taken to prison in Mexico City.[19] Liberal prisoners who had been rounded up in Sonora and Coahuila were handed long jail sentences. By the end of April 1907, it was clear that revolt was no longer feasible, and the main aim of the group shifted to resettling the junta and bringing out a

Figure 13.2 Guard house at Las Vacas. Bancroft Library, U.C. Berkeley.

new paper—ideally, a reissue of *Regeneración*. But Mexico's consular service was hot on Ricardo's trail, and the circle around the junta began closing. In June, Modesto Díaz, who was known to Furlong dectectives as a fervent Magonista, put out the paper *Revolución*, and this helped Mexican consuls and Furlong detectives locate the junta in Los Angeles and move to its final apprehension, which occurred in August 1907, almost one year after the rebellion had been betrayed.[20]

Internal Polarization

The 1906 revolt may have been a disaster, but it was also a formative experience. One precedent set by the 1906 revolt was how to deal with internal dissidence. The decision to stage an armed revolt had always been deeply contentious. Certainly, rebelling was a brave and noble thing to do, but was it wise? Was revolution viable? Was violence justifiable? Not all of those who sought to overthrow Porfirio Díaz agreed.

In some cases, dissenters could quietly withhold support while avoiding open confrontation with the Liberal junta. Francisco I. Madero, for instance, refused to lend economic support to the 1906 revolt, and the Liberals did not openly attack him for that. Indeed, Antonio de P. Araujo still tried to sound out "Don Panchito" for logistical and financial support for the rebellion in Coahuila as late as March, 1907.[21] Often, tepid sympathies such as those of small-l liberals like Madero were tolerated by members of the Liberal junta, rather than denounced, in hopes of gaining more energetic support from the same source once the struggle developed further.

But when rifts occurred within the core circle, ferocious attacks often came into the open. The two most important cases involving the 1906 revolt were Camilo Arriaga and Juana B. Gutiérrez de Mendoza, who were heads of a faction that had once included people such as Madero, as well as old companions of the Liberals' "first circle"—the Club Ponciano Arriaga—such as Alfonso Cravioto, Santiago de la Vega, Sara Estela Ramírez, and Elisa Acuña.

In these cases, once the political break had happened, Ricardo lashed out in vituperative attacks, insisting that the like-minded close ranks around key points, most particularly around the need for immediate revolution. This uncompromising attitude did generate disillusion, though, even at this early stage. So, for instance, Sara Estela Ramírez, a longtime Liberal militant, a supporter of Ricardo, and the editor in San Antonio of *La Corregidora*, wrote a deeply felt letter to Ricardo letting her "little brother" know that she had decided to remain in Camilo Arriaga's group, but that she hoped that both groups would continue to struggle toward their shared ideals:

> I have been sad and overwhelmed, Ricardo, with such mutual antagonism. I will tell you frankly that I am disappointed with everything, with absolutely everything.... I thought that there was unity and true fraternity in our group; I thought that there was in it a natural and exquisite harmony.... Each disappointment leaves a painful mark in my soul and—can you believe it?—there was even a moment in which I regretted participating in this intimate struggle with insufficient energy to fight against the perils that we set against ourselves."[22]

On the other hand, Ricardo's willingness to embrace conflict does seem to have galvanized a strong identity among the Liberals who remained faithful to the junta—they became increasingly politicized and doctrinaire after 1906. But it also led to the legitimation and proliferation of the use of violent language against alleged internal traitors, language that came to be used all too frequently and sometimes against the wishes of the junta itself.

Camilo Arriaga and Juana B. Gutiérrez de Mendoza were both venerable figures of Mexico's Liberal opposition. Camilo had been the founder of the Liberal movement. It was in his library that

Ricardo and Juan and Manuel Sarabia had first read Kroptkin, Karl Marx, and other radicals. Juana, too, had been a prominent member from the beginning, as well as a well-known editor and teacher. Both of these figures would go on to have careers in the Mexican Revolution. Arriaga was imprisoned in 1908 and participated in the Plan de Tacubaya to depose Díaz in 1911; he worked in the Madero government, was exiled after Victoriano Huerta's coup against Madero, and eventually held government posts after the triumph of the revolution. Juana B. Gutiérrez de Mendoza was imprisoned by Díaz on several occasions, participated in the Madero revolution, and when she becamed disillusioned with Madero, joined Emiliano Zapata and helped draft his Plan de Ayala; she organized several newspapers as well as feminist associations and continued to write for the agrarian cause after the revolution. In short, neither of these people was either cowardly or reactionary.

But Ricardo's attack was calculated to cut all possible ties between them, no holds barred:

> We had thought that the membership of the Partido Liberal had been purified of late and that at the very least, there were no traitors to the cause among the group that expatriated itself in order to combat tyranny in Mexico with freedom. But we were wrong: we still had one desertion pending—perhaps very meaningful to our enemies, perhaps painful to some of our fellow party members—but not to us. We are accustomed to placing principles above persons, and so for us, this desertion is as despicable as any other.[23]

Here is the dividing line—traitor versus patriot—clear and sharp. And Camilo Arriaga was on the other side of that line. He was described by Ricardo as a lazy aristocrat accustomed to exploiting the humble, a sellout who was ready to do business with the Díaz government. and to turn in the junta to the St. Louis consul. Later, Ricardo would rant against Francisco I. Madero very much along these same lines.

I have been unable to find any trace of Arriaga's alleged betrayal of the junta to the St. Louis consul. It may nevertheless have happened, but that seems unlikely, not only because there seem to be no records (and the St. Louis consul was active and ambitious in tracking the junta), but also because if Arriaga had done this, it seems likely that the junta would have fallen to the police earlier than they did. Arriaga did accept a secret commission from Madero to undermine Liberal networks in the United States, but that was after the revolution had triumphed, in 1912, and of course well after Ricardo had publicly insulted him.[24]

The accusations against Juana Gutiérrez de Mendoza were of a different nature. Rather than portraying her as an aristocrat, Juana was outed as a lesbian—a degenerate who was unworthy of being associated with the elevated morality of the cause. Ricardo began his article against Juana by saying that he was responding to her attacks on him and added a note on the substance of their disagreement, which was the problem of confronting Díaz directly (in 1904): "With the excuse that we were fighting for principles, and should not be *personalistas*, they urged us not to run the campaign—that we in the end did—against the sixth reelection of General Díaz."[25] Published in mid-June 1906, though, the article's importance was connected to the looming revolution that was being planned for September.

After indulging in some indiscretions with regard to their correspondence wherein Juana was showed up by Ricardo as a schemer and a hypocrite, Ricardo got to the heart of the matter. The junta had been warned about Juana by friends back in Mexico City, but:

> We couldn't believe that Doña Juana B. Gutiérrez de Mendoza—the person who preached morality, and who calls herself the redeemer of peoples; the one who boasts that she works for the good of the human race and who wishes to redeem the Mexican woman—would take up a quarrel with Nature, which has so wisely created the two sexes, in order to give herself up to the sterile and stupid pleasures of Sapho, along with her companion Elisa."[26]

Not giving credence to these rumors, Ricardo and the group had allowed Juana and Elisa Acuña to accompany them to San Antonio, but there, the men saw the problem with their own eyes, and they were filled with "indignation and shame," because they were in contact with "depraved and odious beings." At that very moment, Ricardo and the boys ejected Juana and Elisa from the group.

Not content with this revelation, though, Ricardo went on to elaborate. Ricardo had heard that when Juana and Elisa were in Belem Prison, the inmates complained that "the 'erotic' excesses of those two scandalized the inmates night after night—they proceeded with no discretion, they could not contain themselves" and that the two women, "dispossessed of all shame, had the run of the Galley at the Department of Women, catechising the poor wretches in order to sacrifice them in the stench-filled altars of Sapphism."[27]

According to Ricardo, the fact that Juana B. Gutiérrez de Mendoza and Elisa Acuña were lesbians was known throughout Mexico City, since "everything that happens in Belem is known in the city." And the women's indulgence in unnatural pleasures was a reflection of deeper degeneration. So, for instance, "Elisa and Doña Juana do not love their parents." And Ricardo went on to quote from a letter that Juana had sent to him in which she admitted that she did not love her parents, who had behaved toward her like executioners. Then Ricardo pontificated: "The child who does not love his parents cannot be a good person."

Not content with this, Ricardo turned on Juana's relationship with her husband, Cirilo Mendoza, a man whom he claimed to have been publicly told of Juana's many affairs and lovers and who chose to live passively with that. No honorable person had dealings with the infamous Doña Juana. No one, that is, except Camilo Arriaga, who, according to Ricardo was now in cahoots with Díaz's vice president, Ramón Corral, and wanted only to betray the Liberal cause: "Like a dead and decomposing animal, Doña Juana lives alone, loveless and angry, with no other company than her vices and ill deeds. Camilo Arriaga encourages to write against us and against the Party because like all cowards, he hides behind women's skirts to make his attacks!"[28]

The strategy of dealing so viciously with internal fractures and dissent was undoubtedly connected to the urge to place a strategic goal—armed revolution—above any other personal or ethical consideration. Following the failed revolution of 1906, this would become a recurrent practice in the Liberal ranks.

Lessons Learned
During the months of clandestinity followed the initial disaster at El Paso and Jiménez, the junta had two goals: supporting a revolution that they thought could still happen—under the military leadership of Aarón López Manzano and Antonio de Pío Araujo, who were stationed in Texas and moving back and forth to Coahuila and Tamaulipas—and regrouping the junta itself, which involved contacting lost

members and also relocating to a new city, reconnecting with militants in Mexico and the United States, and getting back into print.

Regeneración had been shut down in June 1906. That left two Liberal San Antonio papers standing: *El Progreso* and *Resurrección*. The trouble was that there was fierce animosity between the San Antonio factions. The core of the local Liberal leadership, Araujo and López Manzano, distrusted the *Resurrección* group and felt that its leaders, Aurelio N. Flores and Franciso J. Sáenz, were spies whose aim was to get their hands on *Regeneración's* mailing list and turn in all militants.[29] For their part, some of the men in the *Resurrección* faction were refusing to fight under the leadership that had been named by Araujo and so had left their positions in Mexico and returned to San Antonio.[30]

In February 1907, Araujo moved to make *El Progreso* the official organ of the junta.[31] He and López Manzano were the military leaders of the movement at that point, and Araujo had the support of the Sarabia brothers, as well, who were writing for *El Progreso* and working on improving its quality. But Ricardo and Antonio Villarreal were very concerned about the split in the San Antonio leadership, which they believed to be based merely on personal grudges. As a result, Ricardo tried to rein in all language of "treason" and chided Manuel Sarabia for referring to "Trejo" (Sáenz) as a traitor, calling him a sincere comrade instead and insisting that the rift should be recognized as a response to personal animosity.[32] Moreover, in both Ricardo's and Villarreal's view, *Resurrección* was a better paper than *El Progreso*.[33]

On Villarreal's suggestion, Ricardo offered himself as a mediator between the San Antonio factions.[34] But Araujo and López Manzano were adamant and could not be reined in, and they published attacks against "those dogs" barely a week after Ricardo had offered to smooth over relations between the factions. "I will not submit to any arbitrator," Araujo wrote to Tomás Labrada. "Those bastards falsified my signature and used my name to invent a celebration," he said. "I did right to exhibit and denounce them!"[35]

In fact, during the clandestine period, the junta was so weakened that it had to give way to demands made by forces on the ground, and Ricardo was forced to beg and plead to Araujo to stop his attacks: "I beg you once again not to attack our correligionaries of *Resurrección*. Circumstances are truly delicate.... Let hostilities between you cease in favor of our common cause. I beg you truly."[36] But Araujo stood firm. "Those men are working in bad faith. I don't want to fall into the hands of the government [*en poder del bandidaje*], denounced by those wretches," he wrote to Tomás Labrada. "I have labored in every way for the interests of the Junta and the Party. For that I've suffered enough hunger, physical pain, and suffering. The rest is irrelevant."[37] Araujo's autonomy was such that the Sarabia brothers decided not to forward a letter from Ricardo to him, because it contained a positive remark about *Resurrección* that they feared might offend him.[38]

After his attack on Flores and Sáenz, Araujo wrote to Tomás Labrada that he was afraid that they would turn him in: "I'm convinced that I'll be caught by the bandits from Mexico before this month is out. I'm well known there. I will owe that arrest to these fraudulent wretches [*desgraciados farzantes*]."[39] These factional struggles also took their toll on *Resurrección*, which interrupted publication on the days where these atttackes were occurring.[40] Just as troubling, the fragmentation of the leadership, combined with the defeats suffered in Jiménez and El Paso, led some Texas Liberals to think of alternative strategies. Because there were two factions within the Díaz government jockying for position in anticipation of the opportunity to succed Díaz, for instance, some suggested making an alliance with the *científico* faction against the members of the *reyista* faction, who governed in the northern border states and who were the Liberals' oldest and staunchest enemies.[41] In other words, defeat was draining some sympathizers away from the rebel ranks and into the mainstream factions of Porfirian politics.

The example of Texas factionalism made the reestablishment of *Regeneración* fundamental—the junta needed to regain strategic and ideological ascendancy over the movement. Two weeks after Araujo refused to heed Ricardo's call to reign in his attacks, Antonio Villarreal wrote to Manuel Sarabia to inform him that he and Ricardo had decided that *Regeneración* needed to be resurrected and that Manuel would be its new editor. Ricardo and Antonio could not do it, because they were both wanted men, and Librado Rivera had not yet resided in the United States for three years, which made him vulnerable to deportation. Enrique was still at large. This left Manuel as the only junta member capable of rising to the challenge.

Ricardo and Antonio suggested publishing the journal out of El Paso, because it would be easy to smuggle it into Mexico from there and because editor and rabble-rouser Lauro Aguirre had offered them access to his printing press.[42] The fact that they were planning to publish *Regeneración* out of Texas signaled their dissatisfaction with the option of leaving ideological leadership either to *El Progreso*, as Araujo had wished.

More broadly, the persecution that followed the 1906 uprising made the relevance of the junta clear. Its disarticulation spelled disaster for the movement, which was now prey to infighting and ideological drift. The junta had to be protected—this was an imperative. In addition to reviving *Regeneración*, a new home base was needed, now that St. Louis had become uninhabitable. "We need a big place where one can go unnoticed," Ricardo wrote to Manuel. "Maybe we could do alright in San Diego, Cal. I've been told that it's a big city. I think that we could be OK in any big city, except in those in which they suspect we are."[43]

The experience of 1906 had convinced Ricardo that the members of the junta were too valuable to sacrifice—and that they must not venture prematurely into Mexico. Thus, in February 1907, Ricardo wrote to Manuel Sarabia, who had announced that he was going to lead one of the expeditions into Mexico, ordering him not to go. Indeed, Ricardo did not wish either Manuel or Librado to enter Mexico: "We must not weaken the Junta with the further loss of members. We need to realize how important the Junta's role is—the Junta is nothing less than the directorship or head of the movement. If the movement is left without its heads, everything will turn into a pandemonium that no one will understand."[44]

Ricardo's experience under pressure, then, was that without the junta, the movement dissolved into factionalism and disorganization and could even drift into unsavory reformist alliances. Therefore, the junta had to be preserved. Ricardo would remember this strategic conclusion in his instructions for revolt in 1908, when he kept his brother Enrique away from the fray, and again in 1910, when he tried to keep Práxedis Guerrero from the front, and then yet again with regard to his own decision to keep the junta in Los Angeles during the entire revolutionary process.

Fine-Tuning Persecution

The 1906 rebellion left its mark not just on the Liberals, but on the governmental policies deployed to neutralize them. The Díaz government soon understood that the persecution of the rebels involved careful management of bilateral relations with the United States government, including choosing between alternative legal options for prosecution, developing strategies of interinstitutional cooperation, and developing tactics for opinion management on both sides of the border.

The Mexican government had developed an elaborate and relatively efficient information-gathering strategy. Its expanding network of consulates reported regularly to Mexico's ambassador in Washington and to its Ministry of Foreign Affairs in Mexico City. The foreign minister and the ambassador then hammered out policies based on a wealth of local information—at times consulting with Porfirio Díaz, with the minister of internal affairs (*gobernación*), or with this or that state governor. If the U.S. government needed to be brought on board or consulted, that was usually done by the ambassador in Washington, though consuls also learned to coordinate with various local officials—sheriffs, immigration officers, district attorneys, and judges.

This system had effectively allowed the Mexican government to nip the 1906 revolt in the bud. After that successful operation, the government continued to expand its network of consulates in order to achieve better coverage in fractious Mexican communities. New consulates were established in Texas at Del Rio, Waco, and Bridgeport, Texas, in addition to the older ones in Laredo, Brownsville, San Antonio, and El Paso. In Arizona, consulates sprung up at Douglas, Yuma, and Globe—supplementing the work of those in Phoenix and Tucson. In California, offices were set up in Calexico, Imperial, and San Diego.

In addition to this, Mexican consulates learned to work well with specialized private services. The Thomas Furlong Detective Company was used by the consul in St. Louis, sometimes in ways that violated U.S. laws, but with no major consequences for the Mexican government. Other officials at times hired Pinkertons. Furlong and Pinkerton detectives followed, kidnapped, and turned rebels in to authorities on both sides of the border. Moreover, some detectives had privileged relations with the U.S. Postal Service—at least in some localities—and were allowed to open, copy, and then reseal the rebels' mail. This is, indeed, the reason why we have much of the rebel correspondence that I've been citing in this chapter.

A second front of governmental activity was management of the press. The 1906 revolt underscored widespread anti-Díaz sentiment among Mexicans on the U.S. side of the border, and this facilitated an incipient shift in U.S. press coverage on Mexico, which began, at least in some instances, to romanticize the Mexican rebels and to speculate about discontent in Mexico. Reacting to these articles was the business of the Mexican consuls and ambassador, but it was not always obvious just how best to do that. In some situations, a concerted policy needed to be decided on in Mexico City.

So, for instance, one of the reasons why the Mexican government decided to support prosecution of the rebels for violation of neutrality laws, rather than to seek their extradition to Mexico, is that extradition proceedings tended to give the Mexican government bad press in the United States. Mexican judicial institutions were not trusted by the American public. They were seen as venal and incapable of guaranteeing due process. As a result, at extradition trials, attorneys for the defense would invariably claim that Mexico would never guarantee their clients either a fair trial or humane punishment. Mexican prisons were (for the most part rightly) portrayed as dungeons, and not modern reform facilities; courthouses were subservient to executive orders; prisoners were routinely "shot while escaping," rather than tried, and so on. In short, rebels who were tried for extradition would be seen by the American press as underdogs, and as a result, these trials hurt the image of the Mexican government.

Such public-relations disasters could neatly be avoided in prosecutions of rebels for violation of the neutrality laws, because prisoners would then be charged by U.S. prosecutors in U.S. courts, for violating U.S. laws. And indeed, this is why extradition proceedings were not pursued against Ricardo Flores Magón, Antonio I. Villarreal, Librado Rivera, or Manuel Sarabia. By March 1907, after consultations between the Mexican ambassador and former U.S. secretary of state (and former ambassador to Mexico), John W. Foster, and between the Ministries of Foreign Affairs and Internal Affairs and Porfirio Díaz, Foreign Minister Ignacio Mariscal instructed Ambassador Enrique Creel to abandon extradition and deportation proceedings as a routine course of action. The Mexican government would henceforth support U.S. federal proceedings against the rebels for violation of the neutrality laws. Porfirio Díaz also recommended that extradition proceedings could be maintained in cases that were already under way as a way of keeping the pressure on this or that leader.[45]

There were, in addition, other ways to manage the American press that could be leveraged locally by the consuls, including preparing press releases, dictating conferences, or bribing newspapers. So, for instance, Mexico's consul in St. Louis wrote to Foreign Minister Ignacio Mariscal for an interesting consultation in this matter. The *Saint Louis Post Dispatch*, which belonged to the Pulitzer chain, was printing articles favorable to the rebels and contrary to the government. The consul told Mariscal that he had plenty of intercepted rebel letters that could be used to disprove the claims of the *Post Dispatch*, but the consul advised against using them because the content of the letters would tend to confer the status of "revolutionaries" upon a group of individuals that the Mexican government was consistently labeling "bandits." But the consul also warned that bringing those letters to light would put the Mexican government in a precarious position, since they had been garnered by violating the U.S. mail laws.[46]

Rather than supplying the *Post Dispatch* with this privileged, but also tainted information, the consul suggested buying the paper off. Indeed, the consul believed that the *Post Dispatch* was only trying to extort the Mexican government in the first place. It is difficult to assess whether consuls in fact did much purchasing of the American press—consulates generally had limited resources and probably did not influence opinion that much—but it is certain that the Mexican government became convinced that money was critical to gaining favorable coverage in the United States, just as it was in Mexico. That is why Porfirio Díaz gave juicy land concessions to key owners of major U.S. media chains: William Randolph Hearst owned over two million acres of land in Chihuahua, and Harrison Gray Otis owned about half a million acres in Baja California. Maybe old Joseph Pulitzer, who owned the *Saint Louis Post Dispatch*, was just jealous.

As border traffic intensified, the role of money in the management of the American press came to be accepted wisdom in the Mexican government. Thus, by 1919, when revolutionary foreign minister Cándido Aguilar did a tour of the border states on the U.S. side, he discussed the problem of the press's negative coverage of the revolution and reminded President Venustiano Carranza that "it is well known that the majority, if not all, of the press is venal, and that it follows the instructions of those who pay."[47]

CHAPTER FOURTEEN

The Social Life of the Militant

Radical Mobility

Revolutions cannot be made without an everyday reality to sustain them—a structure of labor, a social world, a personal network. The anarchist revolution was the most radical revolution that the Enlightenment spawned. It was a concerted attempt to build a world founded on human cooperation, with no state and no private property. The social conditions that were needed in order to imagine such a possibility and, just as importantly, to strive for it, were rather peculiar, and in the case of the Mexican anarchists, very much shaped by traffic across the U.S.-Mexican border.

The first of these conditions was labor mobility. The degree and form of mobility in the base of the Mexican Liberal Party was really quite remarkable, and it stood in stark contrast with the forms of bonded labor—debt peonage, forced military conscription—to which the Liberals so ardently objected. These forms of labor mobility involved moving from one place to another within the same line of work, or moving between jobs within the same city, or constant changes in both town and occupation.

Some kinds of jobs lent themselves to movement from place to place within the same branch of activity. So, for instance, copper miners often moved from mine to mine, and even marginal differentials between places could spur movement. There is evidence that some workers even got attached to movement for its own sake. Indeed, copper miners and smelter workers in Arizona, Colorado, and Texas—the workers who formed the heart of the radical Western Federation of Miners—stayed in one mine for an average of two years or less.[1]

Migration was also a feature of the Mexican northwest—to such a degree that ambitious young men in the center and south sometimes left white-collar jobs in order to earn some cash in mining and then moved into commerce or politics from there. There were also ways of combining activities and moving back and forth between them. Many Mexican miners in Arizona were also ranchers in Chihuahua and routinely moved back and forth between ranching and mining as part of a pattern of circular migration.[2] All of these mobile networks were the natural base of the Mexican Liberal Party.

Movement between jobs within a city was also a salient dimension of life in the cities of California, Arizona, and Texas. Historian Mario García identifies labor mobility as the key characteristic of Mexican workers in El Paso during this period.[3] Writing about Tucson in the same years, Thomas Sheridan notes:

> Life on the ranches was coming to an end for many families on both sides of the border, and so, in order to survive, they migrated to cities like Tucson, El Paso, Los Angeles, and Phoenix. Men and women who had grown up raising crops and cattle suddenly found themselves in urban settings which demanded new skills and new patterns of living. They had become miners, railroad workers, laundresses, or small businessmen. Most, in fact, mastered a number of trades.... In a community like Tucson, where no single industry dominated the economy during the late nineteenth century, working men and women had to do a little bit of everything to make a living and raise a family.[4]

The lives of the leaders of the Liberal Party were all marked by this combination of precariousness of existence and vast freedom of movement, with agitators such as Blas Lara, Fernando Palomares, Enrique Flores Magón, Práxedis Guerrero, Tomás and Manuel Sarabia, and practically every other leader that one can name or think of moving between, say, agricultural work in the Imperial Valley, construction, work for utilities companies, in lumber mills, mines, on railroads, and more. The combination of precariousness and mobility made for a peculiar kind of sociability, oriented toward establishing relations of support and solidarity between strangers, based on anything from ethnic identification, to politics, to simple "sympathy." In his memoir, Blas Lara tells of his first migration from his native Jalisco to the United States.

Blas Lara

Blas was born to a peasant. Due to a conflict with local landowners, his father was conscripted and packed off to Yucatán, at which point Blas was sent to live with a segment of his family that enjoyed a kind of communistic existence that he nostalgically invoked in his old age:

> A real democracy reigned in that country abode. The help was composed, in addition to those that I have named, of Manuela, who washed clothes; Cuca made the tortillas, and Teodosia, whose offspring were children of love, was the wet nurse—being as she was a good "milk cow." She had no husband and lived separate from the family in the same ranch. Rosaura was an adopted daughter, and she helped Leonor and Lucina with the house chores. Aunt Fidelidad cooked and her sister, Poli, was the house doctor—she knew how to heal with plants. I carried water with a yoke that held a clay jug, tied with a rope on either end, like the Chinese.
>
> Everyone sat at table at lunchtime, with no distinctions between them. The head of the house used to say: "I don't know how to read or write, but I know that this is how democracy should be." A little later, the bohemian Mario also joined the party.[5]

But then again, this was not the only life that Blas knew in his hometown, having had to move several times within the village and between the village and the outlying country. The town itself was dominated by a couple of landholding families and their priest allies, an oppressive situation that eventually led Blas to leave. Thus, the communism that he described was always in a threatened position and was unattainable for most.

From his village, Blas moved to Guadalajara. This occurred at a time when Porfirio Díaz had promoted the so-called Leyes de Pantalonización, which were edicts that forced men to wear trousers, rather than the peasant *calzón* (white pajama) if they were to be allowed to move freely within the perimeter of any Mexican city. When Blas arrived outside Guadalajara with white *calzones* "wide as a woman's petticoat," he bought a pair of threadbare and rotten pants, which he tied on with a string so he could walk into Guadalajara, go to market, and buy some working pants, a shirt, and a vest.

Blas's transformation had only just begun. In Guadalajara, he started work as an unskilled mason and was later promoted to skilled mason. He took evening classes to improve his reading skills and learn basic arithmetic. At night school, he was introduced to trade unionism, socialism, and liberal anticlericalism.

From Guadalajara, Blas moved to Aguascalientes, where he worked at the Guggenheim-owned copper smelter, and from there to Nuevo Laredo to work on the railway. At that point, he crossed the border. On the U.S. side, Blas washed dishes in El Paso and went on to Los Angeles to work on the railroad, then up to Fort Bragg to work in the sawmills. After a few years in the United States, Blas returned to Guadalajara to help a sick sister and got involved in a strike there, which landed him in jail. He then returned to the United States, where he held countless jobs in Los Angeles, Oakland, San Francisco, Berkeley, and Fort Bragg.

Like most other Liberals, this constant movement meant that Blas made a habit of "riding the rails" and that he was used to working in multiethnic settings. On one of his trips, Blas brought some of his kin from Guadalajara back with him, and encouraged them to come to Fort Bragg with the following argument: "We'll feel right at home here. The people are all very fraternal. They are émigrés from southern Russia, with socialist ideals and revolutionary principles." His feeling of kinship was such that Blas had a theory that he himself was of Jewish origin.

Families of the Cause

The occupational mobility experienced by Blas was not unusual among the Liberals. New forms of friendship and family life developed in tandem with this culture of mobility.

Sometimes, domestic units were made up of groups of male coworkers—friends who lived together, stuck together, and ate together, friends who pooled resources and relied on one another for every key kind of support. So, for instance, Blas's decision to go to the United States had actually been made collectively by the four friends who worked, and lived together at the smelter in Aguascalientes:

> Between the four of us, we barely earned enough to eat, pay our rent, and have our clothes washed. At night, we spent hours talking about the misery of the worker.... We four friends had been living together for two months without the slightest difference of ideas between us. As

Felix said: "We lead a pig's life: it's all eating and sleeping. If we work, it is only to get food, which has so little nourishment in it that it all ends up in the toilet anyway."[6]

What they earned amounted to shit, so the cohesive group decided to embark on the journey north.

Sometimes people lived in composite groups that included the elementary particles of a conventional family—a married couple with children, or a group of siblings—but were then almost always supplemented by additional household members, who might be kin or friends or comrades, with or without additional kin.

These novel households were key to the social experience of many of the Liberals, and for the leaders of the junta, they acquired the added intensity of feeling that was generated by the pressures of clandestine work and by their experiences in prison. When they were on the run, trustworthiness was a paramount concern, and all of that bundled together with the complex households that were emerging suffused the world of the comrades with deep ties of affection for those inside these novel, familylike domestic units—very strong feelings—ties that were marked by daily signs of familiarity and inclusion.

Recall that the core that first made up the junta in St. Louis in 1905 was a group of young men who had emigrated together, or at least in a coordinated fashion. The ties between them had been formed by collaborative work in the opposition press. Each of those young men had proved his valor to the others on many occasions. Those experiences helped them build a kind of community or family when they arrived in St. Louis. Historian José Valadés enthusiastically describes their way of life: "They started living in community then. They prepared their own meals, and passed their clothes from one to another, with no distinctions. Within the group there was only the purest feeling of fraternity."[7] His account is not idealized.

When one looks back on the early period of political activity—the years between the creation of the first *Regeneración* (1900) and the group's departure from Mexico (1904)—one is struck by the strong undertones that still carried over from the bohemian life of their younger years. Indeed, the life and adventures of the group from 1901 to 1904 has a kind of Dumasian flavor to it: hating the dictator and the dictatorship, writing exalted or satirical poems, competing on how best to shock political society from the offices of

Regeneración or *El Hijo del Ahuizote* while writing poems and seeking trysts with some idealized maiden.

Manuel Sarabia described how his San Luis Potosí cousin, Juan Sarabia, gently reformed his reading habits, weaning him away from the heroic to the political, in imitation of Juan's own trajectory:

> When Juan came to Mexico City from San Luis Potosí in 1902, he discovered that I was a fan of Ponson du Terrail. I loved Rocambole. Carolina Invernizio, too, robbed me of many hours of sleep. Juan was already done with his Don Juan period [*época tenoresca*], so he took pity on me and tactfully suggested that the fantastic readings by those authors were not so edifying, and that they only spoiled one's sense of taste. Better, he said, that I read serious works, like those of Gorky, Zola, etc.[8]

The two authors that Manuel mentions—Pierre Alexis Ponson de Terrail and Carolina Invernizio—wrote romantic mysteries, thrilling and macabre stories of heroes and villains. The characterization of Juan and his own youth as an "época tenoresca" (in reference to Don Juan Tenorio), sums up what I am trying to conjure here by referring to Dumas, who of these kinds of authors is one of the few who is still remembered today.[9]

It is also significant that the oldest of the Flores Magón brothers, Jesús, after his release from Belem Prison in 1901, told his brothers that he was setting aside his radical activities because of his desire to marry.[10] This was because in Mexico City, the life of the rebel was for the most part a life for unattached young men.

The playful "tenoresco" aspect of these young men's lives gave way to grim determination after migration to the United States. First, the group lost one of its dearest members in the border crossing, the poet Santiago de la Hoz, who drowned while swimming the Rio Grande on his way to join up with the others in March 1904. It was as if Aramis had died in the middle of an adventure: one for all, and all for the one who was now forever lost. The seriousness of the group's commitment, pounded into them by persecution, prison, and by Santiago's death, was then hardened by the empty meaninglessness that the life of an exile in America would have had without the Mexican Cause.

And if anyone doubted the meaninglessness of an American life without the cause, there was Camilo Arriaga to provide an object lesson: Camilo, who had been the founding leader of the Liberal

Figure 14.1 Andrea Villarreal. Courtesy of the Bancroft Library, John Murray Papers.

movement, was found drifting in San Antonio in an aimless exile. Penniless, depressed, and dispirited. Camilo's ambivalence with regard to embracing outright revolution had led to a pointless banishment. Soon, he would have no alternative but to begin to negotiate a peaceful return to Mexico. In the face of such an example and the sacrifices that the exiles had already made, the men committed definitively to revolution as the only honorable alternative.

Except that in a cold and foreign context such as the United States, the creation of something like a hearth and home was fundamental, and yet they had no familial homes on which to fall back. Rather, the sense of home was built around compounds that I am tempted to christen the "Liberal Joint Family System," which included a disparate range of people. When the group was in St. Louis, the sisters and father of Antonio Villarreal helped provide a homely feeling. Andrea Villarreal, in particular, was herself a very active writer and voice, quite popular in the American press and hailed by St, Louis's papers as a "Mexican Joan of Arc" (Figure 14.1) When Regeneración was reestablished in Los Angeles, it had Librado Rivera's wife, Conchita, at the center. Meals were taken collectively, and Conchita was hired to cook for them all.

As the Mexican Liberal Party gained allies, many of these, too, had compound "families" like these—local bases of support that had houses with women and men dedicated to the cause. The El Puente gang in California, the rival groups in El Paso and San Antonio, the pro-Liberal groups in Bisbee, Douglas, Morenci, Del Rio, Waco, Bridgeport, Oakland, and Fort Bragg all had households of this kind as organizational centers that were heart to the Liberal movement.

One of the many expressions of intimacy in the junta group was nicknames, and the group's most charismatic leaders—Ricardo Flores Magón and Juan Sarabia, for example—were invested with a kind of nominative power. Thus, Juan Sarabia was known to the Regeneración family as "El Charal" (a small dried and salted fish). Manuel Sarabia was "El Chamaco" (The Kid). Librado Rivera was "El Fakhir," Rosalío Bustamante was "Caníbal," while Ricardo always called Enrique "Manito," "Little Brother."

These nicknames were not the same as the ones that were used for purposes of clandestine operations (for example, "El Provisional" for Antonio de P. Araujo, "Caule" for Ricardo Flores Magón, "Luis" for Enrique, "Violeta" for Elizabeth Trowbridge, and so on), nor were they the pseudonyms that some of these radicals chose to use when writing for the press ("Anakreón" for Ricardo, for instance). They were more like family names, used as signs of intimacy and affection.

The evocative power of these names, their ability to well up feelings associated with the deepest camaraderie, comes through in a letter that Enrique Flores Magón sent to his friend Rafael García in 1923, after the death of Ricardo. In it, Enrique tells Rafael all about his impression of Herón Proal, the leader of Veracruz's tenant movement, who had been much maligned by a number of their comrades. But Enrique had come away with the most favorable impression of Proal. When describing the man to Rafael, summing up the kind of quick tie of kinship that they felt, Enrique identified Proal with Ricardo by way of intimacy of address, combined with generosity of access. Proal had immediately and spontaneously offered Enrique the chance to take over the movement's newspaper, which bore the ominous, but not atypical name of La Guillotina: "'Go on, manito!' Proal said, using manito the same way Ricardo did. 'Here's an opportunity to spill your poison, lending your personality to this paper and providing guidance to our people.'"[11]

We have only a few first-hand descriptions of day-to-day life in the office of *Regeneración*, but they all paint it as a place of deep comradery, reminiscent in some ways of Thomas More's "hospitals" and other utopian communities. So, for instance, Blas Lara recalled:

> All of us worked for our food. No one received a salary of any kind. When Owen (who was Mexico's Thomas Paine) attached himself to the Mexican Revolution, he quit a paying job reading proofs in a bourgeois paper, preferring what that apostate called our "exquisite delicacies": soup, beans, and *tortillas* with chili peppers. Concha cooked for all, and the families of the other comrades lived in such poor dwellings that they never paid more then $10 rent. Harmony reigned among us all."[12]

Ethel Duffy Turner, who was a member of *Regeneración*'s staff in the most exciting days of the journal, just as the revolution of 1910 finally erupted, recalls their collective work in that golden age, before the group split into pieces:

> There was remarkable camaraderie in those days. I had my typewriter in the main office. Sometimes I took my baby there with me; others, I'd leave her with a German sitter. I chose news items from the papers and wrote articles in the office, Antonio Villarreal helped me set the English page for the press.
>
> At lunch we all came round a big table, which was in a spacious room at the back, near the kitchen. Librado's wife, Concha, and other women prepared the meal. At table, Librado was very quiet, as usual, but when he spoke he did it with sincerity. Years earlier, Juan Sarabia had given him the nickname of El Fakhir, because he had a Hindu Fakhir's gift for remaining unmovable, and he took on that role completely when it came to the revolutionary cause. Ricardo spoke little, and he was friendly when he was in small groups, because he enjoyed listening to others. Práxedis was brilliant and ingenious in conversation.[13]

In a 1965 letter, Ethel mentions that these *Regeneración* offices had several bedrooms and that an undefined number of people slept there, including Ricardo, Librado, Anselmo Figueroa, and Enrique.[14]

In its final years, between 1915 and 1918, *Regeneración*, very much in decline due to every kind of pressure, moved to Edendale, just outside Los Angeles, where the group finally found a more worldly opportunity to become the sort of community that it in some ways always had been. The inhabitants of the colony included Enrique, Teresa, and her five children. As Blas Lara recalled,

Ricardo lived in the colony with his *compañera* [María Brousse] and their grandson Carlos; so did José—Anselmo L. Figueroa's son-in-law—with his daughter, Babe. Rivera lived there with his son and daughter. So did comrades Atanacio and Tachita, Doctor Ochoa and his *compañera*, Maria.... Comrades Vale, Ralf ("Texano"), Villota, Floritos, and I were all bachelors. There were usually two or three others who knew that when they found no work in town, there was always some work that could be done for the paper for a day or two, and they would be fed."[15]

Suspicion

Communism, in short, had a real social base. It was not "utopian," because it was built on real circumstances and on everyday solutions to everyday problems by groups of workers who pooled resources, shared rooms, and supported one another and composite new families that could, under certain conditions, morph into veritable colonies. Communism was an ideal, certainly, but it also existed, right there, as real, lived experience. This, in the end, was why many workers felt robbed when the state appropriated these forms, in Russia, for example. The soviets had been betrayed. The state was not a union of soviets, but an armature that had been raised above them and that exploited even their name, only to turn around and call the small-c communists "utopians."

But I am getting ahead of myself.

If working for a capitalist was a *yugo*, yoke, work for the Mexican Cause was work for freedom. The women and men who combined both kinds of work—the libertarian communists who struggled under capitalism—were "slaves of freedom," but this does not mean that communism was something that existed only in their imaginations. It was an everyday reality, created by their need to pool resources, by their need to explode traditional family structures so as to admit perfect strangers to the most intimate situations, and by their need to build transcendental goals in the face of the breakdown of traditional morality, customs, and habits.

The life of the freedom slave was full of love. It was a love for humanity that emerged from an everyday practice of love for the comrade or openness to the comrade. Blas Lara provides fascinating detail in his experience of solidarities built upon his arrival to California—solidarities that cut across national boundaries and even class boundaries. So, for instance, the person who invited Blas to stay at his house when he first arrived in Los Angeles was from a wealthy Jalisco family who had turned his back on his family's politics and opened the first Spanish-language bookstore in the city. But Blas's portrayal of everyday communism among the new migrants is perhaps best captured in his experience working in railroad construction. In that labor camp, composed of two hundred workers, with Mexicans a small minority, Blas discussed the formation of a union. Among the various characters in the camp—an elderly Frenchman who introduced Blas to libertarian communist ideas, a guitar-strumming youth from Chihuahua who sang to lyrics by Victor Hugo, an accordionist from Cananea, Sonora—there was also the following cameo:

> Ignacio García of Aguascalientes was a communist without knowing it. One day, his cousin Jesús said to him: "Hey Nacho, on my next payday, I'll return the money that you loaned me the other day." To which García responded: "What money did I loan that you feel you owe me? If it's the cash I gave you when you got here all fucked up [*fregado*] from Mexico so that you could eat and buy clothes, then you owe me nothing."[16]

On the other hand, because the freedom slave was full of solidarity, he or she was also always nagged by suspicion. The salience of suspicion in the freedom slave was connected to the relationship between work and freedom, or, to put it more broadly, to the relationship between emancipation and the status quo. Given the magnitude of these individuals' sacrifices—they led passionate, open, giving lives—they could easily suspect that they might be being taken advantage of. Indeed, when militants left the cause, they sometimes retrospectively lamented their lack of selfishness during their years of militancy.

So, for instance, when Antonio de P. Araujo left the Liberal Party after more than ten years of risking everything for it, he is said to have said to an old Liberal comrade, Cecilio Garza, that "I regret having been a militant in the company of the Flores Magóns. Had I spent that time in other political parties, by this time, I would be enjoying a juicy government job."[17] Araujo did not sell out the Liberals, but he is reported by Blas as having allowed himself to be duped by them.

Of course, not everyone was disillusioned, but suspicion was fairly widespread among believers, and it could take many forms.

A comrade could be suspected of using his militancy to create a political career for himself. Another might be suspected of cashing in on fund-raising drives. A woman could be accused of using the libertarian communist ideal as a front to satisfy her lust or to prostitute herself. This had happened in a very ugly way when Ricardo and Juana Gutiérrez de Mendoza publicly broke off political ties and Ricardo denounced Juana as a lesbian, justifying his group's break with her and her lover, Elisa Acuña, by saying things such as: "What kind of love for humanity can two women who offend and despise it with their sterile and odious vices have? Not even animals want what they want."[18]

The sources of suspicion between militants were founded on the fact that the life of the libertarian was transgressive—it confronted the status quo and sought to create an alternative to it. If an individual only pretended to lead that life, but did not believe in its goals sincerely, he or she could reap advantages in the "establishment" (to use a useful word from another time) by taking from the generosity of the worker.

People who engaged in this kind of two-faced exploitation were robbing the sacred gift of workers' love and solidarity. They were making prostitutes of free women. They were making slaves of free workers. They were, in other words, traitors, and like Judas, they always betrayed with a kiss. They had to, because the only way to dupe a comrade was with a nod and a bow to the libertarian communist ideal.

And beyond suspicion of exploitation, there was the broader question of selfishness, of lack of sensitivity to the common cause, of lack of attention to the collective interest, and the question of the connection between the sacrifice of the militant and the life choices of his or her fellow workers. Ricardo himself expressed this sentiment on several occasions when he wrote to his beloved María from prison. So, for example, writing from the county jail in Los Angeles in 1908, Ricardo argued: "More than tyrants, it is our friends who have us in jail, because of their laziness, their indolence, and the lack of initiative that ties them down. They do nothing."[19] Twelve years later, writing this time from Leavenworth Federal Penitentiary and from what was in effect a life sentence, he expressed the same idea in a more theorized, but also more definitive and bitter fashion:

When I was free, anyone with a need came to me, looking for help, and I had to sacrifice everything.... And now that I'm afflicted, no one remembers me.

That's how it has always been. Selfishness is a poison lodged deep in our bones. It is the outcome of century upon century of individualistic education and training for the masses. The primordial human instinct of cooperation and mutual aid has been suppressed in favor of an individualistic education."[20]

Espionage

In addition to these internal forms of betrayal, there was also the problem of betrayal that was orchestrated by the Liberals' sworn enemies: the government and the rich.

As soon as they arrived in the United States, the leaders of the Liberal Party had to confront the problem of infiltration. They would live intimately with it forever after. Because this aspect of the Liberal's lives is in some ways the most "colorful" for contemporary readers and because spying and policing generated records to which historians can easily refer, this dimension of the social world of the anarchist has been quite amply discussed: Furlong guards ransacking the offices of *Regeneración* in St. Louis in 1906 and kidnapping Librado Rivera Pinkertons kidnapping Manuel Sarabia in Douglas, Arizona, and handing him to the *rurales* in Sonora.[21] Spies tracking Ricardo and Enrique into Canada, where they first went when they escaped from St. Louis. The U.S. Postal Service hijacking mail from militants in Texas and Arizona. Mexican consular offices acting as spying agencies, orchestrated from the Mexican Embassy in Washington. Los Angeles Police Department plainclothes detectives cooperating with Mexican officials and with their hired detectives. El Paso, San Antonio, Douglas, and Tucson police officials doing the same thing.[22]

The story, covered by historians who can at times be about as flat-footed as the policemen that they are tracking, is still waiting for a Mexican John LeCarré to bring it into its own. But that is not my aim here. For the purposes of our inquiry, we can say, in a nutshell, that the Liberals knew that they operated clandestinely, knew that they were constantly being watched, and had ample and early evidence that many of these spying operations were successful.

Every militant knew that there were spies around. Their presence is constantly overheard by any reader of their correspondence: fleeting references to suspicion or lack of trust punctuate the Liberals' letters. Often, their presence is implied. "I just saw you go by," Ricardo wrote to María and Lucía from the L.A. County Jail, "but I couldn't call out to you because the window was down.... There was an olive-skinned man following you two. Did you notice him?"[23]

The correspondence between Liberals is loaded with passages like this. X is not to be trusted. Y is not one of ours, but can be trusted. And a reading of the records from the Mexican foreign service and the American Bureau of Investigation shows that although they were good at detecting police, the Liberals did not always succeed in pinpointing traitors, and they did, at times, wrongly suspect people who were loyal.

Militants such as Tomás Sarabia Labrada, Manuel Sarabia, Librado Rivera, and Ricardo Flores Magón expended a fair amount of effort and attention on developing clandestine methods, including secret codes, pseudonyms, and various styles of allusion in their letters. What they did not know, however, was that the U.S. Mail was in fact capturing, reading, and then releasing a very significant proportion of their correspondence (Figure 14.2). They did not know this, but they felt its effects.

The spy and the traitor were part of the social world of the militant. This had a dual effect: it sharpened the boundary between those who could and those who could not be trusted, and it made available an extreme mode of rejection when a falling out occurred between comrades. There was, after all, a difference between being self-serving and being the servant of your class enemies.

Love
It is not possible to describe the role of love in a fashion that is as general to the entire group as we were able to discuss with regard to the diffuse logic of suspicion. Love is a private subject that varies widely between individuals, and historical sources for a direct discussion of love are fewer and often limited to rather prominent people. Still, something needs to be said about the subject, for along with the much discussed and very public "love of the people," there was also always the theme of romantic love between a man and a woman and the love between intimate same-sex buddies. The

Figure 14.2 Ministry of Foreign Relations report on one of the Liberals' secret codes. The state is part of the clandestine revolutionary's intimate world, not only as antagonist but also as party to his or her closest secrets. Courtesy of the Archivo Secretaría de Relaciones Exteriores.

relationship between these forms of love was neither simple nor unproblematic.

The issue that we need to consider here was first identified for general sociology by Georg Simmel, who discussed the different kinds of social dynamic that emerged between "dyads" (romantic love is one sort of dyadic relationship) and "triads," which are relationships that involve third persons.[24]

When we try to analyze the social world of the Mexican libertarians, we find, first, strong relationships of personal loyalty and solidarity between groups of migrants—coworkers, *compañeros*, and *compañeras*. These are "triads" in Simmel's terms, because these friends' key spaces of sociability were in household groups, in meetings, or on the job. Ties of solidarity were built around work, around the practical chores that went along with political agitation, or around migratory movement itself.

These sorts of solidarities were characterized by what Blas Lara described as "being a communist without being aware of it," but the concrete solidarities—friendship, love, camaraderie—that developed in these contexts suffered some transformation once politicization set in. One of the keys to politicization was the abstraction of the worker's concrete situation into a broader, world-historical story. This form of storytelling involved the elaboration of abstract categories, such as "the people," "the proletariat," "the worker," and an abstract and exalted love could be professed to "the worker" that was different from what could be publicly pronounced for the companion and friend. In short, a language of romantic love for the *pueblo* was accepted and could not easily be transferred to a concrete individual.

So, for instance, María Brousse wrote to Ricardo in prison, saying "I no longer have any faith except in the people. I don't believe in anyone else."[25] But of course, the *pueblo* is not a person or a single actor with the kind of intentionality that a sentence like this would appear to imply. What we have, rather, is the abstraction or sublimation of a day-to-day love of a comrade or comrades into an exalted fictional subject: the people. In such an operation, the people or the general good become a transcendental object. What I mean by this is that sacrifices are made for it: hard-earned money is donated to "The Cause"; the scarce leisure time of the proletarian is dedicated to it; lives are risked for it. But the strength of feeling for the cause is fed by suffering and longing for real loved ones of flesh and blood (Figure 14.3).

So, for instance, the great Liberal leader Práxedis Guerrero emigrated to the United States with his friend, Francisco Manrique. Each of these young men was the son of *hacendados*; they came from neighboring haciendas in the state of Guanajuato and grew up together as children. Práxedis and Manrique left their families in order to live with the working people. They suffered with them and foreswore their fortunes and inheritance in order to redress the wrongs that their class had wrought. Práxedis later led a band of rebels into Mexico and to his death, in part because he had lost Manrique in the 1908 revolt. Práxedis, who had gone into battle against Ricardo's wishes, owed going always into battle to Manrique.

Jack London captures this connection between intimate love and the general cause in the person of his fictional boxer, Rivera, who conjures the image of his parents being butchered by Díaz in order to steel himself for the prize fight that he was compelled to win: "He saw the flat cars, piled high with the bodies of the slain, consigned to Vera Cruz, food for the sharks of the bay. . . . His mother he especially remembered—only her face projecting, her body burdened by

Figure 14.3 María Brousse, represented in the Los Angeles press as a romantic and dangerous anarchist mastermind and would-be assassin, based on a plot in which she would have murdered Chihuahua governor Enrique Creel when the 1907 rebellion was still in the works. This newspaper drawing is from an unknown source. It is the only image of María Brousse found from this period. *Los Angeles Daily Times*, September 19, 1907. Courtesy of the Bancroft Library, John Murray Papers.

the weight of dozens of bodies. Again the rifles of the soldiers of Porfirio Díaz cracked.... To his ears came a great roar, as of the sea, and he saw Danny Ward, leading his retinue of trainers and seconds, coming down the center aisle."[26]

At the same time that the cause of "the people" was made into a transcendental cause, however, the actual social world of the militant tended to get more laden with suspicion. That is why María "trusted no one but the people." The specters of selfishness, betrayal, and treason grew more menacing as more and more sacrifices were made for the cause. Because of this dynamic, the more single-minded the devotion to the cause, the greater the tendency to withdraw from the regular world of social relations, particularly of triads, since triads involve observers, and observers could be snoops or selfish weaklings.

That dynamic contributed to the creation of a rather peculiar romantic field. What I mean by this is that the ideology of the romantic couple was very different among Mexico's anarchists than it was for the principal leaders of revolutionary movements inside Mexico (Madero excepted—since the construction of "the people" that developed under the mystical doctrines of Spiritism was similar to that of the anarchists). The military *caudillos* of the Mexican Revolution were leaders of men who proved their courage and their military ability under fire. They were not steeled in the discipline that the Liberals developed in the United States—a life devoted to sacrifice, to work and saving, to clandestine propaganda under police surveillance. The military revolutionary leader was stereotypically prone to wasteful expenditure and debauchery. Polygamy was common. Promiscuity, sexual exploitation, and recklessness were characteristic.

Our anarchists, on the contrary, were disciplined men and women, capable of skimping and saving in a manner that would have made Benjamin Franklin blush. They were used to being trusted with wiring money for the cause without pilfering a penny to spend on drink; they held day jobs and dedicated nights to political activism. Love, conjugal love, was much more important to them, both as an ideal and as a daily practice, than it was for the Villas and Zapatas, the Obregons and Pascual Orozcos.

Moreover, because Liberal exiles operated under conditions of chronic suspicion, the dyadic connection, the relation in which one's secrets were kept safe and guarded, was also the most prized social relationship. The militant gave everything and therefore could be disappointed by the fact that this or that comrade was weak, lazy, or untrustworthy. This led to an affirmation of the transcendental goal, an ideology of sacrifice for the people, but also to a penchant for realizing deep communion in either intimate friendship or romantic love. This, I believe, is the meaning of Ricardo's best-known romantic letter: "if there is anything sacred and sincere in me, it is the love that I have for you as a woman and for the revolution as an ideal. María and the revolution: that is what fills my heart."[27]

There were almost equally torrid relations between intimate friends. I don't mean to imply that these friendships involved homosexual relations—there is no way of knowing whether or not they did. What matters here is the intensity of the dyadic bond and its connection to the general struggle.

Thus, while Juan Sarabia and César Canales were jailed in San Juan de Ulúa, they fell out with one another for reasons unknown to us. Juan's despair seems to have reached such a pitch that his friends feared a suicide. After receiving a long letter from Juan, Manuel Sarabia wrote to Antonio Villarreal from England, pleading that Antonio intervene with César Canales's family: "It is urgent that we take measures to avoid a suicide, for this is what Juan intends to

Figure 14.4 Enrique kept the heart-felt notes that "boy comrade Ramp" wrote on strips of brown paper. Presumably many notes circulating between inmates were written on strips of brown-paper wrapping like this. Writing paper had to be purchased from the prison store. Numbers of sheets usable in weekly outgoing letters were restricted to two. Courtesy of the Casa de El Hijo del Ahuizote, Mexico City.

do. What is happening is sad and deplorable. Contrary to what we expected, Juan has survived a long imprisonment and all kinds of privations. He must not now succumb to such trifles."[28]

In a similar key, one Floyd Ramp, a "Red" who shared prison with Enrique Flores Magón in Leavenworth, regularly wrote little notes to him in the prison—these were notes of deep appreciation and concern, philosophical notes of political commitment, and impressions on readings. In one of these, Ramp (who at times signed off as "Your boy Comrade Ramp. #12702") began with reflective mournfulness: "We Americans—especially we who are proletarians have never really learned to love each other. Our mothers never had time to love us, because the struggle was so severe, so we never learned to love openly. We just grew up, either too calloused to feel fine things or too self conscious to express them." He then went on to explain the sentiment that was growing in him for his comrades and particularly for Enrique, whose company was the thing that Floyd most valued in prison:

> There is developing within the ranks of rebels a finer friendship and a deeper love, and this is bound to grow till it becomes one of our greatest assets. No movement can become really great until it has aroused in its members a devotion which binds them together as lovers are bound ["are bound" is crossed out, but still legible]. Until we are ready to make the supreme sacrifice for that which we believe, will our great cause ever really begin to grow and become an important factor in the world's history.[29]

Such emotional intensity, in which love and the cause were inextricably intertwined, seems to have been present in many intimate friendships: in the relationship between Juana B. Gutiérrez de Mendoza and Elisa Acuña, the friendship between Práxedis Guerrero and Francisco Manrique (Figure 14.4), and between Librado Rivera and Ricardo Flores Magón. In relationships like these, trust was such that anything might be sacrificed for the other.

The Junta on the Eve

Liberation

On August 4, 1910, Ricardo Flores Ma
and Librado Rivera were released from
They had been locked up for three ye
went out to meet them and returned v
les. They arrived at Arcade Station th
hundred people were assembled there a
cheers and embraces. "Seeing that th
them the three men, with tears in the
Women embraced the men. There were c
'Villarreal!' 'Rivera!' that could be hea
moving trains."[1]

At the head of the reception committ
de Lara and his wife, Hattie, and F. H.
suffered a brief arrest as collaborator ir
Lázaro welcomed the three Liberals on
that had struggled so hard to free them.
his wife, Conchita, his daughter Cuca (Re
Antonio, age seven. They had moved to Fl
rado during his time in prison. Villarreal v
while Magón and the Rivera family went
The papers do not mention whether María
tion. Possibly she was not, since the paper
family reunion, but probably she was there
because she and Ricardo were not "proper

Three days later, on August 8, a mass ra
Temple. Brief speeches were given by Libra
(translated to English by Lázaro Gutiérrez

r, Gutiérrez de Lara himself, and lawyers Job Harriman and A. R.
on. About two thousand workers showed up, and they took up a
tion that accrued $414 for the purpose of starting a revolution-
per in Los Angeles: "This paper will be named *Regeneración* and
nded to advocate the cause of constitutional liberty in Mexico,
ing the right to free speech, free press and speech making,
r schooling and the right for public assemblages."[3]
his speech, Turner, who was by then the most famous of these
in the United States, that is) and who got a prolonged ovation,
red:

my mind the freedom of Villarreal, Magon, Rivera and De Lara is
e to mass against class. They are free tonight, yet Díaz, the "Czar
Mexico," wants them. Two years ago [District Attorney] Oscar
wler stated that there were eleven indictments against these men
d that when they were released from the Arizona prison, they would
re-arrested. Only two months ago United States Attorney General
ickersham indicated that it was the desire of the government to go
with their prosecution.

These men are armed for revolution. Why? Because they can't get
y expression any other way.... I predict that if the United States
aves them alone for six months, they will have accomplished enough
ork to make Díaz get off his horse."[4]

lutionary Strategy

Mexican situation was radically different when the junta leaders
imprisoned, in August 1907, than when they were released,
in August of 1910. What had changed?

irst off, the revolutionary situation itself. In the view of the
a, there were two main causes for failure in 1906: betrayal of
leged information and lack of a sufficiently generalized ground-
l of simultaneous, coordinated revolt. In part, these two causes
e connected: espionage and the persecution of propagandists
e United States and in Mexico kept the revolutionary message
spreading properly. Spies intercepted information, and the gov-
ment anticipated Liberal actions, allowing the Díaz government
epress them effectively, even before the start of the revolt.

ehind the junta's understanding of the causes of its failure there
a vision: Mexicans all over the country were thought to be fed up

with the dictatorship and ready to rebel. This conviction was built out of the everyday practice of editing *Regeneración*, which from its inception in 1900 was one of the very few venues to which people across Mexico could write to complain about legal trespasses and injustice. Precisely because the dictatorship did not provide sufficient venues, *Regeneración* was flooded with correspondence from the start.

The letters to the editor that the journal received from all over the country built in its editors and readers an image: Mexico was a seething cauldron. Each town was ready to boil over into revolution, and the only thing that was needed to effect this revolt was coordination, communication, and intellectual leadership. This was, however, a distorted picture.

There was at least one major flaw in the Liberals' diagnosis of the viability of revolution, and this was their refusal to grant any importance of Mexico's electoral calendar as a factor. Indeed, the pressures that the junta faced in exile seem to have led the leadership to forget or to ignore the organization's own past. The key figures of the junta had been initiated to Mexican politics in 1892, an election year. *Regeneración* and the Gran Congreso Liberal had deliberately been launched immediately after what they expected would be Díaz's final election, in 1900. The group's imprisonment in 1903 occurred, again, in the frame of electoral politics, and there was a reason why Díaz came down harder on the opposition on or near election years. Elections were moments when widely diffuse discontent could conceivably come together and gel into an organized oppositional force.

One often ignored detail when considering the Liberals' failed strategy in 1906 and 1908 is that when the core of the group committed to revolution, in Texas in 1904, Díaz had just been reelected, this time to a six-year term (after a change in the constitution), and with a vice president who was equally unsavory to the Liberals. But waiting six years to initiate revolutionary activities was impossible from an existential point of view—lingering that long in Texas or Missouri without a clear propaganda objective meant being condemned to dispersal as a group. Abandoning the electoral calendar in their plans for revolution was not so much a consequence of cold political analysis as an existential imperative. Waiting six years in the United States with no real activity was political death.

However, abandoning the electoral calendar also meant adopting a voluntaristic attitude toward the revolutionary process. That position was founded on an image of collective emancipation: throwing off shackles. Mexico was a country of slaves. Given the opportunity and a fighting chance, the slaves would rise against their masters and be free, independently of bourgeois conceits such as elections.

This vision contrasted with local political dynamics in Mexico. In each municipality, district, and state, there were political groups that had been marginalized by the prolonged stability of the Díaz dictatorship. These alternative groups did not necessarily believe that the revolutionary program of "Land and Freedom" was attainable or even necessarily desirable, but they did want a change of regime and at least some reform. The Liberals had grown progressively more radical, so they emphasized economic oppression as the key motivational factor for revolt. Gaining control of local, state, and federal governments was not for them a goal in itself. In this, they made a big mistake.

But when the leaders of the junta finally arrived to Los Angeles as free men, Díaz was eighty, and discontent in Mexico was widespread. And 1910 was an election year. In short, the junta was released from prison at a time when the conditions for revolution were finally ripe.

Regeneración *on the Eve of Revolution*
As a result, the impetus of *Regeneración* was never stronger. In the United States, the journal had support from Mexican workers, from their friends in various unions, among the Wobblies, and in the Socialist Party. In Mexico, the journal and the junta had prestige in opposition circles, and the men of the junta were poised to seize the moment.

As a result, the start of this fourth era of *Regeneración*, the four months between the men's release from prison and the outbreak of the revolution around December 1910, offered a unique moment of unity. The journal had an all-star team of collaborators that included the full junta, with talented and charismatic writers such as Práxedis Guerrero, Ricardo and Enrique Flores Magón, Antonio Villarreal, Lázaro Gutiérrez de Lara, and John Kenneth Turner. The journal's quarters, as described by Ethel, were also satisfactory. Located on the corner of Fourth and Town, "they had the whole building and some of them slept and ate there."[5]

However, despite the heady activity, excitement, and optimism of those days of revolution, the situation on the ground in Mexico was no longer in sync with the Liberal's political strategy, though this was not yet entirely apparent to them. This is because another social movement, focused mainly on political rights and the vote, had managed to articulate a much more extensive, better communicated, and more effective organization. Under the leadership of Francisco I. Madero, the Anti-Reelectionist Party had built a nationwide network of political clubs, many more in number than the clandestine Liberal clubs. Moreover, by 1910, Francisco Madero was better known and fresher in the minds of the people than Ricardo, who, though a moral leader, was not even a presidential candidate. And he had been in jail during a critical time.

While the junta leaders languished in prison, Madero had embarked on feverish political activity. He had ample personal funds and the courage to tour the country and lead political rallies. His willingness to take risks and make real personal sacrifices became public and catapulted his fame across the nation. Madero and his collaborators spent long hours making contacts, writing and responding to letters, and engaging the press. Magón, in the meantime, was locked up in Florence, Arizona. Lest the reader be unsure of what that implied for Ricardo's ability to engage in agitation, let us listen to what Antonio I. Villarreal wrote about their life in the Yuma and Florence Penitentiaries. "This was our daily life," wrote Antonio, "at 6 o'clock we rose, made our beds, and were marched to breakfast. Following this came the disgusting job of emptying slops and at 7 we were taken to the workshops. Dinner was at 11, and as soon as it was over we went once more to work. Supper was at 4:30 and at 5 we were locked in our cells."

The cells were so small and crowded that there was no room to walk in them. Prisoners had to stay in their beds for a full thirteen hours, bearing the atrocious heat, which routinely hit 120 degrees. In Yuma, the cells were also mosquito ridden because of the proximity of the Colorado River. Finally, "talking was forbidden and was dangerous, as the guards were perpetually on the watch. Reading was out of the question. It was a daily thirteen hours' inferno of compulsory inactivity."[6]

Conditions were mildly better at the new penitentiary in Florence than they were in Yuma. There, cellmates could talk among themselves after lockdown until 8:00 p.m. Other than this, there was no substantial difference between life in the old adobe prison and in the new, steel-frame cells at Florence. Neither prison had a real library. Books, newspapers, and journals that were kept in the prison reading room were either religious in nature or out of date. Correspondence was, of course, limited in number, monitored, and censored, as was any reading material that was sent from the outside.

In short, while Madero rallied, wrote and read letters, and traveled throughout Mexico, Magón was little more than a ghost, a venerated name, true, but also somewhat of an abstraction, a man who had been out of Mexico for six years and in prison for the last three of those. Even some of Ricardo's closest lieutenants, such as Práxedis Guerrero, did not really know the man, because they had entered the movement around the time of his imprisonment.

It is true that Madero was intellectually less impressive than a Ricardo Flores Magón or a Juan Sarabia, but he had a more elitist education than they, was a good speaker, and had proved to be fully capable of writing a courageous and best-selling, though awkward, book, *La sucesión presidencial de 1910*.

Finally, although Madero's social program was indeed ambiguous, and although his social extraction from the wealthy class justified the Liberals' skepticism regarding the depth of his commitment to economic reforms, Madero understood something that had slipped from the attention of the Liberals: the importance of the democratic contest and especially of the struggle over access to political offices, from the presidency all the way down the chain. And when Madero finally made his very reluctant call to arms, it was after having built up a political machine and having run a political campaign throughout Mexico.

CHAPTER SIXTEEN

Puntos Rojos

Maderismo had begun to take shape after a famous interview with Profirio Díaz by the Canadian journalist James Creelman that was published in the March 1908 issue of *Pearson's Magazine* in which Díaz announced (falsely, it turned out) that he would not run for reelection and that Mexico was ready for democracy. But Francisco Madero did not truly emerge into public view until the publication of his book, *La sucesión presidencial de 1910*, at the end of that year. By 1909, the anti-reelectionist movement had gotten started, and in June of that year, the Anti-Reelectionist Party began publishing the weekly *El Anti-Reeleccionista* under the editorship of José Vasconcelos.

But even at that point, the aim of the Madero movement was to attack Díaz's choice for the vice presidency, Ramón Corral, rather than Díaz's reelection itself. The dictator was about to turn eighty, and no one expected him to live through another six-year term—as indeed, he did not. The Anti-Reelectionists also attacked General Bernardo Reyes, who was the most popular establishment successor of Díaz. In other words, the Anti-Reelectionist Party was, at that point, neither revolutionary nor even directly opposed to Díaz, or indeed opposed to Díaz's finance minister, José Yves Limantour, who was a respected friend of the Madero family and who was spared direct attacks in *El Anti-Reeleccionista*.[1] Rather than the overthrow of the decrepit dictator, The Anti-Reelectionists sought at first to interrupt Díaz's plans for his own succession and to introduce a democratic process.

The timing, logic, and aims of Partido Liberal Mexicano organization were entirely different. The party had consistently called for armed revolution since 1906, it was unabashedly anti-Díaz, and it was militant in its opposition to both of the factions that were poised to succeed Díaz, both pro-Reyes *reyistas* and pro-Limantour *cientíjicos*. The party's commitment to democratic process and elections was emphasized in its 1906 manifesto, but a prominent fraction of the leadership had turned against voting and elections since that time.

After Rivera, Villarreal, and Magón were imprisoned in 1907, organization of the Liberal groups had fallen to a second circle of militants that included Enrique Flores Magón, Antonio de P. Araujo, Anselmo Figueroa, Manuel and Tomás Sarabia, Jesús Rangel, Prisciliano Silva, Fernando Palomares, and Práxedis Guerrero, among others.

Of these, Práxedis was the most charismatic and energetic—though all were rather impressive. The phrase *Puntos Rojos* (red dots) was the title of a newspaper that Práxedis published out of El Paso at a time when *Regeneración* and its short-lived successor, *Revolución*, had been shut down. The same title was later used for Práxedis's column in *Regeneración* during the heady months between its reappearance in September 1910 and Práxedis's death while leading an armed incursion in Mexico in December of that same year. Práxedis Guerrero's work during the years of the junta's confinement combined organization and a poetic effort to bring converging points of resistance into public view: these were his *puntos rojos*.

Práxedis's rhetorical and poetical abilities were comparable only to those of three other Liberals: Santiago de la Hoz, who had perished in 1904, Juan Sarabia, who was locked inside the nitrous-saturated dungeons of San Juan de Ulúa, and Ricardo Flores Magón. His *Puntos Rojos* column in *Regeneración* combined brief political commentary with punchy phrases geared to steeling readers for rebellion. The section was structured as a set of news flashes, each of which was so nicely phrased that, decades later, Ethel Turner still took to copying them out by hand:

> In Guanajuato, thousands of proletarians eat only cactus pears and herbs [*quelites*].
>
> If vegetarianism is proof of refinement, then it must be admitted that Mexico is the most educated nation on earth, by dint of the effort of tyrants and the bourgeoisie.[2]
>
> At this coming September carnival [a celebration of Mexico's independence], 30,000 children will get the crowns of their heads soaked in the same pool in which Miguel Hidalgo was baptized. It would be nice to get a hold of the ceremony's program so as to add to it a sacrifice to

Huitzilopoxtli, for he, too, was one of the good gods of our forefathers.[3]

Soon Belem Prison will close down. Tyranny is getting civilized: it is building itself a new house for barbarity."[4]

Alongside this sort of pithy epigram, Práxedis informed *Regeneración* readers of world events. He had a knack for making the connections between international and local affairs clear, either explicitly, as in the case below, or implicitly:

> Alfonso, the murderer of Monjuich, has sent Porfirio Díaz, the butcher of Rio Blanco, the Great Collar of Charles III, which had been worn by the late Edward VII. According to the court's heralds, it is a great treasure and honor. It bears the Latin inscription: "Virtuti e meriti."
>
> But the Revolution also knows how to reward merit and virtue, and it is preparing a separate collar for the Hero of Peace [Díaz]. This one is made out of indigenous materials: a necklace of twine [*ixtle*].
>
> Which of the two will suit the august neck better?[5]

Finally, Práxedis poured effort into promoting a kind of revolutionary spirit, an ethos of rebellion. He did this in the form of aphorisms, in *Puntos Rojos*, but also with writings that are perhaps the best prose poetry produced by this group, especially the pieces titled "Sopla" and "¡Escuchad!" "Sopla" represents a man, a fighter, alone, facing the gale of a coming revolution and in mental dialogue with it. Toward the end of the literary fragment, the hero asks the gale where it comes from:

> —I come from each of the world's corners. I bring the righteous future. I am the breath of Revolution.
>
> —Blow hurricane. Comb my hair with your terrible fingers. Blow gale. Blow over cliff and valley and in the abyss. Turn and encircle mountains. Bring down those military barracks and those churches. Destroy those prisons. Shake that resignation. Dissolve those clouds of incense; break the branches from which the oppressors have built their lives; awake that ignorance; tear out those coins that stand for a thousand misfortunes. Blow hurricane, whirlwind, blow. Raise the passive sand that snakes and camels trample and turn them into burning projectiles. Blow, blow, so that when the soft breeze returns, it does not find the horrible anguish of enslaved humanity still trapped in my hair.[6]

Written barely six weeks before the outbreak of the revolution, these are among the most beautiful political verses to have been composed for Mexico's proletarian readership.

Although *Regeneración* flourished alongside the early development of mass literacy, followers of the paper included a significant but undetermined number of illiterates. Literacy rates in Mexico went from 17.9 percent in 1895, to 22.3 percent in 1900, to 27.7 percent in 1910.[7] Readers, in other words, were very much a minority, and even within the literate sector, there were many new readers with little background or experience with books or journals. *Regeneración* recognized these facts. The journal provided lists of recommended readings and advertised vendors where readers might purchase the works; it also occasionally published advertisements for dictionaries, inviting its readers: "Teach yourself to talk and to write with propriety." As the revolution approached, the journal provided readers with instructions about how to share the journal's contents with illiterate comrades.[8]

Much has been made of the multiplying effect of oral transmission in the case of *Regeneración*. In part, the magnification of its effects was an illusion of those who wrote the magazine, but the image of a worker or a peasant reading out loud to a circle of listeners also became an emblem of the revolutionary community as seen by revolutionary vanguards for many years thereafter. And indeed it was true that the magnification of print culture by oral transmission was at the very heart of revolutionary popular culture, a "folk culture," to use the expression of anthropologist Robert Redfield, that spread in a prolific cascade of ballads (*corridos*), often printed as loose sheets and disseminated in songs and verses that shaped the regional cultures of revolutionary Mexico.[9]

Nonetheless, the breadth of *Regeneración*'s ripple effect remains very difficult to assess, requiring patience and diligence in trying to reconstruct the movement of cultural innovations through space. Moreover, as Redfield pointed out based on his fieldwork in the 1920s and 1930s, the dynamics of distinction between the literate and the illiterate—between what he called the "urban" and the "folk" cultures—was a fundamental organizing principle across regional space.[10] As a result, the indirect impact of literature was at once structurally guaranteed and diffuse.

I am not concerned with resolving this complex matter here. For our purposes, what matters is that there was deep heterogeneity among followers of *Regeneración* and of the other radical papers and that a segment of these papers' public was made up not of readers, but of tellers and listeners. For this reason, the poetic abilities of a Práxedis Guerrero, of a Ricardo Flores Magón, or of a Juan Sarabia mattered quite a lot. Ingenuity, generally, was much cultivated among those who worked in propaganda. It was not only a matter of keeping readers interested, but also a question of writing material that could be remembered and then reported or retold—not necessarily in the exact same words, but sometimes exact words were useful, and their repetition could be achieved through the rhyme and meter of closed poetic forms such as the *décimas* and the *octavas* that are typical of *corridos*.

Given the expectations about the oral retransmission of writing, there was a subtle, never emphasized, but also very real distinction between the first-generation Liberal proletarian or peasant writers and comrades who were either more schooled or more talented and more dedicated writers. The distance between better and worse writers is often quite dramatic and obvious to anyone who has handled the original letters and writings of the Liberal comrades. Among those writings there are many by authors who were clearly also "new readers," that is, individuals who had little or no schooling before their politicization and for whom reading and writing developed as part and parcel of politicization. In this, the Liberal movement was not unlike Mexican Protestantism, which, as Jean-Pierre Bastian has shown, developed around schools and schooling, and schools were often a key point of attraction for those drawn to the religion.[11]

The Liberals' correspondence is crowded with letters written with no punctuation marks and saturated with unconventional spelling that reflects oral pronunciation, but that is sometimes difficult for habitual readers to interpret. At times, even important leaders wrote like that. Women, for instance, were sharply divided between those who were schoolteachers—and who sometimes wrote in the most elaborate and baroque prose—and those who had received little or no formal education and learned their letters in politics. A couple of examples clarify the point.

Mariana Gómez Gutiérrez, a Liberal schoolteacher living in Presidio, Texas, wrote a letter to Enrique Flores Magón at Leavenworth Federal Penitentiary, an extract of which reads as follows:

Dearest comrade in the cause of Land and Liberty. Greetings!

This letter has as its only object to visit you in the great enclosure of your laborious prison.

It comes to greet you from remote and distant places, where you have several brothers, dispersed like the Wandering Jew of legend.

It comes to hear from your lips and your instruments the bellicose and classical songs and hymns that will be sung—in the key of a Universal music—on the day of Promise, in the universal country, of the world society. Do you want to sing? The material world—which is perishable, vile, and contemptible—hears not what is great and sublime, but the spirit—that marvelous motor of all that moves—does perceive it, and hears the mysterious songs of the heroic sentiment at any distance.

Sing, then, in the confines of your ample and painful prison.[12]

The contrast between this sonorous and beautifully penned composition and the scrawling letters of Enrique's own wife, Teresa Arteaga, could not be more stark. I reproduce the first lines of one of the many letters that she wrote to her husband at Leavenworth:

> my dear husband I cannot portray the pleasure [misspelled] with which I received [misspelled] the day it came [misspelled] your letter in Spanish Ithought that it was [misspelled] the first thatIreceived since youleft because I can't get used to thing withanothers' [misspelled] head [misspelled] my love [misspelled this letter was [misspelled] with the news [misspelled] that I am crazed with pleasure [misspelled] Maria Andrade and Ramon have given you a violin [misspelled] so that you learn during the time thatremains for your release Matilde got hitched [misspelled] with her old [misspelled] boyfriend [misspelled] their union is the other [misspelled] news [misspelled] that Vale is here [misspelled] with us send his greetings.[13]

It is important to note, though, that, despite the chasm between these two women's education, both were respected militants.

It is true that "poor writing" was even more dramatic among women than men, because one could find women who had been denied educations that their brothers had received, but in the fundamentals, the breach was equally important among the men. In such a context, a man such as Práxedis Guerrero, who was the son of an *hacendado* and who had read Tolstoy, Victor Hugo, and the socialists in his own father's library, a man who could credibly take on many disguises and who was at the same time truly committed to the cause and willing to expend every ounce of his literary and organizational talent on comrades who were either rather rudimentary writers or illiterate, was a precious rarity. Little wonder that Ricardo saw in Práxedis the son that he never had.[14]

Organizing Liberal Clubs

Most of Práxedis's efforts since 1906 had been in the field of organizing. In Douglas, Arizona, he had shared rooms with Manuel Sarabia, and both men were involved in the organization of political clubs and in unionizing, not only at the Copper Queen smelter that the Phelps-Dodge corporation operated there, but also in mining camps in Morenci, Metcalf, Miami, Globe, and elsewhere. We know something of the activities of these local groups because they were infiltrated. A brief aside on this is in order here.

Perhaps the most poignant example of the extent to which our knowledge of these events relies on police records is that of Ricardo's quite famous love letters to María, written on strips cloth and smuggled in and out of jail with the laundry (Figure 16.1). Ricardo often complained of the pains of writing on that medium, interjecting phrases such as "My love I can't write on this rag," or "tell my daughter Lucía that I don't write because this rag is no good."[15] He also went to lengths to instill caution in María so that their method of communication would not be discovered. So, for instance, on an occasion when Ricardo wished María to show a letter to Elizabeth Trowbridge (code name Violeta), he wrote: "Read the letter my love, and send it to Violeta. Beg her not to tell anyone that it is written on a rag because if she does our enemies will guess how I get letters out."[16]

And yet, all along, Ricardo's notes were being intercepted, photographed, and inconspicuously reinserted into the laundry. Thus, on October 30, 1908, the consul in Los Angeles wrote to his superiors in Mexico City: "On the afternoon of Saturday 10 of this month, I found a letter in the clean clothes that María [Brousse] Talavera sent to Flores Magón. It was of no importance, since it mainly lamented their separation and expressed the love she has for him. On the following Monday, the 12th, I found a note in Magón's dirty clothes, and I have the honor of remitting to you a photographed copy of that."[17]

The historian eavesdropping on the eavesdroppers only adds a second level of titillation—something between fascination and guilty complicity with the police—to our reading of the love letters, while it helps explain, too, why we have none of Ricardo and María's many letters from the Leavenworth or McNeill penitentiaries: they were written at a time when the Mexican government had lost interest in tracking the Liberals' movements. By then, they were of secondary importance. So the fact that we know something of Práxedis's and Manuel Sarabia's activities in these years means that this was a time when the governments of Mexico and the United States still worried about these men.

What were the Liberal organizers doing during the years when Librado, Antonio, and Ricardo were in prison? The letters of Manuel Sarabia, written from Douglas, Arizona, provide a useful glimpse of the work being developed.

At the local level, Manuel worked to wrench the representation of the Mexican community from pro-Díaz community leaders. By September 1907, he had succeeded, or so he wrote to fellow militant Marcelino Albarra:

> in the past few days, I was very occupied in the organization of the [Mexican] national holidays in this place. I was elected President of the Patriotic Junta, but I had to bear the burden of organizing the events entirely on my own. I had to confront a thousand obstacles laid before me by the magnates who own these celebrations here and to breach the tremendous difficulties that the envious sympathizers of the P. Díaz dictatorship laid before me. But I triumphed in the end and managed to raise our flag high. All of the speeches that were pronounced were by Liberals."[18]

Figure 16.1 One of the rags used by Ricardo Flores Magón to write to María Brousse, photographed by the Mexican consul in Los Angeles and sent to Mexico's minister of foreign affairs. Dialectical image: purloined photos of purloined letters are presented here as a memento mori both of the tragic hero and the government spy. At one level, they are icons of the futility of the hero's pains and the restless guile of his oppressors; but at another level, they are tokens of a heroic beauty that can never be apprehended. They bring to mind the inevitable death of both the revolutionary hero and the secret serviceman. Archivo Secretaría de Relaciones Exteriores, Mexico City.

María:

[texto en gran parte ilegible]

... Estoy muy ... que si
... mande ... sublime ...
... certificado de ...
... médico sobre ...

... se ... de ...
... que no le ...
... médico ... que el ...
... porque no le ...
... médico ...
... estoy enfermo y ...
... necesito que me vea
un médico. Dile a
Harriman que es ne-
cesario que ese certi-
ficado esté en Washing-
ton antes del 1º de Oc-
tubre. Yo estoy muy
enfermo y no pue[do]
negarme la libertad
bajo fianza porque ...
... tanto como ...
... estoy ...
... enfermo de ...

...cho ... Los ...
... de los ingleses po-
... hacer muchas ...
... Por ... estas ...
... que no lo ha-
cen ... pueden ha...
... las calles ... un
no asunto, protesta
... contra la ...
... cación. ¿Por qué
... de hacer? La
... incomunicación ...
completamente ile-
gal. Lo que me entris-
tece es que ...
... que ... la
... Te ...
... que mi co-
... para lo del
médico. Dile a ...
... que no le
escribo porque no ten-
... mucho ...
... No la vi para el 16. Lo
... para la ...
de Buena Vista. Dile ...
... a que ... los ...
... pasar para
estar pendiente. Me
... con que termi-
na pienso en ti. Mi
admiración por ti es
inmensa. Recibe
en tu boquita mil
más ardientes ...
... Tuyo Ricardo

Gaining control over patriotic festivities—principally Independence Day (September 16), but also May 5 (commemoration of the Battle of Puebla) and at times March 21 (Benito Juárez's birthday)—was an important goal for militants. In American border towns, it was indeed crucial, because it meant that those places could safely be considered bastions of anti-Díaz militancy. As a result, Liberal speakers were at times kept from delivering their speeches there or even run out of town. So, for instance, the Mexican vice-consul in Solommonville, Arizona, reported that a group of Liberal Party members were run out of Metcalf "for having loudly proffered insults the President, on the May 5th celebrations."[19]

We do not have too many specifics about the contents of Liberal speechmaking on those occasions, except that they were stridently anti-Díaz. We do, however, have some of the lyrics that were sung on September 16 by Liberals in proletarian and radicalized sectors of Guadalajara. These anarchist hymns are mostly forgotten today. The first is a proletarian version of the Mexican national anthem, written with its same rhyme and meter and made to be sung to the same tune. I do not know the tune of the second song:

> Proletarios al grito de guerra,
> Por ideales luchar con valor,
> Y expropiad atrevidos la tierra
> Que detenta nuestro explotador;
> Y expropiad atrevidos la tierra
> Que detenta nuestro explotador.
> Proletarios, precisa que unidos
> Derrumbemos la vil construcción,
> Del sistema burgués que oprimidos
> Nos sugeta con la explotación
> Que ya es tiempo que libres seamos
> Y dejemos también de sufrir,
> Siendo todos iguales y hermanos
> Con el mismo derecho a vivir.

> [Proletarians arise to the war cry,
> With valor come and fight for ideals.
> And daringly expropriate the land
> That is held by our exploiter;

And daringly expropriate the land,
That is held by our exploiter.
Proletarians, we need to unite
To bring down the vile construct
Of the oppressing bourgeois system
That subjects us with exploitation.
For it is time that we be free
And that we also stop suffering
And all be equal and brothers
With the same right to live.]

The second song was sung on the eve of September 15:

Para que cambie el sistema
Y termine tu mal,
Hay que acabar con el clero,
Gobierno y capital.
Esos buitres de sotana,
Que no tienen compasión,
Embrutecen a millones
Con su infame religión.

[So that the system changes
And your ills come to an end,
We must finish off the clergy
capital, and authority.
Those befrocked buzzards
Who have no compassion
Stupify millions
With their vile religion.][20]

Songs such as these were supplements to the staple "El hijo del pueblo," whose first stanza is:

Hijo del pueblo, te oprimen cadenas
y esa injusticia no puede seguir.
Si tu existencia es un mundo de penas
antes que esclavo prefiere morir.

247

[Son of the people, the chains oppress you
And that injustice cannot go on.
If your existence is a world of sorrows
Then choose to die before being a slave.]

Events and meetings generally concluded with a singing of rallying cry of all Jacobins, the "Marseillaise." Singing was a way to
galvanize sentiments of collective belonging that usually followed
speech making against Porfirio Díaz, against slavery, and so on. It
could be performed only when the Liberals actually dominated a
public event, as Manuel had managed to do in Douglas in 1907.

A second kind of activity that we find in Manuel Sarabia's intercepted letters is monitoring and sharing thoughts and experiences
about the best way to conduct the Liberal press. So, for example,
Manuel writes to Antonio de P. Araujo and to his own brother,
Tomás Sarabia Labrada, from his prison in Yuma, lauding their
paper, *Reforma, Liberad y Justicia*, and then offering a word of advice:

> May I suggest that you moderate your language if you want your paper
> to get registration and to operate without difficulties? Bear in mind that
> *Revolución!* is currently facing two suits for libel: one for having called
> a goon a "gorilla!!!" and another because it said that another goon who
> is bowlegged acquired that trait riding stolen horses in his youth. Here,
> anything can be called libel, just as in our country, goons are used to
> finish off publications.[21]

Speaking from experience with libel laws used on multiple occasions against both *Regeneración* and its short-lived successor, *Revolución*,
Manuel warned Araujo and Labrada that the "big fish" never brought
libel suits directly against the press, because they did not want to
call attention to themselves, but rather used low-level politicians for
that purpose. Both warnings were well attuned to the policy of the
Mexican government and indeed to joint U.S.-Mexican governmental
strategies used against the so-called *revoltosos*. Indeed, Internal Minister Ramón Corral had written to the Foreign Ministry approving the
U.S. undersecretary of state's suggestion that the Mexican government
promote a libel suit against the journal *Revolución* as the most effective
way of shutting down that venue: "at that point, the government of the
United States would provide firm, though indirect support in order to
promote and expedite proceedings in the courts."[22]

Manuel also offered other kinds of advice to sister publications. Writing to a Mr. Torres Delgado, publisher of the Douglas paper *El Progreso*, Sarabia criticized the paper's new literary page: "I agree that a serious paper like *El Progreso* should concern itself with literary matters, but it will not do to insert 'Verses of Love.' I think that it would be better for you to take fragments from Vargas Vila's *Verb de admonition y combated* or from any other revolutionary author and publish them weekly. Or else, if that won't do, then publish a literary page, but with heroic poetry."[23]

Finally, the leadership organized groups of resistance. This included creating political clubs such as Morenci's El Partido Liberal Club, founded by Práxedis Guerrero, which had around fifty members, according to the Mexican Consul in Tucson. It also involved taking up collections to support leaders in prison or their families, to purchase arms for revolution in Mexico, and to support various Liberal papers (Figure 16.2). Organizers were also much concerned with information management—warning comrades against spies, offering strategic advice, and so on.[24]

Práxedis Guerrero and his buddy, Francisco Manrique, along with Manuel Sarabia, Enrique Flores Magón, Fernando Palomares, Antonio de P. Araujo, and Tomás Labrada Sarabia, were among the most active leaders in this phase. Their prolonged grassroots organizing, which began around preparations for the 1906 revolt and continued through the release of the junta leadership in 1910, meant that some of these organizers were better known on the ground even than Ricardo Flores Magón himself. There is no question that Ricardo was more famous than Práxedis Guerrero—his role in Mexican public life had made him a national icon there, which Guerrero was not. But in the Texas, Arizona, and California border communities, Práxedis, Enrique Flores Magón, Antonio de P. Araujo, and Manuel and Tomás Sarabia were better known in the sense that they were known directly, face to face. They were also the agents who dealt most regularly with the local leaders of the Liberals in the Southwest: men such as Laura Aguirre, a Liberal editor in El Paso, Prisciliano Silva, head of a rebel clan in South Texas, and Jesús Rangel, a store owner in Waco. When Antonio, Librado, and Ricardo were finally released, and they returned to the helm of a refurbished and much energized *Regeneración*, they briefly brought this leadership back together as a single unitary force.

Figure 16.2 The Liberal Party's bond issue for supporting the revolution, featuring Ricardo Flores Magón, Antonio Villarreal, Juan Sarabia, and Enrique Flores Magón, and commemorating the 1908 revolution. These bonds were probably issued between August and December 1910 — certainly no later than that. The design of these bonds ties the credit of the PLM to the personal honor of the men of the junta. The faces are all emblematic of the Liberal Party at this point. The date of the bond's emission — June 26, 1908 — is also emblematic, since it was the scheduled time of the second Liberal uprising against Díaz. The gaze of each leader is not directed at the buyer of the bond, but rather to an invisible cause. This is the gaze of "the men that Díaz fears." Courtesy of the Bancroft Library, John Murray Papers.

Regeneración *1910*

The period between the release of Ricardo, Antonio, and Librado on August 4, 1910, and early December of that year was a brief and golden moment that would never be repeated in the long history of *Regeneración*. It was a time when all forces, Socialist and anarchist, American and Mexican, worked together under their natural leaders, the freed men of the Junta Organzadora. Congressional inquiries into the persecution of Mexican refugees, wedded to the uncertain future of the Díaz regime wrought by Madero's anti-reelection movement, provided the Los Angeles junta with a brief moment of respite with regard to persecution by the U.S. government. And revolution was in the air. It was a fact.

This brief period was devoted to rallying opinion and to trying to give shape to a unitary revolutionary movement. The anarchist convictions of a key portion of the junta leadership had not yet translated into a new Liberal Party platform, so the 1906 manifesto, which was by no means an anarchist document, was still officially in place. As a result, there was some ambiguity about the goals of the Liberal revolution—a useful ambiguity, perhaps, since there were many shared goals among revolutionaries, and so open differences were not emphasized.

All Liberal factions pitched in and participated in *Regeneración* during the fall of 1910. Antonio I. Villarreal published a three-part series denouncing prison conditions in Arizona; there were notes on the reception and impact on American opinion of John Kenneth Turner's *Barbarous Mexico*; Práxedis Guerrero brought his *puntos rojos* to the pages of *Regeneración* and wrote weekly to give shape to the spirit of revolt. Práxedis, Enrique, and Ricardo wrote stories memorializing Liberal martyrs and the 1906 and 1908 movements. Subscriptions to *Regeneración* and volunteer work increased so much that Práxedis had to develop a new system to manage them.[25]

The role of political collaboration with non-Mexicans was also now openly recognized with the publication of an English-language page in *Regeneración*, edited by a dedicated German volunteer, the Socialist Alfred Sanftleben. The work of Turner, in particular, had attracted many American and some European volunteers to the cause, and this brought along a new readership. John Turner wrote pieces in the English section. So did Job Harriman and a few others.

Missing from this scene were Manuel Sarabia and Elizabeth Trowbridge. Their escape to England had initially caused friction between Manuel and many of his old comrades, including Lázaro, Enrique, and Práxedis, who disapproved of Manuel for having given priority to his relationship with Elizabeth over militancy in the revolution. Only Antonio defended Manuel on the staff of *Regeneración*. Manuel thanked Antonio for his support and added that "one day, I'll show those who have doubted my loyalty that I am worth more than they."[26]

However, the rift between Práxedis and Manuel, at least, seems to have been mending, perhaps thanks to Ethel and John's mediation, since they were close to both men. In her notes, Ethel reports that Práxedis had finally responded to Manuel's correspondence and was reconciled with him. Ricardo, who, as we will see, had developed stronger negative feelings toward Manuel, preferred to say nothing of them publicly. He had bigger fish to fry.

Moreover, despite their unseemly escape, Manuel and Elizabeth were proving to be useful, since they were publicizing Mexican conditions in Europe and gaining valuable friends for the cause there. In England, John Turner's book had found the commercial publisher that it was denied in the United States, and it made quite a splash. Manuel and Elizabeth helped broker and promote John's work in England. The British antislavery league took an interest in Mexico, for instance, and the British press sent an envoy to Mexico to investigate Turner's claims and report.[27] His findings confirmed Turner's allegations.[28] Pressure from British public opinion, stoked by Manuel and Elizabeth and by the antislavery society, forced the British consul in Merida to produce an account for her majesty's government.[29]

Manuel and Elizabeth took an active role in the British and French press, challenging official statements by Mexican diplomats and publishing pieces on the Mexican situation. In England, they contributed to the dissemination of John's work in venues such as *Fry's Magazine* and the *Labour Leader*. In France, they were in contact with the editors of prestigious anarchist and socialist publications such as *Le Temps Nouveaux* and *La Société Nouvelle*, and they were also active in Spain, Germany, and Belgium.[30]

Their efforts made Mexican conditions, the Liberal Party, and *Regeneración* known to radical readers in Spain, France, and England.[31] Ricardo and Librado, for their part, had built a close relationship with Emma Goldman, Alexander Berkman, and Voltairine de Cleyre since their St. Louis days, and Goldmans's journal, *Mother Earth*, as well as Berkman's *The Blast* published pieces that were sympathetic to the Mexican Revolution. Spanish, South American, and Italian anarchist circles, too, were well informed of the activities of the Mexican group. By 1910, the Mexican Liberal Party was internationally famous.

On the Socialist side, connections were, if anything, stronger still, thanks to the intervention of Job Harriman, Mother Jones, John Murray, John Kenneth Turner, Eugene Debs, and others. The pages of the *Appeal to Reason*, the *New York Call*, and other journals were broadly sympathetic to the Liberals and to the Mexican Revolution in this period. So Manuel and Elizabeth's presence in London starting in 1909 was in some ways timely, since it magnified the impact of John's book and built bridges between the Liberals to the anarchist and socialist press in Europe (Figure 16.3).

Figure 16.3 Coverage of Mexican affairs
in *The New York Call*, 1909 (no exact date).
Courtesy of the Bancroft Library, John
Murray Papers.

Manuel's European writings are said to have changed Leo Tolstoy's once positive view of Porfirio Díaz, for instance, and Parisian communists' interest in Mexico's revolution extended to the publication of a French edition of Juan Sarabia's prison poems.[32] In his introduction to that collection, Manuel tipped his hat to Práxedis, probably hoping to accelerate their reconciliation: "When I invited my dear friend and comrade Práxedis G. Guerrero to write this forward, I was sure that his gallant pen would uplift the work. He responded that he would write it with pleasure, but time is upon us, and his forward has not arrived. There is nothing for it but for me to write it, which displeases me a little, because I cannot judge Juan impartially."[33]

In addition, Ricardo was still asking Elizabeth for financial support. The two remained in correspondence with one another in the final months of 1910. The trouble was, though, that Elizabeth had spent most of her money, so she could not send much. That worried Manuel, and in several letters to Antonio Villarreal, which the latter was at times asked to show to Ricardo, Manuel bent over backward to detail Elizabeth's finances as best as he could. "I assure you, my dear friend, that neither you nor anyone else has a full idea of what Eliz spent for our cause. I myself, as I have said elsewhere, know more each day, but still do not know the full extent." Elizabeth was not entirely ruined, Manuel continued, because she still stood to inherit eight or nine thousand dollars, but beyond that, they were broke, and Manuel had taken a job as translator in a British law firm to pay the bills. Still, he worried that he might be perceived as having diverted Elizabeth's support from the cause to further his own private interests: "It would pain me if any of you were to think that I have become selfish—that being in a position to provide monetary aid, I prefer to the comforts of plenty; that witnessing *Regeneración* in agony, I close my eyes and ears to your anguished pleas and separate Eliz from her path as benefactress."[34]

Everyone, in short, was working toward a common goal, and divergences on revolutionary methods and goals seemed to be secondary or surmountable in this brief, four-month period. Still, there were some important tacit—and at times explicit—differences between the people who were converging on *Regeneración* in the months between the journal's reappearance and the revolutionary outbreak. These can be understood by way of an analysis of goals and tactics and of short-term versus long-term goals.

Perhaps the most important divergence concerned attitudes toward revolutionary violence itself. Madero, as mentioned, was inimical to violence. He saw violence as truly a last resort and believed in prioritizing legal methods. This attitude was long known to be in sharp contrast with that of the Magóns. So, for instance, Madero had declined a 1907 invitation to join a San Antonio, Texas, Liberal political club precisely because of this issue: "As you know perfectly well, I, too, reject the current state of affairs in our country, but we don't agree on how to remedy the situation. I have always believed that our struggle should occur within the limits set by the law, in the next elections. Everything induces me to believe that if we proceed energetically, we will triumph."[35]

When Madero finally became reconciled to the need for an uprising, he did so reluctantly and was much invested in reining in revolutionary violence. Thus, the Plan de San Luis, which he issued on October 6, 1910, calling for the nullification of Díaz's election and for Mexicans to take up arms against the government, justified revolution on a constitutional basis, given the impossibility of changing things via the vote, which had been tried, and the failure of all possibilities of legal recourse to nullify its results. The Plan de San Luis also made an effort to promote adherence to the laws of war: it punished the shooting of prisoners and looting and called for the strictest military discipline. Indeed, the plan lavished substantially more attention to the rules of war than it did to land distribution, for instance. And during the battle of Ciudad Juárez, Madero followed through on his instinct of reining in violence, ordering his generals to shoot any looters among the troops and, most controversially, ordering Pascual Orozco and Pancho Villa to refrain from executing the hated Porfirista General Juan Navarro.[36]

This attitude contrasted with Ricardo's, who was convinced that elections were never an option—at least not since 1904. Only bullets, and not the ballot, could change Mexico. The revived *Regeneración*'s editorial in the first, September 1910 issue set the tone forthrightly: "Here we are, announcing war: with the torch of revolution in one hand, and the Program of the Liberal Party in the other. We are not whining messengers of peace. We are revolutionaries. Our ballots will be the bullets fired by our rifles.... They want to subdue us with bullets; let's conquer them with bullets, too."[37] The junta then hammered the point home in articles with titles such as Antonio I.

Villarreal's "Mexicano, tu mejor amigo es el fusil" (Mexican: Your best friend is a gun). This conviction was shared by Socialists and anarchists at the start of the revolution. There were, however, some subtle, but important differences between PLM leaders.

The first involved taking direct military leadership roles versus taking the role of ideological leadership. When Antonio I. Villarreal wrote that the Mexican's best friend is a gun, what he had in mind was leading an army to topple Porfirio Díaz. Ricardo, however, had a different idea. Although he was discreet, indeed, outright mysterious when it came to expressing his position openly, his actions followed a different logic. For Ricardo, the revolution's three enemies were capital, government, and the clergy. Therefore, revolutionary strategy could not be geared simply to toppling a regime on the basis of a professional or would-be-professional army. Instead, his proposed strategy was to invite peasants and workers to take property directly and to topple the system by a vast movement of direct appropriations.

Given this strategy, intellectual work—"propaganda work," as they called it—was fundamental, while battles would be won and lost. The revolutionary tide would be unpredictable. Keeping an even keel on the ideological plane was the only way to avoid disaster. And yet Ricardo felt, in these early months, that he could not say this in public. As a result, he sometimes seemed mystical in his insistence on the sacred role of *Regeneración*.

For Villarreal and for most leaders, however, the strategy was not direct action. At least not principally or exclusively. True, both Villarreal and Lázaro Gutiérrez de Lara would promote something like direct action at different times, inviting peasants to take the land, for instance. However, for them, Mexico was a backward country with only incipient industrialism and a largely "feudal" countryside. Socialism was not immediately attainable, but would need a long process of progressive economic development. Their aim, therefore, was to change the government and then engage in a protracted democratic struggle that would progress in tandem with industrialization.

As a result, these leaders were soon won over by the Madero side. A compromise with Madero would give Socialists some political clout, while new democratic conditions would allow unionization and land reform to get a start—not without conflict, certainly, but at least it would be possible to begin to move forward. Gaining a foothold in a liberal democratic state, then engaging in sustained conflict with the bourgeoisie was the way to go.

To the Socialist and democratic leadership, Ricardo's position appeared contradictory, for he exalted armed revolution, but held himself back from it, keeping *Regeneración* in the comparative safety of Los Angeles. Writing at a time when the anarchist group led by Ricardo had split from both Madero and the Socialists, and trying to bring some of the Socialists back into the fold, William C. Owen tried to minimize the depth of these differences by claiming that a portion of the Socialist leadership had sold out, and trying to claim the rest for their camp: "What," he wrote, "do the Mexicans know of these fine, scholastic distinctions between Socialism and Anarchism? What, for the matter of that, do the rank and file of the Socialist Party know about them? Nothing, absolutely nothing."[38] But differences did not stem from the fine points of anarchist and Socialist philosophy. They were fundamental strategic differences and could not be easily reconciled, with or without Madero.

Violence for Vegetarians

Attitudes toward revolutionary violence are the best way to understand the differences that shattered the short-lived harmony that the Liberals found in the months prior to the revolutionary outbreak. The fragmentation of the Liberal Party cannot be understood if it is reduced to ideological differences between anarchism and Socialism or between anarchism, Socialism, and Liberalism. William C. Owen's skepticism regarding the relevance of any finely drawn ideological debate was well placed in this regard. In the Mexican Revolution, as in the feminist movement of the 1970s, "the personal was the political." It is with this in mind that we can proceed to the analysis diverging attitudes toward violence in Ricardo's most intimate circle.

Práxedis Guerrero was twenty-eight in 1910; Ricardo was thirty-six. But after three stints in prison in Mexico and one even longer one in the United States, Ricardo was a very mature thirty-six. Besides, he was famous. When John Murray went to Mexico to do his reporting in 1908, he discovered that Magón was "worshiped next to Juárez."[39] An exaggeration, surely, but not by much. Moreover, Ricardo had no parents to whom he could go back. His youthful womanizing days had forever been put behind him, and his single-minded loyalty to the cause had long been sealed.

Práxedis, for his part, was like a shooting star—a young man whose febrile activity never rested. When he left his parental home, the hacienda Los Altos de Ibarra in Guanajuato State, he worked as a peon in the fields and then as a stableboy. These jobs allowed him to see his natal social class from the viewpoint of its servants. Práxedis then turned to more independent forms of labor. He worked as a carpenter and as a mechanic in a railway shop before crossing the border into the United States. By then, he was committed to labor organizing and propaganda.

Práxedis had begun writing for the press in Guanajuato, when he was still an *hacendado*'s son. He had also briefly joined in General Bernardo Reyes's civil militia, the Segunda Reserva, with an officer's rank. Práxedis therefore had some military training. In short, he had all the elements with which to be a revolutionary leader: an upper-class education, deep proletarian and popular knowledge and commitment, and experience in the press, as an organizer, and in the army.

In the United States, Práxedis started several combat papers, even as he moved across the Southwest. He worked in lumber mills in Texas and in coal mines; he was a railroad section hand; he cut wood along the Mississippi; he worked on the docks and in the Arizona copper mines. This dizzying movement across the entire field of proletarian experience was spurred by a keen rejection of injustice and of human suffering. In her notes on her friend Práxedis, Ethel scribbled: "usually dressed in overalls. He was a vegetarian, as for humane reasons he did not believe in eating meat."[40]

For vegetarians, violence is always a complicated thing, so Práxedis had given much thought to the matter, particularly since he was such a passionate advocate of armed revolt. To Práxedis, revolutionary violence was a thing of nature, like a red dawn. Writing the story of the 1908 revolt, in which his dearest friend Francisco Manrique was killed, he began: "It was dawn. On June 26, 1908 the sun announced itself with blood-colored strips on the horizon. The Revolution was awake, with its fist in the air"[41] Revolutionary violence was necessary, even beautiful. But it should be done without hatred. Writing just a few weeks before departing to the revolution and to his death, Práxedis admonished: "Hatred is not required to fight for freedom. Tunnels are dug without hatred, and dikes are made on rivers without it. Hatred isn't needed to wound the earth in order to plant grain. Despotism can be annihilated without hatred. One can embrace even the most violent act when it is needed for human emancipation."[42]

In another article, one of his very last, he wrote a more extended argument about the ends and the means of the revolution: "We are going off to a violent struggle without making violence our ideal and without dreaming of the execution of our tyrants as if that was the supreme victory of justice. Our violence is not justice, it is simply a necessity."[43] Práxedis was also careful to point out that being peaceful was not the same as being good. In this, he was a Nietzschean. "Passivity and tameness do not imply goodness, just as rebelliousness is not the same as savagery."[44]

Though Ricardo may have agreed with at least some of this, he and Práxedis had quiet, but important differences. In particular, they differed on the need for a revolutionary leader to risk his own life on the battlefield, as well as on role of hatred in revolutionary violence. Ricardo did not write much about hatred in the months preceding the outbreak of the 1910 revolution. He concentrated his energy on trying to smash the prestige of pacifism. "Preaching peace is a crime" is the way that he put it.[45] And with this Práxedis agreed. But perhaps because Ricardo was not preparing to go to battle himself—preparing to kill and preparing for his own death, as Práxedis was—Ricardo said little about hatred, the way Práxedis repeatedly did, and he regularly indulged in hate speech, moving easily from the use of biting sarcasm—common to practically all of these writers—to true vitriol against his opponents.

Práxedis envisioned violence as a practical necessity, like opening the ground to plant a seed, whereas Ricardo saw the war as a long and open-ended process that needed hatred to fan it and keep it going: "This Revolution is not one of those that last six months. This one has to be of very long duration. It will last years and years, since it is not about bringing down a president to place another in his stead, but rather to change economic, political, social, and moral conditions."[46]

This vision, too, is what justified the second, more explosive difference between them, for whereas Práxedis felt that he must absolutely go into battle, that he could not ask others to lay down their lives without leading them in the field, Ricardo was against going into the field himself, and he also wished to keep Práxedis from going.

Here we enter a murky terrain that has been of concern for all serious students of Ricardo Flores Magón.[47] Two questions have arisen with some insistence. Was Ricardo selfish, or even cowardly, in his decision not to go to battle while urging others forward? And had Ricardo become estranged from Práxedis when the Liberal Party's favorite son insisted on going into battle himself? I will deal with the second question first.

The literature on Ricardo generally portrays him as having deep affection and partiality for Práxedis. Everything indicates that this was in fact the case. Ethel, who was present on a routine basis during the short months when the two men shared a daily routine at *Regeneración*, says that Práxedis was recognized by all as second only to Ricardo and that Práxedis was like a son to him. Práxedis's prominence made itself felt in three ways: first, in the pages of *Regeneración*, which benefitted greatly from his eloquence, energy, and charisma; second, in the daily life of the *Regeneración* "family"; and third, in the mixture of sentiments that his decision to go to the front produced.

Recall a fragment of how Ethel painted the lunches at *Regeneración* in 1910: "Ricardo spoke little, and he was friendly when he was in small groups, because he enjoyed listening to others. Práxedis was brilliant and ingenious in conversation."[48] One can intuit a kind of paternal delight in Ricardo's habit of bearing witness to the excited conversations occurring at *Regeneración*'s family table. This was a man who had just come out of three years of prison, including many months incommunicado. During all those years, he had worked only to ignite a revolution, which was finally beginning to happen. And he was there to witness it—and to lead it.

As early as 1899, Ricardo had chosen the newspaper as his weapon of choice. Now he was ready to use it, and with a great team behind him. It is, I think, in this frame that we might best interpret the secret conflict between Ricardo and Práxedis regarding the decision to go to war. For unlike Ricardo, Práxedis felt obligated to go to war. He framed this obligation in general ethical terms. Indeed, one of the aphorisms that he wrote up for his *Puntos Rojos* seemed to have been written for *Regeneración*'s editorial board itself: "The word, in order to unify tendencies. The act, in order to establish those principles in practice."[49]

The ethical reason to move from words to action was defended philosophically in Práxedis's writings. His *Regeneración* piece "Soy la acción," for instance, is adamant on the subject. It begins: "I am action. Without me, the concepts of the human brain would be but a bunch of humid matches in a moldy match box." And it ends: "Progress and Liberty cannot be without me. I am action."[50] Given the essay's emphasis on action over thought uncoupled from action, one can feel the spurs of the argument digging into *Regeneración*'s editorial office as much as into a passive citizenry.

But in addition to his philosophical reasons, Práxedis had a compelling personal motive to go to war. His best friend had perished in the quixotic and foolhardy 1908 incursion to Palomas, Chihuahua. Manrique had followed Práxedis at every turn and into any scrape (Figure 16.3). Together, they had renounced their inheritances. Manrique had given up a good government job in the state of Guanajuato to live, with Práxedis, the miserable life of the worker; he had gone across the border with him, and had followed every one of his friend's initiatives. And together, they went to the revolt of 1908, where Manrique was killed.

Práxedis retold Manrique's death in the pages of *Regeneración* as part of an effort to bring the heroism of the revolutionary past into the present and could not exclude himself from its implications. Manrique, Práxedis wrote, loved two things most of all, his mother and the revolution. Manrique was a man of truth, but he died telling a "sublime lie." He had been mortally wounded, but was still alive when the federal troops captured and questioned him. In order to protect his comrades, Manrique told them his name was Otilio Madrid:

> It was that very Otilio Madrid whom they called the chief of the bandits at Palomas. That was the man who lived for the truth and who died shrouded in a sublime lie and whose pale lips spoke two names in their final shudder: the name of his dear mother, and mine—his brother, who still lives to make justice in his honor and to continue the struggle for which he spilt his blood. His brother, who lives to bring the people's passivity to a close with the youthful and heroic silhouette of the one who was sacrificed at Palomas."[51]

the principals were dead, Enrique claimed in detailed accounts to have taken part in the campaign."[54]

According to Liberal rumor transmitted to Albro, Enrique had shot himself on purpose. Albro then shows that Enrique communicated to Práxedis Ricardo's own sense that the intellectual heads of the junta should not risk their lives in battle. Albro does not believe that this caused a rift between Ricardo and Práxedis. There is, however, no doubt that there was tension there. Ethel herself recalls the months before the outbreak of the revolution as being dominated by the drama of Práxedis's decision to go to war: "In memory, that period before the revolution is revived by one event—the departure of Práxedis Guerrero.... of his talents and revolutionary spirit, was easily in second place. I remember how reluctant the Junta members were to give him permission to leave when he declared his intent to take a personal role in the fight."[55]

Ethel did not pick up on the barbs that Práxedis sent the junta in his *Regeneración* writings on the primacy of action, but when he finally left for the front, in November 1910, he left the junta with a challenge. Jesús González Monroy, who was a member of the junta at that time, said that he and the other men living in the *Regeneración* offices felt the barb sharply: "Plus, we had nailed in our minds and our conscience the one fiery word that Práxedis left for us, by way of an *adieu*, written on the windows that looked onto the street. It was: [are you] MEN? [¿*HOMBRES*?]"[56]

The fact that the challenge also stung Enrique Flores Magón is suggested, once again, in a careful reading of Enrique's self-glorifying memoir, which was composed when there were no living witnesses to contradict it. According to that version, Práxedis and Enrique set out to the 1908 revolt together, and Enrique masterminded the plan of attack, with Práxedis enthusiastically following his lead. Enrique led the attack on Palomas and held Manrique in his arms while the great Patroclus expired: "With sobs drowning in my throat, I leaned over Francisco Manrique. There was no longer any sign of life in him. I left with my soul in agony. Silently, our small group left the damned place where Death hunted down my dear comrade, and where Chance ruined my plan."[57]

Enrique then went on to explain that Práxedis's 1910 revolutionary attack in Chihuahua had been done in exact imitation of the strategy that Enrique had devised for the revolution in 1908. As in 1908, it was a noble and necessary sacrifice: "Prax left without consulting us, on an adventure that was as foolish as the one at Palomas. But he decided that something had to be done to keep the Revolution that the Liberal Party wanted from extinction." Práxedis's heroic action at Janos then relit a revolutionary fire that was about to die out: "Prax's attack, and his assassination, are what saved the Revolution!"[58]

In short, Enrique claimed that Práxedis's departure, though unauthorized by the Magón brothers, was supposed to have replicated a strategy that had been devised and put in practice by Enrique in 1908. These contorted mnemonic acrobatics strongly suggest a feeling of guilt and shame with regard to Práxedis, for we know that Enrique did not participate in the 1908 attack on Palomas and was nowhere near Manrique when he died. And Manrique's death scene in Enrique's arms, too, is stolen from Práxedis.

I suspect that Ricardo may not have felt as personally wounded by Práxedis's attempt to shame the men into action, except perhaps with sadness. He could not come out in the open and say that to him, some men were more valuable than others, just as he could not say that in his view, *Regeneración* was of greater long-term relevance than fighting at the front. He who had said that the bullet was his ballot could not turn around and express all of this openly. So with much regret, Ricardo and the junta named Práxedis general commander of all Liberal forces in the field and let him go.

The tension between "father" and "son" seems to have found final expression in Práxedis's choice of executor for his final will. It was Ethel, and not Ricardo. "One afternoon in November," Ethel wrote,

> he came to our apartment. I was there alone. John was on his gun buying adventure. I was somewhat surprised to see Práxedis, who handed me a small japanned tin box, which contained all the treasures he possessed. "Send it to my sister Eloisa," he said, "if I don't come back," he said. "And I know I'm not coming back." As he spoke those dark prophetic words I could not speak. I was frozen with horror. He gave me Eloisa's address, and we bade each other goodbye."[59]

In December 1910, Práxedis G. Guerrero led a military incursion into Chihuahua. He and his men took Casas Grandes and then Janos, where, on December 30, he was shot dead.

CHAPTER SEVENTEEN

Revolutionary Commonalities

and Their Limits

Trying to Retake the Lead

When *Regeneración* finally reappeared, in early September 1910, a consensus was beginning to emerge in broader sectors of Mexican political society about the need for an armed uprising. Earlier that year, Francisco Madero had campaigned for the presidency and had been met by crowds of supporters across the country. Porfirio Díaz, who in 1908 had promised that he would welcome democratic opposition in this election, threw several thousand of Madero's supporters in jail while the elections were being held. Madero himself was imprisoned in San Luis Potosí's penitentiary on June 10 and was still in jail when the first issue of the new *Regeneración* appeared.

The junta of the Liberal Party made the best of this situation, using it to come out shooting, so to speak. Ricardo Flores Magón, Antonio Villarreal, and Librado Rivera were free and supported by an entirely novel notoriety in the United States, founded on a strong public denunciation of the Díaz regime as a slave autocracy. In Mexico, in the meantime, the dictatorship was crumbling. Maderista disaffection needed political expression, and the Liberals were in a strong position to call for revolution, since they were in the United States and so not immediately available to the Díaz police. Their leadership now had at least a measure protection, thanks to a host of American supporters.

Regeneración's gamble was simple. Madero had succeeded in rallying a broad electoral up-welling, supported by an ample network of anti-reelectionist political clubs. And yet, they believed, the man was weak. Madero had hoped, against reason and experience, that Díaz would respect the ballot. Now he and many of his supporters were in jail. It was time for Mexico to listen to the Liberals, who had been calling for armed revolt consistently since 1906.

The Liberal junta issued its call to arms with occasional barbs directed at an (unnamed) Madero, trying to remind readers of *Regeneración* that only the Liberals combined a deep understanding of political facts with the courage to do the manly thing—the courage to step up and shoot. So, for instance, on October 8, *Regeneración* published a piece remarking on the Mexican Congress's refusal to accept Madero's formal petition to declare Díaz's election null and void. The Liberals' position is perfectly summarized in this statement:

> This was foreseeable; there was no other way for the farce to conclude. Everyone, even the pacifists, even the ones who want peace at any price, knew how the electoral campaign would end: with prison for some of Díaz's opponents, death for some others, exile for yet others, and a cynical pronouncement of the election's legality by the lackeys of the dictatorship.
>
> The Liberal Party did not take part in this campaign. The Liberal Party knows, from its own experience, that peaceful struggle is entirely useless in Mexico and that the only route that is left for the people's improvement is armed revolt."[1]

This propaganda was intended to convince all those who just wanted peace—who, in the end, are always a majority—that peace was in fact not an option and to paint Maderismo as lacking in either realism or courage, or in both. The attack on Maderismo was implied, rather than explicit, because the Liberals still hoped to attract Madero's supporters. The propaganda also reminded readers that only the Liberal Party stood for the redistribution of agrarian property.

The Liberal strategy was well thought out, well timed, and well executed. A broad-based revolutionary sentiment was indeed rising in Mexico and among Mexicans in the United States. Nor did Liberal calls for social justice fall on deaf ears. There was, however, an obstacle standing in the way of the junta's ascent. Thanks to the intervention of Finance Minister José Yves Limantour, who was a family friend of the Maderos, Francisco Madero was allowed to escape from prison, and he entered the United States on October 6h, 1910, crossing the border to San Antonio disguised as a railway mechanic. Quick to take the pulse of the situation, Madero issued a revolutionary plan immediately after his arrival in San Antonio and backdated it to October 5, so that it would appear as having been issued from within Mexico, rather than from the United States, always a point of vulnerability for the junta, as well.

In that call to arms, Madero reminded his readers that the Anti-Reelectionist Party had tried every legal method within its reach: "Imitating the wise customs of the republican nations, I crossed the republic making a call on my compatriots. My campaign tours were veritable triumphal marches, because everywhere the people—electrified by the magic words '*Sufragio Efectivo, No Reelección*' [True Suffrage, No Reelection]—offered proof of its unbreakable commitment to obtaining these redemptive principles."[2]

After Madero's imprisonment, the Anti-Reelectionist Party had appealed to the Mexican Congress, asking that the elections be declared null and void, and their petition was spurned. Because the Mexican people are sovereign and their rights were denied by the dictatorship, Madero proclaimed that the election of 1910 was illegal and declared himself provisional president of the republic while the people toppled Díaz and carried out a new, free, and fair election. Madero then "designated Sunday 20 of November next, so that from six P.M. forward, all of the localities of the Republic arise in arms under the following Plan."

As a result, the Liberal junta enjoyed barely one month of being the only party that stood openly for revolution. As of early October, it had to compete with Maderismo, which had at its back a much broader base of political clubs, an effective, widely publicized presidential campaign with a brave leader, Madero, at its head, and the indignity of the Díaz reelection, during which the popular candidate had been jailed. In short, the Liberal junta had been released from jail too late. It did not have time enough to develop a political organization that might truly compete with Madero's.

Simultaneity

One peculiar fact about Mexico's Liberal revolutions (1906, 1908, and 1910) is that they were supposed to be responses to a convocation. The liberal leaders always envisioned a simultaneous uprising throughout Mexico.

Regeneración had provided the Liberals with the conviction that every town in every state of the nation had its oppressed peoples, suffering under the boot of the same system of exploitation and ready to rise at the call of a brave leader. Madero had gained a similar conviction by other means—his Spiritism led him to conceive of his historic role in messianic terms, and his experience during the presidential campaign, in which his personal courage corresponded with an upsurge of popular support, sealed that conviction, making it seem true incontestable. Revolution would be like a brushfire. Fast, uncontrollable, unquenchable. But a close look at these engagements to revolt provides useful clues as to the differences in strategy between Madero and the Liberals.

In 1906 and 1908, the Liberals chose the date of each revolt carefully, following a logic of vindication and, often, of revenge. The 1906 revolution was set for September 16, Independence Day, as a vindication of national independence. In 1908, when the Liberals tried again to rise, they set the date for June 25, in commemoration of—and as revenge for—the Veracruz Massacre of 1879 perpetrated by Díaz against supporters of his former rival, Sebastián Lerdo de Tejada. The Liberals chose such emblematic dates because they were not revolting in accordance with an electoral calendar. The rebellion needed some kind of pretext, and that could be found only in the vindication of a patriotic memory.

In 1910, on the contrary, the call to revolution was dictated by the upheaval generated by the election—there was no need to wait for a symbolic date. For the Liberals, though, setting the date for revolt was still a delicate matter, because they needed to coordinate with the Madero people, who were by far in the majority and so were in a position to dictate the timing of the simultaneous outbreak. And, indeed, it was Madero who set the date for November 20, although the Liberals scrambled to present the decision as if it had been made jointly. They tried to hide their weakness by emphasizing their own internal process of deliberation.

So, for instance, one of Ethel Duffy Turner's proudest moments—one of the times when she felt she had truly gained the trust of the inner circle of Liberal decision making—was precisely the time when the Junta "decided" upon the date of the uprising. Here is how Ethel told it:

> One afternoon Ricardo and Enrique Flores Magón, Librado Rivera, and Práxedis Guerrero invited John and me to go into an inner, very private office, as they had something to tell us. What do you think it was? The date of the Revolution!

They had such confidence in us that they told us November 20 would be the date the Revolution would start....

You know, it's one of my proud memories that they had such confidence. It did start on November 20, although it didn't get on its way so quickly. They had the same date with Madero. They had made an agreement."[3]

But it was Madero, and not the Liberals, who had decided the starting date. Ricardo Flores Magón admitted this in an article in which he explained the differences between the PLM and Maderismo: "The revolution that is now going on in Mexico and that seems, at this moment, to be extending its influence, has our heartiest endorsement. Hundreds of the men in the field are members of the Liberal Party. Many of the officers are Liberals. Our own personal representatives are on the ground. This is true, although the revolution was precipitated by Madero and his friends."[4] The backroom decision that Ethel wrote about with such gravity and emotion was in fact a rear-guard action of minor consequence: the junta was compelled to follow Madero's lead or else be condemned to irrelevance.

Thus, in its November 16, 1910, military instructions to the Veracruz leader Donato Padua, the Junta Organizadora explained:

> it seems that Madero is preparing a "personalist" movement that will start on the 20th of this month, or on December 1 at the latest, and if the movement takes place, we Liberals will have the best opportunity that we will get to rebel as well. For this reason the Junta recommends that you prepare yourself and that you recommend to your friends that they be ready, so that if Maderista perturbations begin, we make the best of the ensuing confusion to stage a general Liberal uprising.[5]

In the end, then, and despite his pacifism, it was Madero, and not the Liberals, who "precipitated" the date for revolution, and the solemn junta "decision" to start the revolution on November 20 meant very little indeed. Madero's choice of date, on the contrary, was determined by the need to strike while there was still electoral indignation and before Díaz could settle matters with President Taft and either prosecute him in Texas for violation of the neutrality laws or extradite him because he had escaped from prison in Mexico. Thus, the revolution was quickly set for November 20—a date that was dictated by very immediate tactical considerations.

Commonalities and Differences

If the Mexican Revolution were an alcoholic beverage, it would be a port—a mixture, in other words, of something fermented (a wine) and something distilled (a brandy). The ferment was caused by the strain on Mexican agrarian life, on villages, on families, and on individual peasants. The distillate that gave the peasant ferment the medium to coalesce by way of ideology and by providing occasions to rise up together, was prepared by people who were generally literate (though they were often new readers and writers) and who were often geographically mobile or living in what some historians have called "transitional modes," as ranchers who were also seasonally miners, schoolteachers who did skilled manual labor, artisans who had been proletarianized, peasants who worked in commerce.

From a cultural point of view, the mobile and literate milieu was distilled from a variety of brews, manifested in a number of competing or complementary "isms": liberalism, modernizing Catholicism, nationalism, Protestantism, Spiritism, Jacobinism, Socialism, and, in the case of Ricardo and his closest group, anarchistic communism.

When we read in the lives of many of the individuals who made up what I refer to here as the revolutionary "distillate," which could also be called the more modern wing of the revolution (as historian François Xavier Guerra had it) or the more ideological wing, we find quite a lot of movement between these various persuasions and often a combination of them in a single individual.[6] Did these differences matter much? Were there shared elements between them that allowed for their reconciliation?

Spirituality

Much has been made of the fact that Francisco I. Madero was Kardecist Spiritist. Novels have been written about that and psychological portraits of the man seldom fail to emphasize it. And, in fact, understanding that Madero was a Spiritist is important. At the same time, it was by no means as singular or as eccentric a persuasion as is sometimes imagined, and neither were the various forms of spirituality as divorced from the worldview of radical revolutionaries as one might think.

Práxedis Guerrero, for example, who had become the poster boy of the Partido Liberal Mexicano by 1910, had flirted with Protestantism and Spiritism, was influenced by Tolstoy's spiritual renunciation, and eventually espoused revolutionary violence and anarchism. And it is not the case that sectarian spiritual beliefs were simply stepping stones on the road to atheistic enlightenment and radicalism. People could also move in the opposite direction or maintain various practices simultaneously. Práxedis Guerrero remained a vegetarian, for example, despite his exaltation of armed revolt.

Elizabeth Trowbridge remained a Socialist Party member from her youth until her death in 1934, but she was also a vegetarian and a Theosophist throughout that entire period.[7] Sometimes one of these tendencies was used to modulate the other. So, for instance, Elizabeth wrote to Ethel in 1925, "I've been studying somewhat, chiefly along theosophical lines.... I think that I am more radical than ever though I have more toleration than formerly for the opinions of others."[8] Other times, a spiritualist tendency was what gave a sense of humanity and purpose to militancy. Vegetarianism, for example, stemmed from a love of animals and a concern with suffering, both of which were of a piece with the defense of the human and especially with commitment to sacrifice for the lowly and for the defenseless.

Elizabeth was reflective on the interplay between spiritual belief and radical behavior. I quote from her at length because explicit meditations on this subject are rare in this group, and yet Elizabeth's ideas on the subject reflect a broader tendency that can be found not only with regard to spiritual practices such as Theosophy, vegetarianism, or Spiritism, but also with regard to art and aesthetics.

> I believe, however, that, either through my own feelings or those of persons close enough for me to "sense it" all, I've known about every feeling that a rebel can experience—I whose truly greatest desire is to serve Humanity intelligently under the direction of persons or powers better and wiser than myself! It isn't "authority" that I object against, it's authority that one can't trust. And I'm not a "lamb" (though Manuel used to call me one). It takes more than talk to "put things over" me.
>
> Really, Ethel, I believe that persons like you and me who are interested in matters beside our purely personal matters need a belief in something beyond the material aspects of events more than the average individual needs it. Most mortals have at least a few periods when they're not in difficulties but the great surge of human unrest is always there for those who can feel it. The only spiritual belief that has ever

touched me is Theosophy—and that has held through every storm. Whatever balance and reasonableness I have or ever hope to attain is due to it.[9]

Much is said in these two paragraphs: the feeling of connection between kindred spirits who are cruelly separated and often facing "self-inflicted" difficulties alone, but who are also always making sense of their hardships and triumphs in mental dialogue with one another. This sense of unity in separation, of a shared and common sense and purpose, also helps account for the respect and salience of love in this group of revolutionaries, which stands in such stark contrast with romantic attachments that seem to have characterized *la bola*, that is, the roaming revolutionary peasant bands that swarmed through Mexico.

Here, revolutionary activity implied a cultivated interiority, an ascetic quality that led to an almost Neoplatonic form of spirituality—Theosophy, Spiritism, vegetarianism, astrology. There, in the revolutionary bands that were scattered across the Mexican countryside, the sentiment was more of one who has been uprooted by a powerful gale—enmeshed in the tumbleweed of *la bola*—and who finds communion not in the stars, but rather in the violent confusion of the revolutionary mass.

In a remarkable passage, Martín Luis Guzmán described *la bola* as a pulsating and amorphous life form. He was in Culiacán, Sinaloa, with the victorious troops of the revolution. It was night, and the city was hollow, a ravaged and empty shell, hidden beneath the luxuriant vegetation. Martín Luis had made his way to meet Carrasco's men, who were massed together in a house. When he entered the dark room, a strong arm threw itself over his shoulder and pinned him there. He was helpless. His inebriated companion put a bottle to Martín Luis's mouth. "I felt the cold and sticky mouth of the glass bottle against my lips, and the mezcal ran down my breast. He then withdrew the bottle from me and drank from it in big gulps."

The mass was at once silent and connected through chaotic murmurs and songs. The blackness of the night was punctuated by red flashes of guns occasionally being shot into the air:

What a strange mass inebriation, as silent and sad as the darkness in which it hid! A gregarious and lightless drunkenness, as if of termites, happy in their shared stench and touch. It was the brutality of the mezcal at its fullest, put in the service of the most rudimentary needs of liberation and of inhibition. Splashing about in the mud, lost in the shades of both night and conscience, all of those men seemed to have resigned their humanity the moment they came together. They formed something like the soul of a monstrous reptile, with hundreds of heads and thousands of feet, dragging itself, clumsy and drunk, between the walls of a murky street, in a city with no inhabitants.[10]

That was the "ferment," momentarily enveloping and over-whelming the "distillate," pinning it down, putting mezcal to its mouth and threatening to dissolve it completely. But our protago-nists, our movement in the United States, at this time, at least, were still a relatively unadulterated distillate, still in their purest form.

María Brousse, too, like Elizabeth, was a member of the Socialist Party, though she had stronger anarchist leanings. We learn from her letters to her niece, Teresa, that she, too, became a Spiritist. At least she was that by the 1930s. Thus, she writes to her niece from Colima:

> Tere let me know if Jacintita is with you I want to write to her so that she talks to Teja to ask if she knows the school of Joaquín Trincado it is more advanced than that of Allan Kardec and the practice of this new school is very vast and fast it has many public conferences in the "*Eraldo Espírita*" [sic].... I'm very happy with the knowledge I've acquired.... [W]e started to practice and got very good results from things that the Brothers from Space [*hermanos del Espacio*] told us.[11]

Perhaps María turned to the "Brothers from Space" after the deaths of the two people who were dearest to her—Ricardo and her daughter, Lucía. I do not know. But what is certain is that María's turn to Spiritism did not come at the expense of her political activ-ism. She continued to be a militant throughout her life. Militants such as Enrique Flores Magón, who was not a Spiritist, nevertheless also were open to believing in its powers. Thus, Enrique recounted how he was saved from being captured in El Paso by editor Lauro Aguirre's wife, a Spiritist and medium, who ran to Prisciliano Silva's house to "tell me that I was going to be arrested by secret service agents if I didn't clear out of there in five minutes' time. She left, while, out of curiosity, I observed from a nearby house and saw that, in fact, what she said happened just when she said—it was no fiction."[12]

Though not a persuaded Spiritist, Enrique was a Freemason, and he came to have a high rank in his lodge. So were Fernando Palomares and Filomeno Mata, the editor of Mexico City's *El Diario del Hogar*, who had taken the three Flores Magón brothers under his protection and wing at the start of their journalistic careers. And many, many others. Librado Rivera was originally a Protestant and a Spiritist;[13] Juana B. Gutiérrez de Mendoza, the radical editor of the Mexico City journal *Véspers* and close ally of Ricardo in the early years, was originally a Methodist.[14] Provided that it had no connection with the Catholic clergy, spirituality, in short, was a background element—not universally shared, but common—in the lives of these revolutionaries.

Ideological Tensions

By the end of 1910, an ideological fracture divided the great Liberal family into three positions. The most moderate, led by Francisco I. Madero, sought democratic reform: free and fair elections, freedom of association and of the press, freedom to unionize, and some—quite vague—acknowledgment of the need to redress injustice around land distribution.

Madero's Plan de San Luis made it very clear that it stood for legality and for institutional stability and was against revolution except as final recourse, with Articles 8, 9, and 11 devoted to following the laws of war, avoiding the summary execution of counterrevolutionaries, avoiding damaging the lives and properties of foreigners, and disciplining militia members who engaged in looting or killing prisoners. In short, the moderate position sought to instate a democratic system and to protect individual rights. Its social demands were vague.

The second position, best represented by socialists such as like Antonio Villarreal, Jesús Flores Magón, Lázaro Gutiérrez de Lara, and Juan and Manuel Sarabia, was that although the ultimate goal of collective political action was socialism, Mexico was a backward country that could not realistically aspire to make such a leap in a single bound. Socialists needed to support industrialization alongside unionization. This position saw the fulfillment of program of the moderate (Madero) wing as a necessary, but insufficient condition to attain its goals. The moderate position needed to be supplemented with a militant approach to labor organizing and a real commitment to social and agrarian reform. The Socialists sought a government that would foster investment, but curb the power of foreign trusts, curtail support for foreign capitalists who had favored the enslavement of Mexico's population, fight monopolies, and improve competitive conditions across the board.

The Socialists and the moderates shared something else: they both had concluded that contrary to the official image that was so constantly touted, Porfirio Díaz had not been a very effective modernizer. John Kenneth Turner put the matter most convincingly:

> Did Porfirio Díaz "make" modern Mexico? Is Mexico modern? Hardly. Neither industrially nor in the matter of public education, nor in the form of government is Mexico modern. Industrially, it is at least a quarter century behind the times; in the matter of public education it is at least a half century behind the times; in its system of government it is worthy of the Egypt of three thousand years ago.... The fact is that whatever modernization Mexico has had during the past thirty-four years must be attributed to evolution—that is, to the general progress of the world—instead of to Porfirio Díaz.[15]

This sentiment was shared by Madero, who was a modernizing entrepreneur himself—Berkeley-educated in agronomy, Paris-educated in politics and philosophy—Madero had practiced a modernizing and humane sort of entrepreneurship in his estate at San Pedro de las Colonias, Coahuila, and he was certain that a different approach to labor relations was possible. However, Madero and the Socialists parted ways when it came to social reform. So, for instance, Jesús Flores Magón, who was brought into Madero's cabinet belatedly to appease disgruntled radicals, resigned his post as minister of interior in 1912 after an altercation with the president over whether or not the revolution had accomplished its mission with the latter's democratic reforms.[16]

The third Liberal ideological position was also the most minoritarian: anarchism. That faction had its ideological heart with Ricardo Flores Magón, and its most powerful armed faction eventually identified with Emiliano Zapata. Anarchists were against elections because they saw voting as an instrument of the state. The "three-headed hydra" that they sought to destroy was "Capital, the

State and the Clergy." Their strategy was "direct action," that is, seizing the means of production.

Anarchists sought to combine a communism that they believed was still in the living memory of Mexico's peasants with the benefits of progress and civilization. Like the socialists, they favored equality between the sexes, progressive education, and enlightenment, though they were against education that gave students titles of privilege. They believed in the universality of labor.

Before the outbreak of the revolution, however, the anarchist position had not yet published a program of its own. Rather, the junta still officially subscribed to the 1906 program of the Liberal Party, published out of St. Louis. Written by Ricardo Flores Magón, Juan Sarabia, and Antonio I. Villarreal at a time when their differences were not yet so great, the 1906 program called for reforms to the democratic apparatus (reducing the presidential tenure back to four-year terms, eliminating the office of the vice president, and suppression of compulsory military service and conscription), compulsory universal public education for all children under fourteen, shutting down all Catholic schools; all foreigners who acquired property in Mexico became by that fact Mexican citizens, and, so they could be governed by Mexican law; confiscation of all ill-gotten properties of government functionaries; forcing landowners to make their lands productive or lose them to the state; and restoring lands to the Yaqui in Sonora and to the Maya on the Yucatan Peninsula.

The 1906 program was indeed a remarkable document, because its seven sections and fifty-two points offered a set of precise social demands that were by no means limited to the purely political. At the same time, it was decidedly not an anarchist document, insofar as it proposed to reform, rather than to abolish, the state and to curtail, rather than abolish, private property.[17]

Indeed, there was no explicit anarchist program written up as a party platform until the September 23, 1911 manifesto, which was published after the military defeat of the PLM in Baja California and Chihuahua and at a time when the key members of the junta were under indictment and once again awaiting trial. In some ways, it was precisely the military defeat of the Liberal organization that allowed the junta to express its ideas publicly, hoping thereby to energize and guide the most radical revolutionary elements who were operating in the field.

Accordingly, the September 23 manifesto begins with a call to abolish private property and, as a corollary, to abolish all the political, economic, social, religious, and moral institutions that came together to stifle the free association of human beings. The Liberal Party "recognizes that all human beings—by the mere fact of existing—have a right to enjoy each and every advantage that modern civilization has to offer, because these advantages are product of the effort and sacrifice of the working classes of all times."[18] The junta then called for direct action—taking the land, taking the factories, eliminating the mediating role of the church and the state.

Criminal Inversion

On the eve of the revolution, then, there was a call for a simultaneous uprising in all of Mexico, dated for November 20, 1910, at 6:00 p.m., with three families of Mexican Liberals—moderates, Socialists, and anarchists—coming together briefly. Close beneath the surface of that confluence, however, there were tensions between revolutionaries who wished to achieve a quick restoration of political order, others who planned to push the new government to embrace difficult, but popular economic reforms, and yet others who were interested in the destruction of the state and private property altogether.

These differences were made apparent around the issue of legality and criminality. Alongside the ideal of simultaneity of rebellion, there was always the image of revolution as societal inversion. The whole of Mexican society had been turned into slaves; honorable citizens had been turned into animals; men had lost their virility. So, for example, the feminist Liberal paper *La Voz de la Mujer*, published out of El Paso, called on Mexico's women to refuse sex until their men rebelled:

> We should renounce contact with men who are slaves and so avoid having cowards for children. The duty of bequeathing an inheritance of liberty to our offspring comes before our domestic happiness. Our nature should not be spent raising eunuchs! Our existence should not exhaust itself feeding parasites! Our cares and worries should not be devoted to raising ailing serfs!
> "The Fatherland needs heroes!"[19]

These radical women refused to have children with slaves. In a kind of inversion of *Lysistrata*, editor Isidra de Cárdenas called on women to deny sex to all men *except* to those who would go to war.

This sense of social inversion touched the problem of criminality, too. Indeed, criminalizing opponents was a fundamental resource both during the Porfiriato and during the revolution—so much so that Blas Lara used the neologism *criminar*, to signify the procedure of transforming a subject into a criminal by way of labeling. Thus, when his father, Beliserio, escaped from Yucatán, to which he had been deported, and managed to return to his village, he expressed his dislike of priests to a neighbor, who responded: "You're right to say that rather than love, those people hate. They are capable of making a poor person criminal [*criminar*] even for not doffing his hat."[20] Similarly, Blas's grandfather warned that "when the man who is charged has money, he is let go; when he is poor, he goes to prison or to the gallows. There are many innocents in jail while men who should be there run free. Earthly justice is purchased with money."[21]

This habit of incriminating—very literally making criminals of one's opponents—was maintained during the Mexican Revolution. All men in arms were *bandoleros* to the established governments. Revolutionary factions often referred to one another as "bandits" once they came into direct conflict. So, for instance, in the Carrancista press, Pancho Villa's followers, who had been "revolutionaries" as long as Villa formed part of Carranza's Constitutionalist army, instantly turned into "bandits" once the two factions confronted one another.[22] Similarly, Liberal and Orozquista rebels soon turned into *bandoleros* in the eyes of the Madero government. The United States press, for its part, referred to practically any Mexican revolutionary as a "bandito."

Indeed, the criminalization of opponents was so commonplace that factions that were routinely targeted as bandits—the Zapatistas and the Liberals, for instance—at times came to defend the label and even to adopt it as a badge of honor. "Take the land!" was the Liberals' motto during the revolution, and it was understood as an act whereby proletarians took back property that had been stolen. Property was theft; recovering it was justice.

Jack London, too, captured this spirit of transgression in his speech of support for the Liberal campaign in Baja California at the beginning of 1911:

We Socialists, anarchists, hobos, chicken thieves, outlaws and undesirable citizens of the U.S. are with you heart and soul. You will notice that we are not respectable. Neither are you. No revolutionary can possibly be respectable in these days of the reign of property. All the names you are being called, we have been called. And when graft and greed get up and begin to call names, honest men, brave men, patriotic men and martyrs can expect nothing else than to be called chicken thieves and outlaws.

So be it. But I for one wish there were more chicken thieves and outlaws of the sort that formed the gallant band that took Mexicali.

I subscribe myself a chicken thief and revolutionist.[23]

Internationalism in the Solidarity Movement

Ricardo Flores Magón is said routinely to have spent eight hours of each day attending to correspondence. Indeed, all of the men of the junta engaged their correspondents for many hours each day. The junta's need for allies brought it into conversation with political allies, political parties, and unions. Most important among the latter was the IWW, which had been formed in 1905, and the Western Federation of Miners, which had begun admitting Mexicans into its ranks after 1903. Among the anarchist newspapers that mattered most were Emma Goldman's New York–based *Mother Earth* and Alexander Berkman's San Francisco paper, *The Blast*.

The junta's connections with Europe became more important in this period, too. The unionization of Mexicans in the United States generated a working-class cosmopolitanism that was rare among workers in Mexico and also quite distinct from Mexican upper-class cosmopolitanism (Figure 17.1). Indeed, this working-class cosmopolitanism extended beyond union relations per se and into various spheres of life, sometimes in unsuspected combinations, as, for instance, in the case of hundreds of single Punjabi migrant men who married Mexican women and begot cohorts of "Punjabi Mexicans."[24] Mexican workers in California and in Washington State often had some familiarity with Italian, and maybe spoke a little Yiddish, too. It was in the United States that Enrique and Ricardo Flores Magón learned English, French, Italian. and Portuguese.

I do not mean to say that there was no international element among Mexico's factory workers. Mexico's rising new industries—railroads,

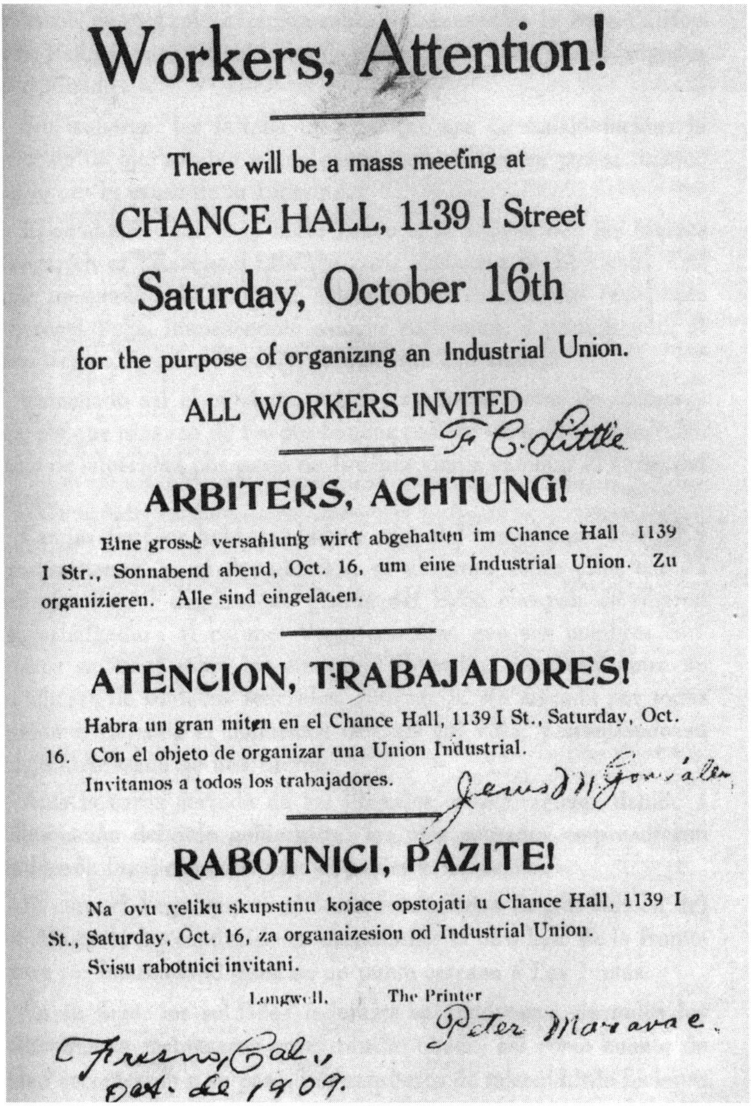

Workers, Attention!

There will be a mass meeting at

CHANCE HALL, 1139 I Street

Saturday, October 16th

for the purpose of organizing an Industrial Union.

ALL WORKERS INVITED

F. C. Little

ARBITERS, ACHTUNG!

Eine grosse versahlung wird abgehalten im Chance Hall 1139 I Str., Sonnabend abend, Oct. 16, um eine Industrial Union. Zu organizieren. Alle sind eingelaoen.

ATENCION, TRABAJADORES!

Habra un gran mitęn en el Chance Hall, 1139 I St., Saturday, Oct. 16. Con el objeto de organizar una Union Industrial. Invitamos a todos los trabajadores. *Jesus M. Gonzáles*

RABOTNICI, PAZITE!

Na ovu veliku skupstinu kojace opstojati u Chance Hall, 1139 I St., Saturday, Oct. 16, za organaizesion od Industrial Union. Svisu rabotnici invitani.

Longwell. The Printer *Peter Maravae.*

Fresno, Cal., Oct. de 1909.

Figure 17.1 A multilingual flyer for a meeting of workers in Fresno held by the Industrial Workers of the World. Proletarian cosmopolitanism has been at the heart of the Mexican experience in the United States for more than a hundred years. From Jesús González Monroy, *Ricardo Flores Magón y su actitud en la Baja California* (Mexico City: Editorial Academia Literaria, 1962).

steel, glass, breweries, mining, and oil—regularly imported skilled labor from Europe and the United States. But because these foreign workers were a labor aristocracy there, their unions and associations were adamant about keeping Mexicans out. Indeed, foreign workers in Mexico probably formed the single most racist sector of the foreign population in that country.[25]

On the American side of the border, the playing field was a bit different. Unions had rules about keeping out non-European migrants, especially Mexicans and Chinese, and Mexicans in the Southwest were generally paid less—often substantially less—than "Anglos" doing the same jobs, but at least some all-white unions were under pressure to admit Mexicans, because keeping them out meant that Mexicans would undercut union wages. Also, closing off the Mexican border was a lot harder than closing off the ports on the Pacific, so seeking something like the Chinese Exclusion Act, but for Mexicans, was not realistic. Nor was there much support for it. As a result, there were two diverging strategies emerging in the unions in this period—either maintain an all-white policy and use union muscle to dissuade employers from hiring Mexicans, or support Mexican organizations. Both strategies had supporters.

Beyond official union policies, however, labor mobility in this period generated a lot of informal communication between workers, and although this communication was sometimes received with suspicion and prevented by the segregation of living quarters in labor camps, Mexican workers often developed good relations with Italian, Spanish, and Russian workers, for instance, and learned words in their languages, as well as organizing practices and ideologies, including anarchism and socialism. Beginning around 1907, labor-oriented papers such as the New York *Call*, the *International Socialist Review*, the Kansas City publication *Appeal to Reason*, and the Western Federation of Miners' *Miner's Magazine*, as well as local Socialist papers in Los Angeles, the Imperial Valley, San Francisco, and elsewhere, then the anarchist press—*Mother Earth*, *The Blast*, and others—began to cover Mexican affairs, albeit occasionally.

The significance of these relations came to be such that when *Regeneración* was reissued in September 1910, it appeared for the first time with an English-language page and an English-language editor. There were three English-language editors in the life of *Regeneración*: Alfred Sanftleben (for a four-month period in 1910),

Ethel Duffy Turner (for a seven-month period in 1910 to 1911), and William C. Owen (starting in mid-1911 for roughly for a six-year period). Each of these editors had connections to political organizations outside the Mexican sphere—in the Socialist Party in the United States (Sanftleben and Ethel) or with members of the European and American anarchist movement (Owen). For a four-month period in 1911, after the capture of Ricardo, Enrique, Librado, and Anselmo Figueroa, an Italian-language section of *Regeneración* was published under the editorship of Ludovico Caminita and was an expression of the depth of Italian union support for the Liberal revolution, particularly in its early phase.[26]

It is important to underline two conclusions about the international character of the revolution and the Partido Liberal Mexicano. First, "international relations" were vital for the junta, and they involved the grassroots mobilization of opinion in the United States and beyond. This contrasted with the situation both of the Mexican government and of Mexican revolutionary groups operating within Mexico, who had to concern themselves keenly with relationships with various governments (especially the U.S. government, but also those of Germany and Great Britain), but who often did not rely crucially on mobilizing public opinion. Second, the junta's cosmopolitanism was sensitive to the broader experiences of the Mexican working class in the United States, an experience that was not shared by working classes in Mexico.

PART FOUR

High Tide (1909–1912)

CHAPTER EIGHTEEN

El Coronel de los '41

The Split with Madero

Ricardo's break with Madero produced a deep rift inside the Liberal Party from which it would never recover. The division could be presented two ways: Maderistas versus true Liberals, or alternatively, anarchists versus the Socialist Party. After the split, the Partido Liberal Mexicano, headed by Ricardo, was finally free to present its goal, the abolition of property, openly. But this development also made the party eccentric in relation to Mexico's principal revolutionary movement. After the split, the Liberal organization moved from the heart of the revolution to its margins, even while its call for direct action and "Land and Freedom" moved toward the center of the revolutionary aspirations of many people. Ricardo himself was left in a position reminiscent of one of Bob Dylan's verses, learning that "there's no success like failure, and that failure is no success at all."

The split occurred in three stages. The initial moment involved an attempt to establish something like a "separate, but equal" policy with regard to Madero's anti-reelection movement.

The junta tacitly recognized that Liberals were in the minority with regard to Madero's Anti-Reelectionist Party. Liberals in Mexico were losing ground to the Madero movement, with old Liberal sympathizers such as Antonio Díaz Soto y Gama and journalist Paulino Martínez shifting to the Madero side, while staunch Liberal supporters such as Hilario Salas and Donato Padua of Veracruz had to negotiate with the Maderista clubs and play second fiddle in strategy and planning.

As early as July 1909, Hilario Salas, who was trying to spread Liberal influence to Puebla, Tlaxcala, and Mexico City from the Liberal stronghold of southern Veracruz, wrote from Atlixco that his strategy was to try make alliances with anti-reelectionist clubs with the understanding that each group would keep its own ideology and that the Liberals would not support any "personalist candidate" (meaning Madero), but only their 1906 platform of reform. However, in that same letter, Salas described how the anti-reelectionists shunned his proposal. The Liberals were left with few options other than to join Madero or be excluded.[1]

In his memoir on the Liberal movement in Guerrero, Francisco Campos tells how the local Liberal organization got sideswiped by Johnnies-come-lately, rebels with no ideological formation, such as Ambrosio Figueroa, who allied themselves with Madero. Because of the strength of the Liberal organization in that region, Madero tried to bring Campos over to his cause, and when he failed, due to their differences over the issue of land reform, Campos reported that "in a huff, Mr. Madero said to me in San Lorenzo, Tehuacan, Puebla, that I was a demagogue and that he was not and never could be." However, Campos philosophized, "one has to be a demagogue to be a revolutionary. How could I be a revolutionary and not be a demagogue? Only by being a social counterrevolutionary."[2] By April 1911, the Madero allies under general Figueroa had the upper hand in Guerrero State.

Despite these early setbacks, the junta was confident that its radicalism would eventually gain their movement competitiveness with Maderismo. They were not entirely wrong about that, either. After all, Madero's plan was concerned almost exclusively with democratic reform, while the Liberals were calling for land distribution and workers' rights. The junta believed that if it could retain autonomy from Madero, they would eventually gain the upper hand.

But this "separate, but equal" policy was not what Madero and the Anti-Reelectionist Party wanted. Their aim was to topple Díaz, and doing that involved leading a unified movement. Madero knew that the Liberals were the most venerable symbol of anti-Díaz militancy, and so he sought a rapprochement. Emissaries were sent, and an electoral formula that included Ricardo Flores Magón as vice presidential candidate was explored. However, Ricardo rejected any participation in a Madero-led government, and *Regeneración* insinuated that political reform was nothing but the substitution of one dictator with another.

And the strategy of separate and distinct, but equal movements joining together for the same putative ends was problematic even within the Liberal camp, because some Liberals shared Madero's priorities regarding the toppling of Díaz and wished to coordinate with the Anti-Reelectionists in the military campaign. This, in fact, is what *Regeneración*'s English-language editor, the Socialist Alfred Sanftleben, believed, and it is what he printed in the English-language page in the early weeks of December 1910, only to be told by Ricardo the following week that this was no longer the policy. Because there was considerable ambiguity on this point among the Liberals, Ricardo's reaction surprised Sanftleben, who, unsure now that he understood or shared the ideals of the Liberals, resigned his post (Figure 18.1).

And the separation between the two movements posed an immediate problem on the ground: the organization of a coordinated military campaign. This quickly led to a split between the Liberals and the Maderistas. Madero had announced November 20 for the start of the revolt. As a result, the Díaz government was prepared for the uprising, and the Anti-Reelectionist movement was nipped in the bud across Mexico's network of cities, starting with the massacre of Aquiles Serdán and his family in the city of Puebla on November 20 itself.

Consequently, the Anti-Reelectionist revolt shifted from the city to the country, and especially to the Chihuahua-Durango region, where Pascual Orozco, Pancho Villa, and other, until then little-known local leaders, took charge. This development presented a challenge for Madero, since he now had to negotiate with a distinctly new set of actors. In such a context, Madero could ill afford to have a second group of active belligerents—the Liberals—with an alternative party organization, since they were bound, in the end, to compete for the loyalty of these same figures. In his Plan de San Luis, Madero had taken on the mantle of provisional president (he had, after all, been cheated of elections by Díaz) and had called for a new election after Díaz's fall. At that point, he had claimed, the Liberals would be able to participate as an independent political force, but Madero insisted that they should not function independently during the military campaign.[3]

In addition to the problem of competition for alliances with the new revolutionary warlords from Chihuahua, Madero was concerned with military discipline. His Plan de San Luis committed his troops to respecting the law, and he was adamantly against the application of "revolutionary justice." The Liberal Party, though

Figure 18.1 Alfred Sanftleben. This photo of Sanftleben seems to have been taken in Los Angeles later in his life. The cat, I think, betrays the sensibility of a romantic. Courtesy of the Bancroft Library, Ethel Duffy Turner Papers.

somewhat ambiguous on these points in the early weeks of revolution, very soon called for confiscation of property, a policy that included land invasion, shaking down capitalist firms for money, and looting. Madero understood that coordination in military matters with the Liberals therefore would involve violations of the regime of law and order for which he claimed to stand.

There could be no "separate, but equal" policy under these conditions of competition concerning both the end and the means of the rebellion. And indeed, as these strategic considerations unfolded very quickly into action, the tensions between Madero and the Liberals as led by Ricardo from Los Angeles came to a head.

The crisis occurred in mid-February 1911 with the first significant Liberal victory (the capture of Mexicali), followed by a military action by Madero in Casas Grandes, Chihuahua, where Liberal troops were invited to join Madero's army or to disband, while their leaders were captured and disarmed.

The open break with Madero was finally declared in the February 25, 1911, issue of *Regeneración* in a strident front-page article titled: "Madero Is a Traitor to Liberty." The article described the trap that Madero had set for the Liberals at the battle of Casas Grandes: how the Liberal General Prisciliano Silva and a few of his captains had been taken hostage, while his men were either disarmed or incorporated by Pancho Villa and how one of the Liberal leaders, Lázaro Gutiérrez de Lara, had betrayed the Liberal Army, switched over to the Madero side, and helped convince many Liberal soldiers to do the same. In that same February 25 issue, Ricardo announced that Antonio I. Villarreal was no longer a member of the Liberal junta. The announcement was reissued regularly in subsequent editions.[4]

In short, the first two stages of the Madero-Ricardo divorce were marked by some internal tear in the Liberal Party. The "separate but equal" stage, which was set forth with much ambiguity, cost the Liberals several leaders within Mexico—people such as Paulino Martínez and Antonio Díaz Soto y Gama—and it cost *Regeneración* its first English-language editor, the loyal Alfred Sanftleben. But even then, a deeper conflict was brewing under the surface, and it came into the open in February 1911, with the open break with Madero and a number of prominent desertions from the Liberal camp, including the second most senior junta member, Antonio I. Villarreal.

Although Antonio had no qualms about separating himself from Ricardo, given the latter's position on an alliance with Madero, he and Manuel Sarabia did in fact make inquiries into the matter of Madero and Lázaro Gutiérrez de Lara's alleged betrayal of Prisciliano Silva at Casas Grandes. Thus, an El Paso merchant named W. M. Love, who was close to the Liberals, responded to Antonio's inquiry on this matter, saying the Prisciliano Silva was a sick man, "very nervous and high tempered," and that Love knew for a fact that Silva had been maligning Madero in such a strident manner that in order to prevent friction between his men and Silva's, Madero had invited Silva to his tent, captured him, and then gone "before the crowds and spoke and informed them of what had taken place and consulted every man's opinion as to whether they wished to go forward or remain with Mr. Silva and the general opinion was to proceed so they did so."[5]

For example, from the Socialists, Ricardo's accusations against Lázaro brought forth an indignant response from Alfred Sanftleben, who wrote a letter of protest to the New York *Call* for having published Ricardo's denunciation of Madero and Lázaro's alleged betrayal. In that letter, Sanftleben protested the "vile attacks upon comrade De Lara who bravely fell in battle for his cause while his vilifiers are safely this side from the danger line."[6] Sanftleben went on to clarify that Lázaro was a Socialist, and not a member of the PLM, and that he had always supported unity in the face of the Díaz dictatorship: "Many times I listened to De Lara's speeches on the plaza and they were all for socialism, but also for unity of all elements." Finally, Sanftleben noted that when Hattie de Lara went to Ricardo to protest his portrayal of Lázaro as a traitor, "Magon admitted to Mrs. De Lara that his tale of the incident did not correspond with the facts, and yet he has not corrected."[7]

In fact, it mattered quite a lot that Ricardo's virulent denunciations of Madero came when Porfirio Díaz was still in office and the final outcome of the revolution was still very much in doubt. As a result, the Liberals would be charged by Madero sympathizers with supporting Díaz or even of being in his pay. Moreover, Ricardo's attack on Madero was believed by some to stem from personal passions—envy and spite. Thus, Manuel Sarabia wrote to Ethel when she reported on the break between Ricardo and Villarreal that the attack on Madero "is too passionate to find the approval of anybody."[8]

In February, the most prominent desertions were those of Antonio I. Villarreal and Lázaro Gutiérrez de Lara, but they were soon joined by many others, not only of the rank and file, but also among those who would go on to take leadership positions in the Maderista military campaign. Indeed, as soon as Ricardo announced Antonio's expulsion, junta member Jesús González wrote to Antonio from the border, asking him to wait for him so that they depart for Texas together.[9] One week earlier, Antonio had received a telegram from his father, Próspero Villarreal, letting him know that he had a lot of sympathizers in San Antonio,[10] and Antonio was able to enlist 160 workers when he arrived to El Paso, which was a sizable number for a Liberal chieftain to raise.[11] Villarreal also received supporters from the group in Douglas, Arizona.[12] In Los Angeles itself, there were Liberal factions that sided with Antonio over Ricardo.[13]

According Jesús Rangel, Villarreal misled forty-six Liberal groups in Mexico and the United States into thinking that he represented the Liberal Party and led them in his campaign to join Madero, including five hundred men that Rangel had raised and armed in Texas and Oklahoma.[14] Whether or not this is exact, it is indicative of the Antonio's pull among an important sector of the Liberals.

With Madero's triumph, in May 1911, the seceding faction would be further joined by Liberals who had been freed from the San Juan de Ulúa prison, including, most significantly, the Liberal "martyr" Juan Sarabia and the two leaders of the Cananea strike, Manuel Diéguez and Esteban Baca Calderón. By May, the bulk of the membership of the American and Mexican Socialist Parties had ceased supporting Ricardo and were rallying to build a post-Díaz Mexico. This included Manuel Sarabia and Elizabeth Trowbridge, who moved to Mexico City from their London exile by way of New York.

The final phase of the Ricardo-Madero drama occurred only a few months after the open break of February—in June 1911, after the abdication of Porfirio Díaz, which was negotiated in the Treaty of Ciudad Juárez after Ciudad Juárez fell to Pascual Orozco. At that time, thanks to some persuasion from erstwhile Liberals such as Juan Sarabia and Antonio Villarreal, Madero tried once again to extend an olive branch to Ricardo. This time, however, the carrot of reconciliation was presented together with the stick of repression.

The only place in Mexico where Liberal troops effectively controlled an area was in Baja California, where they held Mexicali and Tijuana. These two villages—for they were little more than villages at the time—were surrounded by the now Maderista Federal Army. The rebels in Mexicali had agreed to surrender to Madero's negotiators—the former Liberal leaders Jesús González Monroy and José María Leyva—while the federal officer in command decided to take Tijuana by fighting and defeated the Liberals even after they had agreed to lay down their guns.

Ricardo, for his part, received a peace offering from his brother Jesús and from Juan Sarabia, who went together to Los Angeles to negotiate with the junta in person. Ricardo had not seen Juan or Jesús for years, and presumably the meeting was filled with emotion. But Ricardo refused Madero's proposal to enter Mexican democratic politics, and he, Enrique, Librado, and Anselmo Figueroa were arrested by the Los Angeles police immediately following this refusal and charged yet again with violation of the neutrality laws, this time for the invasion of Baja California.

In both cases—the surrender of the rebels in Baja California and the imprisonment of the Liberal junta—Madero proved that he was now effectively a head of state. He had used the Federal Army to take control of Baja California; and he had used Mexican-American bilateral agreements to shut down the junta in the United States.

The Personal and the Political

The rupture inside the Liberal Party separated some of the men who had created the movement, and it separated them forever. Antonio I. Villarreal, who had been secretary of the junta for years, who had signed all of its official communiqués alongside Ricardo since 1906, who had been in prison with Ricardo and Librado in Los Angeles, Yuma, and Florence, Arizona, was forever estranged. So was Juan Sarabia, who had edited *El Hijo del Ahuizote*, who had been in prison with Ricardo in Belem in 1903, and who had been, until Práxedis's death, the Liberals' most beloved martyr, their great poet and a key ideologue. And so was Manuel Sarabia, also a Liberal hero, also imprisoned with the men in California and Arizona. And there was Lázaro Gutiérrez de Lara, not a member of the intimate circle, but a man who had risked his life to guide John Kenneth Turner through Mexico and who, through his agitation, had contributed as much as anyone to the dissemination of the Mexican Cause in the United States and to protecting the men in prison; Lázaro, who had faced the wrath of Díaz in the form of extradition proceedings and of imprisonment on trumped-up charges, who had testified on behalf of the political refugees in front of the Rules Committee of the U.S. House of Representatives in 1910, whose novel *Los bribones* (The scoundrels) had been lavished with praise in the pages of *Revolución* and *Regeneración*. He, too, was lost to the Liberal cause.

And divisions also separated Liberal families. Jesús Flores Magón became Madero's home minister and so a traitor from the viewpoint of his brothers in Los Angeles. Tomás Sarabia denounced his brother Manuel and his cousin Juan as traitors in the pages of *Regeneración*. Antonio Villarreal cast aspersions on the reputation of María Brousse; Ricardo insulted the honor of Antonio Villarreal's sisters, Andrea and Teresa, who were editors of well-regarded Liberal papers in San Antonio. Librado's wife, Conchita, who daily had cooked for the *Regeneración* family, was for a time suspected of treason even by her own husband. The rift, in other words, tore apart the group's most intimate relationships, and so the passionate tenor of these conflicts offers a unique vista to everyday forms of revolution.

A good place to start is the connection between generalized suspicion of infiltrators and personal antipathies. Suspicion and paranoia were part of the everyday life of the militant in the United

States. Militants had to be fearful of agents of the Mexican government, plainclothes policemen, hired detectives, paid informants, and bounty hunters. At various points when they faced interrogations, trials, or narrow escapes, the Liberals were surprised by the identity of some of these spies. After the 1906 St. Louis raid, for instance, Librado Rivera wrote to his wife and warned Conchita of the identity of one of the spies: "Do you remember that short little American who spoke Spanish, and whom we all knew because he was our oldest American friend?"[15] Examples like this—warnings, suspicion—abound in the Liberals' correspondence.

Militants were attentive to their instincts, as well as to rumors, and sometimes they made painful mistakes. So, for example, in October 1907, shortly after the imprisonment of Ricardo, Antonio, and Librado, *Revolución*'s editor, Modesto Díaz, printed an article denouncing Fernando Palomares, allegedly for having turned the men in to the authorities. The language of this denunciation is pretty much typical: "Fernando Palomares. The man is a stool pigeon. He comes not from the race of Judas, but from something even more repugnant. Palomares's lackey soul has never once felt the beautiful impulse of those who love the sublime and who set their sights high. He was born in a crib of abjection, and his life is consecrated to crime."[16]

Palomares, who was one of the most self-sacrificing militants the Liberals ever had, was in Texas when this denunciation was published. He wrote to Modesto Díaz asking to receive a formal hearing, saying that he would drop his work immediately to go to Los Angeles to clear matters up. This letter prompted a consultation between the editorial staff of *Revolución* and the men in prison, who cleared Fernando's name. A disclaimer was printed in the following issue.

At times, suspicions needed to be acted on, even when they were not yet proven. So, for instance, writing to Enrique in preparation for the 1908 uprising, Ricardo considered the case of Néstor López in Texas. Ricardo reminded Enrique that there was no proof that he was a traitor, but it was certain that there was a traitor in the region, and field commander Díaz Guerra did not trust López. As a result, Enrique should deny him information. "Néstor has always behaved like a good friend. One feels remorseful mistrusting him, but we need to heed Díaz Guerra, since he is the chief and the one who is going into battle."[17]

Although personal conflicts did not automatically filter into this space of suspicion, they could tend in that direction. Personal differences were sometimes expressed around degrees of devotion to the cause. So, for instance, Blas Lara, whose memoirs are a delicious source of Liberal gossip, wrote of a couple of Los Angeles politicians who were investing in their relationship with the junta in hopes of eventually reaping profits after the revolution: "Two other two-bit politicians residing in Los Angeles were more active; they dreamed of gaining a juicy government post [*roer huesos del presupuesto*]. One was a music teacher named Avalos, and the other was a Mr. Ortega, who had two daughters. Ortega used to say: 'My daughter Laura, who is the eldest, will marry Ricardo, while Conchita will marry Mr. Villarreal. I will be governor of Jalisco.'"[18]

This sort of gossip also extended to people who had succeeded in gaining access to the "families of the cause." Thus, commenting on Rómulo Carmona, the first father-in-law of Enrique Flores Magón, Blas remarked that the man used his daughter Paula to gain financial advantages in the *Regeneración* group while Enrique was in prison at the McNeil Island Penitentiary in Washington.[19] And if a comrade was thought to be opportunistic and had personal ambitions, that person could be prone to selling out and maybe even to selling out his comrades. For this reason, the line between personal dislikes and suspicions of treason could get thin, and work was required to keep them distinct.

So, for instance, in 1908, María Brousse repeatedly complained to Ricardo about Lázaro Gutiérrez de Lara. María and Lázaro were both members of the Socialist Party, and she believed that Lázaro, who was prominent in the party, was standing in the way of her efforts to organize and lead the Mexican Socialists. Whatever the cause, though, María suspected Lázaro of having embezzled money from his Mexico trip and wanted Ricardo to undermine his influence among the Mexican element.

Ricardo, however, felt that Lázaro, though pompous, was harmless. He should not be allowed into their inner circle, but he should also not be attacked: "Poor Lázaro is just a victim of his bad luck. I know about the trip he made, and I know where he got the money to do it. There's nothing wrong with his trip. Keep Lázaro out of the loop where it comes to secrets, but don't be hostile to him. Though he's weak, he's a man with a good heart."[20]

But Ricardo had no such forbearance for his two prison comrades, Antonio Villarreal and Manuel Sarabia. Ricardo wrote to María that unlike Lázaro, whose main flaw seemed to be his weakness, Antonio and Manuel were "at once evil and cowardly."[21] In 1908, this personal break was not yet publicly aired. As in the case of Lázaro, the most immediate consequence was to keep Manuel and Antonio at a distance from the most delicate plans. Thus, in 1908, Antonio and Manuel were not apprised of the plans for what proved to be a disastrous incursion at Viesca and Las Vacas. "Antonio and Manuel will know neither the date nor the developments of the movement,"[22] Ricardo wrote to Enrique, a few weeks before the scheduled action.

By October of that year, the men appeared to have agreed to a political separation. But it was meant to be amicable, and it did not imply casting Antonio and Manuel as traitors. Thus, Ricardo wrote to his adopted daughter, Lucía Norman: "Antonio is no longer a member of the junta, and Manuel will soon be quitting it, too. Don't worry, though. Those of us who remain are enthusiastic and resolved. And don't think that those friends have betrayed us—they are incapable of that, but they don't share our ideas, that's all."[23]

It is in connection with the effort to exclude former friends from the intimate circle of the "families of the cause" that we get the first violent words from Ricardo regarding Manuel Sarabia, for Manuel had won over Lucía's affections, and Ricardo was adamantly opposed to their relationship. And Manuel then won the heart of Elizabeth Trowbridge, a woman who had been Ricardo's greatest supporter and whom he held in singular regard. Elizabeth, Ricardo had said, was like a mother to him. "She alone has done more than all the rest. She's an angel, as you rightly say."[24] And yet these two women, Lucía, his dear daughter, and Elizabeth, a surrogate mother, were the very ones who were (successfully) pursued by Manuel.

There may have been some jealousy mixed in with Ricardo's distrust. Manuel Sarabia had become a cause célèbre and rallying point for Liberal propaganda when he was kidnapped by Pinkerton detectives in Douglas and taken forcefully across the border. Manuel's abduction and imprisonment generated an enormous show of solidarity among miners and citizens, first in Douglas and then all along the border. His kidnapping became a rallying point in the protest movement against U.S. government collaboration with Díaz. As a result, Manuel became a bit of a poster boy, and he had a lot of fans (Figure 18.2). So, for instance, *Voz de la Mujer* celebrated his release from jail at Hermosillo with a satirical verse against Díaz:

A Manuel Sarabia
Como *papas* te llevaron
Y volviste como hombrote;
Los lacayos se callaron
Y mascaron el garrote
Que de Washington enviaron
Al eunuco guajolote [Porfirio Díaz].

[They took you like potatoes
And you came back a big man;
The lackeys fell silent
And they had to take the beating
That Washington dealt
To the turkey eunuch.][25]

It is unclear whether it was jealousy or a genuine negative opinion regarding Manuel's moral character (or both), but Ricardo was deeply antagonistic to El Chamaco (Manuel) by the time that Lucía began to show interest in him, and Ricardo reserved unusually harsh language for Manuel in his correspondence with María. "El niño," as he now disdainfully called him, (demoting him from his prior nickname of El Chamaco, The Kid), was "a little scoundrel" who wrote "lacrimose letters." He was false and disloyal. At that point, Ricardo still did not foresee that Elizabeth and Manuel would marry, and his principal concern seems to have been to keep Manuel away from Lucía, whom he pressured and cajoled to stay away from Manuel.

In addition to his other offenses, Ricardo complained to María, Manuel was conspiring against Elizabeth:

He's such an ingrate that he mistrusts even Violeta—who is a woman who makes sacrifices to save us, who is an angel—and he's getting her mixed up with his little letters. I've seen the notes with which he's trying to wrap the young lady—who is like our mother—in an atmosphere of mistrust so as to cast suspicion upon her. It seems that these rumors have already reached Violeta's ears, and she is going to take her vengeance like a saint—by helping him!—because she is going to pay

THE BORDER

A Monthly Magazine of Politics, News and Stories of the Border

VOLUME ONE ❧ DECEMBER, 1908 ❧ NUMBER TWO

Tucson, Arizona, U.S.A.   One Dollar a Year

RURALES—THE COSSACKS OF MEXICO

How I Was Kidnaped

Story of My Escape from the Rurales and Hermosillo Penitentiary

Manuel Sarabia

The kidnaping of Manuel Sarabia from the jail at Douglas, Arizona, by the orders of the Mexican Consul, Antonio Maza, caused a furor of popular indignation in Southern Arizona. Public meetings were held, telegrams were sent to Washington, and finally the Mexican government was forced to release its prey. More than all else, has this kidnaping opened the eyes of Americans to the astonishing power of President Porfirio Diaz on this side of the line. Apparently, he can open and close the doors of United States jails at will, give orders to United States officials, and finally protect his secret service system now operating in this country from being punished for its misdeeds.

IN Mexico, the rurales ride like the Cossacks of Russia, threatening, capturing and killing all who oppose the will of their master, the Dictator.

Mexico is accustomed to a military rule that strikes in the dark and gives no reason. To be taken from one's home suddenly and without warrant, imprisoned without having committed a crime, held "incommunicado" because your political opinions differ from those of the ruling power, all this Mexican citizens expect as part of their daily life.

But in the United States, everything is different, and so, when the long arm of President Porfirio Diaz stretches across the border line into this country and kidnaps those whom he fears and hates, it is time for American citizens to be on guard. For this reason, I write the account of my kidnaping.

It began with the red-faced man, who had been watching me from the opposite side of the street, crossing and intercepting my efforts to catch the train leaving Douglas, Arizona, for El Paso. I had a letter to drop into the mailcar and the

---

Figure 18.2 From *The Border*, December 1908 issue, courtesy University of Arizona Libraries.

his bail. Violeta is such as saint! But the rascal doesn't understand that angels exist. He's always looking for an underside.[26]

Ricardo then asked Lucía to refrain from writing to Manuel and not to see him. Manuel would soon be quitting the junta. Ricardo also told Lucía that she was an intelligent young woman who could speak English and so agitate the masses, work propaganda, and save Ricardo: "You, my beautiful daughter [*hijita linda*] know English and can urge the Americans to defend us, and that way you will save Ricardo, who you love as a father, from certain death. I am not afraid of death—it would bring rest to me—but I fear for María. The poor thing would die of sorrow."[27] In other words, Ricardo asked Lucía to be loyal to him, to leave aside her friendship and correspondence with Manuel, and not to interfere in whatever was beginning to happen between Elizabeth and Manuel. I believe that Ricardo would feel some responsibility for Lucía's later psychological instability, due to the sacrifice that he asked of her for his own benefit.

The Judas Cycle

The Judas theme—a vehement discourse of betrayal within the inner circle—burst into full bloom once Ricardo had proclaimed that Madero was a traitor. Before then, Ricardo had tried to keep internal differences low key. So, for instance, when Sanftleben left *Regeneración* after being publicly contradicted by Ricardo regarding the party's Madero policy, Ricardo published a note of personal appreciation and expressed regret for his resignation: "We have always looked upon Alfred G. Sanftleben as one of the best friends of the Mexican cause to be found in this country."[28] This mild and generous way of treating comrades with diverging political positions disappeared completely after the break with Madero. From that point forward, deviation was betrayal.

One might say that the first and most vilified traitor was Madero himself. Starting with the February 25, 1911, issue of *Regeneración*, Madero was called a "traitor," a "murderer," a "dictator," a "second Porfirio Díaz," a "pawn of the Catholic Church," a "slave owner," a "midget," and many things more. He was called these things despite the fact that Madero had once supported *Regeneración* in a time of financial need and that Ricardo had called on Gustavo Madero, Francisco's brother, to provide $800 (a considerable sum) to alleviate his brother Jesús's finances during a health crisis.[29] But the fact that a bourgeois upstart such as Madero could hijack the revolution for which they had all sacrificed so much was too much to bear.

The action that led to the break has not yet been fully clarified by historians of the Revolution. According to Ricardo's version of the break with Madero, after asking for and receiving military support from the Liberals, Madero had forced Liberal troops either to disarm or to join his army; he had apprehended their leader, Prisciliano Silva, and held him prisoner because he had refused to yield to Madero's authority. What is more, according to Ricardo, when the Liberal general called on Gabino Cano for reinforcements from Texas, Madero blew the whistle to American authorities, who captured Cano on the border and accused him of violation of the neutrality laws.

In short, Madero had moved to quash any revolutionary movement that was not under his command and had not shied away even from using the American government itself. Madero, Ricardo clamored, was an opportunist who had reaped the abundant sacrifices of the Liberals for his own benefit: "Madero found everything ready and set for him to make his ascent. The sacrifices of all who have struggled were going to serve him, just because he had spent a few thousand pesos that he had previously stolen from his peons by starving them, the way all landowners do."[30]

The sense that Madero was a rich boy who had robbed the Liberals of their revolution is displayed in a revealing fashion in interviews that Enrique Flores Magón held with General Jenaro Amezcua in the early 1940s. By that time, Enrique was invested in rescuing the glorious stories of the so-called "Precursors of the Mexican Revolution" via an organization with that name that he directed and that was part of the Mexican state. Based on Enrique's story, Amezcua speculated that had Enrique not risked his life and been lost in the Chihuahua desert in the 1908 attack on Palomas (which in fact never occurred, though there were by then no living witnesses to contradict the claim), and had stayed in El Paso, instead, the Liberal captains inside Mexico would have had communication with the revolutionary masterminds in the United States and would have succeeded in revolutionizing Mexico as early as 1908. Moreover, "had Enrique been in El Paso, Texas, the revolution would have caught fire and begun right then, without the mistakes of 1910, because there was revolutionary cohesion behind a single flag and a unitary cause that was advanced and well defined."[31]

In fact, of course, there is no way that the 1908 revolt could have taken root the way that the 1910 revolution did. It was not an electoral year in 1908, and the Liberal clubs had neither the coverage nor the wide base of support that Madero had built up by 1910. But the fantasy is as revealing as it is absurd. In their different ways, Ricardo and Enrique both felt that the revolution had been within their grasp and that it had been stolen by Madero and his rich allies. Madero had betrayed "the cause of liberty" and had usurped the sacrifices of all the Liberals, not least those of Ricardo himself.

But though Madero was a "traitor" and a "Judas" to the revolution, he was not a "Judas" to the Liberal Party itself. That epithet was reserved for insiders. The first of Ricardo's Judases was Lázaro Gutiérrez de Lara, who was also denounced in the February 25 article that announced Madero's betrayal to the cause of liberty. According to Ricardo, Lázaro had betrayed Prisciliano Silva and switched to Madero's side, along with the men who were under his command. This was a betrayal to the Liberals: "Nobody could have suspected that Lara, who had taken money from the Liberals, who had gotten the funds for his trip from the Regeneración Group in Los Angeles, who made speeches in El Paso supporting the Liberal Party, and who pretended to favor the economic emancipation of the proletariat, would jump to the side of Madero with his weapons and dependents."[32]

He was followed in the Judas role by Juan Sarabia, Antonio Villarreal, and Manuel Sarabia, though the epithet was used as well against a number of Liberal military captains who negotiated with Madero or, later, with other revolutionary or counterrevolutionary governments—people such as Lázaro Alanís, Emilio Campa, Antonio Díaz Soto y Gama, Paulino Martínez, and others.

Regeneración Burguesa
The break with Antonio Villarreal and with Juan and Manuel Sarabia produced a contest over ownership of the "Liberal" label. Camilo Arriaga, Juana B. Gutiérrez de Mendoza, Juan Sarabia, Filomeno Mata, and Jesús Flores Magón had been among the original founders or supporters of the Partido Liberal Mexicano in 1901, as much as Ricardo or anyone else. The first editor of *Regeneración*, in 1900, had been Jesús, not Ricardo. Juan Sarabia served as editor of *El Hijo del Ahuizote* in 1903, and he and Antonio I. Villarreal had been founders

of the junta in St. Louis in 1905, alongside Ricardo. They had been major contributors to the 1906 program, which had remained the PLM official platform during the whole of the Madero revolt. And Juan Sarabia had paid for his militancy with prison in San Juan de Ulúa, which was a fate harsher even than what Ricardo had faced. For these reasons, these men felt that they had a legitimate claim on the "Liberal" label.

When Antonio Villarreal left Los Angeles to join Madero, Ricardo published regular announcements telling *Regeneración*'s readers that Antonio was no longer a member of the junta and that Liberals should not follow his directives. From Villarreal's point of view, however, he had as much right to address Liberal militants as Ricardo. After all, many militants agreed with his ideology and strategy, and Antonio had never betrayed the principles of the 1906 Liberal program. He considered himself to be as worthy of bearing the Liberal mantle as Ricardo—and more so, because Ricardo's anarchism was not an original part of the program.

When Maderismo triumphed and Porfirio Díaz departed into exile, Juan Sarabia and other imprisoned Liberals were freed, and they joined with others who had splintered from Ricardo's branch of the Liberal party, including Antonio Villarreal, Camilo Arriaga, Jesús Flores Magón, and Filomeno Mata, to enter the new democratic politics in Mexico with a refurbished Liberal platform.

The group wished to make itself visible beyond the posts that some of them were gaining in the interim, caretaker government of Francisco León de la Barra in preparation for stronger positions in the Madero-led government. Jesús Flores Magón would soon be appointed minister of the interior, Juan Sarabia would be elected to Congress, and Antonio Villarreal was named a colonel in the army, while Camilo Arriaga was given a secret commission as special envoy to the Mexican consulates in the American Southwest.

These men's cohesion as a leftward-leaning coalition in Mexico's new democratic politics involved relaunching the Liberal Party, along with the publication of a new version of *Regeneración*. The idea to relaunch *Regeneración* in Mexico City was suggested by Juan Sarabia and Jesús Flores Magón immediately after their trip to Los Angeles, when Ricardo refused to lay down weapons and return to Mexican democratic politics.[33] The journal was precariously funded by the Ministry of Justice, where Jesús Flores Magón was at that point an undersecretary, and had Juan Sarabia and Antonio Villar-real as editors. It initiated publication in July 1911.

The purpose of the Mexico City version of *Regeneración* was to reclaim the old Liberal mantle for the new political party. It soon gained adherents from the more radical end of the Maderista movement, including leaders of various local organizations in Chihuahua, Sonora, Tamaulipas, Coahuila, Nuevo León, and Puebla, as well as in several border towns on the U.S. side.[34] The party was not strong enough to field its own presidential candidate and so supported Madero's candidacy, but it did have its own vice presidential candidate, Fernando Iglesias Calderón, and was trying to get a union movement and a league of political clubs off the ground.

This project involved working hard to claim and establish true and credible Liberal credentials, an effort that drove yet another nail in the coffin of Ricardo's party. By then, Ricardo and Enrique had been indicted for violating the U.S. neutrality laws for the invasion of Baja California and were awaiting trial in California. Their movement had been defeated militarily, and the influence of the original *Regeneración* was teetering. It was a good time to make the move. The publication of the Mexico City *Regeneración*, which Ricardo first dubbed *Degeneración* and then *Regeneración burguesa*—bourgeois *Regeneración*—generated a final wave of recriminations between the two Liberal factions.[35]

Regeneración burguesa made consistent attacks on its Los Angeles counterpart. Each issue included a block notice that read: "This newspaper is completely unconnected to the weekly of the same name that is published by the anarchist Junta of Los Angeles, California." And each issue contained attacks on Ricardo Flores Magón, in particular. On occasion, this also led people who had complaints against Ricardo to address letters to the Mexico City paper, as well.[36]

Juan Sarabia had published an open letter to Ricardo in *El Diario del Hogar*, and it was translated into English by Manuel Sarabia and printed in the *New York Call*. In it, Juan stood firm in his differences with Ricardo. This earned Sarabia another round of attacks, not only from Ricardo, but also from William Owen, in *Regeneración*'s English language page, and more hurtfully, from Juan's cousin and Manuel's brother, Tomás.

Owen had been most consistent in leading *Regeneración* against the Socialists:

I assumed the editorship of this section April 15, 1911, and the first thing that struck me was that the "People's Paper," of Los Angeles, had become silent on the Mexican question, although the daily papers were full of the triumphs then being scored by the revolutionary forces. The silence was the more remarkable because the "People's Paper' had just become a Socialist Party organ, with John Murray as editor; and John Murray had been prominently identified with the Mexican revolutionary movement, having edited "The Border," for which a Miss Stowbridge [sic] supplied the funds. In my first issue, therefore, I chronicled this silence as singular. [37]

The Socialist Party, Owen argued, wanted to be in with Madero for its own political reasons, and it was willing to sell out the PLM in order to do it. It is likely, though, that John Murray's paper was silent because of the split between the junta and Villarreal. Owen developed his arguments against the Socialist position on Madero and rallied radical opinion for the revolution, including most prominently that of Emma Goldman, who spoke publicly in Los Angeles for the Liberal Party and then wrote: "This is not the special cause of Socialists, Anarchists, Single Taxers, Trade Unionists, or other individual wings of the great army of discontent. It is a straight case of millions of our fellow creatures having been driven from the lands in which they and their forefathers had lived for generations in order that absentee syndicates may reap colossal fortunes by indescribably revolting slavery."[38]

However, this call for unity among the "army of discontent" came too late. By the time of its publication, the Baja California campaign had been lost, and Maderismo was in control of Mexico. In fact, Emma's article appeared in the same *Regeneración* issue that announced the imprisonment of Ricardo, Enrique, Librado, and Anselmo Figueroa, all charged with violation of neutrality laws for the invasion of Baja California. On the other hand, the Mexican Socialists pointed out, very respectfully, that Owen had no clue about the actual reality of Mexico or why they had veered away from the utopian ideology now being championed by Ricardo. Thus, Manuel wrote for the New York *Call* and Mexico City's *El Diario del Hogar*:

Had Mr. Owen ever been to Mexico, his words and concepts would be otherwise. It is a pity that he cannot go there and make close observations of the country and its inhabitants. If he did that, he would find just what

Juan (Sarabia) says: a people who don't know a word about anarchism, socialism, or maybe even liberalism. How can you establish an anarchist community in a country where no one understands anarchist philosophy? Like Ferrer, I think that the people need to be educated first."[39]

Even so, Owen's attacks stung the American Socialists, because a few of them had continued to support the revolution while maintaining a quiet stance toward the Liberals. Turner, in particular, had taken personal risks for the revolution in Baja California and had never spoken out against the junta, despite Ricardo's ferocious attacks on Lázaro Gutiérrez de Lara, Antonio Villarreal, and Manuel Sarabia—all of whom were personal friends of John's. Also, Owen snubbed Ethel Turner, despite her firm loyalty to the junta, possibly for the same reason that he could not find it in him to spell Elizabeth's last name correctly. Despite his many impressive virtues, Owen seems to have been a bit of a male chauvinist and was prone to claiming that his predecessor as editor of the English-language page was the famous John Kenneth Turner, rather than young, unknown (and female) Ethel, who was, as it happened, the editor. Even as an elderly lady, the slight still stung. Thus, Ethel recalled: "It made me so angry when it was later said that John wrote everything! He didn't. I had guidance from everybody, but I wrote most of the articles myself. That gives me prestige in Mexico today, that I was on that paper. My name was on the masthead."[40]

One by one, the Socialist allies of the junta were lost—either because they sided with Madero or because, like Turner, they felt estranged by the virulence of Ricardo's attacks on good friends and comrades.

The most painful attacks on Juan and Manuel Sarabia came from Tomas, who like Manuel, had been in prison in Texas for violation of the neutrality laws, and also like Manuel, had emerged from prison with a case of tuberculosis that would kill him soon enough. In the first of a series of public letters published in *Regeneración* of Los Angeles, Tomás made a painful recitation of how he had once looked up to Juan and how Juan's betrayal polluted their sacred family home. He then concluded: "Admiration and love for Juan Sarabia the martyr, the great hero who died in San Juan de Ulúa. Anathema and divine chastisement for Juan Sarabia, the wicked and contemptible traitor whom the bourgeoisie brought back to life!"[41]

In later months, Tomás's curses turned to Manuel, whom he reproached as a clown ("Tartuffe") and degenerate for having defended Juan Sarabia and for having suggested that Tomás had been manipulated by Ricardo: "I am filled with pity and sadness because you have forced me to descend to a turf that only depraved degenerates tread, blinded by their bastardly ambitions. For in allowing Juan the goon and the two-bit politician to print our private family intimacies, you have put yourself among those who care not a whit for family."[42]

Tomás also accused Manuel of having abandoned a love match in order to marry Elizabeth for her money and of having used Elizabeth as a pretext to abandon his comrades in the Arizona prison and skip bail:

> Later you had the chance to marry for convenience, so you sacrificed the pure and disinterested love of Adelita—who had no millions—and of course, you changed your ideas, too. You became an evolutionist and would no longer share the fate of your comrades, because "had I remained at their side, the prison would have brought a mere rag back to my wife." And so leaving them seemed fair to you.[43]

It was in the context of this campaign against the Mexico City Liberals that Ricardo launched into a virulent attack against Antonio Villarreal and Manuel Sarabia, whom he accused of being degenerate pederasts—homosexuals (Figures 18.3 and 18.4).

El Coronel 41

The attacks on Antonio's and Manuel's sexual integrity and honesty deserve close attention, contrary to historians' routine habit of skirting lightly over them.[44] In his first publication on the subject, Ricardo actually made three accusations against Villarreal: that he was a murderer, an opportunist, and a degenerate—that is, a homosexual. And although he referred to some facts to support his case, he also said that he was holding other facts back, threatening that he would publish them in due course.[45]

In the case of the charge of murder, Ricardo's accusation went back to the fact that Villarreal had killed José Flores in a duel, ostensibly over a literary disagreement, back when Antonio had his first job as school principal in Villaldana, Nuevo León, before his American exile.[46] This duel had been the cause of Antonio's

Figure 18.3 Cosmetically altered photo of the Junta Organizadora of the Partido Liberal Mexicano, December 1910. Left to right: Anselmo Figueroa, Praxedis Guerrero, Ricardo Flores Magón (sitting), Enrique Flores Magón, Librado Rivera. The photo of Praxedis has been pasted in from a different portrait and overlays the image of another person. Praxedis was not in Los Angeles in December 1910. The man who is being covered over by Praxedis is very probably Antonio I. Villlarreal. Courtesy of the Casa de El Hijo del Ahuizote, Mexico City.

Figure 18.4 Photo of Praxedis that was reproduced and pasted on the doctored group portrait of the junta. A photo of the doctored portrait of the junta, which is more blurry and so less obviously forged, was published in Jenaro Amezcua's biography, *¿Quien es Enrique Flores Magón?* (Mexico City, 1943). Photo courtesy of the Casa de El Hijo del Ahuizote, Mexico City.

imprisonment—he spent almost four years in jail in Villaldana and then in Monterrey—and when Villarreal was later persecuted in the United States by Díaz's agents, the Mexican government had tried to get him extradited by charging that he was guilty of this murder. At that point, the Liberals' lawyers had rather easily thrown out the case for extradition, and *Regeneración* itself had published defenses of Villarreal against these charges.[47]

Ricardo thus was willing to make an accusation that had been used against Villarreal by the dictatorship and that had earlier been rejected vehemently by the junta. In these accusations against those he regarded as Judases, Ricardo employed a double morality: when the charge was leveled by the state against a comrade, the state was accused of lying; when the comrade was no longer a comrade, the charge was reinstated.[48]

Duels, though illegal, were not uncommon in Mexico, particularly between men who wrote for the press.[49] Ricardo himself had written an indignant letter to Antonio Villarreal when the U.S. authorities sought Antonio for extradition, complaining about the servile and unjust attitude of the American government: "Nowhere can a man who kills in legitimate self-defense be called a felon; nor even is that valid in cases where the homicide occurred in circumstances that deprived the killer of his reason. They are trying to screw you, and that's that."[50] Thus, in his private correspondence, Ricardo had denied that Antonio was a murderer.

Moreover, Villarreal had participated in another duel, against César Canales, before his fatal encounter with José Flores. The two men had emerged from the affair unharmed—which was the most common outcome of these duels—and had gone on to become close friends and political allies.[51] His history of dueling suggested that Antonio Villarreal was a man who was much concerned with his honor, so it was by impugning his honor that Ricardo offended him.

The accusation that Villarreal was an opportunist who sought only self-promotion and was willing to sell out the cause found its emblem in Villarreal's new title of colonel, conferred on him by Madero. In Ricardo's hands, "colonel" was almost a made-to-order insult. For anarchists, the officer class as a whole was an object of derision: a class of leeches and exploiters. Among the Liberals, leadership in the field was democratically decided by comrades, and not centrally appointed. Moreover, within the objectionable officer caste, the rank of colonel was perfectly suited to Ricardo's biting satire: a very high rank, but not the highest, it conjured up the image of a well-fed underling. Antonio had exchanged his leadership in the PLM for a plate of lentils:

> If I were shameless like him, I'd be a member of the cabinet at the very least. Haven't we had peace envoys coming and going, trying to get us to abandon our aggressive attitude? Haven't they begged us in every way to place ourselves on the side of the rich and to turn our backs on the poor? All we had to do was to open our mouths, and we'd have received states to govern, cabinet portfolios, and high and lucrative public posts.[52]

Ricardo's incontinence in his use of the press for venting his spleen did not help his own image or that of *Regeneración*. Thus, remarking on one of Ricardo's defamatory articles against her husband, Elizabeth Trowbridge wrote to Frances Noel from Mexico City:

> I have always been very fond of Lucia [Norman] but have not heard from her for a long time and do not expect to do so again as Manuel and Magon have broken. I cannot understand Magon's extraordinary and ridiculous behavior. It is well enough to disagree with people but when it comes to such lies and foul language as he indulges in, that is another matter. Why doesn't Owen 'shut him up'? He at least should know enough to know that it hurts their paper."[53]

But it is the third component of Ricardo's defamatory attacks on Villarreal that most concerns us here: degeneracy and pederasty. His first article on the subject, titled "El coronel de los 41" (slang for "the homosexual colonel") was addressed to his brother Jesús. Ricardo complained that Jesús was subsidizing Villarreal's *Regeneración burguesa* and that the paper was regularly printing lies and attacks against him. Ricardo claimed to have proof that Antonio was a pederast and degenerate, but that he (Ricardo) was reticent to provide it. Nonetheless, he called on Jesús to look Antonio in the eye and inquire after a certain barber from Lampazos and to ask Antonio about a certain fence behind which he and the barber used to meet. Jesús would immediately see the truth of Ricardo's allegation in Antonio's eyes and immediately throw Antonio out of his post as editor for his degeneracy.[54]

"The Colonel of the 41" is a reference to a famous Porfirian scandal that was still fresh in collective memory. On November 17, 1901, the Mexico City Police had raided an upper-class ball where a group of forty-two "*pollos*," young upper-class dandies, were found dancing with one another, half of them dressed and made up as women. They all were rounded up, compelled to sweep the streets dressed as women amid public jeering, and then many of them were conscripted into the army and packed off to a probable death in Yucatán.[55] All of this without a trial, of course.

The event came to be known as the "Scandal of the 41" because the forty-second man managed to escape the raid. Rumor had it that this forty-second "effeminate" was Don Ignacio de la Torre, a Brummellesque dandy of superior taste who was also Porfirio Díaz's son-in-law. According to Carlos Monsiváis, the event was Mexico's first homosexual scandal, and it remained an iconic point of reference for homosexuality throughout the entire twentieth century.[56]

Calling Villarreal the "colonel of the 41" tarred both Villarreal and his troops with the homosexual brush. Ricardo also intended the accusation to isolate Villarreal in Mexico City. Not only did he ask Jesús to dismiss him from his post, but he claimed in a follow-up article that "it is natural for those who hang out with him to feel ashamed and for them to start thinking that 'he who lives with wolves learns to howl.'"[57]

The Liberal loyalists retained the homosexual epithet for Villarreal for many years. So, for instance, writing to Enrique Flores Magón a dozen years after the Magón-Villarreal split, Rafael García, commenting on Antonio I. Villarreal's campaign for the Mexican Senate, still feminized Villarreal, calling him "Toña": "And speaking of Toña, she is very agitated in Monterrey with her strip of ham—in other words, with her candidacy. You can see her little face lots of places, on large billboards, looking for her yams and potatoes."[58]

The most sensational aspect of the accusation against Villarreal was that it went into intimate specifics. In this, Ricardo's attack was very similar to his 1906 denunciation of Juana Gutiérrez de Mendoza as a lesbian. Ricardo had launched his first Villarreal exposé based on hearsay, accusing him of a homosexual affair with the barber in his home town at Lampazos, and pointing to witnesses from that place. But when the cycle of accusation escalated, with responses to Ricardo from Villarreal and Juan and Manuel Sarabia in various venues, including *El Diario del Hogar, Regeneración* ("burguesa"), and papers in the United States, Ricardo fired away with what he claimed was direct testimony against both Villarreal and Manuel Sarabia, with whom he had been in prison:

> Manuel Sarabia, the man who relieved his hunger by selling himself, by marrying a rich American. He was one of Villarreal's favorites. We often surprised them in each others' arms, stroking one another's moustaches and hair. In fact, on one occasion, our expressions of distaste for these extraordinary and unnatural expansions, which are distinctive among degenerates, so mortified them that they gained us an African hatred from both of these fellows.[59]

Degeneration

The flip side of the call for renewal made via a publication such as *Regeneración* was, of course, a sense of degeneracy—of Mexicans' having fallen away from an ideal. Concerns with emasculation and virility thus were widespread among the Liberals. Slavery was understood as a form of emasculation, and the dictatorship's other instrument, co-optation, was also understood as degrading.

Porfirio Díaz, Ricardo argued, hated the Mexican race because he saw them as generate: "To Porfirio Díaz and the men who are in power, there is no race that is lower, stupider, lazier, more vicious, more immoral or more antithetical to civilization than the Mexican race." Racial degradation was used to convince everyone that the people were unfit to govern themselves, a policy that was enforced by giving privileges to Europeans.

"Do we Mexicans deserve this?" Ricardo asked, and he did not hesitate to answer: "Maybe we do, because we've not known how to punish our oppressors. But it is time to open our eyes, comrades. The Winchester will give us the right to be respected."[60] The call for regeneration was also a call to be more manly—to stand up and fight. Indeed, feminism itself had a manly component for Liberals: it supported radical human equality, yes, but it was also—and sometimes primarily—a movement by women to force their men to stand up. Time and again, Liberal women stepped up and occupied the front row in clashes with police, political rallies or taunted their men into action.

So, for instance, when Enrique Flores Magón returned to Mexico in 1923 and joined the leadership of Veracruz's tenant movement, he wrote an enthusiastic letter to his friend Rafael García, back in Los Angeles: "Moreover, the female element is the most numerous, the most enthusiastic, the most conscientious and resolved, to the shame of so many boastful swaggering revolutionaries [*tanto calzonudo revolucionario de pico*]. Those women and a few men engage the police almost daily, defending the people who are evicted onto the streets. And they always win."[61]

Feminine newspapers had been important among the militants since the early 1900s, and in them, the women called on their men to stand up and not prostrate themselves before the government. Moreover, the wives of the Liberal chiefs were usually important militants in their own right. This was as true for highly educated militants such as Elizabeth and Ethel as it was for the more precariously schooled Mexican *compañeras* such as like Enrique's wife, Teresa Arteaga, Ricardo's María Brousse, and Librado Rivera's wife, Conchita.

I don't mean to imply that men and women were equal. When Elizabeth Trowbridge and Manuel Sarabia had their first and only child, a girl, Elizabeth expressed regret to Frances Noel: "I am sorry that the child is a girl—it is a great misfortune for a progressive person to be a woman today, with the general idiotic prejudice against women, but it can't be helped, and each generation will have a better chance than that before."[62]

But though women were at a disadvantage, they participated consistently and often with powerful voices, as writers and as speakers, in street brawls, and sometimes in military actions. Antonio Villarreal's two sisters each published newspapers in San Antonio; Mariana Gómez Gutiérrez had led troops in Chihuahua, served as secretary to Villa, and eloquently addressed militants in correspondence. When Ricardo, Enrique, Librado, and Anselmo Figueroa went to prison again in 1912, Rosa Méndez traveled to Los Angeles to take up a leading editorial role and help keep *Regeneración* alive. Speakers in the Los Angeles free speech park known as the Plaza de los Mexicanos, or La Placita, routinely included vocal women.

In his memoirs, Blas Lara says quite a lot about those speeches at La Placita. Blas compared the Mexican women, who would come "every Sunday to speak to the workers, rain or shine," with women of the Russian Revolution, and then gave details.

A few months before the Junta was tried and convicted, Francisca J. Mendoza, a revolutionary comrade from Matehuala, San Luis Potosí, came here from the state of Texas. From my first Sunday back in Los Angeles, I saw that she was a good speaker and that she knew the anarchist ideals. Her forum was the Placita de los Mexicanos, where every Sunday I'd watch her get up on her box and harangue against this system of social injustice.[63]

Francisca Mendoza, who briefly took a staff position in *Regeneración*, was usually seconded by María Brousse and Concha Rivera. "Concha," Blas recalled, was a "buena polemista." All of these women at the plaza sold international revolutionary literature: ¡*Tierra!*, from Havana; *Renovación*, from Costa Rica; *Cultura Proletaria* from Montevideo; *La Protesta*, the one from Perú and the one from Buenos Aires; *Cultura Obrera* and *Brazo y Cerebro*, from New York; *L'Era Nuova*, from Patterson, New Jersey; *Cerebro y Fuerza*, from El Paso; ¡*Tierra y Libertad!*, from Barcelona; ¡*Luz!*, from Mexico City, and countless pamphlets with sociological propaganda and postcards."[64]

In short, the call for regeneration had a gender component. "Degeneration" was figured first as debasement of the male, whose role as protector and whose dignity had either been trampled by force (in slavery) or corrupted by money. This is why the term *esbirro* (hired thug, petty officer) is ubiquitous in the writings of the Liberals—any government employee, ally, envoy, informer, or advocate was an *esbirro*, an underling who had exchanged honor for a few crumbs. Virility, in short, was at the very core of the notion of regeneration. Women were stepping up because they were entitled to equality and because by doing so they shamed or encouraged their men to take a firm stand as men.

This context helps understand the importance of homosexual scandal in the late Porfiriato. The "Scandal of the 41" implied that the whole of the Porfirian upper echelon had been corrupted and was now composed of degenerates. It is for that very reason that the government treated those upper-class "effeminates" so very harshly—subjecting them to extralegal public humiliation by making them sweep the streets dressed in drag—and then to deportation to Yucatan as conscripts and practically certain death.

The notion that the Porfirian *científico* elite was effeminate and ineffectual became so prevalent in the last decade of the Porfiriato that we even find it being bandied about by foreigners who had only the most superficial understanding of Mexico.[65] So, for instance, Giuseppe Garibaldi, a grandson of the great Garibaldi and a soldier of fortune and general in Madero's army, seemed to think that all officers of the Federal Army were *científicos*, despite the fact that the so-called Científico Party was in fact entirely absent in the army. But no matter. The point was that they were effeminate:

> About this time two young federal officers joined us, deserting from the federal army across the Rio Grande. This was my first contact with the so-called *cientificos*, an intra-governmental political clique which supplied most of the leadership in the Dictator's army, and I was not impressed. These two were sorry specimens, insufferably conceited and ignorant. They owed their military rank solely to political preferment. If these men were typical of the federal officers who would be arrayed against us, we had little to fear, I felt.[66]

The accusation of degeneracy against Antonio Villarreal and Manuel Sarabia had this same general principle at its heart: corruption was seen as a perversion of virility, which was expressed in "pederasty" (Manuel and Antonio; Juana Gutiérrez de Mendoza, and Elisa Acuña), male prostitution (Ricardo called Manuel a gigolo— *braguetero*—for marrying Elizabeth), and effeminacy.

But there is even more to the Villarreal affair than this, for after the release of the junta leadership in August 1910, Antonio Villarreal had published a three-part article in *Regeneración* denouncing conditions in the Yuma and Florence Penitentiaries. Homosexuality and degeneracy figured prominently in those articles. The penitentiary, Villarreal wrote, was a hotbed of degeneration and perversion. Sexual degeneracy, he wrote, "was habitual in the cells and common in the bull pen, although in the latter, concealment was almost impossible." But when the Liberal leadership tried, in private communications, to denounce the situation to prison authorities, they were told that "the conditions were an inevitable feature of prison life, and we were even informed, with unspeakable cynicism, that such vices served a useful purpose, since they kept the men quiet and submissive."[67]

Indeed, homosexuality was not just tolerated, it was promoted by way of the prison's internal organization. The penitentiary, Villarreal wrote, "was run on the stool-pigeon system, those willing to play the part of spies and furnish the officers with information being placed in positions of authority. It goes without saying that men of that stamp are essentially moral degenerates, and they are almost always sexual degenerates also, of the most appalling type."[68]

As in Mexico, then, "degenerates" were placed in positions of authority, and denunciation of injustice was impossible. Thus, Antonio

> compiled a list, giving the names of forty men who habitually sold themselves, but it fell into the hands of the assistant superintendent who destroyed it.... Publicity is the one thing prison officials seem to dread the most.... Particularly, as it appears to me, this holds good for the prevalence of sexual degeneracy, to which I have alluded and only alluded, since it is a subject almost impossible to discuss in print.[69]

As a result of this conspiracy of debasement and silence, prisoners had to work under conditions of harassment. Indeed, Antonio and Ricardo had themselves labored under the supervision of one such pervert. "We were under the supervision of a degenerate Mexican who made himself exceedingly disagreeable. I myself worked under him nine months, and Magón throughout his term."[70]

The virulence of Ricardo's antihomosexual attack on Antonio and Manuel may well have been connected to these experiences with what the men considered to be the ultimate and paradigmatic form of "degeneration," the renunciation of virility in favor of becoming another man's woman. Thus, Villarreal wrote of the case of a young lad who arrived at Yuma:

> When the prison has succeeded in producing a class of men who have become slaves to unnatural vices, it has constituted itself a school of crime in the fullest and most comprehensive meaning of the term, for it has wrecked character and destroyed manhood beyond possibility of redemption. It is impossible to speak too strongly.
>
> While writing this last paragraph, I have had in mind the case of a young fellow who was obviously a most decent lad when he entered Florence. Within a few months, he was, openly and shamelessly, the boon companion of a notoriously corrupt negro. He will be a criminal for life, beyond all question.[71]

In this case, the subjugation of a young and presumably Mexican worker to a "degenerate" Negro clinched the sense of ultimate loss of virility. The proud young lad had become the woman of a member of society's lowest caste.

And neither were these Ricardo's first experiences with degeneracy and homosexuality, for he had done time in Belem Prison in Mexico City. In his 1906 denunciation of Juana Gutiérrez de Mendoza and Elisa Acuña as deprived "Sapphists," Ricardo had already written: "We have been in jail many times for defending the people, and have taken advantage of our contact with prisoners to make sociological studies from real life, which is better and wiser than books.... The imprisoned men and women who are not strong of will are soon perverted. They slack off to such a point that they spurn human dignity.[72]

Indeed, Belem had been the place where Mexico's first positivist studies of the link between criminality and homosexuality had been carried out. Carlos Roumagnac's study of criminality in Mexico was based on observations in Belem Prison, and the problem of "pederasty" and "degeneracy" was front and center in case after case. Roumagnac distinguished between "active" and "passive" pederasts (called *mayates* and *caballos*, respectively) and viewed the feminized *caballos* as active pederasts, while the masculinized *mayates* were only "passive" pederasts. In his view, degeneracy was a kind of epidemic in Belem. Its only possible remedy, the isolation of the active pederasts, was not possible, given the proportion of isolation cells (*bartolinas*) to prisoners. In Roumangnac's estimation, so-called pederasty was ubiquitous in Belem and practiced by the majority there.[73]

In Belem, effeminacy was often recognized and visible in various ways—from feminine nicknames given to *caballos* to physical concentration of effeminates in a visible portal or patio, to their employment in the prison laundry. In short, relations inside the prison intensified those found in the outside world, with oppression leading to widespread degeneracy, effeminate behavior, and, in the case of the Arizona penitentiaries, at least, with "degenerates" being placed in positions of authority because they were also stoolpigeons. In the face of this staggeringly widespread problem, "regeneration" among prisoners involved claiming one's virility and proving one's trustworthiness in one's intimate circle. As a result, Ricardo's revulsion against same-sex sex developed in an environment that combined harassment and the keen identification of homosexuality with two kinds of moral weaknesses: offering up secrets to authority under pressure, and an insufficiency of ascetic power of the will.

Ricardo's feelings on "Sapphism" and "pederasty" had also

developed in a context in which his own integrity as a man might be called into question, given years spent in various prisons, given the importance of homosocial friendships for the group as a whole, and given the fact that Ricardo had no biological children and an unconventional relationship with a woman who was at times accused of promiscuity.

The Apostle

There was increasing anxiety and bitterness in Ricardo's experience with human weakness. This sentiment, which made Ricardo ever more sour and aggressive, was expressed most bitterly in a story that he wrote immediately after Práxedis's death and that seems inspired by Práxedis's poetic writings. The piece, published in the January 6, 1911, issue of *Regeneración*, is titled "The Apostle."

It is the (fictional) story of a delegate of the Liberal party who, braving danger and suffering hunger and thirst, travels across thorn-infested deserts in order to announce urgent tidings of the coming revolution. Dogs bark as the delegate moves through the half-abandoned country, where only the ham-fisted silence of dictatorship can be heard. That, and the sound of crickets, the distant mooing of a cow, or the rattle of a viper underfoot.

Finally the delegate reaches a hamlet where he hopes to find comrades. He tells the men and women of the village that the revolution has begun and calls on them to sacrifice and to help. At that point, "an eagle passed overhead, swaying in the clean atmosphere as if it were a symbol of that man who, though he had walked among human pigs, always remained on high, very pure, very white."[74]

The men and women of the town react distractedly. An old man sleeps, with flies coming and going freely from his open mouth. No one helps the delegate. No one gives him a cent. In the local tavern, the people purchase drink, "giving to the bourgeoisie what they had denied the revolution." Finally, a worker asks local authorities how much he'd get for turning in a revolutionary.

> The deal was closed. Judas had lowered his price. Moments later, a hand-tied man was pushed to jail. He fell several times on his way, and the henchmen kicked him till he stood back up, surrounded by the laughter of the drunken slaves. Some boys enjoyed themselves throwing fistfuls of dirt in the martyr's eyes—for the man was none other than the apostle who had crossed fields and roads, over thorns and

stones, mouth parched by thirst, but always carrying in his lucid brain the idea of the regeneration of the human race by means of well-being and liberty.

Ricardo was mourning Práxedis, who had died just days before. But "The Apostle" was also saying something of Ricardo's own story of sacrifice for a revolution that was being co-opted by the bourgeois Madero. And having survived Práxedis—having, in some way, led Práxedis to slaughter while surviving—Ricardo would have no compassion for collaborators. He would be a hard man.

CHAPTER NINETEEN

Baja for Beginners

The Facts

The ideological prominence of the Partido Liberal Mexicano was in inverse proportion to its military significance. On the field, the movement foundered from the start. In 1906 and 1908, the Liberal call for revolution was premature in relation to Mexican social and political conditions, and when conditions conducive to revolution finally existed, in 1910, the Liberals were not in a position to take full advantage of them.

The Liberal military offensives collapsed just months after the revolution began. The edifice of their ideology appeared as a kind of holographic illusion: its elegant outlines, volumes, and perspectives had no hard substance. How are we to understand the disconnection between the Liberals' ideological work and the everyday practice of revolution in Mexico? The Liberals' Baja California campaign offers an opportunity to answer this question.

Brief as it was, the Baja California campaign was the Liberals' best-known military offensive, but it was so complex and, above all, so chaotic that even after the publication of a number of in-depth studies, it is still not to easy to summarize, let alone to comprehend.[1]

On January 29, 1911, the Liberals had the first strategically significant victory for which they, and they alone, could take credit: the capture of Mexicali. It was hardly a great epic battle. Total dead: one, an unfortunate prison guard who tried to stop the Liberals from freeing the prisoners who were in his custody. But for the Liberals, the capture of Mexicali happened between two calamities—the death of Práxedis Guerrero on December 31 and the subsumption of their main armed contingent in Chihuahua into Madero's command at Casas Grandes in mid-February. As a result of those twin developments, the victory at Mexicali emerged as the only identifiable front where the Liberals had undisputed leadership.

Despite its modest size of under one thousand inhabitants, Mexicali was a strategic point in a rapidly expanding economy. Indeed, 80 percent of its merchants were Americans.[2] The construction of a canal system on the Colorado River transformed a huge tract of California desert into the agricultural emporium that was freshly baptized the Imperial Valley. The Colorado River canal system had a portion of its infrastructure on the Mexican side near Mexicali, so the town was also of strategic significance for U.S.-Mexican relations.

Thus, the capture of Mexicali was not an insignificant triumph, and the news energized Liberals. Wobblies and volunteer adventurers from the Imperial Valley and beyond began flocking to the towns of Holtville, Brawley, Imperial Valley, El Centro, and Calexico to join the tiny initial force of Liberal fighters. Nevertheless, despite all of this energy and the jump in circulation and funds for *Regeneración*, the Baja campaign stalled due to a leadership crisis.

The Baja Liberals were made up of three main contingents. Mexican Liberals—often coming into Baja from Southern California and Arizona; American sympathizers, mostly Wobblies, often workers from the Imperial Valley towns bordering on Mexicali or from Los Angeles and San Diego; and an assortment of privateers, including veterans of the Spanish-American War and the Boer War in South Africa. As a supplement to their various ideological motivations, volunteers were attracted by Liberal promises of 140 acres of land and pay for all veterans. In addition to these three contingents, there was an assortment of local Baja participants—Cocopah, Diegueño, Papai, and Kiliwa Indians, and some local ranchers, farmhands, and (Mexican and American) merchants.

Naturally, there were tensions between these contingents—Mexicans and Americans, Liberals and Wobblies, Indians and ranchers, ideologically driven revolutionaries and privateers. This was a heterogeneous group with substantial differences in aims and motivations. Anarchist troops disavowed the fundamental principle of traditional armies: the unquestioned authority of the officer class. For them, military leaders were supposed to be elected, and an officer's more controversial decisions would not go unquestioned. The practice of electing officers meant that Americans could be selected to leadership positions and that militarily effective privateers might achieve positions of leadership over socially committed militants. Developments of this sort, which did in fact occur, were public-relations liabilities for the Liberals.

The heterogeneity of the troops' origins and motivations was manifest soon after the victory at Mexicali. At that time, command of the forces was still in the hands of two members of the Liberal Party, both of them Mexicans residing in the United States: José María Leyva and Simon Berthold. Neither of them had military qualifications, and conflicts soon arose between them. As a result, the troops lingered around Mexicali for almost two months. During that time, fissures began to emerge between Berthold loyalists and American volunteers who had had no prior connection to the Liberal Party.

On the other hand, in California, rumors of a possible incorporation of Baja California into the United States began to make headlines, particularly in publications that promoted annexation, such as Randolph Hearst's *San Francisco Chronicle*, as well as in some of the Imperial Valley newspapers. Baja California historian Marco Antonio Samaniego has shown that less than a month after the fall of Mexicali, the term *filibustero*, which in Mexico referred to adventurers who sought to break off a portion of the national territory and make it independent in order later to annex it to the United States, was being used in all the major Baja towns to refer to the fighting men in Baja California and to their supporters in San Diego.[3] By early March, Mexico City newspapers were also denouncing the *filibusteros*.

The tension over military leadership burst into the open after precious weeks lost in inaction, with a good many of the Americans supporting the leadership of a Stanley Williams (also known as William Stanley, but also sometimes known as Cohen and as Robert Lowell). Stanley was a Wobbly who had been in the Spanish-American War and so had the military training that Simon Berthold, who was a union worker at the *Los Angeles Times*, lacked. Leyva, for his part, was accused of corruption and lack of expediency. Tensions grew to such a degree that the Los Angeles junta sent John Kenneth Turner and Antonio de P. Araujo to mediate and ended up sacking Leyva on March 29. After lingering a bit, Leyva joined up with the Maderista army, where he was given the rank of general.

Though the force was "purified" to some degree by this expulsion, the allegiance of the troops was still split between Berthold, who was a Liberal and a Mexican of sorts (born in Nacozari of a Mexican mother and a German father, though now a resident of Los Angeles), and Williams, who was neither, but who was, at least, a member of the Industrial Workers of the World. As a result, the junta granted autonomy to Williams, who operated east of Mexicali. His group, formed principally of an assortment of American volunteers, was sometimes referred to as the Foreign Legion.[4]

But both Williams and Berthold were killed in April, and neither was replaced, either by a Mexican or by a long-standing member of the Liberal Party. Simon Berthold was succeeded by Jack Mosby, a widely respected member of the IWW who had military experience himself, but who historian Lowell Blaisdell described as being militarily ineffective. Stanley Williams was replaced by Carl Ap Rhys Pryce. Pryce was a British aristocrat, adventurer, and veteran of wars in India and South Africa who was working as a Mountie in Canada when a copy of John Turner's *Barbarous Mexico* fell into his lap. Pryce read it and made his way to Mexico to enlist in the revolution.[5] That was how Pryce sometimes told it. Another, more probable explanation, offered by the British Foreign Service in Pryce's defense when he was processed for extradition to Mexico on charges of robbery and murder, was that Pryce had simply responded to an ad in an American paper calling for volunteers.[6] With these changes, leadership of the movement shifted to the soldier-of-fortune contingent, since Carl Ap Rhys Pryce was quite an able military commander.

Under Pryce's leadership, the Baja campaign finally took its second major prize: the village of Tijuana, which fell to his troops on May 10, 1911 (Figure 19.1). Like Mexicali, Tijuana provided the Liberals with revenues from its customs house. It also strengthened the sense among some soldiers that Baja could break off and form an independent republic, because neither Madero nor the Federal Army had control of the region.

From the fall of Mexicali in late January to the fall of Tijuana in May, the Federal Army—which was still Díaz's Federal Army at that point—had more or less stayed put. Its strategy had been to reinforce Colonel Celso Vega at Ensenada as much as possible and to place Colonel Mayol at the Bee River, a tributary of the Colorado, in a position where he could provide the Colorado River Land Company with protection for the dikes and canals that they had built for the Imperial Valley. Mayol's troops also stood in the way of the Baja

322

Liberals, in case they decided to try a move toward Sonora. Finally, Díaz's government had given the Colorado River Land Company permission to arm its workers and set up its own defenses as soon as Mexicali fell, in case the canal system came under any threat.[7]

Basically, the Federal Army's containment tactics worked. Despite Ricardo's haranguing, Liberal troops never moved east against Mayol, because the men on the ground felt that they were not strong enough to try it. Movement against Colonel Vega at Ensenada, which might have succeeded, was at first delayed by the timidity of the Leyva-Berthold team and then weakened by internal fissures among the rebels.

On May 9, 1911, the same day that Tijuana fell, Ciudad Juárez was captured by Pascual Orozco and the Maderista forces. Chihuahua was the key military arena of the revolution, and the fall of Ciudad Juárez prompted the signing of an agreement on May 21, the so-called Treaties of Ciudad Juárez. Following the terms of that agreement, Porfirio Díaz resigned on May 25.

Díaz's resignation caused disarray in the Baja campaign. Ricardo and the junta had already declared that there was no difference between Díaz and Madero and that the revolution would continue, but many combatants disagreed. Historian Marco Antonio Samaniego shows that most Mexicali troops and residents (including those exiled in Calexico) turned Maderistas right after the fall of Díaz.[8]

John Kenneth Turner was among those who retired from the battle after the fall of Díaz. On May 24, days after the signing of the Treaties of Ciudad Juárez, John made a statement to the *San Francisco Chronicle* saying that his participation in the Mexican Revolution had concluded.[9] Soon, Turner found himself being condemned by William C. Owen, allegedly for praising Madero in an article that Turner had published in the *Pacific Monthly*. Turner responded privately to Owen, asking him also to transmit his reply to Ricardo:

> I have tried to do a work that need not take sides between any party fighting Díaz, but you cannot but agree with me that in my writings I have given the Liberal Party more than a shade the better of it, and in what other things I have done all has been done for the Liberal Party.
>
> I have never attempted or desired to make friends with Madero. I do not wish to be thought of as having praised Madero. I have not praised him. I will therefore ask you, in all fairness to me, in your next issue

Figure 19.1 Tijuana viewed from the border, 1911. Today there are two parallel walls all along this border, both built by the United States, with migrant-detecting sensor towers between them. Courtesy of the San Diego History Center.

Figure 19.2 "Tierra y Libertad" over Tijuana. Wobblies and the PLM restore Tijuana to Mexico and the red flag after fellow revolutionaries declared its independence. Courtesy of the San Diego History Center.

either to print an article in which you say on a second reading you went too far in saying that I praised Madero or print all that I said about Madero and the Liberal Party."[10]

Regeneración never printed a retraction. Indeed, by the end of the Baja campaign, *Regeneración* was not tolerating even skeptical agnosticism with regard to Madero. Thirty years later, in a letter written to former junta member Jesús González Monroy, John explained that he had continued fighting on the Liberal side until Díaz fell, but that his emotional separation from the junta had occurred after Ricardo's insults to Antonio Villarreal, which John never forgave.[11] John had fought on the Liberal side in Baja California and never for Madero. He was nonetheless treated as if he had betrayed the cause.

In addition to prompting the desertion of many of the Mexicali revolutionaries, Díaz's abdication caused Pryce to cross to San Diego for a political conference that led to the sudden and improvised declaration of independence of Baja California. That act had plenty of political consequences for Ricardo and the junta, but from a military standpoint, it was just a parting gesture. Shocked into action by the opportunism of the privateers among them, the Wobbly contingent and the PLM loyalists rebelled against the declaration. They removed Pryce and his officers from the movement and raised the red flag over Tijuana once more (Figure 19.2).

But the reunion of whatever remained of the Liberals under the red flag came too late. The association of the Baja campaign with filibustering was already firmly in many people's minds—it had circulated widely in California and Baja, both inside and outside the various groups of fighters, among their supporters and detractors, and even in Mexican national opinion. Indeed, on April 1, Porfirio Díaz had tried to rally support by denouncing the invasion of Baja California on just those grounds. Although the Los Angeles junta never endorsed the idea of a Baja California republic and would have violently rejected annexation by the United States, it had not spent too much energy denouncing those rumors, either—until it was too late.

More importantly, perhaps, given the weakness of the Liberal movement, it could be perceived as supporting American annexation regardless of the junta's declared intentions. The majority of the Liberal troops in Tijuana were American, rather than Mexican; some troops, and even some of the Baja leaders had made declarations to the press to the effect that they were considering the formation of a nominally independent Baja republic, and rumors and musings to this effect had been circulating on and off in California papers since the end of January without provoking more than tepid reactions from *Regeneración*.

Moreover, although the junta adamantly rejected any connection to the intended president of the Republic of Baja California (a Mr. Dick Ferris, about whom we will have something to say in the next chapter), and although Jack Mosby's men had symbolically preempted the formation of the Baja Republic (symbolically, because their own position in Tijuana was so tenuous), the junta and the Liberal Party made no formal renunciation of its ties to General Pryce. On the contrary, on August 20 1911, when Liberal fighters Pryce, Mosby, J. B. Laflin, Samuel Reed, and Pedro Solís were being tried in Los Angeles for extradition to Mexico, the PLM organized a rally in support of all of them, Pryce included. Their petition—reproduced in the pages of *Regeneración*—declared "our firm belief in the honesty and good faith of these men" and said that they had fought solely for the purpose of undoing a tyrannical government.[12] No difference was made in this declaration between the situation of the soldier of fortune Carl Ap Rhys Pryce and that of the Wobbly Jack Mosby, for instance, and the supporters of both of these men rallied together as one at the Los Angeles courthouse.[13]

Because Ricardo was tainted with the charge of filibustering for many decades, the historians who set out to clear his name—Ethel Duffy Turner, Jesús González Monroy, and Agustín Cué Cánovas—draw sharp distinctions between Jack Mosby, whom they paint as a true Liberal and defender of Mexican integrity, and Pryce, who is portrayed as the opportunist who was run out of the ranks of the Liberals as soon as he supported the Baja Republic. Though there may indeed have been a sharp difference in the qualities of the two men, when it came to defending them in public, the junta made no distinction (Figure 19.3).

Among Mexicans, the fear that Baja was being annexed was not confined to the pro-Díaz faction. Nor was it, as Ricardo later declared, "an invention of Madero." Both Díaz and Madero sympathizers protested developments in Baja, and within Baja itself, concern over the filibusters was present in the towns of Ensenada,

Figure 19.3 *Insurrectos* in Tijuana. The word *insurrecto*, spoken out in English phonology, was often used to refer to American revolutionaries in Baja California, and was an index of the projection of the peninsula as an extension of the American frontier. The garb of the *insurrecto* combines the getup of the Western cowboy or miner, the Mexican revolutionary, and the U.S. Army veteran. Courtesy of the San Diego History Center.

Mexicali, and Tijuana, as well as among ranchers of the region.[14] Worries extended to groups of Mexicans in California, as well, and by the middle of May, a number of Mexican citizens in San Diego, supported by the Mexican consul, formed the Sociedad Defensores de la Integridad Nacional. This group split Mexican opinion in Southern California and gained a fair amount of traction in San Diego, as well as a foothold in Los Angeles itself. The Defensores de la Integridad Nacional sought to isolate the junta on the U.S. side of the border and to repel American "invaders" in Baja. They thus sent arms and volunteers to buttress the position of Díaz's Colonel Celso Vega, back in Ensenada.[15]

Ironically, when the men of the Defensores de la Integridad Nacional were ready to embark on a ship from San Diego to Ensenada, Liberal leaders Antonio de P. Araujo, Pryce, and their attorney, E. E. Kirk, alerted the American authorities and demanded that those men be captured for violation of neutrality laws, which the U.S. authorities did, on May 25. The new interim Mexican government that took over after Díaz responded with such outrage, though, that the men were let go on May 31, and they belatedly made their way to Ensenada to reinforce Colonel Vega's troops.[16]

Meanwhile, on June 6, 1911, in Ciudad Juárez, after the treaties were signed, the principal Maderista politician and now governor of Chihuahua, Don Abraham González, formed a commission to pacify Baja California, headed by former Liberals José María Leyva and Jesús M. González. In his signed edict, Abraham González said that the revolution had triumphed completely and that there was now democracy in Mexico, including freedom to organize and to strike. This meant that the Baja rebels were no longer justified bearing arms—they could struggle for their ideals within a democratic order.[17]

In the speech that he pronounced before the assembled Maderista troops at the time of this edict, Don Abraham said that there no longer Porfiristas and anti-Porfiristas, but only Mexicans, who now needed to unite. Don Abraham was also very clear about the connection between the PLM and Baja California's secession from the union: "And now, before your discharge, I would like to ask those of you who are willing to help pacify the country to join the one thousand ex-federal soldiers who are about to leave the City of Chihuahua, so that together you may throw the rabble of anarchists and filibusters out of the Baja California territory, for they are threatening to separate the peninsula from our nation's soil."[18]

In the face of this military project, which would certainly have crushed the Liberal forces, four ex-Liberals volunteered to go to the junta with a peace offering. They were Juan Sarabia, Jesús Flores Magón, Jesús González Monroy, and José María Leyva. Abraham González approved the mission, and so Jesús and Juan went to Los Angeles, while González Monroy and Leyva went to Calexico to negotiate disarmament with the Mexicali men.

On June 13, Jesús Flores Magón and Juan Sarabia met with Ricardo and the junta. We have no direct account of the conversation that transpired between them, but Juan and Jesús left in utter disappointment, to such an extent that Jesús later wrote that his brothers were no longer family to him. According to Ricardo, Juan Sarabia left the junta with a curse, saying that he would do them as much harm as possible.

On the following day, U.S. authorities arrested Ricardo, Enrique, Anselmo Figueroa, and Librado Rivera and charged them with violation of the neutrality laws. A few of the foreign intervention-ists—Pryce, Mosby, Laflin, Reed, Solis, and Dick Ferris—were also charged with the same crime. The men of the junta were imprisoned on June 14, 1911; they were later released on bail, finally brought to trial on June 21, 1912, and sentenced to federal prison at McNeil Island, in Washington State, for a twenty-three-month term.

On June 17, the Mexicali troops came to an agreement with Madero's emissaries. The troops were given ten dollars each, fed at the Chinese restaurant in Calexico, boarded on a train to El Cen-tro, and asked to disperse from that point.[19] When they heard the news, many of the Mexican forces in Tijuana, including the Indian contingent under their captain, Emilio Guerrero, retired into the mountains. Historian Marco Antonio Samaniego has concluded that for Mexican troops fighting in Baja California, "Despite its distance from that place, the Treaties of Ciudad Juárez were a definitive fac-tor in ending the struggle in Baja California, despite Flores Magón's insistence on continuing the fight."[20] Indeed, although fighting con-tinued in much of the rest of the country, the events of 1911 would be Baja's only sustained military campaign in the course of the entire decade from 1910 to 1920. On June 22, Colonel Vega, who had finally gone on the offensive, arrived in Tijuana from Ensenada, which somehow was five-days' journey in those days, and defeated the troops under Jack Mosby (Figure 19.4).

That was the end of the Liberal movement in Baja California, and it represented the defeat of the Liberals as a discrete and indepen-dent fighting force. At the start of the revolution, in November 1910, the Liberals had tried to tack their forces onto the Madero revolt and to thrive alongside that revolution, but they were either absorbed or defeated in Mexico and imprisoned in the United States. Barely one month after Porfirio Díaz's resignation, the Liberal offensive had sputtered out, and the junta was back in prison.

Revolutionary Theory
Ricardo and his closest circle had committed to revolution in 1903, and they had worked tirelessly and without interruption toward that end. Nevertheless, the movement that they built with such sacrifices collapsed in the first six months of a revolution that would last for a decade. Why?

Figure 19.4 *Federales* patrolling the international border during the second battle of Tijuana. Courtesy of the San Diego History Center.

Ricardo and his most ardent followers routinely blamed every-thing on persecution and betrayal. Thus, according to partisans of the movement, the 1906 revolution failed because it had been betrayed. Likewise for the revolution of 1908. The PLM's revolution-ary effort of 1910 had foundered because the U.S. government had failed to capture Madero for violation of the neutrality laws, while it had imprisoned Liberal captains. That revolutionary effort had failed because of betrayal, too—Madero's dishonorable conduct toward the Liberals at Casas Grandes, the betrayal of Villarreal and the Sara-bias, and the weakness and seduction of many other erstwhile Lib-eral leaders, such as Paulino Martínez, Antonio Díaz Soto y Gama, Rosalío Bustamante, Cecilio Garza, Lázaro Alanís, Lázaro Gutiérrez de Lara, Emilio Campa, and a long etcetera. Although it is certainly the case that the Liberal revolutions suffered tenacious persecution, infiltration, and efforts at co-optation, the collapse of the Baja Cali-fornia campaign reveals problems that Ricardo never admitted and that have not been very thoroughly outlined in subsequent histories.

The historiography of Magonismo is a complicated subject in its own right. In the 1920s, both apologies and condemnations of it were published. Rómulo Velasco Ceballos published a detailed history, with a number of primary documents, that was commissioned by former Baja California governor Esteban Cantú, whose purpose was to show that the Magóns were traitors and supporters of filibusters whose ultimate aim was the annexation of the Baja peninsula to the United States.[21] In the opposite camp, immediately after Ricardo's death, an Argentine anarchist Diego Abad de Santillana published the first hagiography of Ricardo, with a foreword written by Librado Rivera.[22] Anarchist printers of the 1920s also published the two plays that Ricardo had written in 1917, ¡Tierra y Libertad! (Land and freedom) and Verdugos y víctimas (Henchmen and victims), alongside essays, poems by Práxedis Guerrero and other Liberal heroes, and so on.

In the 1930s, Enrique Flores Magón participated in the organization of a political association, the Precursores de la Revolución Mexicana, tied to the corporate structure of the governing Partido de la Revolución Mexicana, which later morphed into the PRI. This organization flourished alongside much memorializing and also much concern with the authentication of "Precursor" status, since that recognition provided access to state pensions and other advantages. In addition to serving as an authenticator, Enrique published a weekly column in El Nacional dedicated exclusively to this sort of reminiscence. Writing from Los Angeles for La Opinión, the young historian José C. Valadés also dedicated weekly space to interviews and documents garnered from Mexican political exiles there, who, in those days, included revolutionary leaders of every political stripe, including many Liberals, whom Valadés admired.

In the 1950s, a set of partisan writers, including, most prominently, Ethel Duffy Turner, Jesús González Monroy, and Agustín Cué Cánovas, set about the task of exonerating Ricardo and the PLM from the charge of filibustering and treason. These efforts produced several books and culminated in a raucous 1956 historical congress in Baja California where Pablo Martínez del Río, one of the doyens of Mexican history at the time and himself rather conservative, absolved Ricardo and the PLM of the charge of supporting U.S. annexation of Baja, against the interpretation of Velasco Ceballos, which had predominated (and is still important) in Baja California. In 1945, Ricardo's remains were transferred from the Panteón Francés to the Rotonda de los Hombres Ilustres, which is a kind of national pantheon, thus confirming official support of his memory, at least in some powerful quarters. By 1962, Ricardo Flores Magón's name, written in golden letters, was added to those of the heroes enshrined on the wall of Mexico's Federal Congress, and that finally laid the issue of treason to rest.

Meanwhile, the historiography of Magonismo began to pick up steam in the United States. Contrary to the histories first written on the Mexican side, these interpretations were mainly written by academic historians, rather than by partisans, though intense contestation over the memory of the Liberals continued to ruffle the pages of Hispanic newspapers in Texas, California, Arizona, and New Mexico for many decades.

The first major academic history, Lowell Blaisdell's *The Desert Revolution*, is a well-researched military and political history of the Baja California movement. Its author was no great admirer of the Magóns, though neither can it be said that he was a virulent detractor, like Velasco Ceballos. In the late 1960s, a current of much more admiring, but also empirically rigorous historical works began to appear, beginning with James Cockroft's classic *Intellectual Precursors of the Mexican Revolution*[23] and continuing with W. Dirk Raat's well-documented work on the persecution of the *Magonistas (Revoltosos)*[24] in an arc of research and writing that continued through the 1980s and 1990s and that included works such as John Hart's *Anarchism and the Mexican Working Class*,[25] Collin McLachlan's work on the political trials of Ricardo Flores Magón,[26] and Ward Albro's biographies of Ricardo Flores Magón and Práxedis Guerrero,[27] among others. These are often the work of U.S. scholars who sympathize with Leftist currents in Latin America and who began revision of the Mexican Revolution with the blowback from the Vietnam War and the Cuban Revolution as guiding impulses.

A third front, that emerged almost simultaneously, in the early 1970s, was the recuperation of Magonismo by the new Chicano movement, a move that was initiated by Juan Gómez Quiñones[28] and that is still important, with contributions to our understanding of Magonismo's connection to Mexican-American issues in books such as James Sandos's *Rebellion in the Borderlands*[29] and Benjamin Heber Johnson's more recent *Revolution in Texas*,[30] as well as numerous works on women's participation in the revolution, such as Joel B. Pouwels's work on women in journalism[31] and a number of high-quality social histories of Mexican communities in the cities and towns of the Southwest.

In Mexico itself, the contemporary historiography of Magonismo developed under two principal umbrellas, one in academic history, the other the publication of anthologies and compilations of documents. Academic historians have produced detailed and well-documented works in the regional history of the movement, including Elena Azaola's *Rebelión y derrota del magonismo agrario*,[32] Jane-Dale Lloyd's essays on the regional history of North East Chihuahua,[33] Alfonso Torúa Cienfuegos's *El magonismo en Sonora (1906–1908)*,[34] Josefina Moguel Flores's *El magonismo en Coahuila*,[35] and Marco Antonio Samaniego's *Nacionalismo y Revolución*, among others. Meanwhile, the publication of anthologies and compilations of documents in Mexico has been more or less continuous, because the writings of the movement's principal ideologues have continued to be of interest to important sectors of the Mexican Left. Editorial Antorcha published anthologies and works by many of the movement's major figures—Ricardo, Librado, Práxedis—while other publishers brought out biographies and writings of prominent figures who were once attached to the movement, such as Antonio Díaz Soto y Gama, Juan Sarabia, Camilo Arriaga, Juana Gutiérrez de Mendoza, and others.[36] This work of documentation culminated in the past decade with the indispensable contribution of Jacinto Barrera Bassols, who published a monumental critical edition of Ricardo's complete works and made them widely available through a website.[37] This stratigraphy of historical interpretation must then be supplemented with the voluminous and sophisticated bibliography on the Mexican Revolution as a whole, as well as with the historiography of comparative anarchism.

In short, any account of the collapse of the Liberals' revolutionary organization has to navigate contested traditions of interpretation, and pronouncements of any kind can be objectionable to either supporters or detractors, Mexican or Chicano nationalists, internationalists and anti-imperialists, and more. The choices I make here are guided by the aims of this book, which dovetail with some of the concerns of the Mexican-American literature on the subject, as much as with those that have concerned anarchy, revolution, and transnationalism.

In his appraisal of the Baja California revolution, historian Lowell Blaisdell emphasizes the strategic blunders of the Los Angeles junta: their unwise and inefficient use of funds, directed more toward the work of propaganda than toward support for the military campaign; Ricardo's failure to move the junta into Mexico when the revolution started and to take personal charge of the campaign in the field; and the lack of military experience and talent of many of the Liberal captains and the ideological unreliability and/or foreign nationality of their more capable military chieftains, such as Stanley Williams and Pryce. Indeed, Blaisdell arrives at some harsh, but not unsubstantiated conclusions: "Unlike the talented Trotsky, who was endowed with a rare combination of skills as a writer of theory and as a chief of staff, Flores Magón had no administrative ability whatsoever."[38]

But in addition to the persecution and betrayal to which partisans of Ricardo such as Ethel Duffy and Enrique Flores Magón attributed all failures, and in addition to strategic blunders and military incompetence, there was a final problem that ran even deeper: Ricardo's theory of revolution was built on an illusion. Succinctly put, the Liberals had bought into and even contributed to a view that figured the dictator Díaz as an absolute sovereign. Not a leaf in Mexico's political forest shook without Díaz's approval, or so they claimed. The Liberals imagined that Díaz held a lid on a system of repression that extended down to every village and hacienda, every mine and urban neighborhood. Given a chance, each of those populations would rebel, recognize its own pulsation for freedom in that of its neighbors, and ignite a massive collective transformation.

The problem, however, was that as in all civil wars, once fighting broke out, it ran along the fault lines of already existing local political factions. And the weaker the state, the more important those factions and cleavages are for the revolutionary process.[39] The image of Díaz as an almighty despot, which was buttressed by constant flattery and hero worship, distracted the Liberals' attention from a harder fact, which was that the Mexican state was weak, and so Mexican political factions would be deeply fragmented and diverse under conditions of civil war. Had the Mexican state not been so weak, why would Díaz have had to undertake such a complicated balancing act in making concessions to competing foreign interests? Had it not been weak, why were local *jefes políticos* universally portrayed as petty tyrants? Indeed, had the Mexican state been strong, Porfirio Díaz would not have been in a position to get himself reelected for thirty years. It was always the threat of implosion, factional strife, and revolution that transformed Porfirio Díaz into *el hombre necesario.*

As long as Díaz was in power, it made sense for the Liberals to take aim at the president as the source of all evil and to imagine that once revolution began, a universal emancipatory force would well up, but this was only an expedient fiction. In fact, revolution would depend to a very high degree on alliances with a bewildering variety of local factions, and there, it was the Liberals who were weak, either because they had insufficient local ties or because leaders who did have ties were often compelled to subordinate their ideals to the practical desires and requirements of local factions and so became vulnerable to accusations of treason from Ricardo, back in Los Angeles

Local Diversity

The fulcrum of the early phase of the Mexican Revolution was Chihuahua, but the Liberal militants who had remained loyal to the Los Angeles group suffered early misfortunes there. Práxedis Guerrero lost his life in Janos. Other Texas chieftains were detained by U.S. authorities for violation of the neutrality laws and kept off the field during key months of revolutionary upheaval. In February 1911, the old veteran Prisciliano Silva was arrested by Madero and his loyalists disarmed. Many loyal Liberals had flocked to Villarreal's expedition into Mexico, some of them under false pretenses. In short, though the Liberals had many sympathizers in Texas and Chihuahua, their ability to lead in that critical border region foundered.

This left Baja California as the Liberals' most accessible field for action. Baja was close to the junta's headquarters, and its sparse population of scarcely forty thousand souls was isolated from the Mexican mainland and so relatively easy to hold. Indeed, Baja's very isolation made it attractive as a base from which the Liberals might hope to expand operations as the movement gathered strength. But the very situation that made Baja California a plum for the Los Angeles junta—its proximity to California and its isolation from the rest of Mexico—made the region a focus of international politics. The diversity of actors, economic interests, and cultural situations was such that making the Baja revolution into a single conflict—unifying actors around a shared set of goals—required resources beyond those of the Los Angeles junta.

335

When Baja began to be developed, through copper mining in the mid-1890s, the Díaz government gave mining concessions at Rosarito and El Boleo to French companies, leased the Bahía de Magdalena to the United States for naval exercises, gave major land concessions to the British-owned Mexican Land and Colonization Company, and cheaply sold 832,000 acres of Baja lands that would soon come under irrigation to Los Angeles newspaper mogul Harrison Gray Otis.[40] Despite concessions to French and English capital, though, economic incorporation northward, to California, was progressing at a dizzying speed, driven on the west side by the rise of San Diego (in anticipation of the 1914 opening of the Panama Canal) and in the east by the development of the Imperial Valley, thanks to the irrigation canal system on the Colorado River, which spans the border into Baja California.

These twin developments gave rise to several border towns: Mexicali/Calexico and Tecate/Tecate in the Imperial Valley and Tijuana, across from San Diego. Though these places were still very small, they had come to be of importance almost comparable to Ensenada, the political capital of the district. Indeed, border traffic came to be so important that after the defeat of the Liberals in 1911, the district capital of the Baja California Norte territory was transferred to Mexicali.

Baja California had U.S. capital investments in railroads and in agricultural infrastructure (the Colorado River canal) and a burgeoning cotton and ranching economy in the Mexicali region. Baja was free to import Chinese laborers, banned from California thanks to the Chinese Exclusion Act, to work in the Mexicali cotton plantations. The region was also of growing strategic significance—the Panama Canal project increased international competition for control of ports in Baja California and Sonora. Finally, Baja's proximity to California, its accessibility, and the ascendancy of U.S. interests in the region made it an obvious place for a certain modality of border traffic and commercialization tied to leisure. This was by no means confined to gambling, drinking, and prostitution, though all three were important, especially since the Imperial Valley passed blue laws starting in 1906. The rise of San Diego as a port built to compete with San Francisco—the first U.S. port for ships coming in from South America—stimulated the advisability of giving that new city a Latin face. On the other hand, Hollywood was beginning to emerge as a center of film production in those years, and "Spanish" (largely Mexican) themes would also provide a useful reservoir of themes and images for that industry.

In short, managing a revolutionary force in Baja was complicated, even despite the region's small population, because it was an area with a lot of "future" invested in it or projected onto it. This made the Liberals' programs difficult to assimilate or interpret, both by the local population and by interested parties from without.

So, for instance, Baja California residents seem often to have identified the Liberals either as American "filibusters" who were interested in annexing the peninsula to the United States or as sharing in the same fight as Madero.[41] As a result, local aims and motivations involved in their participation in armed confrontations that involved the Liberal Party are still difficult adjudicate. So, for instance, in the 1960s ethnohistorian Roger Owen did oral histories with the descendants of the 300 to 700 Diegueño, Papai, and Kiliwa Indians who participated on one side or another of the Magonista revolution in northern Baja California. Although elders keenly remembered the events of 1911, Owen concluded that "the Indians were basically unaware of the larger political events in which they were involved.... From the standpoint of the Indians themselves, much of the action in which they were involved was a case of Indian fighting Indian rather than a case of Indians joining a revolution."[42]

The question of the nationality of the rebels and their degree of understanding of Mexican issues was not a negligible issue, either. Most Americans who were attracted to the rebels for ideological reasons might have read John Kenneth Turner's *Barbarous Mexico*, at best. In order to supplement ideological motivations stemming from this reading, volunteers not only were promised land—140 acres—but a bonus of from $100 to $600 if they triumphed, so many volunteers may have learned about the Mexican Cause only after joining.[43] And the junta's ability to control those groups or even to orient them ideologically was limited. This led both to internal problems and to challenges to the Liberals' public image.

One tension of internal relevance was that American volunteers outnumbered Mexican soldiers on the Western (Tijuana) front (Figure 19.5).[44] As we've seen, U.S. volunteers were split between Wobblies who shared many of the Liberals' goals and adventurers

Figure 19.5 American *insurrecto*, standing guard.
Courtesy of the San Diego History Center.

who had only vague ideas of their cause. As we've seen, conflicts between Mexicans and Americans occasionally broke out.[45] More importantly, the command of the two main Liberal "regiments" (the one stationed around Mexicali and the one stationed around Tijuana) at times fell to "Anglos"—Stanley Williams, Jack Mosby, and Carl Ap Rhys Pryce—and so leadership crises, like the one faced in March by José María Leyva, who was ousted by the Los Angeles junta, could at certain moments be given a "Mexican versus American" slant.[46]

This matter was even more delicate for the movement's public image. Thus, the anti-Magonista Baja California historian Rómulo Velasco Ceballos relates that when the Sociedad Defensores de la Integridad Nacional was formed in San Diego shortly after the first battle of Tijuana, a stocky matron named Doña Blasa Manríquez de Marrón got up on the soapbox to harangue the crowd:

> The gringos are killing and stealing! Does that not rouse your indignation? There are babies being orphaned and left in misery! Is there no one to defend them? Even the corpses have been injuriously treated! They've thrown them into this country so that people can make fun of them!...If you all won't do your duty, if patriotism has died in you, if you don't want to prove that you're Mexicans, if you've lost all shame—yes, shame—then we women are here, and we know what to do.[47]

According to Blaisdell, only around 10 percent of the two-hundred-odd troops who captured Tijuana were Mexicans, so it was in fact true that Americans under the command of Anglo captains were killing Mexicans on Mexican soil (Figure 19.6).[48] Moreover, some of the field commanders, including Mosby and Pryce, had publicly entertained the possibility of declaring a socialist republic in Baja California—that is, of secession from the Mexican union—a move that was interpreted by many as a first step to annexation by the United States and that led leaders of the Sociedad Defensores de la Integridad Nacional to accuse Ricardo Flores Magón and his party of playing a role that was akin to that of the Tejanos at the time of Texas' independence: they were pawns of the U.S. government.[49]

Ricardo reacted in two ways to this issue. When Tijuana fell to the Liberal troops, he sent a congratulatory letter to Pryce and the fighting men: "This victory was earned thanks to the intelligence and courage of our men, who knew how to defeat the wretched slaves

Figure 19.6 Porfirista loyalists being executed by American *insurrectos*. Courtesy of the San Diego History Center.

that Capital and Authority sent to their deaths, and this to undermine the rights and prolong the suffering of the human race."[50] The casualties, in other words, were not to be seen as Mexican citizens, the way Mexican nationalists wished, but rather as slaves of "Capital" and of the Mexican state. On the other hand, Ricardo was slow to respond to charges of treason. On June 10—that is, after all was lost, he wrote: "We have said this many times: we do not want to transfer Baja California to the United States."[51] But protesting intentions in this way was not always enough to allay fears of annexation.

Indeed, even within the Liberal Party, the foreigners' shallow understanding of the Mexican Cause could be embarrassing. So, for instance, in an interview with Western cowboy novelist Peter Kyne for *Sunset Magazine*, field commander Pryce confidently listed the crimes of the despot, including the following item: Porfirio Díaz, he said, had deposed the popularly elected Indian President Benito Juárez. Except that Juárez had been dead for four years when Díaz came to power. Lowell Blaisdell summarizes Pryce's shaky understanding of the entire Liberal ideological formation:

> Pryce also denied to Kyne that his enterprise was in any way an attempt to set up a new socialist nation in Baja California: they were 'fighting

out of sentiment to help the Mexican peones to get their rights under the "constitution of 1836 ... or 1858," he was not sure which, but it was an excellent constitution, and a pity that the Díaz regime had not lived up to it.[52]

This kind of gaffe was not uncommon among foreign volunteers in the armies of the revolution, whether Liberal or Maderista. Indeed, a comparison between the Maderista Garibaldi and the Liberal Caryl Ap Rhys Pryce is instructive. Like the Liberals, Madero, too, incorporated a good many foreigners into his army, most of whom were adventurers with military experience spurred to join the revolutionary effort by a mix of (often vague) emancipatory sentiments and a thirst for adventure (or profits). Like the Liberals, Madero, too, was interested in these men because many had military experience. This was the case of both Giuseppe Garibaldi and Ben Viljoen, both Boer War veterans who Madero made generals. And like the Liberal rank and file, Madero's Chihuahua allies were suspicious and resentful of the leadership positions that these men were granted. Moreover, there were concerns that foreign soldiers might receive higher pay than Mexican soldiers, mirroring the inequalities that prevailed among foreign and Mexican workers. Finally, like Pryce, Garibaldi, too, had only sketchy notions of Mexican society, politics, and history.

Nonetheless, the differences between the two cases were significant. In Liberal Tijuana, the Americans were at times fully the majority of the troops, whereas in Maderista Chihuahua, local military captains and troops dominated. Moreover, Madero crossed into Chihuahua and personally led his allied forces from the field. Indeed, Madero's fearlessness in the face of fire earned him the lasting respect and loyalty of local commanders such as Pancho Villa.[53] By contrast, Ricardo's absence from the field meant that command of the Baja troops was largely decided through internal consensus and factional struggle, which opened the door for foreigners such as like Pryce to lead, despite their lack of familiarity with Mexico.

Finally, Madero used the prestige of Garibaldi's name and lineage as a publicity gimmick for his movement: the grandson of the great liberator Garibaldi was now joining Madero and Mexico's fight for liberty. Pryce, on the other hand, was an English aristocrat whose name was unknown in either Mexico or the United States. Jack

Mosby, for his part, was the nephew of a Confederate general, and no one even knew what Stanley Williams's real name was. So the Baja foreign commanders conferred no benefit to the Liberal public image inside Mexico.

Ideological clarity regarding the Liberals' aims in Baja was further complicated by the fact that the junta still officially claimed the PLM's 1906 manifesto as its political program. That document had been written in close collaboration with Juan Sarabia and Antonio Villarreal, who were now siding with Madero. The PLM's new ideological program, much more radical and in tune with the ideas of the junta, appeared only on September 23, 1911, months after Baja California had been lost and when the directorate of the junta was under indictment and awaiting trial.

Overall, one might say that the diversity of constituencies and political interests operating in Baja California overwhelmed the junta. Ricardo would have had to move his entire outfit from Los Angeles, a communications center, to the backwater that was Baja California to have a real chance of cobbling together a coherent movement there. But to leave Los Angeles was to abandon a viable base for a broader propaganda effort. For better or for worse, Ricardo decided not to limit his scope of action in that way. As a result, the Liberals never really gained control of the Baja movement.[54]

Double Strategy

After the defeat in Baja California, *Regeneración* struggled, but it managed to survive. In its heyday, when Mexicali and Tijuana were in Liberal hands, the journal printed 27,000 copies, and money flowed into PLM coffers from donations from numerous sympathizers, including most principally the IWW and a group of Italian labor unions.[55] After the separation of the Socialists, the fall of Porfirio Díaz, the collapse of the Baja campaign, and the imprisonment of the junta, *Regeneración* lost about half of its subscribers, and the finances of the party practically collapsed.[56] Among the Italian unions, there were rumors that the junta had misspent or misappropriated funds—a charge that was echoed in the French anarchist journal *Les Temps Nouveaux*.[57] The Wobblies, for their part, got disaffected because they had lost more men in Baja than anyone else, and they felt that the junta was not providing sufficient funds for the defense of their leader there, Jack Mosby. Wobbly anger boiled when

William Owen, the editor of *Regeneración*'s English-language page (who now had a pivotal role in the journal, after Ricardo's imprisonment), minimized the significance of the Baja defeat, writing that "nothing... could have shown more complete ignorance than the centering of attention on the exceedingly subsidiary movement in Lower California."[58]

The comment was very impolitic and naturally spurred anger among the Wobblies, who had born the brunt of the campaign. But Owen was not entirely wrong. After the Liberals' defeat in Chihuahua, Ricardo's strategy had been to revolutionize Mexico by calling for the immediate and direct appropriation of lands by the poor, summed up in the motto "Tierra y Libertad," while orchestrating a centrally directed military campaign to gain a permanent foothold in Baja California. That strategy involved propaganda and ideological work—making the many spots in which there were spontaneous uprisings visible to one another and providing ideological coherence and direction to a movement over which Ricardo and the junta had practically no military influence. The Baja California front, on the other hand, was supposed to be directed and supported from Los Angeles.

These two strategic fronts required a third, diplomatic effort, geared to avoiding American military intervention and to energizing solidarity with the Mexican Cause in order better to arm and sustain the military campaign in Baja California and, ideally, elsewhere, and thus be effective in the effort to consolidate efforts at "direct action," for "Land and Freedom" throughout Mexico.

The problem was that the three fronts divided the junta's attention. With Práxedis dead and Villarreal and Juan Sarabia gone, there was no leader in the junta who could balance Ricardo's weight as an ideologue. Enrique, though impressive as a militant and thoroughly reliable as a working presence, was more an operations man. So were Antonio de Pío Araujo, Fernando Palomares, and Anselmo Figueroa. The two men left who had stature as strategists and ideologues—John Kenneth Turner and William C. Owen—were foreigners. And although Turner threw himself into the Baja California campaign, he was estranged by Ricardo's dealings with Antonio, Manuel, and Lázaro. John supported the revolutionary cause and "Land and Freedom," but could not serve as a balance to Ricardo. In the end, as we've seen, John felt that once Díaz fell, Madero should be given a chance.[59]

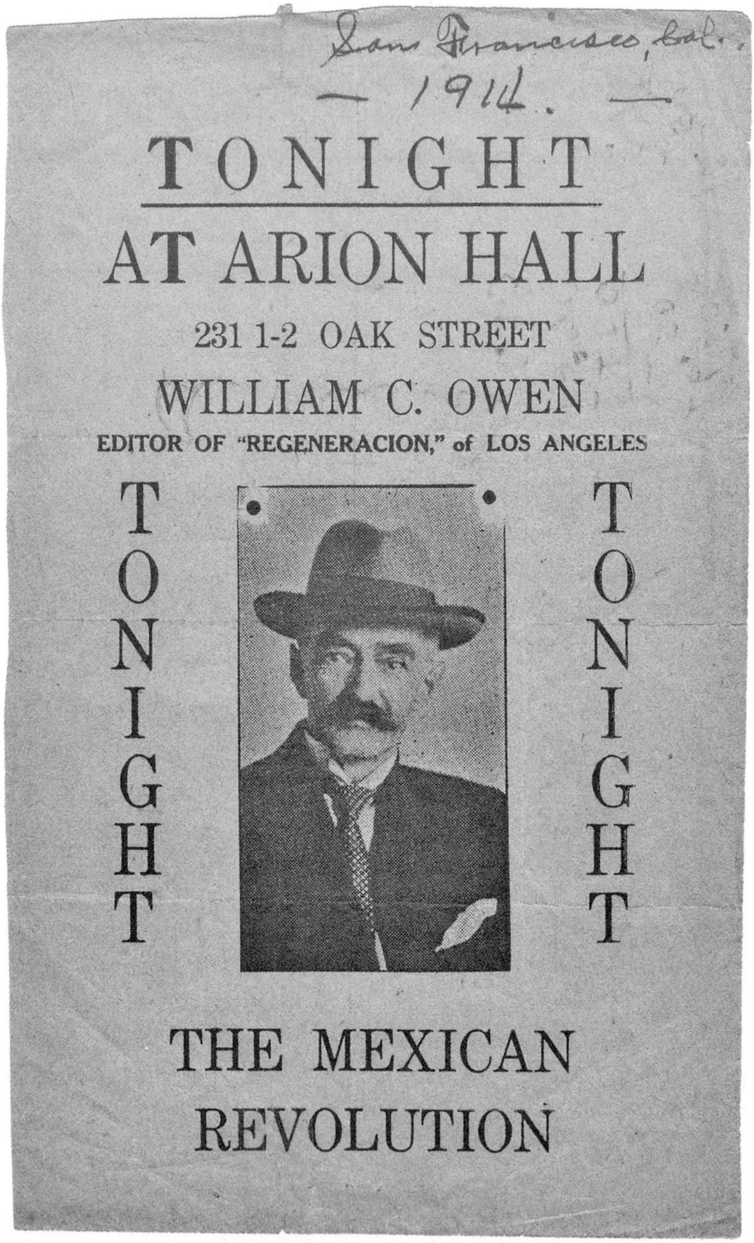

San Francisco, Cal.
— 1914. —

TONIGHT

AT ARION HALL

231 1-2 OAK STREET

WILLIAM C. OWEN

EDITOR OF "REGENERACION," of LOS ANGELES

T O N I G H T

T O N I G H T

THE MEXICAN
REVOLUTION

Figure 19.7 William C. Owen. This is the only known image of the indefatigable Owen, announcing a lecture in San Francisco in 1914. Courtesy of the Casa de El Hijo del Ahuizote, Mexico City.

344

William C. Owen, for his part, served energetically in the ideological battle that was boiling within the American Left with regard to the Mexican Revolution, arguing ferociously against the Socialist line (Figure 19.7). But there were two reasons why Owen could never lead alongside Ricardo. First, he had joined *Regeneración* only in late April 1911, too close to Díaz's fall and Madero's rise to win over a substantial portion of the Socialist camp, and second, as opposed to Turner, Owen was unfamiliar with Mexico and was completely unknown there, so his role was confined to the *Regeneración* editorial office and largely to internecine conflicts of the American and European Left.

After the Chihuahua defeat of February 1911, *Regeneración* of Los Angeles changed its format. From then on, the first page was regularly dedicated to reporting brief news of the revolution's advance from all states of the Mexican Republic. The idea was to produce an image that Práxedis Guerrero might have called *puntos rojos*—multiple flash points of revolution through the entire nation. Internal pages then supplemented the image of a massive, spontaneous revolt—which was, in fact, really occurring—and attempted to provide it all with ideological direction and coherence by way of thematic pieces.

Correspondence for this effort occupied at least eight hours of Ricardo's day, every day, and then he was writing the articles for *Regeneración*, participating in meetings, and doing other work to further the cause. Such a schedule was not compatible with going into the field in Baja to try to direct a military campaign for which, moreover, Ricardo had neither the training nor, perhaps, the physical endurance. So directives from the junta to Baja were general and loosely worded, and funds coming into the junta were not all channeled to Baja, but were often invested in broader propaganda work, instead. The junta harbored the hope, expressed later in William Owen's much-decried article, that Baja was only one among many fronts, although in fact, there was no other region in which the junta actually had military ascendance.

That left one final concern for the junta, which was how best to work to avoid U.S. military intervention in Mexico.

International Relations for Anarchists
Madero's instructions regarding the protection of foreign lives and property were firm and explicit, and Chihuahua field commanders generally understood the significance of this policy. Thus,

Methodist minister Alden Buell Case, whose parish was in an Orozquista hotbed in Chihuahua's Guerrero District, wrote: "It was
well known in town that the commanders of both opposing factions had issued strict orders that their troops should guard against
the molestation of foreigners, and particularly of Americans. Over
the great front entrance of our house during those days waved the
American flag."[60]

Ricardo, too, had understood the critical significance of this
point and had consistently issued instructions to PLM delegates in
the same sense as early as 1906. But beyond protecting American life
and property, the Liberals needed to address U.S. opinion, and there
was no one in the junta who could really do that, not even Owen.

John Kenneth Turner was the man who did the most by far to
steer American opinion against military intervention. John worked
tirelessly against U.S. intervention, even long after his separation
from the Liberals. He repeatedly warned against the temptation,
first, for the United States to prop up Díaz; and later, in 1912 and
1913, for it either to topple or to support Madero. After denouncing
the successful (U.S.-backed) coup against Madero by Victoriano
Huerta in 1913, Turner scathingly reported on the 1914 American military invasion of Veracruz.[61] In 1916, he wrote against the
Pershing punitive expedition against Pancho Villa, despite Turner's
support for Villa's rival, Venustiano Carranza.[62]

The effects of Turner's consistent, poignant, and informative
reporting against interventionism were sufficiently serious for the
State Department to make a formal review of his track record in
1919 and to keep him from traveling to Mexico for more reporting:

> From the above it appears that Turner is an agitator of an extreme type,
> and that if he were permitted to return to Mexico he might again cause
> considerable annoyance to the Mexican authorities as well as to those
> of our own Government. Furthermore, he might by his writings and
> agitation tend to create bad feelings between the Mexican Government
> and that of the United States. I therefore recommend that his name and
> that of his wife be placed on the permanent refusal list.[63]

The State Department denied John and his second wife, Adriana
Spadoni, passports. On that particular occasion, Turner's mission
was to expose the oil interests' intentions to back U.S. intervention,
this time against Carranza. In 1921, he published one of his last major

works, *Hands Off Mexico*, which was a well-informed and polemical exposé of U.S. interventionist intentions.[64]

Ricardo's attention to American opinion was less consistent and less sophisticated than John's. His main efforts were focused on the revolution in Mexico itself. The U.S. government had made its views of the Liberals clear by jailing their commanders. It was obvious that Ricardo had no chance of winning the government over to his side. On the other hand, his limited spoken English (relative to his poignant Spanish) and inability or lack of desire to adapt to the styles and modalities of the American "bourgeois press" meant that he could not persuade U.S. opinion directly, either. In the United States, Ricardo could be a cause, but not an effective advocate.

A second problem was that Ricardo's idea of direct action, summarized in the party's new motto "Tierra y Libertad," could not be put into practice in Baja without provoking U.S. intervention. The most important properties in Baja were owned by Americans. The Liberals shook down property owners by levying a revolutionary tax, but they refrained from expropriation for strategic reasons that were abundantly clear to the field commanders: on the one hand, they needed the income from those taxes, and on the other, they had to maintain relations of goodwill on the U.S. side of the border in order to make arms purchases and to avoid harassment or intervention by the American troops that were stationed there. These considerations were no different from those faced by other, nonanarchist, *agrarista* leaders such as Pascual Orozco and Pancho Villa, for instance, and they tended to blur any real distinction between Liberals and military commanders who were allied to Madero.

This effect was felt among Baja native combatants, most of whom supported the Liberal effort only until the triumph of Madero, but this was perhaps less obvious in Los Angeles, because the junta was removed from the scene of revolutionary action. In the field, the radical ideological coherence of the Liberals became to some degree undone, particularly in the border region, where all factions faced similar strategic dilemmas.

Figure 20.1 Jack Mosby and his troops, surrendering to Captain Wilcox at Fort Bliss. Courtesy of the San Diego History Center.

Figure 20.2 Corpses at a so-called hospital, according to the caption on this American photo. But Mexican anti-*insurrecto* nationalists represented this field as something else. To them, Mexican corpses were being dragged across the border and exposed there for public viewing. Photo courtesy of the San Diego History Center.

CHAPTER TWENTY

The Man from Mexico

Jack Mosby's Tears

"Far inferior in equipment and manpower, Mosby also found himself badly outgeneraled by Vega, with the result that the battle, though hard-fought, ended in a rout after only three hours.... Mosby, overcome with emotion and 'weeping like a child,' and 106 of the non-Mexicans threw down their arms and crossed the boundary as political refugees."[1] That was the final scene of the final battle of the Baja California campaign (Figure 20.1).

For the most part, though, the Baja revolution was a rather dispersed affair, characterized more by low-intensity conflict and occasional skirmishes than by pitched battles. Even so, it produced plenty of anguish and devastation. Death tallies are not known, and the Mexican government of the time was too poorly organized to provide any accurate estimate. When the Mexican government tried to extradite Carl Ap Rhys Pryce and Jack Mosby, in August 1911, it brought charges against them for the murder of the postmaster and the subprefect of Tijuana, for burning Tijuana's bullring, for sacking its general stores, hotels, and curio shops, for the extortion of Chinese merchants in Mexicali, for stealing mules and horses, and for levying a revolutionary tax on American and Mexican ranchers.

There were, of course, many other costs. The Liberals lost a good many brave and beloved men, including some very popular leaders, such as Simon Berthold and Stanley Williams. Berthold had been a union activist in Los Angeles. During the campaign, he once went back to that city for consultation with the junta and stayed the night at John and Ethel's place, where he left behind a poem intended for his girlfriend. Its trite and conventional innocence says something, I think, about the personality of some of the volunteers who lost their lives in Baja:

Quiero llevarte
Para cantarte
Con lira de arco
Canciones mil;
Que solo encuentro
Feliz momento
Contigo estando
En el pensil.
Si Dios quisiera
Niña hechicera
Yo viviría junto a tus pies;
Mas entretanto
Mi triste llanto
Vierto a raudales
Bajo el ciprés.

[I want to transport you
To sing to you
With a viola
A thousand songs;
Because the only time
That I am happy
Is when I'm with you
In the garden.
If God willed it
Bewitching girl
I'd live at your feet;
But in the meantime
My sad tears
Flow in torrents
Under the cypress.] [2]

Nor was the conservative side necessarily less innocent. In Ensenada, fear of Liberal troops invading and of looting led the local population to succumb periodically to wild rumors. A number of the town's residents—many from the local merchant and professional classes—took the steamer to San Diego for fear of remaining in their homes. The American consul in Ensenada, a twenty-five-year-old named George Schmuker, described by Velasco Ceballos as being very closely tied to Ensenada society, lost his mind in fear and anxiety about the nature of U.S. participation in the region. At first, he nervously asked the State Department to provide naval protection for Ensenada, but by mid-May, he had gone mad and cabled the following message to the State Department "To comprehend political and social conditions at present moment, study and apply latter part of the Book of Revelation, Holy Bible," and also: "I have a plan that will result in bettering civilization everywhere and in preventing my own assassination. Answer."[3]

Among the counterrevolutionary Mexicans who came together in San Diego, the complaints against the "filibusters" were magnified by the fact that Tijuana, with its five hundred inhabitants, was a face-to-face community, whereas the Liberal troops had their ranks swollen by volunteers who came from anywhere and everywhere. As a result, practically all Tijuanense casualties were *conocidos*—daily acquaintances—who died at the hands of *desconocidos*, strangers, and American *desconocidos* at that. One of the complaints mentioned repeatedly by Velasco Ceballos, who as a historian was a partisan of these counterrevolutionaries, is the fact that bodies of Tijuana dead were piled unceremoniously on the border: "The Mexican casualties were put on a dirty, miserable cart and taken to the international borderline, and they were heaped onto U.S. territory as if they were trash." Ceballos then describes how portions of the federal soldiers' clothing were taken by onlookers as souvenirs: "The Yankees stole the shoes off the corpse of the head of the post office, and U.S. soldiers [stationed in San Diego] ripped the buttons off his jacket. And that's how they desecrated other corpses, too, ripping off pieces of clothing to keep as 'souvenirs.'... The Yankees don't even respect a Mexican's corpse!"[4] (Figure 20.2)

These hardships found expression in the press because they were transpiring on the border and were suffered by groups that had political representation. Farther inland, though, and further on down the social scale, suffering was no less intense, but is more difficult to track. Thus, historian Lowell Blaisdell tells how antirevolutionary vigilantes shot and killed eleven Indians near Alamo, without ascertaining whether they were or were not allied to the revolutionary effort.[5] American merchants in that same region were unceremoniously shot and killed because, as Americans, they were associated with the Liberal armies. And finally, there was the suffering of the Liberal chieftains who remained loyal to the junta.

After Porfirio Díaz's abdication, anyone could see that the Liberal campaign was done for. Until that time, the Federal Army had concerned itself with Chihuahua and with the spread of the revolution from there to Mexico's heartland. Its strategy in Baja California had been defensive—containment. Now that Madero had triumphed and a peace treaty was signed, federal troops were freed up and could take the offensive. Furthermore, they were reinforced by Madero's revolutionary troops. The Liberal Army at Casas Grandes, Chihuahua, had, after all, been disarmed by Pancho Villa himself, and there was no scarcity of Maderistas who saw the Liberals in Baja as traitors and secessionists. Finally, San Diego's Sociedad de Defensores de la Integridad Nacional also had sent reinforcements to Colonel Vega in Ensenada, whose position had thereby been strengthened. The treaties of Ciudad Juárez dictated that Madero keep the Federal Army pretty much intact. This meant that the Liberals would have to face the combined forces of the revolutionary and the federal armies.

Pryce and many of his men realized this. They were, moreover, dismayed by the lack of material and political support from the Los Angeles junta. A profiteer in Pryce's army named Hopkins wrote to a comrade in hospital on June 1, complaining that the junta had not helped them in any way. The junta's role in the campaign had been limited to sending letters of congratulations. Even when Madero had called them "filibusters," the junta had failed to come to Tijuana to make Mexican leadership of the movement public. John Kenneth Turner, on the contrary, had come down to the border and had conferred with Pryce, letting him know that in his view, they could not win against Díaz's Federal Army and the Maderistas combined. So, Hopkins concluded, "As far as I can see, the game is up—that is, the financial end of it—and I do not feel like risking my life for nothing.... My next move will be either South America or the South Seas."[6]

A lot of desertion followed, leaving the men the choice either of indeed trying a filibuster—the declaration of a Baja republic in the hope that it would find U.S. support and so allow them to fend off Mexico's Federal Army—or remain loyal to the Liberal revolution. Pryce flirted with the former solution; Jack Mosby opted for the latter.

There was no support for the filibuster forthcoming from the U.S. government, so Pryce traveled under an assumed name to San Francisco, where he was captured and then tried, first for extradition to Mexico and, when that failed, for violation of the neutrality laws. Jack Mosby, on the other hand, was a Wobbly, rather than a soldier of fortune, so he stuck it out in Baja, and his men were defeated on the field.

Mosby was then tried and convicted for desertion from the U.S. Army and for violation of the neutrality laws. He died in prison. The men of the junta, too, became casualties of the Baja campaign (Figure 20.3). They were convicted and sentenced to two years in prison in the cold dampness of McNeil Island, Washington, where Anselmo Figueroa's health deteriorated to such an extent that he died shortly after his release. Ricardo's health, too, began its steep decline at McNeil.

Farce and Tragedy

All historical events are susceptible to being told as either tragedy or farce. An event implies transformation, and change always slips from the control of history's heroes. This is history's tragic element—the defeat of the hero's best purposes by the social forces that he or she has nurtured or unleashed. But historical events also have "back stages," places like the back rooms, hallways, and draperies on the sets of eighteenth-century farces. Political actors often hide their own petty motivations behind the grand ideals, the "master narratives," that frame great historical events. In those back rooms, secondary plots are hatched that undermine the grave intentions of the heroes and heroines who grope to occupy center stage, transforming them into instruments and playthings.

In 1910, Mexico was an economic dependency of the United States. It had also invited European capital—particularly British, French, and German—to temper overwhelming reliance on American investment. As a result, American and European powers were like an ample "back stage" in Mexican national history. The embassies and consulates, foreigners' clubs and informal salons that dotted the Mexican landscape, the hotels, restaurants, and business associations in El Paso, Los Angeles, San Diego, New Orleans, Havana, New York, London, and Paris—these were all places where the proclaimed intentions of Mexico's political men and women could be subverted or twisted to another purpose.

Within the image: At Ti Juana, Mex. Before March Gen. Mosby and Adjutant Laflin Insurrectos

San Diego History Center

Figure 20.3 Jack Mosby and Bert Laflin, both beloved Wobbly leaders, suffered imprisonment. Mosby died in prison. Photo courtesy of the San Diego History Center.

Mexican revolutionaries were clear on this point, and they struggled either to keep the United States neutral or to bring it to their side. They needed U.S. government recognition; they needed to avoid U.S. military intervention; they needed to buy and sell goods in the United States, and they needed to buy arms there. Even at the lowest organizational levels, revolutionaries needed access to commerce, police tolerance, grassroots solidarity, and material support on the U.S. side of the border.

The Mexican Liberals never aspired to official U.S. recognition, however. This seems natural, given that they were anarchists and opposed to the U.S. government as much as to any other, but this very fact also suggests how far this political movement was from aspiring to national power in any conventional sense. Francisco I. Madero, on the contrary, had hired lobbyists and personal representatives in Washington as soon as his party became belligerent and had developed ties to U.S. oil interests.[7] Later presidents, Venustiano Carranza, Álvaro Obregón, and Victoriano Huerta all sought this sort of connection, as did Pancho Villa. The Liberals relied on the solidarity of smaller players instead—unions, the Wobblies, the Socialists—and restricted their diplomatic efforts regarding the U.S. government mostly to the fight against the repatriation of political refugees to Mexico.

Moreover, Ricardo was used to jockeying for American public opinion with the Díaz government. For years, the PLM had stood as the only defender of Mexican workers against the dictatorship and the trusts. However, Ricardo was not as ready to compete in the diversified political market that blossomed once the actual revolution had broken out. Until that point, Mexico was only a very occasional item of interest in the U.S. press, but the revolution changed all of that.

Battles on border towns produced a form of spectatorship that soon spread to a much broader market. Those battles were viewed from the safety of the American side (Figure 20.4). Writing only a few years after the events, the conservative nationalist historian Rómulo Velasco Ceballos paints the scene for the First Battle of Tijuana: "On the hills of Tia Juana—on the American side—and near the international borderline the inevitable Yankee public gathered—avid, trembling with emotion, but happy in its own security—and ready to witness the first scenes of bloodshed, which

Figure 20.4 Crowd driving to the border post in order to witness the Battle of Tijuana. Courtesy of the San Diego History Center.

would later multiply in number, thanks to Washington's machinations to ruin the grandeur of the Mexican Republic."[8] Ciudad Juárez, Ojinaga, Mexicali, Tijuana, Matamoros, Agua Prieta... every border town battle of the Mexican revolution had these spectators—perched on promontories that might afford a decent view, cheering for one side or another, generally for the *insurrectos* during the early phase of the revolution, often for the underdog, in any case. As a result, the image and material culture of the revolution began its career as consumable commodity: postcards, souvenirs, and war trophies opened the way to a much broader cultural appropriation in the form of news, newsreels, and as an aesthetic and backdrop in the booming development of California and the American West. Indeed, the revolution had erupted at a time when the U.S. market for Wild West shows had begun to tire, and it breathed a whole new life into that market niche.[9]

However, no one in the junta paid sufficient attention to the broad symbolic potential of Mexico in the vibrant American consumer market, to the consumption of the Latin image—the Mexican bandit, the beautiful señorita, the "Spanish" architectural style, the Aztecs, and, more broadly, the erotic and the exotic freedom that

356

could be imagined in a Land Beyond the Law that was just beyond the nation's political boundary. Turner's and Ricardo's analyses of American policy in Mexico had focused on the logic of "dollar diplomacy." American intervention in Mexico would be determined by American economic interests, they believed, so Turner worked diligently to produce facts that exposed the investments and machinations of the oil, copper, railroad, and ranching interests. But the junta never realized the weakness of "the Mexican Cause" in the face of the broader American consumer economy.

In that context, Ricardo's nickel-and-dime propaganda network was drowned out by a variety of business interests less concerned with ideological competition and political strife and more with sales, image, and reputation. Because Ricardo never left the United States, and because he relied on grassroots support on the U.S. side, his movement was beset on all sides by dangerous "free riders" whose ambitions and interests could easily subvert the PLM's earnest revolutionary aspirations, Ricardo's attempt at a military campaign in Baja California was drowned out by these interests, so it can't be told only as tragedy. In the Baja story, farce overwhelmed tragedy.

A Prescient Thought, Forgotten

Ricardo's limited understanding of the American market dynamic can be seen as a kind of tragic flaw, even though the problem had once been considered by Ricardo himself when he was making preparations for the failed 1908 revolution. On August 9, 1908, during the same days when Lázaro and John were starting their journey into Mexico, a curious item was published in *El País* and *The Mexican Herald*. It was the text of a letter that Ricardo Flores Magón had written in code in the Los Angeles County Jail and sent to his brother Enrique, who was in El Paso.[10]

Both the letter and the code had been intercepted, and Mexico's authorities found its contents worthy of the public's attention. Ramón Corral, Mexico's vice president, wrote to Enrique Creel, then Mexico's ambassador in Washington:

> This letter was written in code and was among the papers that the American police took from the rebels that they arrested there. They managed to capture the key to the code, too, so the letter has been deciphered...and since it includes some very harsh concepts regarding Americans, I think that it would be convenient for you to get it printed

in the newspapers of that capital, as well as New York, Chicago, and other important cities, not forgetting Texas, which is where it's most important that Flores Magon's ideas concerning Americans be known."[11]

In that letter, Ricardo called the United States an "insufferable country" (*este infumable país*). Its president was "a tyrant," and its pachyderm-citizens were incapable of feeling either enthusiasm or indignation. The American people were "cold and stupid." "This is truly a nation of pigs"—"Es éste un verdadero pueblo de marranos," Ricardo wrote.

All of these epithets poured forth because Ricardo wished to discuss how to avoid a U.S. invasion of Mexico in the context of the impending 1908 revolution and to explain to Enrique and to Práxedis why they should not expect strong support from the American public. Americans had no real fight in them, he said. The supposedly great union movement—with the American Federation of Labor at the head of the pack—was incapable of confronting government censorship, judicial injunctions, repression of the unemployed, and rampant militarization. The Socialists were cowards. A people that was so indifferent to its own fate could not get exercised over the fate of another: "If Americans don't get ruffled over their own domestic wretchedness, how can we expect them to care about ours?"

But the hullabaloo about Ricardo's opinion of Americans and the United States diverted attention from a deeper aspect of Ricardo's analysis, an idea that he presented almost as an afterthought, but that proved so prescient that Ricardo himself would forget it: the only way to sway American opinion was by way of spectacle: "Maybe because these animals are always so anxious for news, agitation could prosper after the revolutionary outbreak.... The news of a revolution in progress—yes, I am sure that would attract the gringos' attention—because they will be sensational events and then, if they have not yet invaded us, maybe we could agitate opinion in our favor, and avoid an invasion."

But Ricardo failed to take in the full implications of his own idea, for the problem was not only that spectacle moved American opinion, but that because of this, the issues that were most vital to his cause could be drowned out in a competitive consumer market. It was in the vortex of that market that Ricardo's most concentrated military effort, the Baja California campaign, floundered.

Dick Ferris

The persistent idea of a Baja California filibuster ha
The possibility was underwritten by the important
ence of American citizens and companies in the re
that Baja was just beginning to develop, and by the
dynamism of Southern California. The scenario in v
tionary process that began with the fall of Mexicali
could in fact lead to the secession of the peninsula w
by a variety of factors, ranging from the heterogene
of the Liberal volunteers to the impossibility of wi
fornia against Madero without U.S. support. A nu
field commanders toyed with the idea of a Baja Ca
before abandoning it. But the only open, vocal, and
pion of the idea was a character by the name of Dic

Ferris is most frequently painted as a charlatan
Ethel described him as "the blatant American ty
Lewis has handled with mordant satire. He was the '
at banquets and clubs, associating always with the r
ful; he himself was by no means destitute."[12] Ferris
eccentric, a charmer, and an egomaniac who did thin
his thirty-fifth birthday every year. The U.S. gove
him as essentially harmless—a publicity hound wh
kept gingerly at a distance. The Liberals did not tak
enough—either as an individual or, much more in
symptom. What was Ferris? Historians Lawrence
Hansen, Lowell Blaisdell, and Marco Antonio Sama
vided valuable information for an initial assessment.

Dick Ferris was a publicist—a man who connected
opers, and local governments. He was also an actor, a
businessman. In his youth, he worked as an employe
and for the railroads; he held low-level jobs in the
before moving out of his native Washington, D.C., to
he established the "Ferris Comedians." Taylor Hanse
one point, Ferris owned as many as ten theater com
percentages in many of the great theatrical hits of th
married to a popular actress, Florence Stone, and mo
Los Angeles in 1905, where he started out as a manaş

In California, Ferris diversified his activities as a
involved cultivating relations in the media, in go'

among investors, all of which was done by way of building himself up as a member of the class of the "glitterati." He ran for lieutenant governor of California on the Democratic ticket as part of his generally successful bid for notoriety.[14] Garnering publicity was more the point of these activities than gaining office. Ferris began to organize automobile races and air shows, all of them as part of the general promotion of California's new place in the world.

Most of these activities had the name "Panama" and the name "California" in them, for the great Panama-Pacific International Exhibition was being prepared to coincide with the opening of the Panama Canal in 1915. The cities of San Francisco and San Diego had competed for serving as fairgrounds, and the new San Diego business elite managed to get the plum, because San Diego would be the first U.S. port on the Pacific for ships coming north from Panama.[15]

The matter of Panama in the promotion of California is very relevant to understanding the significance of Ferris for our story, because the promotion of the new California image was predicated on the region's role as the Pacific gateway from the United States to Latin America. Because of this, the great park that was to house the Panama-California International Exposition was named Balboa Park, after the conquistador who discovered, or at least named, the Pacific Ocean after crossing the Isthmus of Panama. The development commission was given to the famous landscape architects John C. and Frederick Lawson Olmstead, but the theme and architectural flavor of the development would be "Spanish," which, in the parlance of the times, referred to an aesthetic composite characterized by any number of winks, affectations, and references to South of the Border quaintness, with a few Moorish touches thrown in (Figures 20.5, 20.6).

There was, in short, a premium on developing a Latin image—a "Spanish" backdrop to the open horizon of California development, and Dick Ferris was poised to become the impresario most capable of delivering that image. Ferris had been named manager of the groundbreaking ceremonies of the exposition, slated for July, 1911. Because of this, he was attentive to developments that might help stir up publicity. The fall of Mexicali to the *insurrectos* on January 29 provided a perfect occasion.

On February 5, 1911, barely a week after the capture of Mexicali, Ferris interrupted his activities at the car races to send a telegram to Porfirio Díaz. In that message, Ferris proposed that Díaz sell Baja

Figure 20.5 Panama-California International Exposition fairgrounds in San Diego: the Prado East as seen from the Economy Building, 1915. As Mexico exploded and imploded in revolution, a supersized neo-Mexican baroque flourished in California. Courtesy of the San Diego History Center.

Figure 20.6 The California Building at the Panama-California International Exposition, 1915. Courtesy of the San Diego History Center.

California to the United States. He insinuated that he had powerful financiers backing the plan and proposed to set up a new republic there. Dick Ferris's flourish as a comedian showed in one final detail of his bold proposal: the new republic would bear the name "the Republic of Díaz." Ferris then went the extra mile and sent a message to General Pascual Orozco, for good measure. Orozco was the main chieftain of the Madero rebellion and was threatening to take Ciudad Juárez, as he later did. Ferris let Orozco know that if he blocked Baja's secession, he would personally lead an expeditionary force from San Francisco to defend it.

Much to Dick Ferris's delight, Porfirio Díaz actually responded to his telegram, energetically rejecting the offer. Those were still days when Mexican government officials had insufficient experience dealing with the complexities of American society—either in the legal realm or in the realm of public opinion and the market. Díaz's response gave Ferris the credibility that he needed to gain national publicity for himself as a kind of West Coast Teddy Roosevelt. Ferris then held multiple press conferences. Aware of the problem of the neutrality laws, he had an agent place announcements in several New York papers that said that "General" Dick Ferris was looking for 1000 volunteers for Baja.[16] Apparently he received a flood of responses from Spanish-American and Boer War veterans, all sent to his hotel room in San Francisco. This got him in the *San Francisco Chronicle*'s headlines for almost two weeks. When the State Department later investigated Ferris for violation of the neutrality laws, it discovered that he had never enlisted a single volunteer.[17]

After this successful publicity haul, Ferris did nothing. In this, he was not so different from the Liberal commanders in Mexicali. After about a month's lull, though, there was a second publicity stunt—more of a teaser, actually. A dashing San Diego lady by the name of Flora Russell rode, like Paul Revere, from San Diego to Tia Juana Springs (Agua Caliente) and planted a specially confected silk flag there after pronouncing a proclamation before two male witnesses who rode with her:

> Lower California, I claim you in the name of equal suffrage and of model government, which I hereby christen as the future "Republic of Díaz." May the Great Ruler of all things nourish the little plant typified in this flag that I raise over this troubled land, and see His goodness

bring to fruition the hopes and dreams of my sex for fullest liberty, symbolized in the scales of equality and justice.[18]

Here, too, we get a taste of Ferris's talents as a publicist: the strategy was to project onto Baja California the imagery that was to be used to fashion the republic that was actually being built in California. Baja represented the enterprise and freedom of the conquerors of the West (Figure 20.7), figured in the image of the American *insurrectos* and their leaders—handsome and colorful, like Dick Ferris and Pryce. Now Baja was also being connected to women's emancipation. In March 1911, California was preparing a vote on women's suffrage, which finally passed in October of that year. Flora Russell's ride again drew attention to San Diego's open future, projecting it onto the city's southern frontier of expansion—Tijuana. In order to avoid any distasteful identification with the more radical feminists, though, Flora Russell clarified: "I am not, however, to be considered as a suffragette. There are many things being done by the suffragettes that I believe serve as an obstacle in accomplishing their dreams."[19]

After this, the Ferris publicity effort went into hibernation again while Dick worked on his San Francisco car races and on its Native Sons Festival. The latter theme, too, played a role in the way that Ferris first figured the idea of a Baja republic. Lower California, Ferris believed, was destined to be a white man's republic or, more precisely, a white man's playground. A "Sporting Republic," as he genially called it. Thus, when his program for the "Republic of Díaz" was first announced, the *Los Angeles Herald* emphasized the projected republic's interest in the pursuit of happiness: "that happiness may take the form of horse racing, prize fighting, bull baiting, or betting where the little ball will fall."[20]

After the fall of Tijuana to the *insurrectos* on May 9, Ferris again stepped into action. He had just moved to San Diego to work on the groundbreaking ceremonies for the Panama-California International Exhibition. From the Liberal point of view, the fall of Tijuana was both a culmination and the beginning of the end, for it occurred on the same day as Madero's military triumph over Díaz. From Ferris's point of view, though, the event presented new opportunities.

There were three main reasons for this. The first was that the Liberal regiment that took Tijuana was the so-called Foreign Legion,

Figure 20.7 Black *insurrectos*—the Baja
campaign was a space of freedom, and Ferris
wanted to cash in on it. The significance of
Mexico as a space for revolution for Black
Americans has yet to be investigated. Courtesy
of the San Diego History Center.

which had a U.S. majority among its troops (Figure 20.8) and which was led by Pryce, a man who had all of the qualities that Ferris could hope for. The second was that the junta was not providing the Tijuana troops with arms or material support nor had it been effective in mitigating the sting of Maderista and Porfirista representations of its army as "filibusters." Finally, the battle of Tijuana had been massively viewed by San Diego's citizens (Figure 20.9). Indeed, San Diego soon became a market for war souvenirs, as well as a place of sympathy for the *insurrectos*. This was, in short, a perfect chance for further publicity for the president of the Panama-California groundbreaking ceremony preparations.

Ferris's first move was to befriend Pryce and his closest associates. Following Ferris's lead on the "Sporting Republic," Pryce responded to the lack of arms and financial support from the Los Angeles junta by installing gambling casinos in Tijuana as a way to raise revenue for the troops. Although this was effective, it ran against the grain of Liberal political traditions, which were emphatically opposed to alcohol and gambling. So, for instance, the Liberal chieftain Rómulo Gallego, who turned to the Madero side after the fall of Díaz, had initiated his revolutionary career in 1909 by protesting against prostitution in his native Mexicali.

Ferris also tried to organize a demonstration and reception for him and Pryce by the Mexicali troops, orchestrated specially for the press and culminating with "Vivas!" for Pryce and for Ferris together, but the execution of that event was bungled. Ferris did manage, however, to get his name recognized among sectors of the Tijuana troops at what for them was a very critical moment, since Díaz's resignation left the Baja armies exposed to a concerted attack from Mexico's Federal Army, now headed by the provisional government of León de la Barra. The Tijuana troops were looking for American allies.

On May 30, Pryce went to confer with the Los Angeles junta. According to the *San Diego Union*'s report, he laid out three alternatives: surrender to the provisional government, negotiating concessions for the troops and positions in the Baja government; strike an alliance with General Ambrosio Figueroa in faraway Guerrero State in order to present a common front against Madero—but this alternative would require arms and money; and dismissing the troops. Given the circumstances, Pryce preferred the third option.[21] The

Figure 20.8 The Mexican Company in the Tijuana Regiment. Courtesy of the San Diego History Center.

Figure 20.9 "Observation Cart" for tourists wanting to visit the war front. Burro, *serape*, and hat, with curio shop in the background: the "observation cart" is the elemental form of touristic life. Courtesy of the San Diego History Center.

junta, however, decided to continue the fight, but had no arms or money to offer. As a result, Pryce resigned his command.

This left a void in the Tijuana leadership, and one of Pryce's officers, a Louis James, moved with his faction to declare independence for Baja. For that he needed to seek support in the United States, and because he lacked time and contacts, the only expedient formula that he could think of was to go and offer the presidency of the new republic to "General" Dick Ferris and to get financial support for the project from San Diego's leading citizen, sugar tycoon Klaus Spreckles, who owned the railroad and a lot of land in Baja, as well as the *San Diego Union*, and so might be interested in annexation.

Always a glutton for publicity, but also careful not to violate the neutrality laws, Ferris declined Louis James's offer, but designed a flag for the new republic and got his tailor to sew it. Ferris also suggested that though it was illegal for him to broach the subject with Spreckles, on account of the neutrality laws, James, as an *insurrecto* officer, could go speak to Spreckles himself. James tried that and was rejected.

In the meantime, Ferris continued to play the press. He was considering the offer of the Baja presidency, he said. He suggested that there were capitalists who were prepared to finance compensation to Mexico for the annexation of Baja. He said that the new republic would bear the name of the Republic of Madero.... But Louis James did not have time to play around with the press like Ferris did, so, in a final desperate move, he tried to force the issue, crossed from San Diego into Tijuana, raised Ferris's flag, declared the republic, and announced Ferris as its first president.

When he was later brought to trial for violation of the neutrality laws, Dick Ferris declared that this final act had been a joke played on him by the Tijuana boys.[22] It was in fact a bold and desperate act, rather than a joke, but done in vain, in any case, since James did not have Pryce's ascendency over the troops, and there were no powerful U.S. backers for the plan in any case, so Louis James and his thirty supporters were hung out to dry. In the Tijuana regiment, Jack Mosby and the Wobbly and Mexican PLM faction now gained ascendancy. They burned Ferris's flag, declared Ferris persona non grata in Baja California, and evicted James and Pryce from the army. Pryce, of course, had in fact already resigned and was in San Francisco at the time. Two weeks later, Jack Mosby faced Colonel Vega's federal troops and was bitterly defeated.

The Sporting Republic

Dick Ferris was a publicity man. His business was to add news to the news—to start rumors and see if they "had legs" and build a sellable image of himself for California. In the process, the status of beautiful, sparsely inhabited, and rapidly developing Baja California was put on the menu of California's boundless resources: How would you like your Baja served, sir? As a republic, or as an appendage?

The Liberals had little clue as to how to react in the face of such a strategy. In February, when Ferris first made his bumptious proposal for "the Republic of Díaz," *Regeneración* responded only on its English-language page (from Ethel, in other words). Responses were very brief, and none took Ferris seriously. "Don't be foolish, Dick," was the first of these, and that was followed in another issue with an entry that said that if Ferris waited a little, Díaz would surely sell Baja, and cheap, but that he would not be in a position to deliver it. So we might say that in February, the junta read Ferris correctly (they knew he was no threat), while Porfirio Díaz misread him and even gave Ferris the undeserved dignity of an official response.

And yet it was in fact Díaz who knew how to react, while the Liberals' Ferris strategy was all wrong. Porfirio's rejection of the "Díaz Republic" gave Dick Ferris wings, that was true, but it also provided Díaz with publicity in Mexico: he was, as always, a true patriot, and the revolution had brought with it a risk of American annexation of Baja California. Madero, too, understood the political sensitivity of this issue, and the Maderistas quickly condemned any and all filibustering expeditions. By minimizing the importance of Ferris, by not reacting early and loudly to his proposal, by forfeiting the little reaction that there was to *Regeneración*'s young English-language editor, rather than making loud declarations himself, Ricardo left his own stance toward national integrity open to question.

Moreover, the problem was compounded by Ferris's publicity strategy, which was based on opportunistic media stunts, rather than on his continuous presence. The Liberals did not imagine something like that. Thus, by the end of February, Ethel wrote ironically that not a peep was now being heard of Dick Ferris's braggadocio. But then two weeks later, Flora Russell made her dramatic ride to Tia Juana Springs, and Ferris had again gained the headlines. Porfirio Díaz again condemned the act and threatened to prosecute Flora.[23] The Liberals, once again, did not take the matter seriously.

And yet they should have, for they were open to the charge of collaborating with Baja secessionists—whether wittingly or not. The Liberals were not perceived as being strong enough on their own to hold Baja against U.S. annexationists, and they were fighting both the Federal Army and Madero and so were weakening the two forces that could conceivably have the strength to protect Mexico's territorial integrity. Finally, the proportion and military rank of the Anglos in the Baja army opened the PLM's national loyalties to question. Indeed, by May 1911, the soldier of fortune Pryce, their most charismatic military commander, was chums with Ferris and might easily have been won over to secessionism, had there been material support for that within the United States. The Liberals were in fact very vulnerable to the "filibuster" label, and they failed to respond to Ferris in an effective way.

There was, moreover, a final ambivalence that made them susceptible to the charge of favoring annexation, and this was that neither the junta nor the Industrial Workers of the World were nationalists, so, in fact, "national integrity" was not their main concern. This, indeed, was why the Baja effort recruited so many idealistic supporters, and it is also why even faithful Liberal commanders, such as the Wobbly Jack Mosby, at times openly toyed with the possibility of establishing a socialist (rather than a sporting) republic in Baja. Ricardo himself, when he finally did react to the Ferris problem, too late, did so in unreassuring terms, asserting that Baja had long since been ceded to the United States by Porfirio Díaz, that it was entirely owned by foreign capital, and that by gaining it for the workers, the Liberals were retaking the territory.

There were, in short, two competing images for California. One might call them the Countercultural Republic and the Sporting Republic. These two visions coexisted, though in different proportions, even in opposite political camps. Thus, Dick Ferris, who was ready to turn Baja California over to the California developers (he himself became a developer in Baja in the 1920s), nonetheless adored the *insurrecto* image and even spiced it up with a bit of women's suffrage. The Tijuana *insurrectos*, on the other hand, set up gambling casinos when the junta failed to come up with money and arms for the campaign (Figure 20.10).

In fact, the whole of the military effort was vulnerable to this sort of commercialization and thus to being grist for the mill of farce.

Figure 20.10 Birth of the "Sporting Republic," Tijuana, 1911. The businesses are all bars and a curio shop. Courtesy of the San Diego History Center.

Figure 20.11 A very Mexican Tijuana in the days of Colonel Esteban Cantú. Courtesy of the San Diego History Center.

After the defeat of Jack Mosby in Tijuana, for instance, a Lieutenant Lawson went to Hollywood with a group of Wobblies in order to act in a film about the Baja campaign. These same men then went to San Diego, to act as *insurrectos* in the Wild West show that was part of the Panama-California International Exposition.[24]

Even fellow anarchists had to be prodded to take Mexico seriously. Thus, when Voltairine de Cleyre called on the readers of *Mother Earth* to take a good, close look at the Mexican Revolution, she wrote that Americans had a tough time doing that because they were sated with sports and divorce scandals and always presumed that "whatever happened in Mexico was a joke."[25] The American consumer market was a giant next to Mexico's puny political body. All things Mexican seemed amenable to being treated as a "curio" and to being commercialized, either as image or memento.

Like Ricardo himself, the vast hagiography on Ricardo Flores Magón has consistently treated Dick Ferris as a charlatan. They have been very wrong in this. Ferris was a marketing professional, and marketing vanquished Ricardo's Baja revolution in the U.S. consumer market as readily as Ferris might gobble up an hors d'oeuvre.

After the Liberals were beaten, the northern district of Baja California was governed for nine long years by Colonel Esteban Cantú (Figure 20.11). Amazingly, Cantú was able to keep the peninsula on the margin of Mexico's armed struggle for the entire revolutionary decade. First appointed by Madero, Cantú supported Victoriano Huerta's military coup from afar and so kept his position through the 1913 crisis. Then, when Huerta's future clouded, he allied himself with Pancho Villa, but nevertheless refused to send troops against Álvaro Obregón, who was commanding Venustiano Carranza's revolutionary troops in Northwestern Mexico in the revolt against Villa. After Villa's defeat at the Battle of Celaya, Cantú issued a manifesto denouncing Villa and then cobbled a successful alliance with Carranza. In that manifesto, Cantú emphasized that Baja California's loyalties were with all Mexicans who supported Mexico's territorial integrity: "Here, every sincere Mexican has been well received, be he Porfirista, Villista, Carrancista, etc. etc."[26] When Carranza was named constitutional president, in May 1917, he made the northern Baja territory into a state of the Mexican federation and named Cantú its first governor. Cantú survived in that post until 1920.

This story of well-nigh miraculous political survival was accomplished thanks to strict observation of a few principles learned from Cantú's close study of the lessons of the 1911 Liberal revolution. First, Cantú never left Baja California, except to travel to California. If he had gone, say, to Mexico City (and Carranza, among others, tried to get him there several times), he would have been deposed. But because Cantú was in Baja, dislodging him would have cost Victoriano Huerta, Álvaro Obregón, Pancho Villa, or Venustiano Carranza a military campaign that they could scarcely afford.

Second, Cantú could govern Baja with no support from Mexico's central government. He achieved this, first, by careful management of the "Sporting Republic," specifically, by giving permits to the bars, brothels, and casinos of Mexicali and Tijuana and by adding to this tax base the management, taxation, and extortion of Chinese immigrants, a number of whom also got involved in the Sporting Republic (prostitution, gambling, even opium dens).[27] In Tijuana, local government helped set up a Feria Típica Mexicana as a supplement for visitors to San Diego's Panama-California International Exposition in 1915–1916. Tijuana offered visitors a rich stock of "Mexican curios" alongside all sort of sports that were banned in San Diego, such as prizefighting, cockfights, gambling, and bullfights.[28] Soon, California promoters built a horseracing track there. By 1919, when the San Diego-Arizona railroad opened, Tijuana received twenty-two thousand tourists every weekend, drawn mainly by the horse track and the supplementary entertainment.[29] Finally, Cantú was able to support infrasctructure development—roads and the like—that was useful to American investors while also keeping the peace. Because of his autonomy from the federal government, he was able to set up his own taxation system.

In short, Ferris was something of a business visionary. But like so many visionaries, he went too far. His tactics played so convincingly with the threat of an armed expedition to Baja that, much to his own surprise, he was finally arrested by the U.S. government and tried for violation of the neutrality laws alongside Pryce, Mosby, Laflin, and the rest of them. In all likelihood, Ferris had not counted on the denouement of Louis James's desperate act, which resulted not only in the expulsion of Pryce's faction from Tijuana, but also in a showdown between Mosby and the Federal Army and therefore in a bitter and unnegotiated military defeat for the entire movement.

At the trial, Ferris was found innocent. He had never organized an army, had never crossed into Tijuana with a weapon or troops, and had never spent a dime on buying guns. He had never even gone to Klaus Spreckels asking for financial support for the new republic. The whole thing was a publicity gimmick.[30]

The trial did cost Ferris his job at the Panama-California International Exposition, though. Still, he was able at least to reap some benefit out of it. Dick Ferris and his wife, Florence Stone, now starred in a farce, an adaptation of H. A. Du Souchet's *The Man from Mexico*. Unfortunately, I have been unable to find the text of the adaptation, which was done by Willie Collier, but undoubtedly, it added many Tijuana and Baja references to Souchet's original comedy.

That play is about a naughty husband, Ben Fitzhew (played by Dick Ferris) who has cheated on his wife, claiming to have gone on a business trip to Mexico, instead. But Fitzhew's loving wife, Clementina, has catered a "tamale supper" and a dinner party to celebrate his return. During that dinner party, Fitzhew is constantly put on the spot with questions about Mexico, a place about which he has absolutely no clue. He names the Amazon River as crossing Mexico City. Asked if he saw the Alameda, Fitzhew responds that he tried to catch one to bring as a toy for the house. He claims to have attended a bullfight, whose protagonist was a galloping cow that sat down to rest at the end because it was a holiday.[31] An adaptation of this play, with lines and references to the Mexican Revolution, could not have been more apropos for Ferris—the man who used Mexico as an alibi for something altogether more naughty. The play was a great success and played to full houses in all of California's major cities.

The Power of Advertising

In 1913, the United States Senate's Committee of Foreign Relations set up a subcommittee to investigate whether there were U.S. interests inciting rebellion in Mexico, including the Baja California episode. Interrogated by senators Albert B. Fall of New York and William Alden Smith of Michigan, U.S. District Attorneys A. I. McCormick and Dudley W. Robinson shared the results of their investigations during the extradition and violation of neutrality laws trials of the Magóns, Ferris, Pryce, and others. Ferris, they said, had gone into the Baja affair to get advertising for his theatrical business. If the senators cared to interrogate him for themselves, Ferris had his office right across the street and could be brought in for questioning. "I think Dick will tell the truth about it," McCormick told the senators. But District Attorney Robinson interjected, "The only thing about Dick is that he will turn us into an advertisement, too."[32] Grasping the point, the senators decided not to call him to testify.

Ricardo as Traitor

Criticism of Ricardo Flores Magón from former junta leaders came in two kinds: sober and haughty. Among the former was Juan Sarabia's public statement that acknowledged Ricardo's great historical role and then accused him of extreme radicalization, utopianism, and intolerance.[33] Sarabia also debated ideas with Ricardo. For Juan, as for Eugene Debs, Mother Jones, and number of American Socialists, "direct action" was pure folly. Mexico was an agrarian country, and its population was uneducated. Socialism required industrialism and political preparation.[34]

Given Mexico's backwardness, Madero was a decent compromise. He was progressive in his outlook—a modernizer—and a sincere democrat who would make room for unions and legal political opposition. Unlike Díaz, Madero would allow freedom of association and freedom of the press and thereby vouchsafe necessary conditions for the development of a robust socialist movement. Moreover, Madero was not adamantly opposed to at least some form of agrarian reform, so if the progressive movement pushed hard enough, it might gain concessions. Madero, for Sarabia and the Socialists, was the best alternative to dictatorship and to U.S. intervention—not an ideal leader himself, but a realistic means to a higher goal.

This argument was later seconded by Manuel Sarabia:

> Though I don't subscribe to all of my cousin's ideas, I am in complete agreement when he asks whether all ideas that are great and beautiful can be put into practice anywhere and at any time. Will the units who are to build the beautiful edifice be simply improvised, with no prior education or preparation? Socialism and anarchism are founded in scientific principles, and the followers of those doctrines know—if they be conscientious—that they have to confine their acts to those principles, always applying the cold and serene criteria of science, without outbursts of passion or sentimentalism.[35]

Neither Juan nor Manuel Sarabia attacked anarchism as an ideal. They pointed instead to hard factual obstacles for its immediate implementation. Nevertheless, Ricardo's ideals were in fact repellent to at least some of his erstwhile allies. One catches a powerful, if fleeting impression of the repulsion produced by the more intimate aspect of Ricardo's anarchism in a letter from Jesús Flores Magón to Pablo Macedo, a Porfirian politician and friend of Jesús who by the time of this writing was exiled in France. Jesús closed his letter responding to Macedo's inquiry after his two brothers and reported on the condition in which he found them during their June meeting in Los Angeles: "I'm grateful for your letter's expression of goodwill for my relatives. Unfortunately, those boys have degenerated so much, and I found their situation so abject and contrary to the most rudimentary morality, that I preferred to cast a veil on the past and to resign myself to having a family no longer."[36]

Reading between the lines, one can picture Jesús's impression after years of not seeing his two brothers and now witnessing their life in Los Angeles. *Regeneración*'s offices were a kind of commune, where many people lived, ate, edited the paper, and held political meetings in a single shared space. It might also have been difficult for Jesús to see Ricardo in a relationship with a widowed and out-spoken woman with a controversial sexual reputation whose wild and psychologically unstable daughter Ricardo treated as if she were his own. Ricardo's anarchism was so uncompromising, so dismissive of the sensitive waltz of Mexican political relations, and so laden with implications for intimate relations that it had generated a break with a beloved brother. Jesús and Ricardo had once been deeply united, they had suffered together in prison, and Jesús had shoul-dered responsibility for the Flores Magón family like a father.

Toward the end of his life, while he languished in prison, Ricardo reflected rather bitterly on how little recompense he had had for com-mitments that had led him to sacrifice even his nearest relations to the cause he thought was right: "When I was free, anyone who needed help came to me, and I had to sacrifice everything—work myself to death, fight against my own people, compromise my freedom—in order to help them. Now that I'm afflicted, no one remembers me."[37]

The space between intimate behavior and politics was the spot where attacks became most virulent. Villarreal and the Sarabia cousins, whom he had called pederasts, murderers, and traitors, now accused Ricardo of being an embittered coward. Ricardo repeatedly had called for war, but had stayed safely behind the lines. In the 1906 rebellion, he had kept himself from danger, leaving the incursion into Mexico to Villarreal and to Juan Sarabia, and again had refused to lead the bands of Liberal sympathizers into Mexico in 1910 and 1911. Ricardo's cowardice, Villarreal argued, was by now widely known, so he had lost all credibility. This, in the end, was the crucial point, according to Villarreal: bitter, resentful, degenerate, and corrupted, Ricardo now resorted to defamation and libel, a woman's weapons, because they were his only instruments.

> I challenge Ricardo Flores Magón to fulfill his "word of honor," which he pledged years ago, to lead any group of *magonistas*—any one of the many that, he claims, are operating in Mexico...or any new group that he might care to organize. I, for my part, promise to bring together a group of liberals of the same size as any that might support Ricardo Flores Magón and to fight him wherever he wants us to meet.
>
> If I fall in his power, let him hang me; if he falls in mine, I'll spit in his face and turn him in at an insane asylum.[38]

Corresponding in kind to Ricardo's accusation of homosexuality, Villarreal called Ricardo a moral degenerate—an alcoholic with no real friends, a man who "calls himself a communist, but he is that only in the sense that he allows his wife to be the common property of all men of bad taste."[39]

Villarreal also said that Ricardo had blackmailed Francisco and Gustavo Madero, eluding repayment of their substantial loans by threatening to expose them to the Díaz government, and that Gustavo and Francisco Madero, Camilo Arriaga, and Juan and Manuel Sarabia were witnesses to those extortions. Villarreal also accused Ricardo of using money from collections for his own purposes, including cash that had been raised for the benefit of Juan Sarabia's mother while Juan was a prisoner in San Juan de Ulúa.

Finally, Ricardo was accused of asking one of his lieutenants, Emilio Campa, to receive the substantial sum of 50,000 pesos from the hated *científico* faction. Campa, who had been one of the Liberal's successful military leaders, made his peace with Madero and published a letter in which Ricardo had urged him to take the money offered by "the devil," that is, by the *científicos*.[40] According to Villarreal, the letter and the conversation that Ricardo had held with

Campa in Los Angeles prior to it demonstrated that "Ricardo Flores Magón and his little group are following through on what they'd said to Juan Sarabia, when he saw then in Los Angeles, to wit, that they'd recognize the Científicos or even Díaz himself before recognizing the government that sprang from the Revolution."[41]

Villarreal argued that Ricardo's willingness to take *científico* gold explained the survival of *Regeneración*. The Liberals, Villarreal said, had abandoned Ricardo Flores Magón en masse, and canceled their subscriptions to that "filthy paper." How *Regeneración* survived was a mystery, Villarreal continued. Or at least it had been, until Campa's revelations concerning Ricardo's willingness to accept *científico* support. Campa's allegations found further corroboration with the capture of a PLM delegate of Tabasco, Enrique Novoa, who carried documents that proved that Ricardo had received 40,000 pesos from the same *científico* agent, Luis del Toro.[42]

It is uncertain whether Ricardo or any of the various Liberal captains might have taken money from Díaz supporters after that dictator's fall from power. Ricardo vigorously denied it and gave examples of the many places—Yucatán, Morelos, elsewhere—in which the Liberals had directly attacked *científico* interests as proof of the impossibility of such an alliance.[43] Still, the claim was not impossible to believe. Certainly, the Díaz machine had tried to benefit from the faction's split with Madero, so offers of support of this kind may have been made. It is also true that the Liberals were desperate for resources.

Moreover, unholy alliances between extreme Right and extreme Left factions did in fact occur at various points in the course of the Mexican Revolution. The Zapatistas of Morelos, for instance, made an alliance with Félix Díaz in 1916 and 1917; Pascual Orozco and several other agrarian leaders of Chihuahua, including erstwhile Liberals heroes such as Lázaro Alanís and Emilio Campa, took money from the great landowner Luis Terrazas to rise against Madero and later allied themselves with Victoriano Huerta in 1913. Though there was much less risk of a sellout, Ricardo himself had taken money from Francisco and Gustavo Madero back in 1905. In short, though we have no reliable evidence of reactionary financial support for the Liberals of the kind to which that Villarreal referred, the charge cannot be dismissed as impossible, though the allegations are very doubtful, given *Regeneración*'s dire poverty during the period.[44]

In any case, Ricardo was no longer a force to be reckoned with, Villarreal claimed—he was more lunatic than leader. This sentiment would be echoed, though in a more circumspect fashion, by Manuel Sarabia, even before he himself was accused of homosexuality by Ricardo. Commenting on the irrepressible use of personal invective in the pages of the junta's *Regeneración*, Manuel said that despite his own best hopes for Ricardo to mend his accusations and return to the fight for liberty, "every day, Magon exudes more bile.... The Spanish section of *Regeneración* is full of adjectives and derogatory nicknames for all of those who think differently from Magon."[45]

The cumulus of insult found in the pages of *Regeneración* betrayed the isolation of an abandoned man, Manuel claimed. But there was more: Ricardo's anarchism was not only misguided, it was being cynically manipulated to fan his own resentment against Madero. The proof was that Ricardo had adhered to the 1906 program as the PLM's official platform through the entire Madero revolution, and that program, Manuel pointedly declared, called for social and political reform, rather than for anarchy:

> He invokes anarchism, while at the same time he claims to be fighting for the Junta's Saint Louis Program, where one finds clauses such as these:
> "Reduction of the presidential term to four years.
> "Suppression of reelection of the President of the Republic and of State Governors."
> And other clauses like that, all of which add up to a political program, albeit radical.[46]

The hard accusations presented by the Sarabias and Villarreal supplemented Maderista charges that Ricardo was a man of dubious integrity. Mexico City's *Regeneración* ("burguesa") would then print news of other well-meaning Liberals who had been prompted by the junta to do battle while Ricardo held himself back. One such person was the well-known Jesús Rangel, who, according to Villarreal's version, had been sent into battle without sufficient equipment or followers, wounded by Madero's men, and then sent to a hospital in Mexico City. Villarreal summarized Rangel's predicament: "The fault is all that of the swindler of Los Angeles, Ricardo Flores Magón, who, crazed by his infinite failures and political setbacks, tries to organize riots and skirmishes where the lives of men who would be useful to their country are sacrificed, since they think they are sacrificing in defense of noble ideals, rather than for the bastard interests of a cowardly vaudeville revolutionary like Ricardo Flores Magón."[47]

The internal accusations of betrayal were compounded by the charge of filibustering and also by the tenor of the Liberals' legal defense in their widely publicized California trials. So, for instance, after Ricardo made his deposition for the defense of General Pryce against extradition to Mexico, the Mexican consul, Arturo Elías, wrote to the Ministry of Foreign Affairs in Mexico City: "Needless to reproduce here the statement made by the filibuster Ricardo Flores Magon, but I have to say that our country has never seen traitors quite like these, for this individual seems to have every feeling except a patriotic one."[48]

The consul's claim stemmed from a combination of factors, starting with the fact that Ricardo had ceded command in Baja to American generals and moving on to the risks that this implied for national integrity and now to Ricardo's legal deposition to defend those very men against extradition to Mexico. This latter point was touchy, because it had potential racist and imperialist undertones regarding their alleged inability to find justice anywhere in Mexico's political system. Thus, the San Diego and Los Angeles newspapers routinely emphasized that if the United States allowed the extradition to Pryce and his lieutenants, they would not receive a fair trial in Mexico and would be shot. Indeed, defense lawyers Job Harriman and A.R. Holston and the junta itself, Ricardo included, organized a rally in Los Angeles's Mammoth Hall to "protest the methods of the Mexican government," even though this was August 1911 and so no longer the government of Porfirio Díaz, but rather the new provisional government that had been set up by Madero.[49]

Indeed, Holston's defense of Pryce harped more on the lack of justice in Mexico than on Pryce's own innocence. Thus, in its summary of that lawyer's appeal, the *Los Angeles Tribune* reported:

> Pryce, an American soldier of fortune, who had appeared in many countries where stirring times proved attractive to his adventurous spirit, was none the less an American and entitled to the full protection of the American law. To deliver him over to the Mexican government, the speaker declared, would mean that Pryce would be placed against the first wall across the border and shot by a file of soldiers.[50]

Nor had the Mexican Liberals hesitated to employ this strategy in highly visible venues. Thus, when he made his deposition before the U.S. Congress in June of 1910, Lázaro Gutiérrez de Lara asked legislators to intervene and stop U.S. collaboration with the Díaz government, testifying that "I am liable to be arrested again any time and unless you gentlemen help me, they may get me and hang me."[51] And indeed, it was the assertion that justice could be served only in the United States, and never in Mexico, that strongly irritated many Mexicans, including many Mexicans in the United States, who suffered daily the racism that was prevalent against Mexicans in U.S. courts of law. Thus, Velasco Ceballos reproduces an open letter to Ricardo Flores Magón that reads in part: "You should bear in mind that even though you are doing the Yankees favors and letting them butt into matters that don't concern them, they still see you as a member of an inferior race, and they don't stop calling you 'cholo pendejo', 'indio bestia' and other ugly names—because you are as dark and as much of an Indian as I."[52]

Writing in the same vein, a call for a mass meeting on August 13, 1911, in Los Angeles to support the extradition of Pryce and Mosby to Mexico also combined the charge of treason against Ricardo with a note on American racism against Mexicans: "they humiliate and mock us because we had the honor and glory of getting dark skins, characteristic of our race, which is dark to the eye, but is at bottom as immaculate and white as snow. One visible proof of racial hatred against us is the case of the Mexican martyr Antonio Rodríguez, who was so cowardly burned in Texas."[53]

Antonio Rodríguez called here a "Mexican martyr"—had been wrenched out of jail by a mob while he awaited trial on a charge of murder and had been burned alive in Rock Springs, Texas, just the previous year. The protest here was to do with racism and the lack of symmetry and equality between the United States in Mexico: Why should Americans shooting and pillaging in Mexico receive any less justice in Mexico than Mexicans received in the United States?

Some supporters of the Mexican Cause, such as John Kenneth Turner, had often emphasized that the U.S. government was no better than Mexico's. So, for instance, in a March 9, 1911, declaration to the *Washington Examiner*, John had said that the government in Washington was no less tyrannical than Díaz.[54] But now that Baja "filibusters" were being tried for extradition, the inferiority of

Mexican justice was everywhere declared, and even the new Madero government did not seem to merit the benefit of a doubt.

Black Bile

Villarreal's final charge was that Ricardo had repeatedly issued assassination orders against him and Juan Sarabia.[55] Though I have not been able to track the specific documents to which Villarreal referred, there is an order of summary execution issued by Ricardo to one of his field commanders in Baja California, Quirino Limón, that lends credence to Villarreal's claim: "I learned today that Juan Sarabia and Lázaro Gutiérrez de Lara are trying to go there to convince the people to lay down their weapons. As soon as they set foot in Baja California, arrest them and judge them as traitors to the cause of the proletariat. Have no remorse, dear brother."[56]

This is a chilling moment in the intimate history of the Mexican Revolution. Full of spite for the erstwhile friends who had moved away from him ideologically and politically, Ricardo ordered the execution of Juan Sarabia, the dear and admired friend whom he once knew as *El Charalito*, as well as of a man who had sacrificed as much to the cause as Lázaro Gutiérrez de Lara had done. Both men remained good Socialists for the rest of their lives. Apparently, Ricardo feared that Juan and Lázaro would try to convince the Liberals to lay down their arms in Baja California. The order was given on June 14, immediately after Juan Sarabia visited the junta. The Baja campaign was already doomed at the time Ricardo gave his order, and Ricardo knew it, since he had had his meeting with Pryce two weeks prior: the junta was sending no money or materiel to the Baja soldiers, and they could not win against the combined forces of the Federal Army and Madero.

In addition to its having no military consequence, it is also revealing that in the order, Ricardo fingered only Juan Sarabia and Lázaro for execution. He did not include his brother Jesús, for instance, despite the fact that Jesús had been with Sarabia on the Los Angeles mission to persuade him to lay down arms, and he did not target any Maderista or Federal Army commanders in the region. As it turned out, neither Juan Sarabia nor Lázaro was in Baja. The execution order responded to a fantasy of revenge against those whom Ricardo viewed as Judases—people of his internal apostolate who had gone over to Madero.

Figure 21.1 John and Ethel at their Carmel cabin, 1912. It is unclear whether this single-room cabin was their first home or just John's writing cabin. When they first moved to Carmel they lived at George Sterling's house and then they built their own place. Courtesy of the Huntington Library, Noel-Harriman Papers.

Figure 21.2 Ethel painting on the beach at Carmel, with Juanita playing on the side. Courtesy of the Bancroft Library, Ethel Duffy Turner Papers.

CHAPTER TWENTY-ONE

Coda: Carmel

After the fall of Porfirio Díaz, John Kenneth Turner refrained from recriminations toward the junta and took his family to Carmel, California. In those days, the writer's colony was just beginning. The well-known poet George Sterling had been given some land by a couple of real-estate developers who hoped that his presence would attract others, as indeed it did. Sterling and his wife, Carrie, lived in a shingled bungalow at a place called Eighty Acres. Ethel, John, and Juanita moved in there when Carrie and Sterling separated. Later they built a place of their own (Figure 21.1).

In Carmel, you weren't allowed to cut down pines, and people walked back to their cabins from the beach or from the theater treading on a thick bed of needles, lantern in hand, if it was night. To go to Carmel, you took a four-horse stagecoach driven by a fellow known as "Old Sam." It weaved between the redwoods from Monterey to the newly built Pine Inn on Carmel's Main Street, and you walked home from there. As an elderly lady, Ethel's sister Grace reminisced: "In those days, literature was so fundamental a part of life in Carmel, like bread and pine trees."[1] And it was. A number of famous writers and artists settled there—John, Sterling, Grace MacGowan Cooke, Upton Sinclair, and others known and not so well known.

"Most of the writers devoted their mornings to work," Ethel recalled. "Every writer had his 'shack' where he retired until lunch time; no one dared to disturb him in his hideaway. After lunch there was a walk to the post-office. The mail arrived about half past one. There they picked up rejected manuscripts or sometimes checks. When a check arrived, the butcher, the baker, the groceryman were paid; they often had to wait for months."[2] Ethel took up her painting again and took lessons with William Merritt Chase (Figure 21.2).

Figure 21.3 Ethel Duffy Turner and Herbert
Heron in the play *Fire* at the Forest Theater.
Courtesy of Bancroft Library, U.C. Berkeley.

A lifestyle was invented. "We gathered wild blackberries. We hunted pine cones for our fireplaces. We lay on the white sand dunes among the fragrant sand verbena. We found agates on the beach. We saved abalone blisters for Helen Parkes and Stella Vincent to make into jewelry. Sometimes we bathed in the ocean, but the surf was rough and dangerous. The river mouth was better."[3] There was fishing and foraging. There were outdoor birthdays and dinners. Charades, cowboy songs, mountain music, "Barb'ry Allen...."

The center of Carmel life, though, was the theater. An actor and poet named Herbert Heron founded the outdoor Forest Theater. "He and his rather exotic wife Opal, dancer and musician, lived with their little daughter Constance in their house near the theatre. In a time when it was really daring for a woman to have short hair, Opal wore her hair cut close."

Productions were played by the members of the artists' colony and old-time Carmel folk, all mixed together. "Helen Cooke, the strangely beautiful daughter of Grace MacGowan Cooke, played the lead and opposite her was Fred Leidig, groceryman." Plays were written expressily for this venue. They also played Shakespeare...even a Japanese play, which Grace Duffy remembered as being "very moany and long drawn out; probably poetry, but in Japanese."[4] Summer nights, surrounded by pines, the community discovered itself in wonder (Figure 21.3). Grace Wickhem Odhner played Alice's Cheshire Cat, grinning down from the trees. Ethel directed a play by Robert Lewis Stevenson. Another night, John played a sensational Shylock (Figure 21.4).

And here's a final little treasure from the scrapbook (Figure 21.5):

The Famous Abalone Song
Oh! Some folks boast of quail on toast
Because they think it's tony;
But I'm content to owe my rent
And live on abalone.

Oh! Mission Point's a friendly joint,
Where every crab's a crony;
And true and kind you'll ever find
The clinging abalone.

He wanders free beside the sea,
Where'er the coast is stony;

Figure 21.4 John Kenneth Turner as Shylock. John had acted as an American investor shopping for slave plantations in Mexico. After that, doing Shylock may have been relatively easy. Bancroft Library, U.C. Berkeley.

He flaps his wings and madly sings
The plaintive abalone.

By Carmel Bay, the people say,
We feed the lazzaroni
On Boston beans and fresh sardines
And toothsome abalone.

Some live on hope, and some on dope
And some on alimony;
But my tom-cat, he lives on fat
And tender abalone.

Oh! some drink rain and some champagne,
Or brandy by the pony;
But I will try a little rye
With a dash of abalone.

Oh! Some like jam, and some like ham,
And some like macaroni;
But bring me in a pail of gin
And a tub of abalone.

He hides in caves beneath the waves,
His ancient patrimony;
And so 'tis shown that faith alone
Reveals the abalone.

Figure 21.5 Ethel and her sister Jane at Carmel, with abalone shells hanging in the background. Bancroft Library, U.C. Berkeley.

The more we take the more they make
In deep-sea matrimony;
Race suicide cannot betide
The fertile abalone.

I telegraph my better half
By Morse or by Marcone;
But if the need arise for speed,
I send an abalone.

Oh! Some think that the Lord is fat,
And some that He is bony...

{softly—with reverence:}

But as for me I think that He
Is like an abalone.[5]

PART FIVE

Lost Love

Racing against the Odds

Principles and Marginality

On September 23, 1911, *Regeneración* of Los Angeles published a
new program in the place of the famous 1906 Programa del Partido
Liberal. The September manifesto was, at long last, an unrepentant,
explicit, and full-blown anarchist document. Because of its doctrinaire purity, the September 23 manifesto was almost immediately
translated and reprinted in Emma Goldman's journal *Mother Earth*,
and it received an enthusiastic reception from Voltairine de Cleyre,
and other prominent anarchist lights of the day.[1] Although this
radical document has often been admired and touted as proof of
ideological maturation and coherence, it was also a sign of the movement's political marginalization.

It is often said that Ricardo and the junta had retained nominal
allegiance to the 1906 manifesto throughout the Madero revolution
because they did not wish to scare adherents away with the word
"anarchy." Ricardo himself is cited in support of this interpretation.
Thus, in his instructions for the 1908 rebellion, Ricardo wrote to
Enrique and Práxedis: "Only the anarchists will know that we're
anarchists, and we'll ask them not to call us that, so as not to frighten
all those imbeciles who, though they share our same ideals without
knowing that they are anarchists, are used to hear anarchists spoken
of in unfavorable terms. Actually, rather than imbeciles, they're
ignorant. We must not be unfair."[2] The break with Villarreal and
Juan Sarabia in 1911 is at times also cited as having freed the junta up
to take a more radical position.

After the fall of Díaz, old friends of Ricardo's, such as doctor Luis
Rivas Iruz, asked him to return to Mexico to lead the electoral contest against Madero. Ricardo had many supporters in Mexico, Rivas

said, and "if you return to Mexico, abandoning your socialist ideas (which are completely unpractical in our milieu for now—and probably yet for a couple thousand years), we can organize the Great Liberal Party."[3] Ricardo responded by explaining the depth of his commitment to the poor. "I know the Law and how it is applied—with gentleness for the rich, and harshly for the poor.... I want equality, true equality—economic equality, which is the firm foundation of liberty."[4] Ricardo is explicit about the primacy of his commitment to socialism and to a social revolution, but he is not explicit about its implication for his return to Mexico. The implication, though, is pretty clear: Ricardo will not return because he won't be a political candidate in a bourgeois election, and he will not return as a revolutionary because he gives priority to his role as an ideological guide.

There is a logic to all of this, certainly, but there was also always something impracticable about a pure anarchist program. Thus, if we look at the acts of the Liberals in Baja California, where PLM militants and Wobblies were by no means scared of the anarchist label, we see that wielding real political power itself set limits to the radical anarchism of the militants' ideology. In Baja, Liberals could not expropriate American, British, and French investments without courting foreign invasion, so they resorted to taxation, instead. They held on to the customs houses at Tijuana and Mexicali and used them to levy taxes. They tried to give concessions to small ranchers and tradesmen while imposing levies on the larger ones. And there was a long etcetera that made their activities in the region comparable to those of other Mexican revolutionaries. Pryce even set up gambling houses in Tijuana, with no objection from the junta. The troops needed the money, and the junta couldn't provide them with it.

Real power implied making concessions to property—lasting concessions, in fact—and it also implied preserving at least the bare bones of a state: policing, taxing, administering justice. Villa and Carranza printed their own paper scrip, and even the Zapatistas would have had to do that had they not controlled the Taxco silver mines and so had access to their own silver.

The manifesto of September 23 is one of the purest and most beautiful ideological statements of the Mexican Revolution, true, but its immaculate purity had political impotence as its underbelly. By September 1911, the Baja campaign had been lost, Madero had triumphed resoundingly, and the Mexican Revolution had evolved into a dispersed rumble of agrarian dissatisfaction, unionization, and local political jockeying. Ricardo, Enrique, Librado, and Anselmo Figueroa had been arraigned and were awaiting trial, which finally came in June 1912 and put them away at McNeil Island.

And there was more. Madero's triumph initially generated a sense of elation that provided his government the benefit of the doubt from many of the revolution's supporters in the United States. Not all supporters of economic transformation were ready to rally to a cause that was calling for Madero's fall even before he had been elected to office. Nor did the Liberals' defeat in Baja California and the confusion surrounding their national loyalties and credentials help them any. Even in Los Angeles, Ricardo's prestige was badly shaken.

The very virulence of the Los Angeles *Regeneración*'s personal invective against an ever-growing list of traitors also carried local costs for the junta, for public speaking and debate at the Placita de los Mexicanos now included equally injurious counterattacks on Ricardo. So, for instance, the insulted leaders of a Los Angeles Liberal group that favored Antonio Villarreal did not hesitate to pay Ricardo back for his insults, and they certainly did not pull any punches:

> Magón always says in his rag that *Ratón Mojado* [Wet Mouse], *Cara de Hígado* [Liver Face], which is me, and *Cara de Panza* [Stomach Face] are local concessionaries of the "41" [Antonio Villarreal's army of queers]. But in the Placita I tell him what's what: I call him *Palo Blanco* [White Stick], exploiter of prostitutes, syphilitic, bandit, degenerate, coward, orphan of shame, dressed by charitable donations, bayonet-tongued and chickenhearted. I then say what he did in El Paso in 1906; I tell about the bookstore that he opened with the people's money and how he sold out Carmona's daughters. Brave, yes...like a mouse. In El Paso, he hid under a bed for three days at León Cárdenas's house. Liberator, yes...just like Torquemada. Revolutionary, yes...he scratched even his mother's womb, and when she offered him her tit, he bit it.[5]

The group also rounded up 960 signatures on a letter in English dedicated to denouncing Ricardo.[6] Sizing up the situation, a C. Flores had written to Antonio Villarreal as early as June, saying that "Magón goes from bad to worse, and daily looses more of his prestige. No one wants to help him any longer here in Los Angeles."[7] Although the claim was exaggerated, the junta undoubtedly faced a truly urgent crisis, even while its manifesto implied and required a long-term strategy.

Tar and Feathers

One immediate issue that emanated from the principles of the September manifesto was leadership. The Liberals had lost in Baja, and their most successful military chieftains in Chihuahua had been making pacts, one by one, with Madero. That left only Emiliano Zapata in arms, but in 1911 and early 1912, Zapata was still involved in negotiations with Madero, and the junta by no means trusted him to act any differently from the Chihuahua revolutionaries, a fact that can be ascertained in the tone that *Regeneración* took when Zapata declared, in November 1911, that he was ready for a truce. "Let Zapata go ahead and surrender," Ricardo declared, "he'll find someone with a firm hand to stab him in the back for being a traitor. The surrender of one felon has never spelled the death of a deeply felt want."[8]

It is worth noting that Ricardo was ready to call Zapata a traitor and a felon even before his truce with Madero had been consummated. Having been betrayed (in his own mind, at least) by his closest people—Juan Sarabia, Villarreal, and even his own brother Jesús—he was not willing to grant others the benefit of the doubt.

But beyond the bitter and almost paranoid distrust that Ricardo had developed, there was also an ideological point about the question of leadership that concerned him. From the time of its founding, the Mexican Liberal Party had a tradition of denouncing *personalismo*. That antipersonalist position hardened in its implications now that the movement turned openly to anarchism, for whereas the antipersonalism of the early era was designed to give priority to the preservation of law and the constitutional order, anarchist opposition to *personalismo* targeted leadership in and of itself.

That development escalated Ricardo's obsession with betrayal and his glorification of revenge and open-ended revolutionary violence. Indeed, Ricardo's call to violence by no means subsided after the defeat in Baja California. On the contrary, he continued to argue consistently for it. So, for example, on the anniversary of the assassination of the Spanish anarchist educator José Ferrer, Ricardo harangued his audience at a public meeting: "Comrades: may the death of the Teacher help convince the pacifists that the use of force is needed to end social inequality, to kill privilege, and to make each human free."[9]

Enrique, for his part, used the anniversary of Práxedis Guerrero's death to make a broad argument for the beauty, justice, and necessity of violent revenge, even though Práxedis had explicitly argued against hatred and saw the use of violence as justified only as part of an organic moment of social transformation and not as a psychological impulse of revenge. Arguing against Christ's dictum of offering the other cheek, Enrique clamored that "the proletariat's freedom shall be the daughter of vengeance."[10]

The result of Ricardo's venting of hatred was the suffusion of the pages of *Regeneración* with violent and vile language directed against any and all leaders who might be perceived as self-interested or as sellouts of the proletarian cause. In the breathless months that transpired between the junta's arraignment in August 1911 and the mens' conviction in June 1912, a veritable parade of leaders was subjected to *Regeneración*'s verbal insults and calls for lynchings or summary executions, with Ricardo very often lighting the torch.

With regard to insult and invective, there was practically no restraint: Villarreal was a pederast, a homosexual degenerate, and an assassin. Juan Sarabia was a Judas. Manuel Sarabia was a eunuch. The signers of the Plan de Tacubaya, which promised agrarian reforms (Paulino Martínez, Emilio Vázquez Gómez, and others) were idiots. Pascual Orozco, who had purchased weapons in the United States and had run guns to Mexico for the Flores Magóns, but who then supported Madero, was a *baboso*, aslobering idiot. Antonio Díaz Soto y Gama, who had helped found the Partido Liberal Mexicano, was an mentally unbalanced and shameless opportunist. Inés Salazar, Emilio Campa, and Lázaro Alanís, who had led the Liberals' most successful military campaigns in Chihuahua, were bandits and traitors. Camilo Arriaga, the wealthy convener of the first Liberal Congress, was now a slavedriver (*negrero*). And a long, very long etcetera (Figure 22.1). Practically every issue of *Regeneración* contained some invective against Villarreal, Sarabia, and Mexico City's "*Regeneración burguesa*. That was a staple of the journal in 1911 and 1912. And to its denunciations was added any new treason by Madero, or anyone else.

Ricardo's indulgence in mudslinging and insult encouraged imitators. So, to give just one example, publishing in an alternative revolutionary paper in Texas, a José Pérez from Knipps, Texas,

Figure 22.1 Inés Salazar (*left*) and
Pascual Orozco (*right*). Orozco's portrait
captures a laconic northern ruddiness
that is iconic. Courtesy of the Bancroft
Library, John Murray Papers.

denounced a traitor, identifying him as yet another "Judas" and suggesting that he belonged in the ranks of Villarreal's 41s.[11] After the junta went to prison, the new editors of *Regeneración* also felt no compunction in using similar language against traitors and enemies of the cause—denouncing "Judases" here and "degenerates" there.

Verbal insults were not infrequently followed by calls for execution. Pascual Orozco should be summarily shot by the proletariat; the same went for former Liberal heroes Salazar, Campa, and Alanís; Hilario Salas, too, deserved the noose (*mecate*) for having accepted the post of *jefe político*. And—this went without saying, but it was in fact said—so did Madero. Following Ricardo's lead, California Liberal leader Antonio Rincón wrote a public letter to the (now traitor) Emilio Campa: "What a step you've taken!... You went from being a fighter to being a despicable thief.... Emilio Campa, your fate is sealed. You turned in your comrades, you stole the sacred funds of the Party. You shall be delivered to Proletarian Justice by another proletarian."[12]

In short, the Judases of the revolution all deserved to be shot, and Ricardo was at the head of the line of those calling for their execution. The week that he was sentenced, he typed off a parting shot: "Even the best of politicians ought to be tarred and feathered."[13]

Ricardo held up his own example and that of the other junta members as a counter to opportunists. In his farewell letter before going to prison at McNeil Island, he reminded *Regeneración*'s readers:

> Our sacrifice is for your sake. We have not wished to be tyrants or bourgeois. That is our crime!...For my part, I can attest that I have been offered the post of Vice-President of the Republic of Mexico, and I have been offered millions of dollars in exchange for betraying you. I have not wished to be your executioner. I have not wished to sell out my convictions. I prefer prison or the gallows![14]

Fables

After the publication of the September manifesto, the ideological strategy of the PLM can be summarized as follows: to call for generalized, decentralized, armed revolt, with rebels being encouraged to seize the means of production directly, never to cede power to any leader, and to attack any political leader who might draw a salary or collect a bribe. The great enemies of the proletariat, as always, were capital, authority, and the clergy.

Ricardo constantly reminded his readers that they were fighting for an economic revolution and that this implied a protracted struggle. They must not lose heart. On the other hand, the junta's strategy also relied on sustained ideological guidance. It relied, in other words, on *Regeneración*: "the journal must stay alive so that the beautiful revolutionary movement of Mexico does not degenerate into a mere political movement, which would set proletarian emancipation back many years."[15] Ricardo wrote this at the end of 1911, in one of his almost weekly calls for readers to fork over money to save the paper.

A revolt without ideological guidance would lead to its transformation into a "political movement," rather than an economic revolution, and Ricardo's view of each and every local rebel was pretty much that they were politicians in the making—either because they were brigands and opportunists, like Antonio Díaz Soto y Gama and Juan Sarabia, who wished to be elected to Congress, or because they were ingenuous and insufficiently prepared. Even leaders who championed agrarian reform, such as Emiliano Zapata and Emilio Vázquez Gómez, were said to be heading "authoritarian parties." That was why the selfless and mentally disciplined ideological guidance of *Regeneración* was indispensable to the social revolution (Figure 22.2).

And yet *Regeneración* was sinking. When Antonio Villarreal accused Ricardo of taking $40,000 in *científico* money, Ricardo wrote a detailed response, claiming that the accusation was a calumny. However, Ricardo did not wish to make public just how bad things were for the Liberal Party and made the outrageous claim that its membership had doubled, from ten to twenty thousand in the months between June and September, 1911.[16]

In fact, the paper's falling circulation was obvious to any diligent reader and is, indeed, the reason why the accusation that Ricardo took the *científico* money is so very doubtful. So, for instance, in the August 19 issue, Tomás Labrada published a report of his impressions of *Regeneración*'s offices on his visit from Texas. Labrada enthusiastically described fervent activity. The editorial team worked long hours daily, including Sundays. Typewriters clanged out letters and articles one after another; volunteers brought mail and packages to and from the post in a continuous stream. Others revised addresses and added names to subscriber lists. Everyone worked for nothing, and in every

Figure 22.2 Yaqui troops fighting in Carranza's army. Courtesy of the Bancroft Library, John Murray Papers.

face, there was the gleam of the evangelist—"se refleja el entusiasmo de estos obreros de la Buena Nueva. Nonetheless, Labrada was distressed by the economic destitution that he found everywhere visible in the group and called on readers to increase contributions.[17]

By December of 1911, Ricardo himself was crying out that *Regeneración* was dying.[18] He described the conditions of misery in which he and the staff lived. They were mired in debts to landlords, grocers, and friends. But none of that really mattered. The important fact was that they could no longer afford the newsprint, rent for the offices, or printing costs. Ricardo warned that the journal had only two weeks of life left if contributors did not pick up the slack.

During the following weeks, urgent appeals continued.[19] They appear to have had only limited success, though, so on January 13, 1912, Ricardo announced that although the journal was not closing, it would be reducing its run almost to half—13,000 (from 21,000—these are Ricardo's numbers). In short, *Regeneración* was languishing at a time when, according to its own theory, it was needed the most, since the Liberals no longer had armies in the field and thus relied entirely on popular embrace of their message.

It was in this context that Ricardo began to invest more in another writing genre: the fable or allegory. Given the timing of this turn, my impression is that it was part of a larger attempt to increase revenues. One aspect of this effort was fomenting the cult of the martyrs of the Liberal Party, whose anniversaries occupied some attention in the pages of the journal.

The most important of these was Práxedis Guerrero. *Regeneración* took to printing and selling Práxedis Guerrero lapel pins at this time. Indeed, it may have been Práxedis's ghost that inspired Ricardo to write more stories. Práxedis had been the only one in the group to do this kind of writing in the pages of *Regeneración*, and his allegories, especially "Sopla," and "Rojo Amanecer," had become classics of the movement and were reprinted often. Ricardo had written his first allegory immediately after Práxedis's death: "The Apostle,'" which was ostensibly about Práxedis, but also can be thought of as being about Ricardo himself. Now, a year after Práxedis's death and in the face of a long, uphill battle against heavy odds, with enthusiasm low and running mainly on grim discipline and a thirst for revenge, Ricardo returned to the genre.

Significantly titled "The Catastrophe," Ricardo's first moral tale in this period told the story of a miner, Pedro, who makes fun of a certain Juan for scrimping and saving to buy a gun and to make regular contributions to *Regeneración*.[20] Calling Juan a fool, Pedro thinks that he has it good with his employer. "Better to spend it on drink." But then the mine collapses with Pedro and a group of miners inside. Nothing is done by the owners to extract them. Working desperately to break out of the mine, breathing each time with more difficulty, Pedro is suddenly stung by his own earlier words. While Pedro expires in impotence, Juan is out with a rifle, fighting his oppressors. Pedro's wife now will be destitute, his children, sent to prison. This was the disaster that faced the proletariat without *Regeneración*.

CHAPTER TWENTY-THREE

From Transnational Solidarity

to International Relations

The Changing Strategic Significance of the Neutrality Laws
The Maderista revolt of 1910 and the fall of Porfirio Díaz transformed the relationship between Mexicans on the U.S. side of the border and revolutionary activity in Mexico. As the border heated up, beginning around 1907, the Mexican government responded by increasing the number, resources, and activities of its consulates, studying the legal resources that were available to it in the United States and gaining experience in coordinated action with various U.S. governmental agencies.

By 1910, Madero and the Liberal junta had each come to understand how to work within the constraints of the neutrality laws. When Madero issued his revolutionary manifesto, the Plan de San Luis, from San Antonio, Texas, backdating it one day in order to set it fictitiously in San Luis Potosí, Mexico, he did so not only to appear as a revolutionary who was working within Mexico, but also because had Madero dated it October 6 and called his proclamation the Plan de San Antonio, Texas, he might have made himself vulnerable to prosecution for violation of the U.S. neutrality laws. The junta, for its part, was careful not to enlist its soldiers for the Baja campaign in Los Angeles, but directed them instead to the border, where they might register to fight after crossing the line into Mexican territory.

With the fall of Díaz, however the politics of neutrality subtly shifted. The neutrality agreement with Mexico had been signed at the time of the Spanish-American War, as a quid pro quo with President Díaz. Going against important currents of Mexican opinion, Porfirio Díaz had declared Mexico neutral in that conflict. In exchange for that concession, Díaz got a neutrality law that gave his government an instrument with which to contain political agitation by Mexicans operating out of the United States.

Apparently, that arrangement would now benefit Madero, as it in fact did in the case of the 1911 and 1912 trials of Mosby, Pryce, and the members of the Los Angeles junta. However, Madero's government soon proved to be weak. It had powerful opponents, as well as an unsatisfied popular opposition. Madero's weakness, manifested in a series of uprisings in 1912, increasingly made the application of the neutrality laws more an instrument for American policy than a concession to the Mexican government.

This was not good news for the Liberals. In the hearings organized by the U.S. Senate Foreign Relations Committee in September 1913, geared to evaluating the question of how American interests and citizens were aiding revolution in Mexico, Senators Albert B. Fall and William Alden Smith ascertained that although the Liberal Party was no longer a military threat, the effects of its propaganda had nonetheless been considerable.[1] Thus, though the Liberals no longer had troops or leadership in any Mexican region, their propaganda had generated a long-term problem. This view did not change after the election of President Woodrow Wilson, early in 1913.

For the most part, Woodrow Wilson's Mexico policy was very different from that of President Taft's, his predecessor.[2] In particular, Wilson did not support the military coup that Taft's ambassador to Mexico had helped to orchestrate. Since Wilson took office just weeks after that coup, which included the assassination of Francisco Madero, he was in a position to refuse U.S. recognition to Mexico's new president, Victoriano Huerta. And he did just that. On the other hand, Wilson wished to avoid a full-fledged military invasion of Mexico. Instead, he sought to manage Mexico's revolutionary process indirectly and to support an outcome that was neither fully restorative (no counterrevolutionary return to Díaz) nor led by a faction that was inimical to American interests. The category of factions inimical to American interests included the Liberals.

Indeed, one of Woodrow Wilson's early decisions as president was to support the conviction of the junta. As a law professor, Wilson had a reputation as a liberal (in the American sense), and given the various civil liberties organizations' position regarding the discriminatory use of the neutrality laws against Mexican exiles, he was petitioned directly to review the junta's case. Wilson agreed to do this, but found, contrary to the hopes of supporters of the Mexican Liberty Party, that the junta members had indeed been guilty of the crimes with which they had been charged, and they should not be granted a pardon.

Americans and the Mexican Cause: Turner Again

The shaky performance of President Madero in the course of 1912 and then the Victoriano Huerta coup d'état in February 1913 generated an upswelling of sorrow and remorse among observers of Mexico. Those feelings had consequences for the Liberals, for they had taken an uncompromisingly negative stance toward Madero. As Jesús M. Rangel later wrote, "V. Huerta and F. I. Madero, they were all the same to me, because of the perfidious acts that Madero committed against the Liberal Party, which he had abandoned for fear that its 1906 Program would affect his great interests."[4] The Liberals, in other words, were not in a position to react indignantly in the face of the military coup. What could they do, now that Madero was a martyr?

Regeneración had crooned and taunted when Madero fell—*Schadenfreude*. It was not a pretty picture. So, for instance, an article covering the assassination of Madero began: "The first...bourgeois Lady, Sara P. de Madero, along with Angela and Mercedes Madero—sisters of the bloodthirsty man who just fell from the post of First Executioner, threw herself at the stinking feet of the bandit Huerta, arms extended, and implored a pardon for the other bandit."[5]

In fact, it was this hostile attitude toward the mild-mannered Madero and "bourgeois democracy" that had made alliances with Huerta thinkable for former Liberals such as Emilio Campa, Lázaro Alanís, and Inés Salazar in Chihuahua. Basing themselves on the principle that "the enemy of my enemy is my friend," some erstwhile Liberal *caudillos* supported Huerta outright—they could at least find some sort of alliance with him that might gain them temporary concessions in the regions where they were strong.

Even a personage such as Jesús Flores Magón, who had been Madero's minister of the interior, but had always had conflicts with Madero, chose to keep his position as senator during the initial months of Huerta's government and tried to convince old members of the Liberal Party to join a unity government. Indeed, the whole of the Jesús Flores Magón faction—Villarreal, Juan Sarabia, Santiago de la Vega—had had conflicts with Madero over his lack of commitment to social reform and so had flirted with allying themselves to people such as Pascual Orozco, who eventually allied himself with Huerta.[6] In a strongly worded rebuke against this alliance, former Cananea strike leaders Manuel Diéguez, Juan José Ríos, and Esteban Baca Calderón, who were now officers in Álvaro Obregón's insurgent army, which was supporting Carranza's insurgency against Huerta, eloquently responded to Jesús: "You, Mr. Licenciado, because of your enlightenment, your talent and trajectory, your status as senator in the Federal Congress and as an intellectual activist—you, Mr. Licenciado—were much more compelled than us to uphold at any cost the principles that you and your brothers inculcated in us (before they went astray), through those beacons of civic duty that were called *Regeneración* and *El Hijo del Ahuizote!*"[7]

Ríos, Diéguez, and Baca Calderón, who once had taken orders from the Liberal junta, now felt that not only Jesús, but also Ricardo and Enrique had lost their way. They were referring, no doubt, to the junta's role in Baja California, but also to Ricardo's belligerency toward Madero, which had helped Díaz during the revolution and had now helped Huerta topple and murder Madero.

Even more painful to the junta, the Casa del Obrero Mundial workers' federation also took a neutral stance with regard to Victoriano Huerta, at least initially. Mexico's first officially tolerated May Day parade took place under Victoriano Huerta, and with his blessing—a presage, perhaps, of the paradoxical relationship that would later characterize the Mexican state and the union movement.

Toward the end of 1912, John Kenneth Turner decided to travel to Mexico again, this time to write a report about Mexico after Díaz. He wanted to witness life under Madero. Probably he was interested in stories that might counter growing American nostalgia for Porfirio Díaz and what Turner rightly saw as a threat of direct intervention. But it is equally clear from his correspondence with Ethel that Turner was not intending on giving the Madero government a clean bill of health, either.[8]

In December 1912, the condition of Turner's Mexican network was different than it had been in the days of Don Porfirio. Ricardo, Enrique, Librado, and Anselmo Figueroa were now doing time in the penitentiary at McNeill Island. *Regeneración* was being run by Antonio P. Araujo, Blas Lara, Teodoro Gaitán, and William C. Owen.

Liberal Party activity, such as it was, was concentrated in the United States Within Mexico, only Emiliano Zapata had empathy with the junta and identified with the manifesto of September 23, but lines of communication between them were tenuous and had ideological, but little real organizational significance.[9] The junta, in other words, had seemingly become external to Mexican political life.

On the other hand, John's friends in the relaunched Liberal Party in Mexico City were a real presence in Mexican politics. Manuel and Elizabeth Sarabia were living in Coyoacán—Calle Berlín, number 1913—and John stayed with them. Manuel was printing a weekly, *El Socialista*. Juan Sarabia was now a congressman and editor of the prestigious *El Diario del Hogar*. Jesús Flores Magón had by that time resigned from his post as minister of the interior, but was a senator. Santiago de la Vega edited the ferociously anti-Madero magazine *Multicolor*. Finally, the Casa del Obrero Mundial had been created in Mexico City, and among its founders were old Turner acquaintances, including Lázaro Gutiérrez de Lara, Manuel Sarabia, Santiago de la Vega, and Antonio Díaz Soto y Gama. All were working to make their version of the Liberal Party a powerful force in Mexican national politics. All were very critical of Madero, but also committed to democratic politics, and all had succeeded in attaining positions of prominence. Turner, in short, was well connected.

Turner's own political position had never been one of unqualified support for Madero. The president had allowed freedom to unionize, a free press, and had opened the democratic process, but he had not distributed land or changed Díaz's economic policies. The uprising of Pascual Orozco against Madero in 1912 had included a good number of old Liberals. Turner's friends had in the end chosen not to participate in it, because they felt that the revolt had been infiltrated "by elements that are not really entirely progressive," but they were not unsympathetic to the rebels.[10]

Moreover, even Madero's much-touted democratic achievements were limited. Turner knew, for instance, that Manuel Sarabia had been thrown into Belem Prison for libel because he had attacked Morelos *hacienda* owner Iñigo Noriega in the pages of *El Socialista*. Manuel, we recall, suffered from tuberculosis, and Belem was much more humid and dirtier than the prison in Florence, Arizona. Even a few days in that prison would be dangerous to him. When John arrived at Manuel and Elizabeth's home in Coyoacan, several months after Manuel's brief imprisonment, he was distraught by how these tensions had affected Elizabeth: "You wouldn't know her," he wrote to Ethel, "she is so gaunt and pale."[11]

Lázaro, too, had spent short stints in prison under Madero—on two occasions, in fact. The first time was in Torreón, where the consuls of Spain, Germany, and the United States brought a complaint against him because he insulted their national leaders in a public rally.[12] The second was in Mexico City, again allegedly for defamation. Lázaro was organizing the women workers at a textile mill, La Sinaloense, and he publicly called its owner, Congressman Ricardo Otero, a thief. Otero gave Lázaro the choice either of fighting a duel or being thrown in prison. Lázaro chose the latter and was in prison for four days, until his release for lack of evidence—"desvanecimiento de la evidencia."[13]

Even Juan Sarabia, who was a congressman and editor of *El Diario del Hogar*, faced loss of congressional immunity and a trial that threatened to send him to prison on charges of libel, defamation, and calumny for an article printed in his paper against a former Porfirian consul in Texas.[14] In short, in Madero's Mexico, the wealthy and powerful could still avail themselves of the authorities to jail their opponents. Even so, Turner may not entirely have given up on the man.

Madero received John at Chapultepec Castle on January 31, 1913, and spent the better part of an afternoon with him. He praised John for having helped topple Díaz and gave him a signed portrait, inscribed to the "eminent American writer and defender of the Mexican proletariat" (Figure 23.1). Finally, Madero provided John with a letter of introduction for his journalistic mission—a "*carte blanche*," as Ethel put it.

Ten days later, a military coup wreaked havoc in Mexico City and transformed Madero's letter from a boon into a liability. On February 9, Generals Bernardo Reyes, Félix Díaz, and Manuel Mondragón led a military uprising, and Mexico City was bombarded. Bernardo Reyes, who was the coup's most senior officer, was killed in action, but the President Madero and Vice President José María Pino Suárez were captured a few days later, on February 17, the same day that Madero's brother, Gustavo, accused General Victoriano Huerta, who headed the defense, of being in cahoots with the putsch leaders. Gustavo was tortured, mutilated, and murdered that day. Huerta

Figure 23.1 Copy of the photo that Madero
signed for John Kenneth Turner. The photo
is signed January 26, 1913. Madero was
executed a few weeks later, on February 22.
From Jesús González Monroy, *Ricardo Flores
Magón y su actitud en la Baja California* (Mexico City: Editorial Academia Literaria, 1962).

was made president on February 20. Francisco Madero and Vice President Pino Suárez were murdered on February 22.

Days before the coup, Turner had been publishing a series of articles in a Mexico City paper, El País, warning of the imminent danger of an American invasion. Those writings bothered the American community in Mexico greatly. They also irritated the American ambassador, Henry Lane Wilson. A group of self-styled "representatives of the American Community" had strenuously objected to Turner's Barbarous Mexico pieces back in 1909. Now Turner was operating in the open and collaborating with Mexican papers against U.S. interests. Members of the American community reacted yet again, but this time privately, in correspondence with the Department of State.

So, for instance, S. M. Emery, president of the Compañía Azucarera y Mercantil de Vista Hermosa, Oaxaca, sent clippings of the El País articles to Secretary of State William Jennings Bryan, suggesting that "If you have these articles translated...I believe you would find in them much that was libelous and treasonable and that would warrant the deportation of this scoundrel from the U.S."[15] Initially, Ambassador Henry Lane Wilson sent no diplomatic notes regarding Turner's El País articles. The ambassador was busy brokering the military coup against Madero and so had bigger fish to fry. But when Turner serendipitously fell into his clutches, Ambassador Wilson did not fail to exact his revenge.

During the ten days between General Bernardo Reyes's death and the capture and resignation of Francisco Madero, the putchist troops hunkered down in the Ciudadela Military Academy and fought for Mexico City from that base (Figure 23.2). General Huerta, who was supposed to be in charge of President Madero's defense, and the rebel General Félix Díaz were using the conflagration as a smoke screen while they brokered an agreement between them. As an added benefit to their cause, the bombardment of Mexico City's population increased popular clamor in favor of Madero's resignation. The man who orchestrated the agreement between Generals Victoriano Huerta and Félix Díaz was none other than the American ambassador, Henry Lane Wilson, and the pact between them was actually hammered out and agreed to inside the American Embassy.

While all of this was happening, John Kenneth Turner was out and about the town, taking photos and preparing reports. On

Figure 23.2 Soldiers of the military coup standing guard at the Ciudadela Military Academy during the bombardment of Mexico City. Courtesy of the Bancroft Library, John Murray Papers.

February 16, during an armistice, he came a bit too close to the Ciudadela and was captured by a Félix Díaz patrol:

> I was walking on the streets of Mexico, the same as thousands of Mexicans and foreigners did. I carried my camera with which I was taking photographs of destroyed buildings. I was about half a kilometer from the Ciudadela when a Felicista sentry made me a prisoner and took me to the Ciudadela. I was there placed in custody and explaining my actions, which were without doubt innocent, and that I was an American citizen, I was given to understand that I would be set at liberty soon.[16]

At first, Turner made the best of the chaotic situation to get inside information. He was now within the Ciudadela itself and so could observe the coup from its headquarters. The trouble was, he saw too much—or at least American diplomats believed that he had seen too much. Thus, one embassy official reported:

> During the third visit to the Citadel . . . Turner, without speaking to us or calling attention to his presence, sneaked in behind us and took a seat unobserved, and for about fifteen minutes listened to a conversation which he had no right to hear. This occurred before his presence appears to have been discovered by anyone. Then inquiry as to who he was and a statement from us that we did not know man, caused Félix Díaz to nervously take away the camera, field-glasses and other effects of Turner. Díaz then ordered Turner confined. There was, however, no unnecessary roughness, and I did not see any rifles showed at Turner's chest, as he states. He was, however sent out of the room in charge of a sentinel.
>
> After the conclusion of our interview . . . we requested permission to speak to the American who had been confined. He was again brought into the office and I made inquiry as to his name, residence, friends, etc. He hesitated in answering these questions."[17]

Turner's situation turned very dangerous at that point, with Félix Díaz's men regularly letting him know that he would soon be executed. Turner made desperate appeals to the embassy, but it had been Ambassador Wilson himself who had insisted that Turner reveal his identity to his Mexican captors, thereby placing his life in immediate danger. Félix Díaz was Porfirio Díaz's nephew, and John's *Barbarous Mexico* was notorious and obnoxious to him. As Turner later declared, "I am the only foreigner, so far as I know, from whom the protection of the Ambassador from his country was apparently withheld."[18]

From Transnational Solidarity to International Relations

Turner's experience during the coup against Madero was symptomatic of the growing limits on transnational grassroots movement in Mexican-American relations and their progressive subordination to intergovernmental channels. The Baja California experience had already initiated this trend, with Mexican reaction against the presence of American soldiers in revolutionary armies finding support both from the Mexican government, which that mobilized formal diplomatic protest and extradition proceedings, and in the U.S. government's increasing attentiveness to the strategic use of the neutrality laws. The Turner affair of 1913 revealed the web of diplomatic pressures that were now in play around the journalistic enterprise.

In 1908, Turner had traveled to Mexico as an unknown. Now that he was a famous man, or at least notorious, the matter of his identity had to be managed at the governmental level. Thus, Ambassador Henry Lane Wilson compelled Turner to let Félix Díaz know who he really was, with the idea that Díaz likely would have the man shot and that both Wilson and Félix Díaz could easily deny any responsibility over the matter, given the chaos surrounding the coup in Mexico City. But Turner had managed to get a note smuggled out of his prison and telegraphed to Ethel in Carmel. Turner's friends in the United States rallied immediately and bombarded the State Department with letters. Given Turner's reputation, he drew a few powerful supporters in Congress and the judiciary, and so the case moved into formal channels of international regulation.

The telegrams received by the State Department are also the only source that I have found that reveals at least something Turner's family relations, including letters from Turner's mother and from his two brothers. We get an inkling of the personality of John's mother, the feisty Mrs. L. F. Turner, in the letter that she wrote to President Taft and to the secretary of state from Carmel:

> Whatever Mr Turner may have said or done in Mexico, I ask if he is not entitled to the friendly and protective offices of his country's representative in the Mexican capital?
>
> Such he avers he has not had.

Permit me to call your attention to the fact that a large proportion of the citizens of this country over which you have been called most propitiously to rule, are in complete accord with Mr. Turner in his views, fearlessly expressed, regarding the money power wielded practically by the government of these United States in the country on our Southern border.

The fact that Mexico is being exploited by Americans who have been going hand in hand with the government and that Mr. Turner has fought those conditions in his book "Barbarous Mexico", is the real cause for his arrest, subsequent humiliation and suffering and continued detention.

For further reason why Henry Lane Wilson should not remain our Ambassador in Mexico, see editorial in San Francisco Bulletin Thursday evening of March 6th entitled "Our Ambassador in Mexico Condones Dastardly Murder."

Earnestly hoping that you will, at a very early date, give this matter your most careful attention, I remain yours sincerely, Mrs. L. F. Turner (Mother of John Kenneth Turner), Carmel."[19]

There now.

John's brother, R. Izer Turner, of Anaheim, California, wrote a more concise letter to Secretary of State Knox, while his other brother, R. K. Turner, who was an ensign in the navy, wrote a well-composed letter to his senator, William Alden Smith, who then queried the State Department on John's behalf.[20] In addition to providing a glimpse into the personalities of John's family, letters of concern for John's life included queries from three senators, one federal judge, several well-known journalists, and a couple of U.S. citizens and investors with experience in Mexico and a distaste for Ambassador Wilson:

> You cannot get the truth out of Mr. Wilson, our Mexican Ambassador, especially in the case of John Kenneth Turner, as the latter gave out some facts of Mr. Wilson's double dealings. Our ambassador was sent there to protect all Americans and not to further the interests of a particularly strong financial group. I wish you would ask that gentleman how much mining and railroad stock he received from the Porfirio Díaz regime; also ask Charles Taft [brother of the president] what he was promised when he was given the 2,000,000 acres of land down there. Do not forget to ask your friend Willie Randolph Hearst the

same question. They can graft to their heart's content as far as I am concerned, but I protest when they barter away lives for filthy gold.[21]

Coming from a union man, this letter may not have carried that much weight with the State Department, but there were also rumblings from a few investors who did not agree with the dominant tenor of the American colony, and their opinion dovetailed with the negative media reception of the assassination of Francisco I. Madero in the United States. So, for instance, S. W. Scott, a man who described himself as a frequent visitor to Mexico who had large interests there, wrote to his congressman asking for intervention in the Turner case and added:

> I think it high time that the American government was investigating Mr. Wilson, I personally would discredit anything coming from that man and later will have considerable to say about his conduct in Mexico. Is it possible that Wilson without authority from Washington has recognized these cowards butchers and murderers with blood stained hands. How long will this nation stand and look on?[22]

Not all letters sent to the State Department on John's behalf were endorsements. Some had the Pontius Pilate–like purpose of washing their hands of him. Thus, Ralph Easley, a highly placed official of the American Federation of Labor, felt that it was relevant to let the Secretary know that:

> I have no interest in the matter and don't know any of the parties concerned but I do know that if this Turner had any chance to "raise Cain" he would do it. He is not only a Socialist but belongs to the anarchist end of it.
>
> Don't bother to acknowledge receipt of this but throw it into the wastebasket when you are through with it.[23]

Similarly, Judge John Works, who, prompted by John Murray, had written a letter of concern for Turner, when confronted with Ambassador Wilson's stern information regarding Turner, doubled back and replied: "Turner is a fanatic and inclined to be inflammatory in what he writes. I think probably he deserves some wholesome punishment, but I did not think he had ever done anything that would justify the taking of his life, and therefore appealed to you in the matter at the request of one of his personal friends."[24]

In short, Turner's case provided conflicting advice to the secretary of state, and when Woodrow Wilson became president in January 1913, it allowed the new secretary of state, William Jennings Bryan, to recall and investigate Ambassador Henry Lane Wilson.

Responding to the queries in John's behalf, Ambassador Wilson had written to the secretary of state:

> This man is an extremely bad character and is detested by every self-respecting American citizen in Mexico City. He is the author of "Barbarous Mexico" and just prior to the outbreak in this city was writing inflammatory letters to *El País* in which he claimed to have accurate information that the Government of the United States was preparing to seize Mexican territory and to intervene. He has written me an imprudent letter this morning demanding as a matter of right a safe conduct. He is in no danger, needs no safe conduct, and I should be exceedingly loath to give it to him if he did. Will the Department explain this matter to Senator Ashurst and say to him from me that this person is unworthy of his support.[25]

But the reason why Henry Lane Wilson left John in Félix Díaz's hands, where he would in all probability be executed, went beyond the animosity that Turner had provoked with *Barbarous Mexico*. John had believed and had written that there was imminent danger of U.S. intervention in Mexico and, through Ambassador Wilson, the United States had in fact intervened. Not by way of direct military action, as Turner had imagined, but still very decisively, as backers and orchestrators of the military coup that toppled Madero.

The U.S. ambassador knew for a fact that Turner could speak forcefully and that he had directly witnessed a confidential exchange between American embassy officials and Félix Díaz at the Ciudadela during the coup and prior to Madero's assassination. Ambassador Wilson also knew that Turner was well connected in Mexico and that he had been received by Madero not three weeks before. If Turner was simply freed from the Ciudadela, he was perfectly capable of creating a new media scandal, this time with the U.S. ambassador as villain. For that reason, Wilson's plan was probably to let Félix Díaz kill Turner, and in order to achieve this, he forced Turner to reveal his true identity to his captors and made no move to get Turner out of their clutches.

Indeed, though his notes were confiscated and Turner was deported immediately after his release from prison and blocked from making what would certainly have been key interviews about the U.S. embassy's participation in orchestrating the coup that led to Madero's assassination, Turner was still able to write a powerful, moving, and convincing denunciation of Ambassador Wilson's involvement in that atrocity. Beginning with a stirring reconstruction of the way in which Mexico's president and vice president had been murdered, Turner went on to point his finger at the ambassador's complicity in the pact between Félix Díaz and Madero's chief of staff, the turncoat Victoriano Huerta:

> A very definite impression that I received during the first days [of the coup] was that [Felix] Díaz was doomed. He was cooped up with several thousand men within an extremely short radius. There was no food to speak of within that circle. Federal reinforcements were pouring into the city. It seemed only a question of time until he would be cut off and starved into submission....
>
> Who, except themselves or persons in league with them, could say that Huerta and Blanquet would turn traitor? This being the situation, it is putting it mildly to say that I was astounded when told that Mr. Wilson, the American Ambassador, had asked President Madero to resign.[26]

In the face of the barrage of concern for Turner's safety, Henry Lane Wilson claimed that Turner had never been in any sort of danger. He also acquiesced to Huerta and Félix Díaz's decision to expel Turner from the country and did nothing to demand the recovery of Turner's photographic material and notebooks. Indeed, although there is no direct evidence that Wilson asked the new military junta to expel Turner, it is very likely that he did. Certainly, Wilson would have been consulted in the matter, and he must have approved of the plan, given how close he was to the coup leaders. Turner had seen and heard too much at the Ciudadela for Wilson to be comfortable having him stay on in Mexico to make a full report of the coup. Plus, the assassination of President Madero and of Vice President Pino Suárez and the ravaging and brutal killing of Gustavo Madero was a public-relations disaster for Henry Lane Wilson. There was a serious risk that a new set of investigative articles, penned by Turner, could be as fully as sensational as *Barbarous Mexico* had been.

Rather than risk this, Ambassador Henry Lane Wilson did not insist on recovering Turner's effects, although Turner himself had provided Wilson with a "list of possessions taken from the person of John Kenneth Turner, an American citizen, by officers of Félix Díaz at the Ciudadela, February 16, 1913, a part of them having been taken in the presence of Captain Burnside USA and First Secretary of the American Embassy." These possessions included "two note-books of high value to owner, of no value to others," alongside objects of monetary value (but of less journalistic importance), including a camera and tripod, U.S. military field glasses, a Conklin fountain pen, a Savage automatic pistol, a gold watch, and a penknife, all worth a total of $415.86.[27] Wilson made no effort to retrieve the objects and allowed or encouraged President Victoriano Huerta summarily to expel the journalist, with a military escort taking John directly from house arrest to the Texas border.

Once in the United States, Turner traveled to Washington to try to inform the newly sworn-in President Wilson of the Mexican situation. He was received by Secretary of State William Jennings Bryan, who heard Turner, though only up to a point. The State Department sent a journalist, William Bayard Hale, to make an unofficial report on the state of Mexican affairs, and this was followed by a second investigative expedition by John Lind. After suffering the twin humiliation of being publicly doubted by his own government and having the U.S. government deny recognition to a president that the ambassador himself had instated, Henry Lane Wilson was recalled to Washington.

The story of Turner's experiences in the 1913 coup exemplified the growing trend for major U.S. solidarity initiatives to be closely monitored and managed through intergovernmental channels. Turner had at first been condemned and then had been saved by way of intergovernmental negotiations. He had also effectively been kept from his work as a reporter by those same forces and had been received, instead, as a provider of privileged information by the State Department. Turner's ability to move freely between Mexico and the United States and to affect U.S. and Mexican opinion by way of investigative reporting was compromised. Henceforth, he would have to combine independent journalism with direct diplomatic work. Under President Venustiano Carranza and, later, Presidents Adolfo de la Huerta and Álvaro Obregón, Turner became an agent of Mexican government propaganda, devoted specifically to writing work geared to preempting U.S. intervention in Mexico and to denouncing "dollar diplomacy" and the policies of the trusts.[28]

Texas Martyrs

For the Liberals, the final shutdown of the border began in September 1913. The junta was still in prison at McNeil Island. Antonio de Pío Araujo was holding the fort as acting secretary of the junta and was the senior voice at *Regeneración*. The trouble was that at that point, the comrades in the United States needed to participate in the Mexican Revolution in some orchestrated form if they were going to have any participation at all. They could not simply wait for Ricardo, Enrique, Librado, and Anselmo Figueroa to emerge from prison. Why?

First, because the influence of the junta's *Regeneración* had continued to decline. After the junta's imprisonment in June 1912, conflicts emerged over succession and control over the journal. The junta had left Rafael Romero Palacios, Blas Lara, and Francisca Mendoza to run *Regeneración*, with Araujo as secretary of the junta, but by late October, rivalries had developed, and the junta decided to depose Romero Palacios, who was acting as editor. It seems that in addition to there being conflicts between certain members of the staff, the junta was dissatisfied with the finances and operation of *Regeneración*. William C. Owen tried to rectify this impression:

> I must impress on you the fact that you have not left us with a treasury at command or a fully organized business. Four people—Palacios, Sra Mendoza, [Blas] Lara and myself. Then some other help on detail; nearly all of it, I am sure, boyish and utterly inexperienced. Do you remember how hard you all worked, with a much larger force? I think Palacios is working himself to death.... Yesterday Sra Mendoza had a [epileptic] fit, and she has cut her tongue. On what a narrow margin of human energy—which has its very closely-defined limits—are we working! In short, I assure you that, as far as I can judge, and I am here absolutely all the time, every one is working to the limit, Sundays included.[29]

Nevertheless, the junta asked Palacios to resign—quietly. Typically, though, the squabble spilled out into the public and across the pages of *Regeneración* itself, to boot. Francisca Mendoza left in protest over the junta's decision. Even more critically, William C.

Owen, who was at that point the group's most sophisticated and effective writer and editor, also resigned.[30] Owen was persuaded to return in February 1913, but for three months, *Regeneración*'s English-language page was reduced to fillers, a fact that cannot have helped circulation, given inevitable speculation about *Regeneración*'s survival after the junta's imprisonment. Moreover, Romero Palacios and Francisca Mendoza began to write for other radical papers, making critical remarks about the junta and *Regeneración*.

A couple of months later, another conflict emerged within the Los Angeles group between editors Teodoro Gaitán and Blas Lara, on the one hand, and the internationally known Spanish anarchist, editor, and educator Juan Moncaleano, on the other. Together with Rómulo Carmona, who was Enrique Flores Magón's father-in-law, Moncaleano tried to take control of *Regeneración*.[31] Moncaleano and Carmona telegrammed Ricardo in prison in May 1913, saying that *Regeneración* was dying and that they intended to take it over. A conflict ensued, the junta sided with Gaitán and Lara, and Moncaleano and Carmona split off, which again led to recriminations and to the publication of articles that were critical of the Magóns, the junta, and *Regeneración*. This conflict also split a segment of Wobblies off from the movement, and given Moncaleano's international connections, it led to accusations, counteraccusations, and the decline of international solidarity with regard to the movement.[32] In short, the situation on the U.S. side off the border called for some kind of visible action around which the Liberals could rally.

On the Mexican side, too, there were strong incentives and pressures for Liberal revolutionary action. General Victoriano Huerta had taken power in February of 1913, and a new revolution had arisen against him under the banner of upholding the Constitution. Some former Liberals had sided with Huerta, at least during his first months in office, due to the animosity that they had for Madero. *Regeneración* had consistently denounced this course of action, saying time and again that it was against all politicians, and that Díaz, Madero, and Huerta were all the same.

Popular sentiment, however, viewed Madero differently from the decrepit Porfirio Díaz or the assassin Huerta. Madero may have been weak and ineffectual. He may have been feminized by his critics and ridiculed as a Spiritist, but he had had the courage to stand up to Porfirio Díaz, and now he was a martyr for democracy. If the Liberals

Figure 23.3 Jesús María Rangel. Courtesy of the Bancroft Library, John Murray Papers.

could not put some men in the field against Huerta, their reputation as sellouts to Díaz or to Huerta (or to both) would be hard to shake.

It was in this context that Jesús Rangel, who was one of the most senior and respected Texas Liberal fighters, organized an expeditionary force (Figure 23.3).[33] Although little is known of the details of its organization, the project involved an effort by the PLM at large, since the incursion had been preceded by a May conference in Texas that included Liberal contingents from Chihuahua, Coahuila, Durango, Nuevo León, and Tamaulipas, along with junta representatives and the Texas groups.[34] The plan was to make a bold and decisive incursion into Coahuila on September 16, Independence Day, to wrench that region from Carrancista control, and to fight on from there.

Rangel and a group of over twenty experienced fighters were riding from South Texas toward the border to lead the rebellion, and they were expected on the Mexican side by other fighters. But the party was intercepted by a group of Texas Rangers in Dimmitt County who tried to disarm and arrest the revolutionaries, presumably for violation of the neutrality laws. A shoot-out ensued, with two Mexican comrades killed. One of them, Juan Rincón, was from the Los Angeles group. The Mexicans, in turn, killed a deputy sheriff, and wounded some other officers. Rangel and his men were arrested, and a noisy and very tense affair ensued.

Tensions between Anglo Texans and Mexicans had always been high. Texas had earned a well-deserved reputation for very harsh racism against Mexican "greasers." The revolution in Mexico had heightened these tensions, first because there were now more Mexican refugees in Texas (Figure 23.4), but also because there was also now a highly combative, politicized, and armed Mexican sector that was not so easy to push around.

When Rangel and his men were captured, the mainstream press in Texas and California referred to their expeditionary force as "filibusters," trying, undoubtedly, to produce a split in Mexican opinion regarding Rangel's patriotism, but on this occasion, the label got no traction. This was clearly a situation in which Texas Rangers had butted in, with no jurisdiction over the matter, since violation of neutrality was a federal, and not a state offense, in order to stop certain Mexicans—proletarian Mexicans—from taking sides in their own revolution. Mexicans in Texas and throughout the Southwest were absolutely furious.

The Anglo Texans, for their part, were determined to teach the Mexicans a lesson. They could not go around organizing armed parties, and they certainly could not defend themselves against the Rangers, regardless of the latter's lack of jurisdiction. Moreover, Texas wanted to exert at least a measure control over the development of the revolution on the other side of its border. As a result, a 100 percent Anglo jury quickly handed down harsh sentences (nine years, twenty-five years, and ninety-nine years) against three members of the party, while the movement's leaders were moved to San Antonio for trial. The bravado and braggadocio of Texans with regard to Mexicans—felt time and again throughout these years—now resulted in loud calls for a hanging: they wanted Rangel, Charles Cline, an IWW organizer who joined Rangel's expedition, and the other leaders of the party dead. For anarchist libertarians, prison and slavery were considered to be of a form of death, so, as in the earlier case of prisoners such as Juan Sarabia, the defenders of Rangel and his associates had christened them the "Texas Martyrs" (Figure 23.5).

Texas Mexicans and *Regeneración* quickly collected funds for the legal defense of Rangel and company, even as they mobilized protests. Writing for *Regeneración* and as the its acting secretary, Antonio de Pío Araujo said that if Rangel and the others did not get a fair

419

San Diego History Center

Figure 23.4 Refugees, 1913. Written descriptions of Mexican refugees for somewhat later periods—1914, 1915—paint a more desperate picture. Here the refugee women are streaming into San Diego. Elsewhere, refugees of either are described wandering the streets of various border towns, hungry and unemployed. Courtesy of the San Diego History Center.

Figure 23.5 "Texas Martyrs." The two martyrs at the center, Juan Rincón and Silvestre Lomas, were killed in the initial skirmish when Rangel and Cline's men were captured. The other men are presented with their prison numbers. For the Liberals, the dead leaders and the living prisoners were equally martyrs. Courtesy of the Casa de El Hijo del Ahuizote, Mexico City.

trial, the leadership of the Liberal Party in Los Angeles would not sit back and let them hang. Instead, it would take its revolution to Texas: "Violence, bloodshed, and chastisement. That's what those savage mobs of lynchers and murderers need, because in Texas, eighty per cent of the inhabitants who are called 'White' are bandits, pure and simple."[35]

Less explicit, but no less ominously, a list of 121 concerned Tejanos and Mexicans from San Marcos Texas, sent Governor Oscar Branch Colquitt a telegram protesting "against the state of Texas's persecution of revolutionary Mexicans who were arrested in Carrizo Springs this past September 13. Two of them have been convicted—against the law and the evidence—and they've been sentenced to 25 and 6 years in the penitentiary. A third was convicted in Cotulla by a prejudiced jury, and handed the barbarous sentence of 99 years." They declared:

> We will not endure this barbarous state of affairs and issue a call to all Mexicans if your state insists on murdering men who are loyal to the human race and to the liberty of oppressed peoples. We've received news that the other men will be convicted and hanged, and we tell you, Mr. Colquitt, that if this happens, Texas will have to respond before the entire Mexican community for crimes without precedent in the history of justice.[36]

The governor, a little frightened, tried to calm the waters a bit and worked to portray himself as impartial with regard to politics in Mexico and seeking only to protect the law, lives, and property of Texas citizens. But he also made it clear that he would come down hard against the Mexicans if they carried out any violent acts, and José Angel Hernández, the organizer of the San Marcos Defense Committee, was arrested and prosecuted. Moreover, U.S. Postal Service inspectors began making inquiries about *Regeneración* and its editors, putting pressure on the journal, which, due to its poverty, was coming out with only two-page issues in those days.[37]

Nonetheless, *Regeneración* continued to appear and continued to rally support for an armed reaction in Texas if Rangel was convicted and hanged:

> Capitalism believed that the Mexican proletariat in Texas was a mass of peons that would forever remain prostrated at the feet of the masters who rule that barbarous state. The government thought that those

"greasers" would be as submissive as the Blacks under the yoke of the barbarous cowboys. And both monsters of the system have awoken to the reality of the situation, and they exclaim like the magnate in the letter of Louis XVI, who cried before the multitude: "This is no riot, it is a revolution!."[38]

The governments of the United States and the state of Texas had closed the Liberals' passage into Mexico and had excluded them as best they could from the revolution there. In so doing, they also had hardened the racial line between Mexicans and Anglos and so had brought the revolution to Texas.

Veracruz

Contrary to the wishes of some American interest groups, President Woodrow Wilson wanted to avoid a full-fledged occupation of Mexico, but he was nevertheless committed to influencing the revolution's outcome. Mexican governments and Mexican revolutionaries depended on border traffic and ocean trade. They needed exports to buy guns and provisions. Mindful of this fact, Wilson developed a controversial Mexican policy that relied on the regulation of border traffic and of Mexican maritime trade. This involved both the use of law enforcement as a policy instrument (including enforcement of the neutrality laws) and limited military incursions or threats. The most important of these were the invasion of Veracruz in April 1914 and General John J. Pershing's punitive expedition to hunt down Pancho Villa after his raid on Columbus, New Mexico, in March 1916.

Despite the role of the previous U.S. administration in orchestrating the military coup that brought General Victoriano Huerta to power, Woodrow Wilson refused to recognize Huerta. Huerta had deposed and murdered a democratically elected president. Moreover, there was a wide-ranging popular revolt against Huerta. On the other hand, because the United States did not recognize him, Huerta had tried to import guns from Germany, and that opened a possible scenario that the United States could not countenance: the survival of a Huerta government upheld by Germany, a power that was on the brink of a European war that was bound to involve the United States. In order to preempt that possibility, Wilson ordered the blockade of German weapons from Mexican seaports and the invasion of Veracruz.[39]

The U.S. government's ultimate intentions in invading Veracruz were polemical and far from clear to observers of any political stripe. There were strong U.S. interests in favor of extending the U.S. occupation to the whole of the republic, on the model of Cuba after the war with Spain. Journalist James Creelman, who had been an apologist for Porfirio Díaz, called for just such action. Writing for the *Washington Post*, Creelman described the conflict between Huerta and Villa as hopeless; it was like a frontal contest between Tammany Hall (Huerta) and Jesse James (Villa). Mexico, in the meantime, had been ravaged by revolution and was "a dead nation," all because "President Wilson and Mr. Bryan are bewitched by the theory that there should be, and can be, and must be democratic, constitutional government in a country whose political majority consists of ignorant, irresponsible, blanketed Indians who know nothing of the constitution and care less."[40]

The solution was occupation on the Cuban model:

> On my way to Mexico City I paid a visit to President Menocal in the palace at Havana.
>
> It would be hard to imagine a more clean-cut, alert, and direct man than the Cornell University graduate and successful business administrator who now heads the once tumultuous and revolutionary Cuban republic.
>
> "Mr. President," I said, "do you find the restrictions placed on your government by the United States to be onerous restraints to your national life?"
>
> "On the contrary," he replied, "I think they are a very good thing for Cuba and the Cubans."[41]

A position such as this—racist and flagrantly imperialist—would have been simply unthinkable for anyone even remotely connected to the Left back in 1910—but it had begun to sound convincing to some by 1914. As war in Europe approached, the tension between nationalism and internationalism flared within the Socialist camp, and this again affected support for the "Mexican Cause." The contrast between John Kenneth Turner and Jack London, both Socialists, both erstwhile supporters of the Liberals, is an example of these tensions.

Turner denounced the Veracruz invasion as an imperialist act, decided on unilaterally by Wilson with no consultation with any

Mexican leader and done with the purpose of toppling Victoriano Huerta's government and instating Pancho Villa in his stead. The iniquity of the intervention was most keenly brought home when it was contrasted with the inflated concerns over the protection and defense of national sovereignty that had been used later to justify American involvement in World War I:

> The Belgians, at least, had formal warning of the German invasion. But the population of Vera Cruz, Mexico, had no warning whatever. The government of the United States had not declared war on Mexico, nor upon the city of Vera Cruz. In Europe a desperate struggle of nations was going on. But on April 21, 1914, the United States was in no danger of attack. The life of no American was at stake. Nevertheless, we made an aggressive war upon a practically defenseless city, and entirely without warning to the population thereof.[42]

Turner, in short, stayed consistent in his position against U.S. intervention.

Jack London, on the other hand, followed a very different course. By 1914, London had taken an inward turn. Against John Kenneth Turner's accusation that London had been bought by the oil companies, London's daughter Joan wrote that London had been corrupted by the requirements of his lifestyle.[43] But there was more to it than this. As Europe edged toward war, London's nationalism had flared up, and he turned away from his earlier position against the draft. Nationalist sentiment had, in fact, always been an aspect of London's populism, and his "man of the people" folksiness could easily turn to white supremacy. Thus, around the time of the start of the Mexican Revolution, London had already declared the he was "first of all a white man and only secondly a socialist,"[44] a position that was shared by a number of American soldiers fighting in Baja California, in fact.[45]

The combination of growing self-centeredness and a racist nationalism led London to accept a lucrative commission from an old orchestrator of American foreign intervention par excellence: William Randolph Hearst. London was to accompany the American troops on their landing in Veracruz and write laudatory pieces for *Collier's Weekly*. His expenses at Veracruz's Hotel Diligencias were amply covered, including plenty of drink, apparently. In addition London was to receive what was then the extravagant amount of

$1,100 per week, in addition to his expenses and those of his wife, Charmian.[46]

What is most interesting about London's Veracruz sellout, though, is the way in which he turned John Kenneth Turner's arguments about Mexican slavery into a justification for U.S. intervention. American soldiers, he wrote, were practically on a charity mission. "These natives of Mexico have never possessed more than a skeleton of law.... Come now, in the year 1914, from the United States, the white-skinned armed men with an inherited genius for government."[47] U.S. soldiers brought "decency and order" to the city for the first time, he declared, and, incredibly for the Mexicans, they did not do this for graft.

The Mexican peon, London said, "has always been a slave." They had been bred for baseness in exactly the opposite way that London bred horses: "Whenever a peon of dream and passion and vision and spirit was born he was eliminated. His masters wanted lowly, docile, stupid slaves, and resented such a variation.... For the present generation of him there is little hope. But for the future generations a social selection will put a premium of living on dream and passion and vision and spirit will develop an entirely different type of peon."[48]

Selling out the Mexicans was easy for Jack London. The very same arguments about slavery that Turner had developed to decry Díaz could be mobilized from a eugenicist angle to argue that the Mexican nation was not ready to govern itself and that it could hope for nothing better than American tutelage. Nationalism, in London's case, turned an earlier stance of international solidarity into frank support for imperialism and political subjugation.

CHAPTER TWENTY-FOUR

Crumbs

I Shall Be Released

The political marginality of the Liberals after Madero's rise to power is obvious to any archival historian. Whereas Ricardo Flores Magón, Librado Rivera, Antonio Villarreal, and Manuel Sarabia had been subjected to intense spying by the Mexican government between the launch of the 1906 revolution and 1910, we find no corresponding concern after the junta's imprisonment in 1912. We have a good many of Ricardo's letters from the Los Angeles County Jail—including his precious correspondence with María Brousse—whereas we have none of that for the time spent in the McNeil Island Federal Penitentiary, except the prison's own tally of letters sent and received. The McNeil files also do not contain any of the junta's correspondence. Given the fact that prison censors read everything, this suggests that the junta's letters may not have been deemed to merit the warden's attention.

We learn relatively little from the men's scant prison records at McNeil. Ricardo seems not to have been writing or receiving that much mail: he got only seventeen letters in his year and a half in prison, and, oddly, only two of these from María. A good deal of the internal business of *Regeneración* seems to have gone through Librado Rivera, who kept up correspondence with editors Teodoro Gaitán, Blas Lara, and William C. Owen. Unfortunately, the prison records do not include a list of letters sent and received by Enrique Flores Magón or by Anselmo Figueroa, and it seems likely that much correspondence with the journal moved through them, as well.[1] Other than this, all we know is that the prison physician found all of them to be in good health when they arrived.

Ricardo, Enrique, Anselmo, and Librado were released a bit early from McNeil on good conduct, on January 14, 1914. A rally of supporters was organized to meet them, Wobblies, mainly, along with Owen, Blas Lara, and Araujo, who had come up from California. Enrique addressed the crowd, because Ricardo's English was not good enough for public speaking.

As the eternal optimist—a fighter, as he rightly called himself—Enrique later wrote about this moment as a vigorous return. But a lot had happened while the men were in the jail. Madero's presidency had collapsed, as the junta had hoped and predicted, but it had made a martyr of Madero, a symbol of law and justice not unlike Benito Juárez, whose name became a unifying banner for a wide spectrum of revolutionary activity.

Victoriano Huerta had come to power, and the Liberals' old enemies—Pancho Villa and former *reyista* governor Venustiano Carranza—now led the main revolutionary contingents. Only Emiliano Zapata subsisted as a representative of "Tierra y Libertad," but he was penned in his Morelos stronghold, in the South.

Meanwhile, on the home front, the junta faced a set of dire challenges, beginning with their own poverty. The men needed jobs—*yugos*. *Regeneración*'s distribution was way down, and they would need to struggle to keep the journal going. Moreover, there were important losses in their ranks. Anselmo Figueroa was too sick to continue the fight. He went back to his native Palomas, Arizona, and died in June 1915. Owen, for his part, had moved to the Bakunin commune in Hayward, California. He continued to edit the English-language page for *Regeneración*, but from a distance and as an extra to printing his own English-language paper, *Land and Liberty*, which tried to do for the world what *Regeneración* did for Mexico. War was coming in Europe, and that naturally drew Owen's attention. Thus the English-language page, though decent, was thinner and not as rich as it once had been. The same factor affected many of the Wobbly, Socialist, and anarchist supporters of the Mexican Revolution: with war at their own doorstep, they had another and for them more urgent cause.

Finally, the overall political environment in Los Angeles had changed. In October 1910, a bomb had destroyed the building of the *Los Angeles Times* and killed twenty-one employees, and in April 1911, while the Baja campaign was still raging, two union men, the McNamara brothers, were arrested and charged with the bombing. Their trial was very contentious, since people on the left believed that the

McNamara brothers (and, through them, labor) were being blamed unfairly by the reactionary and famously anti-union owner of the *Times*, Harrison Gray Otis. As it turned out, though, the McNamaras had confessed their guilt, though their confession was kept secret by the prosecution so that the trial was played out and timed in such a way that it badly burned their supporters: the union movement, and especially the Socialist Party and the Wobblies.

It very specifically affected Job Harriman, who had been running for mayor and had had a good chance of winning the election. The McNamara trial ended Harriman's political career, since he had been among those who had publicly doubted Otis's charge against the union. Harriman now turned to a back-to-the-land movement and formed the Del Llano agrarian cooperative.[2] The remaining Socialists of the old Los Angeles group—Turner, John Murray, Ethel, Lázaro Gutiérrez de Lara, and Elizabeth Trowbridge—were for the most part no longer in Los Angeles, and some of them had allied themselves to the Carranza faction of the revolution, in any case, because it had successfully built a bridge to Mexico's unions, which had formed military regiments known as the Red Brigades (Figure 24.1).

In short, Los Angeles opinion was now dominated by Harrison Gray Otis's *Los Angeles Times*, which was militantly antagonistic to anarchism and to the Magóns in particular, because of their role in Baja California. The junta had lost its Socialist allies, who were themselves also weakened. Its situation in 1914 and 1915 was, instead, one of poverty, and they saw few alternatives for successful direct action inside Mexico.

Racism

With regard to action in Mexico, the main problem for the Liberals was how to cope with the draconian application of the U.S. neutrality laws against them. Indeed, this affected both the Liberals' strategy for the Mexican Revolution and their politics within the United States. The case of Rangel and the "Texas Martyrs" set the terms for what followed: the endgame of the Liberals in the United States.

Rangel and his men had been caught by Texas Rangers, rather than by federal officers. They had been detained with no search warrant when the men were on their way to Mexico. Yet there was not the slimmest chance of even-handed justice in Texas. The

Figure 24.1 Red Brigade mother and son from Casa del Obrero Mundial, in a photo inscribed to John Murray. Courtesy of the Bancroft Library, John Murray Papers.

right of the Texas Rangers to detain the Mexican party was never questioned, nor was the matter of who shot who first a mitigating factor—as we've seen, the first three Mexicans tried were handed prison sentences of nine, twenty-five, and ninety-nine years, despite the fact that they weren't the ones who had shot the deputy sheriff. And Anglo Texans were calling loudly for Rangel's men to be lynched—calls that Mexicans had learned to take very seriously, particularly since the 1910 lynching of Antonio Rodríguez, who had been pulled out of prison and burned alive, causing riots throughout Mexico and on the U.S.-Mexico border.[3] At the very least, the Texans wanted Rangel and Cline, the leaders of the party, to hang, but they were generally eager to lynch the whole lot.

On the part of Texas Mexicans and *Regeneración*, there were open calls for Mexicans in Texas to revolt if the men were lynched or executed. In *Regeneración*, Antonio de Pío Araujo had said that it was the duty of all Liberals to raise a revolution in Texas if Rangel was killed. Attentive to these tensions, the Texas authorities delayed the Rangel trials and strung them out to allow things cool down a bit. Also, no death penalties were handed out: Texan Anglos and their supporters would have to placate their blood lust with ninety-nine-year prison terms for Rangel, Cline, other members of the expedition.

When Ricardo, Librado, and Enrique returned to Los Angeles in February 1914, the campaign in support of the legal cause of the Texas Martyrs was their most immediate concern. In his writing and public speaking on the issue, Ricardo concurred with Araujo's position—if the men were hanged, the Liberals should revolt—but he was by then less virulent, graphic, extensive, and specific in his comments on revolution in Texas than Araujo had been.

Thus, when Texas was clamoring to lynch Rangel's men, Araujo had written: "The clock of revolution is about to sound in Texas. Let's not avert our eyes to it; let's not refuse to take advantage of it.... Oh comrades! If we don't save those men, we don't deserve to be called revolutionaries. Rangel and the other men must not be allowed to go to the gallows. If they go there, they will go with each and every one of us."[4] Araujo had called for decisive action in support of the prisoners and held up images of Texas aflame in revolution if the men were condemned.

Ricardo, for his part, wrote a deep, stern, and moving denunciation of the case, explaining how it related to the racism that every Mexican in the United States had ever suffered. He called on Liberals to agitate and to struggle, but left insurrection as a final option, rather than as an immediate alternative, as it had been for Araujo: "and if neither strikes nor agitation produce the desired effect of setting the fourteen prisoners free, then let us rebel, let's rise up in arms and respond to injustice with barricade and dynamite. We should count ourselves: there are millions of us!"[5]

The U.S. justice apparatus was calming the waters with a calibrated combination of repression and delay of the judicial process. Those dilatory tactics defanged the Liberals a bit, because what they now had to do was raise money for the Rangel defense, and this confronted them, yet again, with the poverty of their movement and with the weakened situation in which the junta had found *Regeneración*: overburdened with debts and with circulation running too low to pay up. Now several new developments drove the implications of the Rangel affair more deeply home.

The first of these was the Veracruz invasion of May 1914, which occurred when Rangel and the others were still awaiting trial. *Regeneración*'s analysis of Woodrow Wilson's policy was among

Ricardo's clearest and best. Wilson, he said, invaded as a probe—he wanted to see whether the Mexican people would prefer the Americans to Huerta and whether they would perceive the Americans as siding with the revolution or as imperialist invaders. In order to achieve his aims, Wilson pretended to be greatly concerned with social justice in Mexico and to side with the revolution. This, however, should be recognized by Mexicans as the siren song of U.S. imperialism, for, Ricardo convincingly wrote, "if Wilson were sincere in his revolutionary declamations, he would start by hanging the Rockefellers, the Otises, the Guggenheims, the Hearsts—all of the pirates of industry, all the greedy hoarders of the land, all of the bandits of commerce and finance—and leave us Mexicans to do the work of hanging our own executioners."[6]

But Wilson's invasion had been met with a stronger and more generalized anti-U.S. grassroots response than he had anticipated, and it failed to isolate Victoriano Huerta, as Wilson had hoped. Both Huerta and Carranza sent troops to Veracruz to fight the Americans, and as a result, Wilson was forced to turn to international mediation to seek an advantageous and honorable way of out Veracruz before his marines were thrown out or attacks on U.S. property in Mexico became generalized.

One of the challenges for the junta, though, was how to deal with the implications that the Texas Martyrs affair and the U.S. invasion of Veracruz had for nationalism and race relations. As an internationalist proletarian movement, anarchism was deeply opposed to nationalism and to racism, but the Texas affair and the U.S. invasion of Veracruz heightened the racial divide between Mexicans and Anglos and fomented a nationalist rejection of all *gringos*.

Racial discrimination against Mexicans in the United States was brutal, especially in Texas and the South. Thus, rallying support for the legal defense of the Texas Martyrs, Ricardo had asked:

> Who among you has not received an insult in this country for the mere fact of being a Mexican? Who has not heard tell of the crimes that are committed daily against people of our race? Don't you know that in the South Mexicans aren't allowed to sit in the same table as Americans in restaurants? Have you not walked into a barber shop and, after being looked up and down, been told that Mexicans aren't served there? Don't you know that American jails are full of Mexicans? And have you even

counted the number of Mexicans who have been sent to the gallows or been burned by brutal mobs of white people?"[7]

Ricardo was by no means exaggerating. On the contrary, if anything, he and Enrique had a tempering influence on Mexican rage, always cautioning against a tempting, but disastrous fall into general nationalist prejudice. Thus, in the days of reaction and indignation caused by the Veracruz invasion, Enrique wrote a piece titled "Death to the Gringos? No! Death to the Rich!" in which he cautioned against making war on Americans as such, reminding his readers of Wobbly and Socialist solidarity, of how Mexico's revolution had brave American allies who had consistently stood by them against exploitation, against slavery, against U.S. imperialism, and against the American government in the prosecution of Mexican revolutionaries.[8] Americans were not the enemy. The enemy was "Capital" and "Authority." But there were powerful forces conspiring to make this a race war.

The first and major problem was Texas, in which at that time the largest population of Mexicans in the country was still concentrated and which had the longest and most populated border with Mexico. The feelings of Texas Mexicans against Texan "justice," police, Jim Crow laws, lynchings, exploitation, and Texan and U.S. meddling in the revolution were already running very high. Moreover, Mexicans were no longer the meek peons that they had once been—Mexico was in revolution, and advanced ideas of class struggle were common currency among them. Mexican nationalism had long been consolidated in that region, as well. With the imprisonment of Rangel and his men and wild calls for their lynching, it was clear that the United States would do its best to prevent Texas radicals from weighing in on the outcome of the Mexican Revolution. And Tejanos were perfectly capable of interpreting the significance of this.

The Veracruz invasion of May 1914 heightened animosity considerably, raising it to a new pitch. The expeditionary force against Mexico was launched out of Galveston, with a lot of Texans among the troops, and the U.S. warships were seen off with joy, enthusiasm, and braggadocio that brimmed with racist sentiments and hopes for the humiliation of Mexicans (Figure 24.2).

So, for instance, Jack London reported with delight how the Houston San Jacinto Parade had been unexpectedly empty because

Figure 24.2 The USS *Idaho*, deployed in the invasion of Veracruz, 1914. Courtesy of the Bancroft Library, John Murray Papers.

everyone had rushed to Galveston to go off to war or to see the marines off. The racial composition of the U.S. troops—the invasion of Mexico as an Anglo invasion was very much emphasized: "distinctively American faces, the great majority that laughed to us from the troop train. The percentage of blonds was high, and numbers of them were astonishingly blond. The brunets sparkled amid the blond types—ranged all the way from fairest yellow hair and palest blue eyes down through the richer tones to dark gray eyes and deep brown hair."[9] And among these, he especially idolized the Texan element. Texan soldiers had been ready for this war for more than two years, London reported, and they viewed it as a kind of manly adventure: "They feel they face no giant enemy in the south. They tell over again the tale of the Alamo, and recite with glee how Sam Houston lambasted Santa Anna at San Jacinto." Indeed, all the United States needed to do, was to "turn Texas loose" on Mexico, and Texas alone would "lick them to a frazzled finish".

Except that Mexicans were now not so very ready to be humiliated—either in Veracruz or in Texas—or in Los Angeles either, for that matter. They would let their compatriots in Mexico sink

American fantasies of a Mexican occupation and, for their part, they would defend their own within the United States, starting with Rangel and his men. Thus, Ricardo recited a litany of recent outrages against Mexicans:

> The blood of Antonio Rodríguez has not yet dried in Rock Springs; Juan Rincón's body is still warm; Silvestre Lomas's grave is still fresh; Texas' crossroads are white with the bones of Mexicans; mosses decorate Mexican skeletons in the woods of Louisiana. Do you know how many times a Mexican has received a bullet in the chest when he went to collect his salary from his American employer? Have you not heard that in Texas and some other states in this country, a Mexican cannot travel in the same carriage as a man of white skin? Mexicans are not admitted in restaurants, hotels, barbershops, or on the fashionable beaches. In Texas, Mexican children are excluded from school. In some theaters, there are specially designated sections for Mexicans.[10]

If Rangel's men were put to the rope, the Liberals would take the rope to the necks of the American bourgeoisie.

Anglo racists of the Southwest began to fear the Mexican presence in their midst. Many of those Mexican men and women had union experience and were politicized. By 1914, Mexico's revolution had turned squarely from its initial political concerns to economic demands—land reform and labor rights. And Mexicans had learned to buy and use weapons—profitably being sold both to revolutionaries and to the Federal Army by the tens of thousands in all U.S. border towns. So dark fears, even panic, began to spread as rumors proliferated here and there.[11] Rumors of race war. And these fears were used, yet again, to corral and repress the Liberal movement.

This time, it was in Arizona. On August 1914, the Arizona press disseminated rumors of a Mexican conspiracy to take the towns of Phoenix and Tempe and then to use them as a base from which to launch a campaign into Mexico. Sixteen men were arrested, and one of them was Teodoro Gaitán, who had figured as editor of *Regeneración* together with Blas Lara while the junta was doing time at McNeil. Gaitán had gone to Arizona a few weeks prior in search of work, due to the impoverished situation of *Regeneración* in Los Angeles, and although he was later released because he was in fact unconnected to the conspiracy, the clampdown on the Arizona Liberals was very strong, as it had been in Texas.[12]

435

After a couple of weeks, when matters began to be clearer, Ricardo interpreted what had happened for his readers: a man named Julio Mancillas, who was an agent of the Mexican consulate, had duped a group of innocent, patriotic, and inexperienced Mexicans into a conspiracy and had then turned them over to the Arizona authorities, allowing the latter to arrest other "suspects"—experienced Liberal activists—who had long been a thorn in their side.[13] The arrest of Gaitán was used to suggest a connection between the trumped-up conspiracy in Phoenix and the Los Angeles junta, and Ricardo was awaiting arrest momentarily.

As it happened, the junta was not arrested. Rather, it was put under still more of the pressures that its leaders had been facing since their release from McNeil Island Penitentiary: fund-raising for yet another campaign to support the legal defense of yet another group of prisoners, in addition to sustaining the flagging campaign in support of the Texas Martyrs, all the while trying desperately to keep *Regeneración* alive.

Crumbs

Misery was the junta's most fateful companion. It was its most faithful ally, as well as its most pernicious and persistent enemy.

The junta's poverty was its only truly convincing way of proving that it had never sold out. Since the days before the revolution, one stock argument against Ricardo and the junta was that they lived off of contributions. They were represented as demagogues who duped the proletariat into parting with their hard-earned pennies. Initially, such accusations were mainly circulated by agents of the Mexican government, but once the movement began to split and splinter, they would come from other quarters, as well. Antonio Villarreal had accused Ricardo of taking $40,000 from the *científicos* and had claimed that he had misspent the substantial loan that Francisco Madero had provided to *Regeneración*. After the Baja California defeat, disgruntled soldiers had complained that the junta never sent them money for guns and that the collections that had been made in their name had been misspent.[14] During and after their imprisonment in McNeil, accusations of embezzlement continued to pester the junta. Indeed, each split inside the group came with increasingly petty accusations as the profile of the group itself declined.

Shortly after their imprisonment in McNeil, a split occurred between Rafael Romero Palacios and his wife, Francisca Mendoza, on the one hand, and Blas Lara, Teodoro Gaitán, and Antonio de P. Araujo, on the other. The junta sided with the latter, and after leaving *Regeneración*, Romero and Mendoza repeatedly accused the Junta of dipping into the journal's coffers. Soon after that, with the junta still in prison, there was a second, even greater conflict over control over *Regeneración*, this time between Gaitán and Lara on the one hand, and Juan Moncaleano and Enrique Flores Magón's father-in-law, Rómulo Carmona, a bookseller who distributed Liberal materials, on the other. The conflict had, once again, quite a lot of financial implications.

Moncaleano was a highly respected anarchist union leader and educator who had been expelled from Colombia, Cuba, and Mexico before being taken in by the Liberals in Los Angeles. He had arrived to Los Angeles with great prestige and stood as a kind of successor to the great Spanish anarchist educator and martyr Francisco Ferrer Guardia, who had been murdered a few years before. The junta was in jail when Moncaleano arrived, but their closest associates received him with great admiration. Thus, María Brousse wrote to her niece in those days, saying: "The most admirable thing that we have in Los Angeles are the Moncaleanos! They are a model family whose four children have been educated according to anarchist ideals."[5]

And María was not alone in her reverence for the man. The *Regeneración* group as a whole was initially drawn into his orbit and entered willingly into a joint project to purchase a building that would serve at once as a school for Moncaleano's Educación Moderna movement, as a center for his organization—the Casa del Obrero Internacional—as lodging for Mexican workers who needed a place to stay, as a meeting place and auditorium for political purposes, and as offices for *Regeneración*. William Owen enthusiastically described the building, calling for support for the project from the *Regeneración* community:

> Various friends who have inspected the premises, and are regarded as excellent judges, consider that Comrades Carmona and Moncaleano have made a first-rate bargain. The property has a frontage of about 200 feet on each of the streets previously named. The building is a handsome, three-story brick, in two wings. There are, at least, four reception rooms, each of which will accommodate easily from 250 to 300

persons.... There is bedroom and kitchen accommodation for scores of people.... In short, the Latin race has an immense representation in Los Angeles even now, and this will become vastly greater with the opening of the Panama Canal. At present it is largely helpless, and often in great difficulties, because almost entirely unorganized. That misfortune we have now an opportunity to remedy; or, to put it better, we can give those who are suffering from lack of organization an opportunity for remedying the evil for themselves.[16]

The trouble was that Moncaleano and his ally Carmona now tried to take control of *Regeneración*, even while they failed to do any substantial work for the paper. Worse yet, they sent telegrams to the prisoners trying to turn them against Lara, Gaitán, and Araujo. They also mobilized Paula Carmona, Enrique's wife and the mother of his two children, Práxedis and Margarita, and she pressured him by saying that the economic survival of his own family was at stake.[17]

The junta stood with the comrades who were actually writing *Regeneración*, leading to Enrique's immediate divorce and his permanent separation from two children, who were named, significantly, after Práxedis Guerrero, and his own mother, Margarita. When the junta emerged from prison, Enrique's first article in *Regeneración* expressed his deeply bruised feelings and his resolve to remain on the path of anarchy, despite being

> slandered, cursed, insulted, and stabbed in the back by people who I thought were friends and comrades, and who, on the contrary, took advantage of my absence and of the fact that I could not defend myself to rip my heart apart by destroying my household and making orphans of my children, simply to avenge the fact that I did not lend myself to being an instrument of their base passions and bastardly ambitions.[18]

Thus, *Regeneración* and the Casa del Obrero Internacional broke off from one another, and the journal had to seek out new offices in the midst of renewed accusations of embezzlement and mismanagement, this time coming from Moncaleano and from his allies in Texas, Cuba, and beyond.

All of these fractures took their toll on *Regeneración*, which was not doing so very well even before the junta had been sent to jail. Now it was in a desperate position, appearing irregularly, with diminished runs, saddled with debts that the junta members simply could not pay and with an urgent campaign on its hands to raise funds for Rangel in Texas.

In one sense, poverty was the junta's ally in its drives for *Regeneración*'s survival, for who could truly look the junta in the face and say that they were in it for the money? However, *Regeneración* faltered for lack of money through 1914 and 1915—moving from weekly to bimonthly issues and then having to endure periods when the journal did not appear at all. All the while, the journal called desperately for contributions, explaining the significance of its survival for the cause of the proletariat and the revolution.

On October 2, 1915, *Regeneración* printed an issue after a seven-month pause. In it, Ricardo announced that back in June, their friend and former editor Anselmo Figueroa had died. While *Regeneración*'s enemies proffered their accusations of embezzlement, "Anselmo left [prison] tired, sick, wiped out, and, given our misery, he could not get the medical treatment or the nutritious food that this organism required, so he fell at last to his illness in Palomas, Arizona, where he had gone in search of better weather for his health."[19]

Regeneración

Between the arrival of the junta leaders back to work from prison, on January 29, 1914, and the November 14 issue of that same year, *Regeneración* had initiated an almost continuous series of fund drives to try to keep the paper from folding definitively. In March, Ricardo had announced the journal's immanent death, and in June, the paper began appearing only every other week.[20] The type being used also had exuded the journal's poverty, with vowels from different font types used on each page. And for this, the men had sacrificed deeply. In order to save *Regeneración*, Ricardo finally decided to make a full enunciation of those sacrifices:

> For its sake, we suffered undescribable torments in the dungeons of the Nero Porfirio Díaz; we lost material goods and broke family bonds and friendships in order to publish it. Firm in the struggle, we lived for long periods in those dark pits, full of rot, illness, and misery that are known as cells in Belem Prison. And when our Constitutional rights were struck down with a stroke of a pen and we had to emigrate to the United States, the dagger of a Porfirian assassin still looked for our heart in San Antonio, Texas. And the black gates of prison opened up again for us in San Antonio and Saint Louis, Missouri; and the assassins

tracked us all the way to Canada and followed our paths back into U.S. territory, forcing us to go from one place to another with no rest, repose, truce, or mercy; setting ambushes here, there, and everywhere. Putting us in jail in Los Angeles, in Tucson, in Tombstone, in Yuma, in Florence, and again in Los Angeles, till we ended up with our final conviction on McNeil Island.[21]

Nevertheless by July, *Regeneración* was again announcing that it was at death's door and began publishing names of the contributors and pinning hopes on the drives being made for the journal by local liberal groups. Not surprisingly, given racial tensions, indignation over the treatment of Rangel, and the Veracruz invasion, most of the donors were from Texas.[22] Historian James Sandos studied a *Regeneración* subscription list from 1915, dated during these crisis months. He found that by then, paper had only 1,881 subscribers and sold barely 3,076 papers all told. Of those subscriptions, a full 40 percent were in Texas, compared with 17 percent in California, 6 percent in Arizona, and a mere 3 percent in Mexico.[23] Until 1912, *Regeneración* had served as a kind of prosthesis or zombie for Ricardo and Enrique—a dead, but animate body that could operate inside Mexico and that its editors could activate and move from Los Angeles. The closing off of the border—demonstrated in the repression of the Rangel party—undermined any remaining effectiveness of *Regeneración* inside Mexico, for it had lost the networks that were required to have a readership there, while the activities of the journal's U.S.-based networks were now impaired.

On August 22, the Phoenix affair broke out, and *Regeneración* was forced to add a funding drive for the legal expenses of the Arizona prisoners, in addition to its drive for the Texas Martyrs and for the journal's own survival. Finances were again breaking down, and in September, *Regeneración* again starting appearing irregularly, every other week. Tellingly, too, the donations that the journal was able to garner for the Arizona prisoners were simply pathetic: a paltry $5.30. Such a meager result was meaningful because one of the men who was imprisoned there was Teodoro Gaitán, who had been editor of *Regeneración* just eight months prior. In short, the freedom of a well-known figure was at stake.

In desperation, Ricardo clamored: "Five dollars with which to purchase the courtesan! Five dollars for the prostitute known as bourgeois justice! But the villain wants more money. She does not sell herself for five dollars. One has to stuff her muzzle with gold."[24]

The trouble was that the very depth of their sacrifices, the poverty in which they had lived, their debts, their impotence in the face of declining health, their familial sacrifices—separation from Ricardo's mother at the time of her death, the loss of Jesús's friendship, Enrique's loss of his two children—all of that made Ricardo and Enrique stern judges of others and absolute puritans with regard to self-denial. Indeed, if poverty spoke for the honesty, sacrifice, determination, and sense of purpose of the men of the junta, it also spun those men and women into a downward spiral of attachment to asceticism, recriminations against the impure, and progressive collective impotence.

Thus, in a moment of desperation, Ricardo wrote that they as editors were poorer than the poorest of their disinherited brothers and that the workers who failed to support the journal deserved their fate: "Whoever does not sacrifice a few pennies or a few dollars to earn his liberty and well-being deserves to be a slave."[25] *Regeneración*, Ricardo reminded his readers, had been indispensable for the Mexican Revolution. Its accomplishments, which its detractors were so eager to belittle, were in fact immense. *Regeneración* had been the first journal openly to oppose Díaz; it had single-handedly created a revolutionary spirit—now dominant in Mexico—that had until then been dormant; without *Regeneración*, Ricardo said, Madero would have been unable to raise a revolution, and without it, the economic revolution would have been unspoken for.[26] After the paltry showing in support of Gaitán and the other Arizona prisoners, *Regeneración* shut down for six weeks. It closed its Los Angeles offices and moved to reinvent itself for one last time.

Edendale

The *Regeneración* family found a farm in what was then the outlying Los Angeles suburb of Edendale, at 2325 Ivanhoe Avenue. It printed a couple of issues in November and December 1914 and then stopped for three months, printed an issue again in March 1915, but had to wait seven months, until October 1915, to reinitiate in earnest. With a titanic effort, the junta managed to put a down payment on a very rudimentary printing press and to organize collective work and earnings that were precarious, but operational. Blas Lara provides the most vivid description of the arrangement:

> That's why, on October 29, 1915, *Regeneración*'s number 206 came out of Ivanhoe Avenue, near a lake and a rubbish heap in the City of the Angels, on a 5½ acre ranch (give or take 2 acres). The printing press was set up in the stables. There were 40 fruit trees: peaches, apricots and plums. We also planted greens. And all for only $25 per month's rent. Because it was on the city's outskirts, there was no electricity. The printing press cost $490—$100 up front—paid to a two-bit politician who had been devoted to Victoriano Huerta. The whole group—with families—as well as the bachelors lived there. The *LA Times* called it a "free love colony." The place had an artesian well and a pump that drew water, powered by a windmill.[27]

So: no electricity and no running water. An orchard and a vegetable garden. A "return" to the Eden of primitive communism, built with a punk rock–like "back to the basics" gesture after being superseded by contemporary events. A comrade named Santoyo donated his chickens, and one of the commune's members, Primo Ochoa, did double duty as both the commune's doctor and the guardian of the birds. The printing press was a rickety, hand-operated affair that Blas wittily referred to as "The Son of Guttenberg's First Tweak." They had only enough type to print two-page editions of the paper.

The colony was a full-blown realization of the sort of new family structure that had been at the base of the Liberal Party. Regular inhabitants of 2325 Ivanhoe Avenue included Ricardo, María, Lucía Norman, and her son Carlos; Enrique with his new wife, Teresa Arteaga, who was María's niece, and her five children—Esperanza, Santiago, Estela, Pedro and José—plus Enrique junior, the son that she had with Enrique; Librado Rivera, who was now a widower, and his two kids; the late Anselmo Figueroa's son-in-law, José, with his daughter, Babe; the chicken keeper and medical doctor, Primo Ochoa; a pair of comrades called Atanacio and Tachita; and the (then) bachelors Blas Lara, Rafael García, "Villota," and "Floritos," along with two or three others.[28]

But the joyous and bucolic element that was certainly an aspect of everyday life at the Edendale commune was also blighted by poverty and persecution. Campaigns for saving *Regeneración* started in tandem with its new era of publication. Because of the rudimentary nature of their printing press, the men needed to work late nights, and sometimes all night, to generate their modest product. Between the work of writing, printing, and administering, Enrique, Librado, and Ricardo, at least, could not spare time to get paid work, so others in the commune had to compensate for that, even while they, too, contributed to Regeneración's work. The debt outstanding on the printing press remained mostly unpaid, and as of February 1916, the paper began to publish inserts letting readers know that $190 was still owed on it and that Regeneración's printing press might be repossessed at any moment. As Blas Lara put it, as time progressed, "poverty took root among them like a toothache."[29] In those days, too, they had the policy of privileging the expenses of print even over groceries and medicine, because Regeneración would lose its second-class postage privileges if it appeared irregularly.[30]

Indeed, since the release of the men from McNeil Island, a truly organic connection between the journal's life and that of its editors became increasingly evident. In December 1915, Ricardo had a severe health crisis, which was followed, soon thereafter, by news of Enrique's own faltering health. In order to meet their needs, collections were again raised through Regeneración. The very lives of Enrique and of Ricardo were as much reliant on community support for Regeneración as, say, the legal defense of the Texas Martyrs.

One of the many articles explaining the journal's desperate straits, published by Enrique, was titled "$26.41." In it, Enrique explained that the group was everywhere hounded by creditors, that their families lacked even dry bread on some days, that he and Ricardo could not afford the medicines that had, in fact, been helping them earlier, nor could they get any rest from their work without killing the journal. They slept very little and had to plead for credit to buy paper; they were ruining their eyes working at night with insufficient oil for lighting; and they even had half of last week's run of Regeneración piled up, because they could not afford postage to send it out. It was the twenty-first of the month, and they had still not paid that month's back rent, or even the seventy-five cents owed for water. And in the midst of all of that, Regeneración had taken in a paltry $26.41 the prior week. "How can we go on?" Enrique asked. "How?"[31]

CHAPTER TWENTY-FIVE

A Stake in the Heart

Final Conviction

On February 16, 1916, Ricardo and Enrique were arrested. Bail was set high, at $5,000 each, so neither man could leave prison, though both were very ill. Ricardo, in particular, was truly very sick at that time. Enrique and Ricardo were tried and convicted in June 1916, but their lawyers appealed and, thanks to a funding drive organized by Emma Goldman, they were released on bail and were back at their posts at *Regeneración* in Edendale in July 1916. They continued their publication as best they could, for about a year-and-a-half. However, on February 4, 1918, the U.S. Circuit Court of Appeals confirmed Enrique and Ricardo's guilt and meted out sentences of three years for Enrique Flores Magón. In Ricardo's case, the sentence was soon compounded with a new charge of violation of the Espionage Act for a manifesto that he published along with Librado Rivera in the final issue of *Regeneración*, which was published on March 16, 1918. That brought Ricardo a sentence of twenty-one years, and fifteen years for Librado Rivera. Given Ricardo's poor state of health, this was a death sentence, and everybody knew it.

Since their arrival to the United States, the men of the junta had been convicted on various charges on various occasions, but the charges against them now were of a different tenor. The junta's earliest experiences in U.S. prisons—brief stints between 1904 and 1906—had been brought about by the Mexican government by way of third-party libel suits, provoked confrontations, or brawls. Enrique had been held for assault against a man who had tried to murder Juan Sarabia; Ricardo and Enrique were held for libel against a petty Oaxaca *jefe político* and against Cananea owner Colonel William Greene. In 1907, Ricardo, Librado, Antonio, and Manuel had been prosecuted for violation of the neutrality laws, and this same charge was leveled again in 1911, after the Baja California campaign.

This time, though, the charges against them were of a different nature. *Regeneración* was first investigated by the U.S. Postmaster General and denied second-class postage rates on the grounds that it contained obscene material, a strategy that was being used widely against anarchist and Socialist papers that were opposing U.S. entry into World War I and particularly the draft. As early as September 1914, the San Francisco journal *Fuerza Consciente* was retired from circulation for having printed a photo of czarist troops stripping the bodies of anarchists whom they had slain. The charge was that the photo was immoral.[1] By mid-1916, governmental repression against anarchist publications was at full throttle, and *Regeneración* denounced not only its loss of mailing privileges, but also that of sister publications such as *The Woman Rebel*, *The Alarm*, *The Blast*, *Voluntad*, *Revolt*, *Volné Listy*, and *Temple Talks*.[2] The move to imprison "Reds" such as the Magóns occurred in tandem with the attack on the circulation of anarchist periodicals, often with the charge of obscenity.

Ricardo and Enrique were charged with inciting homicide, printing obscenities, and violating the Espionage Act. The manifesto of March 16, 1918 that earned Ricardo what was in effect a life sentence and Librado Rivera a staggering fifteen-year term was a brief declaration trumpeting the coming of world revolution—a kind of parting shot before Ricardo went to prison to serve time for his other sentence. That manifesto argued for workers' strikes against the war: "The worker goes on strike with no regard for patriotic interests—he is conscious that the fatherland is not his property, but rather the property of the rich."[3]

In other words, the men were now being prosecuted for the content of their writings against American participation in World War I, rather than for leading an "invasion" into Mexico, and they were being persecuted by the U.S. government and only secondarily by Carranza, who, having emerged from the power struggle that followed the overthrow of Huerta, was now president of Mexico. Carranza was happy to use the Magóns as scapegoats in its dealings with the U.S. government, but may not have been too directly concerned by them otherwise. These developments were due to the changing contents and political strategy of *Regeneración* after

Enrique and Ricardo's release from McNeil Island in early 1914 and especially after the journal's survival of the changed political situation that resulted from the upheavals of 1914–1915 in Mexico, the marginalization of the PLM, *Regeneración*'s financial difficulties, and its subsequent move to Edendale.

Ricardo's theory of history always posited that the darkness of the storm was in direct proportion to the brightness that was destined to follow. Thus, after Huerta's fall in July 1914, the revolutionary factions had faced off against one another—Pancho Villa and his allies against Venustiano Carranza and his. This was a very unsettling and confusing state of affairs for Mexican exiles, but Ricardo encouraged his readers to take the long view:

> The break between the two bandits spells chaos—that is true—but it was out of chaos that the worlds and the suns were born. Animals and plants came to life out of chaos. It was from the chaos of History's revolutions that man has achieved the modicum of liberty that he currently enjoys. The current chaos, worsened by the struggle between Villa and Carranza, will give birth to a more effective liberty for the Mexican people, because it shall be built on economic freedom.[4]

Even so, current events must have been unsettling. The brief moment when accord between the factions was being explored, at the Convention of Aguascalientes, could not have brought Ricardo solace, since the president of the convention was none other than "the pederast" Antonio Villarreal. Moreover, the other traitor, Juan Sarabia, had moved to El Paso immediately after the failure of the convention and had started a pro-Carranza press campaign there.

Contrary to Ricardo's bellicose advice, which saw Carrancistas and Villistas as being destined to destroy one another, Sarabia wrote to Villarreal that in El Paso,

> general opinion tends against Villismo, because of its violence and its persecutions in Mexico, and if we proclaim a more moderate program—not in terms of principles, but rather with regard to procedures—if we provide more guarantees, if we show ourselves more humane and conciliatory, we will conquer an avalanche of supporters here that can be mobilized effectively for what is our most fundamental immediate concern: to remove Villa's domain of Chihuahua and close this border to him.[5]

Indeed, although Villarreal's mission at the Aguascalientes Convention had failed, the shape that alliances took thereafter were no great consolation to Ricardo: Zapata had made an alliance with Pancho Villa, an enemy of the Liberals since the time of Madero and someone they viewed as a bandit, butcher, and supporter of the bourgeoisie. Finally, and most disturbingly, the union movement in Mexico—the Casa del Obrero Mundial and other unions—had thrown their weight behind Carranza and his ally Álvaro Obregón, thus splitting off from the peasant movement—represented by Zapata—which was its natural class ally.

It was against this situation that Ricardo would write his second and final play. Titled *Verdugos y víctimas* (Henchmen and victims), it featured a chorus of maimed paupers—former workers who had enlisted in Carranza's Red Battalions, who had helped the bourgeoisie against Zapata, and who now found themselves abandoned, defenseless, and in penniless misery. *Verdugos y víctimas* dangled the specter of hopelessness and despair before the workers who had collaborated in their own demise by fighting against "Land and Freedom."

The bitterness that inspired that piece was fanned by two new worries: Woodrow Wilson's decision to institute a draft and enter World War I, a move that would once again mean that workers would be massacring one another for the benefit of "Capital" (though this time on a vast and universal scale) and a second, lesser, but for the Liberals important set of developments on the Texas-Mexico border. Those two deeply unsettling developments were counterbalanced in October 1917—that is, months before the men's final conviction, with the glow of hope that was the Russian Revolution. So despair competed with elation in a kind of frantic race for the finish line.

To the European War, the junta responded in a way that was consonant with that of the rest of the various American anarchist and socialist movements, resisting the draft and denouncing patriotism as a bourgeois ruse. This made the junta and *Regeneración* vulnerable to the same forms of persecution as the rest of the American Left—the so-called Red Scare—which involved the enforcement of a newly minted Espionage Act (1917) and a set of supplementary policies about collaboration with the enemy—including resistance of the draft—that paved the way for press censorship and the prosecution of militants. This was later buttressed by the Sedition Act of May

1918, which came down even harder on freedom of speech, including "any disloyal, profane, scurrilous, or abusive language about the form of government of the United States."[6]

Not surprisingly, then, the World War I years were a time when fences were mended between the anarchists and the Socialists. Once again, the lawyers defending Enrique and Ricardo were Socialists from Harriman's group—James H. Ryckman and Ernest E. Kirk. And when the *Los Angeles Daily Times* attacked John Kenneth Turner for his writings against U.S. intervention in Mexico, William C. Owen came out in his defense.[7] Even P. D. Noel came out of the woodwork to lead a free-speech campaign in defense of *Regeneración*.[8] Ricardo, too, closed ranks with the Socialists, especially around the time of the outbreak of the Russian Revolution, with regard to resistance against the draft.[9] And, indeed, Socialist leaders such as Eugene Debs would soon be prison companions of Librado, Ricardo, and Enrique.

In short, what got the men into jail this time was their militancy against the draft, against World War I, and for universal revolution. Like so many others, Enrique and Ricardo were convinced that the world was not witnessing either a "Mexican" or a "Russian" revolution but rather the eruption of forces that would usher in a new era for the whole of humanity, or, as Ricardo put it, "Mexico and Russia are the first craters announcing the awakening of millions from misery and hunger. Very soon all the peoples of the Earth will follow Mexico and Russia"[10] For this reason, they were subjected to the same persecutions as other socialist and anarchist agitators, who were censored, imprisoned, or deported as America prepared for war in Europe.

But there was a second factor that led the U.S. government to persecute these men, and that was the situation in Texas and, more broadly, the internal implications for the United States of changing international relations with Mexico. The Texas affair had a complex background: there had been rapid economic development of the lower Rio Grande Valley, with concomitant demographic growth, displacement of Mexicans, decline of interracial marriages in the region, and hardening of anti-Mexican sentiment in Texas. And ties between Mexican revolutionaries on both sides of the border were an added complication, as was the contest between Carranza and Villa for U.S. recognition.[11] Mexicans in southern Texas had been socialized in the Liberal tradition, and as historian James Sandos has shown, by 1915, they were the most loyal remaining readers of *Regeneración*.[12] In other words, they had access to an ideology and a fighting tradition that provided them with a strategic vision of how to resist the economic displacement, political marginalization, and social discrimination that economic development and in migration brought to the lower Rio Grande Valley.

Historian Benjamin Johnson has shown that alongside this penchant for resistance, increased racism against Mexicans also generated a desire to prove loyalty to the United States among Texas Mexicans, and American preparations for World War I provided a perfect occasion for that.[13] Thus, the exacerbation of racism against Mexicans in Texas produced a twin effect: resistance against Anglos and a fracture within the Mexican community. In the Rangel incursion, for instance, the deputy sheriff that the Mexicans had shot and killed, providing the aggravated circumstances that led to incredibly harsh sentences, had the not so Anglo-sounding last name of Ortiz. Similarly, one of the persecution cases denounced by *Regeneración* during its campaign against the draft was that of one Román Farrell Gallegos of Tucson, who was speaking up loudly against the draft. A Mexican-American man in uniform tried to intimidate him, first by arguing, then by pulling out a gun and shooting Farrell. Wounded, Farrell pulled out his knife and killed his attacker. For this, Farrell was sentenced to life in prison.[14]

As this Arizona example suggests, the alternative between resistance and submission was by no means confined to South Texas. So, for instance, the infamous abduction and deportation of over a thousand striking Mexican miners at Bisbee, Arizona, in 1917, also took on the jingoistic language of patriotism and loyalty on the part of the company, and Bisbee was practically run by a "Loyalty League" that had Wobblies and Mexicans under surveillance.[15] The problem of loyalty, which was always already complicated for Mexicans and Mexican-Americans in the United States, given the fact that the Southwest territories once belonged to Mexico, was complicated even more by the dynamics of revolution on the Mexican side, as well as by the connections between Mexican exiles in the United States and the Mexican Revolution.

The Rangel affair showed that the United States was selectively blocking movement by Mexicans into Mexico. But once Mexicans began resisting U.S. authorities on the American side, Mexican revolutionaries could also affect policies inside the United States. Specifically, Carranza's troops had taken control of Matamoros, and with it, a good portion of the Tamaulipas-Texas border. General Nafarrete, who was the commanding officer there, was sympathetic to the conditions of Mexicans in Texas and willingly gave them logistical support.

There was more than grassroots transnational solidarities at stake in this game. Carranza was eager to wrench U.S. government support from Pancho Villa and to gain U.S. recognition for his own movement. For this, he needed to appear as a convincing alternative who might credibly restore stability and negotiate concessions and guarantees for U.S. interests in Mexico. Carrancista presence on the Texas border allowed Carranza's officers to levy a price for American support for Pancho Villa by providing quiet support for Texas Mexicans against their Anglo oppressors. Meanwhile, the Carrancista press referred to the Texas resisters as "revolutionaries" and expressed sympathy for their cause.[16]

This explosive situation helped encourage a Texas uprising, known as the Plan de San Diego (Texas), which led to what was perhaps the most brutal example of ethnic persecution in U.S. history after the extermination of Native Americans, with several thousand Mexicans shot, hanged, or lynched, but the event also led to U.S. recognition of Carranza, who, in turn, immediately ceased to provide logistical support for the rebellion and began to collaborate with the Texan and U.S. governments.[17] In fact, Pancho Villa's 1916 raid on Columbus, New Mexico, can be understood as a brash reaction to his loss of U.S. recognition—except that, unlike Carranza, who had provided only quiet and easily deniable support to Mexican rebels in Texas. Villa invaded New Mexico in person and so burned any remaining bridge to U.S. recognition.

Villa had also by that time lost any chance of dominating Carranza on the battlefield, so his act of bravado appeared as revenge, whereas the Carrancistas' policy toward the Texas rebels gained Carranza political leverage. In both cases, the problem of loyalty for Mexicans in the United States became increasingly vexed, and once the United States entered World War I, Mexican workers and organizers of every stripe became vulnerable to being branded as un-American.

450

This affected the Liberal junta directly. Several of the leaders of the Plan de San Diego were longtime subscribers to *Regeneración*, and one of them, Aniceto Pizaña, had collaborated with the junta from as far back as their arrival in Texas in 1904.[18] On the other hand, because the revolt caused such a panic in South Texas and such a ferocious crackdown against Mexicans, information on the nature and the complex international dimension of the conflict was very scarce. What Ricardo knew for sure was that there was a panic in Texas created by an odd and suspicious-sounding plan that called for butchering all Anglo males older than sixteen, marrying off Anglo women to Mexicans, blacks, and Chinese, and breaking several states off from the United States and giving them back to the Mexicans, Indians, and blacks. Ricardo smelled some sort of ruse there.

For Ricardo, the plan, if it actually existed, was obviously a concoction being used by the Texas whites to persecute and execute Mexicans. More than five hundred Mexicans were killed in Texas on the final months of 1915 according to *Regeneración*'s estimates. Historian Benjamin Johnson puts the figure in the low thousands.[19] Ricardo knew some of the families and political groups involved in the initial uprising and claimed that the outbreak had been a defensive reaction against an abusive Anglo sheriff, rather than a response to some pie-in-the-sky plan to recover the states that Mexico had lost in 1848. That plan was clearly designed to terrify Texans and so to justify the widespread repression of Mexicans.

Plan de San Diego historian James Sandos argues that Ricardo was so obsessed with the revolution in Mexico that he failed to notice and support a revolution that was happening in Texas. Perhaps. But it also seems possible that Ricardo felt that any Mexican revolt in Texas was doomed to a quick and bloody end. Indeed, one can find some support for this interpretation by going back to Ricardo's reaction to the Rangel affair, in which Ricardo had sounded a much more cautious note than Antonio de P. Araujo and generally had refrained from strident calls to burn down Texas. It is also likely that Ricardo suspected some sort of conspiracy or ruse around the plan de San Diego document and the negotiations that might derive from reactions to it. If he did, he was not entirely wrong, since it seems that the Plan de San Diego was printed in Mexico with logistical support from Carrancista officers. And once Carranza received U.S. recognition, he came down hard on the Texas rebels and personally supported the immediate extradition of Aniceto Pizaña, who had been hiding in Mexico, to the United States.[20]

Ricardo and Enrique were then captured and prosecuted for instigating rebellion in Texas barely two weeks after Carranza agreed to extradite Pizaña. U.S. authorities were prompted to act against them by Mexican consuls in Texas, who provided them with allegedly incriminating texts from *Regeneración* supporting the Texas rebels that the consulate translated from the Spanish in order to prompt prosecution. *La Prensa* of San Antonio reported the presence of a secret commission sent by Carranza to accuse Ricardo Flores Magón of being the Texas revolt's intellectual author. In September 1915, the press printed Mexico's San Antonio consul's claim that the PLM was responsible for the revolt, and his consular officers presented U.S. postal officers with articles that the consulate had taken it upon itself to translate from *Regeneración*.[21] Summarizing the implications of those facts, Ricardo concluded: "Simply put, Carranza wants us to be hanged, for that is the penalty that the whore-mongering law applies to those who rebel against the state."[22] Years later, Enrique Flores Magón claimed that it was Carranza's "brutal persecution" that sent them to prison at Leavenworth.[23]

James Sandos offers details on Carranza's exchanges with Washington on this matter. Once he gained American recognition, Carranza moved to protect General Nafarrete from suspicion of having supported the Texas rebels by relieving Nafarrete from his command at Matamoros and stationing him far away from the border region. The Carrancista papers also suddenly toned down their support of the Texas rebels, whom they demoted from the status of "revolutionaries" to that of "bandits" after U.S. recognition of Carranza.[24] To lend further support to Carranza's contention that his own government had had no involvement in the Plan de San Diego revolt, Carranza quickly complied with the request of Texas's governor and captured the Liberal Aniceto Pizaña.[25]

Carranza or his Sonora officers may also have fanned or supported the persecution of Liberals in Arizona, where an old Mexican government agent, Julio Mancillas, promoted a rumor of a Liberal assault on Tempe and Phoenix that led to a crackdown and the imprisonment of a number of leaders in August 1914. I have found no "smoking gun" to suggest that the Mexican government did in fact orchestrate that event, but Mancilla had been an unusually effective agent in 1911 and 1912, with deep connections in the Liberal Party, and had also built up solid relations with U.S. prosecutors involved in the Baja California affair.[26] In other words, the old Porfirian network of intergovernmental intelligence was still being used to persecute Liberals after the fall of Huerta and during the Carranza years.

Though Ricardo and Enrique were not hanged, as Ricardo thought they might be, they were nonetheless charged in February 1916 and later convicted for publishing an article defending the Texas rebels and for a piece calling on Carranza's soldiers to turn against their leader, the politics behind these two accusations led Ricardo to conclude that "Carranza is another Díaz, another lackey of the White House, and they work together to subject the Mexican proletarian and turn him over to the foreign and domestic capitalist class, tied hand and foot."[27]

Thus, Ricardo was not wrong in suspecting political foul play in the public management of the Plan de San Diego. He knew that the repression that was being meted out to Mexicans in Texas would be implacable, brutal, and impossible for them to defeat. Rangel's men in prison, for instance, had become the objects of harassment and torture by the prison guards, and two of them, Lucio Ortiz and Pedro Perales, were beaten to death by the guards at Perry Landing around the very time of the Plan de San Diego uprising.[28]

As a result, Ricardo decried the Texas repression as a hardening of Texas racism against Mexicans, who were now not allowed to defend themselves in the face of any casual abuse by Anglos or official abuse by sheriffs. The uprising that was being led by men such as Pizaña had been done in a spirit of self-defense, since the law was being used to support whites against Mexicans. And the best that Ricardo could do for the cause was to decry and defend: "The Texas revolutionaries should be given justice, not gunfire. And of course all of us must demand that persecution of innocent Mexicans cease and that the revolutionaries not be executed. It is the Rangers and the mob of bandits who accompany them in their depredations who should be shot."[29]

Ricardo's incensed call for justice to the Texas Rangers, combined with *Regeneración*'s stance toward Carranza and the revolution in Mexico, offered just the pretext that the United States government sought to arrest and convict Ricardo and Enrique.

The Death Knell of Regeneración

It is likely that U.S. officials had expected *Regeneración* to die in 1915. The journal had been revived for a time before then in terms both of quality and regularity, due to Ricardo and Enrique's return from McNeil Island in February 1914. Ricardo's guidance as an analyst was very relevant and very much needed if the journal was going to confront the three main developments of that period: World War I, the deepening and confusing civil war in Mexico, and the hardening of Mexicans' situation in Texas and Arizona.

But as we've seen, *Regeneración*'s finances were in a terrible state, and by June 1914, the journal's publication faltered, appearing only every other week for a couple of months. Then there were no issues in October and only one in December. The next year, 1915, began with no *Regeneración* at all. The junta was able to scrape together money for one issue in March, then again interrupted publication completely until October, when the Edendale period began.

Clearly, U.S. authorities were unhappy with the fact that the journal survived these tribulations, because the charges that the federal government brought against Ricardo's articles and against Enrique (charged as editor of the journal) and William C. Owen (charged as editor of its English-language page) were based on articles published immediately after the move to Edendale, that is, as soon as it became clear that *Regeneración* had survived the closing of its Los Angeles offices.

The *Regeneración* articles that the federal government chose as the basis for the crackdown were also revealing. The first was Ricardo's October 2, 1915, article decrying the Texas killing spree against the Plan de San Diego rebels. The federal charges were based on a sentence that read: "It is the Rangers and the mob of bandits who accompany them in their depredations, that should be shot."[30] The other two were November and December 1915 articles against Carranza, with the federal charges focused on two particular paragraphs. The first claimed that Carranza was the lackey of Woodrow Wilson and of U.S. capital and that he would betray Mexico's proletariat and deliver it to the clutches of American capitalists. The second paragraph called on soldiers fighting in Carranza's army to turn against their officers and to kill them: "what you should do at that point—or before then, if possible—is to rebel and to turn your gun on your officers and chiefs and shoot them, without letting your pulse tremble, because they are your enemies, since they want the institutions that provide them with a life of privilege to perdure."

The charges against Ricardo for the Texas statements suggest that the U.S. government's intention was to proceed against him no matter what and to shut down the journal, since Ricardo's Texas article had not made a call for revolution in Texas, the way that Antonio de P. Araujo's 1913 articles responding to the capture of Rangel's men had, but were rather a denunciation of the killings that were transpiring by the hundreds.

The prosecution against Ricardo for the anti-Carranza articles is also interesting, since by the end of 1915, the United States had finally given formal recognition to Carranza. The timing of Ricardo's prosecution supports the conjecture that Carranza had made a deal with U.S. authorities whereby he was to shut down support for the Texas Plan de San Diego rebels—who were now chased down in Mexico and no longer supported either by Carranza troops or papers—while public responsibility for the rebellion was to be placed at the feet of the members of the Los Angeles junta, who now stood (unfairly) accused of having instigated the Texas rebellion. In other words, after receiving diplomatic recognition, Carranza supported the United States against the Texas rebels, while the junta was saddled with the blame.

Washington was now prosecuting the junta both for its (alleged) support for the Texas rebels, and for its (very real) antagonism to Carranza. The U.S. government had not prosecuted *Regeneración* earlier, when it had actually called for revolution in Texas in retaliation for the violence done to the Rangel expedition, because at that point, it wanted to defuse Mexican outrage over its political use of the neutrality laws to manage and control the outcome of the revolution in Mexico.

In short, *Regeneración* had been run out of Edendale for barely three months when its offices were raided by the police, on February 18, 1916, and Ricardo and Enrique were taken to jail. William C. Owen, who was living in Hayward, California, received news of his impending arrest and fled to England. Being unusually explicit regarding his own motivations, Owen, who continued to publish his *Regeneración* page by mail, offered his readers his reasons for escaping:

> First: I have no love for the martyrdom of prison, and an even greater abhorrence of troubling others to furnish bail or funds for my defense.

Secondly: I am opposed, on principle, to surrender. We should fight. We should not surrender.

Thirdly: in my opinion the ordinary jury is quite incapable of rendering an equitable verdict in political cases. To do so presupposes an adequate education on the subject. This the ordinary juryman does not possess....

Fourthly: Outside the jail I can write. Inside I cannot.[31]

Ricardo and Enrique remained in jail for four months before getting out on bail. During those four prison months, *Regeneración* continued to appear regularly through the end of April and irregularly in May and June. Those issues of the journal provide a glimpse into the Edendale commune and of the Magón brothers' still loyal base of support in Los Angeles, for whereas *Regeneración* at that point was composed almost exclusively of articles by Ricardo, Enrique, and Owen, as soon as those men were in jail or on the run from the law, a whole new roster of writers stepped up to replace them.

Immediately after they were imprisoned, Ricardo's daughter, Lucía, wrote a call to arms, and her boyfriend, Raúl Palma, a young Mexican activist who was quickly becoming *Regeneración*'s new pinup boy, also wrote.[32] Enrique's adopted daughter Estela Arteaga also began to write for the paper, and his wife, Teresa, wrote a piece on Magarita Magón. Rafael García, another member of the Edendale commune, stepped up to support the English section while Owen was on the run. A few non-Edendale Angelenos, such as Celso Marquina, also participated actively and regularly.

Public collections and rallies were made for Enrique and Ricardo. One of these events, scheduled in March at the Labor Temple in Los Angeles, featured as public speakers Teresa Arteaga (Enrique's wife), and Raúl Palma (Ricardo's son-in-law), then one speech in English by Sam Adkinson and one in "Hebrew" (more likely it was in Yiddish) by Chaim Shapiro.[33] In short, there was a vibrant show of solidarity for Ricardo and Enrique, but what *Regeneración* gained in communal solidarity it lost in grit and analysis. Only Owen's page continued to provide a reliable reference to key events beyond the immediate plight of the Liberal community, but it was now written from London and so lagged with regard to Mexican affairs.

Earlier mainstays of *Regeneración* were gone: Anselmo Figueroa was dead; Antonio De Pío Araujo had joined Zapata's forces in

Mexico; Teodoro Gaitán and Blas Lara had each been compelled to find work elsewhere. And while the new generation—particularly Lucía Norman and Raúl Palma—wrote ardent articles, they displayed no eye for conjunctural analysis or for the overall organization of each issue. Though they were capable of sparking dramatic public scenes and were effective public speakers, Lucía and Raúl lacked Ricardo and Enrique's knowledge of news and newsprint and were not capable of carrying *Regeneración*.

As an organizer, Lucía had made headlines back in June 1912 when she led a street riot protesting the verdict that sent the junta to McNeil Island. The *San Francisco Chronicle* began its coverage of that event with the following lede: "Spurred on by the shriek of their women leaders, a mob of several hundred Mexicans and their sympathizers made what the police declared to be an organized attempt to rescue Ricardo Flores Magón, Enrique Magon, Anselmo Figueroa and Librado Rivera."[34] Lucía had been arrested and was held for some days.

Indeed, Lucía had been primed to act as a militant since she was a girl, both by María and, later, by Ricardo. María had used Lucía to transcribe the correspondence that she and Ricardo wrote on Ricardo's prison linen during his confinement in the Los Angeles County Jail. These were not merely clandestine love letters; they were also letters confiding and coordinating political strategy, and Lucía was privy to all of that and thus was a direct accomplice not only in Ricardo and her mother's very passionate relationship, but also in their political plotting.[35]

Ricardo had interfered in Lucía's love life, asking her to abstain from having any relationship with Manuel Sarabia and to be a militant in order to save his life: "We need someone to agitate the American people," Ricardo had written from prison, "and you can do that, dear child. When a woman talks, men get convinced. Above all they feel ashamed not to be brave. You are intelligent and beautiful and you know how to rouse, if you put the fire that's in your heart in your words. You can prepare speeches. Someone will guide you, and you will speak, won't you. The Republican Party puts my life in danger."[36]

After Lucía's ascent to notoriety in 1912, she, like her mother, her aunt Teresa Arteaga, and Anselmo Figueroa's daughter, spoke regularly and distributed propaganda at the Plaza de los Mexicanos, and this may well have been where she met Raúl Palma, a young man of eighteen or nineteen years who was a regular speaker there. By that point, Lucía had a young son, Carlos, from her first husband or companion, whose last name was Guideras. Palma seemed a suitable man for Lucía. He displayed all of the most strident elements of public courage that she admired in Ricardo. Indeed, Palma was not only an ardent and brave speaker, but he was also thrown into prison barely two weeks after Ricardo and Enrique's arrest for speaking out at the Plaza de los Mexicanos and calling on Mexicans to arm themselves, lest they be slaughtered like their brothers in Texas.[37] Palma's cause was immediately taken up by *Regeneración*, and it would later be taken up by Ricardo. It was implicitly a cause related to Ricardo's own succession and to his support for his loving daughter.

Final Days of Freedom

Enrique and Ricardo's four-month imprisonment in 1916 was one strong blow that was compounded with several others. The first was the blow that the two men's health suffered. Both had sustained serious illnesses due to hunger and overwork, the long-term effects of imprisonment at McNeil Island, and the stress associated with their job in moments like these, with civil war and class strife raging in Mexico, Mexican Texans being massacred by the hundreds, family conditions strained, and the United States preparing to enter the World War. Ricardo, in particular, had twice found himself at death's door and was too sick to make a speech in court when the men were first convicted, in June 1916. Enrique attempted to speak for the two of them. Almost equally worrisome, Ricardo was losing his eyesight, a development that the men attributed to the long night hours that they had worked, most often with improper lighting due, again, to pecuniary stress.

In March 1916, the U.S. Postal Service had denied *Regeneración* second-class postage rates. Initially, the pretext used was that the journal was issued only irregularly and that the paper was not "a newspaper within the meaning of the law."[38] Soon after that, the Post Office classified *Regeneración* as "obscene matter." The loss of second-class postal status effectively doubled *Regeneración*'s expenses. By May, the journal had been forced to revert to bimonthly appearances, and by January 1917, it was appearing even more irregularly, usually once per month and occasionally even every other month.

Finally, the U.S. government's offensive against the Magóns was of a piece with its persecution of radicals more generally—anarchists, socialists, and unionists—anyone opposing the draft. It closed anarchist papers and imprisoned activists. Prison brutality against Rangel's men also sent a clear message. In July 1916, Ricardo declared that "there was not torment to which they [the eleven Texas prisoners still alive] are not subjected, or one humiliation that they are spared."[39] In September, Ricardo announced that another of the leaders of Rangel's expedition, Eugenio Alzalde, had been beaten to death by a prison guard.[40]

Indeed, pressure on Mexicans to show loyalty had increased even more in those days, due to Pancho Villa's March 1916 raid on Columbus, New Mexico. Villa's response to the decision by the United States to withdraw support for him and to recognize Carranza added a whole new level of angst for Mexicans in the United States. True, the Liberals had never been Villa supporters, and they were adamantly against imperialist invasions, so in principle, they did not support Villa's invasion of Columbus. Nevertheless, their loyalty to the United States was always under pressure, and Villa's invasion intensified this. The Liberals took the occasion to remind Americans that Villa's invasion of the United States was in fact less severe an infringement on national sovereignty than the recent invasion of Veracruz by the United States. Thus, Owen reprinted an Alexander Berkman article from *The Blast* that presented a column of facts under "Villa" and another under "Wilson" and compared the two men. Berkman concluded: "There is only this difference between them: Villa had the courage to do his own vengeance, taking the risks and profiting nothing himself. Wilson sits safely in the White House and orders others to do the dirty work."[41]

American jingoists did not appreciate that line of argumentation and ratcheted up pressure against Mexican militants. In May, Raúl Palma was arrested and briefly jailed for agitating for Los Angeles' Mexicans to arm themselves. Los Angeles Mexicans were now being submitted to the kind of pressure against public speaking that had been deployed in San Diego after the fall of Tijuana, in February 1912, when Wobblies and anarchists were run out of town and a mob of vigilantes stripped Emma Goldman's lover and partner, Ben Reitman, branded him, beat him, threatened to castrate him, and made him crawl naked on his hands and knees to kiss the flag and sing "The

Star-Spangled Banner." Reitman was so terrified and humiliated that he abandoned both his political activity and Emma Goldman.[42]

Lucía Norman, too, was under pressure and was put on the stand by the prosecution to testify against her own adopted father at his trial. Lucía refused to respond to the district attorney's interrogation and so was vulnerable to being charged with contempt of court.[43] Less than one year later, her lover, Raúl Palma, was again arrested for preaching anarchy, together with Odilón Luna. And soon after that, Palma was arrested yet again, on a trumped up accusation of having committed a murder two years before.

These various causes—the trial of Ricardo, Enrique, and Librado, the plight of the Texas Martyrs, the cause of sister anarchist publications, fund-raising for each issue of *Regeneración*, defending free speech, denouncing arrests of fellow anarchists and Socialists, taking up collections to pay for Ricardo's and Enrique's medical expenses—absorbed almost all of the energy left in the staff of *Regeneración*. As 1917 unfolded and the date of the junta's appeal came closer, Ricardo focused increasingly on preserving an esprit de corps, a clear sense of the cause, and on the reproduction of the libertarian communist family.

To achieve these goals, he turned to experimentation with the theater. In April 1917, at Los Angeles' Lyceum Hall, the community opened Ricardo's play *¡Tierra y Libertad!* The actors were all from the Edendale community: Raúl Palma played Juan, a peon; Lucía Norman played Marta, Juan's lover; Enrique Flores Magón played the part of another of the peons, and María Brousse that of his female companion. Other actors included Zoraida, who was one of Anselmo Figueroa's daughters, and Ralph García.[44] The play was preceded by collective singing of a set of anarchist songs, with lyrics also composed by Ricardo, such as the song "Tierra y Libertad" and the "Marcha Regeneración." The event was a great success, both for the public—who flocked to see it, despite torrential rains—and for the Edendale community.

Blas Lara lovingly remembered the performance, also sharing the group's pride in its workers and artisans.

> All of the improvised actors came to Los Angeles from afar, every night, rain or thunder, to practice the dramatic art.... The sets for "Road Through the Forest," "Tilling Field," "Interior of a Hut," "Two Cells in a Prison," "Field on the Edge of a Hamlet," "Office of a Great Personage," and "Mountainous Place" were all painted by Nicolás Reveles,

from Jerez, Zacatecas. He worked in Los Angeles for a theater utility company. He charged only $16, when his regular price would have been $50.... The artwork of that comrade was on view at the San Francisco World Fair of 1915.[45]

¡Tierra y Libertad! began to be played in a number of places, most notably in Morenci, Arizona, where Mexican miners staged it on the second anniversary of their 1915 strike and got an audience of five thousand, distributed over two performances (Figure 25.1).[46] Workers at nearby mines in Clifton and Miami also staged the play, though the local priest complained to Arizona's governor and got it blocked. The drama also began to circulate in Mexico, with a presentation by the Casa del Obrero Mundial in Tampico.[47]

Attracted by drama's power to shape communal determination, education, and participation, Ricardo dedicated some of his final hours of freedom to writing his second play, *Verdugos y víctimas*, and announced its existence in the second-to-last issue of *Regeneración*, with prison impending. The drama was directed against worker support for Venustiano Carranza. Ricardo had written feverishly before leaving for prison, in the heady aftermath of the October Revolution in Russia. Librado Rivera recalled that the entire play was written in one week.[48] Ricardo characterized the work thus:

> All of the victims of the capitalist system appear in this play.... There is the poor young woman, seduced by the rich man; there is the prostitute, torn from the popular classes to serve as pleasure meat in the brothels of our masters; there the beggars, who came into their state thanks to the system's injustice; there the workers, paying with jail for their lack of foresight in arming themselves; there is the proletarian, suffering in jail for having stolen crumbs from the treasures that he has produced and that the bourgeoisie has stolen; and above all of these victims, there is the bourgeoisie, the powerful, the priest, authority, the pimp, the soldier, the legislator, and the cop—corrupting, trampling, exploiting, and celebrating their triumph over the confident people with bacchanalias.[49]

A Stake in the Heart

On February 9, 1918, *Regeneración* sounded its death rattle. Alongside a piece on the imminent coming of the universal revolution—

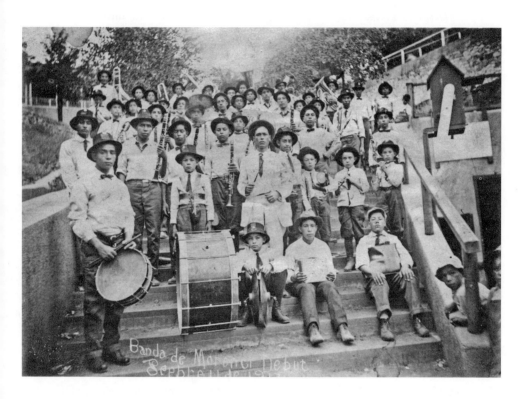

Figure 25.1 Mexican band at Morenci.
Courtesy of the Bancroft Library,
John Murray Papers.

announced by the Russian Revolution and the final throes of the World War—an article denouncing the trial and conviction of Emma Goldman and Alexander Berkman, and yet another effort to rally support for the cause of Raúl Palma, Ricardo published two unusual notes, both of them deeply stirring.

The first was a plea for his daughter. Lucía Norman, who had been supposed to take charge of the English section of *Regeneración*, had been hospitalized. Her long-standing nervous condition had taken a turn for the worse, thanks to the imprisonment of her lover, Raúl Palma. Now she was on the verge of madness. Ricardo explained his despair—full of work, his daughter on the brink, and with no money. He begged support from his friends for her medical treatment.[50]

The second article was a notice titled "Separation" that announced, without comment, that Enrique and Teresa Flores Magón and three other Edendale comrades—Rafael B. García, Trinidad Villarreal, and José Flores ("Floritos"), had decided to leave *Regeneración*. The specific reasons for their separation were not given—a disagreement regarding "some of the details of the struggle." The departing comrades planned to create their own group in order to continue with the struggle on their own terms. *Regeneración*, for its part, would now be headed by Ricardo, Librado, and María Brousse.[51]

Coming just weeks before their appeal and in what turned out to be *Regeneración*'s next-to-last issue, the separation of the two brothers was a sure sign of agony for the group as a whole. But what had happened? Why did the two brothers, who had been inseparable from their youth, decide to make a public break at a juncture that was, in all probability, marking the end of Ricardo's career and probably of his life?

We do not know, exactly, though aspects of what happened can be reconstructed. The rift between Enrique and Ricardo has not commanded much attention from historians, most of whom seem to have been influenced in their opinion by the views of key surviving militants to the effect that Enrique was a bit of a buffoon and guided by jealousy. Thus, in a life history recorded when he was an old man, Nicolás Bernal, who was in contact with Ricardo in those final years, summarized the problem thus:

> [Enrique] tried to organize a group of *pendejos* [jerks] in Los Angeles— people who had no ideas—half a dozen *pendejos*. We said to ourselves "Who's going to join Enrique?"

He invited Blas Lara, me, and others to join him, but Enrique did not have the same intellectual level as Ricardo or the same ideology. Enrique broke with his brother because he was jealous of him, because he wanted to be as well known as Ricardo or more so, but he lacked Ricardo's personality and intelligence.[52]

Bernal's view has been influential because he was one of the people who corresponded with Ricardo when Ricardo was in the federal penitentiary at Leavenworth and who survived long enough to serve as a historical informant and resource. Moreover, Enrique's memoirs, first published weekly in *El Nacional* and then in the form of an extended oral history recorded by Samuel Kaplan, are unreliable, analytically weak, and prone to self-glorification, thereby lending credence to Bernal's diagnosis of Enrique's need for recognition and the ineffectiveness of his presence in the cause.

But in fact, the matter is much more difficult to reconstruct, and we may never have all of the pieces of the puzzle at our disposal. Nicolás Bernal was not a direct witness of the events in question, in any case. Given how acrimonious the brothers' separation became, Bernal's account cannot be allowed as the only version. Certainly, not everyone believed that Enrique was the fool that Bernal says. William Owen, for instance, worked closely and regularly with both brothers during those years and was highly educated, intelligent, and perspicacious. He had a high opinion of Enrique, as well as of Ricardo. Thus, Owen wrote to Enrique shortly after Enrique's release from Leavenworth:

> First, I am most sorry to read such a bad account of your health, and of your economic situation.... I am tempted to wish you would get offices in some labour organization which would support you in the activities which are so essentially natural to you, but I think you cannot do that, it not being in you to do the scheming and make the compromises necessary. Most fortunate, of course, for your character and usefulness in this great movement that you are not of that type; but it comes very hard.[53]

Three years later, Owen still praised Enrique's seriousness of dedication, comparing it favorably even to his own: "Your energy, Enrique, is admirable, and I confess it shames me. I speak, but only occasionally as the opportunity offers.... I write about 3 columns a week for the '*Middleton Guardian*,' and usually have about 2 pages in '*Freedom*.' That, with a speech now and then, is about all."[54]

Moreover, it is certain that key militants of the period did not take the break between the brothers lightly or shrug it off as the excision of a handful of "*pendejos*." So, for instance, Fernando Palomares wrote to Enrique from El Paso in consternation. If it came to a break, Fernando said he would side with Ricardo, but "as a member of the Partido Liberal Mexicano, and one who knows both you and Ricardo, I feel wounded and deeply hurt by your division. Everyone is surprised and in complete confusion. They say that it would be understandable if the cause were political. People on the street are saying that the Patriot Licenciado Don Jesús Flores Magón may have persuaded you."[55]

Rumor and gossip spread widely, but the people most authorized to report on what actually happened died relatively early—Librado Rivera died in 1932, Lucía Norman in 1924—and did no public speaking or writing on the issue. (Enrique never spoke about it, except privately.) As a result, only a reconstruction of the context and analysis of the facts by way of their effects is possible at this time.

We begin with Enrique. Enrique's life had suffered important developments between his imprisonment in Leavenworth in 1912 and his split with Ricardo early in 1918. Imprisonment at McNeil Island gave Enrique a publicity that he had not had since his arrival in the United States, since he had not shared prison with Ricardo and the others in 1907–1910 and so had not been mentioned in the campaigning on their behalf. Also, McNeil had cost Enrique dearly, since it led to the junta's break with his grasping father-in-law, Rómulo Carmona, which led in turn to Enrique's split with his wife, Paula, who took his two children away from him. Enrique never saw them again.

As a result, Enrique emerged from prison more grim and determined, and he was ferociously active during the years that followed. Owen describes both brothers as emerging directly from prison to their posts at *Regeneración* without even hours of interruption. They again did the same when they were released from prison in Los Angeles in June 1916. Enrique wrote more for *Regeneración* between 1914 and 1917 than at any other time. His articles tended to be general ideological proclamations, rather than close readings of the political situation—the paper relied much more on Ricardo and on Owen for analysis. Indeed, like Lucía and Raúl Palma, Enrique was no substitute for Ricardo, but he was experienced and knowledgeable about the newspaper, very active in its correspondence and in general militancy, and also was responsible for some important initiatives, for instance, in his articles on the rights of women and in his warning against anti-Americanism after the Veracruz invasion of 1914.[56]

But Enrique's personal growth and development also occurred in tandem with an odd mimesis of Ricardo. Enrique's exile in Texas and St. Louis had made his older brother Jesús's life path unachievable—Enrique's departure from Mexico City had lost him his fiancée, his *novia*, and the possibility of returning to a settled life there—living instead on the run and leading the clandestine life of the militant. In 1911, Jesús and Juan Sarabia had visited Ricardo and Enrique on behalf of Madero, and the violence of Ricardo's break with these two important figures of Enrique's youth might have contributed to consolidating Ricardo's absolute ascendancy over him. The bridges to Jesús had been burned twice—and now the fall of Díaz would not reunite them.

After the painful loss of his wife and two children, Enrique married Teresa Arteaga, who was the daughter of María Brousse's sister, a most beloved niece that María had raised. The older brother lived with the aunt, and the younger married the niece. Like Ricardo, too, Enrique adopted Teresa's children (five of them), and raised them as his own. Also, like Ricardo, Enrique developed an exalted romantic relationship and correspondence with his Teresa.

It is my impression that Enrique's admiration and imitation of Ricardo reached such a pitch that it produced a kind of psychosomatic empathy in him. When Ricardo began to develop serious health problems in 1916, Enrique's health declined almost immediately. It's true that both men were overworked and underfed, but Enrique's heart condition seemed to be very sensitive to Ricardo's overall condition, and he felt at death's door when Ricardo died, only to recover his health after that final separation. Indeed, one month after Ricardo's death, Enrique wrote to Rafael García: "For about a month now I've had a constant pain in my heart.... Disappointments, disillusions, poverty, tremendous anguish, and deep sadness—all generated in my twin struggle for the cause and for bread.... All of that has lately made me powerless to bear any physical fatigue.... Physically, I'm a man gone overboard."[57] But, in fact, Enrique went on to lead a full life and died thirty-two years later.

Enrique's twin process of personal growth and identification with Ricardo was probably complicated by the fact that the 1914–1918 period was the first since the two brothers' youth when they lived and worked together on a daily basis, spending long hours together at *Regeneración*, especially when all the families settled together at Edendale. This kind of situation had not existed earlier. In Mexico City, the two men had been bachelors, with Enrique still very much the kid brother; in El Paso, San Antonio, and St. Louis, Enrique had to work days at his *yugos*, and as a newspaperman, he was junior not only to Ricardo, but also to Juan Sarabia and Antonio Villarreal. Finally, after 1906, Enrique had moved on to clandestine activity, while Ricardo spent three years in jail, and the 1910–1911 period had been so active that there was no real domestic existence for any of them. Thus, the post-McNeil period was the first extended time that the two men lived together and collaborated regularly and on an equal footing as adults. Moreover, both men were married and had children, and all lived a communal existence whose strains and hardships lent themselves to gossip and factionalism.

Understanding Ricardo in the period prior to his final imprisonment is harder still than thinking through Enrique's position. Those were momentous times, filled with anxiety and hope. Repression was hardening and pressing down on all sides, but what was going on in Russia convinced Ricardo that world revolution was imminent. It was a matter of holding on.

The trouble was that Ricardo's health was faltering, and the movement was so hard hit that solidarity was insufficient even to keep *Regeneración* going. A new prison term was a practical certainty—only the exact date of the new trial was unknown. As it happened, the prison term that Ricardo received in the end—a whopping twenty-one years—was a death sentence, but even the shorter sentence that Ricardo expected he would receive may have been interpreted by him as a final farewell: he would, very probably, die in prison.

There were thus three things weighing on Ricardo's mind: keeping the Mexican movement alive, leaving a new generation in his place, and protecting María and Lucía.

I suspect that these two final items played a role in the conflict between the two brothers. In particular, it was clear that Ricardo was priming Lucía and Raúl Palma as his chosen successors at *Regeneración*. He had hoped that Lucía would take over the English-language page of *Regeneración*, which by that time was of key importance for the journal. He had been training Palma at Edendale, and the tone of Ricardo's defense of Raúl Palma in the face of police prosecution with the sort of praise that he had once reserved for Práxedis Guerrero: "Our bourgeois masters could not be at peace while Palma was free, because they knew that outside prison, this man would subvert the foundations of the old social structure, whose weight we at the bottom have born for centuries and centuries."[58]

This sort of exalted praise may well have been too much for Enrique. Palma was barely nineteen years old, and though brave and charismatic, he had not yet won enough laurels to merit such individual attention. Was Palma's prominent place in Ricardo's writing during those months not some weak concession by Ricardo to Lucía and to María?

Although we do not know what sparked the break between the two brothers, it is certain that Enrique had a very poor opinion of Raúl, whom he later called a "scorpion," and of Lucía, whom he felt was a drama queen, as well as of María, who would soon be referred to in Enrique's correspondence as "the whore." In his day, Práxedis may have been the object of some jealousy on the part of Enrique—possibly even of Ricardo—but if this had been so (and it may well not have been), the jealousy had been sublimated, due to Práxedis's indisputable merits and sacrifice. Enrique had even named his first son after Práxedis. But Raúl Palma, Enrique knew, was no Práxedis. Maybe he had the flair, but Palma was nowhere Práxedis's match as a writer, as an intellectual, as a strategist, or as a man capable of and committed to operating a clandestine network. The idea that Ricardo was crediting Palma so lavishly, simply because he was his Lucía's lover, must have caused Enrique unease.

The idea of nepotism entering the most consequential decisions of the cause seems to have been a flashpoint for Enrique, given his internal tension between individuation and total fusion with a cause that had always had Ricardo as its undisputed beacon. Enrique's personal sacrifices, including separation from his wife and children, made him absolutely intolerant of nepotism in the cause. And, like Ricardo, he, too, could be implacable with the weak. Enrique, too, was capable of breaking with family. He, too, was capable of putting the cause before everything else.

So, for instance, Raúl Palma's first brief stay in prison had transpired alongside that of another man, Odilón Luna, who had also been charged for his public speaking at the Plaza de los Mexicanos. Ricardo raised a campaign in support of both men and compared their plight to that of proven heroes, such as Jesús Rangel, and the union organizers Joe Hill, Warren K. Billings, and Tom Mooney.[59] In another article in the same issue of *Regeneración*, Ricardo placed the names of Palma and Luna alongside the causes of Emma Goldman, Alexander Berkman, and the rest of the nation's leaders in the movement against the draft.[60]

But barely six weeks later, *Regeneración* found itself responding to charges by Luna to the effect that the junta had stolen money taken in collections for his support and that he had not received prison visits from the comrades of the PLM. It was Enrique who responded to Luna's charges. There had been no embezzlement, and the comrades had not rallied to Luna in prison because he was not a true comrade. Luna, Enrique said, had declared to the immigration authorities, and it was made public in the press, that he was not an anarchist, which was a deportable offense for recent immigrants at the time. But, Enrique chided, "anarchists never deny their convictions, not even before a firing squad. . . . If someone denies his convictions for fear of being convicted, he is a coward and a fraud."[61] And then, he added, with a sideswipe at Palma and perhaps as a reproach to Ricardo: "If this group has done something for the benefit of the Luna-Palma business, it has not done it because of their merits, but to defend the principle of free speech."

Then something happened. Something snapped between the two factions, and it occurred or was confirmed in February 1918 during a group meeting at the house of a certain "Chano," where Ricardo, María, Lucía, Raúl and their supporters confronted Enrique, Teresa, and their supporters.[62] The break either produced or reflected a breakup of the Edendale collective, and Enrique and Teresa and their children, Rafael García, Floritos, Villota, Villarreal, and their own families left Edendale. Most of them set up in a new Los Angeles cluster around Rafael García and José Flores, which is where Teresa and Enrique's children remained during Enrique's three-year prison term. That group was also closely identified with a couple of other Liberal "families" of the region—the El Puente clan and the San Gabriel clan.

But these new arrangements were for the clans—for the families—and no longer for Enrique, Ricardo, and Librado, because all three were sent soon off to jail. Enrique went first, because Ricardo was faced with new charges for the manifesto that he and Librado had published one issue after Enrique's separation from *Regeneración* in that journal's final issue. Enrique was sent to McNeil Island in May 1918, but McNeil was overcrowded, so he was transferred to Leavenworth Federal Penitentiary in June. Enrique was now alone, though accompanied by prominent "Reds" such as "Big Bill" Haywood and Indian revolutionary Tarak Nath Das, who later became a prison librarian, together with Enrique.

Sifuentes

The things that were said in the public confrontation or later in private, or indirectly, between Enrique and Ricardo, were so strong that Enrique would never entirely be reconciled with Ricardo. The gossip and bickering between the families that ensued once the feud had begun involved even the pettiest of items—how Ricardo had left a will distributing things from the Edendale colony that belonged to the collective, leaving the horse and wagon to one ally and the record player to "Raulillo's wench" (Lucía), and so on.[63] Through the first months of Enrique's imprisonment, García kept him informed of Ricardo's "efforts to grab what is left, for the 'poor women.'"[64] Enrique was kept abreast of the gossip and told of how the Edendale colony had ceased to be functional and how there were occasional rumors that "Madam Lucille" and "Raulillo" were going to move—things of that nature.

The "Enriquistas" also took it upon themselves to investigate and denounce Teodoro Gaitán, one of the editors of *Regeneración* from 1912 to 1914, whom they accused of having bilked comrades in Arizona under the false pretense that he was commandeering a broad-based offensive.[65] The Enriquistas tried to force several undecided militants to their side by way of their denunciation of Gaitán—people such as Blas Lara, Fernando Palomares, and Nicolás Bernal. They generally failed in that purpose, but did rally a broad campaign against Gaitán.

Once in Leavenworth, Enrique was eager for this gossip and seemed eager to nurse the pain of his violent break with his revered brother. In his correspondence from that period, Enrique refers to Ricardo in code as "Sifuentes," often refers to María as "The Marquise," and usually diminishes Raúl Palma with a contemptuous

"Raulillo." In one letter intercepted by the federal prison authorities, Enrique let Rafael García know that he believed that Ricardo
and Librado would ask to be transferred from McNeil to Leavenworth in order to attempt a prison break, which they could not do
at McNeil Island, because they were not good swimmers.[66] This
letter, which was brought to the attention of the wardens at both
prisons, seems to have been calculated to avoid the two men's transfer to Leavenworth. Enrique dreaded the idea of having Ricardo at
Leavenworth and expected the factionalism between them to be
reproduced within the prison. Thus, he wrote to Teresa that "with
disgust, I am expecting, too, to have to see here the contemptible
bugs of Sifuentes and his flunky [Librado Rivera], whose deeds I have
told already to Ferrer and Martínez, who, by the way, send greetings
to you all."[67]

Death

Leavenworth

Prison was exceedingly lonely, even for the gregarious Enrique. Despair was, of course, worse for Ricardo. With a twenty-one-year sentence and poor health, he seemed doomed to die in prison, whereas Enrique very much looked forward to freedom. Also, Ricardo's eyesight was really going.

One year after his arrival in Leavenworth, Ricardo wrote about the looming specter of blindness, anticipating that

> one fine day, that to me will be as dark as night, when they see that I shall no longer be a danger to oppression, because my eyes will not be able to guide my pen in the writing of those words which the humble loves and the proud detests, I shall be shoved out into the light.... My weapon—my pen—the only weapon I have ever wielded; the weapon that landed me here; the weapon that accompanied me through the infernos of a thirty years' struggle for what is beautiful, will be then as useless as a broken sword."[1]

But Enrique at least found some small sources of satisfaction in Leavenworth (Figure 26.1). When he arrived at the prison, he described it to Teresa as containing eighteen hundred, of whom only twenty-five were Mexicans. Many were political prisoners—an entirely different situation from the one that had been experienced by Ricardo, Librado, and Antonio in Arizona, where the vast majority of prisoners were Mexicans and blacks, often with no education. Enrique's first job was at the brick plant.[2] He was used to manual labor and did not complain about that.

Soon after his arrival, Enrique asked Teresa to send him his long and his short necktie and his watch and chain. The upbeat tone of his early letters was transparently meant to cheer Teresa, his children, and his friends in Los Angeles, but still, there seems to be at least some sincerity in them:

> As time passes by in my new abode, I find that it was a bargain to have been transferred to this place, mainly because from here, I can write you every week. Besides, we are out in the yard on Sunday afternoons, and Saturdays we have ballgame in the afternoon. Moreover, here we have some more freedom, for we are allowed to have in our cells and play musical instruments, such as the mandolin, guitar, etc., and what is best, there is a convict band that has nothing to envy from those outside in its masterful rendering of any classic, opera, or dance musical number. This band plays for us twice a day, at noon dinner and at supper-time, and to the credit of our band, I'd say that I enjoy their playing."[3]

Enrique was well liked in prison both by inmates and by officials and was soon transferred out of manual labor into various clerical jobs, first to the prison post office and eventually to the library. In the post office, Enrique's hours ebbed and flowed with the prison mail—frenetic on Mondays, short hours some other days, and work

Figure 26.1 Leavenworth Penitentiary. Courtesy of the Bancroft Library, John Murray Papers.

for most of Sunday, a detail that had one distinct advantage, for "it saved me from having to go to church, which is compulsory for every living body here, regardless of whether he believes or not."[4]

Enrique began writing combat and love poems, which he sent to Teresa and instructed her to keep, nurturing the idea of one day publishing a book of them. He also began to teach Spanish in the prison school and used those lessons to discuss the libertarian communist ideal, always in the guise of introducing students to Mexican culture and literature: "Two nights ago, on Friday, I wrote the verses titled 'To the Struggle!' on the blackboard—I had sent them to you in my last letter. . . . I made my students read and translate the poem, and they got all roused up by it. I told them that I was sharing it so that they could learn about Mexican literature." He explained that "in school, I have to shield myself behind the Mexican thing, which in fact lends itself to great and wonderful things—one need only explain the customs of our communities."[5] Moreover, as his comrade Rafael García remarked, the concentration of illustrious political prisoners in Leavenworth was such that "judging from your daily life in that place, it seems that at the same time that you are educating others, you are also receiving a first-rate university education and, from what you tell me, you are now an interpreter in five languages. I believe that you will emerge a first-rate linguist from your 'schooling.'"[6]

There was also a prison paper, *New Era*, which by Enrique's account was lively and of good quality. Taking advantage of the freedoms afforded to the prisoners, Estela sent her adopted father a violin and some teach-yourself manuals, and Enrique began to learn the instrument.[7] This detail affords an entertaining cautionary note on the reliability and proper use of oral history: in his 1958 memoir, Enrique claimed that in 1908, he disguised himself as an Italian musician and "rode the rails" playing the violin in order to go fight alongside Práxedis Guerrero:

> I put on some brown corduroy pants, a long khaki-colored shirt, tied at the waist, and an intensely red herb-patterned kerchief around my neck. A twisted pipe hung from my lips. I had a violin in its case under my arm.
>
> Dressed in this fashion, I entered the Pullman car on the train to El Paso. I took the violin from its case and, with a flourish, I started to play the Ave Maria.[8]

In fact, Enrique began scratching out his first notes on the violin in prison, ten years later. And he never did join Práxedis in the 1908 expedition. The memoir must be read in tension with the facts in order to establish new ones.

On the health front, Enrique had teeth problems that were diagnosed as pyorrhea, but his friends and family were able to send him the cash needed for an operation and treatment. Once, he became ill and was hospitalized, and he commented on the model prison's medical facilities: "Everything is spotlessly clean, well ventilated and lit. Our hospital has nothing to envy the County Hospital there [in Los Angeles]." The food was so nourishing that "one isn't even eager to get well."[9] Ricardo's experience with prison medicine at Leavenworth would be very different, but his difficulties did not arise for a lack of medical facilities per se, but rather from deliberate medical negligence.

Overall, Leavenworth was the best prison establishment that Enrique had known. It embraced modern rehabilitation philosophies and provided prisoners with relatively good resources. Moreover, although the prisoners worked full days, and Ricardo and Enrique did what they could to keep up with correspondence in the world, Enrique and Ricardo actually worked fewer hours than they had worked back in Edendale.

But despite these advantages, Leavenworth was, without a doubt, a prison, and there is nothing more antithetical to an anarchist's acute sense of personal dignity than prison. "Oh, if I only could not think!" Ricardo wrote in response to a letter from Lily Sarnoff.

> But I cannot stop thinking! I cannot! And, consequently, every detail of prison life hurts my feelings: the walls, erected to prevent my communion with my brothers in ideals, with my fellow beings, with Nature; the bars... which make me think of the fear and hatred of those who dread to see me free; the rules, which command me to obey, to obey, to obey... the clubs, whose very sight hurt my dignity as though I were physically struck with them; all, in fine, in my dismal surroundings, makes me realize that I am not a man, but a thing, and this, when I feel myself to be a man yet![10]

Prisoners were numbered, fingerprinted, toothprinted, weighed, measured, and photographed. They were kept track of in files that contained general life information—education, names of spouses, parents, and children, addresses, full medical records, records of days worked and days idle, records of all incoming and outgoing mail, records of gifts received and small purchases made. Prisoners could be reprimanded even for "wasting time" and be "denied privileges." They could bargain concessions in return for information, although Leavenworth did not operate on a "stool-pigeon system," the way that Yuma and Florence did.

We have the prison's records of all of these minutiae. We know, for instance, that between July 1, 1919, and June 30, 1920, Ricardo missed work on seven days. We know the dates and quantities of tobacco, matches, and rolling paper that he bought. We can see that he occasionally bought fruit—grapes, pears, peaches, apples, raisins, nuts. Occasionally a pencil, too. With special permission, he had a photo taken and sent to his family. He bought a magazine and received two books as gifts. We even know which ones he got, too: *Russia 1919* and *The Cry for Justice.*[11]

We know Ricardo's credit balance with the prison store. He started in May 1921 with a credit of $404.95. In May, he spent $2.60 on tobacco, $.50 on stamps, and $.65 on paper. We also know that these were the only three items that he purchased regularly and that by the time he died, his balance had dwindled to $184.88.[12]

Leavenworth had a library, and the men read a number of progressive authors. Some of Ricardo's favorites in this period were Andrew Latzko, Romain Rolland, Anatole France, Leo Tolstoy, Sergei Stepniak, and George Bernard Shaw. Nonetheless, there was also some vetting of the reading materials coming in. Only journals with permission to circulate as second-class postage were supposed to be allowed, so that when Lily Sarnoff (also known as Ellen White) tried to send Ricardo missing copies of William Owen's London paper *Freedom*, the warden blocked it.[13]

We know that in the two years between his arrival in Leavenworth, on November 3, 1919, and his death, Ricardo was feeling ill enough to see the doctor on twenty-two occasions and that he saw the dentist on fourteen.[14] We know the names of each of his correspondents and the dates of letters sent and received. Ricardo wrote to and received letters from María weekly and almost continuously through his two years at Leavenworth, though we have almost none of that correspondence. He corresponded with Raúl Palma between August and October 1920 and had almost no correspondence with

Lucía, which suggests that Ricardo may have continued his earlier prison habit of tacking messages to Lucía onto his letters to María. We know, finally, that Ricardo began an intimate correspondence with Ellen White in January 1921 and continued it regularly until his death.[15]

Alone

Ricardo and Librado had been arrested on March 22, 1918, just days after the publication of their manifesto in what was already quite obviously *Regeneración*'s final gasp. They had spent a few months in the Los Angeles County Jail awaiting trial and had been handed their draconian prison sentences in July. Ricardo and Librado were then moved to McNeil Island and transferred to Leavenworth in November 1919.

By that time, Ricardo must have been feeling abandoned. *Regeneración* had perished by the sword, true, but the cash-starved journal had long been dying. It had been abandoned by its readers—loved by many, perhaps, but not loved enough. And then there was the pain of fractiousness, dissolution, and loss, the nightmare of Lucía's mental fragility, and the anxieties of hope placed on a Raúl Palma, who was passionate and brave, but untried and not really of the stature required to reignite *Regeneración*. There was the breakup of the Edendale collective, prompted by Enrique's need to stand on his own, by Ricardo's concern to protect and favor his loved ones, and by the tensions and antipathies brewing between each of their respective clans. All of that weighed heavily in prison.

When Ricardo arrived in Leavenworth, he made a melancholic gesture of love and understanding for Enrique—a kind of affirmation for old times' sake. We know it only from Enrique's correspondence. If Ricardo ever wrote of it to anyone—and he may not have—he would have written this to Maria, but the correspondence between them is largely missing.

Since Ricardo's arrival in Leavenworth, Enrique had been eluding him, but early in December, Enrique had a shocking surprise:

> Sifuentes came to talk to me. As I indicated in my last letter, I have been avoiding him for a week, and everywhere I went, I thought that I'd come face to face with him. Everywhere, that is, except in the school, because I know that he prefers to be locked up in his cell rather than to

Figure 26.2 The dining hall at Leavenworth Penitentiary. Presumably this was the space that was used between meals for prisoners to teach classes. If so, it was here that Ricardo and Enrique had their first encounter after their break in California. Courtesy of the Bancroft Library, John Murray Papers.

go through the hassle of leaving his cell at night and into the noise that is inevitable in a place where 800 men take classes in the same room [the prison dining hall, Figure 26.2].... Moreover, he knows everything that's taught here. Nonetheless, he registered in a French class. Did he do that to talk to me? Whatever the reason, the fact is that on the last school night, when I was among my students calling roll, he was the last one in. I also saw that he asked someone something, and that person signaled me out with his finger. He came straight to me, offering his hand, with his head slightly bowed, and said: "*Manito!*"

The man before me was no longer the arrogant, aggressive, and haughty person who had brought his ruffians [*la porra*] to Chano's house on February 1918. He looked beaten [*abatido*], ashamed, bearing a white flag.[16]

What was Enrique supposed to do, he asked Teresa, Rafael García, and the clan who read his letters. They had all fully internalized an image of Ricardo as a fallen angel, as selfish and venal. Enrique had thought long about just what he and Ricardo would do when they finally came face to face again. He had expected his brother to be insulting and thought that he himself would react only in self-defense: "I've thought that even though he has sinned of excess rancor, hatred, and wounded pride [*despecho*], that does not authorize me to descend to his same level."[17]

Enrique accepted what he chose to interpret as an offer of "armistice," but he would not—could not—return to their earlier intimacy. Their bond of trust and faith (*confianza*) was forever broken. Enrique's allies, for their part, chose to interpret Ricardo's act as a gesture of surrender. Indeed, Rafael García and the tribe at no point changed their views regarding María, Lucía, and Raúl Palma, and they stepped up their offensive against Ricardo's ally, Teodoro Gaitán, as a fraud and traitor. Almost immediately after receiving Enrique's account of his encounter with Ricardo, Rafael denounced Gaitán to Juan Olmos, head of one of the Liberal clans, appending a copy of Enrique's letter. Ricardo's peace offering amounted to an admission of error, he claimed, and the Enrique clan was now justified in pursuing what was just: "This act of Ricardo's (or Sifuentes, as Enrique calls him) seems to prove that he has admitted his error or, rather, his treachery—because that's what it was—and that he felt very guilty about it. So much so, that he came before his worst enemy (which is a fair thing to say) to show his remorse, even if it were in word only."[18]

Enrique had called Ricardo's gesture an "armistice" and had reported it as a triumph. And he had accepted Ricardo's affectionate gesture so as to avoid "vile rancor and unhealthy hatred that should never fester in a libertarian who preaches human confraternity."[19] But the scene seems rather more melancholic to me. In this delicate moment, Enrique leaned on ideology to justify his unprepared emotional response. All of Ricardo's past actions—his ferocious vindictiveness against even their closest family and friends, his unwillingness ever to give ground—had made the possibility of being presented with a "white flag" unimaginable. Enrique had sacrificed deeply, and he had struggled against his own nature to achieve Ricardo's single-minded determination. He could not tolerate weakness in the person who had led him down this path—not after so much sacrifice. Surprised by his brother's uncharacteristic expression of remorse, Enrique was flustered and disoriented, but he still opted for ideological consistency, which, in this case, meant distance.

I believe that Ricardo understood all of this. He knew that he had undercut and shamed Enrique in order to support Lucía, María, and Palma. He probably felt that Enrique wanted more recognition, and he knew, intimately, that Enrique could not provide ideological leadership for *Regeneración*, despite his many talents and rigorous work habits. Ricardo had hurt Enrique deeply, and in the face of this and of the likely fact that he would die in prison, Ricardo wanted simply to express the perdurance of their fraternal bond: "*Manito.*" That was all that Ricardo had said.

So much for speculative interpretation. After the "armistice," Ricardo and Enrique no longer dreaded bumping into one another, but they saw each other only rarely in the ten months that they shared at Leavenworth and seem not to have had conversations that were worth reporting, for none was reported on either side. "I don't see Ricardo much—only once a week in the patio, for about half an hour in the afternoon. Sometimes two weeks go by without our seeing one another."[20] Enrique was released from prison a bit early, on good behavior, on September 10, 1920, and he sent Ricardo a telegram of birthday congratulations on his arrival in Los Angeles, possibly to confirm indirectly that he had delivered a message to María: "Just reached Los Angeles my best wishes on your birthday."[21] That was the final communication between the two brothers.

Prison was practically the only thing that the two men now shared. Their sense of privacy and independence with regard to one another at Leavenworth was such that each brother had a separate subscription to the *Los Angeles Times*. The paper's owner, Harrison Gray Otis, who had done his utmost to put Enrique and Ricardo behind bars, now had the added satisfaction of selling them two separate subscriptions.[22]

Ellen White

Ten days after his encounter with Enrique, Ricardo wrote despondently to María. "Time goes by slowly, my dear Maria. So slowly, that sometimes it seems not to move at all. No one has written to me, and I feel like the inhabitant of some distant planet."[23]

It was in that period of isolation, of feeling abandoned by his friends, and with his estrangement from Enrique now compounded by his brother's distant response to his overtures, that a new light emerged in Ricardo's life. Her name was Ellen White—or, rather, Ricardo knew her by that name. Her actual name was Lily Sarnoff. She was a Russian Jew, a poet, anarchist, and white-collar worker, twenty-two years old and living in New York. Ellen White began writing to Ricardo without their ever having met. At that time, Lily Sarnoff recalled (writing in 1966, as an elderly lady, in the only letter we have from her subsequent to those she wrote to Ricardo), she was writing letters to eight or nine imprisoned men, presumably all "Reds." Ellen White was only one of the pseudonyms she used in those letters—Lilly Linng and Alice Donald were two others.[24] Sadly, we do not have Ellen's letters to Ricardo, only his to her. There was something about his situation, their shared ideals, or maybe about his writing, that touched her, and they initiated an intimate correspondence that illuminated Ricardo's final years.

Ricardo himself reflected on this on the first anniversary of their correspondence. Ricardo confessed to Ellen that after María and Lucía, she had been his most constant correspondent. He kept track of each of her letters, reminded her that she had missed sending him her weekly report on two occasions during the past 365 days, and then conjured a kind of Dionysian-Christian language in which he compared his spirit to wine: "It is a wine that in my innocent infancy I pledged to the gods, but having not found them in Heaven, nor on Earth, I now offer it to Man. Is it too strong? Drink in nevertheless, my good Ellen, and thus divinely drunk let us sing, let us sing to life."[25]

We have only the smallest fragment of the correspondence between Ricardo and María for this period—though it was copious—so it is Ellen White who provides the best source on Ricardo's state of mind, and indeed, some of Ricardo's best writing is in the two-page letters that he wrote almost weekly, in English, to Ellen. The platonic relationship between them—established through correspondence and deepened in ties between Ellen and Ricardo's friends and family—made for more philosophical exchanges, since there were only a few practical matters to coordinate between them, except during the final period, when Ellen campaigned for Ricardo's release.

Ellen gave Ricardo something precious: her letters were gratuitous. She gave of herself freely, without asking and with few possibilities of ever receiving anything from Ricardo except another letter. "Have you ever seen a blade of grass all a-trembling under the kisses of the sun, and the whispers of the breeze, and that seems to respond with a quiver to the breath of the flowers and the song of the birds, yet [is] dumb to utter a word of appreciation and thankful-ness for the underserved blessing bestowed upon it?"[26] Ricardo was that blade of grass.

There is a novel waiting to be written about Ellen White. Only once in their correspondence is there a hint that Ellen might have wished to explore a romantic relationship with Ricardo—though of course, their correspondence itself was very romantic. The moment came toward the end of Ricardo's life, when his release from prison and deportation to Mexico seemed imminent. Ellen had arranged to go meet Ricardo—it would be their one and only meeting—and she seemed to want to discuss something with him that had not been discussed in their torrential correspondence.

"You want me to be frank," Ricardo wrote. "This morning puz-zles me, for I thought that our natural esteem had as its basis our mutual frankness. I cannot understand the riddle."[27] Ricardo went on to reaffirm the sincerity of all of his sentiments to her while care-fully signing off "with comradely love." Reading between the lines, one senses that Ellen wanted to witness for herself whether there was a chance of a relationship with Ricardo after his release. She had gone to Kansas especially to meet him. Ellen and Ricardo met for fifteen minutes at Leavenworth Penitentiary October 13, 1922. That would be their only time together.

From the very beginning of her correspondence, Ellen sent Ricardo her poems and wrote to him about her feelings and about the oppression she felt in her white-collar job. Some of her letters were typed at "the place," as she called her office. She often sent Ricardo flowers inside her letters—sometimes a rose, sometimes a pansy. Fern leaves. Candy. A telegram on Christmas Eve. They spoke of art, beauty, nature, hope. They worried about one another's health. Ellen communicated often with Harry Weinberger, Ricardo's lawyer, and she corresponded with his supporters in New York and Philadelphia, also with Enrique after he left prison, as well as with María and Lucía.

They exchanged views on the turn of events in Russia—neither approved of Lenin and Trotsky's turn to dictatorship, and Ellen wor-ried about anarchy being drowned out by the Communists, in New York and elsewhere. Ricardo offered his political views. He believed, for instance, that, despite its shortcomings, anarchists such as Ellen should support the syndicalist movement:

One thing I firmly believe we must not do—to be against it.... I do not believe, however, that syndicalism will ever succeed in breaking up the chains of the capitalist system by itself; that will be the work of a chaotic conglomeration of tendencies; that will be the blind work of the masses moved to action by despair and suffering, but then syndicalism can be the nucleus of the new system of production and distribution, and in this role it will be of great importance.[28]

Ricardo denounced Marxist oppression in Russia. "Tyranny cannot but breed tyranny...sooner or later the Marxian intoxication will fade away, and the sobered minds will adopt the Ideal that in their darkness they scoffed at."[29] On the other hand, he was adamantly against the allied invasions of Russia and believed that strategic alliances with Marxists were needed outside of Russia: "I do not agree in declaring war against the Marxists that in all countries are endeavoring the overthrow of capitalism. This would be to insure a victory to the common enemy. I am for presenting a solid front against it, and then, when the monster is dead, to fight against any imposition the Marxists would pretend to carry on."[30]

In Ricardo's letters, some of the myths that inspired him flash up poignantly. Responding to Ellen's Christmas greetings, Ricardo had a presage of his own destiny: "Now, I must close this letter, my good, dear Ellen, wishing you happy hours on this coming holy days [sic], when the Christian world will celebrate the coming into life of a dreamer who got assassinated by the same ones who have made a god out of him, and grovel at his feet."[31] Ricardo often described himself as a dreamer. Elsewhere, he identified not with Jesus, but with Lazarus, waiting to be raised from the dead. Referring to his feelings after he received one of the only two prison visits that he had gotten over the past two years, he wrote: "They went into Life, while I sank into my coffin—my cell—waiting, like the dead leper, for the sacred words which have to send me forth into Live [sic] again, if ever."[32]

Ricardo saw Ellen, for her part, as a human torch—a modern Prometheus, keeping the spark of hope alive, igniting the ideal. She was a symbol of feminine strength and beauty, an Amazon, or a Christian virgin, braving the lions set on her by her employers: "You stand alone, or better, you stand alone with your faith, that poetic aspiration that you call: the Ideal. No one understands you, no one seems to notice the aureoles that encircle you."[33]

In his prison isolation, Ricardo was at last clear on what was fundamental for him, and it was beauty and love. In one letter—and there are many similar phrases—Ricardo wrote to her: "I could not help laughing a little—only a little—at your lovely naiveté. You say that it is superfluous to speak to me of Beauty, and you say this when it is Beauty what I love most."[34] To Socialist leader Winnie Branstetter, Ricardo explained this again: "Man has wronged the Beautiful. Being the most intelligent animal, the one most favored by Nature, Man has lived in moral and material filth."[35] In another letter to Ellen, he shared an imaginary oration to all of his brothers and sisters: "Brothers," Ricardo wrote, "there is one master in the infinite space, and the only law ruling there is mutual love and mutual help, for everyone to enjoy its individual life, it is necessary that it help the others to enjoy theirs, and that law is gravitation, or in other words, mutual attraction, love."[36]

Ellen and Ricardo shared readings. She sent him books and asked his opinions of her writing. Ricardo in those days wanted only "good books," by which he meant beautiful, deep, artfully written books, but not "art for art's sake." He loved Ellen's letters and her poems and writings, and he believed her to be a very gifted artist. At one point, she asked for criticism, and Ricardo responded:

> You want me to be a critic, my good comrade, and I think it sensible to decline such a function. I cannot judge your productions for one simple reason to wit; that I have forgotten all about rhetorical rules. This *Isle of Dreams* you have sent me is very beautiful.... For me, the merit of the composition does not lie in its more or less skillful arrangements of words and phrases, but in the intensity and quality of the aesthetic emotions it stirs in me.[37]

Much of Ricardo's best advice was proffered to Ellen. In the face of Ellen's insecurities and her claim that she "was not an artist," Ricardo chided her: "Of course you, you are exceedingly modest, and I respect your feelings, my beloved comrade, but please do not pamper that modesty till the extent of allowing it to overpower you, and fetter you as effectively as real impotency does. You must be self-confident, Ellen; Trust yourself!"[38]

In that same letter, Ricardo was lovingly firm with Ellen for dismissing the importance of thought and valuing action over words—the quiet conflict that he had had with Práxedis, but this time in the open:

I do not altogether partake of that Olympic contempt you have for words.... Ungrateful creature. Were not words with a sacred meaning that stole into your privileged brain, and kindled in it the Ideal which now urges you to action? Do you think that the Bastille was converted into a heap of reeking debris by the onrush of the Parisian mob? No, it was crushed down under a mountain of words patiently accumulated in one hundred years of incessant preaching.[39]

And indeed, Ricardo's final love—a love that seems not to have substituted for his feelings for María or Lucía, but that appears to have been unique—was made entirely of words. When, on October 13, 1922, Ellen saw Ricardo at Leavenworth, they had only a few minutes together. Ricardo saw her through the mist of his cataracts. "For how long did my tired eyes behold you? Was it a second? It was just a touch of sympathetic wings in the wilderness.... How grateful I feel to you!"[40]

Movement for Return
Ricardo's two years in Leavenworth combined hope and despondency in a kind of race against the odds. Ricardo had four main sources of hope. On the personal front, the usual relationships (with María, Lucía, and his grandson Carlitos) as well as the unusual (with Ellen White). Politically, though, there were three sources of hope. The first was a general hope for humanity—the imprisoned men shared the sense that the world was on the cusp of a momentous transformation. World War I had destroyed the old system. Revolution was afoot: "God Capital bleeds to death after his last crazy adventure—it is a clear case of suicide—and I hear the rumor of spades digging the grave where an indignant humanity will kick him down."[41] The trick was to hold on.

And he had two sources for his own private hopes for liberation: first, the trend, initiated in 1920, of granting amnesty to political prisoners from World War I—sometimes on the condition of accepting deportation. Eugene Debs, who was also in Leavenworth, was pardoned around Christmas 1921, along with two dozen other political prisoners there. Alexander Berkman, Emma Goldman, Bill Haywood, and others were deported to Russia. Enrique would soon accept deportation to Mexico.

The hope of leaving prison came in two waves. The first hinged on a presidential pardon for political prisoners—mainly "slackers," prisoners held for mailing "obscene" materials or for violating the espionage act. This started to stir around Christmas in 1920, but Ricardo was not in the initial list of people pardoned. His lawyer, Harry Weinberger, stepped up the campaign to get Ricardo included among a new batch of amnestied prisoners, making an argument that combined the fact that Ricardo was a prisoner of conscience with a plea based on his state of health, but his application for executive clemency was denied on March 7, 1921.[42]

In a letter to the leadership of the Socialist Party, Ricardo wrote:

> Thus, my fate is sealed. I have to die within prison walls, for I am not forty-two, but forty-seven years old, my good comrade, and a twenty-one year sentence is a life-term for me.... I never expected to succeed in my endeavor, but I felt it to be my duty to persevere, conscious that sooner or later humanity shall adopt a way of social intercourse with love as a basis.... My present and my future are dark, but I am certain of the bright future which is opened to the human race, and this is my consolation, this certainly comforts me.... As a lover of the Beautiful I exult at this prospect.[43]

Not taking no for an answer, however, Weinberger stepped up the political campaign in favor of a pardon for Ricardo and sent a copy of Ricardo's letter to Winnie Branstetter, who was president of the Socialist Party, to Attorney General Harry Daugherty. In April, Weinberger traveled to Washington to take the case up personally with Daugherty, and he added weight to the case, writing to President Harding that "I am afraid that [America] will continue to be the only country in the world that has political prisoners caused by the late war."[44] Unfortunately, President Harding required prisoners to repent for their pardon, and Ricardo refused to comply. Shortly after reviewing the materials that Weinberger had left with him, Attorney General Daugherty replied that Ricardo was considered a dangerous man who was determined to violate the laws of the United States and that because he showed no sign of remorse, he could not be freed before his first eligibility for parole.[45]

At the same time, Daugherty queried Warden Biddle at Leavenworth on the state of Ricardo's health. The warden seems to have suspected that the whole effort to get Ricardo out on health reasons was not much more than a lawyer's trick. He had Ricardo examined by the prison doctor on two occasions and concluded that "his health seems to be good for a man of his age." Moreover, the warden added, Magón had been given work at the prison library, which was a cushy job as far as prison work went. The long and the short of it was that "Magon is now serving his third term in prison. He is a well educated, cunning Mexican, who has made false statements relative to his physical condition."[46]

Thus, the first route for liberation, a presidential pardon as a prisoner of conscience, failed, and Ricardo's health was not allowed as a mitigating circumstance. However, a second avenue to freedom opened up shortly after that one closed, and it came from Mexico itself. Until Álvaro Obregón's ascent to the presidency at the end of 1920, Mexico's governments had been uniformly hostile to Ricardo and supportive of his imprisonment in the United States. Díaz had tried to extradite him in 1907 and had supported his prosecution for violation of the neutrality laws when that failed. After Ricardo had spurned Madero's offer of incorporation into Mexican electoral politics, Madero, too, had supported the United States in its prosecutions for violation of the neutrality laws. The junta was in prison for most of Victoriano Huerta's presidency, but when it emerged from McNeil Penitentiary, it stood adamantly opposed to both Pancho Villa and Venustiano Carranza.

Carranza's politics toward the junta were both more opportunistic and Machiavellian than Díaz's or Madero's. Until 1917, he did not view the junta as a great threat to his government, but rather as a useful bargaining chip in his relationship with the United States. Carranza moved to shut down radical politicking across the border and to separate the Liberals from any legal status they might enjoy in the United States. Around the same time that he had helped get Ricardo arrested (February 1916), Carranza also had cracked down on the Casa del Obrero Mundial inside Mexico, thus asserting internal control over the union movement while doing his utmost to undermine the free movement of radical unionists across the border. While Carranza was president, Ricardo could hope for no intervention from the Mexican government on his behalf.

All of this changed with the assassination of Carranza and the rise of Obregón. Carranza had defeated Zapatismo and killed Zapata, and he had proved that he could dominate labor and maintain some calm on the U.S. border. Obregón brought the Zapatistas and the labor unions back into government, and thanks to Carranza's previous work, he could do so from a position of power, balancing out the various factions. One of these, led by various unions and by a number of former Liberals who were now in positions of influence, decided to bring pressure on the United States for the release of Mexico's political prisoners.

Mobilizations began by way of the union sector. In May 1921, the Mexican Federation of Labor, the Comité Regional de Obreros Mexicanos (CROM) of San Luis Potosí, wrote to President Harding protesting the imprisonment of Mexican socialists in U.S. jails. Other union confederations followed suit.[47] These letters were preceded by rallies in public squares and so were observed by American consular officers, who tracked the rise of anti-American sentiment, a trend that was of particular concern because of tensions between U.S. oil interests and the Mexican government and the public denunciation of the oil interests by John Kenneth Turner, among others.[48] Mobilization by labor was later followed up by diplomatic efforts by the Mexican Congress and other public institutions on behalf of the prisoners.

In June 1921, Mexico's ambassador to Washington, Manuel Téllez, interceded in favor of the release of the prisoners.[49] Negotiations moved very slowly, though. In September, Weinberger queried Ricardo, asking whether he would agree to be deported from the United States as a condition for his release, to which Ricardo replied in the affirmative, provided he was given some time to gather his effects and help move his family—María, Lucía, Raúl Palma, and Carlitos.[50] Ricardo signed the State Departments' forms to initiate a review of the case under these conditions, stating that because the attorney general "does not put repentance as a condition for release...this is why I signed the document this time."[51] In December 1921, Weinberger was getting ready for a meeting with President Harding on behalf of the various Mexican prisoners and was also preparing to meet with Álvaro Obregón in Mexico City. He believed that Harding was thinking of pardoning the men on Christmas Day.[52]

That, however, did not happen. Weinberger wrote that he thought that this was because the U.S. government was afraid that Magón could make trouble for them in Mexico. Sensitive to these dynamics, Weinberger "hesitated about asking President Obregón because I thought he might refuse because of the ticklish relationship between the United States and Mexico at this time, but he did ask that the Governor of Texas in my Texan case to release the five Mexicans and one American."[53] On the other hand, the Mexican Federation of Labor, with four hundred thousand members, passed a resolution on behalf of the men's release, and the Mexican Congress offered the men a pension, which Ricardo refused on the ground that he could take money offered freely by workers, but he could not take money extracted from them forcibly by the state. In short, the case was building momentum, but the United States was still negotiating recognition of the Obregón government, so movement on the issue was slow, while Ricardo's health continued to deteriorate. By late August 1922, Ricardo himself did not believe that he and Librado would be released at all.[54]

And yet, in September, things seemed to get moving again, and release and deportation seemed imminent, prompting Ellen White's visit to Ricardo in October and her asking him "to be frank." On November 3, 1922, Weinberger wrote to Ricardo that he expected them to be freed and deported within thirty days. Early in November, a new set of mass rallies were held in support of the release of the men. In Veracruz, workers demonstrated, and a twenty-four-hour strike was called. In Progreso (Yucatán), the rally was more massive, and aggressive to the U.S. consulate. Calls were made to boycott U.S. products.[55] Some picketing had started in Washington, too.[56] On November 18, Weinberger wrote to Ricardo saying that the deportation hearings had successfully concluded, and he was waiting only for the pardon attorney to make his report to the attorney general. He believed that release and deportation were imminent.[57]

Twilight

In terms of his personal prospects, Ricardo's two years in Leavenworth can be described as extended pessimism, punctuated by periods of hope about his possible release—hopes that he verbalized only in the final weeks of his life.

During his years in prison, Ricardo's main source of personal despair was his illness. "Health," he had once written to María, "is the only wealth of the poor."[58] It was something to be nursed, nurtured, and cared for. So, for instance, when Ellen White wrote to Ricardo saying that she had "the blues," Ricardo protested at length against giving way to any and every sort of dejection, but he also did not fail to ask whether she was not in fact sick and admonished her about the importance of getting physical exercise.[59]

Ricardo had been seriously ill since 1916. When he arrived in McNeil, the prison doctors concluded that he had high blood sugar, and his cataracts were getting worse. Shortly after Ricardo's arrival in Leavenworth, he was again inspected by an ophthalmologist, who concluded that the cataracts were not yet advanced enough to be operated on—Ricardo would have to wait for his eyesight to worsen, almost to the point of blindness, before being eligible for this operation. In the meantime, though, his eyesight was very bad. By mid-1921, he used a magnifying glass both for reading and for writing. "That I can easily recognize a person about ten feet of me depends on the light, for I can see better in subdued light, under the sunshine I cannot recognize a person in about three feet of me."[60]

Starting around October 1920, Ricardo's overall health became seriously compromised. He developed a cold and a cough that he could not shake. He had constant headaches and toothaches. Ricardo was occasionally spitting up blood and was convinced that he was developing tuberculosis. He had lost weight and began to insist—directly, in prison, and through his lawyer—that he was most grievously ill. By March 1922, he added chest pains to his list of symptoms.

It seems likely that the connection between health and freedom being promoted so actively by Harry Weinberger led to the warden's obstruction of proper medical attention for Ricardo. Weinberger argued that Ricardo had tuberculosis, that he needed sunshine and fresh air, and so he had to be out of prison. When this humanitarian intervention was compounded with the allegation that Ricardo was a prisoner of conscience, jailed in connection to legislation that had expired after World War I, and that the Mexican government itself was no longer adverse to him but that, on the contrary, it actively sought his release, it all added up to a strong argument for freedom.

For this reason, the warden suspected—or claimed to suspect—a ruse on the part of Ricardo, the "cunning Mexican." Warden Biddle had the prison doctor examine Ricardo, and he found no tuberculosis or diabetes and, other than the cataracts, which were not totally impairing and would be operated in good time, "when they ripened," he found Ricardo in good general health. Ricardo was a third-time, unrepentant convict. Why should he be given special considerations?

Ricardo objected strenuously to this diagnosis. If the doctors in McNeil had found high blood sugar, there was no reason to think that his diabetes had magically disappeared. The chemical analysis of his sputum, done in a lab at Topeka, had not been made available to him or to his lawyer. He had lost forty pounds. He was occasionally spitting up blood. He had chest pains. But the prison doctor and the warden stood firm in their views. They found no medical reasons for releasing him.

In June 1922, Librado Rivera was so alarmed by Ricardo's state of health and by the doctors' lack of attention to his ailments that he tried to denounce the situation to the movement's allies. On June 1, he wrote a letter to Gus Teltsch:

> I am sorry to say that his sicknesses have not suffered any favorable change for he is not subject to any medical treatment; so the illnesses are left free to undermine his body, which looks now just a gloomy semblance of what Ricardo was when you knew him years ago. He is out from the hospital; he was discharged three days after he was received in there. According to the physicians of this institution Ricardo is enjoying good health—he has nothing for what to be complaining. But while they are affirming on one side, the facts are denying on the other. The cough has not diminished, he feels fever very often, specially on evenings. He feels a strange malaise in his whole body, besides the cataracts which are totally covering his eyes. It seems that a great conspiracy among natural forces and the tyrants of the poor is what is carrying out the complete destruction of this good Comrade, whose presence of mind and firmness are as high as his endowed intelligence."[61]

This letter was marked "Not Permitted," and it was never delivered. It had been one of several that Librado had sent out denouncing the prison doctor. Thus, Warden Biddle explained to Harry Weinberger, "his mail privileges were suspended indefinitely because he wrote improper letters about the prison physician, the last one after he had been warned by the Warden not to repeat the offense."[62] In late August, Ricardo was haunted with presentiments. "I feel so melancholy," he uncharacteristically wrote to Ellen, "It seems as though the severe colds that greatly torment me are degenerating into a dreadful, loathsome malady.... I know that in one way or other one has to die, but I cannot help feeling sad nevertheless."[63] Still, as late as October 16, 1922, after a new examination, the prison doctor recertified that Ricardo's general physical condition was good and that he was standing his confinement well.[64]

On November 7, Nicolás Bernal, who corresponded regularly with Ricardo during this period, disseminated among the Liberals the contents of a letter that he'd just received from a Mexican just released from Leavenworth. The imprisoned comrade wrote:

> My object is to let you know that Magón is in very critical condition. He is developing tuberculosis and is going blind. The institution's medic, Dr. Yobe, is dissembling, negligent, and a quack. He plays with men's lives as if he were playing with dolls.... Warden W. I. Biddle took Rivera's mailing privileges because in them he referred to Magón's condition. Mr. Biddle has called Magón twice and he has told him: "I'm going to observe you closely in the future, and the first time I catch you sending reports about yourself I'll take away all your time for good behavior and will put you in Section 2."[65]

Ricardo had by that time accumulated more than seven years' time off for good behavior, the writer continued, so that Warden Biddle's threat carried weight. After reproducing this report verbatim, Nicolás Bernal concluded that "all of this shows how urgently we need to redouble our efforts save our comrade, though we don't expect that he'll come out of that brutal prison alive."

Ricardo died at 4:30 A.M. on November 21, 1922. The cause of death was said to be angina pectoris.

Redemption Song

These songs of freedom
Are all I ever had.

Patriation

Because Ricardo's illnesses had been a recurring issue for Warden Biddle, the prison doctor immediately wrote to him, detailing the circumstances of Ricardo's death. Indeed, the day after Ricardo's death, the warden had a letter from the U.S. attorney general asking how reports of Ricardo's death of heart disease "squared with the [earlier] reports of the prison physician."[1] Given this concern, the physician produced a brief explanation. At 4:15 A.M., the prison hospital's night attendant was called in by a guard named Lewis. Ricardo had a strong pain in the heart. The attendant ran back to the hospital for medication, but by the time he returned, Ricardo was dead. "Prompt service was rendered Magon and he was not neglected in any way," the prison doctor declared.[2] Ricardo had had a heart attack, which is always an unpredictable event.

Aside from the doctor's report, the closest testimony that we have of the circumstances of Ricardo's death is a letter from Librado Rivera to Blas Lara, dated January 7, 1923, that is, six weeks after Ricardo's death. The letter was marked "Not Allowed" by the prison authorities and was never delivered. Although Librado's mailing privileges had been reinstated shortly after Ricardo's death, this letter was detained, probably because it complained yet again of the prison's doctor.

Here is Librado, reporting in English, for the benefit of prison censors:

On November 21, at 5 o'clock in the morning, he left us forever. He died just in his same cell, that is all what I at first know. Unfortunately he was removed a few days previously from his first cell, that was close to mine, to another one from where I could not hear him. But we always looked at each other and lined up to go to the dining room and come back to our dark holes as usual. The last time that I saw him was the 20 in the afternoon, 4 1/2 at supper time. That day he came out from his daily work. We talked about our possible release if the initiated movement of Progreso, Yuc could be carried out all over Mexico as well as all over the world developing its initial program of boycotting etc., for we had considered that that was the only possible way to gain freedom and set a firm foot for the future in our struggle for a better world.[3]

Librado then notes bitterly that the same doctor who had only just recently denied that Ricardo had a heart condition and who had asserted that Ricardo was in good enough health to live out his twenty-one-year prison term pronounced the cause of death to be heart failure.

Poor Ricardo did all he could in order to be cured. He was affected not only by heart disease, he was suffering from diabetes also, tuberculosis, cataracts, etc. Although he never knew that he was affected by heart disease, nevertheless he always felt keen attacks in his heart, and complained very often for it, but he never was heard.

I myself did all I could to save him; I went to the point of breaking the rules and laws of the prison—by doing so I was cruelly punished—but all was useless. I could not save so dear life. What the laws could mean to me if I could save my friend's precious life? My human sentiments and love for humanity are above every law. The law is made in order to protect the rich's interest. It is a whip for the poor.[4]

Later, the story that Ricardo had been murdered in his cell gained such currency that Librado himself chose to deny that he had died due to medical negligence. But let us track the corpse before following the myth.

Los Angeles
There were offers by various supporters to help pay for Ricardo's burial expenses in Kansas, but his body was shipped by rail to Los Angeles, to María, and it arrived there a few days after Ricardo's

death. But already, another drama was unfolding between María and Enrique and their respective factions, whose rivalries again came out—as these things do—around the matter of funerals, commemorations, and legacies. By the time Ricardo's corpse arrived to the Bresee Brothers funeral home on Ninth Street and Figueroa, November 25, 1922, there was drama afoot regarding its management. We have only Enrique's version of the event, but its is quite telling, since it comes from letters written to Rafael García in the days in which the action was transpiring and so is not quite as prone to forgetfulness or falsification as later memorializations.

María was keeping Enrique in the dark as regarded Ricardo's body's whereabouts and the day and time of his its arrival in Los Angeles. She was planning to accept a petition from the Mexican government, made by way of Congressman Antonio Díaz Soto y Gama, to have Ricardo buried in Mexico. But that gesture was understood by Enrique and others as tantamount to handing the body to President Obregón in order to buttress his power. One militant, Epigmenio Zavala, came crying to Enrique: "Manito, don't let them take him to the government," he pleaded.[5]

The image of what had happened at Peter Kropotkin's funeral in Russia was fresh in the minds of the Mexican anarchists: a state funeral, orchestrated by Lenin, had been a nail in the coffin of Russian anarchism, which first had suffered implacable Communist persecution and now had to live with the state's symbolic appropriation of its most revered leader. Similarly, President Álvaro Obregón had already wrenched control over a key sector of Mexico's labor movement from the anarchists, and now, they feared, he would use Ricardo's body to the same effect as Lenin had used Kropotkin's. Enrique received a telegram from the Mexico's anarchist-leaning Confederación General del Trabajo, which was not in Obregón's control, asking him to avoid turning the body in to the president.[6] He took that telegram to María, to prove to her that her plan amounted to handing Ricardo over to Obregón.

Fortunately for Enrique, Lucía Norman agreed with him for once, so María desisted from ceding the corpse to the Mexican government. Enrique then sent telegrams to unions and newspapers: "We will not turn Ricardo's body in to any government, only to the workers." Enrique's move of going public in the family's rejection of the Mexican government's offer was designed to cajole independent unions into action and to turn Ricardo's funeral in Mexico into a statement of independence with regard to the state. However, the unions seemed to be taking their time about it. So what to do with the body in the interim?

The truth was, they weren't sure. Burying Ricardo in the United States was problematic for several reasons. First, Enrique wrote to Rafael, María was very anxious that Ricardo not be interred in the United States, "the country in which he had been persecuted and murdered." Many comrades agreed.[7]

Moreover, Mexico's workers had only recently organized several mass demonstrations for the liberation of Ricardo, Librado, and the Texas Martyrs, while the movement in the United States had been so deeply repressed by President Wilson's witch hunt and the nationalism that accompanied World War I that despite significant solidarity around Ricardo's death, there was not much hope of stirring up a real movement, whereas moving back to Mexico and continuing the fight there was now a real and viable possibility.

The question was, how to bury Ricardo in Mexico with the desired political mobilizations, but without turning him over to the state. There was no quick solution to this problem, because Mexico's union movement was not reacting. By November 28, Ricardo's body was starting to decompose, so the group decided to take it to the cemetery, thinking initially that they would have it cremated, but at the last minute, the comrades made a collection of $100, which allowed them to embalm the body and preserve it perhaps for a month, until the complex politics of the Mexican event could be settled.[8]

Given all of this, the possibility of interring Ricardo in Los Angeles resurfaced, and at a certain point, it became clear that a Los Angeles funeral at least needed to be observed, regardless of the final destination of the corpse. After all, the men had lived in or around Los Angeles since 1907. Their families were in Los Angeles. Ricardo's beloved grandson, Carlos, Enrique's brood, the former inhabitants of the Edendale commune, the tribes of Los Angeles Socialists, trade unionists, and anarchists—they needed to commemorate the event.

So a memorial with a temporary depositing of the corpse in Evergreen Cemetery was organized. The trouble was that by that point, Enrique was feeling very ill himself. His heart was troubling him. He was unable to do the organization, and María was likewise distraught, and Teresa was ill, so Enrique handed the organization of the event to comrades Kotch, Kneffler, and Lerner so that they "organize the burial together with our Spanish-speaking comrades, so that it be an international protest, and that they accompany the body and deposit it in a vault at that cemetery."[9]

When the day of the funeral came, Teresa and Enrique got out of their sickbeds—they had to support one another in their weakness—in order to assist. According to Enrique, there was still fear of repression of Reds by the government, a fact that compounded by rain, diminished the numbers present at the funeral—both of foreigners and of Mexicans. Still, on December 1 at 3:00 P.M., around three hundred and fifty people congregated at the cemetery to celebrate funerary honors. The program began with a collective singing of "El Hijo del Pueblo" around Ricardo's body. Teresa's daughter Estela and three other girls

> stood guard (two on the sides, one at the head and the other at the feet). They were dressed in white, with broad red sashes crossing their breast and floating to the side, and red hats. Next to them, Enrique Jr., also in white and with a red sash across his breast. All of them held flowers in their hands, while many garlands and flowers rested on the casket, and were piled on the sides. [10]

There was a speech pronounced by a girl, Isabel Rangel, and another, in English, by Mr. H. Bell. Then a funerary oration by F. Velarde and another one by Enrique, followed by yet another by his wife, Teresa Arteaga. Finally, they all sung the "Marseillaise," "each in his language: Spanish, English, Yiddish, Russian, Polish, Italian, etc,"[11] and the corpse was deposited in vault number 16, while matters regarding Ricardo's final resting place were negotiated.

As is clear from these details, Enrique's clan had taken charge of the Los Angeles funeral. Not one of the speeches were given by the leaders of Ricardo's faction—María, Lucía, or Palma—although all were seasoned speechmakers. Carlitos is not mentioned as one of the children flanking the casket. Were any of them there at all? It is hard to say. Possibly there was a second Los Angeles funeral about which we know nothing. Possibly they were there, but waiting for real interment in Mexico, since María, in particular, was adamantly against a U.S. burial. Possibly they simply stayed home.

In his letter to Rafael, Enrique mentions that Mrs. Shea (Lázaro Gutiérrez de Lara's wife, Hattie) was at the funeral. What was she feeling at the funeral of a man to whom she and Lázaro had once been so attached, but who had so maligned her husband? It's impossible to know.

Lázaro

Four years earlier, around the time that Ricardo, Librado, and Enrique were convicted, Sonora's governor and chief of military operations, General Plutarco Elías Calles, had sent a telegram to President Venustiano Carranza that read as follows:

> I am honored to inform you that Lieutenant Colonel Camargo captured the famous agitator Lázaro Gutiérrez de Lara today, when he was trying to enter Sonora by the Altar District.
> I already ordered that he be executed immediately.
> Respectfully,
> The Chief of Military Operations.[12]

Lázaro had gone missing since the first days of January, and rumors of his death circulated from the very day of his execution, on January 8, 1918. Letters of concern from Lázaro's wife, Hattie, his brother, doctor Felipe Gutiérrez de Lara, who was then living in exile in San Antonio, and from numerous trade unionists prompted Arizona's governor, George W. P. Hunt, to send a letter of inquiry to his Sonoran counterpart. Gutiérrez de Lara was in fact friendly with Governor Hunt, for he was a vice president of Arizona's State Federation of Labor and had been a key player in the Mexican miners' recent and bitter strikes in Metcalf and Morenci. Hunt, for his part, was a rare bird in Arizona politics: he was prolabor and rather sympathetic to Mexicans.[13] According to one source, Hunt received his reply from one of Calles's subordinates, who responded with a kind of laconic "Sicilian message": "De Lara was killed while crossing the district of Altar. General de Lasa sends you affectionate greetings from General P. Elias Calles."[14]

Why had Lázaro gone to Mexico? The border papers that covered the shocking story of his execution provide two different, though not incompatible versions. According to the Los Angeles *El Heraldo de México*, Lázaro had decided to go on a kind of self-motivated diplomatic mission to "establish a better understanding between this people and that, an endeavor that he thought he could carry out by way of public speeches and conferences, as well as interviews with businessmen and professionals, seeking to broaden commercial relations between the two countries, especially between Southern California and Mexico's west coast."[15]

Probably closer to the mark, Felipe Gutiérrez de Lara declared to *La Prensa* of San Antonio that his brother had gone to Sonora "with the purpose of discussing matters related to the strikes occurring in some of Arizona's mining centers with the workers of that state [Sonora]."[16] Lázaro had contacts in Cananea and other Sonoran mines that went back to his participation in the 1906 strike, and his leadership among both the Western Federation of Miners, who had had bitter strikes in 1915, 1916, and 1917, and the Mexican strikers who had been deported from Douglas in 1917 meant that Lázaro was in a position to try to coordinate labor policy across the border.

But Lázaro chose a dangerous moment to try this. On the American side, unwanted border crossings had been rigidly discouraged since the 1913 Texas Martyrs affair, and now that the U.S. government had settled with Carranza, it was even less open to the political activity of loose canons such as Lázaro. But as inauspicious as things were for Lázaro was on the U.S. side, it was in the end the Mexicans who did not hesitate to pull the trigger. At the time of Lázaro's crossing, Sonora was in a very turbulent situation, with governor Calles undermanned, fighting a Yaqui rebellion, and struggling to avoid a break in his alliance with the local unions.

On the very same day that Lázaro, a mysterious Russian colleague, and their guide crossed the Altar desert to Saric, Sonora, Calles had wired Carranza stating that the local situation had worsened to such a degree that it would become untenable: "I now consider it an absolute necessity to declare a state of emergency [*estado de sitio*] in Sonora, suspending individual guarantees. Without this measure, the situation will become very difficult."[17]

Since 1916, Carranza had suspended the rights of the workers' unions who had been his key allies in 1915 against Villa, declaring martial law against a general strike. Although Lázaro had been Carranza's agent in the United States, doing propaganda for the revolution at a time when the Wilson government supported Pancho Villa, Lázaro was now operating as an independent union agitator with ties and resources in the United States that could conceivably complicate the delicate balance in Sonora. Once before, with Madero, Lázaro had found himself persecuted by the very regime that he had helped instate, and it had twice landed him in jail. Now he was up against a more ruthlessly pragmatic opponent. On January 18, 1918, Lázaro Gutiérrez de Lara was unceremoniously placed before a firing squad and shot.

The only indirect testimony of the event that we have was taken down by Ethel when she was an elderly lady: "According to the story which was told to Ethel D. Turner in the home of Lic. Rafael Trujillo of Los Angeles, the wife of Lic. Trujillo was in Saric at the time. She saw De Lara marched by soldiers to the graveyard. She followed, and placed a sheet over his dead body."[18]

This was the end of the man that Ricardo had called a Judas and whose execution Ricardo had himself ordered in 1911. This was a man that Ricardo had lambasted as "the working class's worst enemy."[19] Yet Lázaro had risked his life to produce Turner's exposé of Mexican slavery; he had gone to battle alongside Madero, despite being a peace-loving man that Ethel once described as "emotionally not constituted for military warfare.... He could not bear even to pick a flower, so sensitive was he toward all living things. This was not a pose; it was very real."[20] Lázaro had faced persecution in the United States and in Mexico, despite having the education, the linguistic skills, and the talent to make a decent living. At an earlier time, before Ricardo had denounced Lázaro as a traitor, Ricardo had written to María calling the man unlucky: Lázaro was a "victim of his bad star."[21]

What was Mrs. Shea feeling at Ricardo's funeral—at the funeral of a man who had shared so many battles with her and her husband, but who had publicly excoriated her husband as a traitor to his class? What did she feel about her husband's sacrifice? Impossible to say. We only know that Mrs. Shea burned all of Lázaro's papers—a harsh act for the wife of an intellectual.[22]

The Return of Ricardo

Having bought some time for Ricardo's funeral, thanks to the science of embalming, Enrique continued to negotiate with the Mexican labor confederations—the progovernment Confederación Regional Obrera de México (CROM), the anarchist Confederación General del Trabajo (CGT), and the independent rail workers' union—and worked to stoke competition between them so that they might finally spring into action. Enrique also provided the unions with details of what would be needed in order to carry out a proper funerary pilgrimage of repatriation—the requirements of the sanitation department, tickets for María to accompany the corpse, money for meals and hotels for the rest of the entourage, and so on. A total of $740 U.S. would be needed. "Finally, I called their attention to the possibility that stung by my rejection of their proposal to hand Ricardo's body to them, the Obregón government might place obstacles for the return of the body."[23] Enrique encouraged the unions to consider a general strike if they did in fact meet with government opposition regarding funeral plans.

Not all the unions immediately rallied to the cause. The CGT initially responded to Enrique's telegram saying that they were fine with the funeral that Ricardo had received in Los Angeles and were not bent on bringing the corpse back to Mexico.[24] Nevertheless, when they learned that their rival, the CROM, might jump into the void, they changed their tune. Enrique succeeded in using the competition between the unions to get the workers to rally around Ricardo, and in the end, the Los Angeles groups jointly decided to hand the corpse over to the rail workers' union.

In this way, although Enrique and María and their respective clans did not turn Ricardo over to the government, they did not marginalize the government from participating, either. The CROM, which was an arm of Obregón's power, was in fact key to bringing the anarchist CGT on board for the funerary pilgrimage, so they were in the mix practically from the start. And there was more. President Álvaro Obregón's conflict with the Catholic Church was coming to a head in those days, and he expelled the papal nuncio, Monsignor Fillippi, practically at the same time that Ricardo's corpse arrived in Mexico City—the Obregón government thus supported the pro-Ricardo rallies, in part as a show of popular force against the church.[25] Also, in January 1923, Obregón was still involved in some saber rattling vis-à-vis the United States, which had not yet recognized his government. Supporting an event that would inevitably turn anti-American was a way of rallying popular support prior to engaging in diplomatic negotiation. Thus, Obregón sent a much remarked-upon wreath for Ricardo's casket, and a funerary oration for Ricardo was pronounced in Congress by Deputy

Antonio Díaz Soto y Gama. The notion that Ricardo's return would pit the labor movement against the government was conceptually flawed—Enrique and María both needed the government unions and support, even to mobilize the anarchist leaning CGT.

Unfortunately, there are no extant documents on Ricardo's return from María or her tribe, who accompanied Ricardo on the train to Mexico City, and Enrique did not accompany the body, because he was being deported from the United States at the time and had to organize his family's permanent departure. So the only testimony that we have from one of the group is from correspondence of Rafael García to Enrique, since Rafael and Nicolás Bernal had recently moved to Mexico City and set up a commune on its outskirts, in Ticomán.

Rafael's first letter on this subject was mailed in January 15, shortly after Ricardo's body arrived to Mexico City (Figure A.1).

> Engine number 910 came in with the front draped in a black and red flag, and with smaller red and black decorations below the cabin window. It was conducted by the machinist Eduardo Vanegas, and the stoker Emilio Rodríguez, whom I greeted with utmost pleasure. Behind the locomotive was a cargo car with the body. It had lanterns fixed on the side and head of the coffin, and it was also decorated with red and black sashes. There was a multitude of big garlands and bouquets surrounding and encroaching the coffin.[26]

Rafael and Nicolás Bernal had been trying to work the Mexico City end of things in the hope of orchestrating a significant political result from Ricardo's interment. However, at the time of the corpse's arrival, Rafael was still skeptical about outcomes. Animosity between various labor unions and confederations made coordination very difficult, and sometimes Rafael despaired of the unions' lack of initiative. Still, on that January 15, he was surprised that participation picked up steam at the last minute and that there were contingents and standards from about thirty labor delegations, along with a large number of people.[27] Those who received the body were mostly silent or spoke in low voices, with indignation. The twenty-block stretch from the railroad station at Buenavista to the salon where Ricardo's body would be exhibited became a march, with about a thousand workers behind the body and a growing mob of *populacho* on the sides. The procession was headed by about fifty

Figure A.1 Train that transported Ricardo's
corpse. Courtesy of the Casa de El Hijo
del Ahuizote, Mexico City.

railroad workers who had brought the corpse in from Ciudad Juárez, alongside members of the press and Rafael García.

Rafael then described his impression when the lid was taken off the casket and Ricardo's body was exposed for viewing. He and Enrique were still deeply resentful and estranged from Ricardo, and especially from María, Lucía, and Raúl Palma. I think it is that feeling of estrangement, mixed with a deeper love and admiration, that comes forth in this macabre description:

> When they opened the lid, the aspect of Ricardo's face seemed so strange that it had no resemblance to the person he had been in life. Since the body has dried out a bit, his teeth were bared and his skin was a lot darker than it was. He had an ugly countenance, bearing a smile that was somewhere between the serious and the cynical that gave him the appearance of a vulgar and lower-class bandit [un mero bandidazo de baja estofa y de proceder vulgar]. The poor man looks even uglier when seen from the salon's upper balcony. His appearance is of a scandalous drunkard whose just hurled some sarcastic gibe. He has nothing of the noble, serious, and friendly countenance of Ricardo in his day. Of course, all of this is because of the body's decomposition, and so I told all of those who were surrounding me that Ricardo's face now had no similarity to the one who lived.[28]

Rafael had lived in the Edendale commune. The comment is thus written from a space of deep recognition in which Rafael was in a situation of having to explain things to the people surrounding him, for whom Ricardo had, until that moment, been more myth than man. As people began to mill around Rafael for explanations—no one in Mexico had dealt with Ricardo for almost twenty years—Rafael also pulled out a picture of Enrique to show them: "Since people were crowding me in as I explained things to those whom I knew, I took the occasion to show them your most recent picture, and they were all surprised to see you so drained."

Second Funeral

Rafael begins his report on the funeral itself with a note of foreboding regarding the state's control over Ricardo. Rafael was unpleasantly surprised to discover that the railroad workers' leadership had made a last-minute decision to stage a silent funerary march, rather than a vocal and rambunctious "manifestación viril."

The decision was suspicious, because as Rafael put it, the rail workers who had accompanied Ricardo's body on its journey from Ciudad Juárez to Mexico City had practically lost their voices from so much shouting and speech making along the way. At Torreón, for instance, the rally had been held in front of the American Consulate, and the speaker had so inflamed the crowd that the consul had to shut himself indoors.[29] Demonstrations in Chihuahua City and Aguascalientes, too, had been massive (Figures A.2 and A.3).

But the cause of the rail workers' decision was soon apparent to Rafael. In order to avoid Catholic protests on the day that Obregón had expelled the papal nuncio, he had banned all political rallies for the day, so Ricardo's event would have to take the form of a funeral procession. But what was also clear to Rafael was that the union leadership had heard and respected Obregón's demands and requirements: "If instead of the reigning opposition between working-class groups there had been even a little solidarity and agreement, a mere signal would have been enough to have paralyzed the whole nation for a day of protest."[30]

Even so, the event was massive and nothing short of impressive. It was moving for Rafael to see how their anarchist ideal, which had been unpronounceable for so many years, could now be expressed openly, and with real force. Moreover, the workers were not abiding by their promise of silence—they did not make speeches against the government, true, but the procession did find its way to the American Embassy on its way to the municipal graveyard. A man named Quintero, whom Rafael described as a "revolucionario de opereta," an "operetta revolutionary," pronounced a burning speech in front of the embassy "alluding to Ricardo and Enrique as the precursors of the Mexican Revolution and cheering *Regeneración* as a beacon of light that illuminated the whole world with its elevated ideals, a fact that made it, and its editors, immortal."[31]

Already here the sweet was mixed in with the bitter. Ricardo and Enrique were being honored by a revolution that they were supposed to have prefigured, yes, but that they had not shaped. But Mexicans can be very sensitive to the power of this kind of melancholic truth, and in this case, they turned themselves over to it, fully and fervently.

By the time the procession began, it was three in the afternoon, and the salon and a long stretch of road was full of people. The number of

Figure A.2 Crowds Receiving Ricardo's Body
in Aguascalientes. The pilgrimage began in
Ciudad Juárez and made stops in Chihuahua
City, Torreón, Aguascalientes, and Mexico City.
Courtesy of the Casa de El Hijo del Ahuizote,
Mexico City.

Figure A.3 Salvador Rodríguez, railroad union
leader, haranguing the crowd, diagonally
across from the U.S., consulate in Torreón,
Coahuila. Courtesy of the Casa de El Hijo
del Ahuizote, Mexico City.

garlands was such that they were stacked one on top of the other on all sides of the salon. The smallest of these was three feet high, and the largest, offered by the Railroad Workers Confederation, was more than ten feet tall. When the procession was formed, there was such an agglomeration that the demonstrators found their places with difficulty, as did the cars of the various workers' delegations, that were transporting the flowers.[32]

Rafael was most moved by the banner of the contingent that took the lead in the procession, a group of "young communists and peasant comrades" that had improvised a great red banner that read: "He died for Anarchy." But Rafael also did not fail to notice that prominent among the floral offerings were a number of large and prominently labeled garlands from the "generous masters of politics"—including President Álvaro Obregón, Generals Plutarco Elías Calles and Adolfo De la Huerta, and a number of the "festive boys" of the Chamber of Deputies and the Senate.

The funerary cortege began at 3:00 P.M. and wound its way from downtown Mexico City to the outskirts, at the Panteón Francés. María, Lucía, and grandson Carlitos were in a car behind the hearse (Figure A.4). The procession took more than four hours to arrive to the cemetery, and it was night by the time that Ricardo was finally interred. Many speeches were pronounced, some of them deeply impressing even the jaded Rafael García. Floral offerings were piled so high on the grave that they made a veritable monument.

Zapata Lives, Ricardo Was Murdered

Ricardo died alone, with no witnesses other than perhaps a prison medic. The official cause of his death—heart failure—was an embarrassment for Leavenworth's warden and a liability for the U.S. attorney general, as well as for the State Department, since the U.S. embassy and consulates in Mexico now had to face intense anti-American demonstrations. Within the United States, it fueled union protests with regard to other remaining "Reds" in prison.[33] Indeed, the indignation produced by Ricardo's death in Leavenworth also gave the Obregón government some leverage to the extent that it could whip up or temper anti-American sentiment at a time when the United States and Mexico were involved in delicate diplomatic negotiations over reparations to U.S. citizens for damages incurred

Figure A.4 María Brousse descending from the train to join the Mexico City funerary cortège. Courtesy of Casa de la Hijo del Ahuizote, Mexico City.

to their property during the revolution. Ricardo's death in prison had been vocally foretold by various organizations since the time of his conviction, and the deterioration of Ricardo's health had produced letters of concern and campaigns for his removal from prison that had never been heeded. Ricardo's heart attack proved beyond a doubt that prison authorities had deliberately neglected his condition.

Still, Ricardo's survivors felt that this explanation was not entirely satisfying, and soon, a rumor began to circulate with such insistence that even those who had initially believed the medical report—including Librado Rivera and Enrique Flores Magón—came around to subscribing to it. Ricardo, it was said, had been murdered. It was simply not credible that the man died when he seemed finally just about to be released. Plus, there was an additional suspicious circumstance: a few weeks before his death, Ricardo had been moved from a cell that was right next to Librado's to another cell across the aisle from him, where the men could see one another, but not hear each other. And, above all, there was the will to assert a motive: the American government was unwilling to see such a dangerous man walk free in Mexico. Ricardo had to have been assassinated.

The story that began to circulate was that Ricardo had been murdered by a prison guard and that his assassination had caused such rage in prison that one of the Mexicans there, a man named Martínez, took his revenge and stabbed that prison guard to death. The story is apocryphal, because the prisoner Joe Martínez stabbed and killed prison guard A. H. Leonard on November 14, 1922—that is, one week before Ricardo's death—but the rumor that Ricardo had been murdered soon became an established social fact that could not be doubted.[34]

There was, I think, some complex work of collective mourning that was invested in this interpretation of Ricardo's death. Assassination emphasized Ricardo's power vis-à-vis the United States. The man was very frail and practically blind at the time of his death, the movement that he led had only limited influence in Mexico, and it had none in the United States. But by asserting assassination, rather than death by negligence, the living power of the ideal was emphasized.

And there was more. Ricardo's imprisonment—like the imprisonment of Librado and the Texas Martyrs—produced a feeling of guilt among revolutionaries who were, as Antonio Díaz Soto y Gama said in his funerary oration, enjoying the rich banquet of the revolution. Assassination by American hands assuaged that guilt, since it provided Ricardo's survivors with a collective identity and purpose. It also allowed divisions within the movement to be papered over in order to emphasize unity in the cause, instead. But all of these benefits came at a price: Ricardo's humanity, which had once been so emphatically asserted in the Liberals' rejection of *personalismo*—the sense, once articulated by Tomás Sarabia, that Ricardo was simply one more comrade—was set aside in favor of the image of Ricardo as haloed martyr.

There is a telling comparison to be made between Ricardo's case and that of the other great martyr for "Land and Freedom," Emiliano Zapata. Zapata was shot in an ambush, in front of many witnesses, and his body was displayed for public viewing in Cuautla, with photos circulating widely in the press. Nevertheless, a rumor soon surfaced to the effect that the man who had been exhibited was not in fact Zapata, but a *compadre* who had taken the bullet for him. The continued vitality of Zapata's movement was asserted in the idea that Zapata lived—and that Zapatista communities were still his latent supporters, awaiting his second coming.

An assassination by the Mexican state (Zapata's case) was seen as the defeat of a powerful movement. It had to be denied. An assassination by the American government (Ricardo's case) was proof of the power of a leader and a movement that was struggling to claim the place that it had lost almost from the start of the revolution, while the assassination also absolved the shared guilt of the revolution's victors.

Ellen White

Ellen White was in Kansas City, Missouri, when Ricardo died, barely five weeks after the two had finally met. Ellen was deeply distraught by the news and tried to organize a memorial for Ricardo. But as she reminisced decades later, Kansas City was not "a very favorable place for such a meeting." So Ellen went to Hobo Hall, where the hoboes congregated. It was supposed to be a dangerous part of town, but Ellen found that "though they were rough men, they were really more courteous than some of the more polished people."[35]

The hoboes helped Ellen book a space in the basement of a church, and a memorial was held. Ellen looked for speakers and got a couple who were Communists, but who knew or cared little about Ricardo.

"The men helped, but the chairman I got for the meeting turned out to be what I didn't like—or wanted—he spoke more for Russia (you remember it was 1922)—than for Ricardo—I felt sorry I had asked him, I thought I could have done better myself.... But it was still a memorial meeting for R. F. M. the only one around that vicinity."[36]

Enrique

Although Rafael García complained of lack of unity in the labor movement, the union leadership, in turn, was itself surely disconcerted by the lack of unity and political jockeying among Ricardo's mourners, a fact that was apparent to them almost immediately. Ricardo's body was escorted to Mexico by María, Lucía, and Raúl Palma, but also by two of Enrique's stepdaughters, Esperanza and Ana. The night of their arrival in Mexico City, Ana and Esperanza met with Rafael, who then reported back to Enrique that their journey had been very good, "except for the hostile attitude that María and Lucía displayed toward you, even in their conversations with the comrades leading the convoy."[37]

In the weeks and months that followed, the conflict would move from the realm of gossip and hearsay into the public, with manifestos published by María against Enrique and by the Enriquistas against María. In June 1923, María published an open letter in *Excelsior* in which she said that Enrique had never been prominent in the fight against Díaz, that his work for *Regeneración* had never amounted to much, and that he never supported Ricardo's cause, either materially or intellectually. The only thing Enrique ever wanted, she claimed, was to live at the expense of workers' contributions, using the halo of his martyred brother for his own benefit. María warned all workers' organizations against those who sought to profit from the prestige of The Martyr, and Enrique specifically was said to be at the head of the group.[38] María signed herself as Ricardo's widow—"María B. viuda de Flores Magón"—so the matter of control over Ricardo's legacy was explicitly in play.

The slanderous parts of María's attacks on Enrique (that he had never contributed to *Regeneración*, that he had never struggled against Díaz, and that he sought only to live off the workers) were mixed with accusations that were true and that must have been both painful and shameful to Enrique. Specifically, María charged that Enrique had left *Regeneración*, taking a contingent of its members with him, and that since the 1918 split, Enrique had not looked after or even inquired after his brother, and yet now he presented himself as a chief mourner and heir. Enrique's split with Ricardo, which was known in Los Angeles, where both Ricardistas and Enriquistas were marginal to the Mexican Revolution as it progressed, was much harder to explain back in Mexico, where Ricardo and Enrique were hailed as long-lost leaders from the past, revolutionary martyrs, and where Enrique wished to stress that he and Ricardo were equally important and part of the same thing. Indeed, even to this day, school children are taught about "the Flores Magón brothers" and are generally hard put to distinguish between Jesús, Ricardo, and Enrique.

On the other hand, María, too, was mobilizing Ricardo's prestige for her own purposes, and that prompted counterattacks. So, for example, María tried to unauthorize the publication of Ricardo's letters and works by the anarchist group Ricardo Flores Magón, led by Nicolás Bernal. This prompted a riposte from that group that included reminding everyone that María was not Ricardo's real wife, nor was Lucía his daughter, and that they were using Ricardo's prestige to pervert his ideals as an anarchist, which included preventing the dissemination of his work for free, because it belonged to the proletariat that had paid integrally for *Regeneración* and in no case to María. Letters of support from venerable moral leaders such as William C. Owen and Librado Rivera showed, too, that the split with María had far-reaching effects.[39]

Printed attacks were being distributed by each of the parties. So, for instance, Enrique was deported to Mexico with his family in March 1923, and he and Teresa immediately resumed their militancy, touring hotbeds of political activity such as Veracruz City. When they arrived in that port, Enrique wrote to Rafael asking for 100 copies of the manifesto that the Los Angeles comrades had published "against the whore" [*contra la ramera*], by which he meant María.[40]

Gaining moral authority over the movement and control over the Flores Magón label overshadowed everything else for both factions at that point. Thus, even when Rafael wrote to Enrique informing him of Lucía's premature death, in August 1923, Enrique's response was anything but sympathetic. He was concerned above all with severing María's claim to being Ricardo's heiress:

> Thanks for the information on Lucía's death. Did you notice the way the funeral notice was written up? It doesn't mention the stinking name

of the slut at all [*el nombre hediondo de la ramera*], but it does state: "Her parents wish to participate, etc." "Her parents"? Which parents? Why not "her mother"? And they added "Flores Magón" to the name of Lucía Norman. Did she do that in order to get people to believe that she is one of our daughters, and so get some contributions? The old lady is such a scoundrel that I think her capable of making the best even of her own sorrow to get money.[41]

In that same letter, though, Enrique cheered the Los Angeles "tribe" with his own political success in Veracruz, where he had befriended the tenant movement leader Herón Proal and had been handed the editorship of the movement's journal, *La Guillotina*. As proof of a popularity that was, in the exiles' fantasy, their due, Enrique joyously shared the lyrics of a rumba that had been composed in his honor and that was all the rage around town:

Rumba Flores Magon
(composed by Pedro Hernández)

Cuando vino Flores Magón
A la Heróica Veracruz
Toda la gente decía
Ya llegó otro luchador.

Todo el pueblo grita '¡Viva Flores Magón!'
Todo el pueblo grita ¡Viva!

Flores Magón se fue al campo
Con gusto y alegría
Para hacer la propaganda
Contra de la burguesía

Todo el pueblo grita '¡Viva Flores Magón!
Todo el pueblo grita '¡Viva!'

Ya llegó Flores Magón
con su bandera en la mano
Y se llevó la simpatía
Del pueblo veracruzano

Todo el pueblo grita, ¡Viva Flores Magón!
Todo el pueblo grita, '¡Viva!'

La que ustedes escucharon
La rumba del compañero,
Debemos comunicarles
Que la compuso tío Pedro.

Todo el pueblo grita, 'Viva Flores Magón!'
Todo el pueblo grita, '¡Viva!'

[When Flores Magón came
To the Heroic Veracruz
Everyone proclaimed
That a fighter had arrived.

All the people shout
Long live Flores Magón!
All the people shout Viva!

Flores Magón went to the country
With happiness and good cheer
In order to make propaganda
Against the bourgeoisie

All the people shout (etc.)

Flores Magón has arrived
With his flag in hand
And he won over the sympathy
Of the people of Veracruz

All the people shout (etc.)

What you have all just heard
The rumba of the comrade
We must communicate
Was composed by tío Pedro.

All the people shout (etc.)][42]

Still, the harm of open fissures over the Flores Magón inheritance was done. As Librado Rivera put it in his letter from prison to Nicolás Bernal's Ricardo Flores Magón Group: "The arguments that are being brandished against you are known to me. They ring in my ears like the echo of a long nightmare." Librado recalled that

Ricardo, too, had been accused of making fortunes off the backs of the workers and concluded:

> Nothing makes the struggle harder for we who suffer the heavy load of the oppressors than to triumph over obstacles that are frequently placed by the oppressed themselves.
>
> The failure of Mexico's revolution is due to these contentions among ourselves—they are mean-spirited differences that the bourgeoisie takes advantage of in order to get stronger and to tighten our yoke even more.[43]

For Enrique, the path to building a sense of concord eventually led him to embrace the role of memorializer, myth maker, and guardian of the flame. Enrique became the founder and president of the Precursores de la Revolución Mexicana, an organization that was an arm of the revolutionary state (Figure A.6). And María's strategy was not so very different, since she continued to be active in a political life that included association with various government officials, albeit from Colima, and so with no very visible role. Her son-in-law, Raúl Palma, was careful to preserve the final issues of *Regeneración*, where Ricardo had praised him to the skies. He became an aid to the Zapatista General Gildardo Magaña, who was then governor of Michoacán.

By the 1930s, María and Enrique were back on speaking terms and were equally interested in the memorialization of Ricardo. Thus, María wrote to her "Dear brother Enrique":

> I like very much that you criticize the newly minted so-called revolutionaries who are taking advantage of the sacrifices made by the true martyrs of the revolution. I hope that Cárdenas listens and that the remains of my Ricardo are put where they deserve to be. They are very sad and ignored at the French Cemetery, but the more ignored he is by those vulgar despots who are hungry for power and money, the more immense his luminous figure grows, showing the way to the pariahs who venerate him in their pained souls and who fall to their knees before his sublime and redemptive Work."[44]

Pompous Mexico

In 1955, the journal *Problemas Agrarios e Industriales de México* finally translated *Barbarous Mexico* into Spanish, a full forty-five years after

Figure A.6 Precursors of the Mexican Revolution. Enrique, front row, just left of center;
the other two central figures are Generals
Juan José Ríos and Esteban Baca Calderón.
The status of "precursor" can only be bestowed
once the story of the revolution has been
enshrined. The revolution is a fleeting and
inchoate moment that is then stabilized in
narrative and fixed into a monument. These
elderly men and women were living monuments whose position was fixed with the aid
of authentication certificates, published
memoirs, and state pensions. Courtesy of
the Casa de El Hijo del Ahuizote, Mexico City.

its initial publication in English. The journal's editor was Mexico's distinguished historian and editor Daniel Cosío Villegas, who introduced John Kenneth Turner's text with a singularly unenthusiastic prologue. Cosío had read Turner's book three times, he wrote, but was still unsure of whether the book was worth reading even once.[45] Written without any subtlety by an "elemental mind" whose language, too, was elemental, Cosío claimed, *Barbarous Mexico* pinned all the evils of society on an evil man (Díaz). He complained about the way in which Turner captioned the photos and postcards in his book, taking stock images of a peasant mother and child, for instance, and labeling them "Slave Mother and Child." The only reason why Cosío bothered to offer the work in Spanish translation at all, he went on, was because it served suitably as an example of anti-Porfirian propaganda.

Cosío also puzzled over the nature of the text itself—wondering aloud about what, exactly, it was. He astutely picked up on a number of complicated questions regarding Turner's book: How was Lázaro Gutiérrez de Lara's presence hidden? The book starts with descriptions of Yucatan and Valle Nacional and seems to skip over Mexico City, though it provides photographs of Mexico City. Was Turner in Mexico City? Did Turner know how to speak Spanish, and if not, how did he do his interviews? These mysterious aspects of the book were compounded, according to Cosío, by Turner's faulty English—Cosío went on to provide his readers with a lesson in proper English while ridiculing the English prose of *Barbarous Mexico*, which he found to be disgracefully laced with awkward Latin inflections.

Cosío went on to correct many of Turner's mistakes in historical interpretation of the Porfiriato without acknowledging any of Turner's contributions, which, if I were to summarize them, are that he managed to demonstrate that slavery, genuine slavery, was rather widespread in Mexico and that it was part of a system in which the United States was directly invested. But Cosío preferred to pick at the edges of the argument and corrected mistakes of interpretation regarding the origin of the Yaqui conflict, the existence of an opposition press under Díaz, and the deeper history of debt peonage. Here Cosío was on more solid terrain than in his pedantic appreciation of what constituted good and proper English. (After all, Turner's reportage sold copies by the millions—in English.)

Turner, Cosío complained, exaggerated here, misunderstood there. But Cosío's curmudgeonly reaction, which at times seems to berate Turner for not being an academic historian, was also laced with some existential anxiety, for Turner had in fact managed to put himself in dangerous situations in order to carry out his consequential research, something that rarely happens to historians. Unable quite to fathom how Turner did it, Cosío doubted even that Turner had actually existed and suggested instead that the text was written by a Mexican Liberal in the United States: Why? First, implicitly, because of the "elemental" nature of the book's argument and style. Second, because its English prose "conjures in my mind the image of a Mexican who speaks English, but who stumbles once in a while and who, much to his own regret, must recur to the dictionary.... but then only to choose the most artificial and trite word, and consequently, the one that is least natural or appropriate." But most importantly: "My suspicion that Turner might have been an expatriated Mexican of the Partido Liberal is confirmed by the ignorance that he reveals with regard to the history of Mexico, to say nothing of the history of the United States."[46]

Cosío was soon embarrassed by a number of letters to newspapers that vouched for the existence of Turner. In fact, Ethel herself was living in Cuernavaca and writing a book about Ricardo Flores Magón at the very moment at which Cosío was taking it upon himself to demonstrate that Turner, if he existed, barely knew English as a second language (Figure A.7). Like many people both humble and prominent, Cosío was loathe to admit that he had made a big mistake. Instead, he wrote that his critics were taking him too literally... that he had doubted Turner's authorship, rather than his material existence as a person.... Whatever.

The significant point is that by 1955, Mexico's most prominent modern historian was incapable of conceiving the depth of the personal and political relationships that had breached the divide between Mexicans and Americans and that had in fact spawned the ideology of the Mexican Revolution.

Elizabeth

Shortly after Victoriano Huerta's coup against Madero, Elizabeth and Manuel Sarabia had moved back to the United States with their daughter Anita Katherine, their niece Josefina, and their dog Pokey.

Figure A.7 Ethel acting as Rosalind in *As You Like It* (Forest Theater, Carmel), a character befitting Ethel's own ability to subvert social limitations. Courtesy of the Bancroft Library, Ethel Duffy Turner Papers.

They were in bad financial straits, but were receiving support from Elizabeth's mother at the time. Mrs. Shultis had been fretting about her daughter's situation in Mexico, and thanks to the intervention of Frances Noel, was finally able to help her daughter and son-in-law leave. But Manuel's tuberculosis had continued to develop, and he died in early 1915.

For her part, Mrs. Shultis left provisions in her will for Elizabeth's daughters, but support for Elizabeth herself was conditional on her "good" behavior. Elizabeth refused to be so importuned and moved to Brooklyn once her daughters were in college. There, she made a meager living teaching English to Latin Americans.

"I went to visit her in Brooklyn," Ethel later recalled.

> Elizabeth had talked in her genteel Boston way about her home with a Puerto Rican family. She spoke of the delightful fig tree under which we would have lunch. True, there was a fig tree, but the house was a hut with board floors, no window curtains and a miserable cot for Elizabeth. There were five children and one more on the way. The Puerto Ricans were gracious and friendly, and Elizabeth treated them as her own people, with love and respect. This was the life she had voluntarily chosen rather than a luxurious home in the Boston Back Bay district. Her relatives did not know how or where she lived. She used the Spanish paper that ran her ad as a mailing address.[47]

As the Depression drew on, though, Elizabeth's situation became more desperate. The final images that we have of her are again from Ethel, the first in 1931, at the start of the Depression, and the second from 1934, very shortly before Elizabeth's death.

> In New York I wrote to Elizabeth, who had a Brooklyn address, and asked her to have lunch with us in our rented apartment. I expected to see a not much older version of my friend, rather well-dressed, rosy-face, a little heavy in build.
>
> When I answered the doorbell, I'm afraid the shock I felt showed in my face. A wispy gray-haired woman stood before me. She was wearing a terrible hat and had a long, shabby black coat over her arm. Her gray rayon dress sagged in the back and was faded and too short from many washings. She wore long black stockings and heavy oxfords.
>
> Fortunately, I had remembered her vegetarianism and we had her kind of food.[48]

Ethel sent Elizabeth some money. Elizabeth continued with her teaching and translation and kept her dignity and pride at all times. The second and last time that Ethel saw her, three years later, she went to the Brooklyn house, which was now "much worse" even than it had been at her earlier visit. The Puerto Rican man with whom Elizabeth lodged had begged Elizabeth to seek out the help of her family, but she refused. She was recovering from pneumonia. Ethel paid Elizabeth's bills, left her some money, and promised to send more upon her return to San Francisco. Ethel was now on her way to England, after publishing her novel. She received a stirring letter of thanks from Elizabeth when she was in Ireland and responded, but when she got home to San Francisco, her letter was returned, and marked "Deceased." Elizabeth Darling Trowbridge died of malnutrition in Brooklyn, New York.

Blas Lara

In 1948, after fifty years and a life of exile in the United States, Blas Lara decided to take a trip with his son Orbe. His idea was to go from Berkeley to Los Angeles, where Blas would show Orbe the old haunts of the Liberal Party—the San Fernando building, Edendale, the Plaza de los Mexicanos—and from there go to Mexico and all the way to Yucatán. "The idea of going to Yucatan," he wrote, "though apparently preposterous, was driven by curiosity to see the fields where Porfirian slavery had existed and to visit the archeological ruins of Maya civilization."[49]

These were the twin sources of the Mexican Revolution: the enslavement of a people who had once been great and who could be great again. Yucatán was also the origin of Blas's own politicization, since his father had been deported there when Blas was just a boy. The pilgrimage and return was also a way of breaching a yawning generation gap. Blas's older boy, Américo, had been drafted and set to the Pacific after the bombing of Pearl Harbor. Blas had pleaded with Américo and tried to persuade him to desert and flee. Fighting for nations, killing other proletarians, dying for nations...that was the worst.

Américo didn't listen to his father, though, and he went to war like a patriot. Fortunately, he survived, but Blas's pilgrimage to Mexico was meant both as a sentimental journey for himself and as an education for his younger son. They visited all of the meaningful addresses in Los Angeles: 519 ½ Fourth Street, 914 Boston Street, Court Street, Edendale... with Blas explaining what had once stood where new houses were now built, telling the story of the Liberal Party, and sharing the trajectories of the children of the various comrades.

Once in Mexico, Blas was impressed by the disparities in wealth there and was fond of getting into arguments that involved local history. He had an extended imaginary conversation with Porfirio Díaz, trying to figure what the actual gains of the revolution had been. When Blas arrived in Veracruz, he saw that a group of workers were going to stage one of Ricardo's plays. Blas decided to stay for that. He never made it to Yucatán.

Illegal Alien

Looking through Ricardo's, Enrique's, and Librado's prison records at Leavenworth, I came across a letter from Librado's daughter Cuca (Refugio) to the prison warden. It was dispatched from Los Angeles, on August 7, 1946, sixteen years after Librado's death, and twenty-three years after his release and deportation to Mexico. The letter reads as follows:

> Dear Sirs:
>
> Would appreciated very much if you would send me this information as to my enter to the United States. I think you have record of my father. Librado Rivera. Whom served sentence in this penitentiary. I can't get my citizens paper without this information. Thanking you. Mrs. R. R. Hernández.[50]

The warden's answer was as exasperating as it was true to bureaucratic form: "We are sorry to report that the information desired is not available here."[51]

I imagine Librado watching over his daughter and whispering to her confidentially from the heavens: "Death to Capital, Authority, and the Church!"

Acknowledgments

I like to think that this book was written in solitude, because during the writing process, I did not share or discuss its contents with anyone save, occasionally, Elena Climent. But like much memorializing, this heroic view is both unreal and ungrateful. I did have much difficulty talking about what I was up to during the years in which I wrote *The Return of Comrade Ricardo Flores Magón*. I needed the quiet intimacy that only blank sheets of paper can provide. But even so, I benefitted immeasurably from intellectual companionship and support at every step.

On the institutional front, this book was written with invaluable support from Columbia University, and in particular its Anthropology Department, its Center for the Study of Ethnicity and Race, and its Institute for Latin American Studies. Columbia has been a generous home, intellectually and materially. I am particularly indebted to our doctoral students for their creative example and also to a number undergraduates who labored as work-study assistants at different points during this project, bringing library materials to my office or scanning documents. Juana Cabrera and Marilyn Astwood provided me with consistent logistical support, above and beyond the call of duty.

For several years now, I have benefitted from having a part-time research assistant in Mexico City whose work as been to scour local archives for documents and make digital images for me. During the early stages of this book, my assistant was Ana Santos. I am grateful once again to Ana, who put her own accomplishments as an archival historian to work for my projects and patiently followed up on my whimsical requests, no matter how idiosyncratic. Most of this book was done with the assistance in Mexico City of Diana Rosselly, who took over from Ana and learned the ropes from her very quickly. The Mexican end of this research project relied crucially on Diana's regular deliveries of electronic photocopies of documents.

For the documents found in American archives and libraries, I relied on Columbia University's Butler Library and its interlibrary loan service, as well as on assistance from librarians and curators at the Bancroft Library at Berkeley, the Huntington Library, various branches of the National Archives, the San Diego Historical Society, the University of Arizona Library, and a number of other repositories.

The bulk of the actually writing of this book occurred in the remarkable environment of the Wissenschaftskolleg zu Berlin, where I was a fellow in 2011–12. I owe an immeasurable debt of gratitude to that institution, to its staff, and to my fellow fellows, who provided me with a free, respectful, and sensitive community when this book was at its most delicate stage. Most especially, I am indebted to Ayşe Buğra, Alessandro Stanziani, Jie-Hyun Lim, Jeremy Adler, Gábor Demsky, Philip Kitcher, and Ioana Macrea-Toma for their conversation and company.

Once I had a full draft of the book, I was finally able to face friends and ask for their frank (and often feared) opinions. I have true difficulty expressing the depth of my sense gratitude to the friends and colleagues who accepted my invitation to read this long work and make careful comments: Jesús Rodríguez-Velasco, Sabina Berman, Fernando Escalante Gonzalbo, Rihan Yeh, and Xenia Cherkaev.

In the same vein, I benefitted crucially from the readings and critical comments of my editors at Zone, Ramona Naddaff, Michel Feher, and Meighan Gale. Working with Zone is an extraordinary experience. I also wish to thank Julie Fry for her creative and sensitive work with the images.

I wish to make special mention the deep and exhilarating written exchanges that I had with Jorge Aguilar Mora, who read the book for the press. His views on the Mexican Revolution and on writing on the revolution mean more to me than I can say.

Finally, this book was written in the company of Elena Climent and with the unstinting support of my dear family: Enrique, Elisa, Shiara, Adam, Larissa, Alberto, Tania, and the entire tribe. It is to them, always, that I owe the most.

Notes

DEDICATION

1. *Ulises criollo: La tormenta* (Mexico City: Fondo de Cultura Económica, 1993), p. 395. My translation.

INTRODUCTION

1. Peter Kropotkin, *Mutual Aid: A Factor of Evolution* (1902; Hong Kong: Forgotten Books, 2008), p. 140.

2. Librado Rivera, "Mi decepción de la revolución rusa," *Sagitario*, October 25, 1924. All translations from original sources in Spanish to English are mine unless otherwise specified.

3. Antonio Díaz Soto y Gama, "Discurso pronunciado por el C. Diputado Federal Antonio Díaz Soto y Gama a raíz de la muerte de Ricardo Flores Magón, November 22, 1922," available at http://www.antorcha.net/biblioteca_virtual/politica/discursos/3.html.

4. Juan Gómez-Quinones, *Sembradores: Ricardo Flores Magón y el Partido Liberal Mexicano: A Eulogy and Critique* (Los Angeles: Aztlán Publications, 1973). A vibrant program of Chicano research has followed Gómez Quiñonez's lead, including practically all labor historians working on the history of Mexicans in Texas, Arizona, New Mexico, and California during the twentieth century, as well as feminist Chicano historians working on the region and social historians generally.

5. Ethel Duffy Turner, "Heroic End of Guerrero," *Regeneración*, January 14, 1911.

6. Mariano Gómez Gutiérrez [Blas Lara Cázares], *La vida que yo viví: Novela histórico-liberal de la Revolución Mexicana* (n.p., 1954), p. 1.

7. *Ibid.*

8. *Ibid.*

9. John Mason Hart, *Anarchism and the Mexican Working Class, 1860–1931* (Austin: University of Texas Press, 1987), p. 86.

10. Luis Lara Pardo, *La prostitución en México* (México City: Librería de la Viuda de Ch. Bouret, 1908), p. 19

11. Julio Guerrero, *La genesis del crimen en México: Estudio de psiquiatría social* (Mexico City: Librería de Ch. Bouret, 1901), p. 41.

12. John Murray, "Mexico's Peon-Slaves Preparing for Revolution," *International Socialist Review* 9.9 (March 1909), pp. 648–49.

13. Enrique Flores Magón to Teresa V. Magón, July 13, 1919, AEFM.

14. Jules Michelet, *Histoire de la Revolution Française*, 7 vols. (Paris: Chamerot, 1847–1853), vol. 1, p. v., available at http://babel.hathitrust.org/cgi/pt?id=mdp.3 9015059804792;page=root;view=image;size=100;seq=7;num=i, my translation.

15. William C, Owen to Rafael García, July 31, 1923, AEFM, caja 16, exp. 24.

16. Jesús González Monroy, *Ricardo Flores Magón y su actitud en la Baja California* (Mexico City: Editorial Academia Literaria, 1962), p. 105.

17. Alan Knight, *The Mexican Revolution*, 2 vols. (Lincoln: University of Nebraska Press, 1990), vol. 1, pp. 46–47.

18. James Cockcroft, *Intellectual Precursors of the Mexican Revolution* (Austin, University of Texas Press, 1968), p. 102.

19. Ricardo Flores Magón, "Para los envidiosos," *Regeneración*, November 28, 1914.

20. Committee on Foreign Relations, United States Senate, *Revolutions in Mexico: Hearing before a Subcommittee of the Committee of Foreign Relations United States Senate, Sixty-Second Congress, Second Session, Pursuant to S. Res. 335, A Resolution Authorizing the Committee on Foreign Relations to Investigate Whether Any Interests in the United States Are Now Engaged in Inciting Rebellion in Cuba and Mexico* (Washington, D.C.: Government Printing Office, 1913), p. 2513.

21. Octavio Paz, "De la Independencia a la Revolución," in Octavio Paz and Luis Mario Schneider (eds.), *México en la obra de Octavio Paz*, 3 vols. (Mexico City: Fondo de Cultura Económica, 1987), vol. 1, pp. 207–13.

22. Antonio Díaz Soto y Gama, "Club Ponciano Arriaga: Acta," *El Hijo del Ahuizote*, March 22, 1903.

23. Antonio de P. Araujo, "Calixto Guerra Chico," *Regeneración*, July 5, 1913.

24. Tomás Sarabia, "Para el Judas Juan Sarabia habla Tomás Labrada," *Regeneración*, October 14, 1911.

25. Antonio de P Araujo, "Salazar, Alanis y Campa," *Regeneración*, March 22. 1913.

26. Abraham González to Antonio I. Villarreal, October 9, 1911, AAIV.

27. José C. Valadés, "Una página siniestra de la Revolución Mexicana: A marrazos fue muerto Alaniz," *La Opinión* [Los Angeles], February 21, 1937. Jorge Aguilar Mora provides a remarkable reconstruction and analysis of this event in *Una muerte*

justa, sencilla, eterna: Cultura y guerra durante la Revolución Mexicana (Mexico City: Ediciones Era, 1990), pp. 321–22.

28. Rafael García to Enrique Flores Magón, November 17, 1922, AEFM, caja 50, exp. 10.

29. Arnaldo Córdova, *La ideología de la Revolución Mexicana: La formación del nuevo regimen* (Mexico City: ERA, 1973). For an analysis of the diffuse ideology of peasant autonomy and land distribution, see, for instance, Daniel Nugent, *Spent Cartridges of the Mexican Revolution* (Chicago: University of Chicago Press, 1993) and Knight, *The Mexican Revolution.*

30. Martín Luis Guzmán, *El águila y la serpiente* (1928; Barcelona: Editorial Casiopea, 2000), p. 231.

31. Rafael García to Enrique Flores Magón, July 3, 1921, AEFM, caja 9, exp. 4e.

32. Enrique Flores Magón to Rafael García, December 28, 1922, AEFM, caja 50, exp, 10.

33. For an instance of self-referential use of the formula "slaves of freedom," see Enrique Flores Magón to Teresa Arteaga, July 3, 1914, in AEFM, caja 45, exp. 2.

34. Jack London, "The Mexican" (1911), in *London: Novels and Stories* (New York: Library of America, 1982), pp. 920–44.

35. *Ibid.*, p. 922.

36. *Ibid.*, pp. 937 and 933.

37. Gilles Deleuze and Felix Guattari, *Kafka: Toward a Minor Literature* (Minneapolis: University of Minnesota Press, 1986), p. 18.

38. Ricardo Flores Magón to Ellen White, August 16, 1921, in Ricardo Flores Magón, *Obras completas*, vol. 1, *Correspondencia (1899–1918)*, ed. Jacinto Barrera Bassols (Mexico City: Dirección General de Publicaciones del Conaculta, 2001), p. 243.

39. Ricardo Flores Magón to Enrique Flores Magón, August 16, 1899, AEFM, caja 9, exp. 11.

40. Antonio Rincón to Emilio Campa, August 31, 1911, AAIV.

41. Santiago de la Vega to Antonio Villarreal, January 6, 1915, AAIV.

42. Martín Luis Guzmán to Antonio Villarreal, August 4, 1916, AAIV.

CHAPTER ONE: ETHEL AND JOHN

1. John Langdon to Ethel Turner, September 1, 1965, EDT-Bancroft, box 1, correspondence.

2. Juanita Turner Lusk to Ethel Duffy Turner, January 30, 1964, EDT-Bancroft, box 1, correspondence.

3. John Kenneth Turner, *Barbarous Mexico* (Chicago: Charles Kerr & Sons, 1911).

4. Ethel Duffy Turner, "Writers and Revolutionists: An Interview Conducted

by Ruth Teiser. Regional Oral History Office," 1967, p. ii, EDT-Bancroft.

5. *Ibid.*, p. 2.

6. Ethel Turner, *One-Way Ticket* (New York: Harrison Smith and Robert Haas, 1934), p. 3.

7. *Ibid.*, pp. 179–80.

8. *Ibid.*, p. 24.

9. *Ibid.*, p. 86.

10. Ethel Duffy Turner, "Writers and Revolutionists," p. 5.

11. Ethel Turner, *One-Way Ticket*, p. 65.

12. *Ibid.*, p. 185.

13. Judy Stone, "Mexican Reflections of 'A Wild One,'" *San Francisco Chronicle*, March 14, 1965.

14. Ethel Turner, *One-Way Ticket*, p. 293.

15. *Ibid.*, p. 297.

16. Faustino Domingo Sarmiento, *Viajes por Europa, Africa y América* (1847; Barcelona: Lingua ediciones, 2007), p. 364.

17. Ethel Duffy Turner, "Writers and Revolutionists," p. 39.

18. John Kenneth Turner to Antonio Villarreal, dated Christmas 1918, AAIV.

19. Adriana Spadoni's novels include *The Swing of the Pendulum* and *The Noise of the World*. For a discussion of the participation of women in *The Masses*, see Margaret C. Jones, *Hellraisers and Heretics: Women Contributors to "The Masses," 1911–1917* (Austin: University of Texas Press, 1993).

20. Ethel Duffy Turner to John Kenneth Turner, December 2, 1919, EDT-Bancroft, box 1, folder 3.

21. John Kenneth Turner to Antonio Villarreal, Christmas 1918, AAIV.

22. Ethel Duffy Turner, "Writers and Revolutionists," pp. 27–28.

23. *Ibid.*, p. 49.

24. Stone, "Mexican Reflections of 'A Wild One.'"

25. Ethel Turner, *One Way Ticket*, pp. 315–16.

26. Ethel Duffy Turner, "Writers and Revolutionists," p. 8.

27. Philip L. Fradkin, *The Great Earthquake and Firestorms of 1906: How San Francisco Nearly Destroyed Itself* (Berkeley: University of California Press, 2005).

28. Ethel Duffy Turner, "Writers and Revolutionists," pp. 8–9.

29. Ethel Duffy Turner, untitled manuscript, ch. 5, p. 7, EDT-Bancroft, box 1, folder 6.

30. Ethel Duffy Turner, "On the Life of John Kenneth Turner," EDT-Bancroft, box 1, folder 5.

31. Ethel Duffy Turner, "Writers and Revolutionists," p. 32.

32. *Ibid.*, p. 8.

CHAPTER TWO: THE MEXICAN CAUSE

1. Ricardo Flores Magón and Antonio I. Villarreal, March 28, 1907, SRE, legajo L-E-924 (II).

2. The environment in Missouri was more propitious for propaganda work. St. Louis was home to a powerful labor movement and a press with close ties to the progressive movement in Chicago and the eastern and western United States. Indeed, it was in St. Louis that the Mexican radicals met Emma Goldman, Alexander Berkman, and other prominent anarchists and where Ricardo and Librado cemented their ties to that ideology.

3. Ethel Duffy Turner, "Elizabeth Trowbridge Sarabia" (unpaginated), EDT-INAH, doc. 133.

4. Elizabeth Trowbridge, "Members of the Liberal Party as I have Seen Them in Prison," in *Political Prisoners Held in the United States: Refugees Imprisoned at the Request of a Foreign Government. Revised and Enlarged by the Author from a Series of Articles Published in the "Appeal to Reason," the "Miners' Magazine," and Other Periodicals* (Los Angeles: Mission Press, 1908).

5. Ethel Duffy Turner, "Elizabeth Trowbridge Sarabia," EDT-INAH, doc. 133.

6. Trowbridge, "Members of the Liberal Party as I have Seen Them in Prison."

7. John Kenneth Turner, *Barbarous Mexico* (Chicago: Charles Kerr & Sons, 1911), p. 10.

8. William C. Owen, "Carta de Cuba," July 14, 1913, no newspaper title in the clipping, AEFM, caja 12, exp. 15.

9. Victoriano Salado Alvarez, "Flores Magón," *La Prensa* (Los Angeles), November 28, 1922.

10. Mrs. E. Sarabia, "Topacio," *The Border*, no date and unpaginated. In EDT-INAH, doc. 137.

11. Ethel Turner, *One-Way Ticket* (New York: Harrison Smith and Robert Haas, 1934), p. 32.

12. The early history of the Murray clan is described by Charles Monaghan, *The Murrays of Murray Hill* (New York: Urban History Press, 1998).

13. Biographical information on John Murray is from EDT-INAH, doc. 81, "John Murray."

14. Ethel Duffy Turner, "Writers and Revolutionists: An Interview Conducted by Ruth Teiser. Regional Oral History Office," Bancroft Library, University of California, 1967, p. 11.

15. William Knox Mellon, "Job Harriman: The Early and Middle Years, 1861–1912," Ph.D. thesis, Department of History, Claremont Colleges, 1972, pp. 96–124.

16. Phillip J. Mellinger, *Race and Labor in Western Copper: The Fight for Equality, 1896–1918* (Tucson: University of Arizona Press, 1995), p. 36.

17. Ethel Duffy Turner, "Elizabeth Trowbridge Sarabia." EDT-INAH, doc. 133.

18. *Ibid.*

19. Lowell Blaisdell, *The Desert Revolution Baja California, 1911* (Madison: University of Wisconsin Press, 1962), p. 97.

20. Ethel Duffy Turner, untitled manuscript, undated, EDT-INAH, doc. 196.

21. For a general perspective, see Leela Gandhi, *Affective Communities: Anticolonial Thought, Fin-de-Siècle Radicalism, and the Politics of Friendship* (Durham: Duke University Press, 2006). For a more regional account, see Rebecca J. Mead, *How the Vote Was Won: Woman Suffrage in the Western United States, 1868–1914* (New York: pNew York University Press, 2004), p. 17.

22. Alice Stone Blackwell to Prison Physician, February 9, 1922, U.S. Department of Justice, Bureau of Prisons, Leavenworth Penitentiary, prisoner 14596 (Magon), National Archives.

23. Ethel Duffy Turner, "Elizabeth Trowbridge Sarabia," EDT-INAH, doc. 133.

24. Ricardo Flores Magón to María Brousse, December 6, 1908, in Ricardo Flores Magón, *Obras completas*, vol. 1, *Correspondencia (1899–1918)*, ed. Jacinto Barrera Bassols (Mexico City: Dirección General de Publicaciones del Conaculta, 2001), pp. 499–500.

25. Trowbridge, "Members of the Liberal Party as I have Seen Them in Prison."

26. *Ibid.*

27. *Ibid.*

CHAPTER THREE: HERMANOS FLORES MAGÓN

1. Ethel Duffy Turner, *Ricardo Flores Magón y el Partido Liberal Mexicano* (1960; Mexico City, INEHM, 2000), p. 14; Ward Albro, *Always a Rebel: Ricardo Flores Magón and the Mexican Revolution* (Fort Worth: Texas Christian University Press, 1992), p. 3; Pedro María Anaya Ibarra, *Precursores de la Revolución Mexicana* (Mexico City: Secretaría de Educación Pública, 1955), p. 12.

2. Enrique Flores Magón, *Combatimos la tiranía: Un pionero revolucionario mexicano cuenta su historia a Samuel Kaplan*, trans. Jesús Amaya Topete (Mexico City: INEHRM, 1958), pp. 10–11.

3. "Raza Indígena: Ilustración," *El Demócrata*, April 15, 1893.

4. Matías Romero, *El Estado de Oaxaca* (Barcelona: Tipo-Litografía de España y Cia., 1886), p. 20.

5. *Ibid.*, p. 12.

6. "Constancia notarizada y firmada por el Gral Luis P. Figueroa, 14 agosto 1878," AEFM, caja 52, exp. 1.

7. Teodoro Flores, "Apuntes de las fechas relativas…," AEFM, caja 42, exp. 1.

8. Enrique Flores Magón, *Combatimos la tiranía*, pp. 13–14, emphasis in the original.

9. *Ibid.*, p. 13.

10. The names of Perea and Margarita's two children are given in the meticulous chronology of Ricardo Flores Magón's life compiled by Jacinto Barrera Bassols, "Cronología," in Ricardo Flores Magón. *Obras completas de Ricardo Flores Magón*, vol. 3, *Regeneración (1900–1901), primera parte: Artículos escritos por Ricardo Flores Magón en colaboración con Jesús y Enrique Flores Magón*, ed. Jacinto Barrera Bassols (Mexico City: Dirección General de Publicaciones del Conaculta, 2004), p. 31.

11. Jenaro Amezcua, *¿Quien es Enrique Flores Magón?* (Mexico City: Avance, 1943), p. 30.

12. "Los registros de nacimiento y el secreto profesional," *Regeneración* September 15, 1910; "El registro de nacimientos y el gobierno del Distrito," *Regeneración*, September 23, 1900.

13. Ricardo Flores Magón, "El matrimonio canónico," *Regeneración* December 23, 1900.

14. McNeil Island Penitentiary, Inmate Case Files 1899–1920, file 2198 (Ricardo Flores Magón) and file 2200 (Enrique Flores Magón), U.S, Department of Justice, Bureau of Prisons, RG 129, box 20, National Archives. This is the only mention of Josefa in Los Angeles that I have found.

15. AJFM, caja 25, exp. 9.

16. José C. Valadés, *El joven Ricardo Flores Magón* (1942; Mexico City: Extemporáneos México, 1986), p. 10; Enrique Flores Magón, *Combatimos la tiranía*, p. 17.

17. Bassols, "Cronología," p. 31.

18. "Acta de juzgado, Teotitlan del Camino, 1 mayo 1877," AEFM, caja 52, exp,1, The phrases in italics are archaic land measures: pastures were measured in *estancias de ganado mayor y menor* and farm land was measured by amount of seed—*maquilas de sembradura*.

19. Enrique Flores Magón, *Combatimos la tiranía*, p. 22.

20. Enrique M. Flores, "Mis notas," Mexico City, August 3, 1895, AEFM, caja 6, exp. 51.

CHAPTER FOUR: THE GENERATION OF 1892

1. Gabriel González Mier, "La Juventud," *El Demócrata* March 29, 1893.

2. Francisco Bulnes, *El verdadero Díaz y la revolución* (1920; Mexico City: Ediciones Del Valle de México, 1979), p. 193.

3. *Ibid.*, p. 179.

4. Jacinto Barrera Bassols, "Cronología," in Ricardo Flores Magón, *Obras*

completas de Ricardo Flores Magón, vol. 3, *Regeneración (1900–1901), primera parte: Artículos escritos por Ricardo Flores Magón en colaboración con Jesús y Enrique Flores Magón*, ed. Jacinto Barrera Bassols (Mexico City: Dirección General de Publicaciones del Conaculta, 2004), p. 44.

5. Lázaro Gutiérrez de Lara, "Story of a Political Refugee," *Pacific Monthly* 25.1 (January 1911), pp. 3–4.

6. Bulnes, *El verdadero Díaz*, p. 14.

7. *Ibid., El verdadero Díaz*, pp. 87–88.

8. Gabriel González Mier, "La Juventud," *El Demócrata*, March 29, 1893. See also, in the same journal and on the same date, "Juventud y decrepitud: ¿De quien es el porvenir?"

9. For congressmen, see "Cuando no roncan, charlan: Una sesión del Congreso," *El Demócrata*, April 13, 1893; for judges, Joaquín Claussell and Querido Moheno, "El proceso de *El Democrata*: Conducta de los jueces," *El Demócrata*, April 15, 1893.

10. J. V. Villada to Porfirio Díaz, May 17, 1892, reproduced in *Porfirio Díaz frente al descontento popular regional (1891–1893)*, ed. Friedrich Katz (Mexico City, Universidad Iberoamericana, 1986), pp. 43–44.

11. *El Partido Liberal* tried to explain away the practice, interested as it was in claiming that there was fair electoral competition. See "Los estudiantes y la policía," May 14, 1892.

12. "Picos Pardos," *El Diario del Hogar*, May 21, 1892.

13. See "La Calumnia Tizna," *El Partido Liberal*, May 4, 1892.

14. Bulnes, *El verdadero Díaz*, pp. 70–71.

15. "Club antireeleccionista de estudiantes," *El Diario del Hogar*, May 10, 1892.

16. *Ibid.*

17. Enrique Flores Magón claimed there were thirty-five killed and five wounded. Enrique Flores Magón, *Combatimos la tiranía: Un pionero revolucionario mexicano cuenta su historia a Samuel Kaplan*, trans. Jesús Amaya Topete (Mexico City: INEHRM, 1958), p. 31.

18. Cited in Bassols, "Cronología," pp. 40–41.

19. Ricardo Flores Magón to Gus Teltsch, April 28, 1921, Archivo Electrónico Ricardo Flores Magón, http://www.archivomagon.net/ObrasCompletas/Correspondencia/Cor02/Cor50.html.

20. "Papantla: Episodios históricos y politicos," *El Demócrata*, March 29, 1893.

21. "Terribles sucesos en Chihuahua: Otra sublevación en el Distrito de Guerrero sobre las ruinas de Tomochic," *El Demócrata*, April 11, 1893.

22. "¡Baranda vuelve por su fama!," *El Demócrata*, April 6, 1893.

23. "Prisión de los periodistas independientes: Clausura de 'El Demócrata,'" *El*

Diario del Hogar, April 29, 1893; death notices for Teodoro appeared in numerous Mexico City papers, around April 26, 1893.

24. Bassols, "Cronología," p. 43.

25. AEFM, caja 52, exp. 19.

26. The formula has no simple translation. *San Lunes* ("Holy Monday") refers to the practice of not showing up for work on Mondays because you were dead drunk on Sunday. *Pambazo* is a Mexican sandwich, very greasy and filling, associated with the lower classes. So the formula means, roughly: the [derogatory characterization signaling both popular, festive, and connected to appetite] revolt ended in a badly hungover no-show.

27. "Los santos inocentes," *El Partido Liberal*, May 19, 1892.

28. "Las manifestaciones del domingo y lunes últimos," *El Partido Liberal*, May 18, 1892.

29. "Los santos inocentes," *El Partido Liberal* May 19, 1892.

30. "Escuela Nacional de Jurisprudencia: Una expulsión incalificable," *El Demócrata*, April 15, 1893.

CHAPTER FIVE: LA BOHÈME

1. "Constancia notarizada y firmada por el Gral Luis P. Figueroa, 14 agosto 1878," AEFM, caja 52, exp. 1. Evidence of difficulties exist for 1890 in AEFM, caja 52, exp. 1. For the paperwork involved, see Teodoro Flores, "Apuntes de las fechas relativas...," AEFM, caja 42, exp. 1. That he received at least some of his military pay in the early period of his retirement can be ascertained in "Certificado de la Tesorería General de la Federación, 10 Nov. 1877," AEFM, caja 52, exp. 1.

2. Jacinto Barrera Bassols, "Cronología," in Ricardo Flores Magón, *Obras completas de Ricardo Flores Magón*, vol. 3, *Regeneración (1900–1901), primera parte: Artículos escritos por Ricardo Flores Magón en colaboración con Jesús y Enrique Flores Magón*, ed. Jacinto Barrera Bassols (Mexico City: Dirección General de Publicaciones del Conaculta, 2004), p. 35.

3. Teodoro Flores to Margarita Magón, October 11, 1890, AEFM, caja 52, exp. 20. The relevant portion of the letter reads: "Most likely the boys won't be coming here for their vacations, because I can't stay more than four months...but I'll see what other pleasure I can offer my dear boys that can compensate at least a little for the joy of which they'll be deprived."

4. Teodoro Flores to C. Director del Archivo Gral de la Nación, July 9, 1878, AEFM, caja 52, exp. 1; Teodoro Flores to C. Jefe del Archivo General de la Nación, December 1880, AEFM, caja 52, exp. 1.

5. Teodoro Flores to Margarita Magón, September 24, 1890, AEFM, caja 52, exp. 20.

6. Teodoro Flores to Margarita Magón, October 11. 1890, AEFM, caja 52, exp. 20.

7. Rodolfo (no last name) to Jesús Flores Magón, May 11, 1900, AEFM, caja 52, exp. 29.

8. Ricardo Flores Magón to Enrique Flores Magón, September 20, 1899, AEFM, caja 9, exp, 11.

9. José C. Valadés, *El joven Ricardo Flores Magón* (1942; Mexico City: Extemporáneos México, 1986), pp. 27 and 28.

10. Ricardo Flores Magón. quoted in Bassols, "Cronología," p. 41.

11. John Coatsworth, "Obstacles to Economic Growth in Nineteenth-Century Mexico," *American Historical Review* 83.1 (February 1978), p. 81.

12. Manuel Gutiérrez Nájera, quoted in Vicente Quirarte, *Elogio de la calle: Biografía literaria de la Ciudad de México (1850–1992)* (Mexico City: Ediciones Cal y Arena, 2001), pp. 326–27.

13. Valadés, *El joven Ricardo Flores Magón*, p. 17.

14. *Ibid.*, pp. 17–18.

15. Santiago de la Vega, quoted in *ibid.*, p. 22.

16. Meticulous emphasis on cleanliness also placed the group squarely within the ethos of the Mexico City middle classes, for as cultural historians Herrera Basterra and Ponce Alcocer have written, cleanliness was to Porfirian middle-class identity what luxury was to the class identification of the aristocracy. See Herrera Basterra and Ponce Alcocer, "La limpieza, una práctica de identidad social de la clase media mexicana del siglo XIX," *Historia y Grafía* 19 (2002), p. 53.

17. Enrique Flores Magón to Teresa Arteaga, June 16, 1918, AEFM, caja 45, exp. 13.

18. Timothy Turner, *Bullets, Bottles and Gardenias* (Dallas: South-West Press, 1935), pp. 72–73.

19. John Kenneth Turner, "None Braver or Better," *Regeneración*, January14, 1910.

20. "Simpatías por el General Díaz", *El Partido Liberal*, May 17, 1892.

21. Antonio I. Villarreal, "Reminiscences of my Prison Life" (Part 1), *Regeneración* 2, September 10, 1910.

22. "Notas de una excursion en bicicleta," *El Demócrata*, March 29, 1903.

23. Bassols, "Cronología," p. 42.

24. Enrique Flores Magón to Teresa Arteaga, June 16, 1918, AEFM, caja 45, exp, 13.

25. Juan Sarabia to Antonio I. Villarreal, February 19, 1912, AAIV.

26. Librado Rivera, "Prólogo," in Diego Abad de Santillana, *Ricardo Flores Magon: El apóstol de la revolución social mexicana* (1925; Mexico City: Centro de

Estudios Históricos del Movimiento Obrero, 1978), p. 13.

27. Ward Albro, "Antonio I. Villarreal y 30 años de revolución en México, 1904–1934," *Veritas* (Universidad Regiomontana) 9 (1990), p. 85.

28. Federico Gamboa, Mi diario: Mucho de mi vida y algo de la de otros, 7 vols. (Mexico City: Consejo Nacional para la Cultura y las Artes, 1995), vol. 6, p. 526.

29. "Notas de una excursion en bicicleta," *El Demócrata*, March 29, 1893.

30. Bassols, "Cronología," p. 44.

31. Albro, "Antonio I. Villarreal y 30 años de revolución en México," p. 85.

32. Gonzalo G. Rivero, *Hacia la verdad: Episodios de la revolución* (Mexico City: Compañía Editora Nacional, S.A, 1911), p. 28.

33. Lázaro Gutiérrez de Lara, "El comercio marítimo," thesis in law, defended at the Escuela Nacional de Jurisprudencia, September 5, 1898, p. 5, Universidad Nacional Autónoma de Méxoco, Archivo Histórico de la Universidad, exp. 2355.

CHAPTER SIX: A PASSION FOR THE PRESS

1. Jacinto Barrera Bassols, "Cronología," in Ricardo Flores Magón, *Obras completas de Ricardo Flores Magón*, vol. 3, *Regeneración (1900–1901), primera parte: Artículos escritos por Ricardo Flores Magón en colaboración con Jesús y Enrique Flores Magón*, ed. Jacinto Barrera Bassols (Mexico City: Dirección General de Publicaciones del Conaculta, 2004), p. 40.

2. Instituto Nacional de Estadística y Geografía, *Estadísticas históricas de México, 2009*, "Educación," http://www.inegi.org.mx/prod_serv/contenidos/espanol/bvinegi/productos/integracion/pais/historicas10/Tema3_Educacion.pdf.

3. Ricardo Flores Magón to Enrique Flores Magón, July, 23 1899, AEFM, caja 9, exp. 11.

4. *"Regeneración," Regeneración*, August 7, 1900.

5. "Propongamos nuestro candidato," *Regeneración*, February 21, 1901.

6. "Poca política y mucha administración," *Regeneración*, December 7, 1901.

7. "Un problema," *Regeneración*, December 7, 1901.

8. Horcasitas's separation from the journal seems to have occurred amicably, but clearly, it was timed and in all likelihood a result of the radicalization of the journal. See "Al Lic. D. Antonio Horcasitas," *Regeneración*, December 15, 1900.

9. "Lo que somos," *Regeneración*, December 15, 1901.

10. "Periódico independiente de combate," *Regeneración*, December 30, 1900.

11. "Pongamos nuestro candidato," *Regeneración*, February 21, 1901.

12. "Una comunicación," *Regeneración,* January 7 1901.

13. James Cockcroft, *Intellectual Precursors of the Mexican Revolution, 1900–1913* (Austin: University of Texas Press, 1968), p. 80.

14. Cockcroft, *Intellectual Precursors of the Mexican Revolution*, p. 102 n. 25.

15. Gumersindo Santiago to Jesús Flores Magón, May 1, 1901, AJFM, caja 3, exp. 14.

CHAPTER SEVEN: THE WALL

1. Leopoldo Zea, *El positivismo en México* (Mexico City: El Colegio de México, 1943).

2. "Resoluciones tomadas por el primero Congreso Liberal de la República Mexicana, Instalado en San Luis Potosí el 5 de Febrero de 1901," *Regeneración*, February 28, 1901.

3. Jacqueline Ann Rice, "The Porfirian Political Elite: Life Patterns of the Delegates to the 1892 Union Liberal Convention," Ph.D. diss., Department of History, UCLA, 1979.

4. "Los Congresistas," *Regeneración*, February 21, 1901.

5. James Cockcroft, *Intellectual Precursors of the Mexican Revolution, 1900–1913* (Austin: University of Texas Press, 1968). p. 95.

6. This is the version authoritatively told by Cockcroft on the basis of available memoirs and his interviews with Díaz Soto y Gama and Nicolás Bernal. *Ibid.*

7. See Círculo de Amigos del General Porfirio Díaz, *Informe de los trabajos del Círculo de Amigos del General Porfirio Díaz en el año de 1902* (Mexico City, Imprenta de Mariano Nava, 1902).

8. See Jean-Pierre Bastian, *Los disidentes: Sociedades protestantes y revolución en México, 1872–1911* (Mexico City: Fondo de Cultura Económica, El Colegio de México, 1989).

9. *Ibid.*, p. 196.

10. Fernando Palomares to Ricardo Flores Magón, October 10, 1901, AJFM, caja 2, exp. 5.

11. Ethel Duffy Turner, "Ricardo Flores Magón y el Partido Liberal," typescript, second version of ch. 4, "Sonora," p. 2, EDT-Bancroft. This manuscript is an English-language and unabridged version of Ethel Duffy Turner, *Ricardo Flores Magón y el Partido Liberal Mexicano* (1960; Mexico City: INEHRM, 2000).

12. Ethel Duffy Turner, untitled notes on Fernando Palomares, EDT-INAH, document 157.

13. Aarón López Manzano to Ricardo Flores Magón, March 20, 1907, SRE, legajo L-E-924-II.

14. Ricardo Flores Magón to Aarón López Manzano, April 1, 1907, SRE, legajo L-E-924 (II).

15. Jacinto Barrera Bassols, "Cronología," in Ricardo Flores Magón, *Obras completas de Ricardo Flores Magón*, vol. 3, *Regeneración (1900–1901), primera parte: Artículos escritos por Ricardo Flores Magón en colaboración con Jesús y Enrique Flores*

Magón, ed. Jacinto Barrera Bassols (Mexico City: Dirección General de Publicaciones del Conaculta, 2004), p. 61.

16. Jean-Pierre Bastian, *Los disidentes: Sociedades protestantes y revolución en México, 1872–1911* (Mexico City: Fondo de Cultura Económica, El Colegio de México, 1989), p. 87. We do not know the number of Masonic temples for that date, but in the 1893 census, there were a little over two hundred of them.

17. Cockcroft, *Intellectual Precursors*, p. 102.

18. Michael Meyer, *Huerta: A Political Portrait* (Lincoln: University of Nebraska Press, 1972), p. 9.

19. "Al Presidente de la República," *Regeneración* April 15, 1901.

20. Bassols, "Cronología," pp. 65–66.

21. "Los señores Magones," *Las Dos Repúblicas*, June 16, 1901, AJFM, caja 23, exp. 7.

22. Writing from prison, Jesús and Ricardo thanked a long list of papers for their support. See "Nuestros Colegas," *Regeneración* June 15, 1901.

23. "La Sra. Margarita Magón viuda de Flores," *La Crónica* (Laredo), June 29, 1901, AJFM, caja 23, exp. 7.

24. "Sensible defunción," *El Demócrata*, June 16, 1901, AJFM, caja 23, exp. 7.

25. "Obito," *El Ramillete*, July 7, 1901, AJFM, caja 23, exp. 6.

26. Untitled, *El Diario del Hogar*, June 27, 1901, AJFM, caja 23, exp. 7.

27. Enrique Flores Magón, *Combatimos la tiranía: Un pionero revolucionario mexicano cuenta su historia a Samuel Kaplan.*, trans. Traducido por Jesús Amaya Topete (Mexico City: INEHRM, 1958), p. 57.

28. José C. Valadés, *El joven Ricardo Flores Magón*, (1942; Mexico City: Extemporáneos México, 1986), p. 33.

29. Enrique Flores Magón to Jesús and Ricardo Flores Magón, December 16, 1901, AJFM, caja 9, exp. 16.

30. "Resoluciones tomadas por el primero Congreso Liberal de la República Mexicana, Instalado en San Luis Potosí el 5 de Febrero de 1901," *Regeneración*, February 28, 1901.

31. Enrique Flores Magón to Jesus Flores Magón and Clara Hong de Flores Magón, St. Louis, May 30, 1905, AJFM, caja 9, exp. 18.

32. *Ibid.*

CHAPTER EIGHT: SLAVERY

1. John Kenneth Turner, *Barbarous Mexico* (Chicago: Charles Kerr & Sons, 1911) pp. 10–11.

2. Matías Romero, "Los Jornales en México," *New York World*, December 31, 1891, reprinted in Matías Romero, *Artículos sobre México publicados en los Estados*

Unidos de América en 1891–1892 (Mexico City: Oficina Impresora de Estampillas, 1892), p. 125.

3. For a general discussion of the comparative conditions of foreign workers and Mexicans in Mexico, see Jonathan C. Brown, "Foreign and Native-Born Workers in Porfirian Mexico," *American Historical Review* 98.3, pp. 786–818. For wages in Arizona copper mining, see Philip J. Mellinger, *Race and Labor in Western Copper: The Fight for Equality, 1896–1918* (Tucson: University of Arizona Press, 1995), p. 34. For Sonora, see Miguel Tinker Salas, *In the Shadow of the Eagles: Sonora and the Transformation of the Border During the Porfiriato* (Berkeley: University of California Press, 1997), p. 88. For lower wages to agricultural workers in Texas, even at a later period, see Neil Foley, *The White Scourge: Mexicans, Blacks, and Poor White in Texas Cotton Culture* (Berkeley: University of California Press, 1997), p. 130. For an acknowledgment of labor disparities in Porfirian economic policy debates, see Richard Weiner, "Demons and Deities: Market Metaphors in Porfirian Mexico," Ph.D. diss., Department of History, University of California at Irvine, 1999, p. 127.

4. Romero, "Los Jornales en México," p. 130.

5. "Barbarous Mexico: Three Months in Peonage. In Which the Author Tells How He, with Others, Fell into slavery," *American Magazine* 69.5 (March 1910), p. 633

6. The story of these developments is tracked closely in Armando Bartra, *El México bárbaro: Plantaciones y monterías del sureste durante el porfiriato* (Mexico City: El Atajo Ediciones, 1996), pp. 396–99.

7. Channing Arnold and Frederick J. Tabor Frost, "Personal Observations of Two Englishmen Upon Slavery in Yucatan," *American Magazine* 69.6 (April 1910), p. 830.

8. Interview originally published in *El Socialista*, cited in Bartra, *El México bárbaro*, p. 397.

9. For a historical explanation of the racialization of "the Mexican," see Claudio Lomnitz, "Los orígenes de nuestra supuesta homogeneidad: Breve arqueología de la unidad nacional en México," *Prismas* 14.1 (2010), pp. 17–36.

10. "Barbarous Mexico: Three Months in Peonage," p. 636.

11. *Ibid.*

12. Manuel Sierra Méndez to Porfirio Díaz, Mérida, September 1891, reprinted in Friedrich Katz (ed.), *Porfirio Díaz frente al descontento popular regional (1891–1893)* (Mexico City: Universidad Iberoamericana, 1986), pp. 200–201.

13. Channing Arnold and Frederick J. Tabor Frost, *The American Egypt: A Record of Travel in Yucatan* (New York: Doubleday, Page & Co., 1909), p. 326.

14. *Ibid.*, pp. 326–27.

15. *Ibid.*, p. 327.

16. See Jacques Derrida, "Le facteur de la vérité," in *The Post Card: From Socrates to Freud and Beyond*, trans. Alan Bass (Chicago: University of Chicago Press, 1987), pp. 411–96.

17. Benjamin Kidd, *The Control of the Tropics* (New York: MacMillan, 1898), p.3.

18. For a full account, see John Mason Hart, *Empire and Revolution: The Americans in Mexico Since the Civil War* (Berkeley: University of California Press, 2002).

19. Bartra, *El México bárbaro*, pp. 396–402.

20. Quoted in Bartra, *El México bárbaro*, p. 399.

21. Arnold and Frost, *The American Egypt*, pp. 325–26.

22. Herman Whitaker, *The Planter* (New York, Harper, 1909), p. 278.

CHAPTER NINE: JOHN TURNER'S GUIDE

1. The fact that Lázaro was born in Monterrey was established in his deposition before the Los Angeles Court, October 18, 1909, SRE, legajo 343, exp. 2/14.

2. Lázaro Gutiérrez de Lara, "Story of a Political Refugee," *Pacific Monthly* 25.1 (January 1911), p. 2.

3. "Presentimientos," *El Diario del Hogar*, June 2, 1893. For the paper's protest over the expulsion of Lázaro from law school, see "Expulsión de uno de nuestros compañeros," *El Diario del Hogar*, June 16, 1893.

4. "¡Baranda vuelve por su fama!," *El Demócrata*, April 6, 1893.

5. Elizabeth Howard West, "Diary of José Bernardo Gutiérrez de Lara, 1811–1812, Part 1," *American Historical Review* 34.1 (October 1928), p.65.

6. Lázaro Gutiérrez de Lara and Edgcumb Pinchon, *The Mexican People: Their Struggle for Freedom* (New York: Doubleday, 1914), p. 5.

7. *Ibid.*, p. 6.

8. De Lara, "Story of a Political Refugee," p. 2.

9. Ethel Duffy Turner, "Ricardo Flores Magón y el Partido Liberal," typescript, ch. 5, EDT-Bancroft.

10. De Lara and Pinchon, *The Mexican People*, p. 6.

11. *Ibid.*, p. 10.

12. The influence of Andrés Molina Enríquez, in particular, comes to mind. See Claudio Lomnitz, "Once tesis acerca de Molina Enríquez," in Emilio Kourí (ed.), *En busca de Molina Enríquez: Cien años de 'Los grandes problemas nacionales'* (Mexico City: El Colegio de México, 2009), pp. 65–78.

13. For a full exposition of the history of eugenics in California, see Alexandra Stern, *Eugenic Nation: Faults and Frontiers of Better Breeding in Modern America* (Berkeley: University of California Press, 2005).

14. "De Lara dará una conferencia sobre arte antiguo mexicano," *La Prensa*, March 6, 1915.

15. Francisco Bulnes, *El porvenir de las naciones latinoamericanas ante las recientes conquistas de Europa y norteamérica (estructura y evolución de un continente)* (1899; Mexico City: Pensamiento Vivo de América, 1945), p. 41.

16. Ethel Duffy Turner, "Ricardo Flores Magón y el Partido Liberal," typescript, ch. 4, unpaginated, EDT-Bancroft.

17. The ranchers addressed the following letter of complaint to the governor of Sonora on August 13, 1903: "We, the undersigned, owners of the ranches of Ojo de Agua, Las Peñitas, Los Nogales, Los Ajos, have been illegally fenced in with barbed wire by the Cananea Consolidated Copper Company. Our most elemental needs are being denied, and since no one in this state has any guaranteed rights, we sent a telegram to the Ministry of Fomento and Justice. Because we received no reponse from them, and because there are laws that guarantee the rights of Man, we ask you, in the name of justice, to dictate a brief order so that these humiliations and abuses cease." Quoted in Alfonso Torúa Cienfuegos, *El magonismo en Sonora (1906–1908)* (Hermosillo: Universidad de Sonora, 2003), p. 58.

18. "Los pícaros se confabulan," *Regeneración*, July 8, 1905.

19. As early as 1902, Lázaro was calling for the construction of a rail line southward, to link Sonora with central Mexico and so guarantee Mexican control over the region. See Lázaro Gutiérrez de Lara and Ignacio Corella, "Los ferrocarriles en el Estado de Sonora," *El Porvenir*, March 23, 1902, cited in Miguel Tinker Salas, *In the Shadow of the Eagles: Sonora and the Transformation of the Border During the Porfiriato* (Berkeley: University of California Press, 1997), p. 246.

20. Christine Mathias, "At the Edges of Empires: Race and Revolution in the Mexican Border Town of Cananea, 1899–1917," B.A. thesis, Department of History, Yale College, 2007.

21. "La labor de la tiranía: Cananea se hunde," *Regeneración*, February 11, 1905.

22. Ralph Ingersoll, *In and Under Mexico* (New York: The Century Co., 1924), p. 4.

23. *Ibid.*, pp. 116–17.

24. Práxedis Guerrero, quoted in Ward Albro, *To Die on Your Feet: The Life, Times, and Writings of Práxedis G. Guerrero* (Fort Worth: Texas Christian University Press, 1996), p. 33.

25. "Nuestro falso progreso: La esclavitud del obrero," *Regeneración*, March 1, 1906.

26. Jonathan Brown, "Foreign and Native-Born Workers in Porfirian Mexico," *American Historical Review* 98.3 (June 1993), pp. 793 and 804.

27. "El juego en Cananea, "*Regeneración*, January 28, 1905.

28. *Ibid.*

29. "La labor de la tiranía: Cananea se hunde," *Regeneración*, February 11, 1905.

30. Ricardo Flores Magón to Don Tomás D. Espinsa, August 2, 1906, Archivo Electrónico Ricardo Flores Magón, http://www.archivomagon.net/ObrasCompletas/Correspondencia/Cor95.html.

31. Luis Lara Pardo, *La prostitución en México* (Mexico City: Librería de la Viuda de Ch. Bouret, 1908), pp. 19–20.

32. "Juego y prostitución," *Regeneración*, February 18, 1905.

33. Lázaro Gutiérrez de Lara, *Los bribones: Novela* (Los Angeles: Imprenta de El Popular, 1907), p. 204.

34. *Ibid.*, p. 206.

35. *Ibid.*, p. 141.

36. *Ibid.*, pp. 18–19.

37. "Los honrados," *El Demócrata*, April 11, 1893.

38. "Find: A Sonora Mine Fabulously Rich," *Tucson Daily Citizen*, April 21, 1904.

CHAPTER TEN: "THE PEOPLE WERE THE SACRIFICE"

1. Ethel Duffy Turner, "On the Life of John Kenneth Turner," p. 2, EDT-Bancroft, box 1, folder 5.

2. Ethel Duffy Turner, untitled. EDT-INAH, doc. 132, untitled.

3. Ethel Duffy Turner, "Ricardo Flores Magón y el Partido Liberal," typescript, ch. 6, pp. 9–10, EDT-Bancroft.

4. *Ibid.*

5. Ethel Duffy Turner, "Elizabeth Trowbridge Sarabia," EDT-INAH, doc. 133.

6. Ethel Duffy Turner, untitled. EDT-INAH, doc. 132; Turner, "Ricardo Flores Magón y el Partido Liberal," typescript, ch. 6, p. 9, EDT-Bancroft.

7. Ethel Duffy Turner, untitled, Ethel Duffy Turner Papers, EDT-INAH, doc. 157.

8. Mariano Gómez Gutiérrez, [Blas Lara Cázares], *La vida que yo viví: Novela histórico-liberal de la Revolución Mexicana.* (n.p., 1954), p. 143.

9. Rafael García to Enrique Flores Magón, June 16, 1921, AEFM, caja 9, exp. 4d.

10. "Testimonios concernientes a la conducta de Teodoro Gaitán, recogidos por Rafael B García," AEFM, caja 14, exp. 11.

11. Ethel Duffy Turner, "On the Life of John Kenneth Turner," p. 2, EDT-Bancroft.

12. John Kenneth Turner, *Barbarous Mexico* (Chicago: Charles Kerr & Sons, 1911), pp. 111–12.

13. John Murray, "Mexico's Peon-Slaves Preparing for Revolution," *International Socialist Review* 9.9 (March 1909), p. 646.

14. *Ibid.*, p. 643.

15. *Ibid.*, p. 644.

16. *Ibid.*, p. 652.

17. Armando Bartra, "John Kenneth Turner, un testigo incómodo," *Luna Córnea* 15 (May–August 1998), pp. 80–81.

18. John Kenneth Turner, *Barbarous Mexico*, p. 13.

19. Albert Morawetz to Francis Loomis, Department of State, September 23, 1904, Subject: Yaqui Revolt in Sonora. Dispatches from United States Consuls in Nogales, 1889–1906, roll 4, vol. 4, January 2, 1903–July 26, 1906. National Archives Microfilm Publications.

20. *Ibid.*

21. *Ibid.*

22. Albert R. Morawetz to Robert Bacon, State Department, November 3, 1905, Rebellion of the Yaqui Indians in Sonora. Dispatches from United States Consuls in Nogales, 1889–1906, roll 4, vol. 4, January 2, 1903–July 26, 1906. National Archives Microfilm Publications.

23. Louis Hostetter (Consul, Hermosillo) to Roberto Bacon, Assistant Secretary of State, April 20, 1906. Dispatches Addressed to the Department of State by United States Consular Official at Hermosillo. Dispatches From United States Consuls in Mexico, State Department Files, National Archives.

24. Louis Hostettter to Mr. A. F. Call, January 12, 1906, Dispatches Addressed to the Department of State by United States Consular Official at Hermosillo. Dispatches From United States Consuls in Mexico, State Department Files, National Archives.

25. "Border People Are Jubilant: Rejoice With All Sonora Over Settlement of the Yaqui War," *Tucson Citizen*, June 4, 1908.

26. Edward Spicer, *Pascua: A Yaqui Village in Arizona* (Chicago: University of Chicago Press, 1940), p. 150.

27. Quoted in *ibid.*, p. 22.

28. John Kenneth Turner, *Barbarous Mexico*, p. 37.

29. For a study and account of that story, see Orin Starn, *Ishi's Brain: In Search of America's Last "Wild" Indian* (New York, Norton, 2004).

30. John Kenneth Turner, *Barbarous Mexico*, p. 37.

31. "Editorial: Mexico, Our Capitalists' Slave Colony," *International Socialist Review*, January 1911, p. 364.

32. John Kenneth Turner, *Barbarous Mexico*, pp. 12–13.

33. *Ibid.*, p. 16.

34. *Ibid.*, p. 17.

35. *Ibid.*, p. 107.

36. Quoted in Batra, *El México bárbaro*, pp. 288–89.

37. John Kenneth Turner, *Barbarous Mexico*, p. 110.

CHAPTER ELEVEN: THE BORDER

1. Ethel Duffy Turner, "Elizabeth Trowbridge Sarabia," EDT-INAH, doc. 133.

2. *Ibid.*

3. Ethel Duffy Turner, "Ricardo Flores Magón y el Partido Liberal," typescript, ch. 7, p. 1, EDT-Bancroft.

4. Ethel Duffy Turner, "Writers and Revolutionists: An Interview Conducted by Ruth Teiser. Regional Oral History Office," Bancroft Library, University of California, 1967, p. 15.

5. Ethel Duffy Turner, "Ricardo Flores Magón y el Partido Liberal," typescript, ch. 7, p. 1, EDT-Bancroft.

6. *Ibid.*, ch. 6, p. 10.

7. *Ibid.*, ch. 7, p. 2.

8. Ethel Duffy Turner, untitled, unpaginated, EDT-INAH, doc, 136.

9. Elizabeth Trowbridge to Ethel Duffy Turner, March 5, 1934, EDT-INAH, doc. 730.

10. "Peace Reigns on the Rio Grande Border. Formerly It Was an Inquest Every Monday," *Washington Post*, July 1, 1906.

11. Ethel Duffy Turner, "Ricardo Flores Magón y el Partido Liberal," typescript, ch. 7, p. 2, EDT-Bancroft.

12. Ethel Duffy Turner, untitled, unpaginated, EDT-INAH, doc. 136.

13. *Ibid.*

14. Ricardo Flores Magón to María Brousse, no date (1908), Archivo Electrónico Ricardo Flores Magón, http://www.archivomagon.net/ObrasCompletas/Correspondencia/1908.html.

15. Ethel Duffy Turner, untitled, unpaginated, EDT-INAH, doc. 136.

16. *Ibid.*

17. *Ibid.*

18. *Ibid.*

19. Ethel Duffy Turner, "Ricardo Flores Magón y el Partido Liberal," typescript, ch. 7, p. 2, EDT-Bancroft.

20. "Burglar's Loot the Office of Sarabia, 'El Defensor Del Pueblo' Visited by Thieves," *Tucson Daily Citizen*, January 18, 1908.

21. S. W. Finch to Victoriano Salado Alvarez, May 25, 1909, and León de la Barra to S. W. Finch, June 23, 1909, SRE, legajo 332, exp. 1.

22. Ethel Duffy Turner, "Ricardo Flores Magón y el Partido Liberal," typescript, ch. 7, p. 3, EDT-Bancroft

23. Ethel Duffy Turner, untitled, unpaginated, EDT-INAH, doc. 136.

24. *Ibid.*

25. There is no evidence that Ricardo's, Antonio's, and Librado's sentences were affected by Manuel's flight, though the men may well have feared that it could have done so, and Sarabia's failure to appear in court did cause a sensation. See "Revolutionist Sarabia Fails to Appear in Court When His Case is Called to Formal Order, *Tucson Daily Citizen*, April 26, 1909.

26. "Revolutionist Sarabia Weds Rich Boston Girl," *Tucson Daily Citizen*, December 19, 1908.

27. Ethel Duffy Turner, "Writers and Revolutionists," p. 16.

28. "Sarabia desaparece," *El Labrador* (Las Cruces, New Mexico), February 5, 1909.

29. "Revolutionist Sarabia Fails to Appear in Court," *The Tucson Citizen*, April 26, 1909.

CHAPTER TWELVE: MEXICO IN THE HEADLINES

1. Ricardo Flores Magón to María Brousse, October 4, 1908, Archivo Electrónico Ricardo Flores Magón, http://www.archivomagon.net/ObrasCompletas/Correspondencia/1908.html.

2. Ricardo Flores Magón to María Brousse, February 21, 1909, Archivo Electrónico Ricardo Flores Magón,http://www.archivomagon.net/ObrasCompletas/Correspondencia/Cor287.html.

3. "Defending Mexican Refugees," *St. Louis Globe Democrat*, March 14, 1909.

4. León de la Barra to the Secretaría de Relaciones Exteriores, August 21, 1909, SRE, legajo 332, exp. 3.

5. Consul in Tucson to the Mexican Embassy, Washington, "El socialista L. Gutiérrez de Lara," September 17, 1909, SRE, nota 129.

6. Consulate in Phoenix to the Secretaría de Relaciones Exteriores, May 31, 1909, SRE, legajo 332, exp. 3, reservada no. 71.

7. Secretaría de Relaciones Exteriores, Yuma, Arizona, November 6, 1909, nota 65, orden 130; a number of articles appeared in Arizona papers on the case, see SRE, LGL1909.

8. Embassy to Foreign Ministry, October 29, 1909, SRE, exp. 401.

9. Consulate in Los Angeles to the Secretaría de Relaciones Exteriores, October 27, 1909, SRE, dispatch no. 116–19.

10. "Police Charge Proved a Farce," *Los Angeles Herald*, October 27, 1909.

11. *Ibid.*

12. *Ibid.*

13. "De Lara Close to Freedom on a Heavy Bond," *Los Angeles Herald*, October

26, 1909.

14. "Thousands Rally to Support of Accused Mexican Liberal: Overflow Meeting in De Lara's Defense. Former Judge Works among Speakers," *Los Angeles Herald*, October 24, 1909.

15. "Mass Meeting Will Come to Lara's Aid," *Los Angeles Herald*, October 21, 1909.

16. "De Lara Close to Freedom on a Heavy Bond," *Los Angeles Herald*, October 26, 1909.

17. "Prominent Men Will Espouse De Lara Cause," *Los Angeles Herald*, October 23, 1909.

18. "Police Charge Proved a Farce, *Los Angeles Herald*, October 27, 1909.

19. "Thousands Rally to Support of Accused Mexican Liberal," *Los Angeles Herald*, October 24, 1909.

20. *Ibid.*

21. "Imprisonment of Certain Persons at Florence, Ariz.," Report no. 1037, U.S. House of Representatives, [April 15], 1910.

22. See, for instance, Ambassador León de la Barra to the Minister of Foreign Affairs, no date (September 1909), response to 14133, SRE, 3-19-15.

23. Henry Lane Wilson to Secretary of State William Jennings Bryan, March 13, 1913, State Department Files, National Archives.

24. "Is Mexico 'Barbarous'?: A Protest before Publication," *American Magazine* 69.2 (December 1909), p. 282.

25. "Student Demonstration Degenerates into a Destructive Mob," *Mexican Herald*, November 10, 1910.

26. Charles Q. Davis to Secretary of State Philander Knox, December 2, 1910, State Department Files, National Archives.

27. "Furlong Files Suit for Libel," *Regeneración*, January 7, 1911.

28. Ethel Duffy Turner, "Ricardo Flores Magón y el Partido Liberal," typescript, EDT-Bancroft, box 1, folder 6, ch. 7, p. 9.

29. "Police Charge Proved a Farce," *Los Angeles Herald*, October 27, 1909.

30. *Washington Post*, October 19, 1909, p. 10.

31. The best study of the case is Antonio Saborit's foreword to the Spanish edition of this book, in Carlo Fornaro, *Díaz, zar de México y Abul Hamid y Porfirio Díaz* (Mexico City: Fondo de Cultura Económica, 2010).

32. "De Lara Not to Be Sent Across Mexican Border: Case against Liberal Is Dismissed, *Los Angeles Herald*, November 6, 1909.

33. SRE, oficio 73–21, contains letters to this effect from consuls in New York, Kansas City, and St. Louis.

34. "Díaz Refugees Kidnapped," *The Philadelphia Ledger*, June 12, 1910.

35. León de la Barra to Federico Gamboa, nota reservada, June 6, 1910, SRE, LGL1910, p. 5; León de la Barra a Federico Gamboa, nota reservada, June 15, 1910, SRE, LGL1910, p. 18.

36. "Díaz and De Lara: The One a Necessary Despot, the Other Disturber of the Peace," *San Francisco Chronicle*, June 14, 1910. Johann Most (1846–1906) was a German-born anarchist and communist who emigrated to the United States in 1882.

CHAPTER THIRTEEN: LEARNING FROM 1906

1. Ricardo Flores Magón to Manuel Sarabia, January 31, 1907, SRE, legajo L-E-924 (I).

2. Alfonso Torúa Cienfuegos, *El magonismo en Sonora (1906–1908)* (Hermosillo: Universidad de Sonora, 2003), p. 43.

3. For an account of the 1906 uprising in Veracruz, see Elena Azaola Garrido, *Rebelión y derrota del magonismo agrario* (Mexico City: Sepochentas, 1982).

4. Pascual Rodríguez to Aniceto Moreno, February 11, 1907, SRE, legajo L-E-924 (I).

5. Tomás Labrado to Antonio de P. Araujo, February 17, 1907, SRE, legajo L-E-924 (I).

6. "Villarreal Escapes fron an Inspector," *St. Louis Republic*, February 26, 1907, SRE, legajo L-E-924 (I).

7. Ricardo Flores Magón to Manuel Sarabia, January 17, 1907, SRE, legajo L-E-924 (I).

8. Ricardo Flores Magón to Manuel Sarabia, February 20, 1907 SRE, legajo L-E-924 (I).

9. Camilo Arriaga, Ricardo Flores Magón, Santiago de la Hoz et. al. to Esteemed Friend and Correligionary, February 11, 1904, SRE, legajo L-E-918.

10. *El Puerto de Matamoros*, supplement no. 308, February 22, 1907, SRE, legajo L-E-924 (I).

11. Ricardo Flores Magón to Manuel Sarabia, February 25, 1907, SRE, legajo L-E-924 (I).

12. *Ibid.*

13. Ricardo Flores Magón to Manuel Sarabia, January 31, 1907.

14. Antonio de P. Araujo to Tomás Labrada, March 11, 1907, SRE, legajo L-E-924 (II).

15. Ricardo Flores Magón to Manuel Sarabia, March 25, 1907, SRE, legajo L-E-924 (II).

16. Librado Rivera to Manuel Sarabia, April 16, 1907, SRE, legajo L-E-924 (II).

17. Ricardo Flores Magón to Aarón López Manzano, March 6, 1907, SRE,

7. José C. Valadés, *El joven Ricardo Flores Magón* (1942; Mexico City: Extemporáneos México, 1986), pp. 50–51.

8. Manuel Sarabia, "Prólogo" to "Poesías de Juan Sarabia," typescript, EDT-INAH, unnumbered document. The poems were published in France by Imprenta L'Esperance. Asociación Comunista, Rue de Steinquerke.

9. Antonio Gramsci wrote of the ways in which such authors were assimilated in Italian popular culture and referred to Carolina Invernizio, who was amply translated in Latin America and who he noted was an imitator of Ponson de Terrail, as the "honest hen of popular literature." Antonio Gramsci, *Letteratura e vita nazionale*, ch. 3, "Letteratura populare," Editione Intratext CT, 2008, available online at http://www.intratext.com/IXT/ITA3066.

10. Enrique Flores Magón, *Combatimos la tiranía: Un pionero revolucionario mexicano cuenta su historia a Samuel Kaplan*, trans. Jesús Amaya Topete (Mexico City: INEHRM, 1958), p. 58.

11. Enrique Flores Magón to Rafael García, Veracruz, July 19, 1923, AEFM, caja 16, exp. 26.

12. Gómez [Lara], *La vida que yo viví*, p. 186.

13. Ethel Duffy Turner, "Capítulo 13: *Regeneración* reaparece," EDT-INAH, doc. 171.

14. Ethel Duffy Turner to Paul Friedrich, March 30, 1965, EDT-INAH, doc. 542.

15. Gómez [Lara], *La vida que yo viví*, p. 227.

16. *Ibid.*, p. 113.

17. *Ibid.*, p. 219.

18. Ricardo Flores Magón, "Juana Gutiérrez de Mendoza," *Regeneración*, March 15, 1906.

19. Ricardo Flores Magón to María Brousse, October 25, 1908, Archivo Electrónico Ricardo Flores Magón, http://www.archivomagon.net/ObrasCompletas/Correspondencia/Cor274.html.

20. Ricardo Flores Magón to María Brousse, December 20, 1920, Archivo Electrónico Ricardo Flores Magón, http://www.archivomagon.net/ObrasCompletas/Correspondencia/Cor02/Cor25.html.

21. W. Dirk Raat dedicates a detailed and informative chapter to what he called the "Creel International Detective Agency" in *Los revoltosos: Rebeldes mexicanos en los Estados Unidos, 1903–1923* (Mexico City: Fondo de Cultura Económica, 1988), ch. 7; see also Ward Albro, *Always a Rebel: Ricardo Flores Magón and the Mexican Revolution* (Fort Worth: Texas Christian University Press, 1992), ch. 5.

22. Raat, *Los revoltosos*, pp. 172–76.

23. Ricardo Flores Magón to María Brousse, November 29, 1908, Archivo

Electrónico Ricardo Flores Magón, http://www.archivomagon.net/ObrasCompletas/Correspondencia/Cor266.html.

24. Georg Simmel, *The Sociology of Georg Simmel*, ed. and trans. Kurt H. Wolff (Glencoe, IL: Free Press, 1950), pp. 118–69.

25. María Brousse to Ricardo Flores Magón, September 15, 1908, Archivo Electrónico Ricardo Flores Magón, http://www.archivomagon.net/ObrasCompletas/Correspondencia/Cor266.html.

26. Jack London, "The Mexican," (1911), in *London: Novels and Stories* (New York: Library of America, 1982), p. 888.

27. Ricardo Flores Magón to María Brousse, no date, 1908, Archivo Electrónico Ricardo Flores Magón, http://www.archivomagon.net/ObrasCompletas/Correspondencia/Cor281.html.

28. Manuel Sarabia to Antonio Villarreal, September 10 [1910], AAIV.

29. Floyd Ramp to Enrique Flores Magón, August 14, 1918, AEFM, caja 44, exp. 17.

CHAPTER FIFTEEN: THE JUNTA ON THE EVE OF REVOLUTION

1. "To Renew Fight on Díaz's Regime: Villarreal, Magon, and Rivera Return After Three Years in Arizona Prison," *Los Angeles Herald*, August 5, 1910.

2. "To Renew Fight on Díaz's Regime: Villarreal, Magon, and Rivera Return After Three Years in Arizona Prison," *Los Angeles Herald*, August 5, 1910.

3. "Audience Tosses Coin to Liberals, *Los Angeles Herald*, August 8, 1910.

4. *Ibid.*

5. Ethel Duffy Turner, "Writers and Revolutionists: An Interview Conducted by Ruth Teiser. Regional Oral History Office," Bancroft Library. University of California, 1967, p. 22.

6. Antonio I. Villarreal, "Reminiscences of My Prison Life," (Part 1), *Regeneración*, September 10, 1910.

CHAPTER SIXTEEN: *PUNTOS ROJOS*

1. Stanley Ross, *Francisco I. Madero: Apostle of Mexican Democracy* (New York: Columbia University Press, 1955), p. 78.

2. Práxedis Guerrero, "Puntos Rojos," *Regeneración*, "September 10, 1910.

3. *Ibid.*

4. *Ibid.*

5. *Ibid.*

6. Práxedis Guerrero, "Sopla," *Regeneración*, October 15, 1910

7. Mexican census data on literacy can be consulted in Instituto Nacional de Estadística y Geografía, *Estadísticas históricas de México, 2009,* "Educación," http://

www.inegi.org.mx/prod_serv/contenidos/espanol/bvinegi/productos/integracion/pais/historicas10/Tema3_Educacion.pdf.

8. "No se desanime Usted porque sus compañeros no sepan leer," *Regeneración* October 1, 1910.

9. Robert Redfield, *Tepoztlán, A Mexican Village* (Chicago: University of Chicago Press, 1930).

10. *Ibid.*, and Robert Redfield, *The Folk Culture of Yucatan* (Chicago: University of Chicago Press, 1941).

11. Jean-Pierre Bastian, *Los disidentes: Sociedades protestantes y revolución en México, 1872–1911* (Mexico City: Fondo de Cultura Económica, Colegio de México, 1989), p. 133.

12. Mariana Gómez Gutiérrez to Enrique Flores Magón, July 20, 1918, AEFM, caja 50, exp. 9.

13. Teresa Arteaga to Enrique Flores Magón AEFM, caja 45, exp. 21, not dated, but the letter was written in August 1918. In Spanish: "mi querido esposo no puedes figurarte el justo que yo resibi el dia que bino tu carta en español meparesia que hera la primera queresibia desde que tefuiste pues no puedo acostumbrarme a pensar concabesa agena mi bidita esta carta hera de las notisias que yo estoy loca de justo Maria Andrade y Ramon te regalaron un biolin para que aprendas en el tiempo que tefalta que salir Matilde se en laso con su nobio biego que tenia desde ase 5 annos departe de su mama la famlia medisen que te notisie su union la hotra notisia es que Vale esta a qui con nosotros resaluda mucho."

14. Ethel Duffy Turner, doc. 153, untitled, EDT-INAH.

15. Ricardo Flores Magón to María Brousse, September 20, 1908, Archivo Electrónico Ricardo Flores Magón, http://www.archivomagon.net/ObrasCompletas/Correspondencia/Cor268.html.

16. Ricardo Flores Magón to María Brousse, February 21, 1909, Archivo Electrónico Ricardo Flores Magón, http://www.archivomagon.net/ObrasCompletas/Correspondencia/Cor287.html.

17. Secretaría de Relaciones Exteriores, Oficio 773, Nota Reservada, October 30, 1908, AGN Revoltosos.

18. Manuel Sarabia to Marcelino Albarra September 22, 1907, AGN-Revoltosos.

19. Secretaría de Relaciones Exteriores, Oficio 573, September 25, 1906 [signed by Secretary Mariscal], AGN-Revoltosos.

20. Mariano Gómez Gutiérrez [Blas Lara Cázares], *La vida que yo viví: Novela histórico-liberal de la Revolución Mexicana* (n.p., 1954), p. 62.

21. "Sam" [Manuel Sarabia] to Sres. Araujo y Sarabia, May 26, 1908, AGN-Revoltosos.

22. Ramón Corral to Foreign Affairs Minister, August 28, 1907, SRE, legajo

L-E-918, nota reservada 1377.

23. Manuel Sarabia to Torres Delgado, October 23, 1907, AGN-Revoltosos.

24. Secretaría de Relaciones Exteriores, Oficio 846, reservado, November 10, 1906, AGN-Revoltosos.

25. James A. Sandos, *Rebellion in the Borderlands: Anarchism and the Plan of San Diego, 1904–1923* (Norman: University of Oklahoma Press, 1992), p. 18.

26. Manuel Sarabia to Antonio Villarreal, no date, but probably October 1910, AAIV.

27. Anti-Slavery and Aborigines Protection Society to Manuel Sarabia, September 6, 1910, AAIV.

28. The text is reprinted in Spanish as Henry Baerlein, "Los esclavos de Yucatán," in Friedrich Katz, *La servidumbre agraria en México* (Mexico City: ERA, 1980), pp. 68–76.

29. Manuel Sarabia to Antonio Villarreal, undated (but possibly January 10, 1911), AAIV.

30. Manuel Sarabia to Antonio Villarreal, undated (but probably October 1910), AAIV.

31. Manuel provides details of his activities in Europe in his correspondence with Antonio I. Villarreal. See Manuel Sarabia to Antonio Villarreal, August 31, 1910, AAIV.

32. Ethel Duffy Turner, "On the Life of John Kenneth Turner," unpaginated, EDT-Bancroft, box 1, folder 5.

33. Manuel Sarabia, "Prólogo" to "Poesías de Juan Sarabia," typescript, EDT-INAH, unnumbered document. The poems were published in France by Imprenta L'Esperance. Asociación Comunista, Rue de Steinquerke.

34. Manuel Sarabia to Antonio Villarreal, November 18, 1910, AAIV; see also Manuel Sarabia to Antonio Villarreal, August 31, 1910, and Manuel Sarabia to Antonio Villarreal, January 10, 1911, AAIV.

35. Francisco I. Madero to Eulalio Treviño, February 25, 1907, published in José C Valadés, "Las relaciones de Madero con Ricardo Flores Magón," *La Opinión*, November 19, 1933.

36. Friedrich Katz, *The Life and Times of Pancho Villa* (Stanford: Stanford University Press, 1998), pp. 111–13.

37. "*Regeneración*," *Regeneración*, September 3, 1910.

38. William C. Owen, "No Wonder They Cry 'Anarchism!'," *Regeneración* July 15, 1911.

39. John Murray, "Mexico's Peon-Slaves Preparing for Revolution," *International Socialist Review* 9.9 (March 1909), p. 643.

40. Ethel Duffy Turner, "Práxedis Gilberto Guerrero," EDT-INAH, doc. 64.

41. Práxedis Guerrero, "Episodios revolucionarios: Las Vacas," *Regeneración*, September 10, 1910.

42. Práxedis Guerrero, "Puntos rojos," *Regeneración*, October 29, 1910.

43. Práxedis Guerrero, "El medio y el fin," *Regeneración*, November 5, 1910.

44. *Ibid.*

45. Ricardo Flores Magón, "Predicar la paz es un crimen," *Regeneración*, September 17, 1910.

46. Ricardo Flores Magón, "¿Es usted pederasta o no lo es, señor 'Coronel'?," *Regeneración*, October 7, 1911.

47. For instance, Sandos, *Rebellion in the Borderlands*, p. 26; Lowell Blaisdell, *The Desert Revolution: Baja California, 1911* (Madison: University of Wisconsin Press, 1962), p. 96 and elsewhere; Ward Albro, *Always a Rebel: Ricardo Flores Magón and the Mexican Revolution* (Fort Worth: Texas Christian University Press, 1992), p. 136. Hagiographers such as Ethel Duffy Turner tend politely to sidestep the issue.

48. Ethel Duffy Turner, "Capítulo 13: *Regeneración* reaparece," EDT-INAH, doc. 171,

49. Práxedis Guerrero, "Puntos rojos," *Regeneración*, September 17, 1910.

50. Práxedis Guerrero, "Soy la Acción," *Regeneración*, September 17, 1910

51. Práxedis Guerrero, "Episodios nacionales: Palomas," *Regeneración*, September 24, 1910.

52. Ricardo Flores Magón to Antonio Villarreal, February 2, 1907, SRE, legado L-E-924 (I), 1907, "Extradición de Ricardo Flores Magón y Socios por conato de homicidio, robo y daño en propiedad ajena."

53. Antonio de P Araujo to Fernando Palomares, July 17, 1936, EDT-INAH, doc. 1057.

54. Ward Albro, *To Die on Your Feet: The Life, Times, and Writings of Práxedis G. Guerrero* (Fort Worth: Texas Christian University Press, 1996), pp. 76–77.

55. Ethel Duffy Turner document 153, untitled, EDT-INAH.

56. Jesús González Monroy, *Ricardo Flores Magón y su actitud en la Baja California* (Mexico City: Editorial Academia Literaria, 1962), p. 40.

57. Enrique Flores Magón, *Combatimos la tiranía: Un pionero revolucionario mexicano cuenta su historia a Samuel Kaplan*, trans. Jesús Amaya Topete (Mexico City: INEHRM, 1958), p. 224.

58. *Ibid.*, p. 256.

59. Ethel Duffy Turner document 153, untitled, EDT-INAH.

CHAPTER SEVENTEEN: REVOLUTIONARY COMMONALITIES

1. "La Cámara contesta al Centro Anti-reeleccionista de México," *Regeneración*, October 8, 1910.

2. Francisco I. Madero, "Plan de San Luis," October 5, 1910, http://biblio. juridicas.unam.mx/libros/2/594/14.pdf.

3. Ethel Duffy Turner, "Writers and Revolutionists: An Interview Conducted by Ruth Teiser. Regional Oral History Office," Bancroft Library, University of California, 1967, pp. 22–23.

4. Ricardo Flores Magón, "The Work of Alfred G. Sanftleben," *Regeneración*, December 24, 1910.

5. Junta Organizadora to Donato Padua, November 16, AEFM, caja 13, exp. 76a, 1910; "'Relación cronológica del movimiento revolucionario de 1906, en los cantones de Acayucan, San Andrés Tuxtla y Minatitlán, Ver.' Por Cándido Donato Padua."

6. François-Xavier Guerra, *Méxique: De l'Ancien Régime a la Révolution* (Paris: L'Harmattan, 1985).

7. Ethel Duffy Turner, "Elizabeth Darling Trowbridge Sarabia," EDT-INAH, doc 135.

8. Elizabeth Trowbridge to Ethel Duffy Turner, November 10, 1925, EDT-INAH, doc. 720.

9. Elizabeth Trowbridge to Ethel Duffy Turner, October 4 and October 8, 1917, EDT-INAH, doc, 717.

10. Martín Luis Guzmán, *El águila y la serpiente* (1928; Havana: Casa de las Américas, 1963), pp. 146–47.

11. María Brousse to Teresa Flores Magón, October 20, 1934, AEFM, caja 52, exp. 3.

12. Enrique Flores Magón untitled manuscript, AEFM, caja 13, exp. 51.

13. Jean Pierre Bastian, *Los disidentes: Sociedades protestantes y revolución en México, 1872–1911* (Mexico City: Fondo de Cultura Económica, El Colegio de México, 1989), p. 166.

14. *Ibid.*, p. 227.

15. *Barbarous Mexico*, p. 303.

16. Jesús Flores Magón's resignation was prompted by his public opposition to the government's project of erecting a monument to Aquiles Serdán, the massacred Liberal leader who first rose in arms in Puebla on November 20, 1910. Jesús claimed that building the monument was premature, because the revolution had not yet attained its fundamental goals. "Hace 50 años: 25 Noviembre de 1912," *El Universal*, November 25, 1962.

17. A good early study of this ideology is Eduardo Blanquel, *Ricardo Flores Magón y la Revolución Mexicana, y otros ensayos históricos*, ed. Josefina MacGregor (1963; Mexico City: El Colegio de México, 2008), esp. pp. 41–45.

18. "Manifiesto: Junta Organizadora del Partido Liberal Mexicano,"

Regeneración, September 23, 1911.

19. "Nuestro deber," *La Voz de la Mujer* 1.4, July 21, 1907, AGN Revoltosos, 3.

20. Mariano Gómez Gutiérrez [Blas Lara Cázares], *La vida que yo viví: Novela histórico-liberal de la Revolución Mexicana* (n.p., 1954), p. 43

21. *Ibid.*

22. James A. Sandos, *Rebellion in the Borderlands: Anarchism and the Plan of San Diego, 1904–1923* (Norman: University of Oklahoma Press, 1992), p. 119.

23. Jack London, quoted in Lowell L. Blaisdell, *The Desert Revolution: Baja California, 1911* (Madison: University of Wisconsin Press, 1962), p. 42.

24. Karen I. Leonard, *Making Ethnic Choices: California's Punjabi Mexican Americans* (Philadelphia: Temple University Press, 1992).

25. Jonathan Brown, "Foreign and Native-Born Workers in Porfirian Mexico," *American Historical Review* 98.3, pp. 786–818.

26. Piero Ferrua, *Gli anarchici nella rivoluzione messicana: Práxedis G Guerrero* (Ragusa: La Fiaccola, 1976).

CHAPTER EIGHTEEN: EL CORONEL DE LOS 41

1. Hilario Salas to Ramón Sánchez, July 7, 1909, AEFM, caja 13, exp. 76`, "'Relación cronológica del movimiento revolucionario de 1906, en los cantones de Acayucan, San Andrés Tuxtla y Minatitlán, Ver.' por Cándido Donato Padua."

2. Dr. Francisco A. Campos, "Los revolucionarios en Guerrero en 1910," manuscript. dated "20 de enero de 1937," AEFM, caja 13, exp. 54.

3. Stanley R. Ross, *Francisco I. Madero: Apostle of Mexican Democracy* (New York: Columbia University Press, 1955), pp. 144–45.

4. Although Antonio had no qualms about separating himself from Ricardo, given the latter's position on an alliance with Madero, he and Manuel Sarabia did in fact make inquiries into the matter of Madero and Lázaro's alleged betrayal of Prisciliano Silva at Casas Grandes. An El Paso merchant named W. M. Love, who was close to the Liberals, responded to Antonio's inquiry on this matter, saying that Prisciliano Silva was a sick man, "very nervous and high tempered," and that Love knew for a fact that Silva had been maligning Madero in such a strident manner that in order to prevent friction between his men and Silva's, Madero had invited Silva to his tent, captured him, and then had gone "before the crowds and spoke and informed them of what had taken place and consulted every man's opinion as to whether they wished to go forward or remain with Mr. Silva and the general opinion was to proceed so they did so." W. M. Love to Antonio Villarreal, March 3, 1911, AAIV.

5. W. M. Love to Antonio Villarreal, March 3, 1911, AAIV.

6. [Alfred Sanftleben]. unsigned letter to the New York *Call*, March 12, 1911,

AAIV. Sanftleben's authorship of this letter (and the precariousness of his Spanish) is confirmed in Alfred Sanftleben to Antonio Villarreal, March 13, 1911, AAIV.

7. [Alfred Sanftleben], unsigned letter to the New York *Call*, March 12, 1911, AAIV.

8. Manuel Sarabia to Antonio Villarreal, March 19, 1911, AAIV.

9. Jesús M. González to Antonio Villarreal, March 11, 1911, AAIV.

10. Próspero Villarreal to Antonio I Villarreal, March 4, 1911 AAIV.

11. Ward S. Albro, "Antonio I. Villarreal y 30 años de revolución en México, 1904–1934," *Veritas* 9 (1990), p. 91.

12. José Maldonado to Antonio Villarreal, March 21, 1911, AAIV.

13. See, for instance, Guadalupe M. Viramontes to Antonio I. Villarreal, March 17, 1911, AAIV.

14. Jesús Mendez Rangel, "Continuación y final," AEFM, caja 13, exp. 57.

15. Librado Rivera to Conchita Rivera, November 12, 1906, AGN, Revoltosos, exp. 5, fojas 6, caja 1-A.

16. "Fernando Palomares," Revolución, October 12, 1907.

17. Ricardo Flores Magón to Enrique Flores Magón, June 4, 1908, Archivo Electrónico Ricardo Flores Magón, http://www.archivomagon.net/ObrasCompletas/Correspondencia/Cor263.html.

18. Mariano Gómez Gutiérrez [Blas Lara Cázares], *La vida que yo viví: Novela histórico-liberal de la Revolución Mexicana* (n.p., 1954), p. 203.

19. *Ibid.*, pp. 204–205.

20. Ricardo Flores Magón to María Brousse, November 1, 1908, Archivo Electrónico Ricardo Flores Magón, http://www.archivomagon.net/ObrasCompletas/Correspondencia/Cor275.html.

21. *Ibid.*

22. Ricardo Flores Magón to Enrique Flores Magón, June 4, 1908, Archivo Electrónico Ricardo Flores Magón, http://www.archivomagon.net/ObrasCompletas/Correspondencia/Cor263.html.

23. Ricardo Flores Magón to Lucía Norman, October 25, 1908, Archivo Electrónico Ricardo Flores Magón, http://www.archivomagon.net/ObrasCompletas/Correspondencia/Cor274.html.

24. Ricardo Flores Magón to María Brousse, October 4, Archivo Electrónico Ricardo Flores Magón, http://www.archivomagon.net/ObrasCompletas/Correspondencia/Cor271.html.

25. "A Manuel Sarabia," *Voz de la Mujer*, July 21, 1907, AGN-Revoltosos.

26. Ricardo Flores Magón to María Brousse, *Obras completas*, vol. 1, carta 272.

27. Ricardo Flores Magón to María Brousse (in postscript directed to Lucía), October 25, 1908, Archivo Electrónico Ricardo Flores Magón, http://www.

archivomagon.net/ObrasCompletas/Correspondencia/Cor274.html.

28. Ricardo Flores Magón, "The Work of Alfred G. Sanftleben," *Regeneración*, December 24, 1910.

29. See Ricardo Flores Magón to Clara Hong, June 12, 1905, AJFM, caja 9, exp. 18. Ricardo later revealed that it was to Gustavo to whom he had turned in 1905, and also claimed that Gustavo had not given Jesús the money. Ricardo Flores Magón, "¿Es usted pederasta o no lo es, señor 'Coronel'?," *Regeneración*, October 7, 1911.

30. Ricardo Flores Magón, "Francisco I. Madero es un traidor a la causa de la libertad," *Regeneración*, February 25, 1911.

31. Jenaro Amezcua, "¿Quien es Flores Magón?," (Mexico City, 1943), p. 38.

32. Ricardo Flores Magón, "Francisco I. Madero es un traidor a la causa de la libertad," *Regeneración*, February 25, 1911.

33. Juan Sarabia to Antonio Villarreal, June 28 1911, and telegram from Jesús Flores Magón to Antonio Villarreal, July 6, 1911, AAIV.

34. The Archivo Antonio I. Villarreal has correspondence that shows the extent of the influence of the new, Mexico City version of *Regeneración*. See, for example, Cástulo Herrera (from Chihuahua) to Antonio Villarreal, August 1, 1911, and Enrique Gutiérrez Barragán (from Piedras Negras) to Antonio Villarreal, August 30, 1911, AAIV.

35. Ricardo Flores Magón, "Degeneración," *Regeneración*, August 19, 1911.

36. See, for instance, complaints from former Magonistas from Huejutla, Hidalgo, in Gavino Medina to Juan Sarabia, September 29, 1911, AAIV.

37. "No Wonder They Cry 'Anarchism,'" *Regeneración*, July 15, 1911. The original article against the *People's Paper* was "Such Silence We Cannot Ignore," *Regeneración*, April 22, 1911.

38. Emma Goldman, "No Factional Issue," *Regeneración* June 16, 1911.

39. "Ricardo Flores Magón ante el socialismo: Entre todo los partidos honrados está desprestigiado el embaucador de Los Angeles," *El Diario del Hogar*, October 15, 1911.

40. So, for instance, in the obituary that he published upon Ricardo Flores Magón's death, Owen wrote: "When I substituted John Kenneth Turner as editor of *Regeneración*'s English language section." William C. Owen, "La muerte de Ricardo Flores Magón," translated from *Freedom*, London, December 1922, AEFM, caja 36, exp. 6.

41. Tomás Labrada, "Juan Sarabia," *Regeneración*, July 15, 1911.

42. Tomás Labrada, "A mi hermano el Tartufo," *Regeneración*, October 28, 1911.

43. Tomás Labrada, "A mi hermano el Tartufo (cont.), *Regeneración*, December 16, 1911.

44. A number of very sympathetic accounts of Ricardo fail to mention the accusation of homosexuality at all; others mention it, but do not pause for detailed study or analysis, for example, Ward Albro, *Always a Rebel: Ricardo Flores Magón and the Mexican Revolution* (Fort Worth: Texas Christian University Press, 1992), pp. 135–36, and Lowell Blaisdell, *The Desert Revolution: Baja California, 1911* (Madison: University of Wisconsin Press, 1962), p. 193

45. Ricardo Flores Magón, "El Coronel de los 41," *Regeneración*, September 16, 1911, Ricardo Flores Magón, "Que hable el maricón," *Regeneración*, September 23, 1911.

46. Fortunato Lozano, *Antonio I. Villarreal: Vida de un gran mexicano* (Monterrey, Impresora Monterrey, 1959), pp. 9–10.

47. Ricardo Flores Magón to Antonio I. Villarreal, February 2, 1907, Archivo Electrónico Ricardo Flores Magón, http://www.archivomagon.net/ObrasCompletas/Correspondencia/Cor127.html.

48. This "double morality," was again in play in Ricardo's accusations against Lázaro, when who Ricardo charged him with having spied for the Mexican consul in Los Angeles. In point of fact, Lázaro had publicly volunteered that information before the U.S. Congress, as part of his defense of the junta, while its key members were was still in prison. In that statement, Lázaro had declared that "he himself, in order to learn what his government was doing . . . had accepted employment as a 'spy' in Los Angeles to trace the movements of other refugees. He said he resigned after four days." "De Lara Tells Story to House Committee," *Los Angeles Express*, June 10, 1910. Lázaro stated that he had been paid three dollars per day and that he had given those payments to poor Mexican women of Los Angeles. Despite having personally benefitted from Lázaro's testimony in Congress, Ricardo did not hesitate to take Lázaro's admission out of context many months later in order to fling it into his face.

49. Pablo Piccato, *The Tyranny of Opinion: Honor and the Construction of the Mexican Public Sphere* (Durham: Duke University Press, 2010).

50. Ricardo Flores Magón to Antonio I. Villarreal, February 2, 1907, SRE, L-E- 924-I.

51. Lozano, *Antonio I. Villarreal*, pp. 7–8.

52. Ricardo Flores Magón, "¿Es usted pederasta o no lo es, señor 'Coronel'?," *Regeneración*, October 7, 1911.

53. Elizabeth Trowbridge to Frances and P. D. Noel, June 14, 1912, EDT-INAH, doc. 1123.

54. Ricardo Flores Magón, "El coronel de los 41," *Regeneración*, September 16, 1911.

55. Robert McKee Irwin, Edward McCaughan, and Michelle Rocío Nasser

(eds.), *The Famous 41: Sexuality and Social Control in Mexico, c. 1901* (New York: Palgrave, 2003).

56. Carlos Monsiváis, "The 41 and the *Gran Redada*," in *ibid.*, p. 145. Clemente Villagómez Arriaga has argued that Porfirio Díaz withdrew support from Ignacio de la Torre as a candidate for the governorship of the State of Mexico, as far back as 1892, because he was known to be a homosexual. See Clemente Villagómez Arriaga, "La disputa por la gubernatura en el Estado de México en 1892, entre José Vicente Villada e Ignacio de la Torre y Mier," *Historia y Grafía* 27 (2006), pp. 15–46.

57. Ricardo Flores Magón, "Que hable el maricón," *Regeneración*, September 23, 1911.

58. Rafael García to Enrique Flores Magón, April 21, 1922, AEFM, caja 50, exp. 9.

59. Ricardo Flores Magón, "El Enviado de Madero," *Regeneración*, March 9, 1912.

60. Ricardo Flores Magón, "El odio a la raza," *Regeneración*, November 12, 1910.

61. Enrique Flores Magón to Raf y Tribu Veracruz, August 10, 1923, AEFM.

62. Elizabeth Trowbridge to Frances Noel, no date [1909 or 1910], EDT-INAH, doc. 1104.

63. Gómez [Lara], *La vida que yo viví*, p. 189.

64. *Ibid.*, p. 189.

65. For an analysis of the representation of the *científicos* in Mexican public life, see Claudio Lomnitz, "Anti-Semitism and the Ideology of the Mexican Revolution," *Representations* 110.1 (Spring 2010), pp. 1–28.

66. Giuseppe Garibaldi, *A Toast to Rebellion* (New York: Bobbs-Merrill, 1935), p. 224.

67. Antonio I. Villarreal, "Reminiscences of My Prison Life (Part 3)," *Regeneración*, September 24, 1910.

68. Antonio I. Villarreal, "Reminiscences of my Prison Life" (Part 1)," *Regeneración*, September 10, 1910.

69. Antonio I. Villarreal, "Reminiscences of My Prison Life (Part 3)," *Regeneración*, September 24, 1910.

70. Antonio I. Villarreal, "Reminiscences of My Prison Life" (Part 1)," *Regeneración*, September 10, 1910.

71. Antonio I. Villarreal, "Reminiscences of My Prison Life (Part 3)," *Regeneración*, September 24, 1910.

72. Ricardo Flores Magón, "Juana B. Gutiérrez de Mendoza," *Regeneración*, June 15, 1906.

73. Martin Nesvig, "The Lure of the Perverse: Moral Negotiation of Pederasty

in Porfirian Mexico, *Mexican Studies / Estudios Mexicanos* 16.1 (Winter 2000), p. 15.

74. Ricardo Flores Magón, "El apóstol," *Regeneración*, 6 January 1911.

CHAPTER NINETEEN: BAJA FOR BEGINNERS

1. Studies of the Liberals' Baja campaign include Rómulo Velasco Ceballos, *¿Se apoderara Estados Unidos de America de Baja California? (La invasion filibustera de 1911)* (Mexico City: Imprenta Nacional, 1922); Agustín Cue Cánovas, *Ricardo Flores Magón, la Baja California y los Estados Unidos* (Mexico City: Libro-Mex Editores, 1957); Lowell L. Blaisdell, *The Desert Revolution: Baja California, 1911* (Madison: University of Wisconsin Press, 1962); Ethel Duffy Turner, *Ricardo Flores Magón y el Partido Liberal Mexicano* (1960; Mexico City: INEHRM, 2003); Ethel Duffy Turner, *Revolution in Baja California: Ricardo Flores Magón's High Noon* (Detroit, Blaine Ethridge Books, 1981); Roger Owen, "Indians and Revolution: The 1911 Invasion of Baja California, Mexico," *Ethnohistory* 10.4 (Fall 1963), pp. 373–95; Marco Antonio Samaniego López, *Nacionalismo y revolución: Los acontecimientos de 1911 en Baja California* (Tijuana: Universidad Autónoma de Baja California, 2008); and Lawrence Douglas Taylor Hansen, "¿Charlatán o filibustero peligroso?: El papel de Richard 'Dick' Ferris en la revuelta magonista de 1911 en Baja California," *Historia Mexicana* 44.4 (1995), pp. 581–616.

2. Blaisdell, *The Desert Revolution*, p. 50.

3. Samaniego, *Nacionalismo y revolución*, pp. 235–36.

4. Blaisdell, *The Desert Revolution*, pp. 76–77.

5. *Ibid.*, pp. 99–100.

6. British ambassador T. B. Houle to Monsieur le Sous Sécrétaire B. Carbajal y Rosas, August 26, 1911, SRE, exp. 19, Jack Mosby y socios, 2° parte.

7. Documentation is reproduced in Velasco Ceballos, *¿Se apoderara Estados Unidos de America de Baja California?*, p. 121.

8. Samaniego, *Nacionalismo y Revolución*, p. 133.

9. Jesús González Monroy, *Ricardo Flores Magón y su actitud en la Baja California* (Mexico City: Editorial Academia Literaria, 1962), p. 102.

10. John Kenneth Turner to William C. Owen, June 12, 1911. The letter is reproduced in Committee on Foreign Relations, United States Senate, *Revolutions in Mexico: Hearing Before a Subcommittee of the Committee of Foreign Relations United States Senate. Sixty-Second Congress, Second Session, Pursuant to S. Res. 335, A Resolution Authorizing the Committee on Foreign Relations to investigate Whether Any Interests in the United States are Now Engaged in Inciting Rebellion in Cuban and Mexico* (Washington, D.C.: Government Printing Office, 1913).

11. González Monroy, *Ricardo Flores Magón y su actitud en la Baja California*, p. 102.

12. William C. Owen, "Rally to Aid Revolutionists in Jail," *Regeneración*, August 26, 1911.

13. "Near Riot Stirs Hearing of Four Liberal Leaders," *Los Angeles Tribune*, August 23, 1911.

14. Samaniego, *Nacionalismo y Revolución*, p. 133.

15. Velasco Ceballos, *¿Se apoderara Estados Unidos de America de Baja California?*, p. 162; Blaisdell, *The Desert Revolution*, p. 137.

16. Blaisdell, *The Desert Revolution*, p. 137.

17. Official Edict, signed and sealed by Abraham González, Provisional Governor of the State of Chihuahua, June 6, 1911, AAIV.

18. Don Abraham González, quoted in González Monroy, *Ricardo Flores Magón*, p. 137.

19. Blaisdell, *The Desert Revolution*, p. 176.

20. Samaniego, *Nacionalismo y Revolución*, p. 550.

21. See n. 1.

22. Diego Abad de Santillana, *Ricardo Flores Magón; el apóstol de la revolución social Mexicana* (1925; Mexico Ciry: Antorcha, 1988).

23. James Cockcroft, *Intellectual Precursors of the Mexican Revolution* (Austin: University of Texas Press, 1968).

24. See, for example, W. Dirk Raat, *Revoltosos: Mexico's Rebels in the United States, 1903–1923* (College Station: Texas A&M University Press, 1981); Raat, *Mexico and the United States: Ambivalent Vistas* (Athens: University of Georgia Press, 1992).

25. John Mason Hart, *Anarchism and the Mexican Working Class, 1860–1931* (Austin: University of Texas Press, 1987).

26. Colin M. MacLachlan, *Anarchism and the Mexican Revolution: The Political Trials of Ricardo Flores Magón in the United States* (Berkeley: University of California Press, 1991).

27. Ward Albro, *Always a Rebel: Ricardo Flores Magón and the Mexican Revolution* (Fort Worth,: Texas Christian University Press, 1992); Albro, *To Die on Your Feet: The Life, Times, and Writings of Práxedis G. Guerrero* (Fort Worth: Texas Christian University Press, 1996).

28. Juan Gómez Quiñones, *Sembradores, Ricardo Flores Magon y el Partido Liberal Mexicano: a eulogy and critique* (Los Angeles: Aztlán Publications, 1973).

29. James A. Sandos, *Rebellion in the Boarderlands: Anarchism and the Plan of San Diego, 1904–1923* (Norman: Oklahoma University Press, 1992).

30. Benjamin Heber Johnson, *Revolution in Texas: How a Forgotten Rebellion and Its Bloody Suppression Turned Mexicans into Americans* (New Haven: Yale University Press, 2003).

31. Joel B. Pouwels, *Political Journalism by Mexican Women During the Age of Revolution, 1876–1940* (Lewiston, NY: Edwin Mellen Press, 2006).

32. Elena Azaola, *Rebelión y derrota del magonismo agrario* (Mexico City: Fondo de Cultura Económica, 1982).

33. Jane-Dale Lloyd, *Cinco ensayos sobre cultura material de rancheros y medieros del noroeste de Chihuahua, 1886–1910* (Mexico City: Universidad Iberoamaericana, 2001), and "El Partido Liberal Mexicano y la rebelión ranchera chihuahuense," in Javier Garciadiego and Emilio Kouri (eds.), *Revolución y exilio en la historia de México: Del amor de un historiador a su patria adoptiva. Homenaje a Friedrich Katz* (Mexico City: El Colegio de México, Ediciones Era, 2010).

34. Alfonso Torúa Cienfuegos' *El magonismo en Sonora (1906–1908): Historia de una persecución* (Mexico City: Hormiga Libertaria, Nosotros Ediciones, 2010).

35. Josefina Moguel Flores, *El magonismo en Coahuila* (Coahuila: Gobierno del Estado de Coahuila, Comité de los Festejos del Bicentenario de la Independencia y Centenario de la Revolución, 2006).

36. See, for example, Gloria Villegas Moreno, *Antonio Díaz Soto y Gama: Intellectual revolucionario* (Mexico City: Universidad Nacional Autónoma de México, 2010); Eugenio Martínez Núñez, *Juan Sarabia: Apóstol y mártir de la Revolución Mexicana* (Mexico City: INEHRM, 1965); Alicia Villaneda, *Juana Belén Gutiérrez de Mendoza, 1875–1942* (Mexico City: Documentación y Estudios de Mujeres, 1994); Narciso Bassols Batalla, *La inquietud liberal de Camilo Arriaga* (Mexico City: Secretaría de Educación Pública, 1968).

37. Ricardo Flores Magón, *Obras completas*, ed. Jacinto Barrera Bassols, 6 vols. (Mexico City: Dirección General de Publicaciones del Conaculta, 2003) and http://www.archivomagon.net/ObrasCompletas.

38. Blaisdell, *The Desert Revolution*, p. 41.

39. The best theoretical explanation of how this works is Stathis Kalyvas, "The Ontology of 'Political Violence': Action and Identity in Civil Wars," *Perspectives in Politics* 1.3 (September 2003), pp. 475–94.

40. Blaisdell, *The Desert Revolution*, p. 35.

41. Samaniego, *Nacionalismo y Revolución*, p. 11.

42. Roger Owen, "Indians and Revolution: The 1911 Invasion of Baja California, Mexico," *Ethnohistory* 10.4 (Fall 1963), p. 385.

43. Blaisdell, *The Desert Revolution*, pp. 44–45.

44. This is a controversial issue among Baja historians. Ethel Turner Duffy claims that Americans were never more than one-fourth of the Liberal troops in Baja, but this obscures the composition of the divisions; Blaisdell more usefully distinguishes between the Western Division, where U.S. troops far outnumbered Mexican volunteers, and the Eastern Division, where Mexicans predominated.

45. Blaisdell, *The Desert Revolution*, p. 100.

46. *Ibid.*

47. Velasco Ceballos, *¿Se apoderará Estados Unidos de América de Baja California?*, p. 148.

48. Blaisdell, *The Desert Revolution*, p. 122.

49. Antonio Sola, open letter to Ricardo Flores Magón, May 12, 1911 reproduced in Velasco Ceballos, *¿Se apoderará Estados Unidos de América de Baja California?*, p. 158.

50. Junta Organizadora de El Partido Liberal to Tijuana Troops, May 10, 1911, reproduced in Velasco Ceballos, *¿Se apoderará Estados Unidos de América de Baja California?*, p. 141.

51. Ricardo Flores Magón, "La Baja California," *Regeneración*, June 10, 1911.

52. Blaisdell, *The Desert Revolution*, p. 103.

53. Friedrich Katz, *The Life and Times of Pancho Villa* (Stanford: Stanford University Press, 1998), p. 101.

54. As Baja California historian Marco Antonio Samaniego recently put it: "It isn't right to classify the armed movement in Baja California as 'magonista.'" Samaniego, *Nacionalismo y revolución,* p. 8.

55. For finances and circulation figures for *Regeneración* through this period, see Blaisdell, *The Desert Revolution*, pp. 98–99, and Sandos, *Rebellion in the Boarderlands*, pp. 58–59.

56. Sandos, *Rebellion in the Borderlands*, pp. 58–59.

57. *Ibid.*, p. 39.

58. William C. Owen, quoted in Blaisdell, *The Desert Revolution*, p. 185.

59. John Kenneth Turner to William C. Owen, June 12, 1911, EDT-INAH, roll 3.

60. Alden Buell Case, *Thirty Years with the Mexicans: In Peace and Revolution* (New York: Flemming Revel Company, 1917), p. 137.

61. John Kenneth Turner, "Inside Story of the Taking of Veracruz Reveals That American Marines Looted, Outraged and Murdered Helpless People," *Appeal to Reason*, July 10, 1915.

62. John Kenneth Turner, "Mr. Wilson, US Troops Must Leave Mexican Soil," *Appeal to Reason*, April 22, 1916.

63. Passport applications of John Kenneth Turner and wife, February 19, 1919. State Department Files, National Archives.

64. John Kenneth Turner, *Hands Off Mexico* (New York: Rand School of Social Science, 1920).

CHAPTER TWENTY: THE MAN FROM MEXICO

1. Lowell L. Blaisdell, *The Desert Revolution: Baja California, 1911* (Madison: University of Wisconsin Press, 1962), p. 181.

2. Simon Berthold, untitled poem, EDT-INAH, doc. 278.

3. George Schmuker, quoted in Lowell L. Blaisdell, *The Desert Revolution: Baja California, 1911* (Madison: University of Wisconsin Press, 1962), p. 165.

4. Rómulo Velasco Ceballos, *¿Se apoderara Estados Unidos de America de Baja California? (La invasion filibustera de 1911)* (Mexico City: Imprenta Nacional, 1922), p. 139.

5. Blaisdell, *The Desert Revolution*, pp. 167–68.

6. Quoted in Blaisdell, *The Desert Revolution*, p. 145.

7. John Skirius, "Oil and Other Foreign Interests in the Mexican Revolution, 1911–1914," *Journal of Latin American Studies* 35.1 (February 2003), p. 28.

8. Velasco Ceballos, *¿Se apoderará Estados Unidos de América de Baja California?*, p. 125.

9. Paul Reddin, *Wild West Shows* (Urbana: University of Illinois Press, 1999).

10. "Los sucesos de la Frontera: Infames proyectos de los agitadores. Carta de Ricardo Flores Magón a su hermano Enrique." *El País, Diario Católico*, no. 3449. Mexico City, August 9, 1908.

11. Ramón Corral to Enrique Creel, August 6, 1908, in J. E. Moguel Flores, *El magonismo en Coahuila* (Saltillo: Gobierno del Estado de Coahuila, 2006). The Mexican consul in Tucson had articles published about and with excerpts from the letter in Tucson, Phoenix, Bisbee, Clifton, and Yuma, and he printed 500 copies of his own to distribute in various places. SRE, legajo 332, exp. 3, Cónsul Arturo Elías to SRE, nota reservada 43, April 8, 1909, and reservada 61, April 21,1909. The full text of the letter was published in "Magón's Plans for Mexican Revolution," *The Mexican Herald*, August 6, 1908.

12. Ethel Duffy Turner, "Ricardo Flores Magón y el Partido Liberal," type-script, ch. 13, unpaginated, EDT-Bancroft.

13. Lawrence Douglas Taylor Hansen, "¿Charlatán o filibustero peligroso?: El papel de Richard 'Dick' Ferris en la revuelta magonista de 1911 en Baja California," *Historia Mexicana* 44.4 (April–June 1995), p. 583.

14. Blaisdell, *The Desert Revolution*, p. 60.

15. Richard Amero, "The Making of the Panama-California Exposition, 1909–1915," *Journal of San Diego History* 36.1 (Winter 1990), http://www.sandiegohistory.org/journal/90winter/expo.htm.

16. Taylor, "¿Charlatán o filibustero peligroso?," p. 590; Blaisdell, *The Desert Revolution*, pp. 61–62.

17. Blaisdell, *The Desert Revolution*, p. 87.

18. *San Diego Union*, reproduced in Blaisdell, *The Desert Revolution*, p. 88.

19. "Mexico Asks for Arrest of Woman," *San Diego Union*, March 19, 1911.

20. Quoted in Blaisdell, *The Desert Revolution*, pp. 62–63.

21. *San Diego Union*, June 1 and June 3, 1911, cited in Lawrence D. Taylor, "The Magonista Revolt in Baja California: Capitalist Conspiracy or Rebelion de los Pobres?," *San Diego Historical Society Quarterly* 45.1 (1999), available at http://www.sandiegohistory.org/journal/99winter/magonista.htm.

22. "Dick Ferris in Bad at San Diego," *San Francisco Chronicle*, June 17, 1911.

23. "Mexico Asks for Arrest of Woman," *San Francisco Chronicle*, March 19, 1911.

24. Taylor Hansen, "¿Charlatán o filibustero peligroso?," pp. 605–606.

25. Voltairine de Cleyre, quoted in James A. Sandos, *Rebellion in the Boarderlands: Anarchism and the Plan of San Diego, 1904–1923* (Norman: Oklahoma University Press, 1992), p. 41.

26. Esteban Cantú, quoted in Marco Antonio Samaniego, *Los gobiernos civiles en Baja California, 1920–1923: Un estudio sobre la relación entre los poderes local y federal* (Mexicali: UABJ/Instituto de Cultura de Baja California, 1998), p. 36.

27. *Ibid.*, pp. 33 and 41–50.

28. *Ibid.*, p. 54.

29. *Ibid.*, p. 57.

30. Taylor Hansen, "¿Charlatán o filibustero peligroso?,", pp. 598 and 604.

31. H. A. Du Souchet, *The Man from Mexico: A Farcical Comedy in Three Acts* (New York, Samuel French, 1897).

32. Committee on Foreign Relations, United States Senate, *Revolutions in Mexico: Hearing Before a Subcommittee of the Committee of Foreign Relations United States Senate. Sixty-Second Congress, Second Session, Pursuant to S. Res. 335, A Resolution Authorizing the Committee on Foreign Relations to investigate Whether Any Interests in the United States are Now Engaged in Inciting Rebellion in Cuban and Mexico* (Washington, D.C.: Government Printing Office, 1913).

33. Juan Sarabia, "Carta abierta de Juan Sarabia a Ricardo Flores Magón," *El Diario del Hogar*, June 4, 1911.

34. *Ibid.*

35. Manuel Sarabia, "Ricardo Flores Magón ante el socialismo: Entre todo los partidos honrados está desprestigiado el embaucador de Los Angeles," *El Diario del Hogar*, October 15, 1911.

36. Jesús Flores Magón to Pablo Macedo, July 20, 1911, AEJM, caja 25, exp. 6.

37. Ricardo Flores Magón to María Brousse, December 20, 1920, Archivo Electrónico Ricardo Flores Magón, http://www.archivomagon.net/ObrasCompletas/Correspondencia/Cor02/Cor25.html.

38. Antonio I. Villarreal, "Una requisitoria y un reto: Ricardo Flores Magón es chantagista, estafador, cobarde y degenerado," *El Diario del Hogar*, September 27, 1911.

39. *Ibid.*

40. Manuel Sarabia, "Ricardo Flores Magón ante el socialismo: Entre todo los partidos honrados está desprestigiado el embaucador de Los Angeles," *El Diario del Hogar*, October 15, 1911.

41. Antonio I. Villarreal, "El anarquismo magonista, fomentado por el oro de los científicos: Luis del Toro tiende su mano amiga a Ricardo Flores Magón," *Regeneración*, August 26, 1911.

42. Antonio I. Villarreal, "La horca para Villarreal y Sarabia," *Regeneración*, August 26, 1911.

43. Ricardo Flores Magón, "Patadas de ahogado del pederasta y asesino Antonio I. Villarreal," *Regeneración*, September 2, 1911.

44. Ricardo Flores Magón, "El coronel de los 41," *Regeneración*, September 16, 1911.

45. Manuel Sarabia, "Ricardo Flores Magón ante el socialismo: Entre todo los partidos honrados está desprestigiado el embaucador de Los Angeles," *El Diario del Hogar* October 15, 1911.

46. *Ibid.*

47. "¡Otra víctima del Magonismo!: Jesús M. Rangel." *Regeneración*, September 30, 1911.

48. Cónsul Arturo Elías to the Secretaría de Relaciones Exteriores [435–43], September 30, 1911, Jack Mosby y Socios 3˙ Parte, 1911 [17735]; nota reservada, SRE, exp. 19.

49. "Mexican Methods to Be Condemned," *Los Angeles Tribune*, August 20, 1911.

50. "Motion for Dismissal of Pryce Charges Are Denied," *Los Angeles Tribune*, August 25, 1911.

51. "De Lara Tells Story to House Committee," *Los Angeles Express*, June 10, 1910.

52. Luis G. Lara, "Open letter to Ricardo Flores Magón, May 12, 1911, read in the Placita de los Mexicanos, Los Angeles, by Sr. Antonio Sola, 14 de mayo de 1911," reproduced in Velasco Ceballos, *¿Se apoderara Estados Unidos de America de Baja California?*, p. 158.

53. "Jack Mosby y Socios 2˙ Parte, Incitativa al Pueblo Mexicano," signed by "Trabajadores A. M. Villarreal, J. Robledo, A Cantú," Los Angeles 13 agosto 1911," SRE, exp. 19.

54. John Klenneth Turner, quoted in Marco Antonio Samaniego, *Nacionalismo*

y Revolución: Los acontecimientos de 1911 en Baja California (Tijuana: Universidad Autónoma de Baja California, 2008), p. 307.

55. Antonio I. Villarreal, "Una requisitoria y un reto: Ricardo Flores Magón es chantagista, estafador, cobarde y degenerado," *El Diario del Hogar*, September 27, 1911.

56. Ricardo Flores Magón to Quirino Limón, June 14, 1911, Archivo Electrónico Ricardo Flores Magón, http://www.archivomagon.net/ObrasCompletas/Correspondencia/Cor338.html.

CHAPTER TWENTY-ONE: CODA

1. Grace Duffy Zubler to Ethel Duffy Turner, February 17, 1966, EDT-Bancroft, box 1.

2. Ethel Duffy Turner, "Notes on Early Literary Carmel." EDT-Bancroft, box 1.

3. *Ibid.*,p. 6.

4. Grace Duffy Zubler to Ethel Duffy Turner, February 17, 1966, EDT-Bancroft, box 1.

5. The only surviving written copy has a handwritten inscription by Ethel that reads: "to be sung to the pounding of spiked hammers used to tenderize this sea food. This version was approved by George Sterling shortly before his death. He originated it; others added verses as they thought of words to rhyme with Abalone."

CHAPTER TWENTY-TWO: RACING AGAINST THE ODDS

1. James A. Sandos, *Rebellion in the Boarderlands: Anarchism and the Plan of San Diego, 1904–1923* (Norman: Oklahoma University Press, 1992), p. 41.

2. Ricardo Flores Magón to Enrique Flores Magón and Práxedis Guerrero, June 13, 1908, Archivo Electrónico Ricardo Flores Magón, http://www.archivomagon.net/ObrasCompletas/Correspondencia/Cor265.html.

3. Doctor Luis Rivas Iruz to Ricardo Flores Magón, May 28, 1911, Archivo Electrónico Ricardo Flores Magón, http://www.archivomagon.net/ObrasCompletas/Correspondencia/Cor329.html.

4. Ricardo Flores Magón to Doctor Luis Rivas Iruz, June 3, 1911, Archivo Electrónico Ricardo Flores Magón, http://www.archivomagon.net/ObrasCompletas/Correspondencia/Cor333.html.

5. A. M. Villarreal to Antonio Villarreal, October 6, 1911, AAIV.

6. *Ibid.*

7. C. Flores to Antonio Villarreal, June 23, 1911, AAIV; see also Máximo Ortega to Antonio Villarreal, July 31, 1911, AAIV.

8. Ricardo Flores Magón, "El Zapatismo," *Regeneración*, November 18, 1911.

9. Ricardo Flores Magón, "Discurso que pronunció Ricardo Flores Magón en el mitín internacional en memoria de Ferrer," *Regeneración*, October 21, 1911.

10. Enrique Flores Magón, "Venganza," *Regeneración*, January 6, 1912.

11. José Pérez, "A un Judas," reprinted in *Regeneración*, December 21, 1912.

12. Antonio Rincón to Emilio Campa, August 31, 1911, AAIV.

13. Ricardo Flores Magón, "Notas al vuelo," *Regeneración*, June 22, 1912.

14. Ricardo Flores Magón, "Nuestro proceso," *Regeneración*, June 22, 1912

15. Ricardo Flores Magón, "Regeneración muriendo," *Regeneración*, December 23, 1911.

16. Ricardo Flores Magón, "Patadas de ahogado del pederasta y asesino Antonio I. Villarreal," *Regeneración*, September 2, 1911.

17. Tomás Labrada, "Mi llegada a Los Angeles," *Regeneración*, August 19, 1911.

18. Ricardo Flores Magón, "Regeneración muriendo," *Regeneración*, December 23, 1911.

19. "Muerte de Regeneración," *Regeneración*, December 31, 1911; "Por la vida de Regeneración," *Regeneración*, January 6, 1912.

20. Ricardo Flores Magón, "Una catástrofe," *Regeneración*, January 13, 1912.

CHAPTER TWENTY-THREE: FROM TRANSNATIONAL SOLIDARITY TO INTERNATIONAL RELATIONS

1. Committee on Foreign Relations, United States Senate, *Revolutions in Mexico: Hearing Before a Subcommittee of the Committee of Foreign Relations United States Senate. Sixty-Second Congress, Second Session, Pursuant to S. Res. 335, A Resolution Authorizing the Committee on Foreign Relations to investigate Whether Any Interests in the United States are Now Engaged in Inciting Rebellion in Cuban and Mexico* (Washington, D.C.: Government Printing Office, 1913), p. 246.

2. The finest account of Wilson's policies toward the Mexican Revolution is still Friedrich Katz, *The Secret War in Mexico: Europe, the United States, and the Mexican Revolution* (Chicago: University of Chicago Press, 1981).

3. Woodrow Wilson to John Nolan, July 22, 1913, cited in James A. Sandos, *Rebellion in the Borderlands: Anarchism and the Plan of San Diego, 1904–1923* (Norman: University of Oklahoma Press, 1992), p. 50.

4. Jesús Mendez Rangel, "Continuación y final," AEFM, caja 13, exp, 57.

5. A. Narquista, "El moderno Nerón Huerta-Díaz aplica la 'Ley de Fuga' a Madero," *Regeneración*, March 1, 1913.

6. Juan Sarabia to Antonio Villarreal, February 19, 1912, AAIV. Sarabia reported that "there are many Liberals—of our Liberals—as I said before, who have taken up arms [against Madero], especially in Chihuahua and Coahuila, and Alanís tells me that they are backing Emilio Vázquez [Gómez] because they have no

other banner under which to congregate, but that they fight for the Liberal Party."

7. Coronel Manuél Diéguez, Mayor Juan José Ríos, and Mayor Esteban Baca Calderón to Lic. Jesús Flores Magón, August 12, 1913, AJFM, caja 25, exp. 3.

8. Ethel Duffy Turner, "On the Life of John Kenneth Turner," p. 9, EDT-Bancroft, box 1, folder 5.

9. Jesús Rangel tells of his visit to Zapata after being released from Belem Prison, thanks to Victoriano Huerta's coup. Rangel had long conversations with Zapata and introduced him to the September 23 manifesto, which, Rangel said, Zapata approved. Jesús Mendez Rangel, "Continuación y final," AEFM, caja 13, exp. 57.

10. Juan Sarabia to Antonio Villarreal, April 9, 1912, AAIV.

11. John Kenneth Turner to Ethel Duffy Turner, undated, EDT INAH, doc. 131.

12. Juan Manuel Romero Gil, "Lázaro Gutiérrez de Lara: Socialista con fusil de palabras," in Lázaro Gutiérrez de Lara, *Los bribones: Novela situada en Cananea, Sonora, 1907* (Hermosillo: Instituto de Cultura Sonorense, 2010), p. 45.

13. "Gutiérrez de Lara no quiso dar satisfacción al diputado Otero," *El Tiempo*, December 1, 1911; "Las costureras huelguistas volverán a sus trabajos," *El Tiempo*, January 2, 1912; "Gutiérrez de Lara en libertad," *El Tiempo*, December 4, 1911.

14. Juan Sarabia to Antonio Villarreal, January 9, 1913, AAIV.

15. S. M. Emery to Secretary of State William Jennings Bryan, March 18, 1913, National Archives, Record Group 812.00, Records of the Department of State Relating to Internal Affairs of Mexico, 1910–29, Mexican Political Affairs.

16. "Mr. Turner Speaks," *El País*, February 23, 1913, translated by the State Department, National Archives, Record Group 812.00, Records of the Department of State Relating to Internal Affairs of Mexico, 1910–29, Mexican Political Affairs.

17. "Comment" attached to translation of *El País*, February 23, 1913, "Mr. Turner Speaks," National Archives, Record Group 812.00, Records of the Department of State Relating to Internal Affairs of Mexico, 1910–29, Mexican Political Affairs.

18. John Kenneth Turner, "Under Fire in Mexico: My Torture and False Imprisonment by Félix Díaz," *Washington Post*, May 11, 1913.

19. Mrs L. F. Turner to President William Howard Taft, March 15, 1913, National Archives, Record Group 812.00, Records of the Department of State Relating to Internal Affairs of Mexico, 1910–29, Mexican Political Affairs.

20. R. K. Turner (ensign, U.S. Navy) to Senator William Alden Smith, no date, National Archives, Record Group 812.00, Records of the Department of State Relating to Internal Affairs of Mexico, 1910–29, Mexican Political Affairs.

21. J. C. Casselman to Secretary of State William Jennings Bryan, National Archives, Record Group 812.00, Records of the Department of State Relating to

Internal Affairs of Mexico, 1910–29, Mexican Political Affairs.

22. S. W. Scott to the Hon. W. F. Borland, U.S. House of Representatives, Washington, D.C., February 26, 1913, National Archives, Record Group 812.00, Records of the Department of State Relating to Internal Affairs of Mexico, 1910–29, Mexican Political Affairs.

23. Ralph Easley, Chairman of the Executive Council of the National Civic Federation to Secretary of State, March 8, 1913, National Archives, Record Group 812.00, Records of the Department of State Relating to Internal Affairs of Mexico, 1910–29, Mexican Political Affairs.

24. Judge John Works to Secretary of State Philander Chase Knox, February 28, 1913, National Archives, Record Group 812.00, Records of the Department of State Relating to Internal Affairs of Mexico, 1910–29, Mexican Political Affairs.

25. Ambassador Henry Lane Wilson to Secretary of State Philander Chase Knox, February 24, 1913, National Archives, Record Group 812.00, Records of the Department of State Relating to Internal Affairs of Mexico, 1910–29, Mexican Political Affairs.

26. John Kenneth Turner, "Under Fire in Mexico," *Appeal to Reason*, May 11, 1913. The article was printed simultaneously in fourteen U.S. papers.

27. John Kenneth Turner to Ambassador Henry Lane Wilson, February 23, 1913, National Archives, Record Group 812.00, Records of the Department of State Relating to Internal Affairs of Mexico, 1910–29, Mexican Political Affairs.

28. President Carranza was directly involved in dealings with Turner; indeed, it was because of an objection to Carranza's summons of Turner to meet with him in Mexico City that the State Department decided to deny John and his second wife, Adriana Spadoni, their passports in 1919. See Consul Ramón P. De Negri (New York) to Minister of Foreign Relations Cándido Aguilar, February 21, 1919, SRE, 3-19-15, folio 4. Mexico's Ministry of Foreign Relations files also show payments to Turner made in 1917 and 1919, and the documents carefully track the publication and distribution of Turner's *Hands Off Mexico*, published in 1920, SRE, 3-19-15, folio 1 and folio 4, and Consul De Negri to Minister of Foreign Relations, February 24, 1920, SRE, exp. 1262.

29. William C. Owen to Enrique Flores Magón, August 23, 1912, AEFM, caja 5, exp. 53.

30. Rafael Romero Palacios, "Protesta," *Regeneración*, October 26, por; Francisca Mendoza, "Observación," *Regeneración*, November 2, 1912; William C. Owen, "Important to our English Readers," *Regeneración*, November 2, 1912.

31. Antonio de P. Araujo, "La campaña contra Regeneración," *Regeneración*, May 10, 1913. For a narrative of the events, see Mariano Gómez Gutiérrez [Blas Lara Cázares], *La vida que yo viví: Novela histórico-liberal de la Revolución Mexicana*

(n.p., 1954), pp. 197–209.

32. Critical articles were published in León Cárdenas's El Paso journal *Cerebro y Fuerza*, as well as in the Latino section of the Los Angeles Wobblies' journal, and the criticism seems to have extended beyond this. See Antonio de P. Araujo, "La campaña contra *Regeneración*," *Regeneración*, May 24, 1913. Thus, Owen found it necessary to reply to Moncaleano's accusations against Ricardo in Havana that were still circulating a year after the expulsion of Moncaleano and Carmona. See William C. Owen, "Carta de Cuba," July 14, 1913, AEFM, caja 12, exp. 15.

33. Like Práxedis Guerrero, Rangel was the son of a Guanajuato *hacienda* owner who turned against his natal class. In addition to his own long-standing credentials as a rebel in Texas from 1905 forward, Rangel was one of the Liberals with a family pedigree in his struggle against Díaz, since he was related on his wife's side to General Trinidad García de la Cadena, a Zacatecas governor who was assassinated for presuming to run against Don Porfirio. See Antonio de Araujo, "El Conato de Revolución en Tamaulipas en 1906," May 1932, AEFM, caja 13, exp 50, and El suscrito [Jesús M. Rangel], "Proyectos biográficos," February 5, 1940, AEFM, caja 13, exp. 57.

34. Antonio de P. Araujo "La campaña contra Regeneración," *Regeneración*, May 10, 1913. Jesús Rangel's account of the event is "La verdad de los acontecimientos en el condado de Dimmitt, Texas," December 30, 1913, AEFM, caja 12, exp. 20.

35. Antonio de P. Araujo, "Acción en Texas en caso de una convicción," *Regeneración*, November 8, 1913.

36. Antonio de P. Araujo, "Estamos listos," *Regeneración*, December 13, 1913.

37. "¿Un nuevo golpe?," *Regeneración*, December 6, 1913.

38. Antonio de P Araujo, "Estamos listos," December 13, 1913.

39. For an account on the diplomacy of the invasion, see Katz, *The Secret War in Mexico*, ch. 5.

40. James Creelman, "Armed Intervention in Riven Mexico by United States Alone Can Stop Battle for Power and Plunder, says James Creelman in Message from Huerta's Capital," *Washington Post*, March 1, 1914.

41. *Ibid.*

42. John Kenneth Turner, *Shall It Be Again?* (New York: B. W. Huebsch, 1922), p. 209.

43. Joan London, quoted in Elisa Ramírez Castañeda, "Introducción," in Jack London, *México Intervenido: Reportajes desde Veracruz y Tampico, 1914* (Mexico City: Ediciones Toledo, 1991), p. 18.

44. Jack London, quoted in Lowell L. Blaisdell, *The Desert Revolution: Baja California, 1911* (Madison,: University of Wisconsin Press, 1962), p. 43.

45. Blaisdell, *The Desert Revolution*, p. 149.

46. Jeanne Campbell Reesman, *Jack London's Racial Lives: A Critical Biography* (Athens: University of Georgia Press, 2009), p. 277.

47. Jack London, "Lawgivers," *Collier's Weekly,* June 20, 1914.

48. Jack London, "Mexico's Army and Ours," *Collier's Weekly*, May 30, 1914.

CHAPTER TWENTY-FOUR: CRUMBS

1. McNeil Island Penitentiary Inmate Files, 1899–1920, Bureau of Prisons, RG 129, box 20, National Archives. Ricardo's file is 2198, Enrique's is 2199, Librado's is 2200, and Anselmo Figueroa's is 2201.

2. See Job Harriman's introduction to Ernest Wooster, *Communities Past and Present* (Newllano, LA: Llano Co-operative Company, 1924).

3. For an analysis of the role of Antonio Rodríguez's lynching in the hardening of the idea of Mexicans as a "race," see Claudio Lomnitz, "Los orígenes de nuestra supuesta homogeneidad: Breve arqueología de la unidad nacional en México," *Prismas* 14.1 (June 2010), pp. 17–36.

4. Antonio de P. Araujo, "Acción en Texas en caso de una convicción," *Regeneración*, November 8, 1913.

5. Ricardo Flores Magón "La intervención y los presos de Texas," *Regeneración*, June 13, 1914.

6. Ricardo Flores Magón, "Cantos de Sirena de Woodrow Wilson," *Regeneración*, May 30, 1914.

7. Ricardo Flores Magón "La intervención y los presos de Texas," *Regeneración*, June 13, 1914.

8. Enrique Flores Magón "¿Mueran a los Gringos? No; ¡Mueran los ricos!" *Regeneración*, June 13, 1914.

9. Jack London, "The Red Game of War," *Collier's Weekly*, May 16, 1914.

10. Ricardo Flores Magón, "El miedo de la burguesía causa la intervención," *Regeneración*, July 11, 1914.

11. Jorge Aguilar Mora, *Una muerte justa, sencilla, eterna: Cultura y guerra durante la Revolución Mexicana* (Mexico City: Editorial ERA, 1990), pp. 329–43.

12. Ricardo Flores Magón, "La Revolución en Arizona," *Regeneración*, August 22, 1914.

13. Ricardo Flores Magón, "Los presos de Phoenix," *Regeneración*, September 12, 1914.

14. Lowell L. Blaisdell, *The Desert Revolution: Baja California, 1911* (Madison: University of Wisconsin Press, 1962), p. 185.

15. María Brouse to Teresa Arteaga, January 23, 1913, AEFM, caja 52, exp. 34.

16. William C. Owen, "Our New Home," *Regeneración*, February 1, 1913.

17. Mariano Gómez Gutiérrez [Blas Lara Cázares], *La vida que yo viví: Novela histórico-liberal de la Revolución Mexicana* (n.p., 1954), pp. 204–205.

18. Enrique Flores Magón, "¡Viva la anarquía," *Regeneración*, January 31, 1914.

19. Ricardo Flores Magón, "Anselmo L. Figueroa," *Regeneración*, October 2, 1915.

20. Ricardo Flores Magón, "Hacia la muerte," *Regeneración* March 7, 1914.

21. *Ibid.*

22. See, for instance, Ricardo Flores Magón, "La muerte de *Regeneración*," *Regeneración*, July 11, 1914.

23. James A. Sandos, *Rebellion in the Boarderlands: Anarchism and the Plan of San Diego, 1904–1923* (Norman: Oklahoma University Press, 1992), p. 59.

24. Ricardo Flores Magón, "Los presos de Phoenix," *Regeneración*, September 26, 1914.

25. Ricardo Flores Magón, "La crisis," *Regeneración*, November 14, 1914.

26. Ricardo Flores Magón, "Para los envidiosos," *Regeneración*, November 28, 1914.

27. Gómez [Lara], *La vida que yo viví*, p. 220.

28. *Ibid.*, p. 227.

29. *Ibid.*, p. 221.

30. *Ibid.*, p. 226.

31. Enrique Flores Magón, "¡$26.41!," Regeneración, January 22, 1916.

CHAPTER TWENTY-FIVE: A STAKE IN THE HEART

1. Jaime Vidal, "'Fuerza Conciente' Secuestrada," *Regeneración*, September 12, 1914.

2. "En nuestro puesto," *Regeneración*, July 8, 1916.

3. Ricardo Flores Magón and Librado Rivera, "Manifiesto," *Regeneración*, March 16, 1918.

4. Ricardo Flores Magón, "El caos," *Regeneración*, June 27, 1914.

5. Juan Sarabia to Antonio Villarreal, December 23, 1914, AAIV.

6. David Kennedy, *Over Here: The First World War and American Society* (New York: Oxford University Press, 1982), pp. 65 and 80.

7. William C. Owen, "Notes," *Regeneración*, March 3, 1916.

8. P. D. Noel, "Shall the Free Be Throttled?," *Regeneración*, April 1, 1916.

9. Ricardo Flores Magón, "En vísperas de la Gran Revolución," *Regeneración*, June 23, 1917.

10. *Ibid.*

11. The two most important works on this episode are James A. Sandos, *Rebellion in the Borderlands: Anarchism and the Plan of San Diego, 1904–1923* (Norman:

University of Oklahoma Press, 1992), and Benjamin H. Johnson, *Revolution in Texas: How a Forgotten Rebellion and Its Suppression Turned Mexicans into Americans* (New Haven: Yale University Press, 2003). My account here is based on their research.

12. Sandos, *Rebellion in the Borderlands*, p. 59.

13. Johnson, *Revolution in Texas*, pp. 144–75.

14. "Un caído," *Regeneración*, June 23, 1917.

15. John H. Lindquist and James Fraser, "A Sociological Interpretation of the Bisbee Deportation," *Pacific Historical Review* 37.4 (November 1968), p. 405.

16. Sandos, *Rebellion in the Borderlands*, pp. 119–20.

17. *Ibid.*, pp. 123–24.

18. *Ibid.*, p. 72.

19. Johnson, *Revolution in Texas*, p. 120.

20. The file on the Pizaña extradition is SRE, legajo 30963, exp. 1294.

21. Sandos, *Rebellion in the Borderlands*, pp. 125–26.

22. Ricardo Flores Magón, "Los levantamientos en Texas," *Regeneración*, October 9, 1915.

23. Enrique Flores Magón to Gral de Div. Juan José Ríos (Iguala, Guerrero), confidencial, November 17, 1939, AEFM, caja 13, exp. 14.

24. Sandos, *Rebellion in the Borderlands*, pp. 117–25.

25. "Crescencio Barrera y Aniceto Pizaña, 1916," SRE, exp. 1294.

26. "Movimiento Revolucionario" Mancillas, Julio—Agente secreto, SRE, exp/R104-15, 1912. For Ricardo's interpretation of the Arizona affair, see Ricardo Flores Magón, Los presos de Phoenix," Regeneración September 12, 1914.

27. Ricardo Flores Magón, "Asalto a las oficinas de Regeneración," *Regeneración*, February 26, 1916,

28. Ricardo Flores Magón, "Barbarie Texana," *Regeneración*, January 1, 1916.

29. Ricardo Flores Magón, "Los levantamientos en Texas," *Regeneración*, October 2, 1915.

30. Ricardo Flores Magón, "Asalto a las oficinas de Regeneración," *Regeneración*, February 26, 1916.

31. William C. Owen, "The Way I Judge Invasions," *Regeneración*, March 25, 1916.

32. Lucía Norman, "Rebelémonos," *Regeneración*, February 19, 1916; Raúl Palma "Una idea," *Regeneración*, February 19, 1916.

33. "Gran Mitin Internacional, sábado 18 marzo 1916, en el Labor Temple, 8 PM," *Regeneración*, March 10, 1916. Archivo Electrónico Ricardo Flores Magón, http://www.archivomagon.net/Periodico/Regeneracion/CuartaEpoca/PDF/e4n230.pdf.

34. "Tries to Rescue Mexican Leaders: Rebel Mob Battles with Police in Los Angeles When Ring-Leaders Get Sentence," *San Francisco Chronicle*, June 26, 1912.

35. María Brousse to Ricardo Flores Magón, September 17, 1908, Archivo Electrónico Ricardo Flores Magón, http://www.archivomagon.net/ObrasCompletas/Correspondencia/Cor267.html.

36. Ricardo Flores Magón to María Brousse and Lucía Norman, October 25, 1908, Archivo Electrónico Ricardo Flores Magón, http://www.archivomagon.net/ObrasCompletas/Correspondencia/Cor274.html.

37. "Raúl Palma, arrestado," *Regeneración*, May 13, 1916.

38. William C Owen, "Regeneración Barred from the Mails," *Regeneración*, March 13, 1916.

39. Ricardo Flores Magón, "Los mártires de Texas," *Regeneración*, July 8, 1916.

40. Ricardo Flores Magón, "Eugenio Alzalde," *Regeneración*, September 16, 1916.

41. Alexander Berkman, "Villa or Wilson—Which is the Bandit?," *Regeneración*, March 25, 1916.

42. Emma Goldman, *Living My Life*, 2 vols. (New York: Knopf, 1931), vol. 1, pp. 500–501.

43. "El jurado falló en contra de los hermanos Magón," *Regeneración*, June 17, 1916.

44. Program, *¡Tierra y Libertad!*, March 14, 1917.

45. Mariano Gómez Gutiérrez [Blas Lara Cázares], *La vida que yo viví: Novela histórico-liberal de la Revolución Mexicana* (n.p., 1954), pp. 229–30.

46. "El drama 'Tierra y Libertad,'" *Regeneración*, October 6, 1917.

47. Gómez [Lara], *La vida que yo viví*, p. 232.

48. Librado Rivera, notes on "Ricardo Flores Magón," EDT-INAH, doc 92.

49. Ricardo Flores Magón, "Nuevo drama," *Regeneración*, February 9, 1918.

50. Ricardo Flores Magón, "Enferma," *Regeneración*, February 9, 1918.

51. Ricardo Flores Magón, "Separación," *Regeneración*, February 9, 1918.

52. Píndaro Urióstegui Miranda, "Entrevista a Nicolás T. Bernal," Biblioteca Virtual Antorcha, http://www.antorcha.net/biblioteca_virtual/historia/entrevista_bernal/presentacion.html.

53. William C. Owen to Enrique Flores Magón, October 11, 1921, AEFM, caja 5, exp. 53.

54. William C. Owen to Enrique Flores Magón, June 8, 1924, AEFM, caja 5, exp. 3.

55. Fernando Palomares to Enrique Flores Magón, March 18, 1918, AEFM, caja 50, exp. 9.

56. Enrique was unusually explicit about the unjust oppression that was

marriage for most women. See, for instance, Enrique Flores Magón, "Levanta, hermana!," *Regeneración*, January 13, 1911. For his warning against anti-Americanism, see Enrique Flores Magón, "¿Mueran los Gringos? No; ¡Mueran los ricos!," *Regeneración*, June 13, 1914.

57. Enrique Flores Magón to Rafael García, December 28, 1922, AEFM, caja 50, exp. 10.

58. Ricardo Flores Magón, "Por la justicia," *Regeneración*, March 16, 1918. This is the text of a speech read by Ricardo at a rally in February 1918.

59. Ricardo Flores Magón, "En vísperas de la Gran Revolución," *Regeneración*, June 23, 1917.

60. Ricardo Flores Magón, "No debemos callar," *Regeneración*, June 23, 1917.

61. Enrique Flores Magón "Aclaración," *Regeneración*, September 1, 1917.

62. Enrique Flores Magón to Teresa Arteaga, December 16, 1919, AEFM, caja 45, exp. 58.

63. Rafael García to Enrique Flores Magón, September 24, 1918, AEFM, caja 50, exp. 10.

64. Rafael García to Enrique Flores Magón, July 8, 1918, AEFM, caja 50, exp. 10.

65. "Resumen testimonio Ignacio López, tocante a Gaitán. Dado ante compañeros Villarreal, Teresa V. Magón, Luis Pérez, R. B. García y Rafael Covarrubias," AEFM, caja 13, exp. 67; and "Testimonios concernientes a la conducta de Teodoro Gaitán, recogidos por Rafael B García," AEFM, caja 14, exp. 11.

66. Report by E. Kosterlitsky, Re: Ricardo Flores Magon and Librado Rivera, former publishers of "Regeneración" Anarchists, Los Angeles, December 17, 1918, file no. 1675, Leavenworth Penitentiary, Enrique Flores Magón file, National Archives.

67. Enrique Flores Magón to Teresa Arteaga, July 7, 1918, AEFM, caja 45, exp, 41.

CHAPTER TWENTY-SIX: DEATH

1. Ricardo Flores Magón to Ellen White, December 27, 1921, in Ricardo Flores Magón, *Obras completas*, vol. 1, *Correspondencia (1899–1918)*, ed. Jacinto Barrera Bassols (Mexico City: Dirección General de Publicaciones del Conaculta, 2001), p. 301.

2. Enrique Flores Magón to Teresa V. Magón, June 14, 1918, AEFM, caja 45, exp. 12.

3. Enrique Flores Magón to Teresa V. Magón, June 16, 1918, AEFM, caja 45, exp. 13.

4. Enrique Flores Magón to Teresa V. Magón, September 28, 1918, AEFM, caja

45, exp. 24.

5. Enrique Flores Magón to Teresa V. Magón, October 20, 1918, AEFM, caja 45, exp. 26.

6. Rafael García to Enrique Flores Magón, January 3, 1919, AEFM, caja 4, exp. 26.

7. Enrique Flores Magón to Teresa V. Magón, September 4, 1918, AEFM, caja 45, exp. 23.

8. Enrique Flores Magón, *Combatimos la tiranía: Un pionero revolucionario mexicano cuenta su historia a Samuel Kaplan*, trans. Jesús Amaya Topete (Mexico City: INEHRM, 1958), pp. 201–202.

9. Enrique Flores Magón to Teresa V. Magón, November 7, 1918, AEFM, caja 45, exp. 27.

10. Ricardo Flores Magón to Ellen White, October 6, 1920, in *Correspondencia*, pp. 47–48.

11. Record of Articles Received by Prisoners, U.S. Department of Justice, Bureau of Prisons, Leavenworth Penitentiary, prisoner 14596 (Magon), National Archives.

12. Balance Sheet, U.S. Department of Justice, Bureau of Prisons, Leavenworth Penitentiary, prisoner 14596 (Magon), National Archives.

13. Warden to Ellen White, August 1, 1921, U.S. Department of Justice, Bureau of Prisons, Leavenworth Penitentiary, prisoner 14596 (Magon), National Archives.

14. Sick Report, U.S. Department of Justice, Bureau of Prisons, Leavenworth Penitentiary, prisoner 14596 (Magon), National Archives.

15. Letters, U.S. Department of Justice, Bureau of Prisons, Leavenworth Penitentiary, prisoner 14596 (Magon), National Archives.

16. Enrique Flores Magón to Teresa V. Magón, December 16, 1919, AEFM, caja 45, exp. 58.

17. *Ibid.*

18. Rafael García to Juan Olmos, December 24, 1919, AEFM, caja 9, exp. 4c.

19. Enrique Flores Magón to Teresa V. Magón, December 16, 1919, AEFM, caja 45, exp. 58.

20. Enrique Flores Magón to Teresa V. Magón, December 21, 1919, AEFM, caja 45, exp. 59.

21. Telegram from Enrique Flores Magón to Ricardo Flores Magón, September 16, 1920, U.S. Department of Justice, Bureau of Prisons, Leavenworth Penitentiary, prisoner 14596 (Magon), National Archives.

22. Enrique Flores Magón to Teresa V. Magón, December 1, 1919, AEFM, caja 45, exp. 57.

23. Ricardo Flores Magón to María Brousse, December 20, 1920, in

Correspondencia, p. 85.

24. Lili Sarnoff to Mollie, March 26, 1966, EDT-INAH, doc. 1092-A.

25. Ricardo Flores Magón to Ellen White, October 18, 1921, in *Correspondencia*, p. 282. The originals of Ricardo's letters to Ellen are all in English.

26. Ricardo Flores Magón to Ellen White, December 28, 1920, in *Correspondencia*, p. 85.

27. Ricardo Flores Magón to Ellen White, September 17, 1922, in *Correspondencia*, p. 438.

28. Ricardo Flores Magón to Ellen White, September 5, 1921, in *Correspondencia*, p. 249.

29. Ricardo Flores Magón to Ellen White, February 22, 1921, in *Correspondencia*, p. 118.

30. Ricardo Flores Magón to Ellen White, September 19, 1921, in *Correspondencia*, p. 263.

31. Ricardo Flores Magón to Ellen White, December 14, 1920; in *Correspondencia*, p. 74.

32. Ricardo Flores Magón to Ellen White, November 30, 1920, in *Correspondencia*, pp. 65–66.

33. Ricardo Flores Magón to Ellen White, January 11, 1921, in *Correspondencia*, p. 94.

34. Ricardo Flores Magón to Ellen White, January 24, 1922, in *Correspondencia*, p. 314.

35. Ricardo Flores Magón to Winnie Branstetter, March 24, 1921, in *Correspondencia*, p. 139.

36. Ricardo Flores Magón to Ellen White, February 14, 1922, in *Correspondencia*, p. 328.

37. Ricardo Flores Magón to Ellen White, August 16, 1921, in Correspondencia, p. 243.

38. Ricardo Flores Magón to Ellen White, April 5, 1921, in *Correspondencia*, p. 148.

39. Ricardo Flores Magón to Ellen White, April 5, 1921, in *Correspondencia*, pp. 147–48.

40. Ricardo Flores Magón to Ellen White, October 15, 1922, in *Correspondencia*, p. 441.

41. Ricardo Flores Magón to Ellen White, April 5, 1921, in *Correspondencia*, p. 148.

42. Harry Weinberger to Ricardo Flores Magón, March 11, 1921, *Correspondencia*, pp. 130 and 130n.

43. Ricardo Flores Magón to Winnie Branstetter, March 24, 1921, in

Correspondencia, p. 139.

44. Harry Weinberger to Warren Harding, April 23 1921, reprinted in *Correspondencia*, p. 173 n. 80.

45. Attorney General Harry Daugherty to Harry Weinberger, April 18, 1921, reprinted in *Correspondencia*, pp. 163–64 n. 75.

46. Warden William I. Biddle to Attorney General Harry Daugherty, June 9, 1922, U.S. Department of Justice, Bureau of Prisons, Leavenworth Penitentiary, prisoner 14596 (Magon), National Archives.

47. Comité Agrupación Regional Obrera, San Luis Potosí, to President of U.S., May 3, 1921, State Department Files, Dispatches From United States Consuls in Mexico, case 812.00, subnumbers 1601–1880, National Archives.

48. "Aids Anti-American Campaign in Mexico," *New York Times*, April 29, 1921.

49. Ricardo Flores Magón to Harry Weinberger, June 9, 1921, in *Correspondencia*, p. 210.

50. Ricardo Flores Magón to Harry Weinberger, September 12, 1922, in *Correspondencia*, p. 256.

51. Ricardo Flores Magón to Harry Weinberger October 12, 1921, in *Correspondencia*, p. 279.

52. Harry Weinberger to Ricardo Flores Magón, Librado Rivera and Manuel Rey, December 6, 1921, in *Correspondencia*, p. 299.

53. Harry Weinberger to Ricardo Flores Magón, February 1, 1922, Archivo Electrónico Ricardo Flores Magón, http://www.archivomagon.net/ObrasCompletas/Correspondencia/Cor02/Cor93.html.

54. Ricardo Flores Magón to Ellen White August 25, 1922, in *Correspondencia* p. 425.

55. Telegram from Consul Wood to Secretary of State, November 8, 1922; Undersecretary of State to Mr. Hanna, November 10, 1922; O. Gaylord March to Secretary of State, November 8, 1922, State Department Files, Dispatches From United States Consuls in Mexico, case 812.00, subnumbers 1601–1880, National Archives.

56. Harry Weinberger to Ricardo Flores Magón, November 13, 1922, in *Correspondencia*, p. 459.

57. Harry Weinberger to Ricardo Flores Magón, November 18, 1922, in *Correspondencia*, p. 461.

58. Ricardo Flores Magón to María Brousse, August 6, 1921, in *Correspondencia*, p. 240.

59. Ricardo Flores Magón to Ellen White March 8, 1921, in *Correspondencia* p. 125.

60. Ricardo Flores Magón to Harry Weinberger, November 5, 1922, U.S.

Department of Justice, Bureau of Prisons, Leavenworth Penitentiary, prisoner 14596 (Magón), National Archives.

61. Librado Rivera to Gus Teltsch, June 1, 1922, U.S. Department of Justice, Bureau of Prisons, Leavenworth Penitentiary, prisoner 15416 (Rivera), National Archives.

62. Warden William I. Biddle to Harry Weinberger, June 17, 1922, U.S. Department of Justice, Bureau of Prisons, Leavenworth Penitentiary, prisoner 15416 (Rivera), National Archives.

63. Ricardo Flores Magón to Ellen White, August 25, 1922, in *Correspondencia*, p. 423.

64. Dr. Langworthy, October 16, 1922, U.S. Department of Justice, Bureau of Prisons, Leavenworth Penitentiary, prisoner 14596 (Magon), National Archives.

65. Nicolás Bernal to compañeros, November 7, 1922, AEFM, caja 36, exp. 14.

AFTERWORD: REDEMPTION SONG

1. Attorney General Harry Daugherty to Warden William I Biddle, November 22, 1922, U.S. Department of Justice, Bureau of Prisons, Leavenworth Penitentiary, prisoner 14596 (Magon), National Archives.

2. Prison Physician [signature illegible] to Warden William I. Biddle, November 21, 1922, U.S. Department of Justice, Bureau of Prisons, Leavenworth Penitentiary, prisoner 14596 (Magon), National Archives.

3. Librado Rivera to Blas Lara, January 7, 1923, Bureau of Prisons, Leavenworth Penitentiary, prisoner 15416-L (Rivera), National Archives.

4. *Ibid.*

5. Enrique Flores Magón to Rafael García, 1 December 15, 1922, AEFM, caja 50, exp. 11.

6. *Ibid.*

7. Enrique Flores Magón to Rafael García, December 16, 1922, AEFM, caja 50, exp. 11.

8. *Ibid.*

9. *Ibid.*

10. *Ibid.*

11. *Ibid.*

12. The document is from the Archivo de la Defensa, but reprinted in Carlos Macías Richard, *Vida y temperamento: Plutarco Elías Calles, 1877–1920* (Mexico City: Fondo de Cultura Económica, 1995), pp. 231–32.

13. Marjorie Haynes Wilson, "Governor Hunt, the 'Beast' and the Miners," *Journal of Arizona History* 15.2 (Summer 1974), pp. 119–38, available at http:// www.library.arizona.edu/exhibits/bisbee/docs/jahwils.html.

14. "De Lara Killed in Zaric, Mexico," *Arizona Labor Journal*, February 8, 1918.

15. "Como fue la muerte del lic Gutiérrez de Lara," *El Heraldo de México*, February 14, 1918

16. "Se ha confirmado la muerte de Lázaro Gutiérrez de Lara," *La Prensa* (San Antonio), March 2, 1918.

17. General Plutarco Elías Calles to President Venustiano Carranza, January 2, 1918, Archivo de la Defensa, Estado de Sonora, caja 137, exp. XI/481/5/275.

18. Ethel Duffy Turner, "Lázaro Gutiérrez de Lara," EDT-INAH, doc 59.

19. Ricardo Flores Magón, "Lázaro Gutiérrez de Lara," *Regeneración*, June 8, 1912.

20. Ethel Duffy Turner, "Lázaro Gutiérrez de Lara," EDT-INAH, doc 59.

21. Ricardo Flores Magón to María Brousse, November 1, 1908.

22. Ethel Duffy Turner, "Lázaro Gutiérrez de Lara," EDT-INAH, doc 59.

23. Enrique Flores Magón to Rafael García, December 16, 1922, AEFM, caja 50, exp. 11.

24. *Ibid.*

25. "10 mil parade follows Magon's body to burial," *Los Angeles Express*, January 16, 1923.

26. Rafael García to Enrique Flores Magón, January 15, 1923, AEFM, caja 16, exp. 68.

27. *Ibid.*

28. *Ibid.*

29. Rafael García to Enrique Flores Magón, January 18, 1923, AEFM caja 16, exp. 68c.

30. *Ibid.*

31. *Ibid.*

32. *Ibid.*

33. For instance, the prison refused to transmit a telegram of solidarity to Librado from the dress makers' union, which expressed just such a sentiment. Leavenworth, Dress and Waist Makers' Union to Librado Rivera, November 27, 1922, U.S. Department of Justice, Bureau of Prisons, Leavenworth Penitentiary, prisoner 15416-L (Rivera), National Archives.

34. "Convict Stabs Five Guards," *Belleville Hews-Democrat*, November 14, 1922; "Mexican Murder Convict Stabs Guard to Death—Joe Martinez, in Federal Penitentiary at Leavenworth." *Albuquerque Morning Star*, November 15, 1922.

35. Lili Sarnoff to Mollie, March 26, 1966, EDT-INAH, doc. 1092-A

36. *Ibid.*

37. Rafael García to Enrique Flores Magón, January 15, 1923, AEFM, caja 16, exp. 68.

38. María B., viuda de Flores Magón [María Brousse], "El líder Enrique Flores Magón es exhibido ante los obreros," *Excelsior*, June 16, 1923.

39. "Como juzga el compañero Librado Rivera la actuación del Grupo Cultural 'Ricardo Flores Magón', y las imputaciones de María Brousse y camarilla de traidores." San Luis Potosí, February 19, 1924, EDT-INAH, doc 1161.

40. Enrique Flores Magón to Rafael García, July 18, 1923, AEFM, caja 16, exp. 26.

41. Enrique Flores Magón to Rafael García and tribe, August 10, 1923, AEFM, caja 16, exp. 32.

42. *Ibid.*

43. Librado Rivera, "Como juzga el compañero Librado Rivera la actuación del Grupo Cultural 'Ricardo Flores Magón' y las imputaciones de María Brousse y camarilla de traidores," February 19, 1924, EDT-INAH, doc. 1161.

44. María Brousse to Enrique Flores Magón, undated [possibly 1935], AEFM, caja 9, exp. 9.

45. Daniel Cosío Villegas, "Lección de la Barbarie," *Problemas agrícolas e industriales de México* 7.2 (1955), p. 189.

46. *Ibid.*, pp. 190 and 191.

47. Ethel Duffy Turner, "Elizabeth Darling Trowbridge," EDT-INAH, doc. 133.

48. *Ibid.*

49. Mariano Gómez Gutiérrez [Blas Lara Cázares], *La vida que yo viví: Novela histórico-liberal de la Revolución Mexicana* (n.p., 1954), p. 237.

50. Mrs. R. R. Hernández to Department of Justice, August 7, 1946, Federal Bureau of Prisons, Leavenworth Penitentiary, file of Librado Rivera, 15416-L, National Archives.

51. Warden Walter A. Hunter to Mrs. R. R. Hernandez, August 19, 1946, U.S. Department of Justice, Bureau of Prisons, Leavenworth Penitentiary, prisoner 15416-L (Rivera), National Archives.

Index of Names

Zone Books series design by Bruce Mau
Typesetting by Meighan Gale
Image placement and production by Julie Fry
Printed and bound by Maple Press